Cragg

LISSON GALLERY

Germano Celant

Cragg

CHARTA

Graphic Design
Gabriele Nason

Editing Supervisor
Emanuela Belloni

Researches, Apparatus and Translations
Anna Costantini

Translation of the Text by Germano Celant
Stephen Sartarelli

Press Office
Silvia Palombi Arte & Mostre, Milan

Production
Amilcare Pizzi Arti grafiche,
Cinisello Balsamo, Milan

Cover
Island, *1993*

This paperback edition reserved for the art galleries is not for sale.

Hardcover edition is published and distributed by Thames and Hudson Ltd, London-New York

ISBN 88-8158-067-5

Edizioni Charta
9, via Castelvetro – 20154 Milan
tel. 39-2-33.60.13.43/6
fax 39-2-33.60.15.24

Printed in Italy

Acknowledgements

Many people were involved in this publication, the first full monograph on the work of Tony Cragg. The artist himself was a constant source of stimulating ideas and information, which enabled us to reconstruct the chronological development of his ideas to give a historically accurate interpretation of his work.
We are grateful to him for always being available to discuss things with us. By the same token we would like to thank his assistant Sabine Klaproth-Falk who gave us much valuable help in tracking down archive material.
A word of thanks also to Werner Baumuller, Werkstatt Kollerschlag, Vienna; André Buchmann, Galerie Buchmann, Basel/Cologne; Vivian Bobka, Marian Goodman Gallery, New York; Lisson Gallery, London; and Sophie Pulicani, Galerie Chantal Crousel, Paris, who supplied us with documents, photographs and bibliographic information. Finally, we were truly fortunate in being able to draw on the invaluable scholarly attitude of Anna Costantini who left her unmistakeable imprint on the final form. Carlotta Bettanini and Alessandra Carrea both assisted her on this project.
So our thanks to everyone, including those who preferred to remain anonymous.

Germano Celant

Table of Contents

Tony Cragg: Material and its Shadow

Mater Materia

The history of the materials used in art in this century, from the historic avant-gardes to contemporary experiments, can be divided into two periods: the first, which runs from the end of the 19th century to the 1940s, is the period of fecundation and gestation; the second, from the 1950s to the present day, can be defined as the birth and development.

In the first phase, material grows inside the comforting womb of painting and sculpture and their traditions. It is represented by pigment, by pastel and watercolor, by marble and bronze, by iron and canvas. It is used to lend density and reality to the vision of the artist, who still considers it within the familiar framework of the painting, the window on the world, or that of sculpture and volumetrical construction, considered a mimesis of three-dimensional reality.

From Impressionism to Expressionism, from Cubism to Futurism, from metaphysical painting to Surrealism, the artistic material is in fact embraced as a system for establishing a way of perceiving life within art.

Up until the middle part of our century, the material always changed in accordance with a latent circularity that led it to feed on its own flesh, on reflections of itself. It was beginning to show signs of life, but in silence, enclosed within the space of its own genesis. Since thus far there has been no break outside of the body, its shift occurs within a closed space. It is a force beginning to "evoke" external life, to dream of its movement and its logic. It is preparing the skin that will bind it to things and reality, while forever remaining inside a self-fecundating substance. Here the material is a homogeneous figure, belonging to the same bloodline as ancient art, sharing its family tree.

In this sense, artistic material is a food nourishing the embryo of sight within the womb of an established, certain history. Thought becomes superimposed on it, feeding it with energetic, dynamic explosions, with conscious and unconscious notions, with rational and mystical suggestions; but these are always enclosed within the limits of a framework or base, the outer reaches of an illusory plenitude. Within these limits, the pilgrimage toward the multiplicity of materials is extremely varied and fanciful. With Dada and De Stijl, the errant power of the artist striving to represent the everyday led beyond colors, marbles and bronze — which can be manipulated and shaped according to his will — to the discovery of ready-made objects and industrial materials. The perspective, however, still remains internal: material is a generative power, on the human scale, *imprisoned* in the cauldron of painting and sculpture. It helps one to escape fixity, becoming an incandescent object in itself for Vincent van Gogh and Franz Marc, a space-time vortex for Pablo

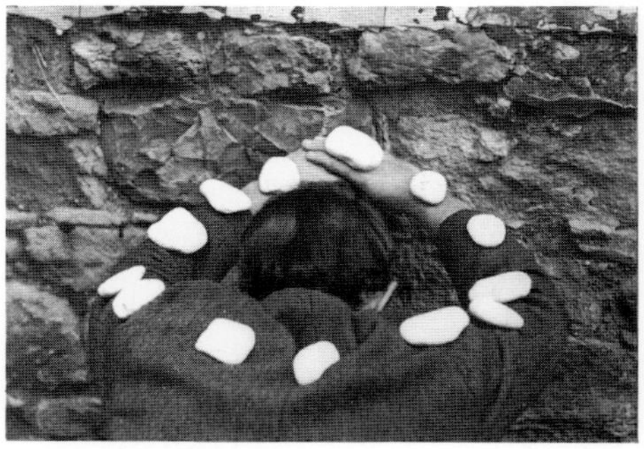

Untitled, 1971

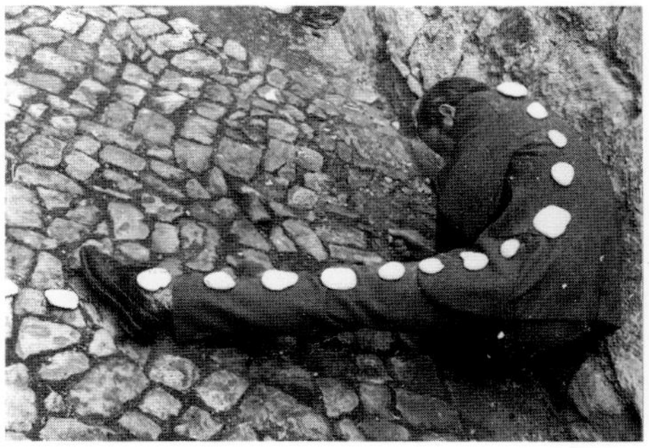

Untitled, 1971

Picasso and Georges Braque, an exploration of the void as formal universe for Kazimir Malevich and Piet Mondrian, a strategy of disintegration for Marcel Duchamp and Salvador Dalí.

Even while it attempts to deviate as much as possible from the norm in its use of materials, art does not depart from its status until after the Second World War, working — through collage and assemblage — instead on reabsorption, on inclusion and fusion. It self-fecundates and transforms itself, but remains within its techniques and its genetic and historical labyrinth. And while it seeks passage into other cultures — primitive and Eastern — it does not venture into an "elsewhere," but rather remains within its womb.

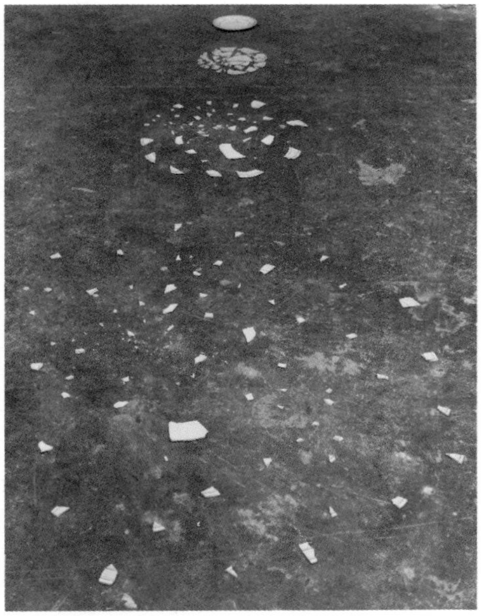

4 Plates, 1977

By the end of the 1940s, the material body is born, revealing its mass and vitality. With American action painting and European *art informel*, the material comes into the light. It emerges from the womb and begins to live a life no longer passive and silent, but active and strident.

Its presence becomes magnetic and hypnotic, seducing the gaze and making one forget representation. Under the banner of vital energy, the material grows and develops: the painting and its surface broaden, refusing the status of window and transforming themselves into territory and arena, capable of housing the artist's gesture and action. The canvas thus may present itself as the ritual field of the painterly ceremony, as in the work of Jackson Pollock, or as the limit to be transgressed and transpierced in search of "another" state, as in the work of Lucio Fontana.

Material art eventually swallows up individuality and the human scale, or at the very least succeeds in opening a two-way dialogue. It is a *magmatic* being that grows alongside its enactor, the artist. By the late 1950s, the material phase of art reached the point — with the neo-Dada and Pop work of the likes of Yves Klein, Piero Manzoni, Jasper Johns and Robert Rauschenberg — of glorifying the *lower* materials of the world and society. Such materials might include a body or its organic traces, or a fetishization of the icons of mass communication and consumption to be found within the urban fabric or carried by the mass media.

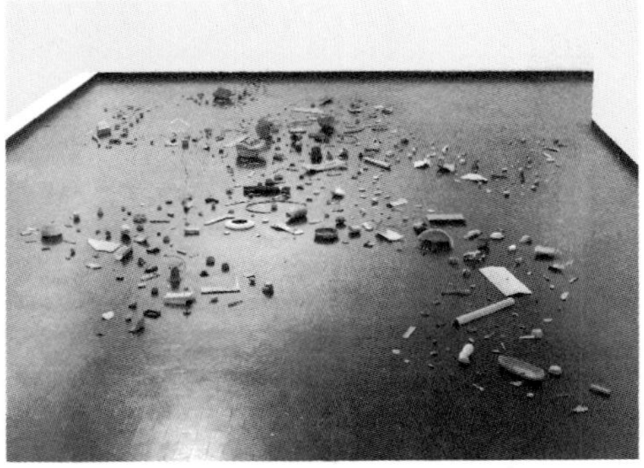

Redskin, 1979

Painting and sculpture get sucked into the vortex of objects and things, of actions and bodies, passing through it and re-emerging transfigured and transmuted. A viscous material cloaks them like a second skin, to the point of occupying space with its inhuman reality and presenting itself as *environment*. It defines an almost theatrical stage, where the artist and the spectator, no longer "directors" of the sight and manipulation of materials, become "actors."

Things begin to break loose. In the 1960s, growth and development become feverish. The material seethes and boils, gushing forth everywhere. Freed of all its armor, it identifies with the landscape and saturates it. It becomes transfused into macroscopic objects — as with Claes Oldenburg — that vie with the world of images, or else it is transcended in images of itself, as in the work of Andy Warhol.

Elsewhere its dark power and density are overturned and subjected to a negative valency: here material discovers its own *immateriality*, and its chaos becomes rigor and structure. In minimal and conceptual art, its eruption seems about to come to an end, engulfed by absence and the void. We are at the apotheosis of logic and the project, as in the work of Donald Judd and Joseph Kosuth, where art designates a pure state of consciousness where neither subject nor object exists and process emerges to determine structures and thoughts.

Running counter to this quasi-metaphysical credo is the development of an art that comes to consider material the *totality* of the world, especially its primordial elements — air, earth, fire and water — and its earthly expanses: deserts and mountains, fields and rivers. The enchantments and portents of *arte povera* and land art — from Jannis Kounellis and Joseph Beuys to Richard Long and Michael Heizer — issue from an effluvium of material that fascinates and awakens the spectator, putting him in touch with the impetus and breath of *nature* — but nature seen as a magical and anthropological whole.

After the emergence into the world, then, comes the return to the self: the material of the personal, material that hatches a second birth marked by the right to be different and multiple. From Vito Acconci and Bruce Nauman to Louise Bourgeois and Robert Mapplethorpe, this material energetically carries the charge of an enigma, the gaze from within, which can be evoked by the formulations of an art that is either gentle and ironic or profound and transgressive. Finally, there is aerial, technologized material, that which slides over the absent surfaces of the television screen or the billboard — that which serves to give shape to the invisible and imperceptible, to electronic ghosts and dreams. It is a mental material, fluid and swift, which cannot be physically grasped, but rather accepts being fraught with images, the images of the nightmare of the present.

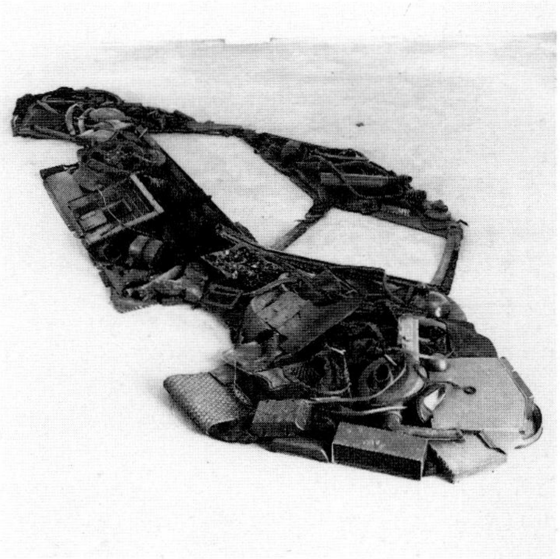

Car, 1980

The gesturality and energy developed by these artists bring with them a revision of the concept of material in art, one that involves the primitive and archetypal dimension of perceptible, physical data. The infinite multiplicity of data and images almost always remains at the tautological and monistic level, as though material were assumed as pure form — in the minimalists — or as pure force — in *arte povera* and antiform art. The urge to measure and isolate, to classify and identify the archetypal principles of feeling, has nevertheless driven this work toward a fragmentation and parcelization of the material vision. The fire has been isolated as well as the concept, the water as well as the line, the light as well as the form, the metal as well as the image — to call attention to individual sensory data. The result, however, has been an absolutization and institutionalization of the fragment, based on the *impersonal* and *univocal* dimension of sight and perception. Between minimalism and conceptualism a certain "mysticism" of the logic and philosophy of sight has served to sustain an immaterial physics, as though the breath of form and the concept sufficed to conceive the universe of forms and artistic discourse.

The generation of artists who were formed and came of age during the historic period from 1968 to 1975, while close to the *evolution* of material as an archetypal principle of art, believes that all its transformations are also *organicistic*, that is, they cannot be imposed from without, but only lived from within. The assumption is that one has emerged from a metaphysical situation and entered an individual condition where material, having come into being in the 1960s, now finds it has become *identity*, with all its internal and external characteristics ready to turn fluid and move about freely. For such artists as Rebecca Horn, Robert Gober and Tony Cragg, the abstract classification of the vast variety of forms and definitions, of materials and phenomena, in fact gives way to a language of personal experience, where material acquires a multidimensionality that contains neither straight lines nor perfectly regular forms, nor processes of universal and symbolic energy. What matters is the deciphering of an experience which, not being based on abstract classifications or the great ideologies, manages to bring to light a reality difficult to describe or to present with words or concepts — an individual meditation on the state of *existence* of people and materials.

Substance Lies on the Ground

The problem of the *genesis* of things and their component parts first seized Tony Cragg's attention while studying at Technical College and during his first experiences working in a laboratory at the Natural Rubber Producers Research Association, where he came into contact with atomic and subatomic phenomena as well as with biochemistry. Here his mode of perception becomes honed with an *introspective* vision of material illuminated from within. The interpretation of the physical and chemical properties of metals and of natural and artificial composites, in the dialectic between abstraction and intuition in the map of knowledge of the real, becomes a way of *seeing* the substances of images.

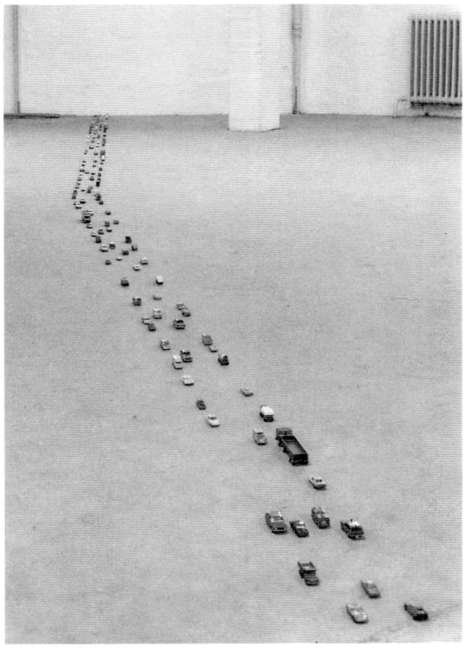

Autobahn, 1979

Thus when he moves on to art in the 1970s, the need to *grasp* the organic and inner multiplicity of things, whether they are objects, bodies, images, or events, becomes directed towards the identification of a visual language that might synthesize the multiple visual situations produced by analysis.

In 1971, in *Untitled* (pl. 1), Tony Cragg has himself photographed next to a drawing of his figure traced in the sand on a beach, with the sun behind him, so that his shadow lines up alongside the silhouette traced in the ground. The work is highly emblematic of the future course his art will take.

First of all the *photograph*, an artificial, technological document organized by human sight, tends to document the synthesis of all possible *figurations*: the figure as plural reality of the material, immaterial, and signic body. For Cragg, art as the science of representation should be identified *only* with one of these three aspects, but must aim at involving them all, or better yet, must seek to seize them all together. From the very start, he opts not for painting, two-dimensional and signic like the silhouette traced in the sand, nor for sculpture, understood as an erected material, but rather for something midway between the two, something that might encompass the *shadow*,[1] that is, the unknown and immaterial dimension that exists parallel to the bodies of material individuality and its representation. But what does the presence of the shadow mean in Cragg's work, and what does it produce?

Its image is linked to the theme of the individuality of persons as well as materials; it runs parallel to them and transcends their limits. It is a variation of their appearance aimed at developing not easily "physicalizable" zones. By including it in his art, Cragg appears to broaden the meaning of the presentation and visual representation of materials. He begins to point to *other* fruitions, which act between the poles of the positive and the negative, the conscious and the unconscious, the physical and the non-physical, the accepted and the unaccepted.

Clearly this expansion and broadening is such only if brought into the light, if made up of waves emanating from a source. For this reason individual intensities will find a power of extension in relation to the individual sources of material. They will

spread according to unknown, unforeseen internal figures, with the result that for Cragg material will be able to dream and fantasize.
Finally, working on the lower part that is *on the ground*, between the body and the image of the identity of beings and things, Cragg will find his substances in the *low* part of the material universe, among discarded, castoff elements, the refuse of society, and among the dense, compact matrices of nature, the rocks and trees, or the artificial magmas of industry. The sought-for experience will be that of a child who "is going to have to learn to consider what possibilities it has for change as opposed to changing the material around it, to consider the qualities and the properties internal to itself, thereby changing the demands and expectations it will place on its exterior circumstances."[2]
The dialectic between high and low, between body and material as life-blood for play as well as for art, becomes, between 1971 and 1973, an emblem of the close reciprocal relationship between self-portrait and objects.
In the two-year period that found him still at the Royal College of Art, shuttling between Wimbledon and central London, Cragg made many photographs that portray him together with a *double* of himself: a cap with ear-flaps raised or turned down (*Untitled*, 1971); a row of white stones arranged along his extended arms and forming a circle (*Untitled*, 1971); the curve of his hip (*Untitled*, 1973); and finally the composition consisting of a long plank of wood for which the artist serves as support or pivot (*Untitled*, 1973).
The search for a metamorphic flux between wood, fabric, stones, and person thus comes to mark a *necessary* relationship between organic and inorganic materials, between soft and rigid, animate and inanimate materials, between found object and created subject. And the grafting of opposites reconciles elements which, while divergent — like the found stool and the cubes cut into wood to form a frame, in *Untitled*, 1972 (pl. 2) — combine to produce a *visual wager* based on equilibrium and surprise, on chance and the aleatory. With this integration of contraries,

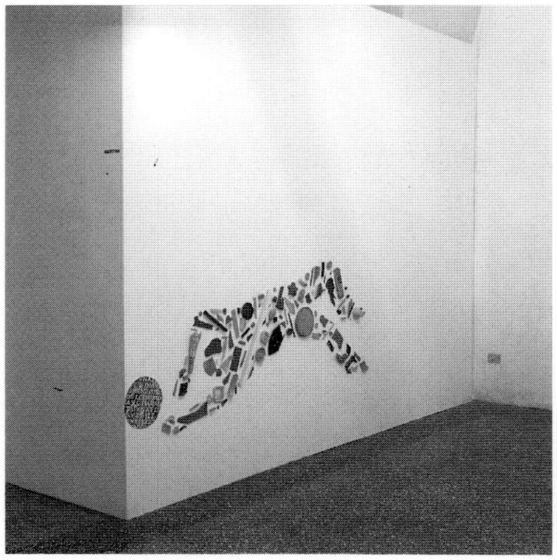

Torwart, 1981

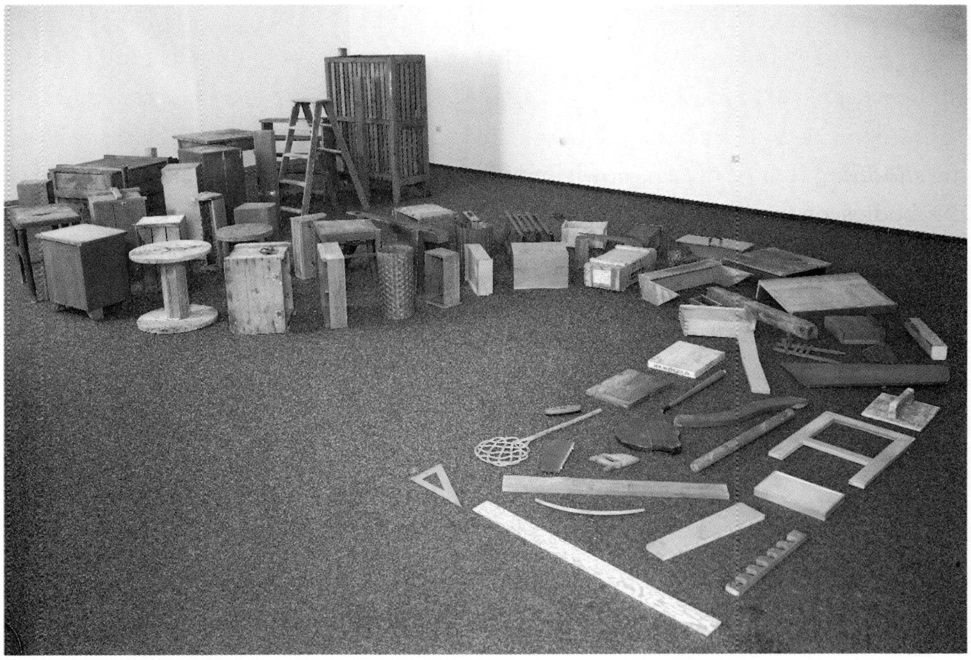

Mittelschicht, 1984

achieved through an unexpected harmony, Cragg effects a linguistic *leap* in sculpture with respect to the conceptual and minimalist manner of Donald Judd, Richard Long, Robert Smithson and Barry Flanagan. In a departure from their rational and analytical approach, he actually reproposes *le hasard*, the Surrealist plunge where "the subject, in order to know the object, must identify himself with it. The individual must first of all project his whole consciousness into the thing to be known, to metamorphose into it through fascination, and thus to integrate it into himself."[3]

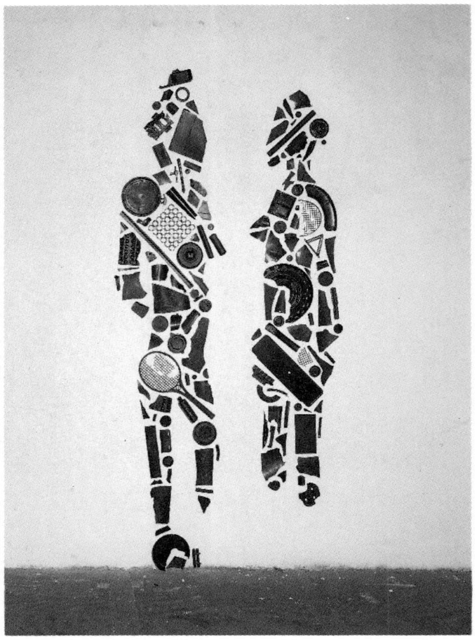

African Sculpture, 1984

This amounts to the same thing as Cragg's declaration: "The need to know both objectively and subjectively more about the subtile fragile relationships between us, objects, images and essential natural processes. [...] It is very important to have first-order experiences — seeing, touching, smelling, hearing — with objects and images and to let that experience register."[4]

In portraying himself in his work, Cragg establishes a parallelism between identities, as well as a transcendence of the boundaries between the animal, vegetable, and mineral conditions. By hybridizing beings and materials in their variations of appearance, his goal is to develop functions and phenomena of *another nature*. The notion is that of a certain *metaphysics* aimed at transcending the idea of an inanimate materiality, a metaphysics that might instead pulsate with a vitalizing energy that would regenerate the very core of matter. Cragg from the very start has always had a fascination for the path between the surreal and the metaphysical, where materials and objects come to throb with a "virtual fire."

The bodies of things and artifacts are thus assumed as inertia and heaviness, though imbued with an internal, alchemical, instinctive power whose fluidity makes it possible to integrate diverse and contrasting materials and to transform boundaries and forms. Such events occur in works like *Lens*, 1985 (pl. 55), *Echo*, 1984, *Plough*, 1990 (pl. 149), and *Social Situation*, 1992 (pl. 159), where the object's skin is extended through graffiti, hooks, and thorns, or works such as *Two Positions*, 1983, and *Mortar and Pestle*, 1987 (pl. 69), where the materials — wood, stone, metal, plastic — are mixed and combined.

Contrary to the external definition and the monolithic volumetrics and materiality of the minimalists, the fullness that Cragg is dealing with is a magmatic birth where energies cease to be oppositional — as in *Stack*, 1976 (pl. 6) — and recognize one another in an "other whole", the *non-object* and the *non-I*, the shadow-side of the object and the I: the mind materialized and material made animate.

Here the explosive power associated with the shadow and its disaggregating double becomes manifest, dissociating unity and form, setting in motion the breakdown of finite and limited entities to open up a continuum of energy based on the *transformation* and *osmosis* between opposites: masculine/feminine, conscious/unconscious, natural/artificial, full/empty, art/science.

In 1976, after five years of exploring the terrain of integrating visual hypothesis and physical gesture, the process of defining an art on the *threshold* of fluidifying materials moves from the summary stage, still grounded in dissociated or at least antithetical entities, to a *regeneration* of the full-whole of material in its shadow. In *Untitled*, 1976 (made up of fragments of cement and brick) and *4 Plates*, 1977 (a sequence of four plates in different stages of wholeness and fragmentation and of territorial expansion), leaving aside the interpretations that identify these works as an "attack" against conventional[5] sculpture, the distinction as well as the coexistence between the object entity and its possible shadow begin to take shape. Their existence as emblem of the explosion of sculpture and the acceptance of an unexpected presence of volumes and forms as separate realities becomes enriched with an idea of fullness, a plunge into the flux of things whole and fragmented, fused or embedded, smooth or perforated. It is a dialogue between existence and living, from the inside out, or from the whole to the particular, where the crux between mind and matter, between conscious and unconscious, between organic and artificial, reconstitutes itself.

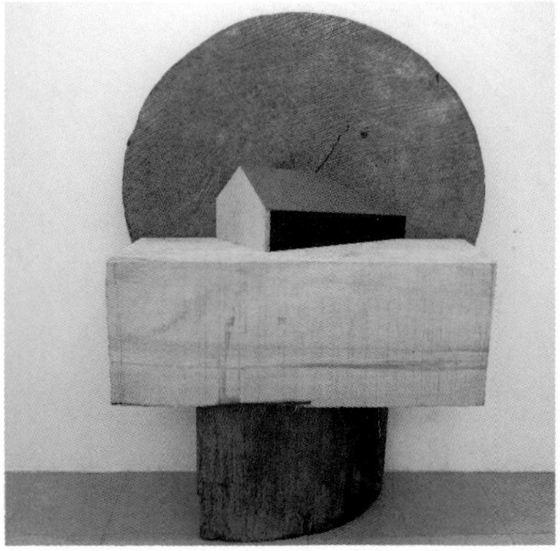

Silent Place with Dwelling, 1984

Castoff Molecules

To restore the life-force one must rise back up from the low to the high, that is, from the place of contact between body and shadow. Cragg, between 1977 and 1981, after having worked on the energy arising from the negative metamorphosis of a figure, body, or object that goes from the state of wholeness to that of fragmentedness, from volume to line, from wheat to chaff, moves on to a generative, positive dimension, whereby the figure, situated between body and shadow, is constructed from waste and fragments, from trifles and pieces.

This transition from the immateriality of the shadow to the physical figuration of the body — thus from the impalpability of dust or light materials to the image — occurs in a series of works from the 1970s. In 1971, in *Untitled*, Cragg drew a sequence of numbers with seaweed, whose shape is reminiscent of the shape of numbers on a computer or calculator. He thus established a visual fusion between nature and artificial representation, where what is divided and dispersed unites and gathers to *compose* the image. If we go back to the *4 Plates*, 1977, the reading process turns from unity to fragmentation and vice versa: the process may therefore be assumed to be a *de-composition* and a *re-composition*. In 1977 Cragg began to unearth images and representations from industrial scraps. The material collected from beaches generally includes fragments of plastic in its various iconographic and chromatic manifestations as toy or tool, container or conductor, ranging in color from industrial hues to monochrome red, yellow, or green.

In 1978, having moved to Wuppertal, in the industrial Ruhr valley in Germany, Cragg began to work with the sort of scraps that are the final result of a further metamorphosis — that of artificial material transposed into form and then consumed until it is mere waste. These are, in fact, splinters and fragments of toothbrushes, toy soldiers, cans, dolls, toy cars, dishes, tubes, bottles, vases, pot-covers — which the artist has chosen for their color and then re-used and indeed regenerated into sculptures on the ground and on the wall. They come to form *other* figures and *other* images, such as the airplane, *Flugzeug*, 1979, and the running Amerindian, *Redskin*, 1979. In being recycled, these waste products of our industrial world are purified and return to being signs, by virtue of being assumed as chromatic and physical material which is then organized and shaped into new images.

And since the collection of fragments often results in a totemic representation of industry and plastics — such as the bottle — Cragg draws inspiration from this and rebuilds the same image, in a game of mirrors that once again brings the shadow into play. In fact, *Flugzeug* and *Redskin* are inspired by two toys. The procedure moves from within, finding inspiration in the core of the material, in its unconscious, so that the figure will generate itself through its hidden, inner identity.

Compared to Richard Long's arrangements of natural materials, Cragg's figurations, rather than abstract images such as the circle and the square, are *found profiles*, derived from the prefabricated object. This object is never unique, and for this reason the potential configuration of the scraps becomes multiple. The shadows and figures present in the finds may well be diverse.

The imagination, for Cragg, is *prefigured*; it does not depart from the real through abstract or geometrical forms but *already exists*. One need only look for it in the universe of *bodies*.

This would appear to be a risky assertion, as it seems to say that the ungraspable lies not only in the unknown, but also in the known, which is already given. Opening one's eyes means accepting the aesthetic and ecstatic gift of natural as well as artificial reality. Many artists, from Long to Smithson, have found this gift in meadows and mines; Cragg instead has discovered it in the urban detritus that accumulates ruined and unusable objects. In his work, the castoff sacrificed by consumption is reified — as difference and diversity — into the castoff of art: the aesthetic sacrifice resacralizes the industrial sacrifice. Moreover, the fact that the collected whole potentially possesses a *multiplicity* also gives rise to a multiplicity of analysis.

Given Cragg's biological and scientific interests, one may perhaps speak of free molecular compounds, which find their structural arrangement depending on the *exposure* to the heat of the exhibition or the public place. It is as though the artist had explored urban refuse with a microscope, as if he had extracted its DNA and from

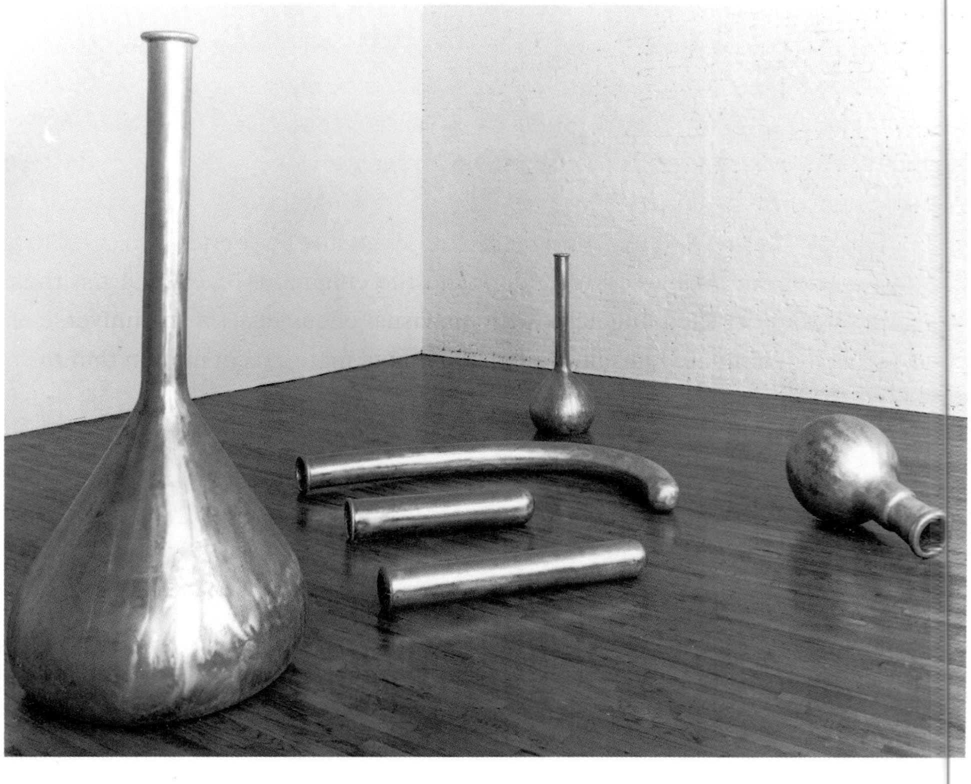

Oersted Sapphire, 1987

this had managed to reconstruct the identity of a given figure.
In *Green Bottle II, Yellow Bottle II, Red Bottle II, Orange Bottle II, Blue Bottle II*, 1982 (pl. 30), the subject of the fluidification between the object and its shadow is confronted from various perspectives.[6] First of all, the bottles, as containers of fluids, imply a circulation from outside to inside and vice versa. Moreover, in ancient symbology they are a sign — and for this reason are often used by Joseph Beuys — of secrecy and the unknown. They display something fragile and separate from the world, something that must be protected because it is unusual. The bottle, for Cragg, is therefore the allegorical place of the imagination; it holds the elixir, the potion, that makes the public fall in love and transforms the beloved. In this respect the bottle is similar to art; it leads to revelations and secret knowledge. In Cragg it is made of plastic, and for this reason the artist may rely on it to find the imagination of the artificial universe.
As container of an imaginary wealth, the bottle thus becomes the motif in a proliferation of images and figures in fragments of colored plastic, iron, steel, aluminum, wood, glass, granite, plaster, and styrofoam. We find such variations as these in *Oersted Sapphire*, 1987, *Eroded Landscape*, 1987 (pl. 64), *Spill*, 1987 (pl. 70), *Bestückung*, 1987-88 (pl. 72), and all the way up to *Blood Sugar*, 1992 (pls. 176, 177), and *Glass Hybrids*, 1992 (pl. 171).
In its dialogue between inside and outside, the bottle is a metaphor of the passage and the projection between conscious and unconscious; it is the container of an oneiric material whose variety is projected in the form of a shadow on the walls — as in *Green Bottle II, Yellow Bottle II, Red Bottle II, Orange Bottle II, Blue Bottle II*, 1982. As carrier of psychophysical fluids, it identifies an unreproducible, unique singularity, that of the broadening of the self.
The artist, too, is a container or carrier of images, so much so that in 1980 he portrayed himself as a collection of industrial scraps — *Self-Portrait with Sack*. In 1982, in *Self-Portrait with Bottles and Bricks* (pl. 26), he established a strict correlation between his own presence and the protective universe of objects, especially bottles and bricks. His silhouette here is protected by an initiatory hail of fragments and colors, the one reflecting in the other.
The *unio mystica* between the human figure and industrial products is a visual ceremony that still functions according to the ancient alchemical relationship with an *other world* that enables us to understand the enigma of life. The artist thus becomes an esoterist shedding light, with his visual chemicals, on the universe of things, so as to illuminate himself. He sets the flux of materials in motion that they might yield secrets and knowledge wavering between object and subject: "The artist is a specialist in a field he defines for himself. This field is a mixture of objectivity, irrationality, and subjectivity. In inventing a denser, more complex vocabulary, the artist contributes to an understanding of the world. He is simply a very small fragment of the universe. Torn between himself and his images, he is a grain of organic material in a universe where man cannot grasp his own insignificance. Trying to transcend his own smallness, using all his power to do so — like an eagle — the artist is constantly torn between these two feelings: his smallness in time and space on the one hand, and his eagle's greatness on the other. He sees the banality of so many activities, the stupidity of many preoccupations. He can observe the universe,

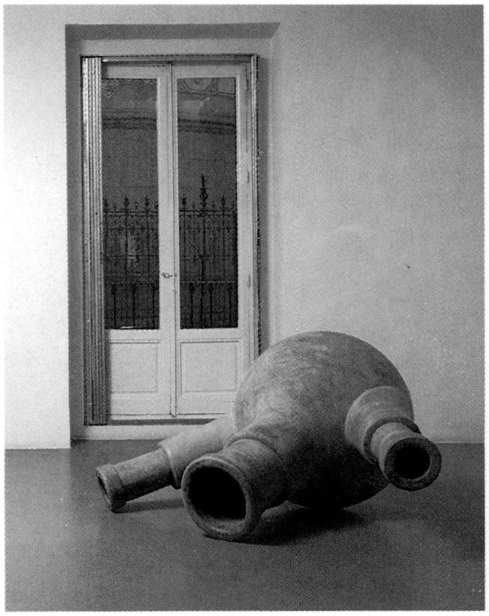
Mother's Milk I, 1987

and knows the value of an intellect which can reflect upon its own existence. In fact it is a celebration of life which, I think, is his main contribution."[7]

The Weight of the Shadow

The integration of the shadow is an important moment in the process of individuation, as well as the requirement for a definitive conquest in the area of linguistic identity — for Cragg as an artist and person who turns his own *projections* into a field of discovery and fantastical investigation. In 1981 the phenomenology of the visual story in Cragg broadens, becoming a narrative and acquiring an imagistic rhythm of fabulistic dimensions, going so far as to make discoveries about the environment surrounding it.

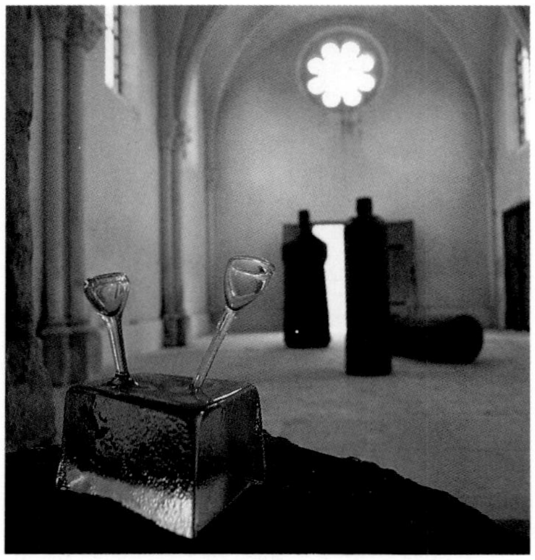

Spore n. 4, 1988

The works that express this outlook are the great orchestrations of figures, in which Cragg tells stories about the present — as in *Policeman*, 1981 (pl. 19), and *Riot*, 1987 (pl. 65) — or evokes natural and urban landscapes — as in *Large Mountain*, 1983 (pl. 34), and *Three Modern Buildings*, 1983 (pl. 39); at times, as in *George and the Dragon*, 1984, and *New Figuration*, 1985 (pl. 49), he even ventures into the world of legend and comic-book fantasy. The interpretation is at times almost caricatural, as though the artist wanted to paint an ironic portrait of his times, bearing witness to its strange customs and perverse imagery. Naturally, it is the harmonious agreement of the scraps used which pushes these figurations into the realm of the burlesque even while it exalts them through the apotheosis of the *marvelous*, in the mannerist tradition of Arcimboldo, Bernini, Rych, and Peeters.

The polymorphous vision, of mannerist origin, serves as further evidence of the artist's abandonment of the minimalist and conceptualist perspective, which was based on stable, fixed points, in favor of a heterogeneity and multiplicity of sight and of making art. Indeed, starting in the 1980s, Cragg's procedure seems to explode in many directions, leaving definitively behind the linear, the balanced, and the coherent, in favor of an intentional dissolution of the univocal and monotonous nucleus. The compositions start to become fluid, not only in the materials, but in the surrounding spaces as well. From *S*, 1984 (pl. 42), and *Mittelschicht*, 1984, to *Echo*, 1984, and *Lens*, 1985 (pl. 55), the works become *landscapes* of scraps or fragments of wood, lead, stone, or cement, as if wishing to confirm their vocation of dominance over space and architecture. They enter the stage and take possession of it, no longer accepting the volatility of the plastic that makes light and fragile figures, but rather presenting themselves as magnetic phenomena, emanations of force. The shadow assumes weight and dimension.

And since it still remains in the realm of the different and unusual, Cragg's transition, following the work rooted in fragmentation and the assemblage of industrial scraps and waste, is toward compactness and unification, thanks to the choice of a single material, which is shaped and molded to create new forms and new images.

If in the beginning there was chaos and self-reflexiveness, the scenario suggested after 1985 is that of a controlled totality, mirror of a gradual growth in which the sculptor takes back upon himself the awareness of a thing not *found* but *created*. The transition is thus towards a non-ephemeral projection of dimension, triggered by the chance functioning of found objects as a kind of sculpture responsible for its own existence and survival, in control of its own techniques and forms. At this point, the shadow becomes autonomous, acting as a whole with a density and corporeality of its own: it is cast in bronze, iron, steel, ceramics, or glass, and assumes the appearance of a modeled object. More than a recuperation of negative value — the scrap, the castoff — this phase of Cragg's work proposes a value. It lays claim to a uniqueness and assumes responsibility for being-in-the-world as an instance of plastic, visual culture. These works are born after the series of *Culture Myths*, 1984, in which the shadows of African and European sculpture appear as an awareness of cultural identity.

With the iconographic emergence of a formative, cultivated plasticity, Cragg succeeds in recuperating craft and manual labor. He once again makes the effort necessary to shape forms and volumes. He turns to the classical tradition of sculpture, integrating it into his own scientific and biological experiences, and thus succeeds in creating an encyclopedic landscape of his own activity and movement about the world: "People say there's a great deal of variety in my work, but I'm not so sure that's true ... It's like making a complete landscape with all the parts in it: there is the urban world, architecture and so on, there's the organic world, there's the atmosphere, and there's the geological structure."[8]

The dynamics of this break from the dissection and loss implicit in the found material, and of the reacceptance of intellectual and physical artifice, lead to a recuperation of fire as the means for shaping the synthesis of new images that are ever more individualized in a technical as well as iconographic sense. The potential relationship that can be established between the incandescent and the solid, as Cragg sets about casting the glass, bronze, steel, or aluminum, leads him to favor masses and membranes. By eschewing fragmentation and segmentation, the telluric force of the material builds up and forms *solid*, *heavy* entities.

From the image of skin we then pass to that of the womb in gestation, the alembic, vase, mortar — cores of material transformation and alchemical process. In 1986, Cragg uses glass, symbol of transparency and fluidity, to create such works as *Mortar*

Huddled Groups, 1989

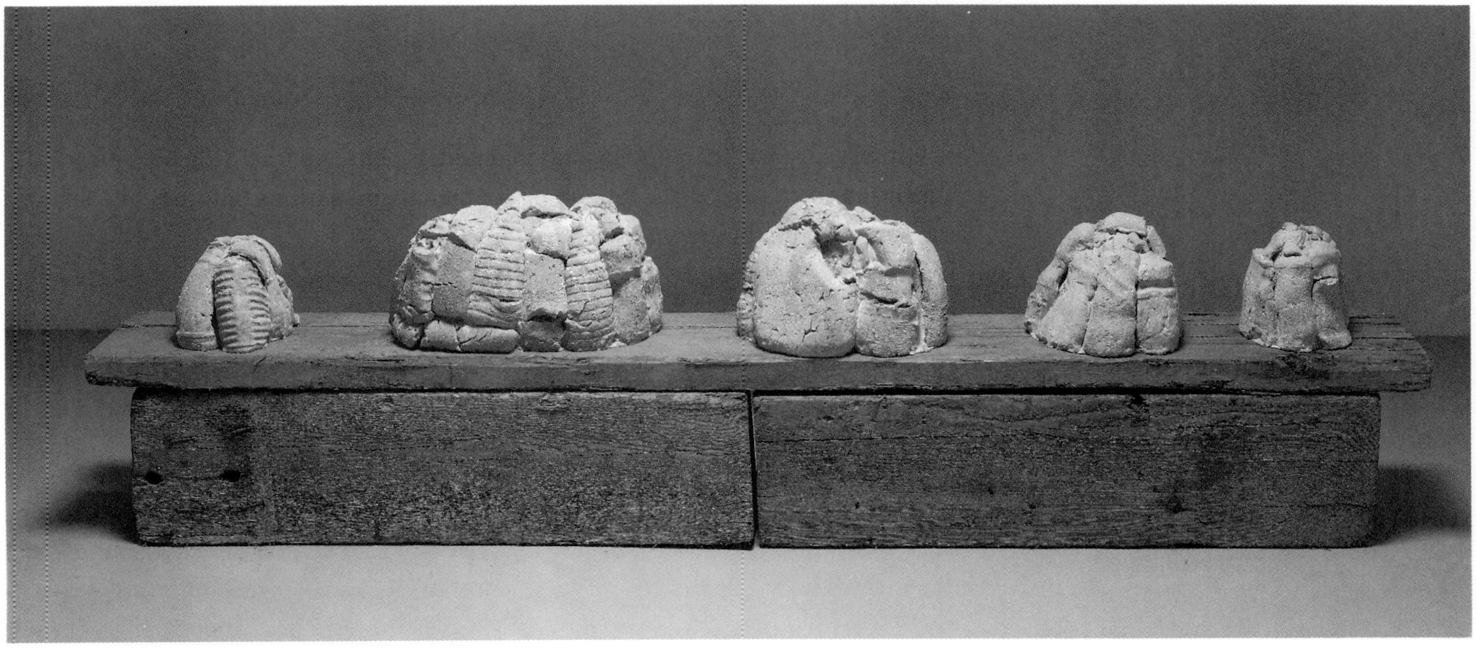

and Pestle, *Eye Bath*, *Glass Horns*, *Sandblasted Glass*, and *Snow Provision*; after these comes the technique of casting, and the instruments of the chemical laboratory: *Oersted Sapphire*, 1987, and *Spill*, 1987 (pl. 70). The iconography of the forge opens up an imagination that will generate other hollows and bowls, symbols of an interiority irrigated by a dense, ferrous, liquid fire: *On the Savannah*, 1988, *Trilobites*, 1989 (pls. 101, 102), and *Emergence*, 1992 (pl. 166).

The topography of these hollow but fluid-bearing forms (womb, breast) feeds their underlying symbology of feminine fertility, as in *Mother's Milk I*, 1987 — an indication of Cragg's new turn, after the flat and volumetric figurations typical of the 1970s and 1980s, to visceral forms and fissures, a swelling of lips and organic cavities. Also from 1986 is an entire series of works concerning the vascular and muscular systems of the human body — *Wooden Muscle*, 1986 (pl. 63), and *Stomach*, 1986 (pl. 60) — where the definition of the shadow now seems focused on the labyrinth of the bodily structure.

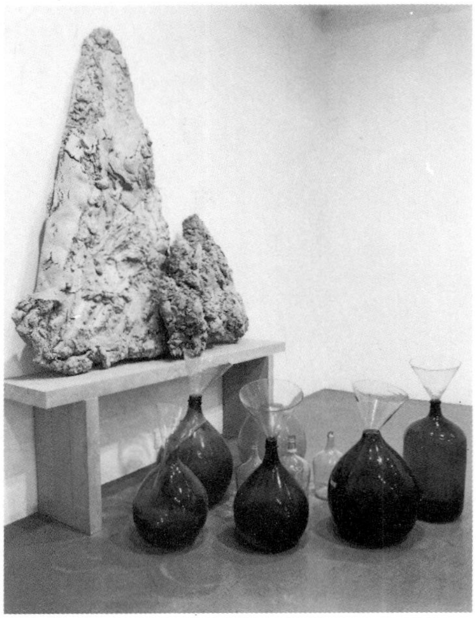

Spring, 1989

In this construction of a vocabulary of the body, the chain of associations relating to dissection calls to mind the dissecting table — an image of Lautréamont important to the Dada and Surrealist approaches — on which fortuitous objects and materials come to lie, objects and bodies capable of forming a new body or landscape. In this vein, *Eroded Landscape*, 1987 (pl. 64), and *Silicate*, 1988, display a sense of the *marvelous* in a panorama of everyday objects: bottles, cruets, alembics, dishes.

Compared to the plastic works, which are characterized by a history and a crumbling that brings out their buried and rediscovered energies, the glass works are like reproducing cells. They carry life's matrix within themselves; they liberate material and, as embryos, foreshadow a mountain of signs. They are similar to human bodies, representing the intermediary surface between the visible and the invisible. When they become transparent or colored — like *Spore n. 4*, 1988, and *Vessel*, 1991 (pl. 115)— they beam with an immateriality, becoming the delicate womb of an opening and closing of consciousness and the soul.

In the glass works, the manifest virtuality of the inside is visible because of the material; but when the material is opaque, like plaster, bronze, ceramic, or stone, this dialogue between opposite realities — between inside and outside, conscious and unconscious, the manifest and the obscure — cannot fail to take place. In the series of *Forminifera*, 1989-90 (pls. 91, 96), Cragg unites polarities by perforating the plaster.

The perforation is an opening onto the unknown. It announces potentiality and the revelation of an unexpected presence. It is a path to biological and spiritual fertility. *Two Tigers*, 1990 (pl. 121), *Invisible Particle*, 1992, and *Spear*, 1990 (pl. 181), are three manifestations of a deep gaze that penetrates into the womb of matter and things.

In achieving a sense of unexpectedness and unknowability, Cragg's aim is not to offer an ontological affirmation, but to exorcize his own existence: "Perhaps I should be frank and say that I'm trying to improve the quality of my life. To find myself a way of dealing with it ... It's a self-defining situation."[9]

Alongside this interpretation, which strives to understand the natural dynamics of the self and its shadow, Cragg's art and sculpture, in their flow and movement, may also be seen as a *galaxy* alternately small and vast in size, made up of heterogeneous

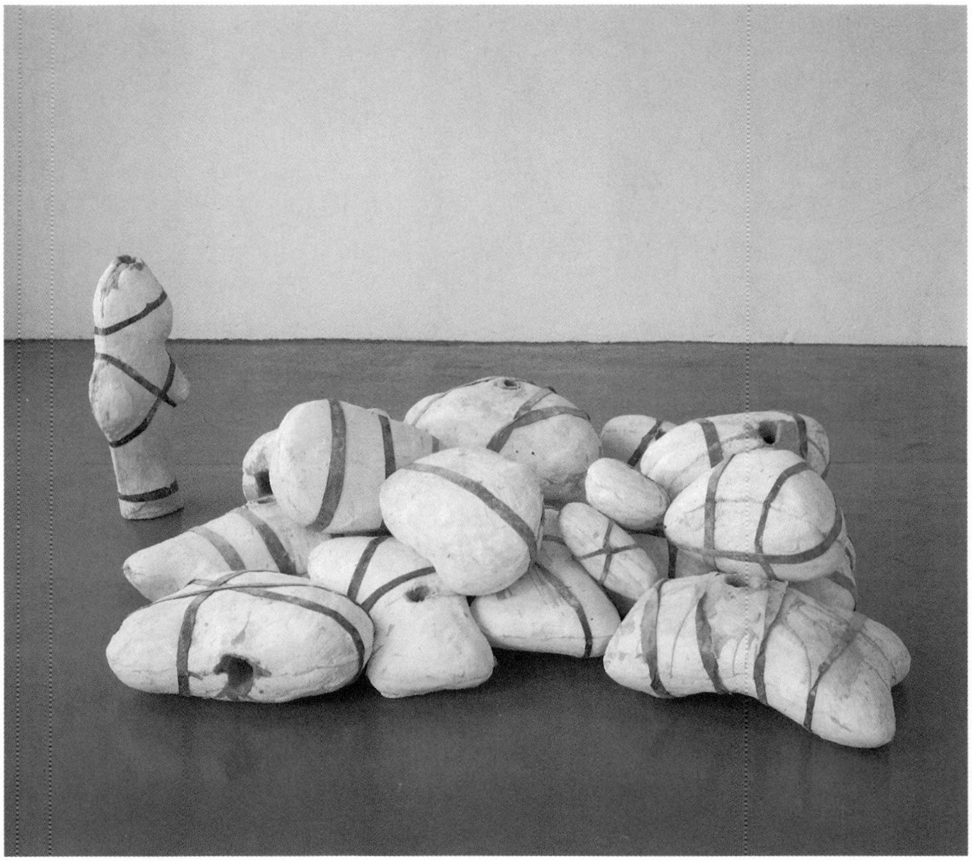

The Hunter, 1991

materials that one can only study and decipher through the use of powerful telescopes: *Terris Novalis*, 1992 (pl. 172). This galaxy, made up of clouds of gas and fire, burns in the universe of sculpture, spinning in the outer space of museums and galleries, consuming itself and expanding, contracting and exploding. Its forms are many and various — disks, plates, spheres, spirals — and they are never in a state of rest. Thus tree cellulose can serve as the visualization of its own bark — as in *Administrated Cellulose*, 1992 (pl. 179) — even while it represents a model of evolutionary cosmology based on the memory of its own material being, as in *Cellulose Memory*, 1991 (pl. 154).

The outside viewpoint, seen through the spy-glass, establishes an astral vision that astonishes because it reduces the artist to a cosmonaut and psychonaut[10] capable of giving shape to our earthly system as sculptural, plastic material. He has the power to depict the urban landscape, the maps and topographical features, to fix them and put them back into artistic circulation. As early as 1979, in *Autobahn*, Cragg had already defined, as a game, an urban motif that would return again in 1984 with a more insistent look at the city, in *Autobahn-Hildener Kreuz*, and in the series that includes *Japanese House*, 1984, and *Two Small Houses and a Village*, 1985. This finally leads up to the *earthly* scenes, the earthmoving achieved with cranes and bulldozers: *Mountain Maquette (Quarry 'T')*, 1989 (pl. 103), and *Quarry Purofer*, 1990 (pl. 104).

But from the infinitely vast world, the universe seen from afar, we return to the infinitely small world, the universe of submicroscopic size, taken down to the level of atoms and nuclei: *Bacchus Drops*, 1985 (pl. 50), for example, redefines from within the

Taking and Giving, 1992

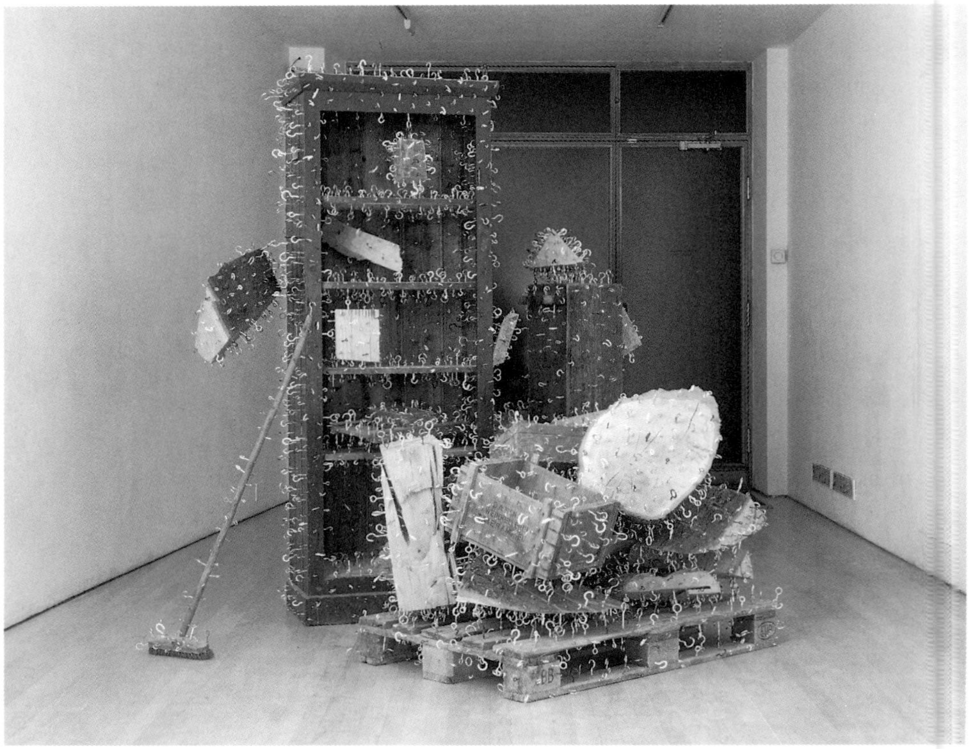

structure of atomic nuclei, while in *Messages*, 1993 (pl. 186), the exploration of DNA confers structures on the outer texture of wood.

Penetrating the deepest strata of material alters one's perception of it. It brings in the value of energy and its range of dilation and expansion. Accordingly, objects become *active* for Cragg; they change shape and become covered with hair, thorns, and other protuberances, as in *Unschärferelation*, 1991 (pl. 151), *Plough*, 1990, *Taking and Giving*, 1992, and *Gazelle*, 1992 (pl. 161). They become transformed into *animal species* with a twofold bodily polarity that represents their innermost, secret existence.

In 1994, the experience of breathing concrete, physical life into the continuum of body/shadow and objects, to make their molecular and material properties combine and interweave, gives rise to a series of new works entitled *Fast Particles*, in which the human figure becomes a three-dimensional shadow on which fragments of reality and energy accumulate as on a magnet. They are images of ice and salt that teem with visual references to the esoteric repertory of vitrification and transmutation. In them Cragg glorifies the connection between art and life and between art and the human mind; at the same time, however, he evokes the notion of the psychic, carnal, and spiritual forces corresponding to the object traces, here intended as projections of the unconscious as well as cosmic energy. One of the metaphors on which Cragg's work rests in fact involves the vitreousness and crystallization that form a unique constellation between the human being and the artificial entity. He suggests a continuity between their elastic, vital flows, delineating their twofold status between states of stiffness and spontaneity, paralysis and driving mobility, as though the universe inhabited by both were at the point of imminent explosion. Or as though the world were a vacillating aggregate of bodies and things on the verge of decomposing and melding together into a myriad of fragments and unexpected balances. Objects thus infiltrate the interstices of the human body, just as the latter with its fluids mingles with the fullness of things. Each imposes itself on the other, burning the other out: they are exemplars of a double being that dries up life's waters and turns all into lime or marble or plaster. It is an experience of aridity that leads to a realm beyond the heavens, where coagulations of flesh become coagulations of things. They possess one another mutually in the dryness and cold, through the current of fluids common to both.

This fullness as flux and outflow clearly serves the artist as a promise of creative and visual fecundity, one that enables him to "pass from a real to an imaginary order; I use material as a means to blaze a trail toward other types of content. This is how ideas and aesthetic solutions come to light."[11]

The unexpected explosion of such encounters is thus a mercurial process, cold and logical, aimed at the crystallization of aesthetic production. In standing the notions of the meeting and melding of materials on their heads, Cragg is seeking metaphors of inventive and visual transparency, where each combination becomes the vector of an unexpected, luminous presence. The definition of this new condition of sight and perception is, however, always "open"; the combinations are bifrontal, with a polarity of light and shadow, like the two faces of one same coin. They present themselves as divided and divisible, and for this reason their condition, both as beings and things, does not offer any certain, comfortably enclosed identity.

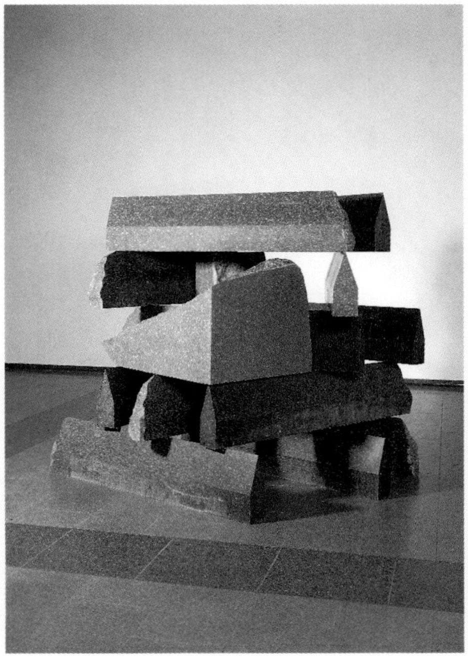
Tun, 1989

And here we may have another perspective from which to interpret Cragg's tense, open sculpture, which is never affirmative, but almost always assumes the appearance of an antagonistic and at times aggressive system. For if the premises of life lie between light and shadow, between the carnal body and the industrial body, then their impervious dialectic must pass through the tension and breakdown of the various parts. There can be no moments of rest, because the one never extricates itself from the other, but can only be doubled in the other. This explains the hard, aggressive quality of *Species*, 1990 (pl. 150), and *Under the Skin*, 1994, in which the soft materials and gentle lines are subjected to the harsh bite of the thorns. It is a mortal embrace, one fraught with a sense of suffocation, in which the iconic "vehicle" — here the bicycle and mobile — vanishes, ushering in a loss desired by a higher, evil will, that of a demiurgic materiality responsible for all transformations. The *Unholy Ghosts*, 1993 (pl. 187), likewise play on the tension between the fullness of the human figure and the molecular chaos of the suspended assemblages. Here the small glassy bodies, scattered about a cohesive space, constitute limbs and fleshly tissue. Translating into a beautiful fabric devoid of aggressiveness and laceration, they are regenerative, so much so that they become dazzling to behold: white, petrified figures. The fusion is positive here, and thus the itinerary of molecularity is one of continual ascent. The theme of the unconscious depths — connected to the discharges of objects — returns again, this time transformed into an artificial, resounding flow of blood, images, and materials.

What Cragg has discovered here is the mechanism of an existence situated between human beings and objects, which are not antagonistic polarities but examples of coexistence. They may at times come to lacerate or aggress one another, as in *Angels and Other Antibodies*, 1992 (pl. 178); at other times they converse and merge, as

Messages, 1993

Flock, 1995

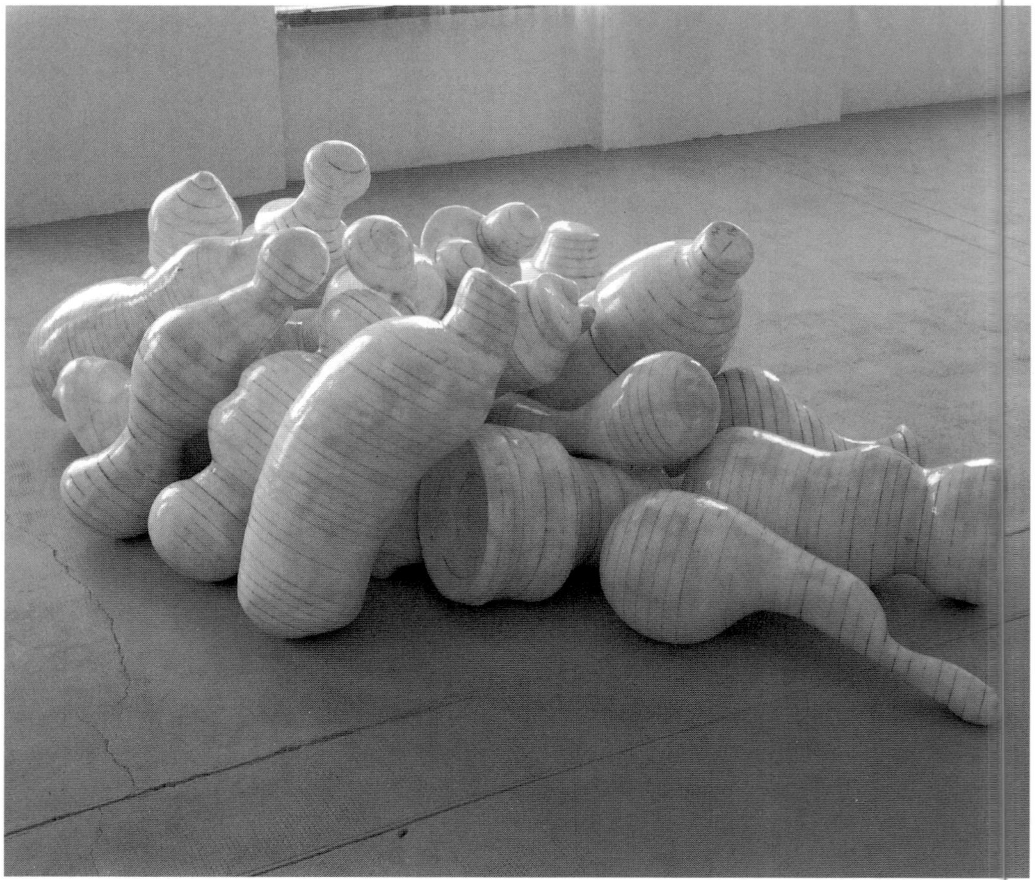

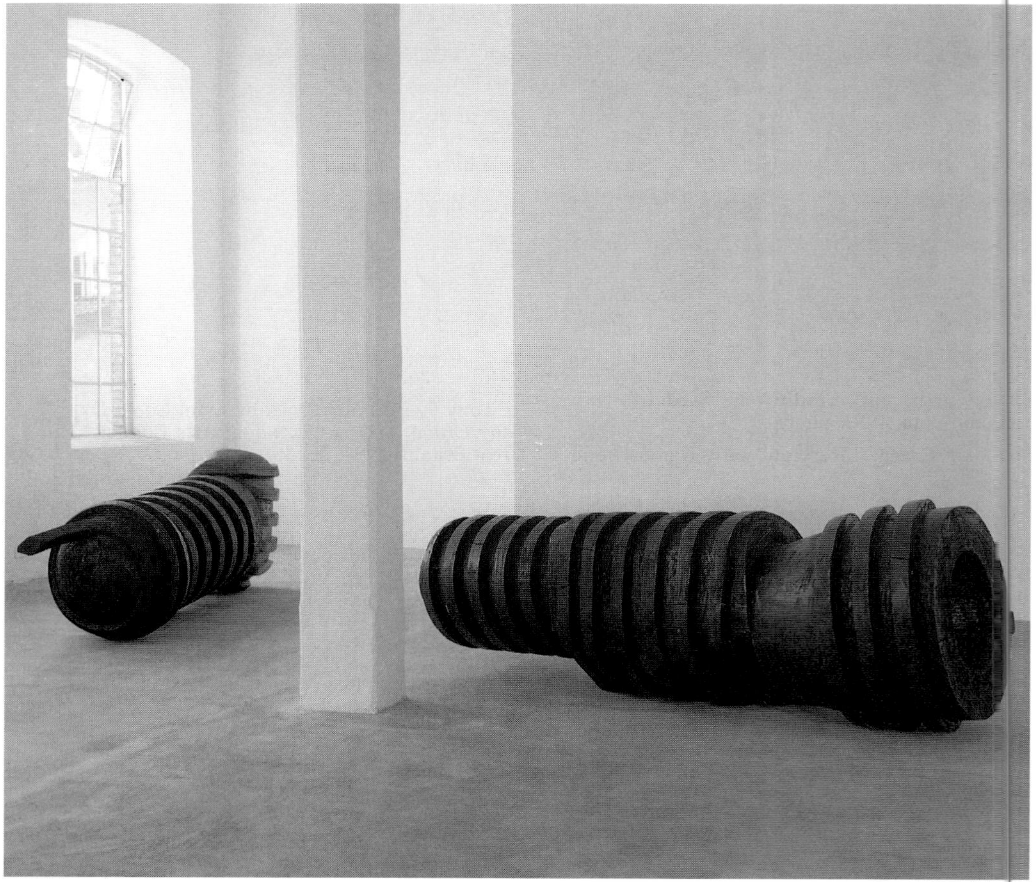

in *Island*, 1993 (pl. 183). At times the encounter becomes a kind of dramatic ceremony — as in *Wildlife*, 1995 (pl. 190) — in which animal and anthropomorphic images magnetically enter into a dreamlike, ecstatic dialogue with the object.
The title of *Wildlife* further underscores the fermentation underlying creation — the double principle, the violent, swirling element that unleashes an unstoppable subterranean energy. Cragg succeeds in capturing this energy, building it on a balance of opposites so that the surreal may enter everyday life and organic and dynamic life may yield to the stasis and immobility of the object. The final goal is to create a whole that is at once a revelation and a transfiguration.
In this sense, the language of Cragg's most recent work attests to the asphyxiation of sculpture: it is the space of passion, where the object does not shun organic and erotic discourse. It expresses itself as a body in the larval state, capable of growing and expanding, arriving at the ultimate experience. This is why the artist subjects things to a fierce process of alteration, reviving the spasm of their feline corporeality. The object is an entity without organs, but also the active pole of a mingling and subdivision that breaks down the perfect, passive body of sculpture. Cragg makes it proliferate through the sandwiching and entanglement of bodies, in an attempt to find liberating alternatives: "We talk about freedom but there is very little freedom. Freedom is becoming less and less and what freedom we do have is basically between our ears. To improve the quality of what's between our ears, and I mean quality and not just quantity, one can make an erotic response to the external world. In one's erotic appreciation of the material world, or one's poetic appreciation, there is obviously something which is expressive as well."[12]

[1] Mario Trevi, Augusto Romano. *Studi sull'ombra*. Venice: Marsilio, 1975.

[2] Tony Cragg. In *Carnegie International*, exh. cat. Pittsburgh: 1991.

[3] R. Gilbert-Lecomte. "L'horrible révélation ... la seule," 1930. In *Le Grand Jeu*. Milan: Adelphi, 1967, p. 236.

[4] Tony Cragg. In *Documenta*, exh. cat. Kassel: 1982, p. 340.

[5] Mark Francis. "Full Circle: Tony Cragg's Work, 1977-1981." In *Tony Cragg*, exh. cat. Newport: Newport Harbor Art Museum, 1990, p. 42.

[6] David Batchelor. "Liquid Containers," in *Tony Cragg*, exh. cat. Eindhoven: Stedelijk van Abbemuseum, 1991, pp. 6-10.

[7] "Tony Cragg. Interview with Demosthène Davvetas," in *Tony Cragg*, exh. cat. Brussels: Palais des Beaux-Arts, 1985, p. 34.

[8] Tony Cragg. In *Tony Cragg*, exh. cat. Newport: Newport Harbor Art Museum, 1990, p. 110.

[9] "Tony Cragg Interviewed by Lynn Cooke." In *Tony Cragg*, exh. cat. London: Arts Council of Great Britain, 1987, p. 20.

[10] Alberto Boatto. *Lo Sguardo dal di fuori*. Bologna: Cappelli, 1981, p. 8.

[11] Heinz-Norbert Jocks. "Tony Cragg: 'Dieses Kleinzeug wirkt dann wie ein Angenfang, vergleichbar den Warzen auf der Haut'." *Kunstforum*, no. 122, 1993, p. 369.

[12] "Tony Cragg Interviewed by Lynn Cooke." In *Tony Cragg*, exh. cat. London: Arts Council of Great Britain, 1987, p. 14.

Plates

1. *Untitled*, 1971

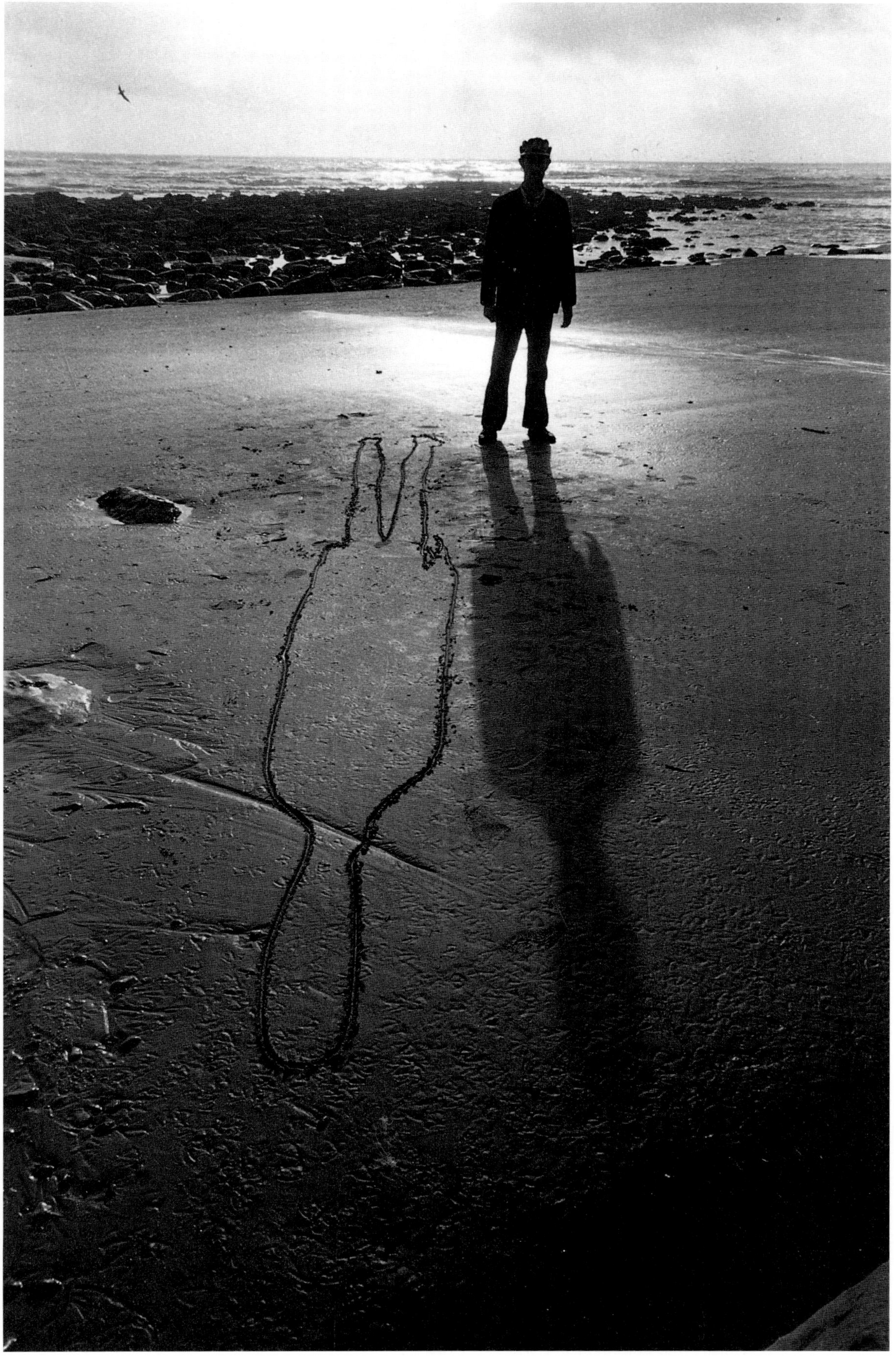

2. *Untitled*, 1972

3. *Untitled*, 1973

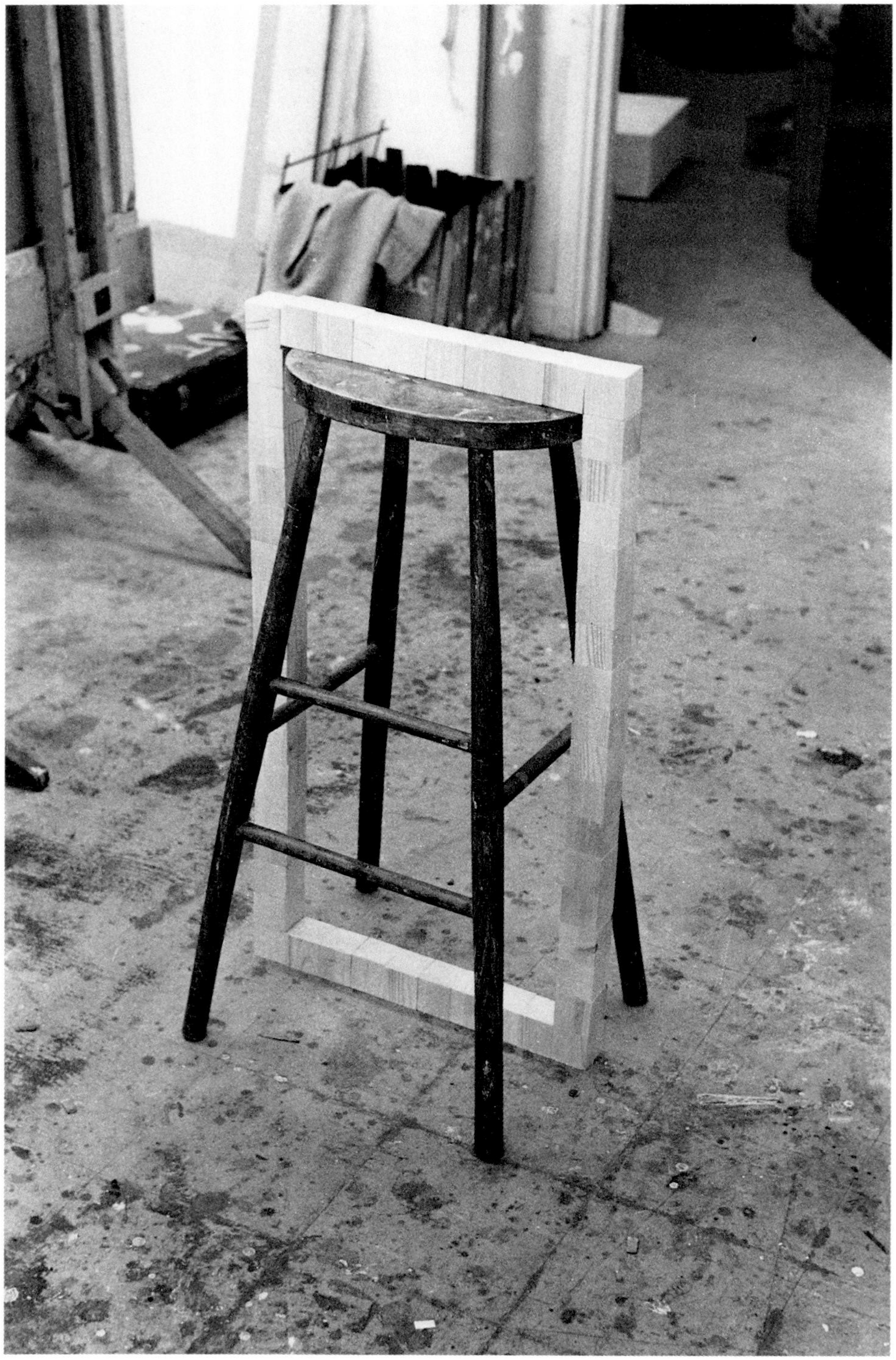

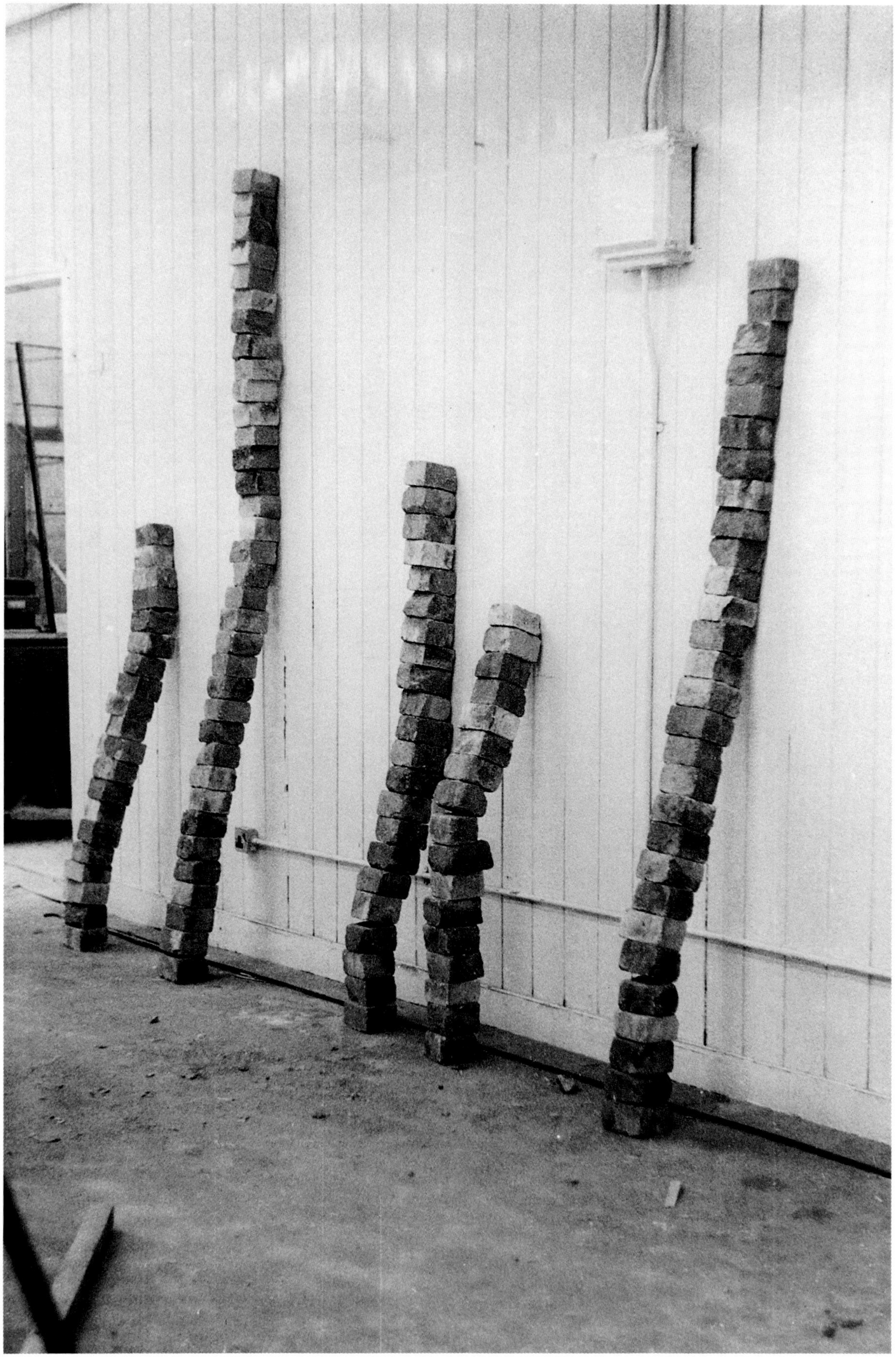

4. *Untitled*, 1974

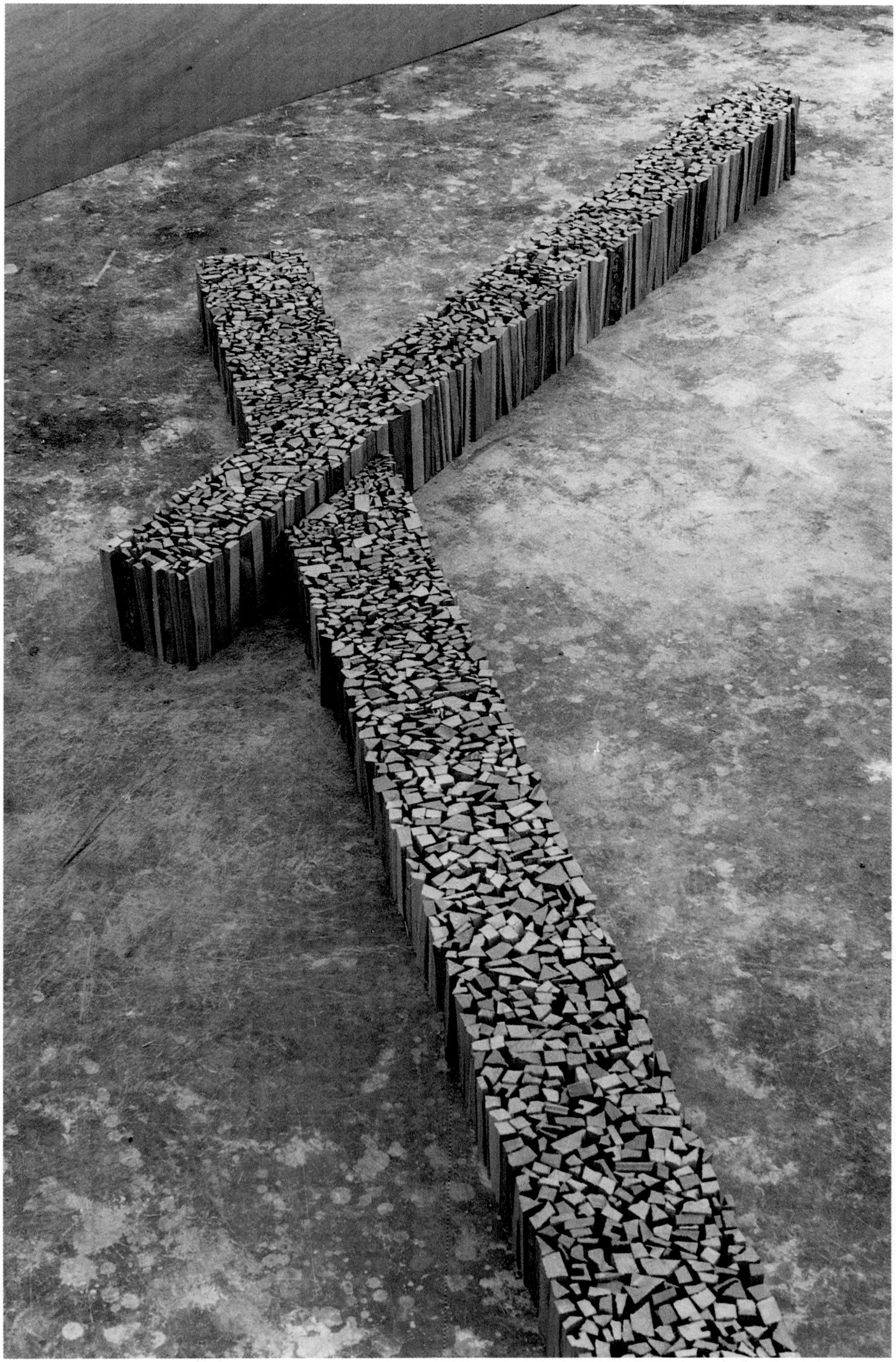

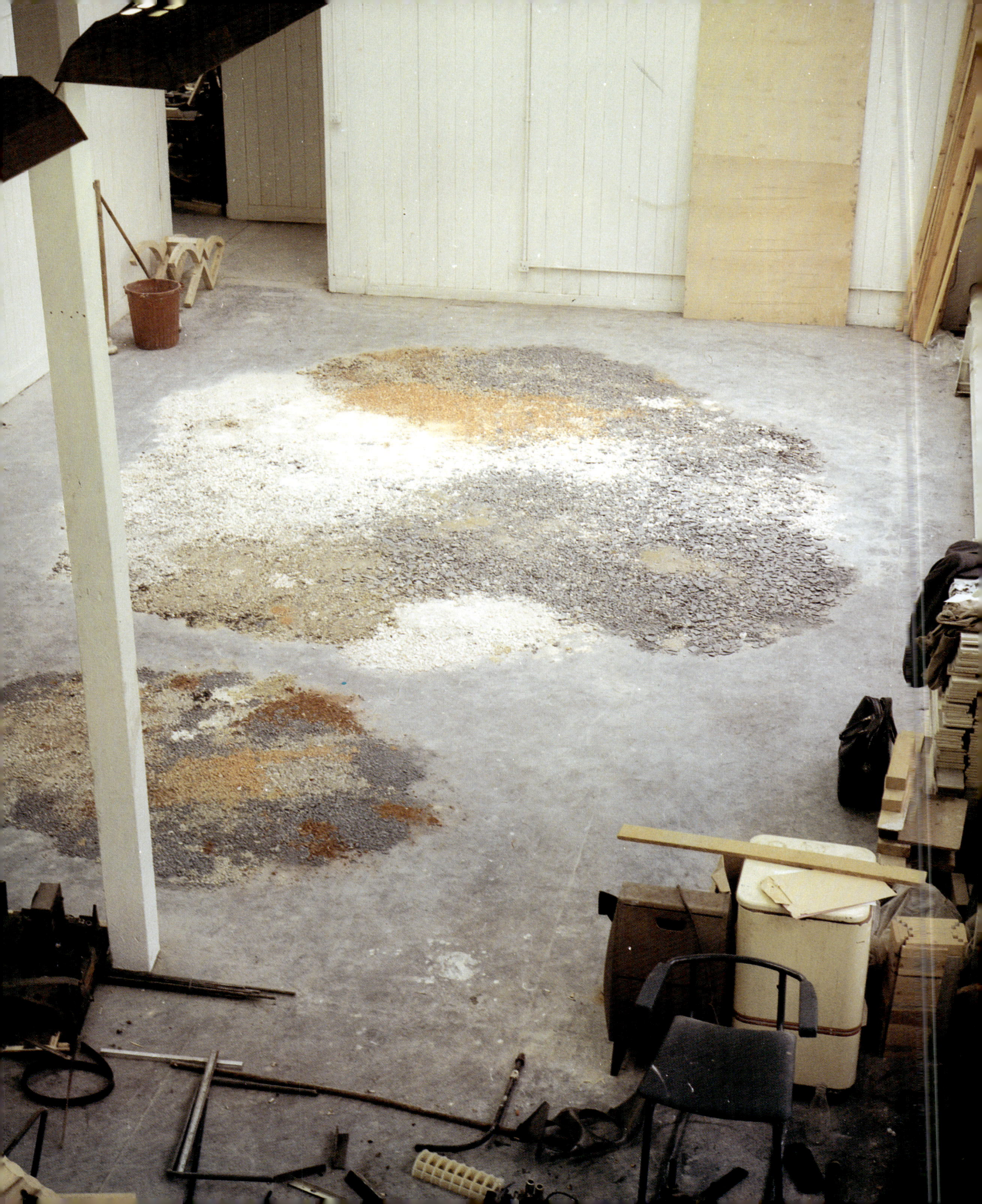

5. *Untitled*, 1975

6. *Stack*, 1976

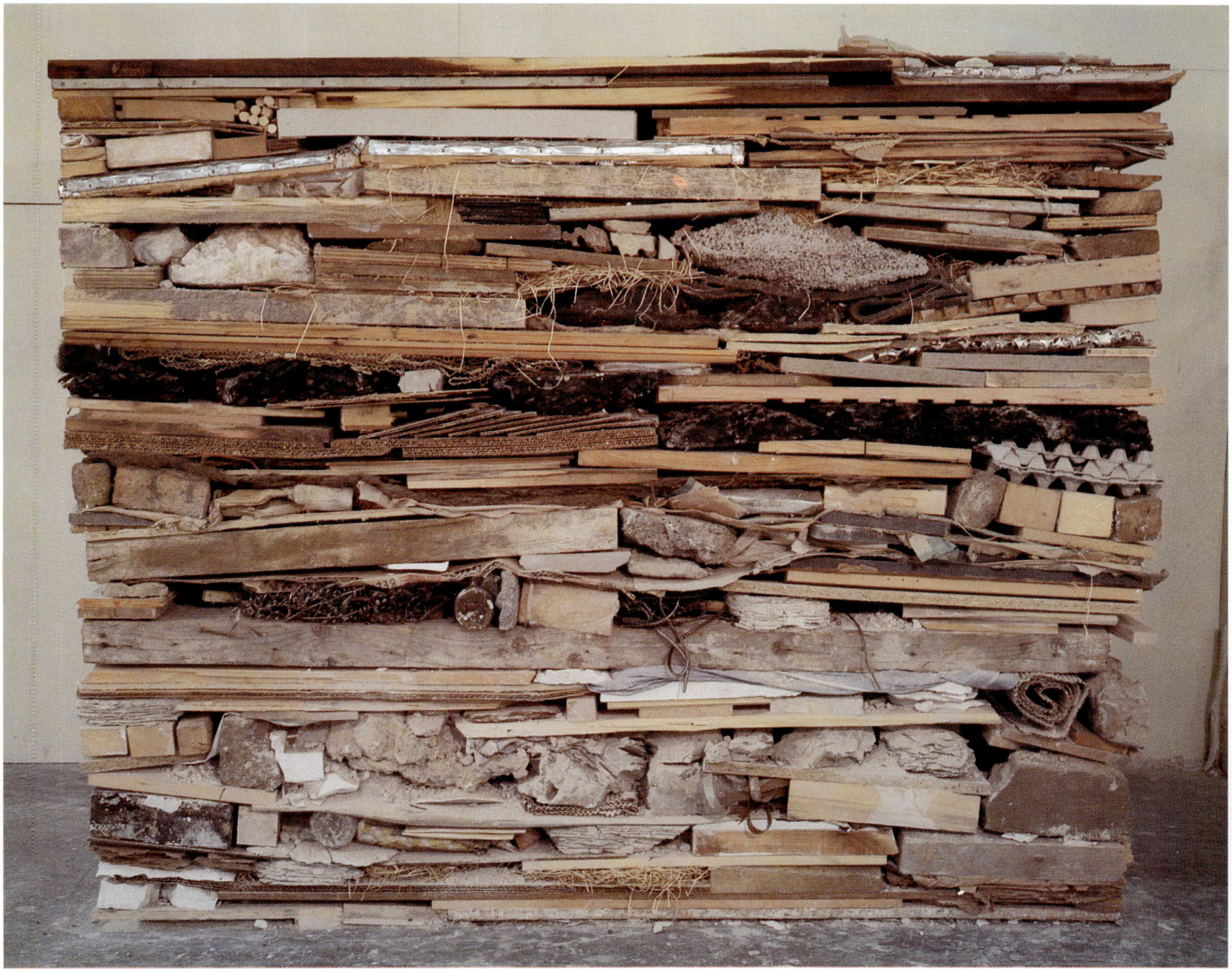

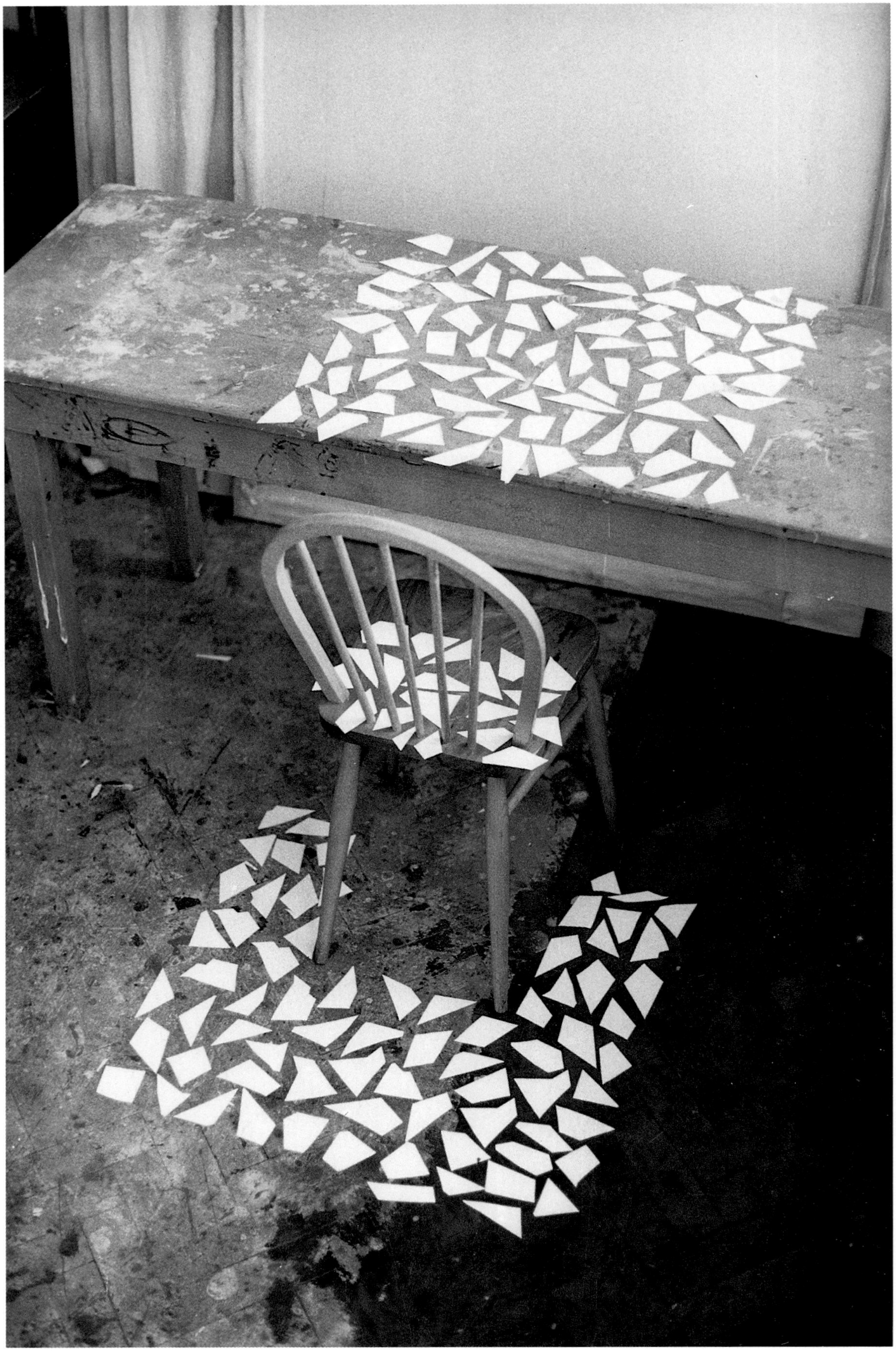

7. *Untitled*, 1977

8. *New Stones-Newton's Tones*, 1978

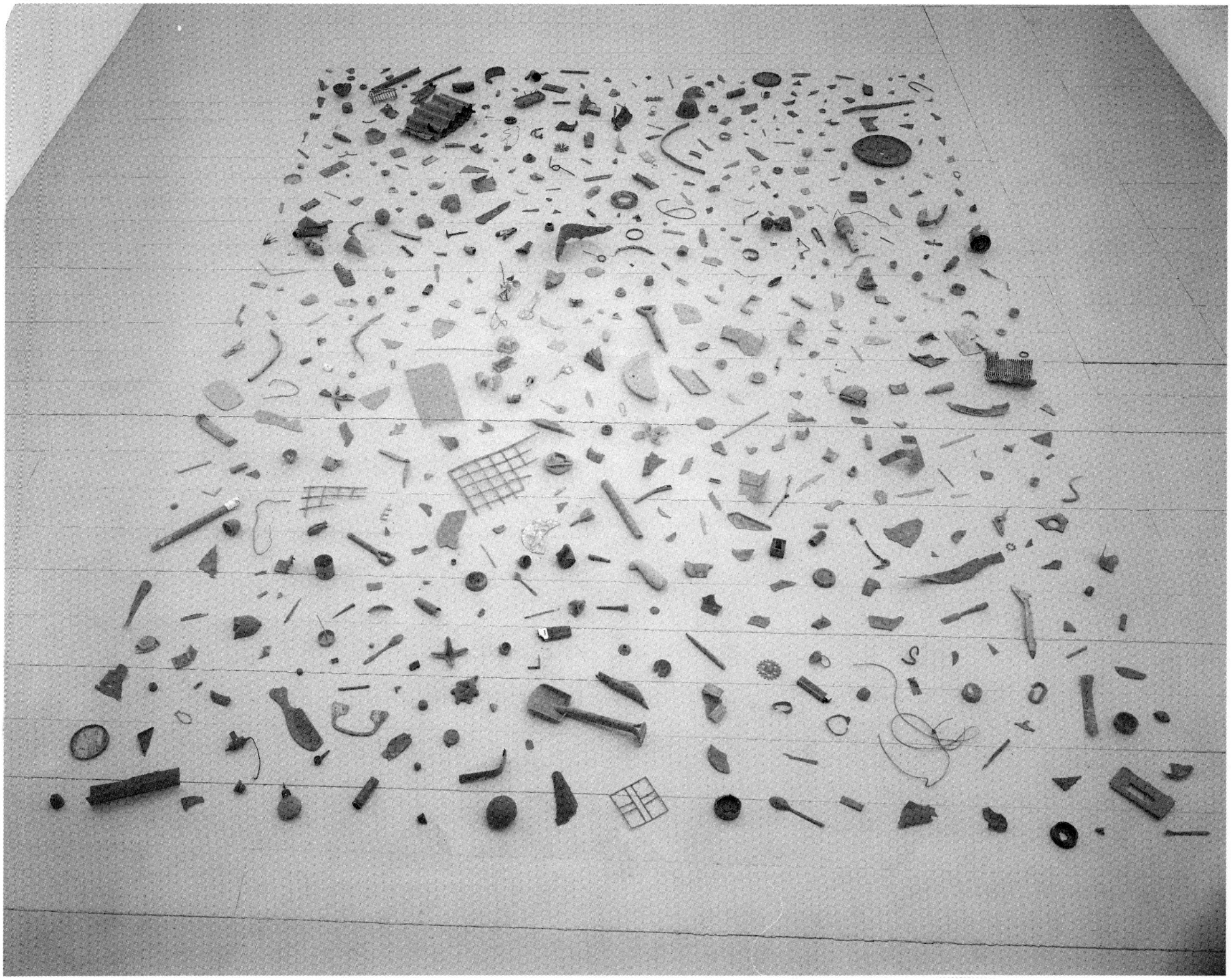

9. *Spectrum*, 1979

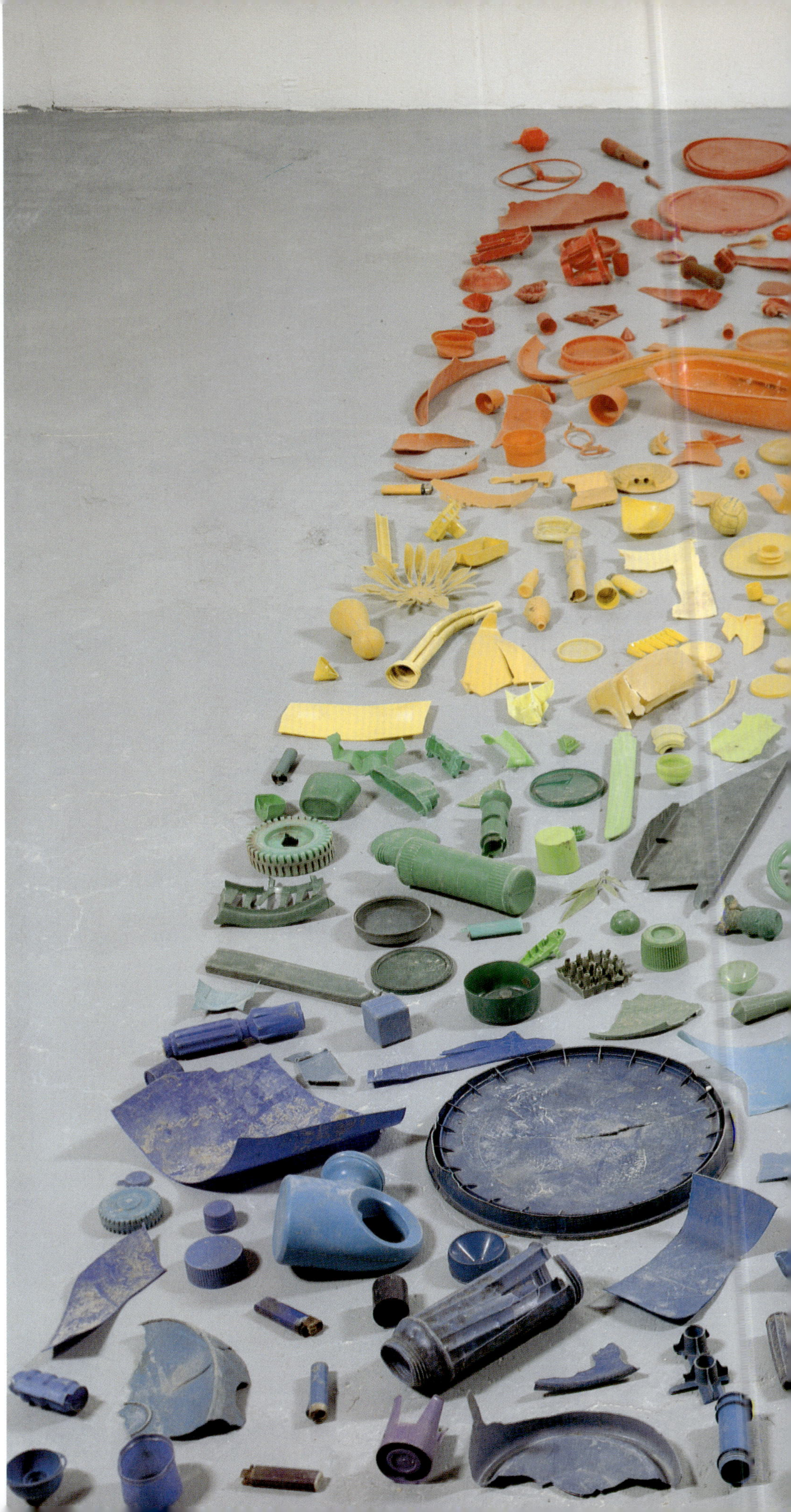

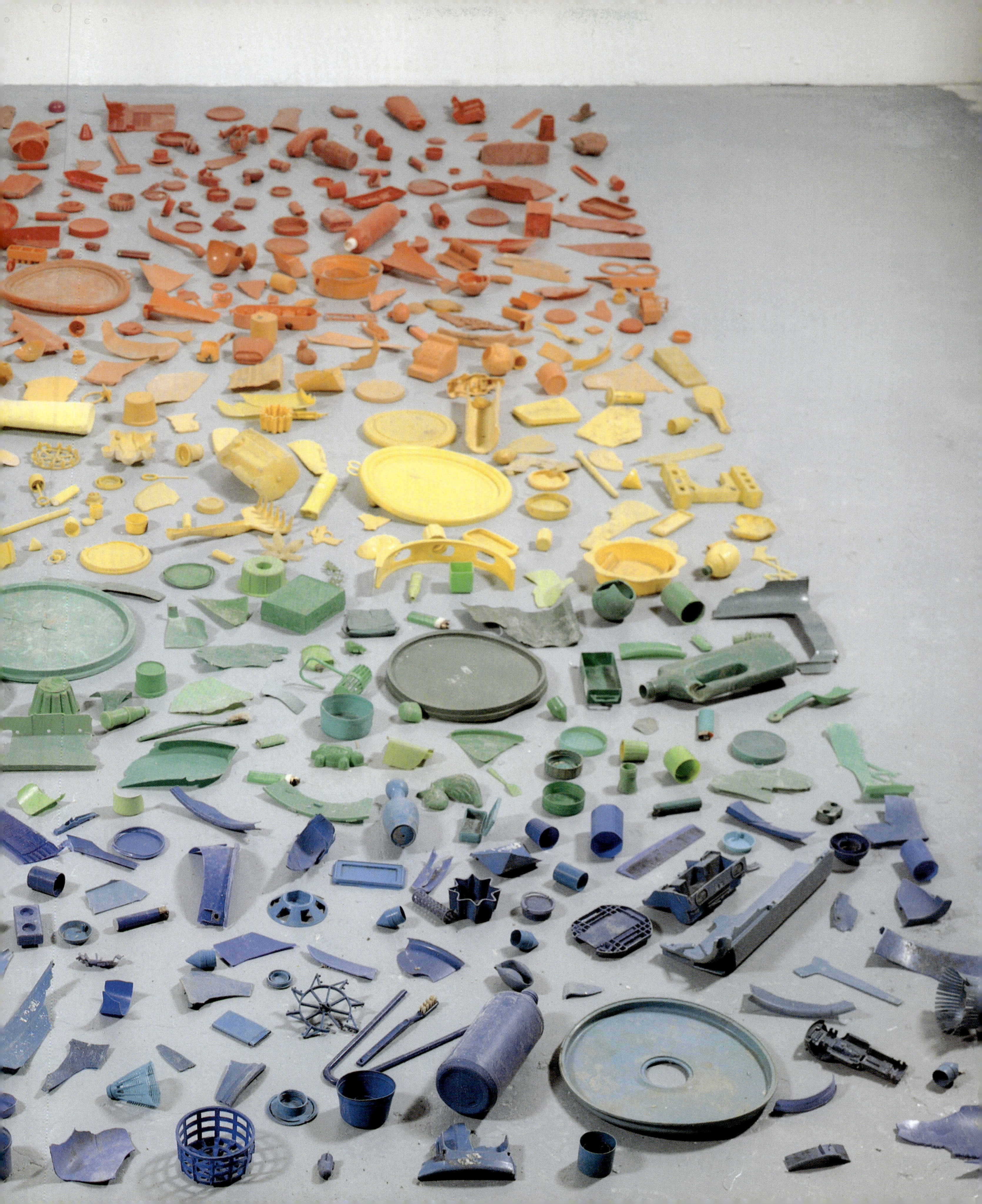

10. *Self-Portrait with Sack*, 1980

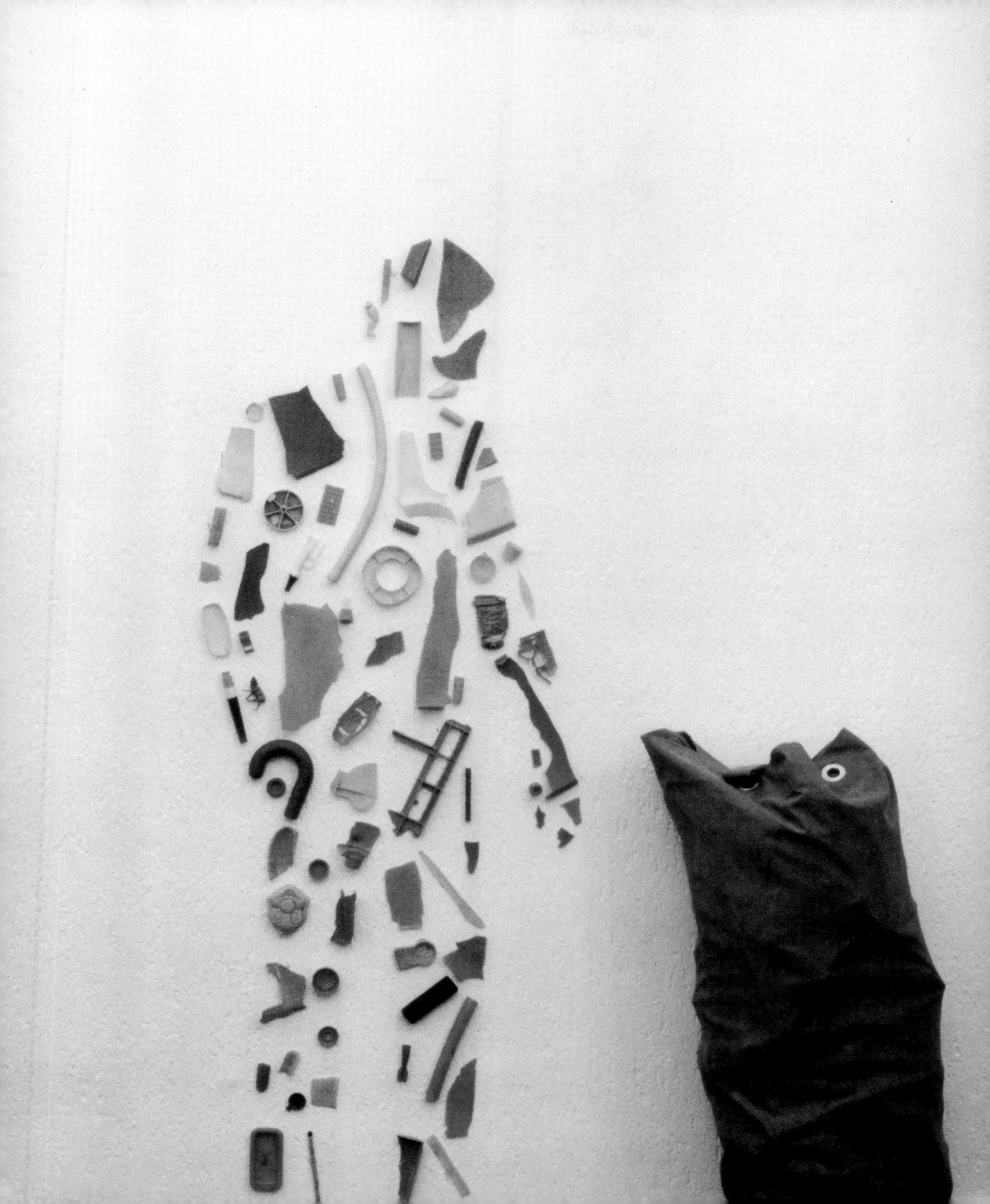

I am not interested in romanticizing an epoch in the distant past when technology permitted men to make only few objects, tools etc. But, in contrast to today I assume a materialistically simpler situation and a deeper understanding for the making processes, function and even metaphysical qualities of the objects they produced. The social organizations which have proved to be most successful are productive systems. The rate at which objects are produced increases; complementary to production is consumption. We consume, populating our environment with more and more objects, with no chance of understanding the making processes because we specialize, specialize in the production, but not in consumption.

First published in *Documenta 7*, exh. catalogue. Kassel: 1982, vol. 1, p. 340.

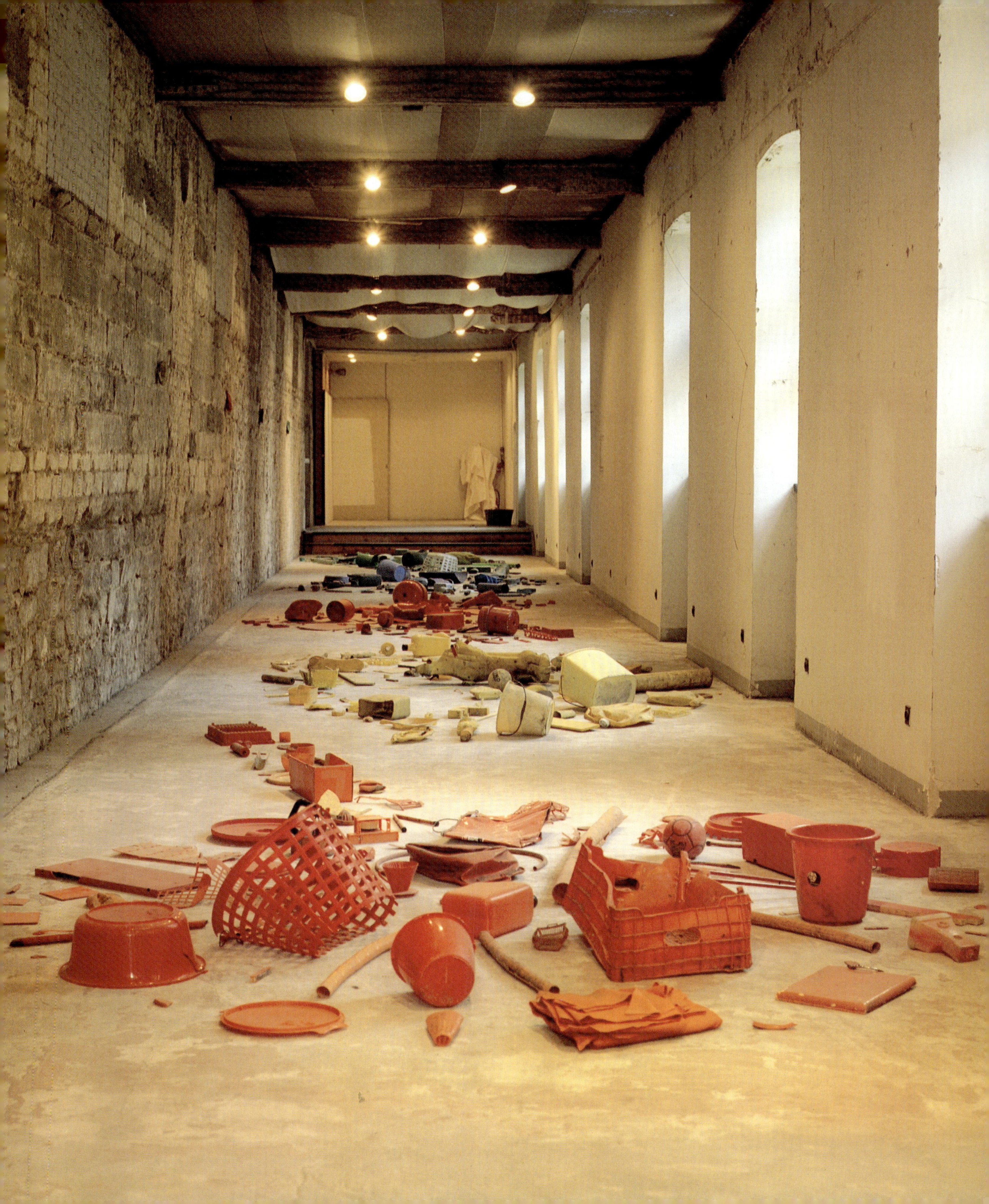

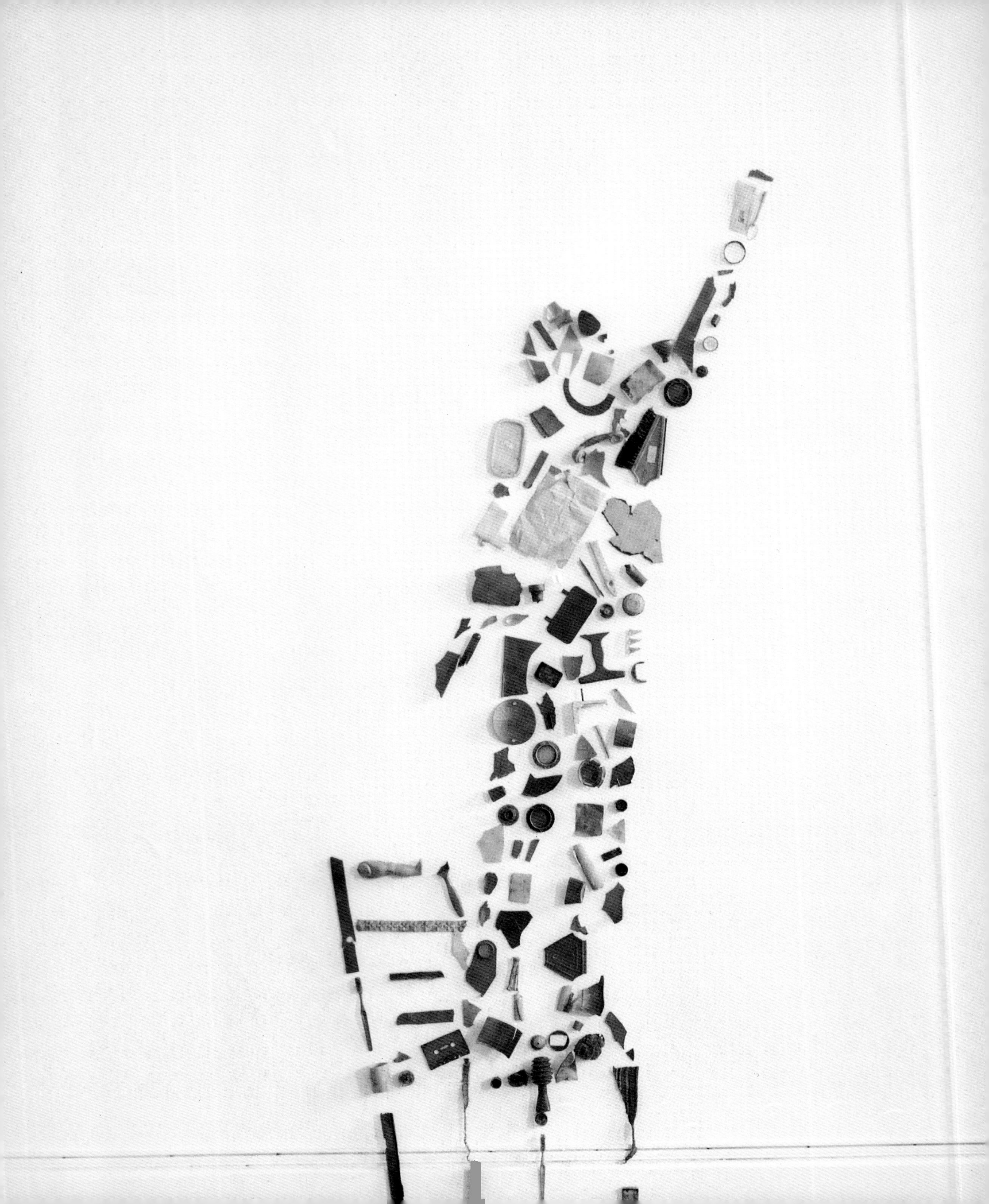

12. *Self-Portrait on Chair*, 1980 13. *Tree*, 1980

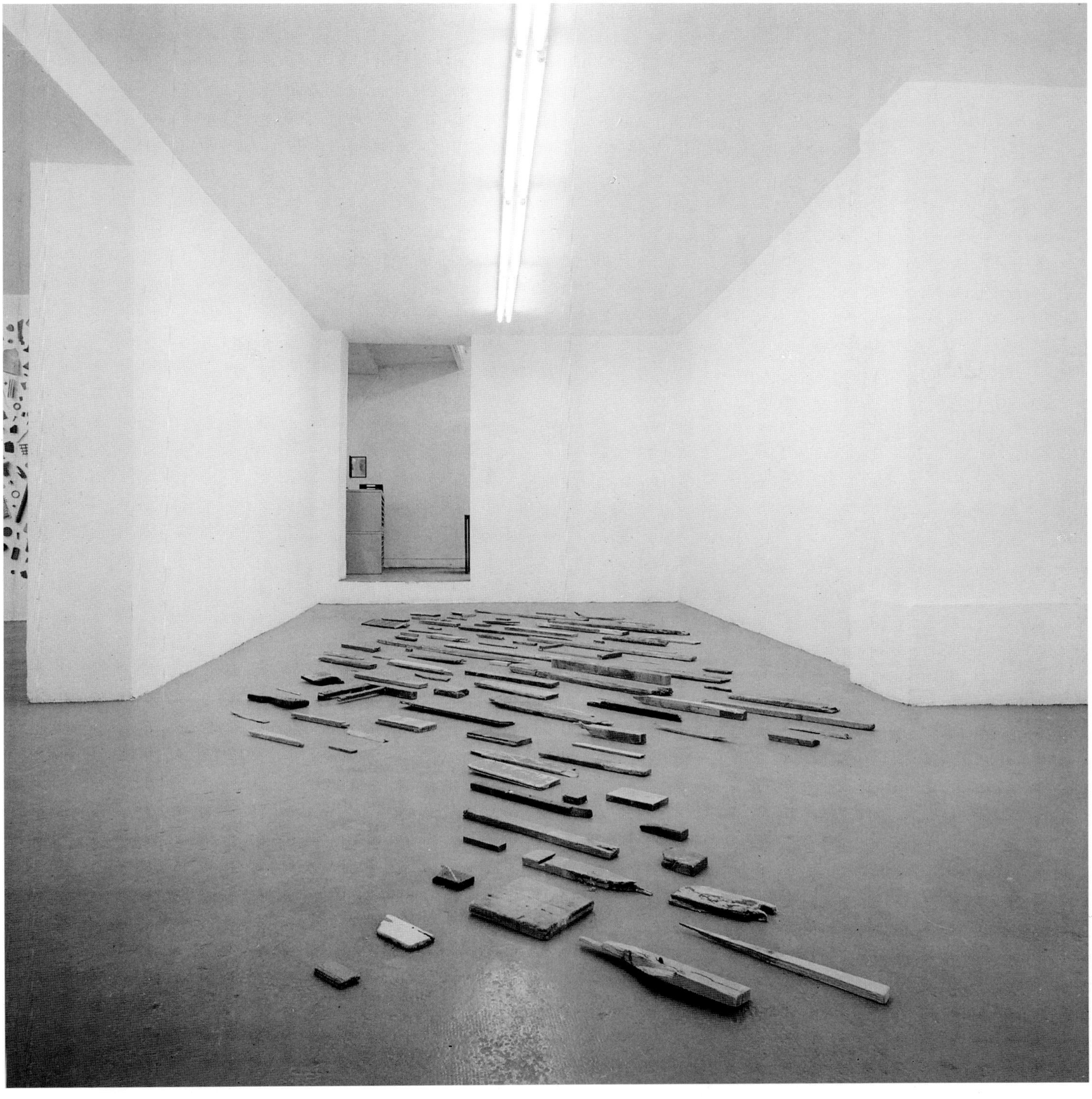

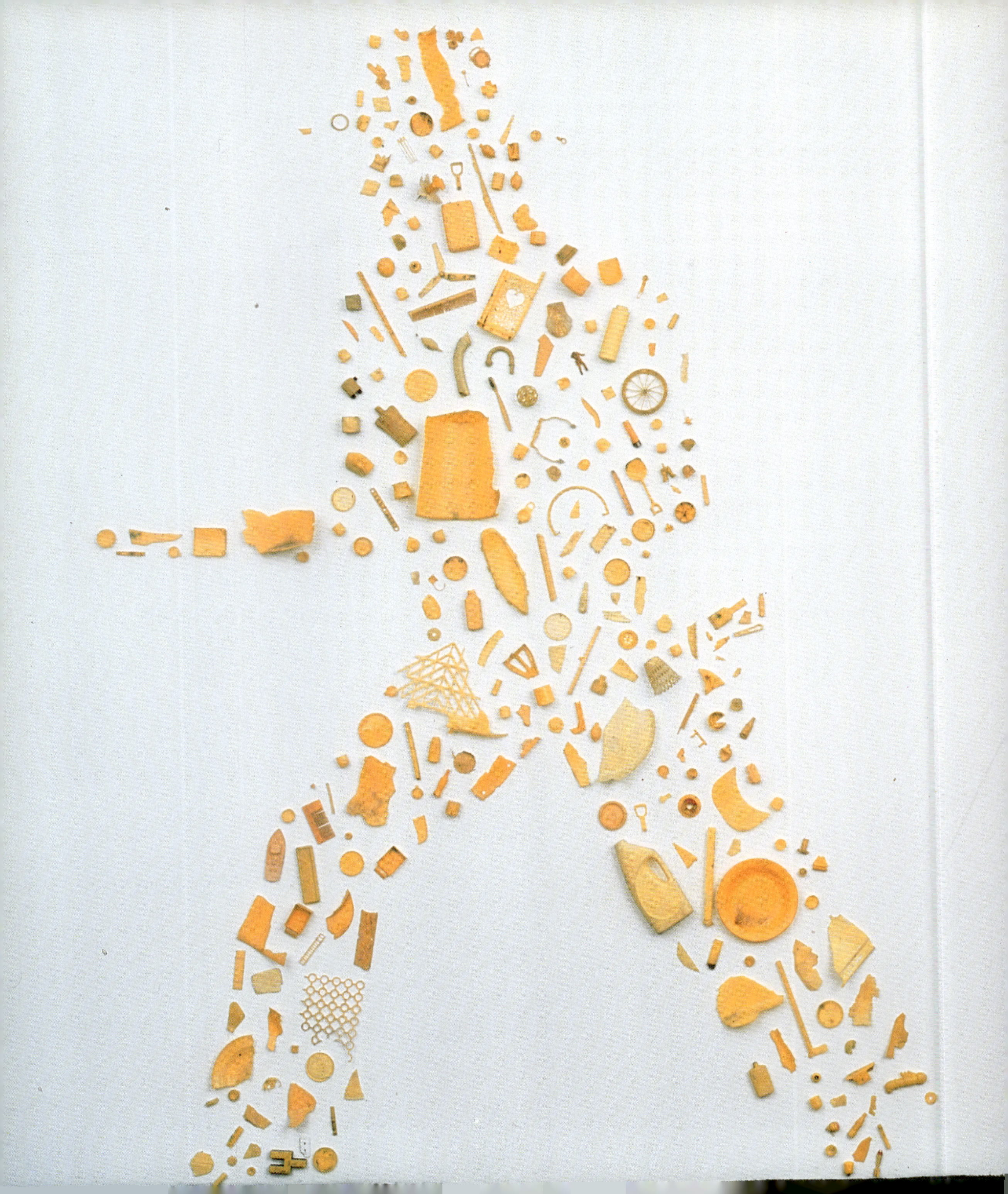

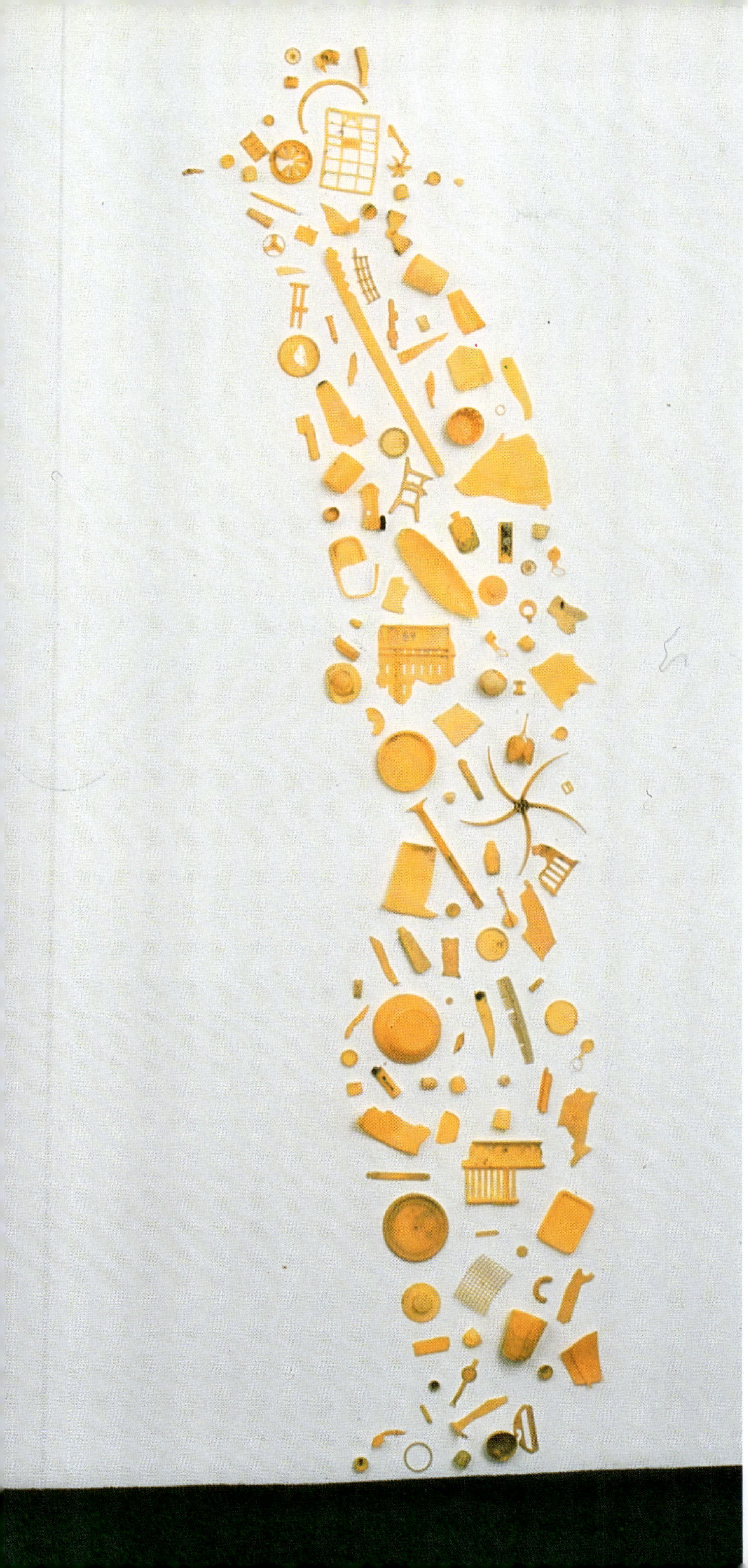

14. *The Street Are Full of Cowboys and Indians*, 1980

15. *Black and White Stack*, 1980

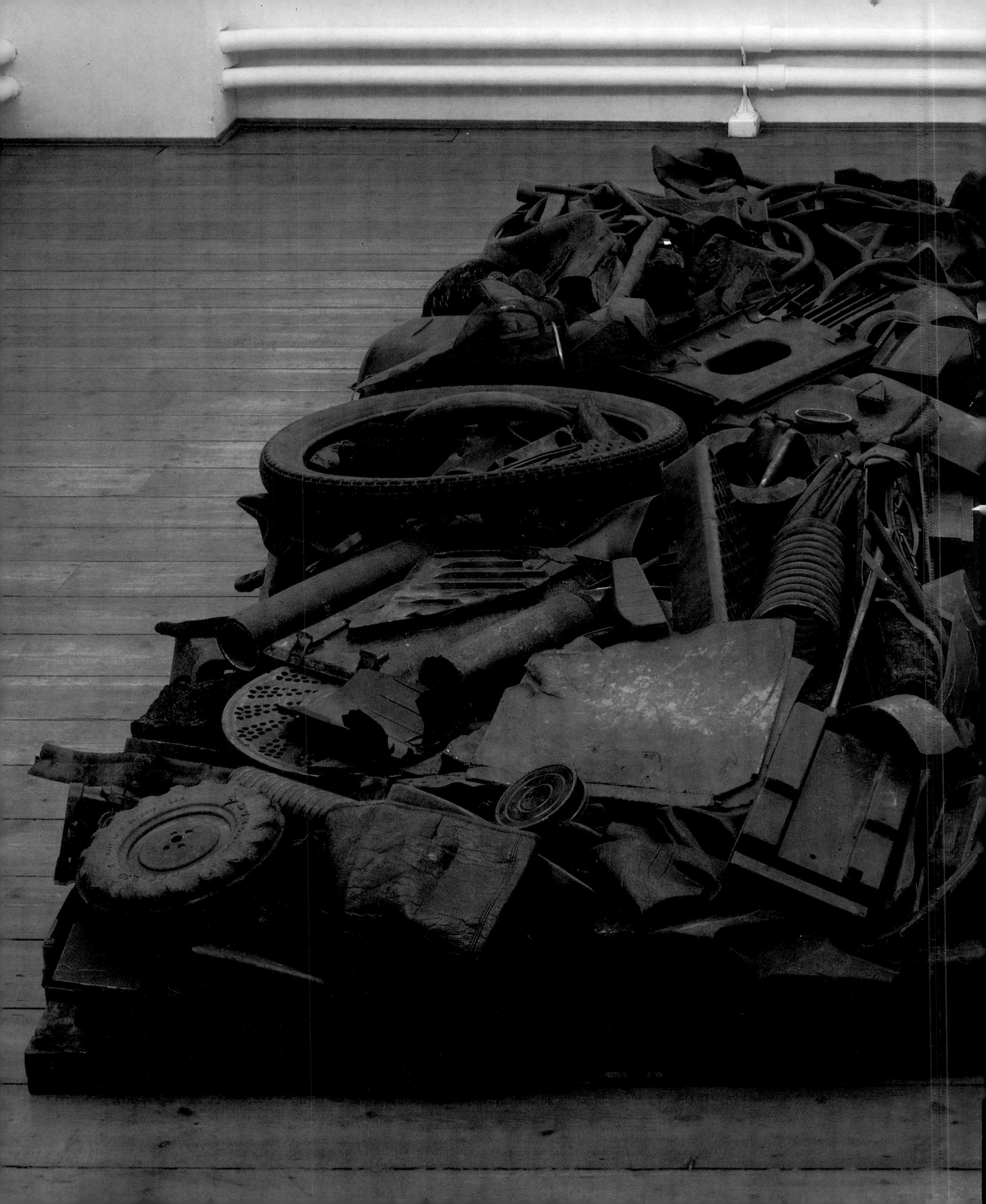

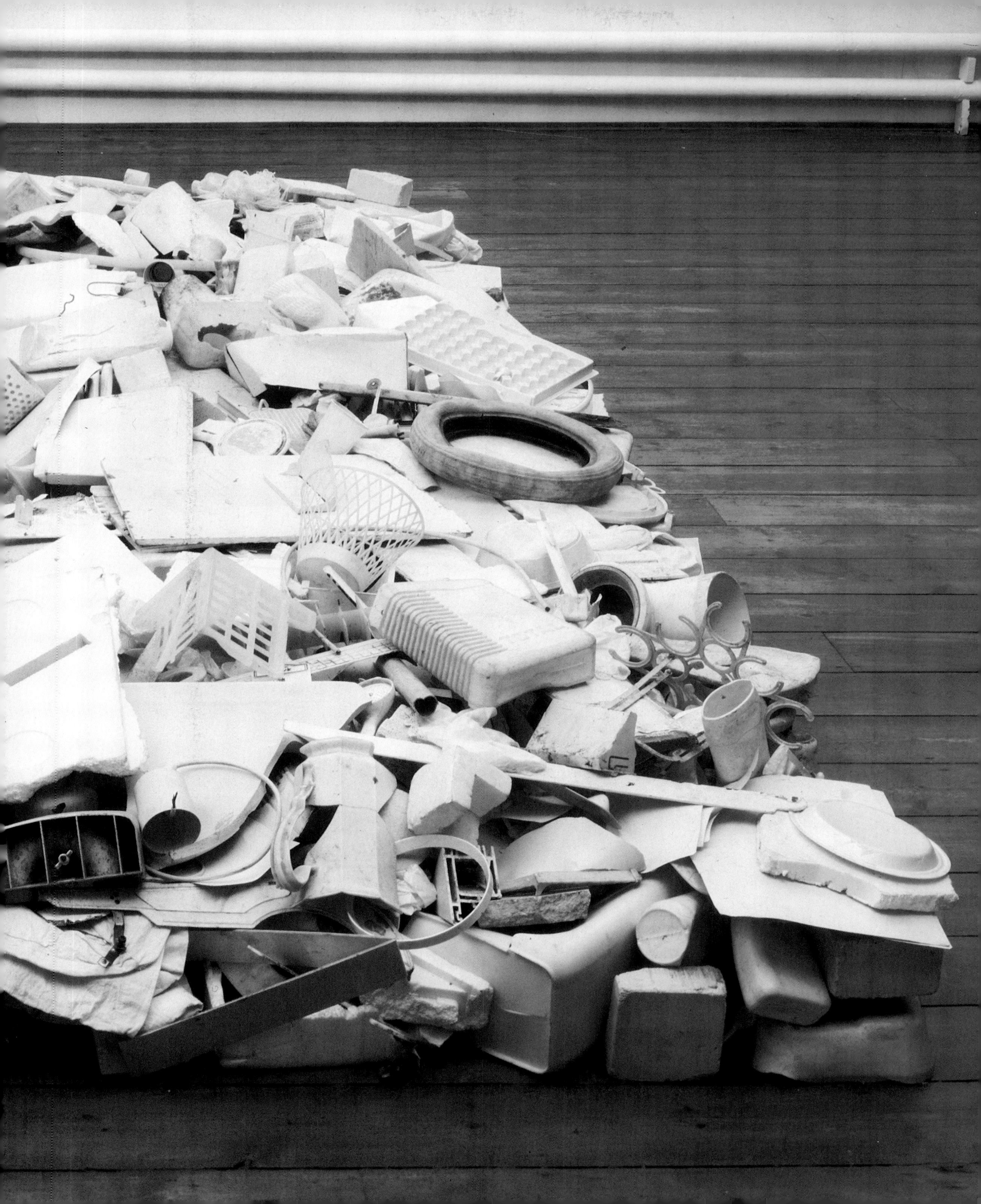

16. *Boat*, 1980

17. *Bird*, 1980

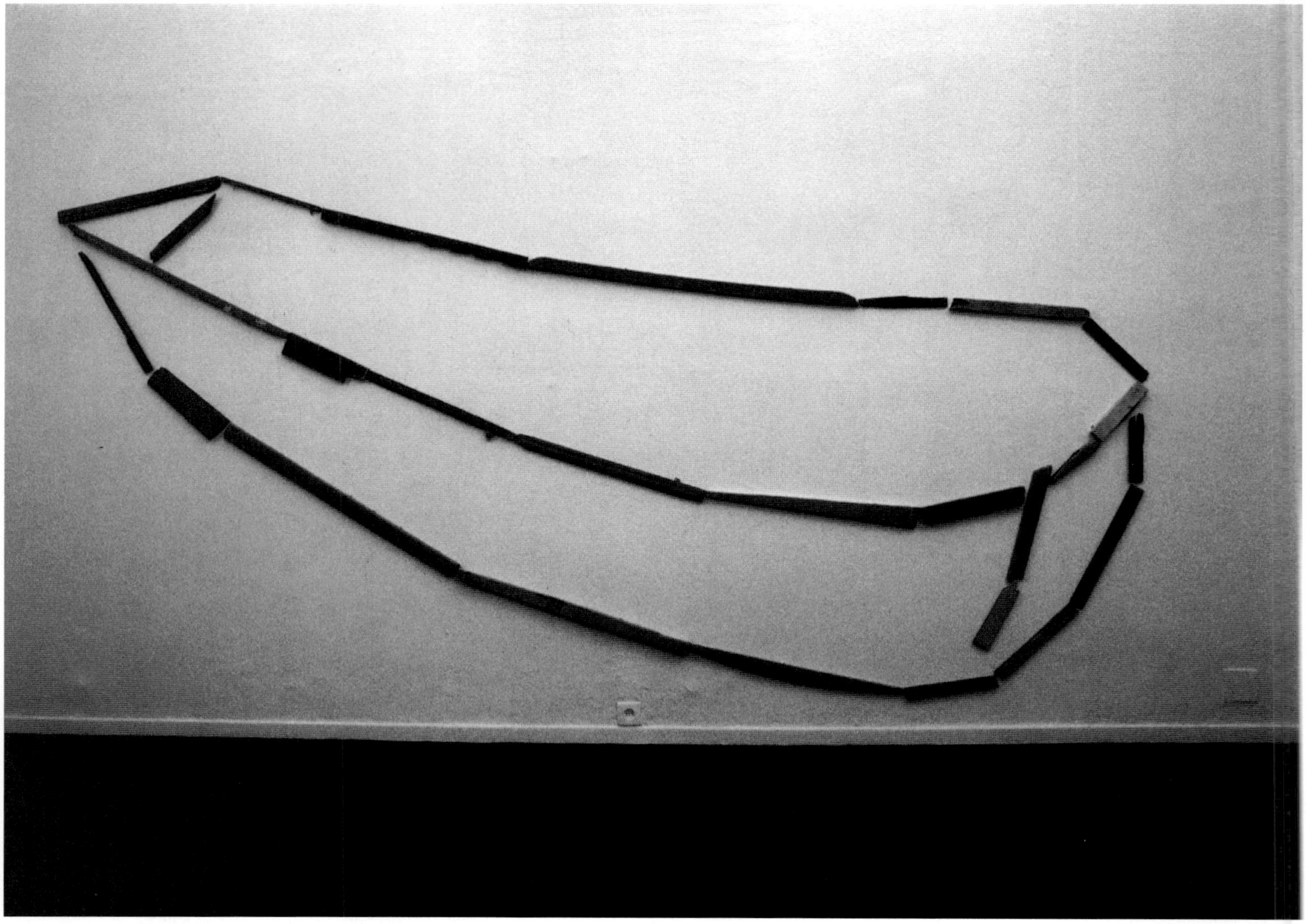

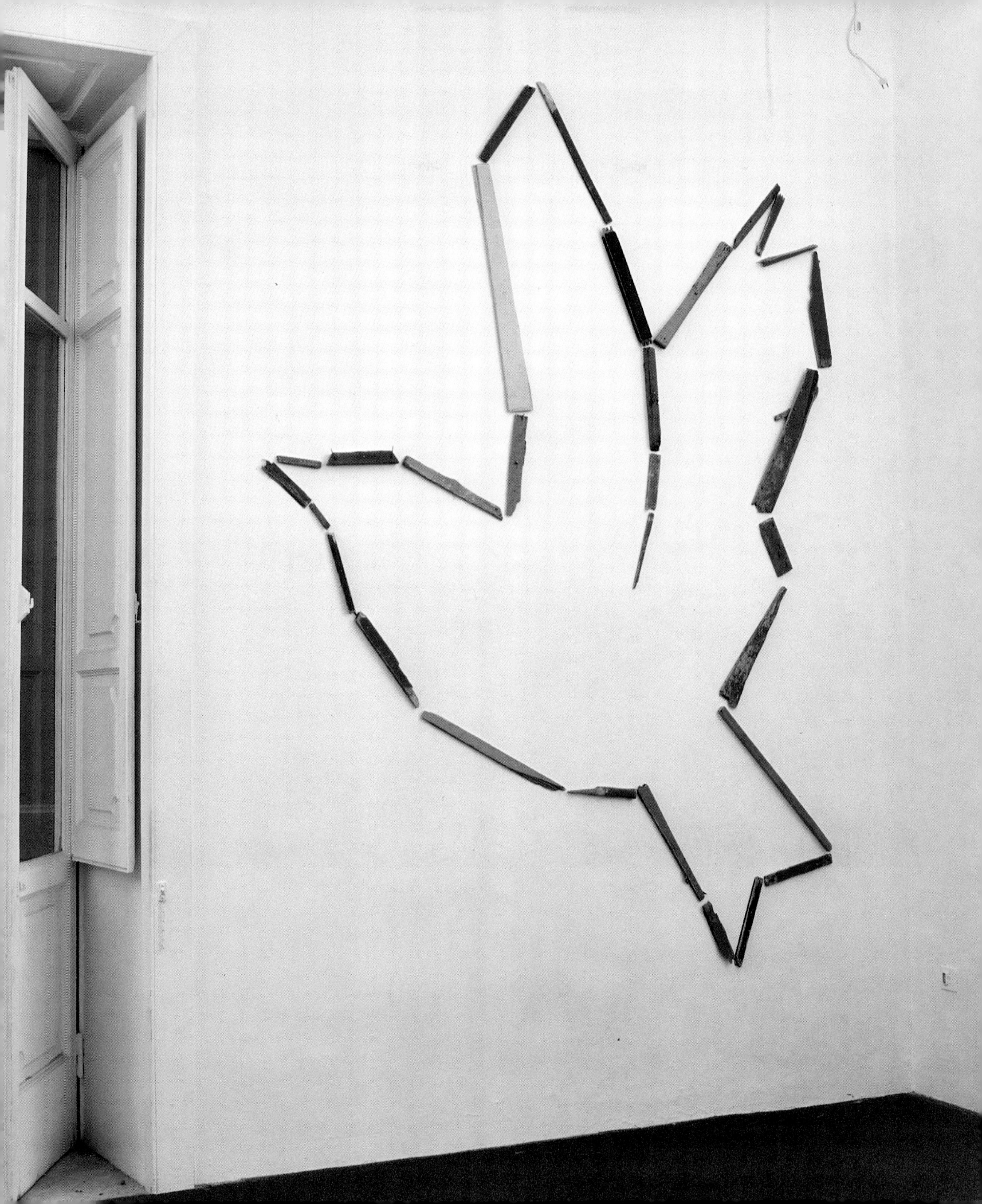

18. *Polaris*, 1981

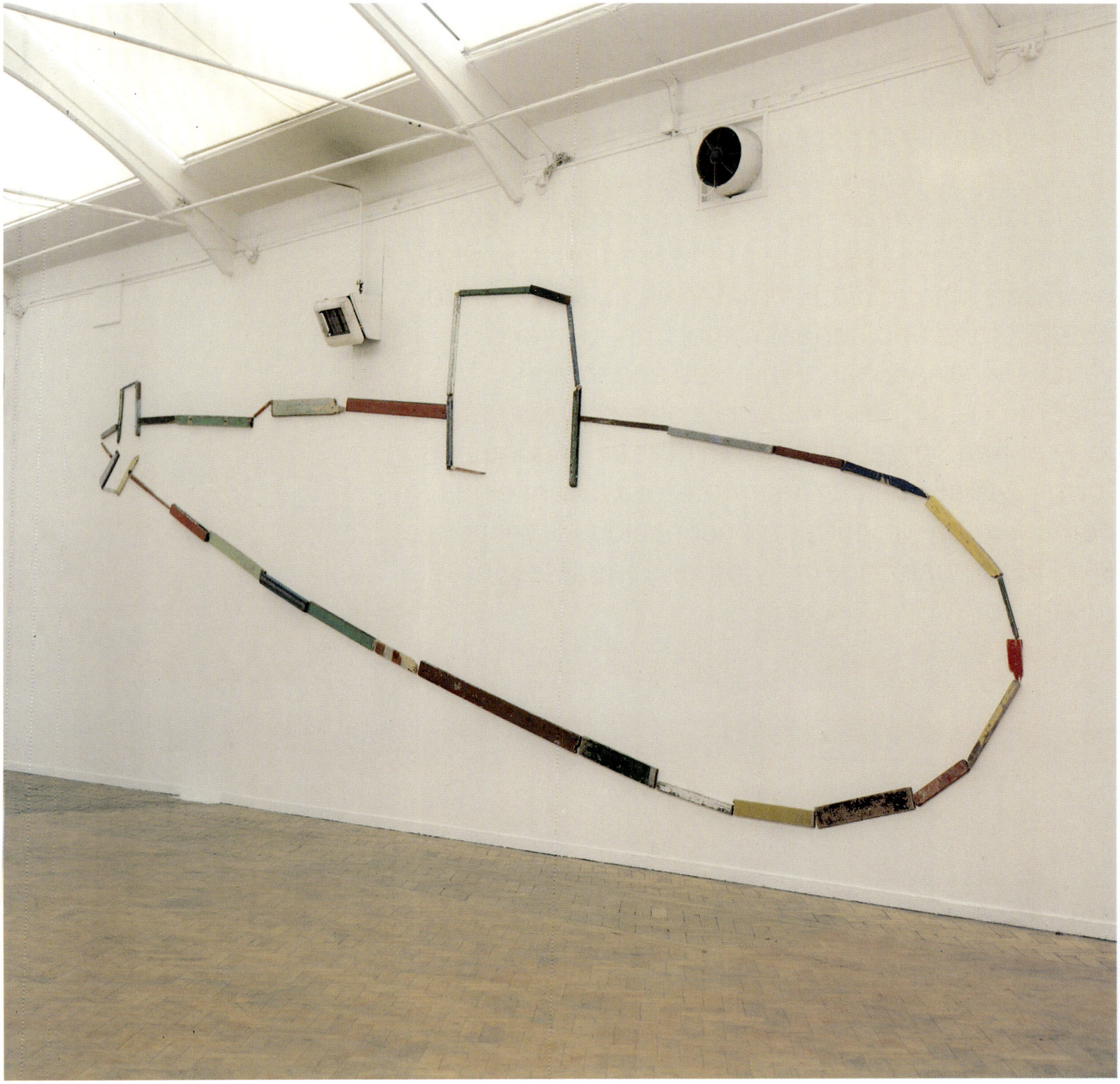

19. *Policeman*, 1981

The use of various materials, stone, bronze, iron etc. has been used as indications of technological development. Our use of materials goes as far as radioactive elements and biochemical substances of the most complex nature. Particularly exploitable have proved to be chemically stable polymers – plastics. Due to the long relationship between man and such materials as earth, water, wood, stone and certain metals, they evoke a rich variety of emotional responses and images. The experience of these materials alters, however, as they appear increasingly in synthetic, industrial forms. What does it mean to us on a conscious, or, perhaps more important, unconscious level to live amongst these and many other completely new materials?

First published in *Documenta 7*, exh. catalogue. Kassel: 1982, vol. 1, p. 340.

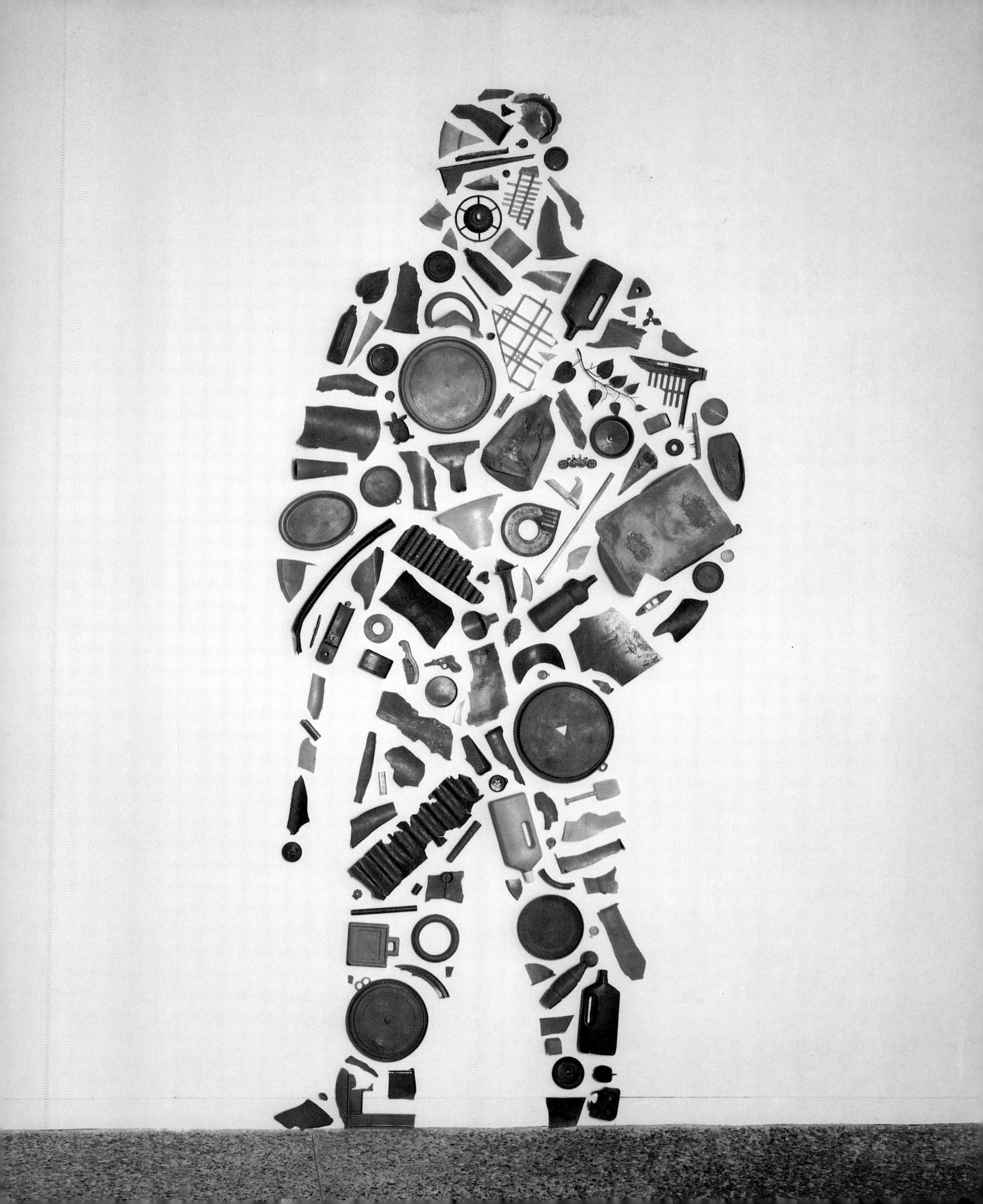

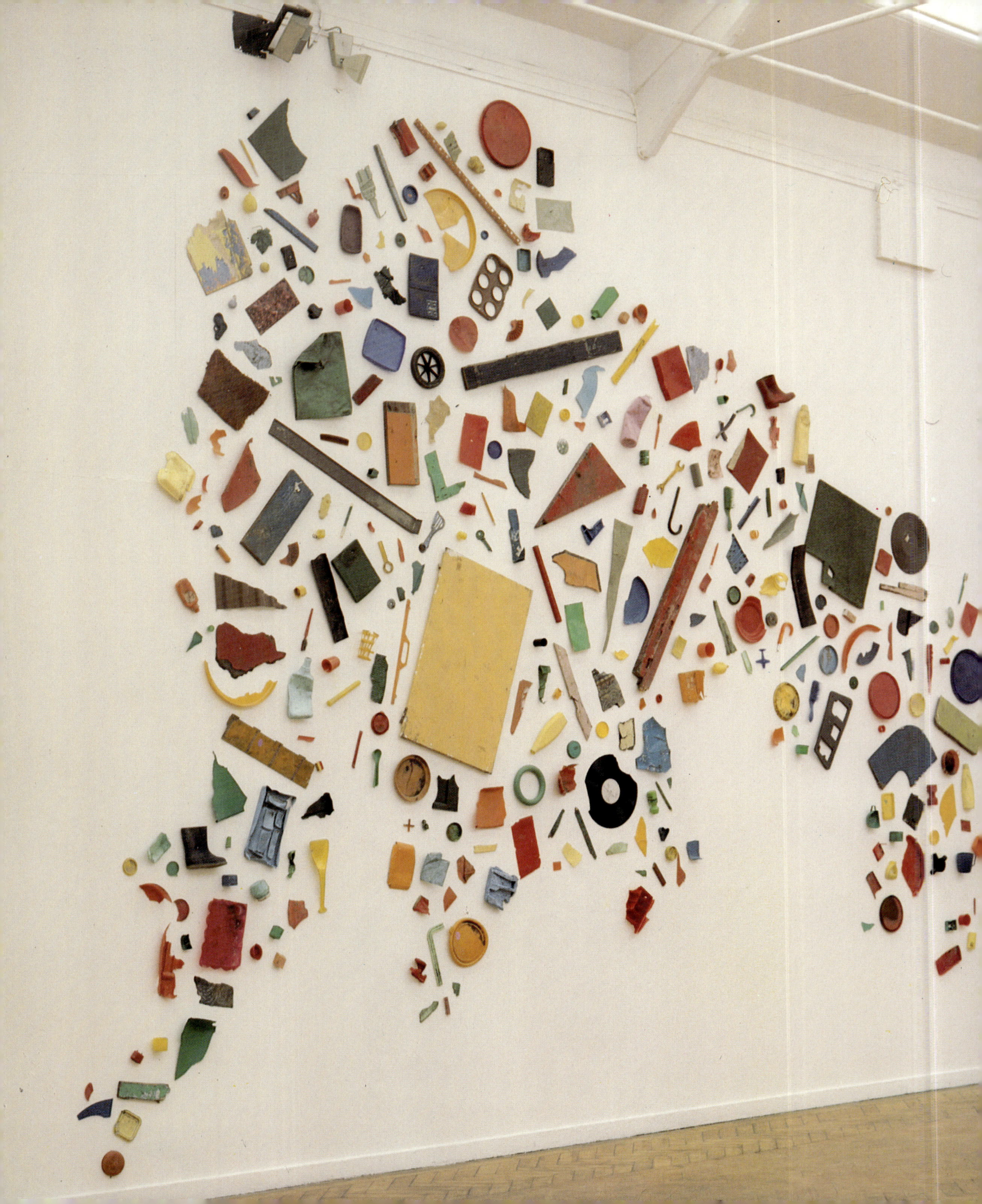

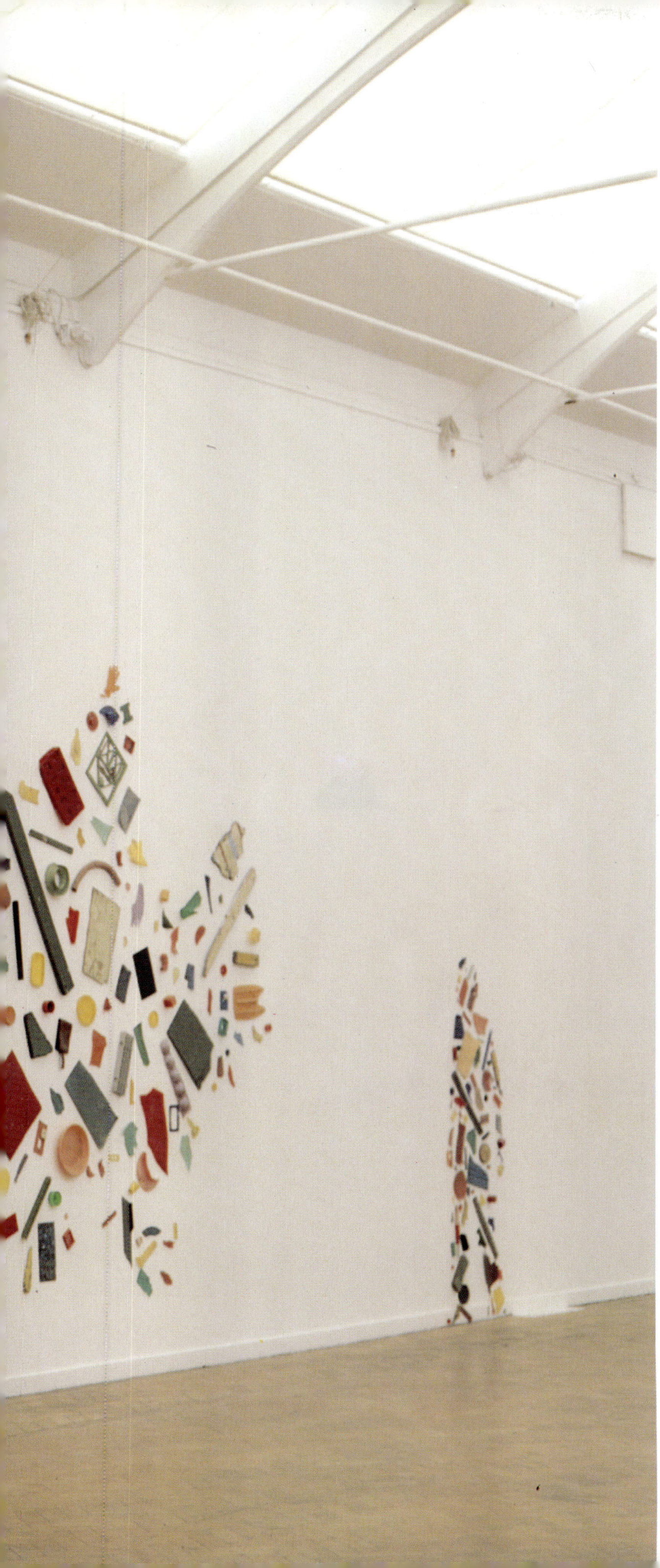

20. *Britain Seen from the North*, 1981

21. *Factory Fantasies I*, 1981

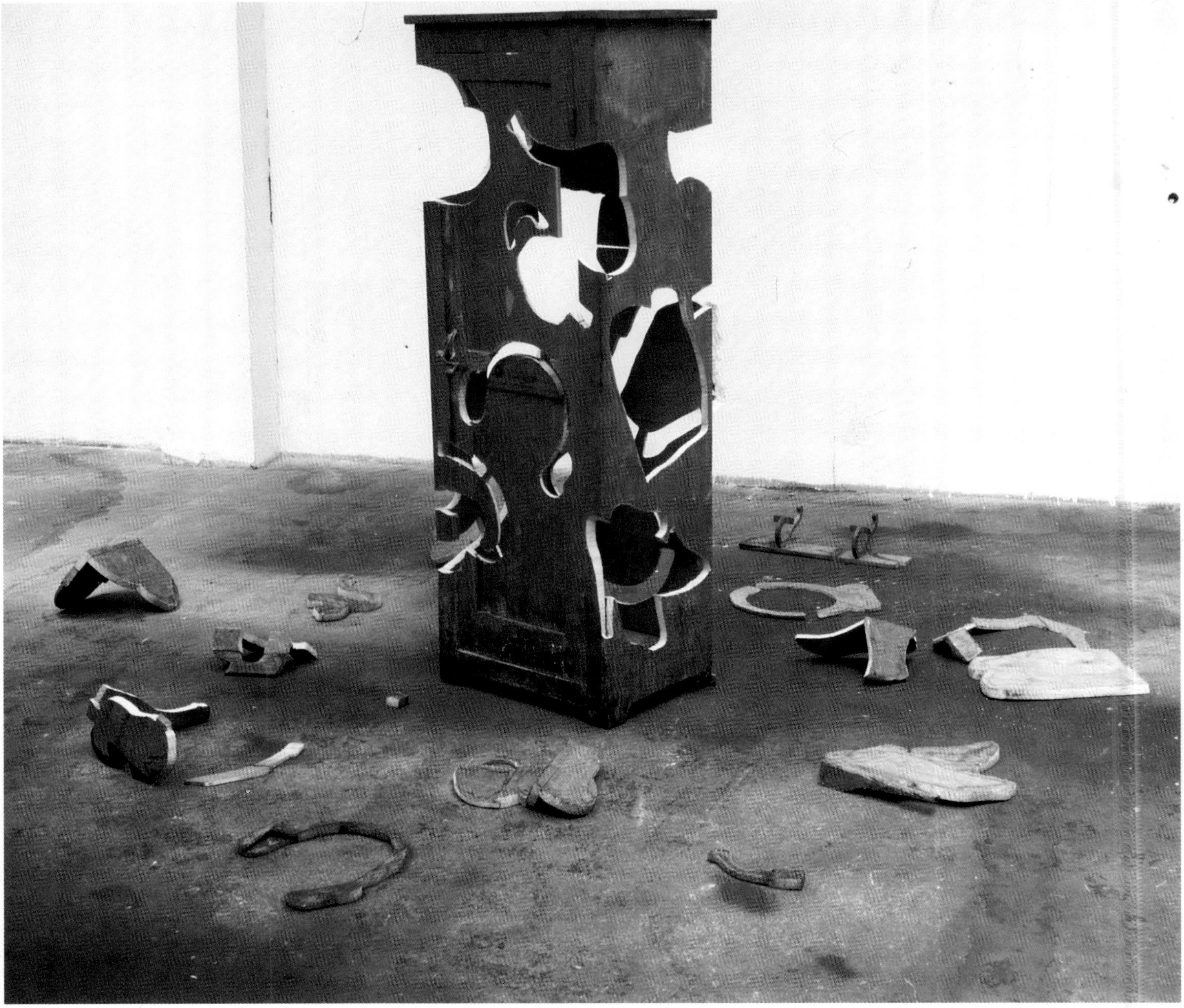

22. *Farbfernseher*, 1981

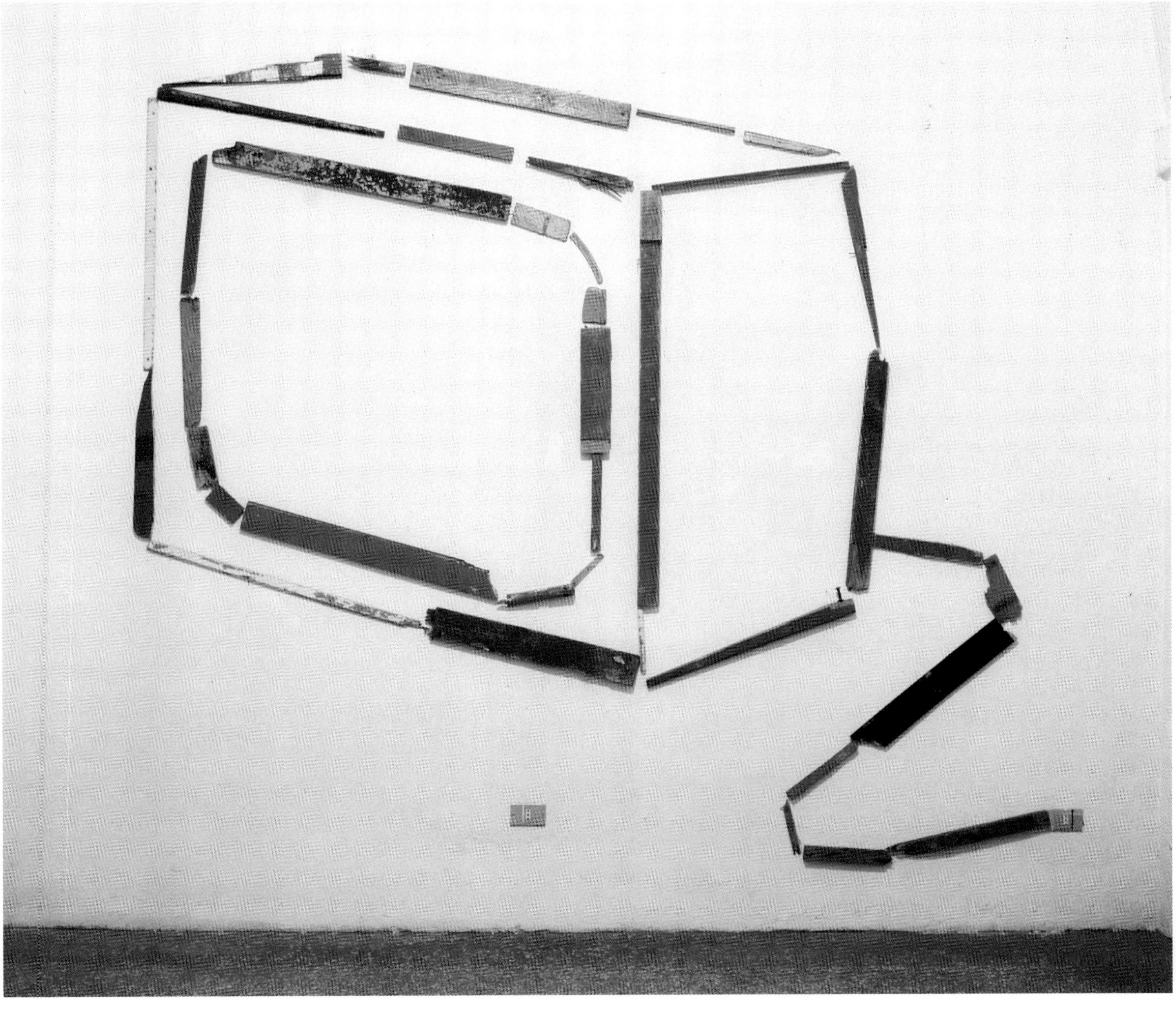

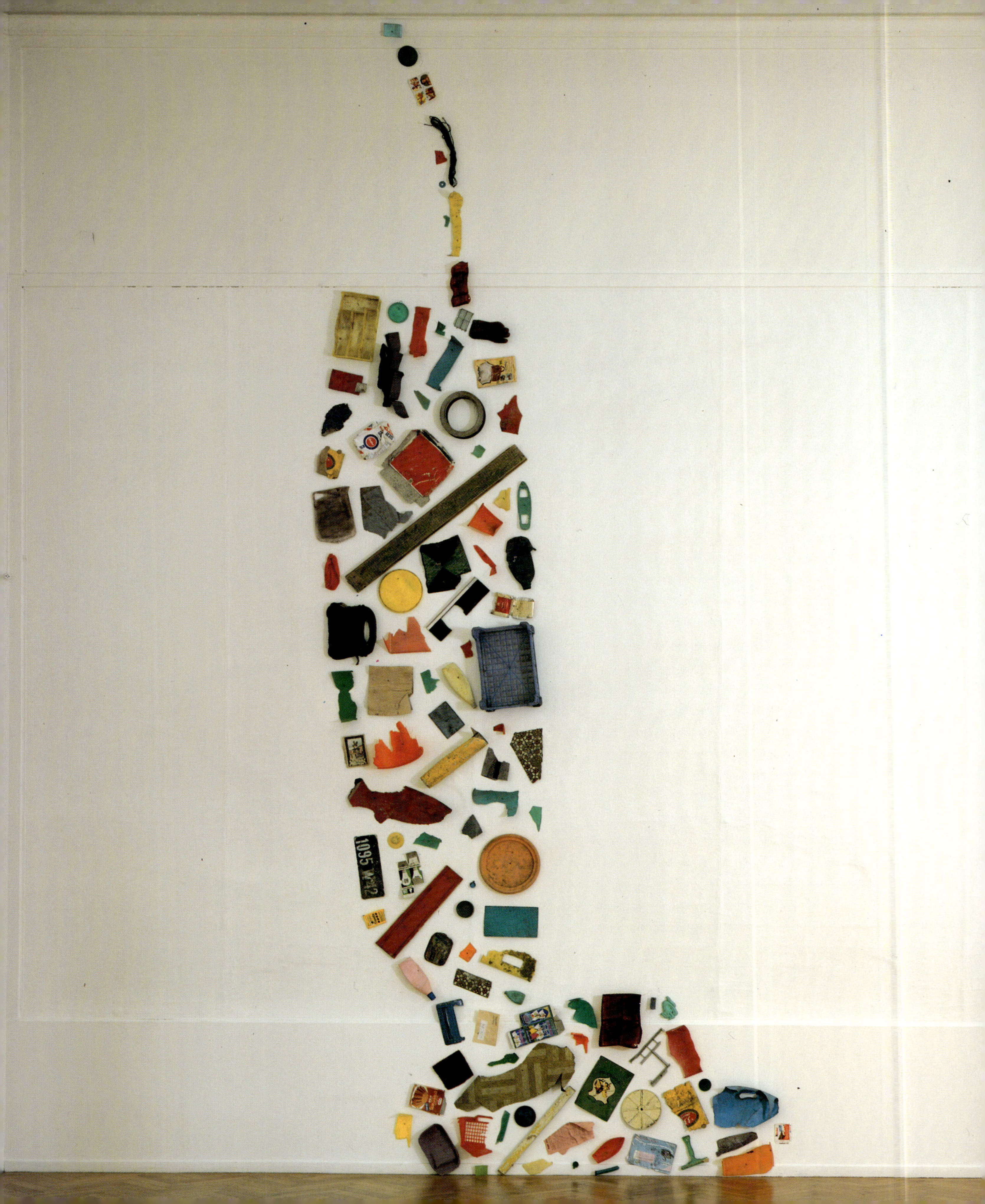

23. *Staubsauger*, 1981

24. *Postcard Union Jack*, 1981

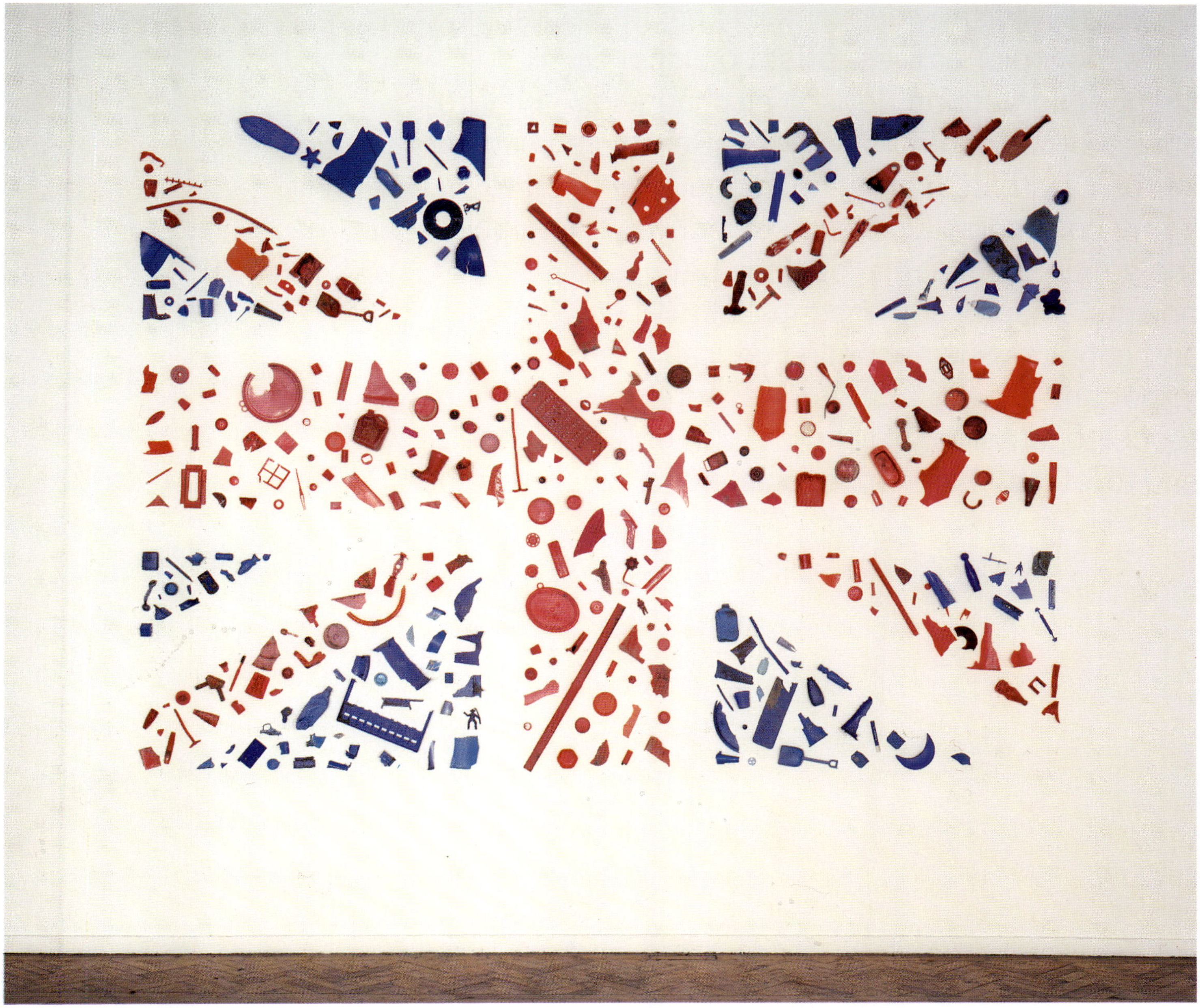

Celluloid wildlife, video landscapes, photographic wars, polaroid families, offset politics. Quick change, something new on all channels. Always a choice of second-hand images. Reality can hardly keep up with its marketing image. The need to know both objectively and subjectively more about the subtle, fragile relationships between us, objects, images and essential natural processes and conditions is becoming critical. It is very important to have first order experiences – seeing, touching, smelling, hearing – with objects/images and to let that experience register. Art is good for that.

First published in *Documenta 7*, exh. catalogue. Kassel: 1982, vol. 1, p. 340.

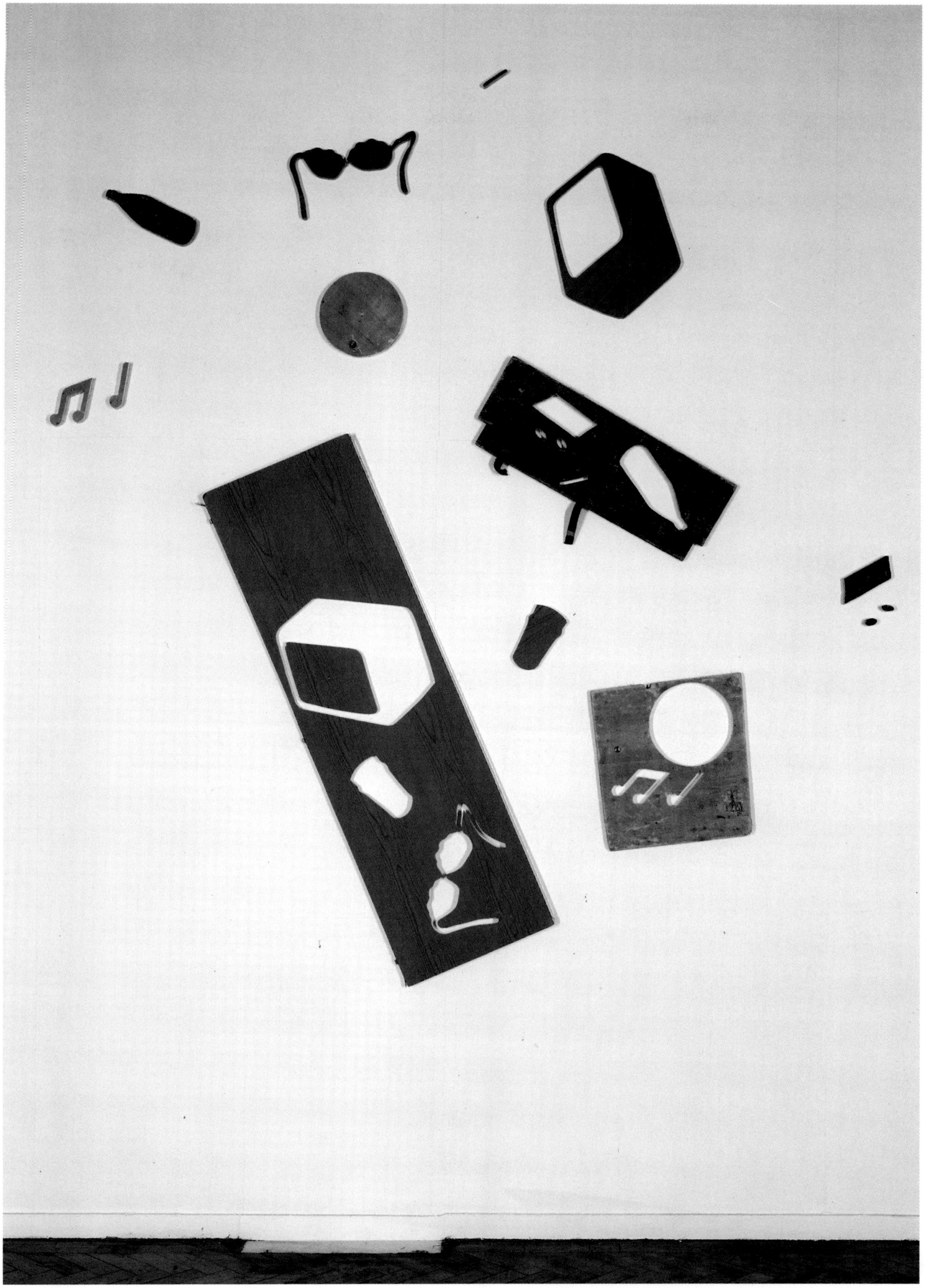

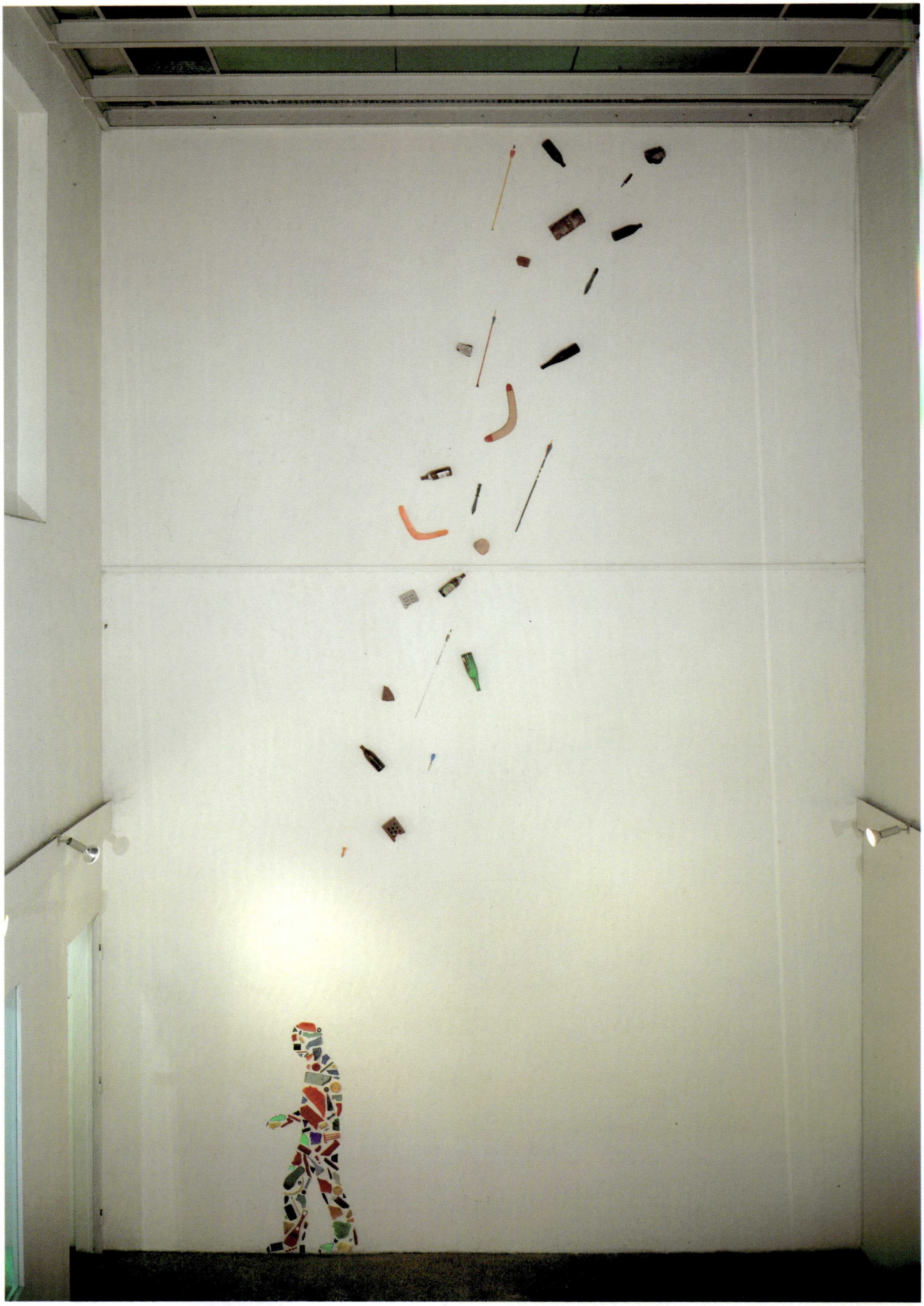

26. *Self-Portrait with Bottles and Bricks*, 1982

27. *Indian Moon*, 1982

28. *Dining Motions*, 1982

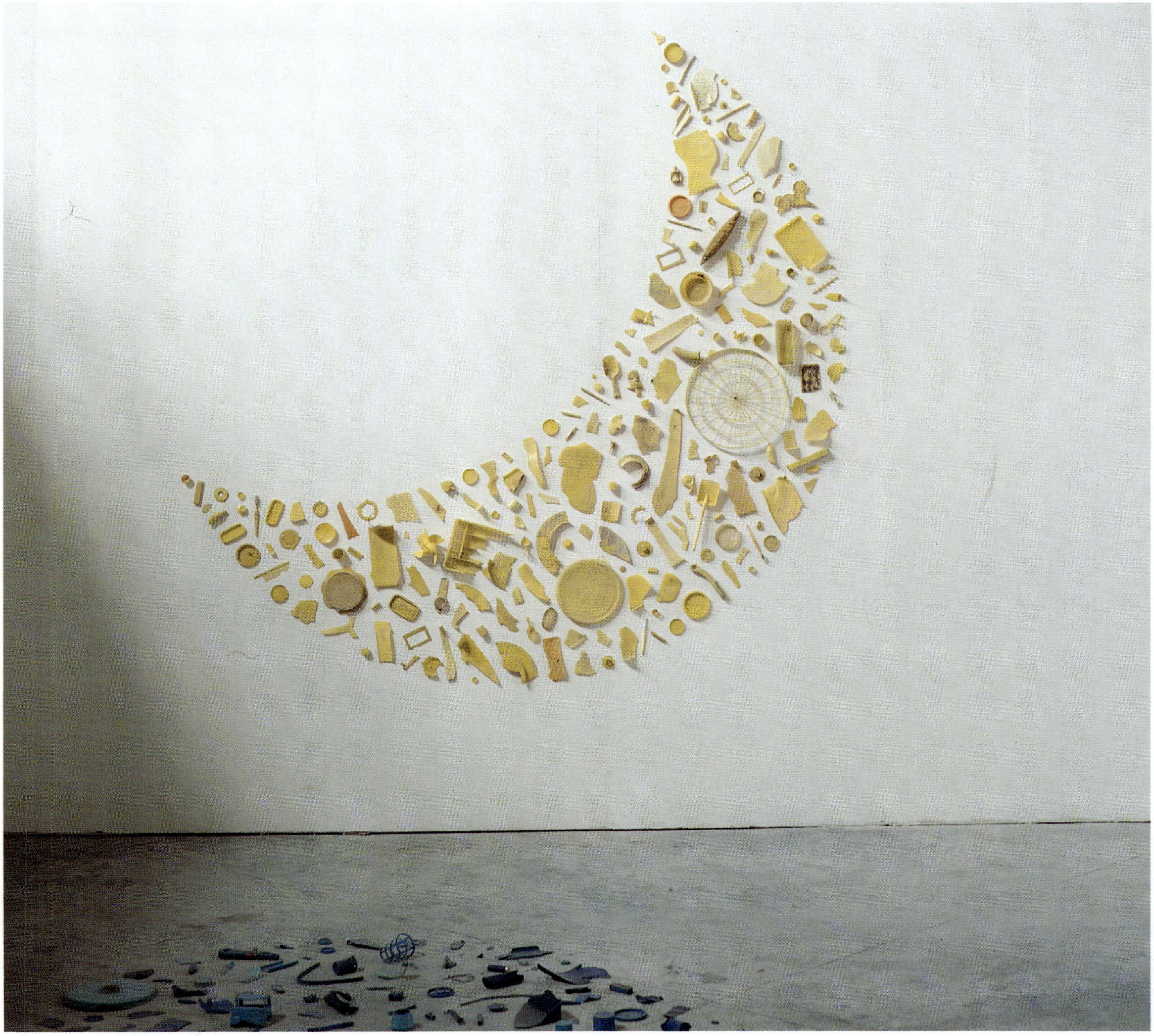

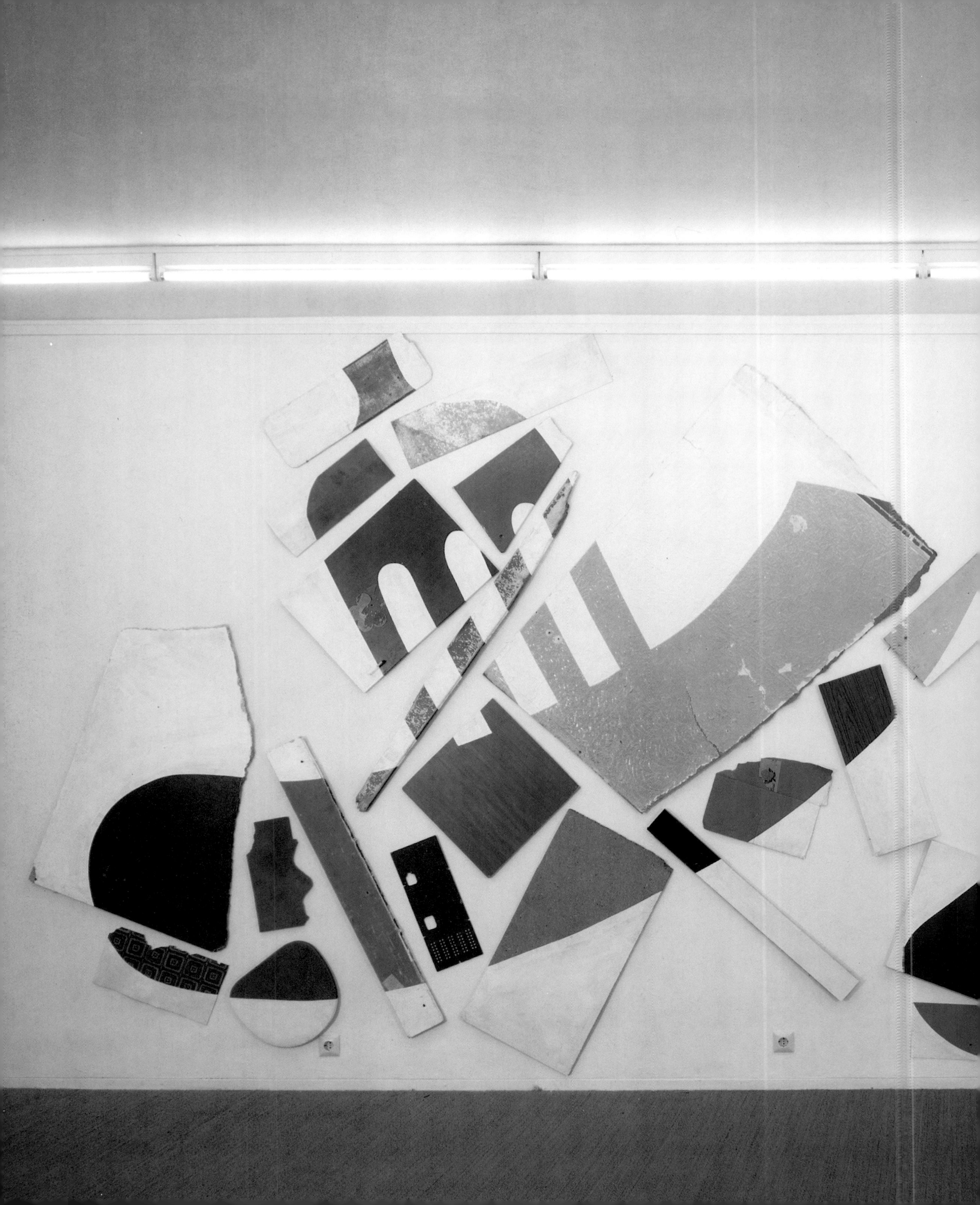

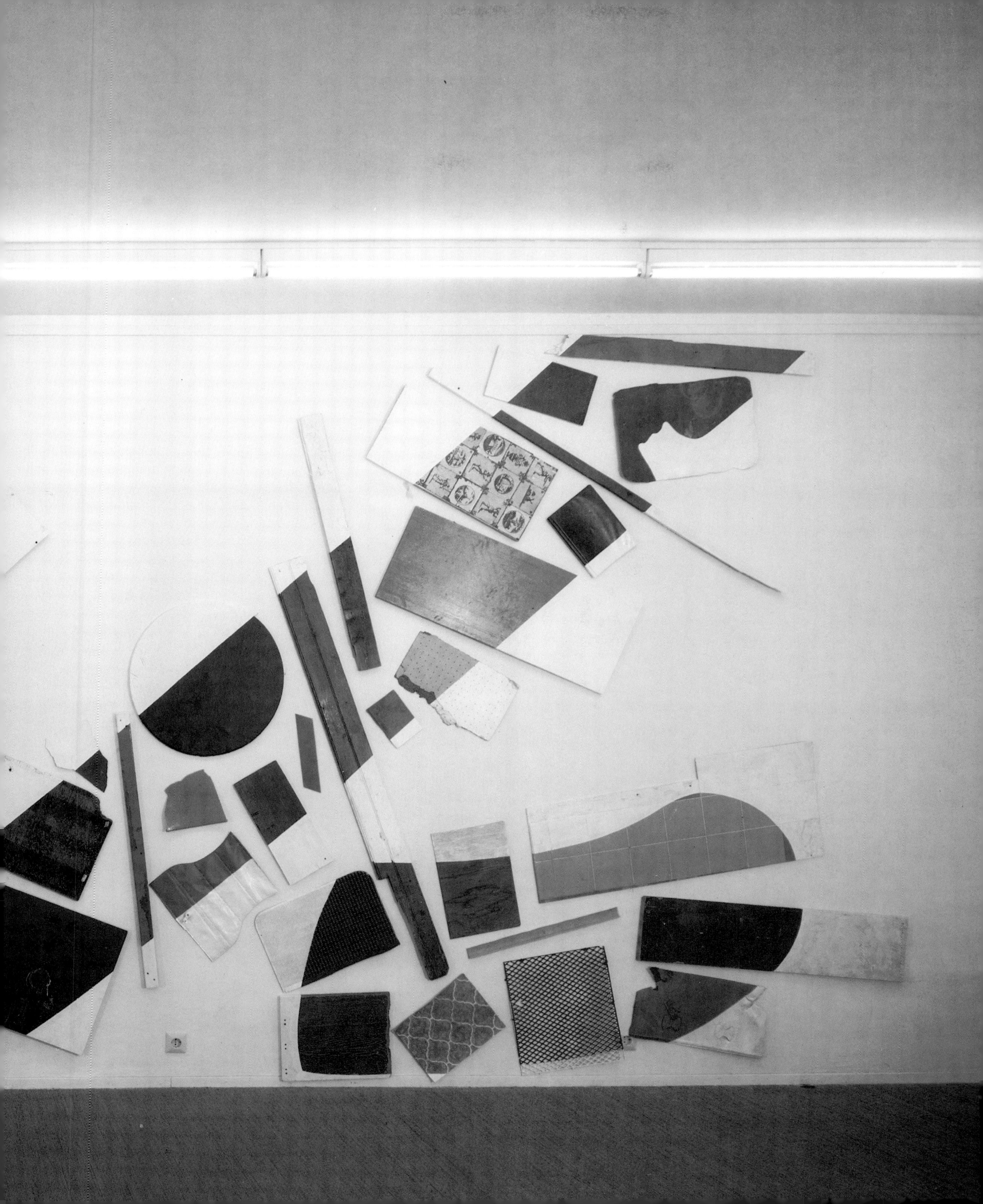

29. *Five Bottles on a Shelf*, 1982

30. *Green Bottle II, Yellow Bottle II, Red Bottle II, Orange Bottle II, Blue Bottle II*, 1982

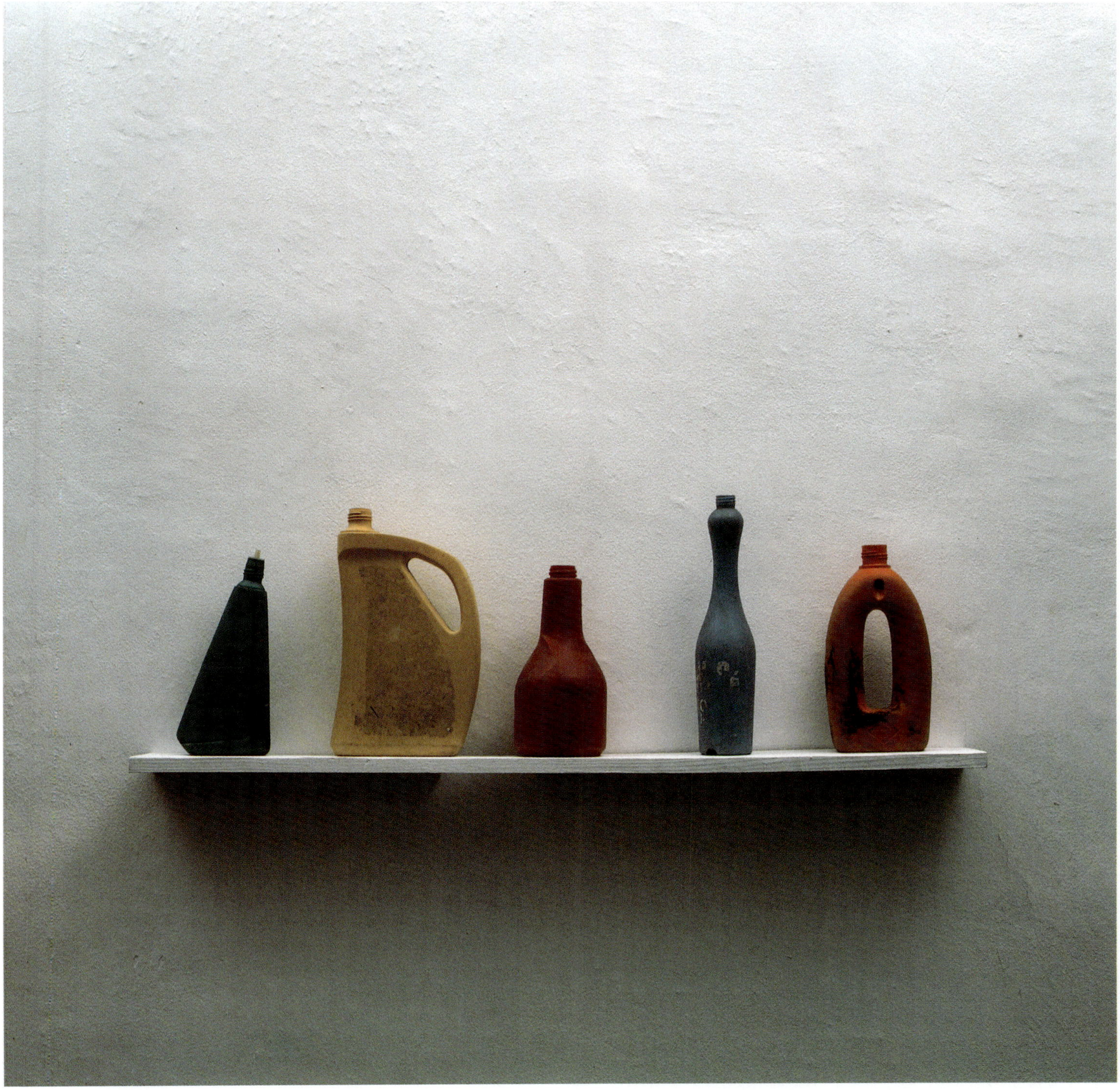

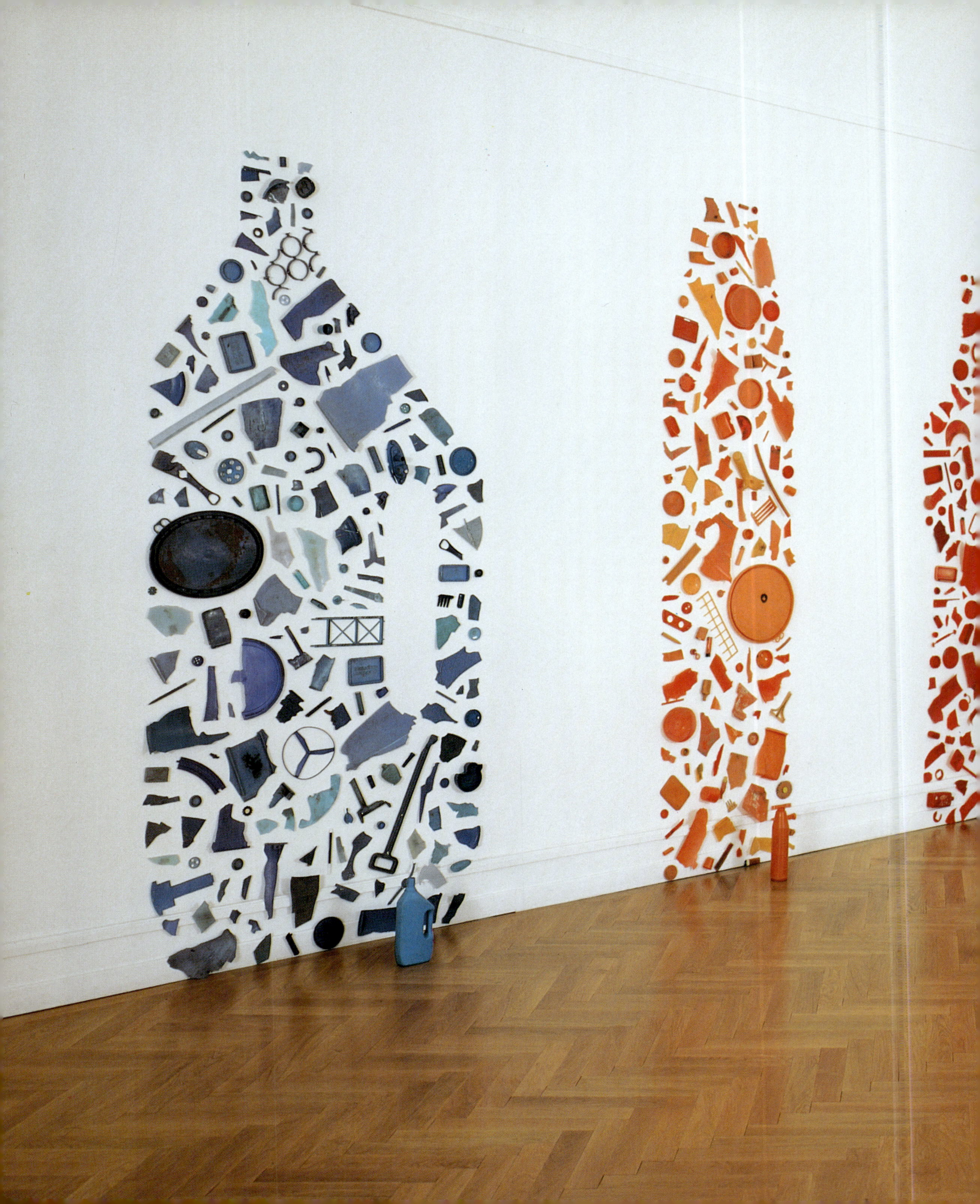

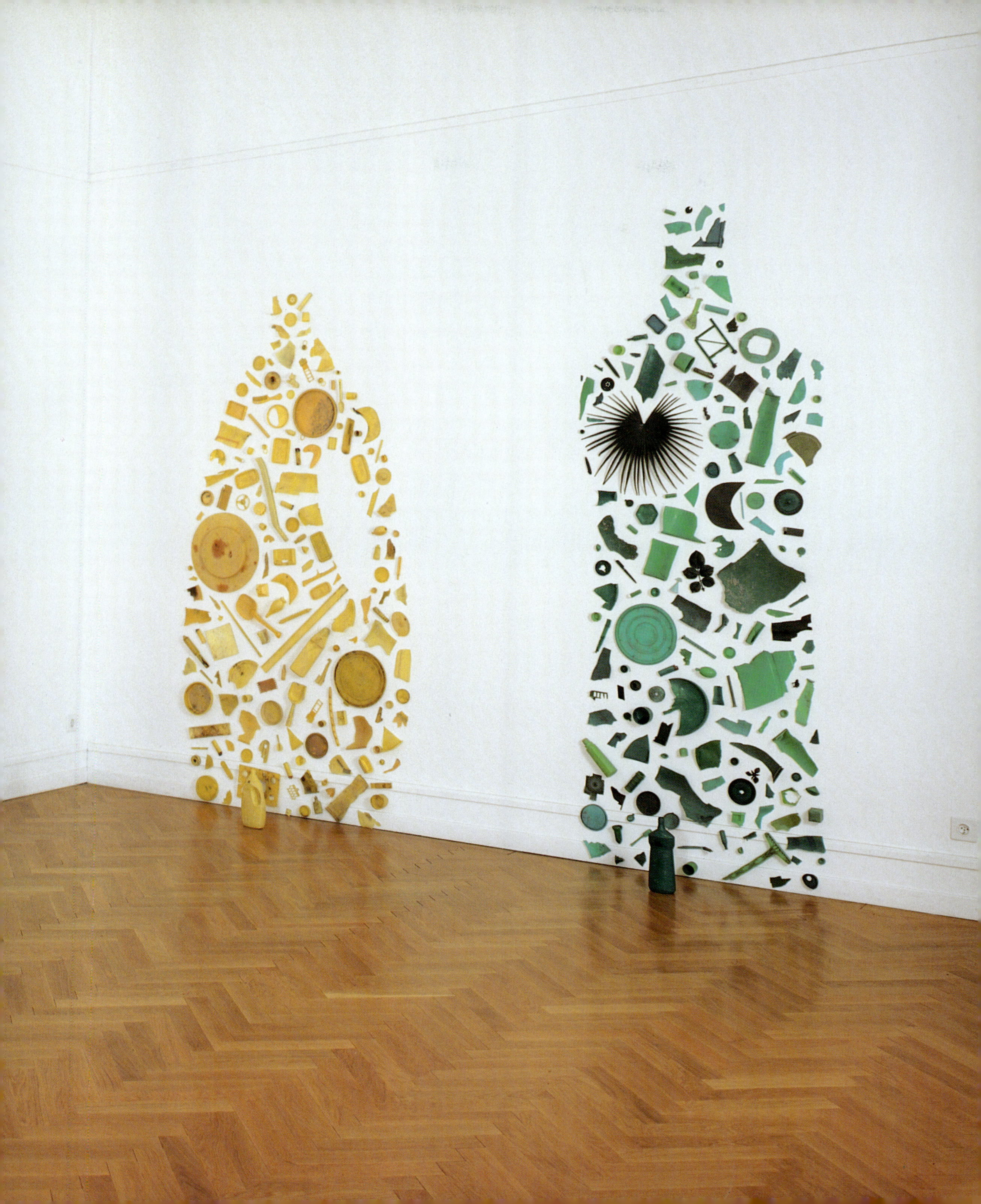

My initial interest in making images and objects was, and still remains, the creation of objects that don't exist in the natural or in the functional world, which can reflect and transmit information and feelings about the world and my own existence. They are not intended as dogmatic statements but as propositions, for me an essential distinction. The impulse comes directly from my observations and experiences in the world around me and rarely results out of literature or cultural history.

First published in *Tony Cragg. Skulpturen*, exh. catalogue. Hanover: Kestner-Gesellschaft, 1985, p. 39.

31. *House*, 1982; *Trough*, 1982; *Mercedes*, 1982

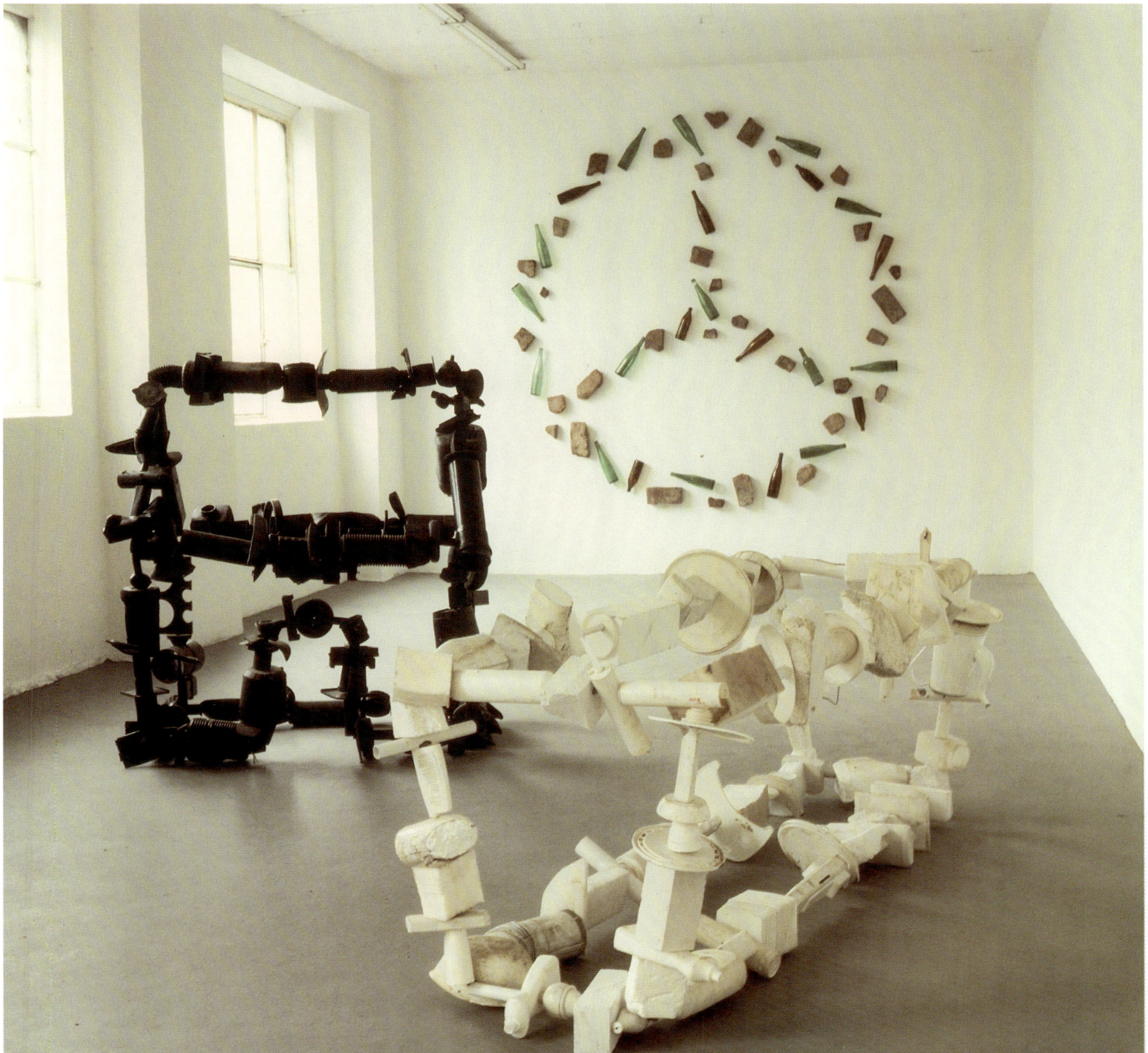

32. *Grey Container*, 1983

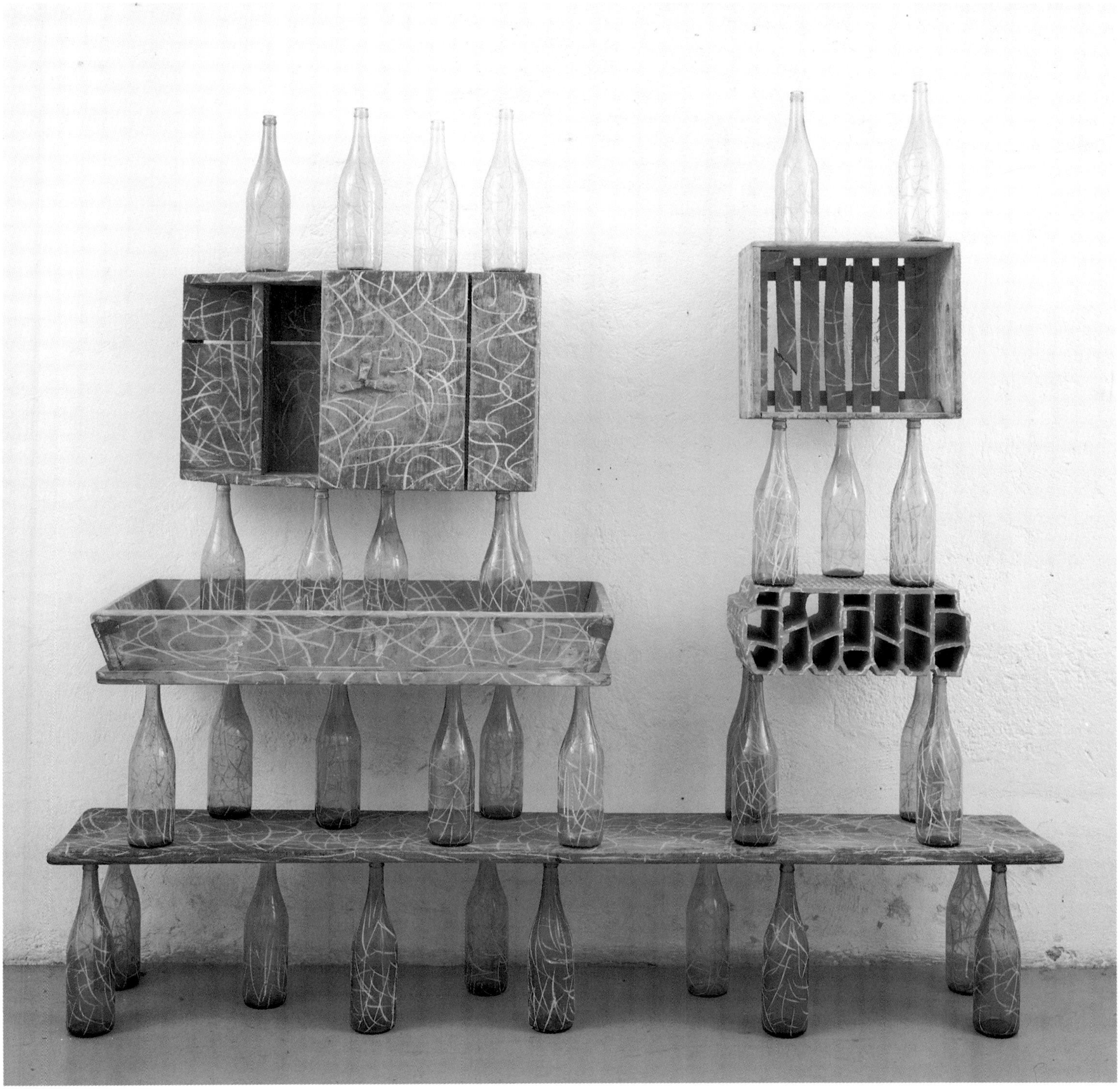

33. *Taxi!*, 1983

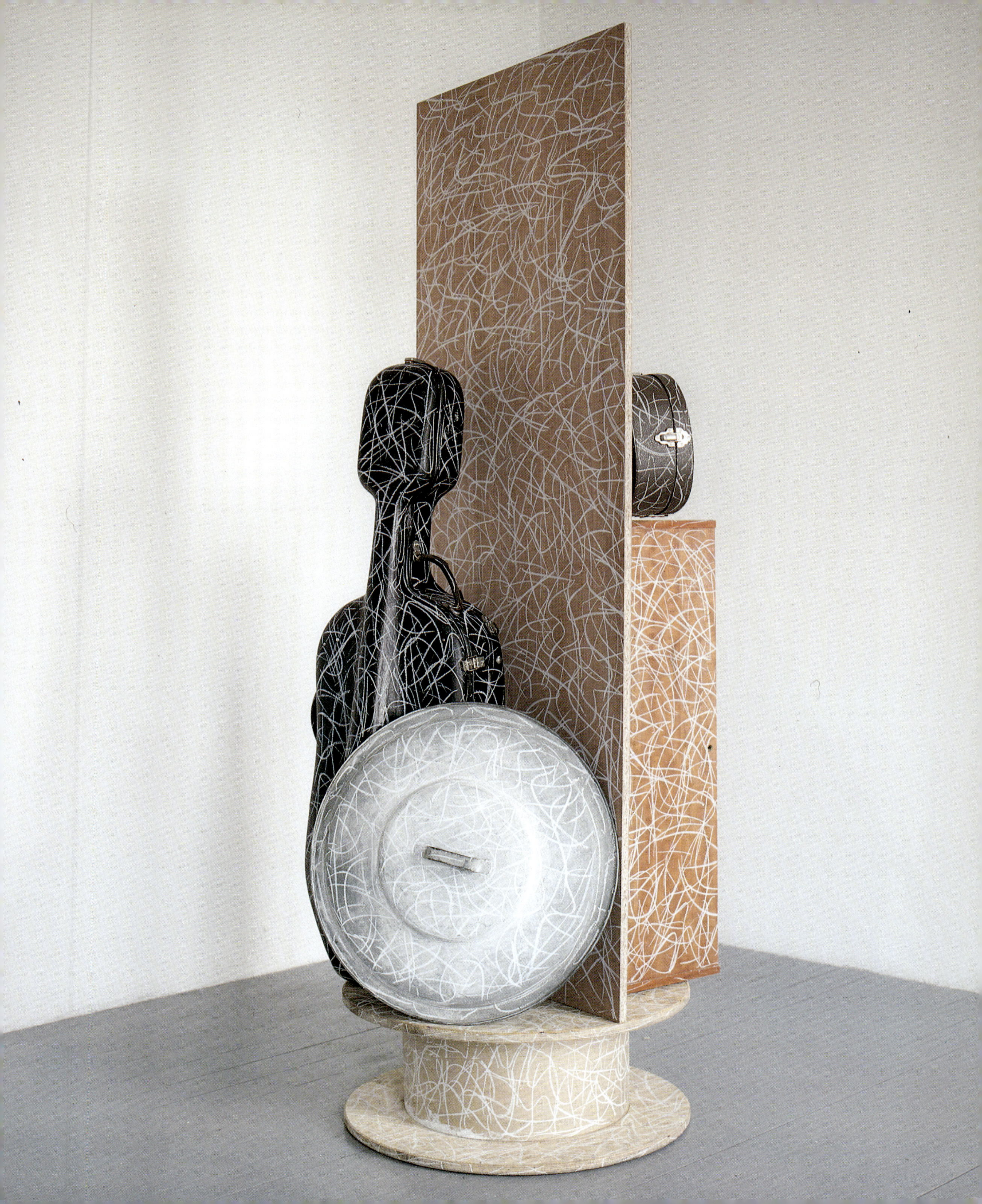

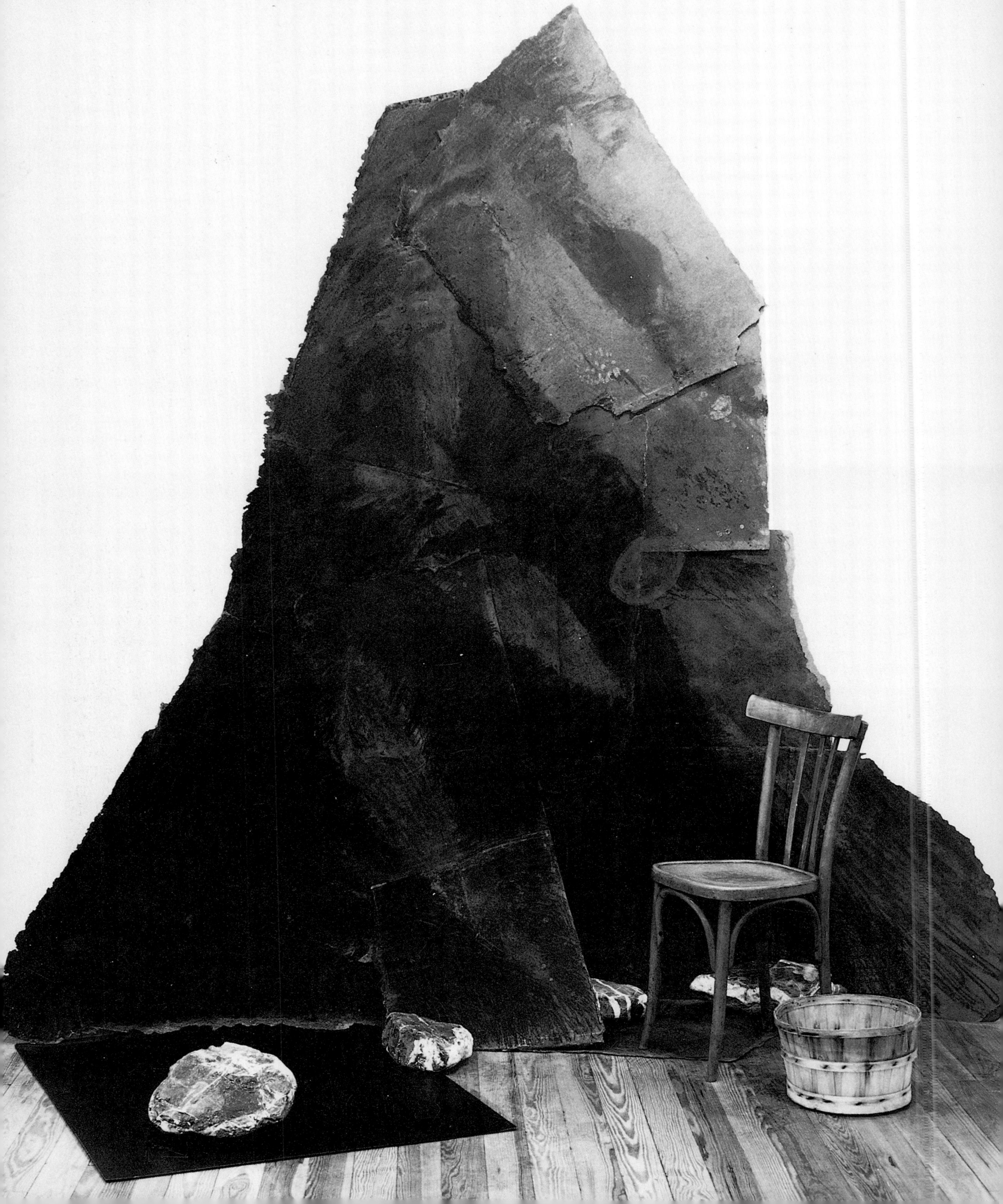

34. *Large Mountain*, 1983

35. *Untitled*, 1983

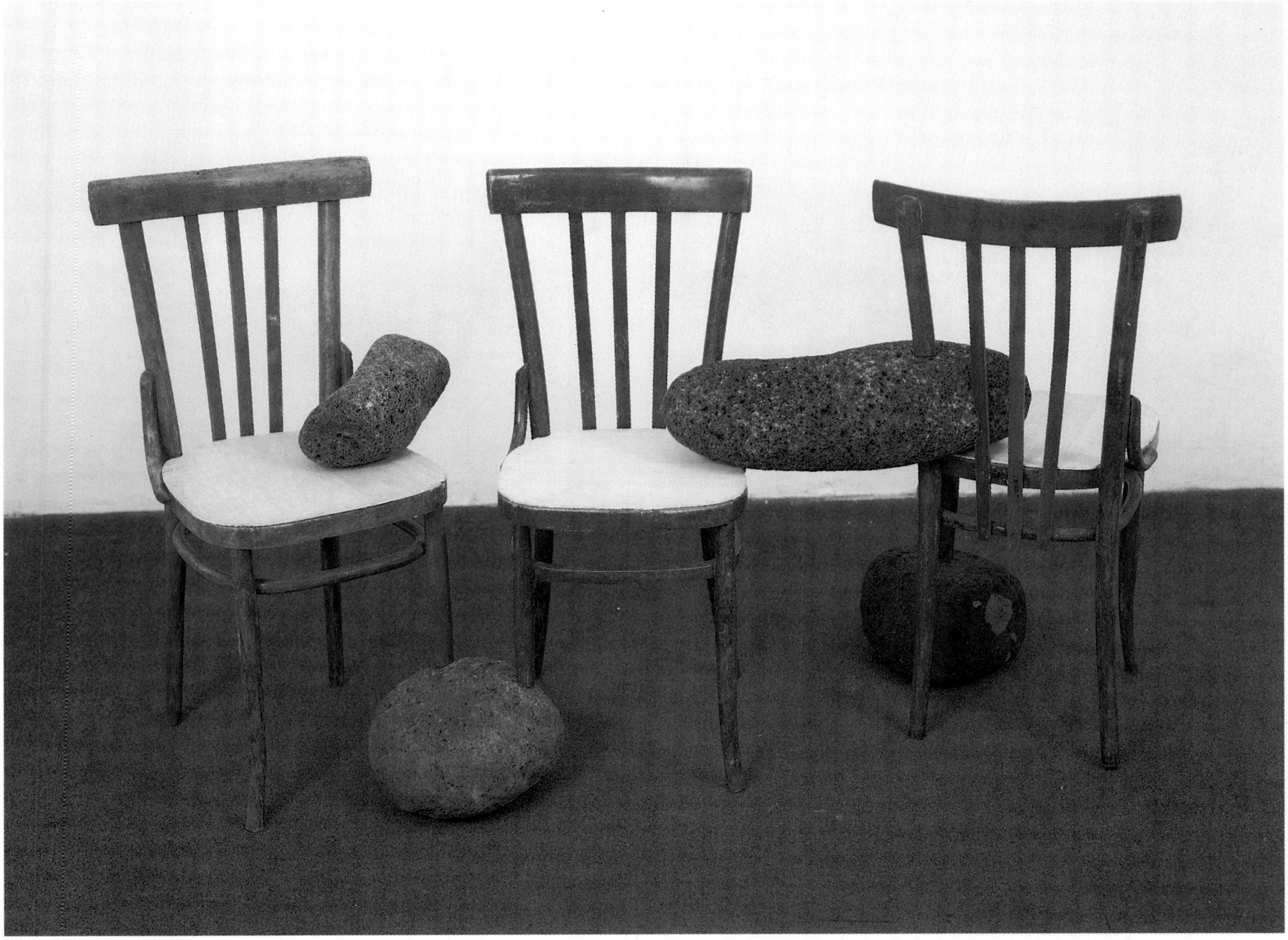

36. *Palette*, 1983

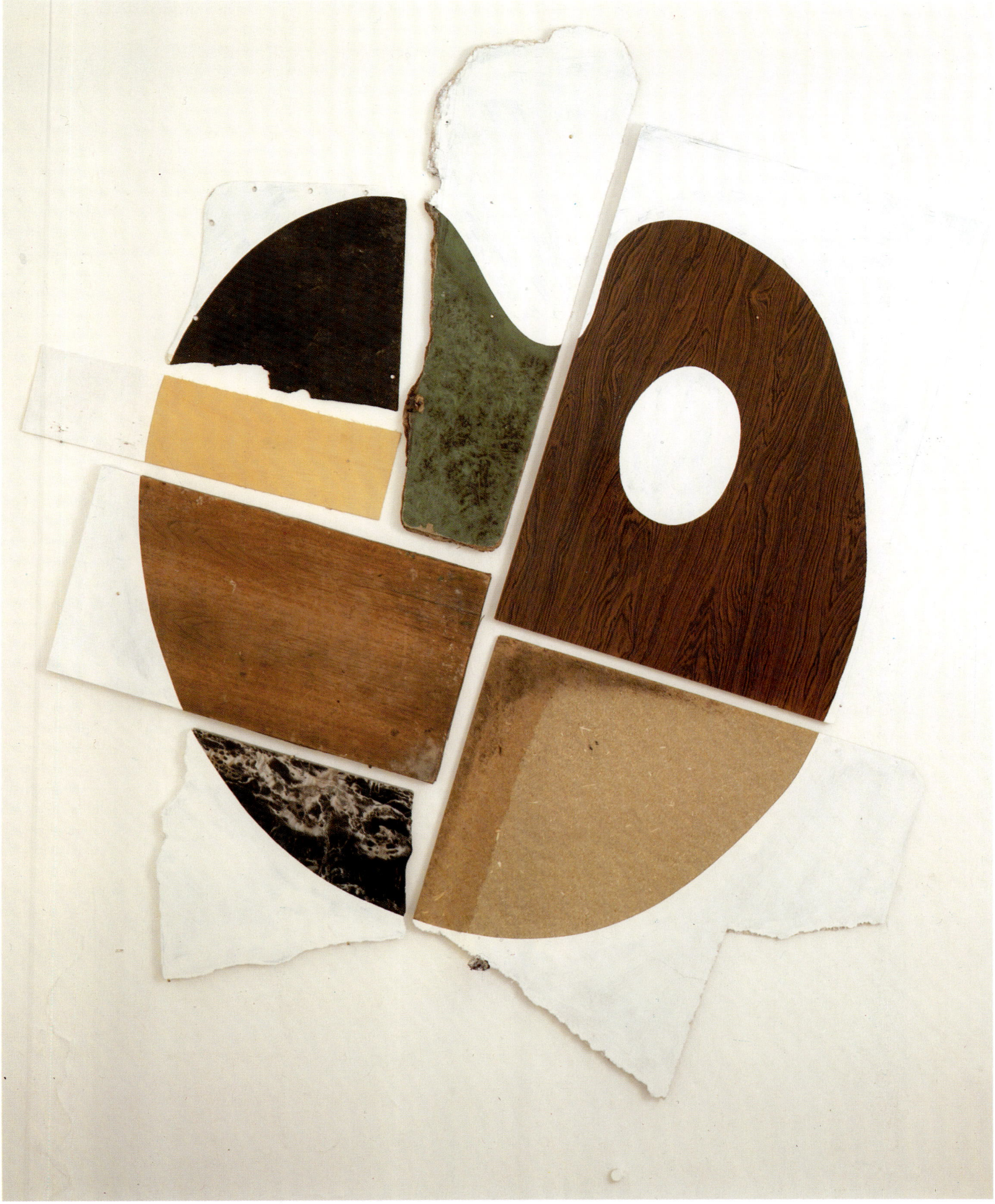

37. *Element Plane*, 1983

38. *Untitled*, 1983-84

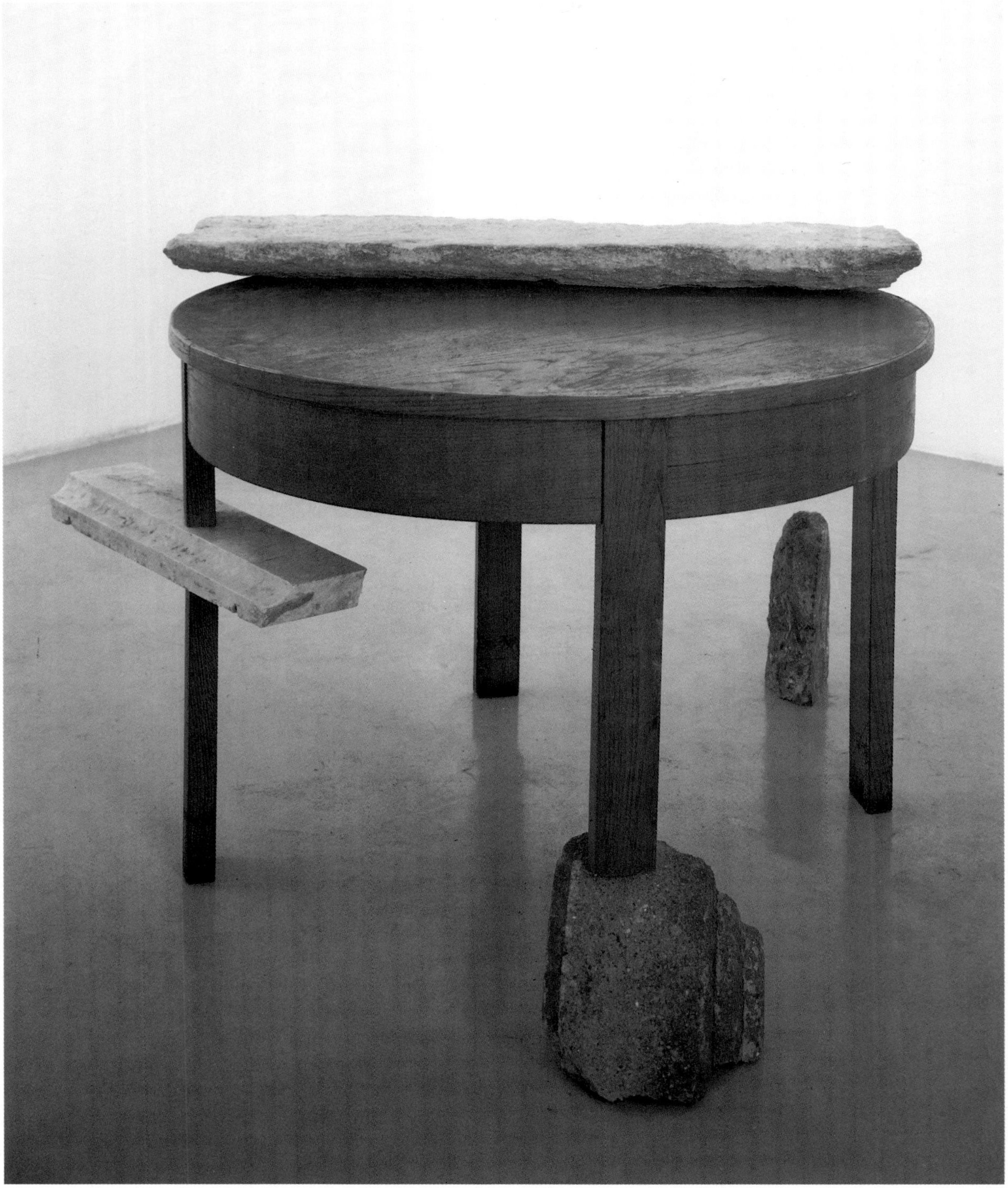

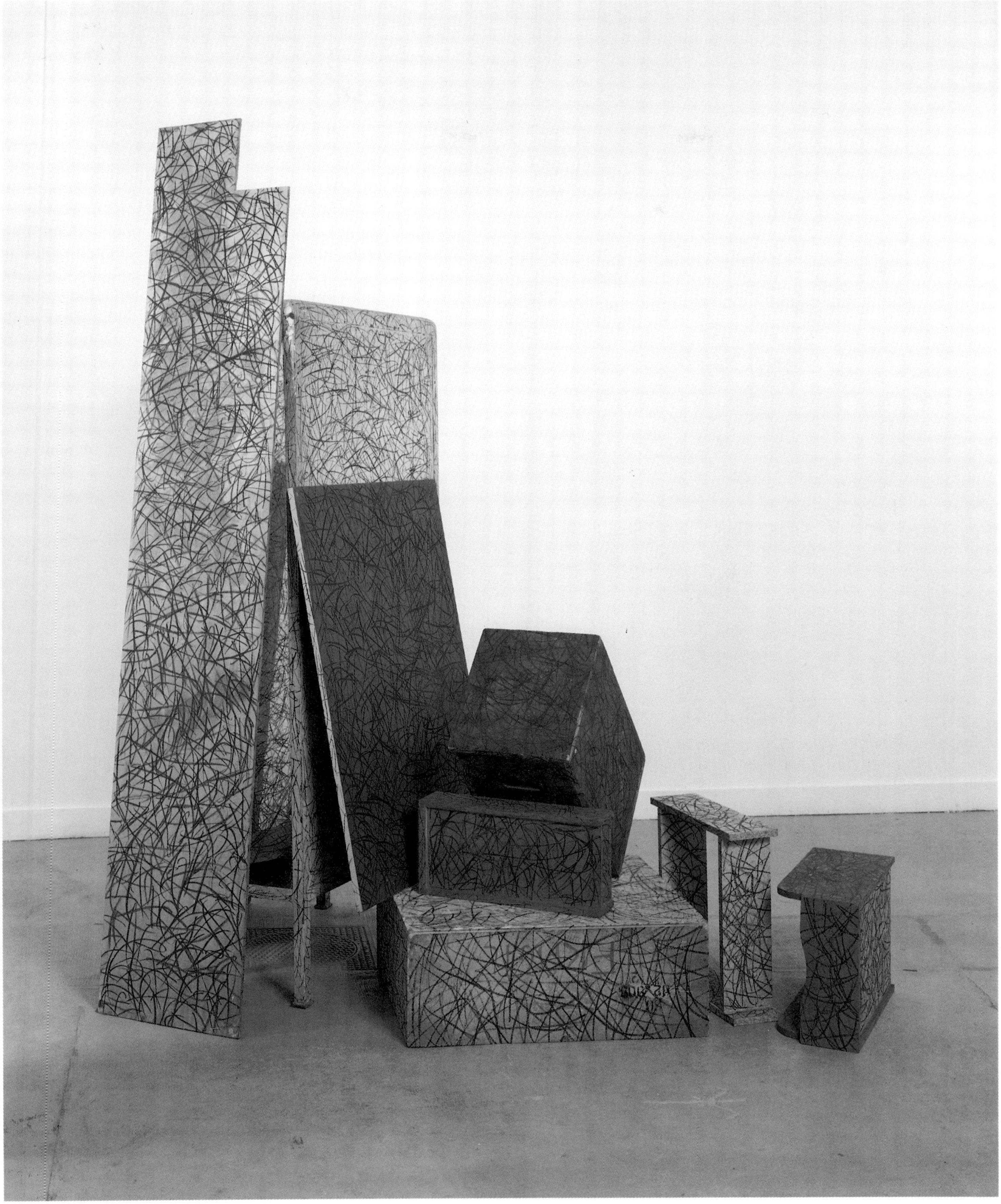

39. *Three Modern Buildings*, 1983

40. *Moonshadow*, 1983;
Silent Garden, 1983

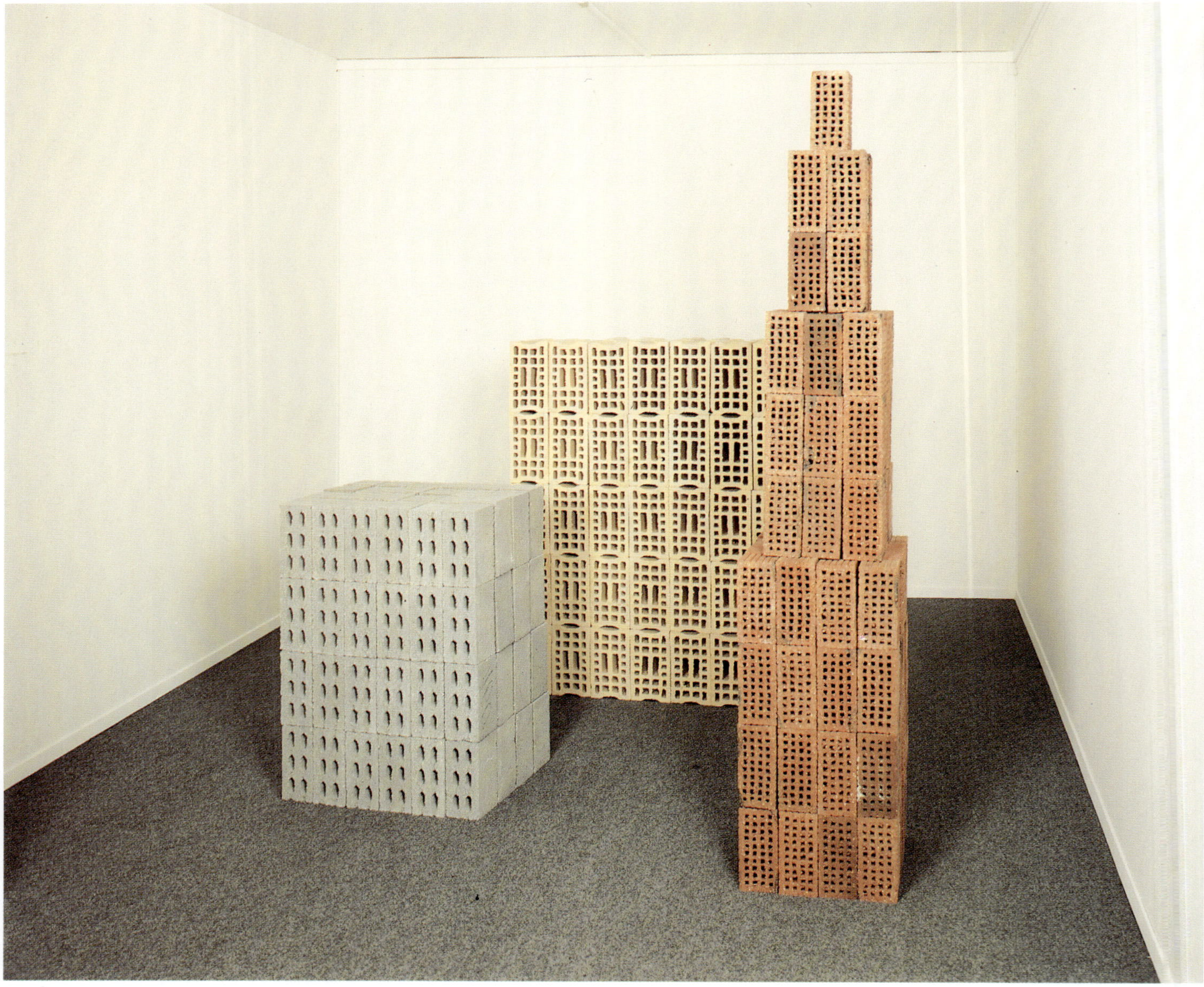

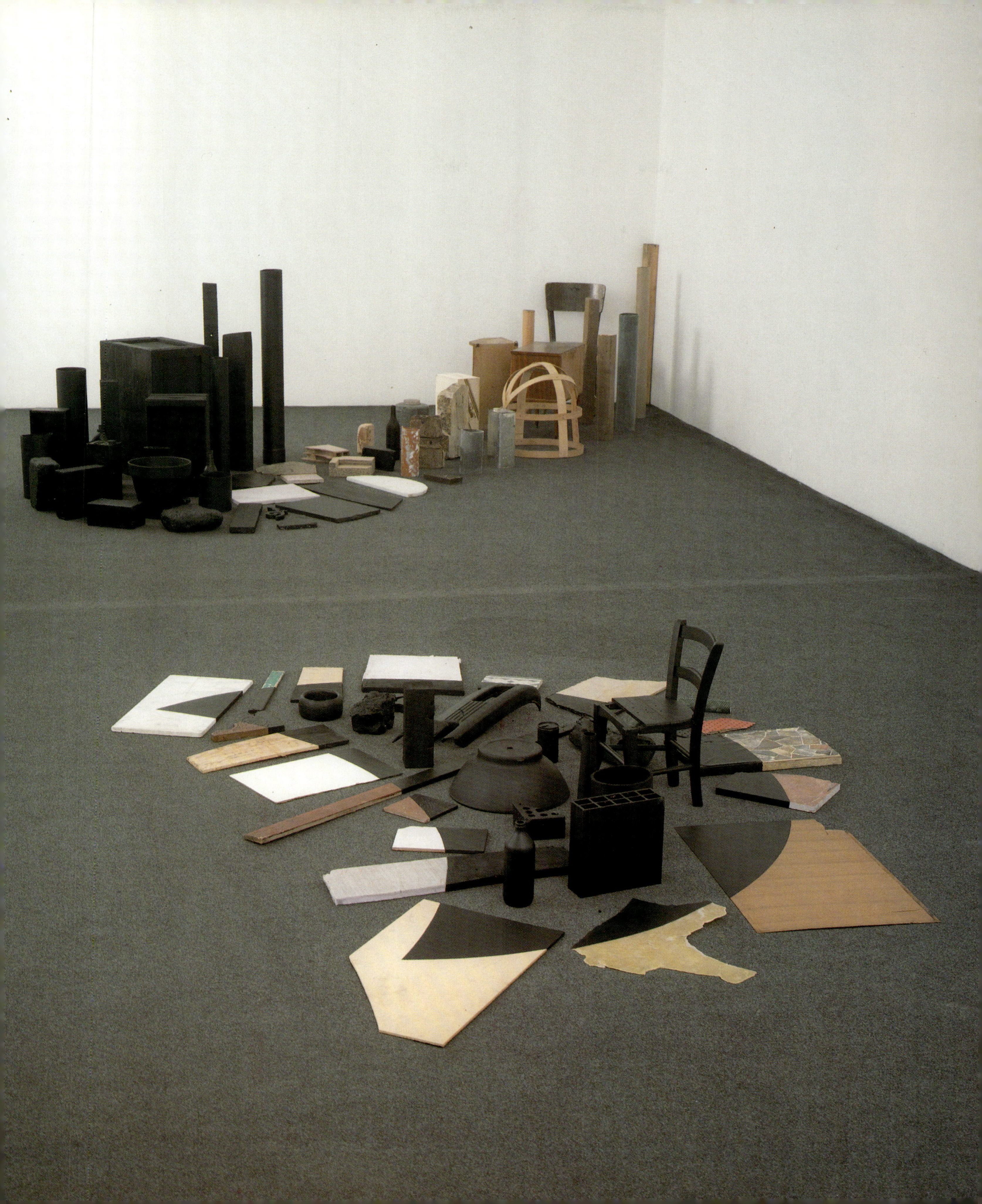

The materials, because of their physical characteristics and the emotions and ideas they bring with them, play an essential role in the forming of the work. A pre-condition for working with man-made materials is that they are equally worthy of carrying significant meanings as natural materials. Many new materials originated for economic reasons as substitutes for natural materials, and as such have automatically been valued as inferior. And many others as parts of practical constructions and industrial systems have assumed an everyday, banal function. This banality provides a hurdle that is essential to overcome in order to start a dialogue with the work.

First published in *Tony Cragg. Skulpturen*, exh. catalogue. Hanover: Kestner-Gesellschaft, 1985, p. 39.

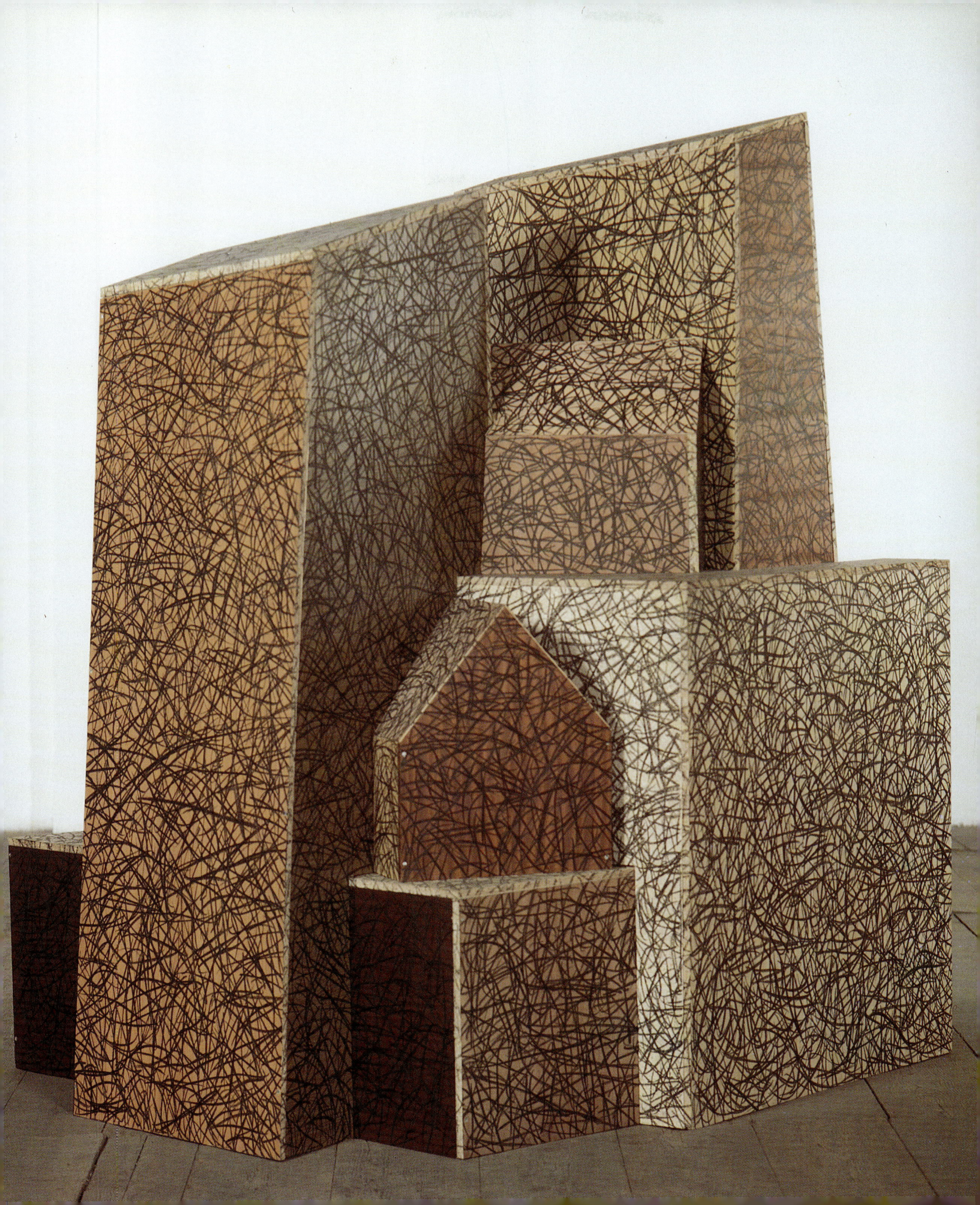

42. *S*, 1984

43. *Shed*, 1984

44. *Village*, 1985

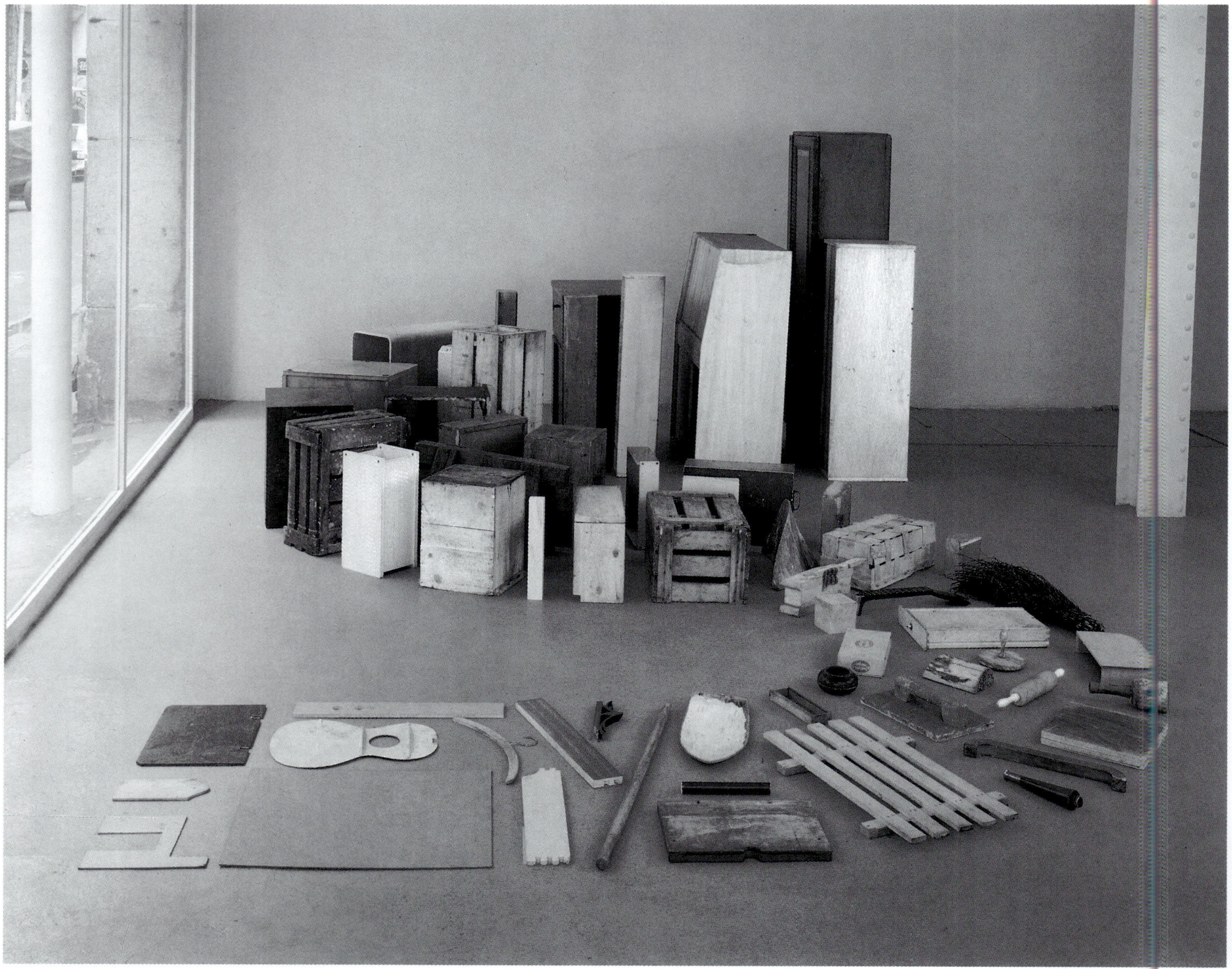

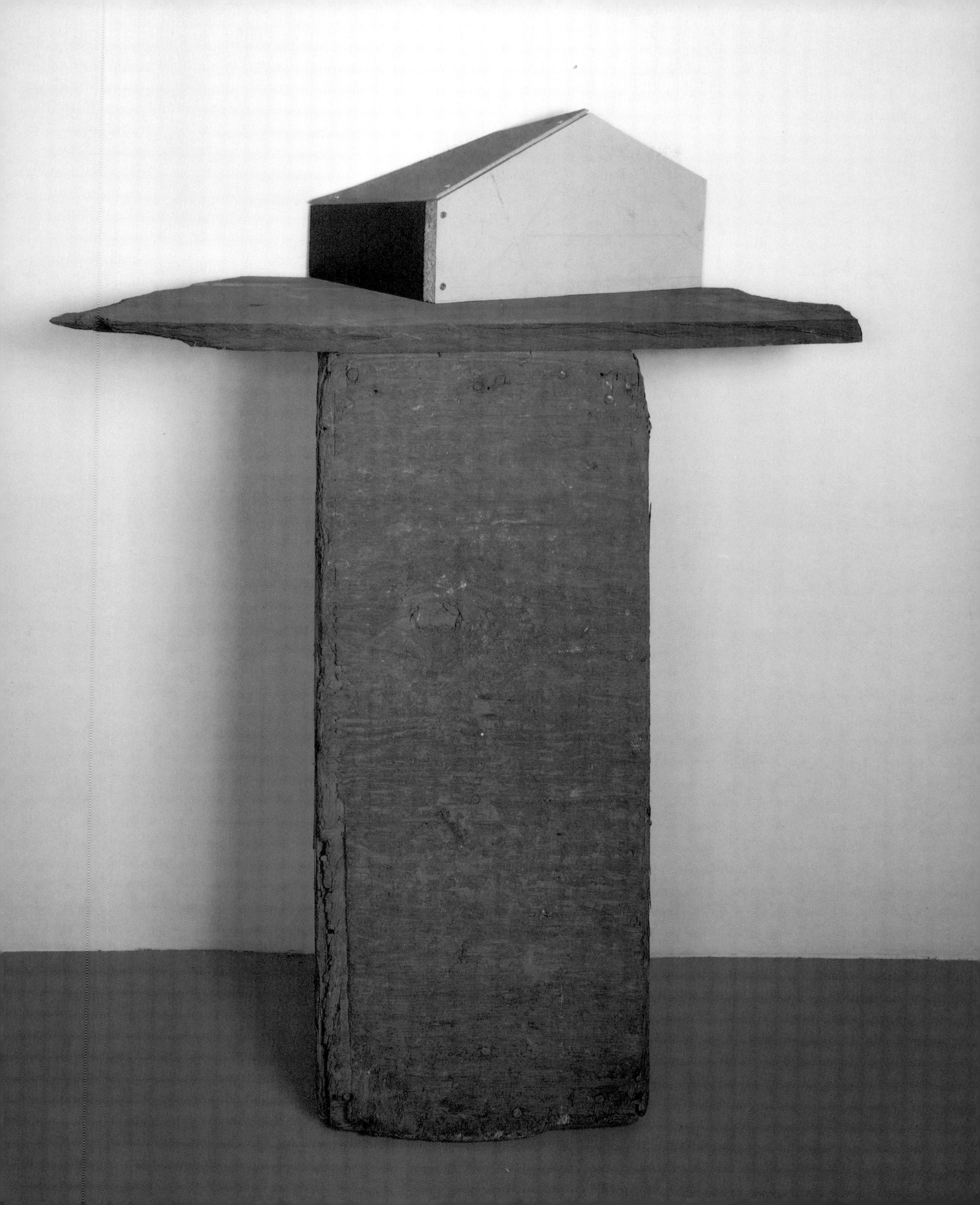

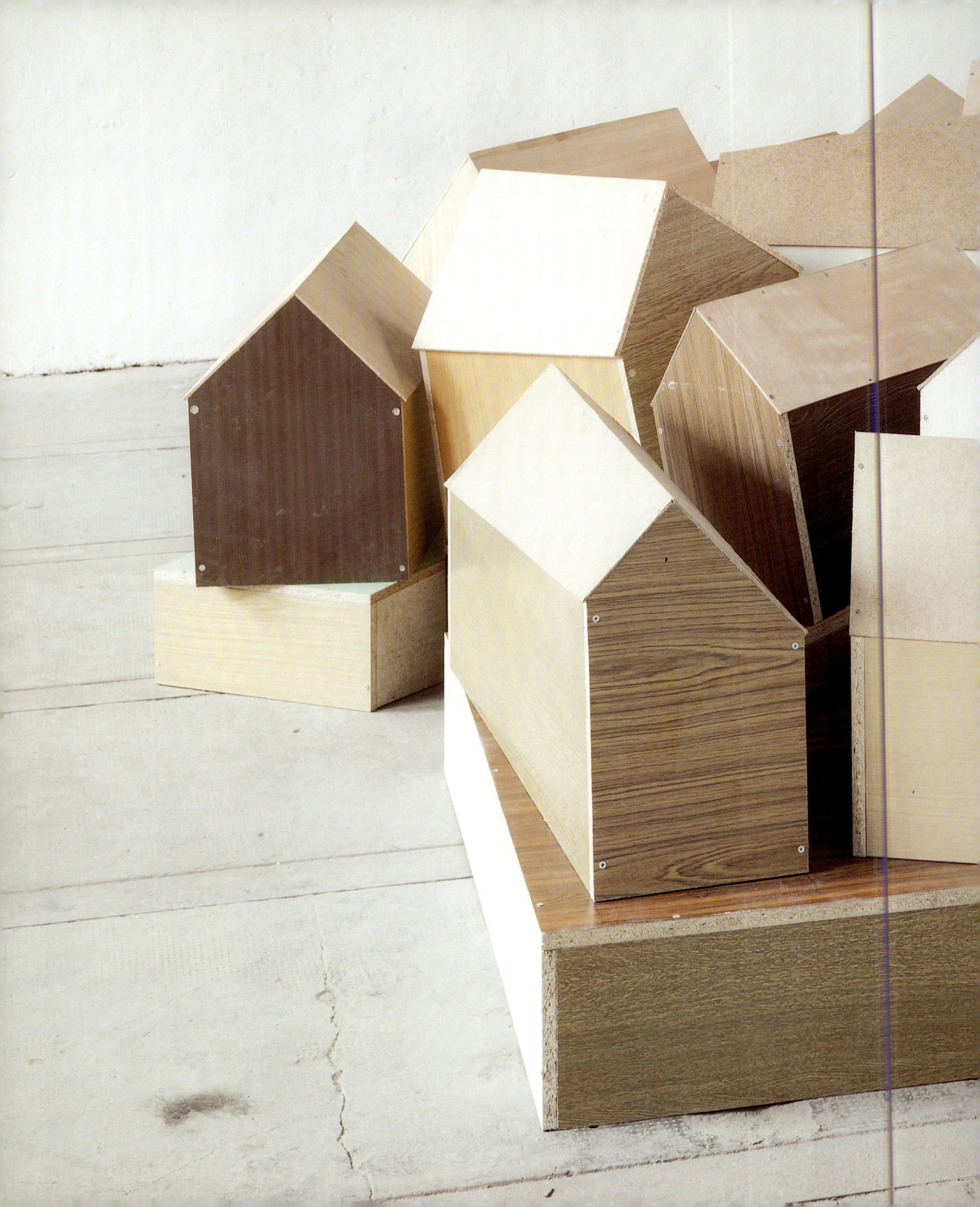

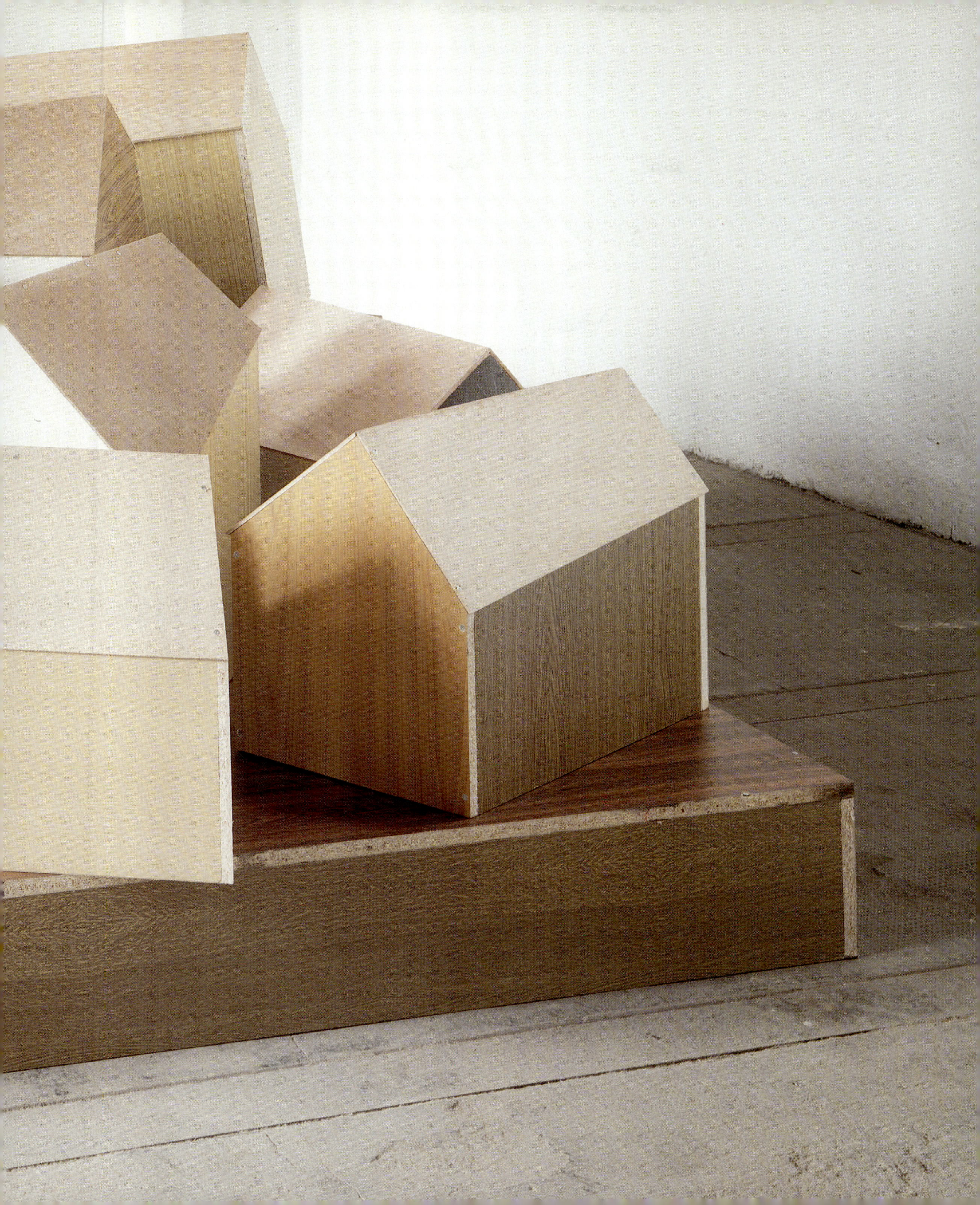

45. *Birnan Wood*, 1985

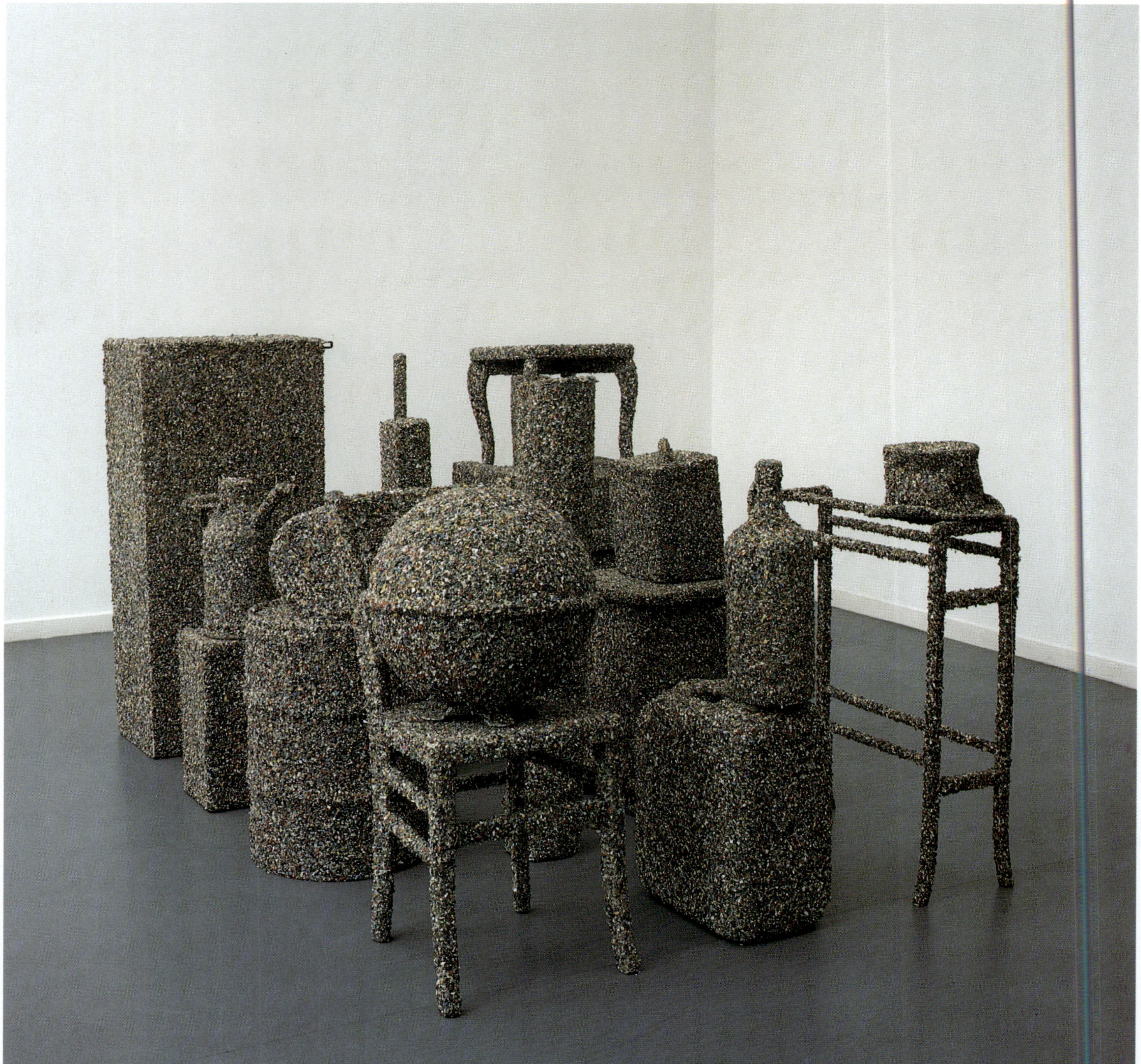

46. *Mortus and Pestal*, 1985

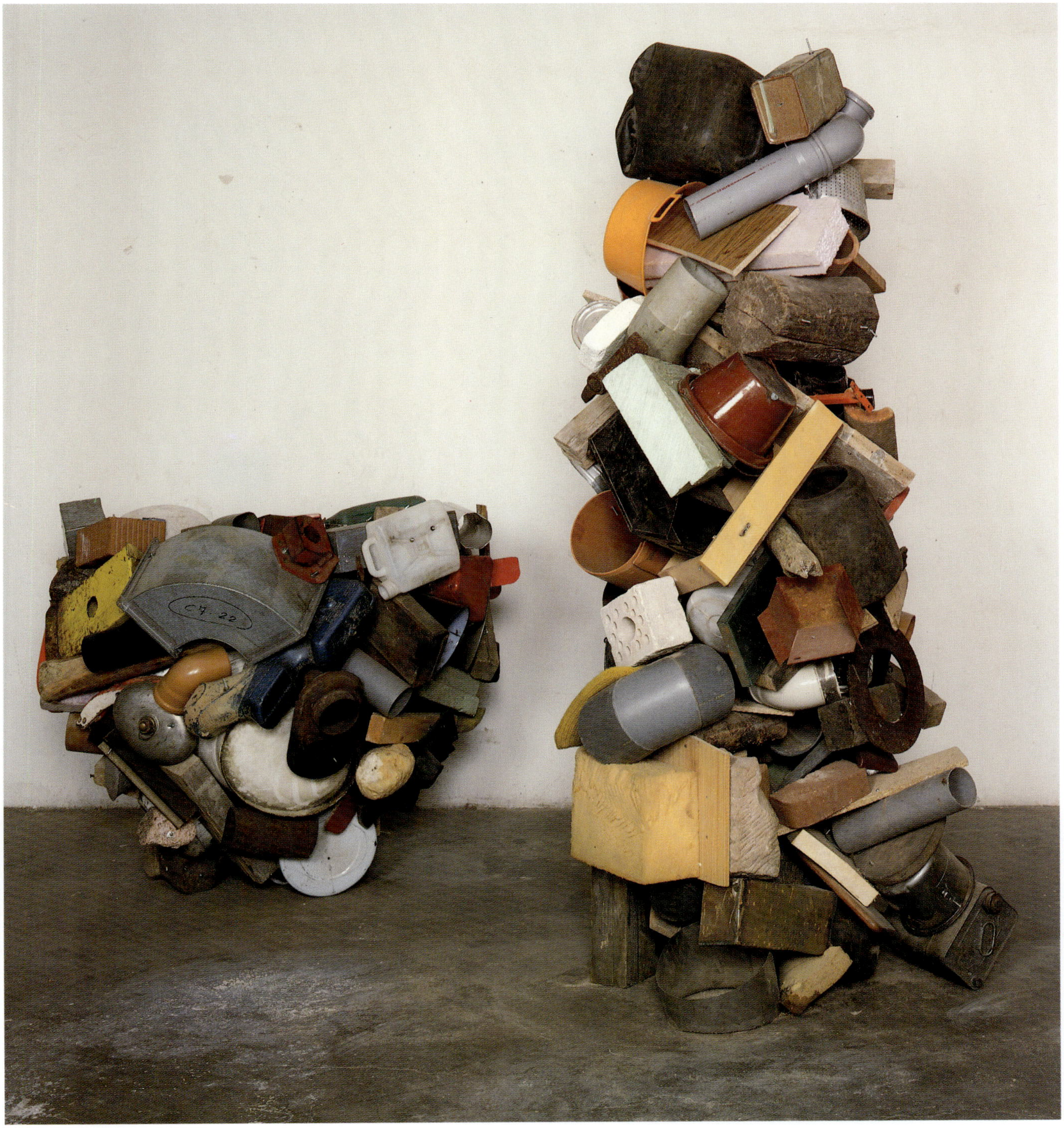

47. *Circles*, 1985

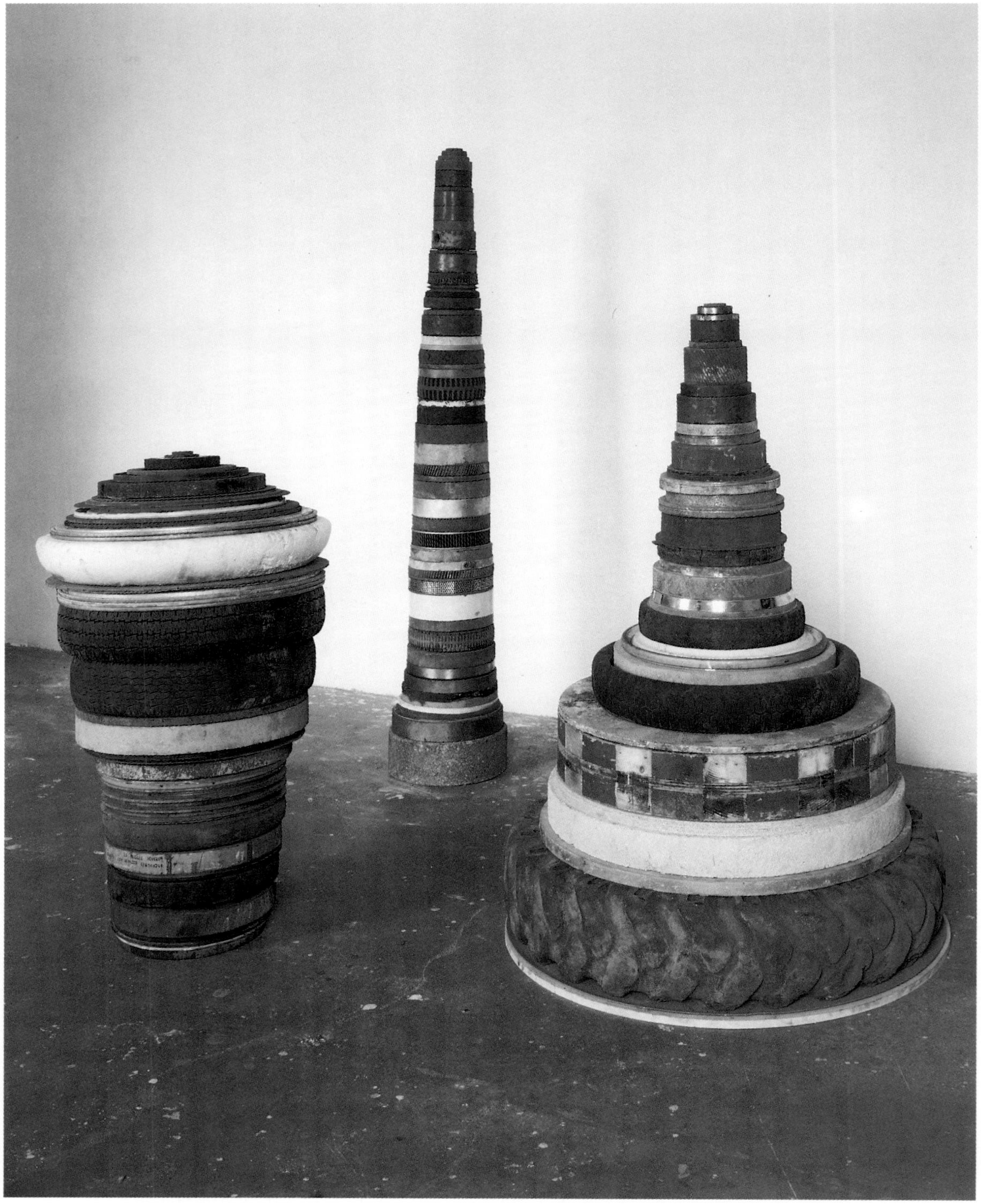

48. *Berg und Ring*, 1985

49. *New Figuration*, 1985

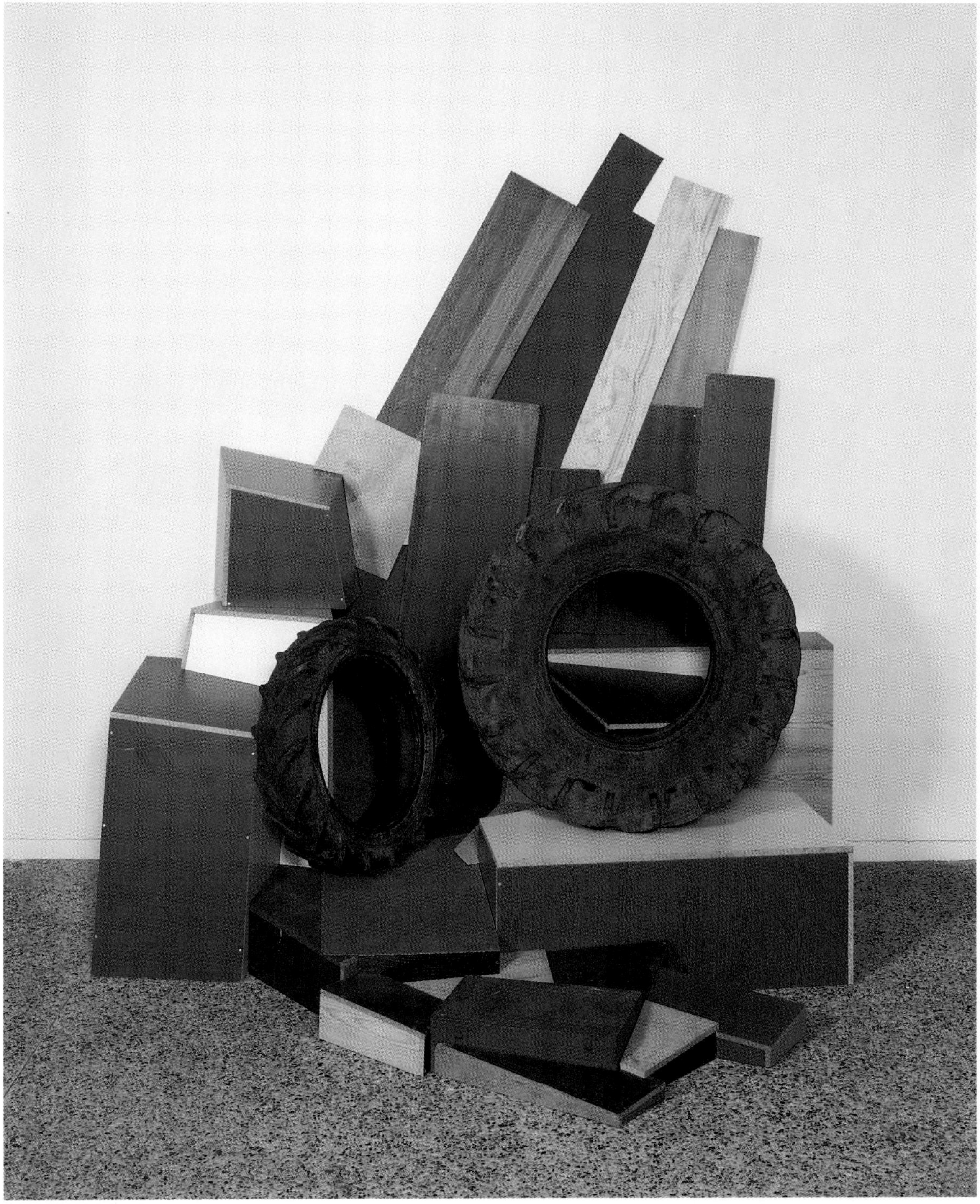

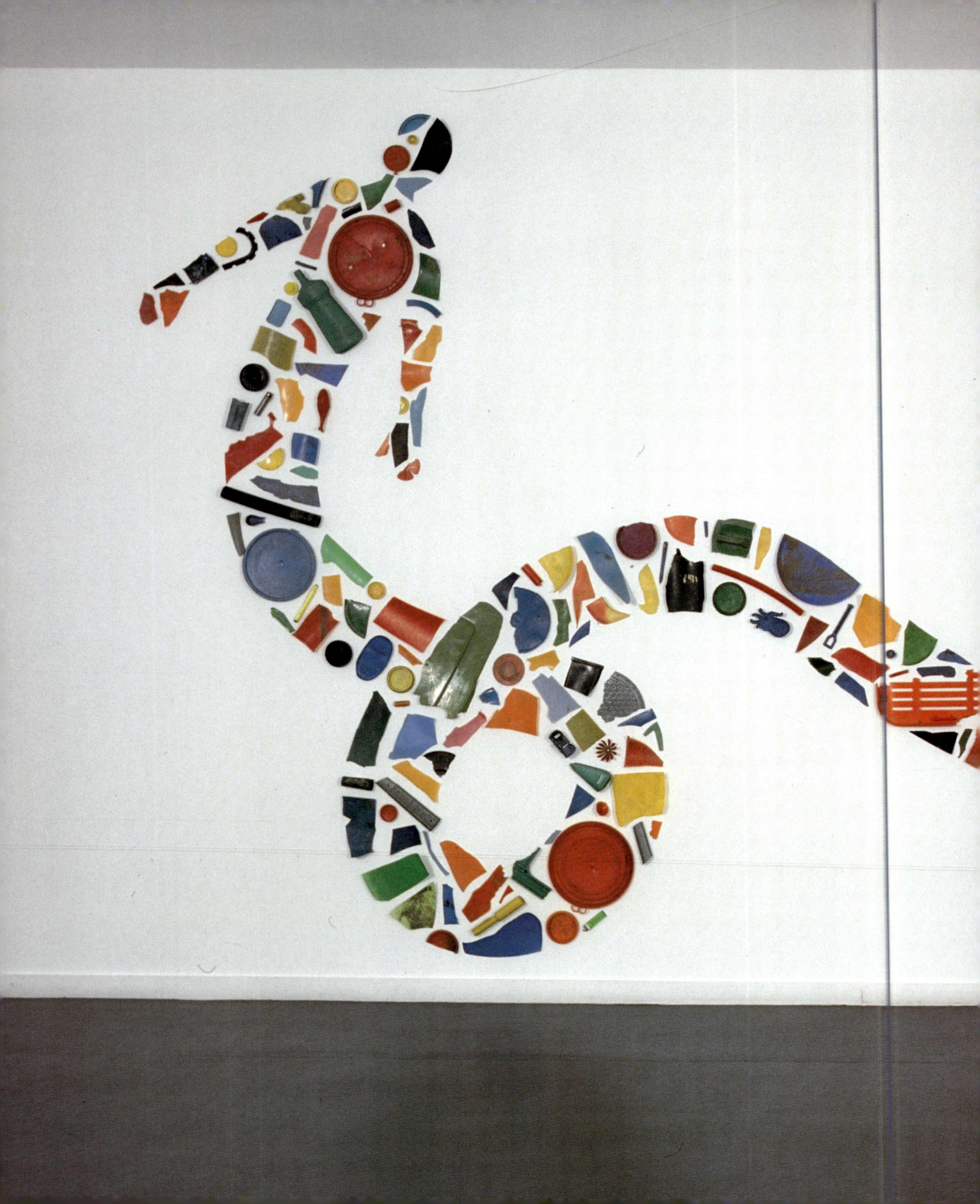

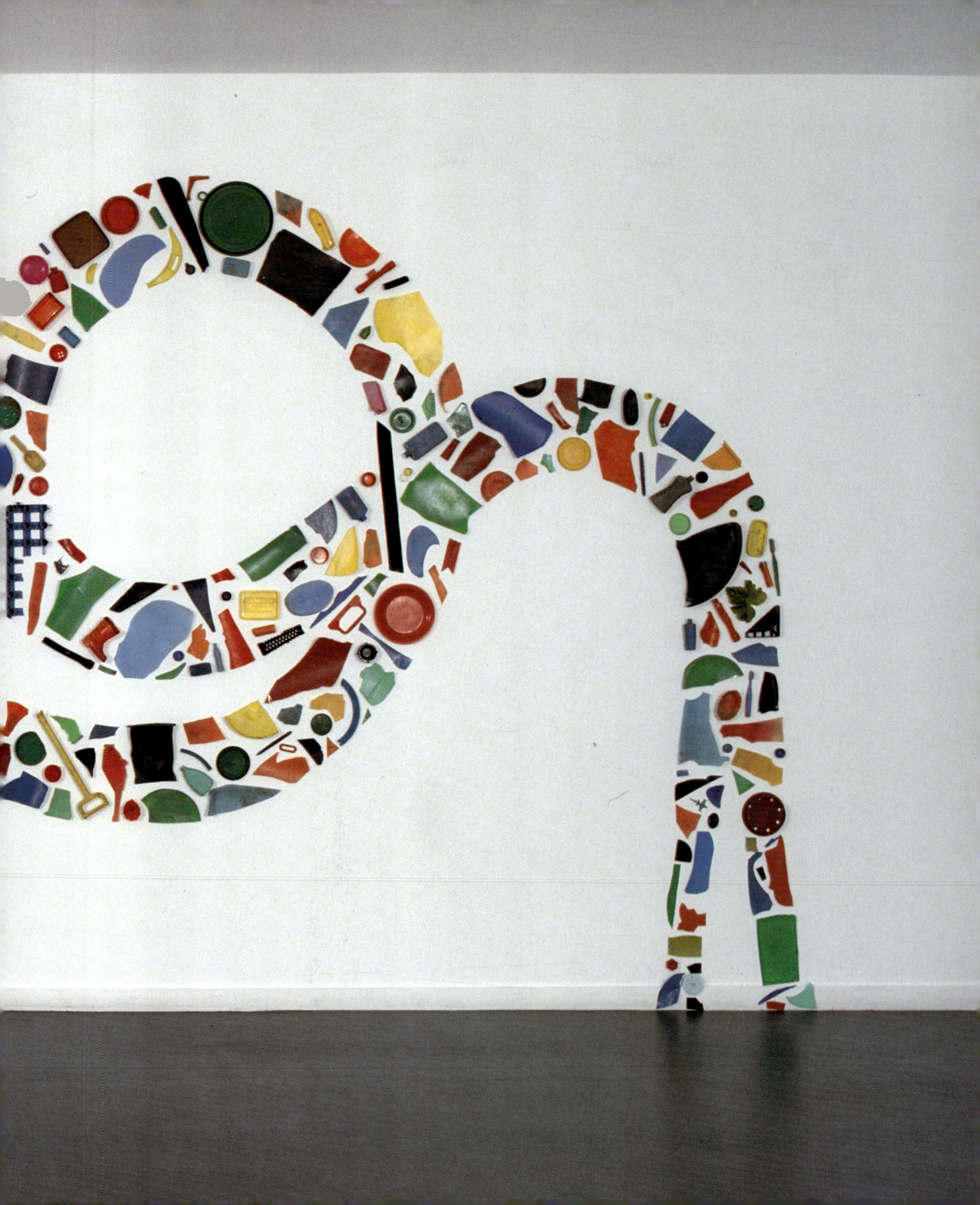

50. *Bacchus Drops*, 198

The materials I use are man-made or at least man-modified and as such belong to a huge category of materials/objects which are integral to the physical, intellectual and emotional lives of men. Though, in fact, one has to emphasize the physical relationship, which is parallel to the already mentioned notion of progress; a progress almost entirely of a materialistic nature. And we have such a bad physical relationship to the objects and materials we produce that it is almost embarrassing to consider the metaphysical, the poetical, the mythological.

First published in *Tony Cragg. Skulpturen*, exh. catalogue. Hanover: Kestner-Gesellschaft, 1985, p. 40.

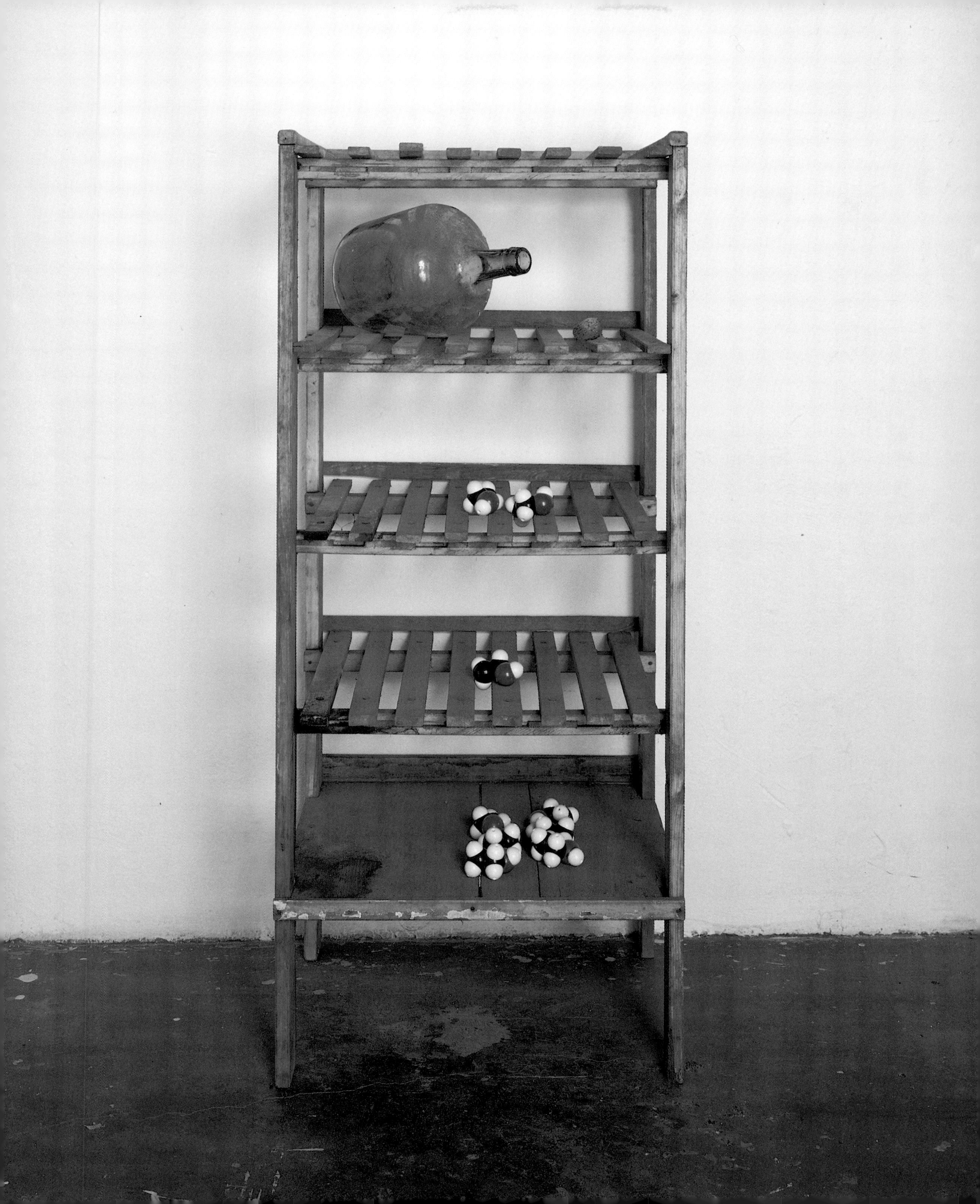

51. *Twenty-four Hours Cycle*, 1984

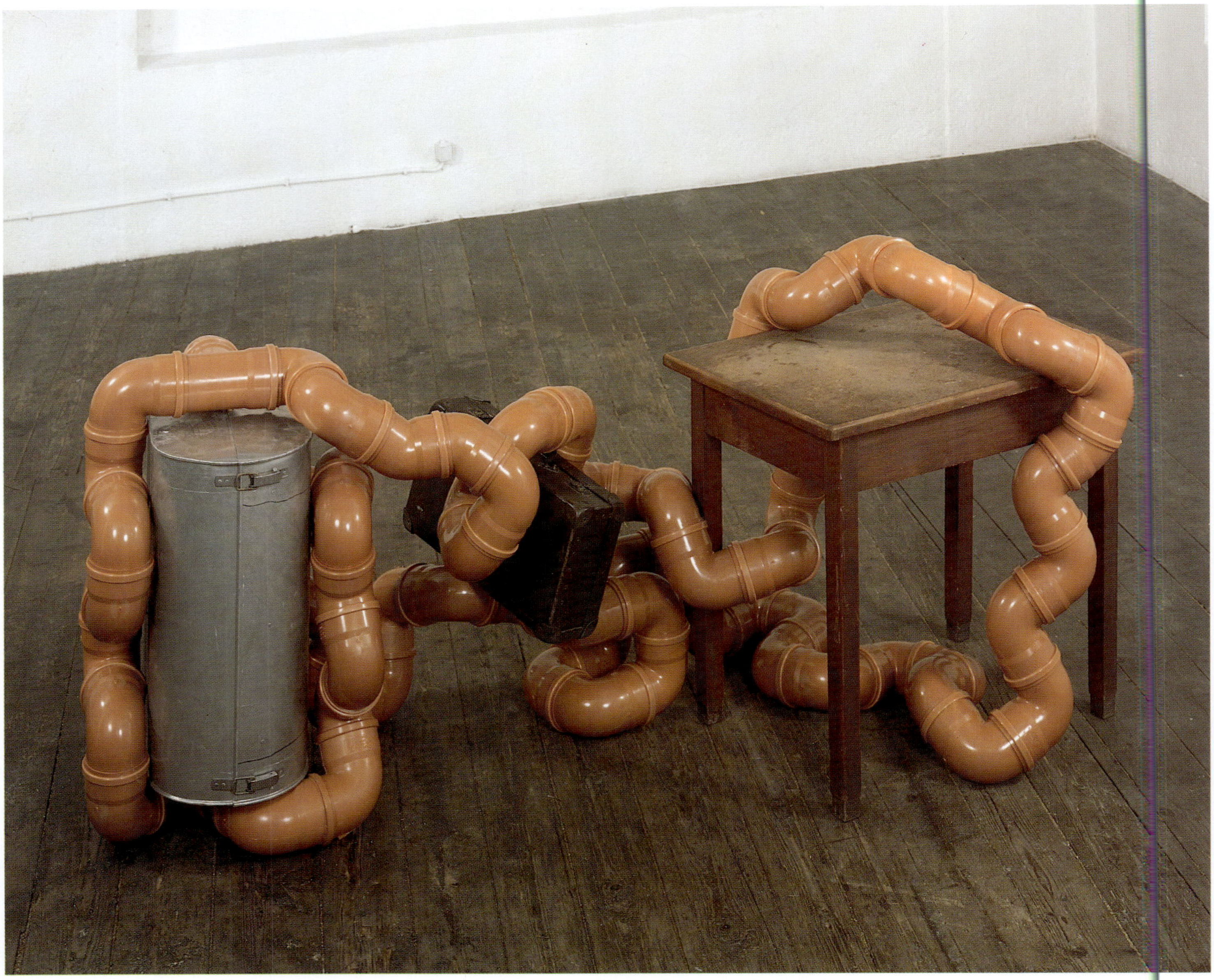

52. *VoltAmpOhm*, 1985

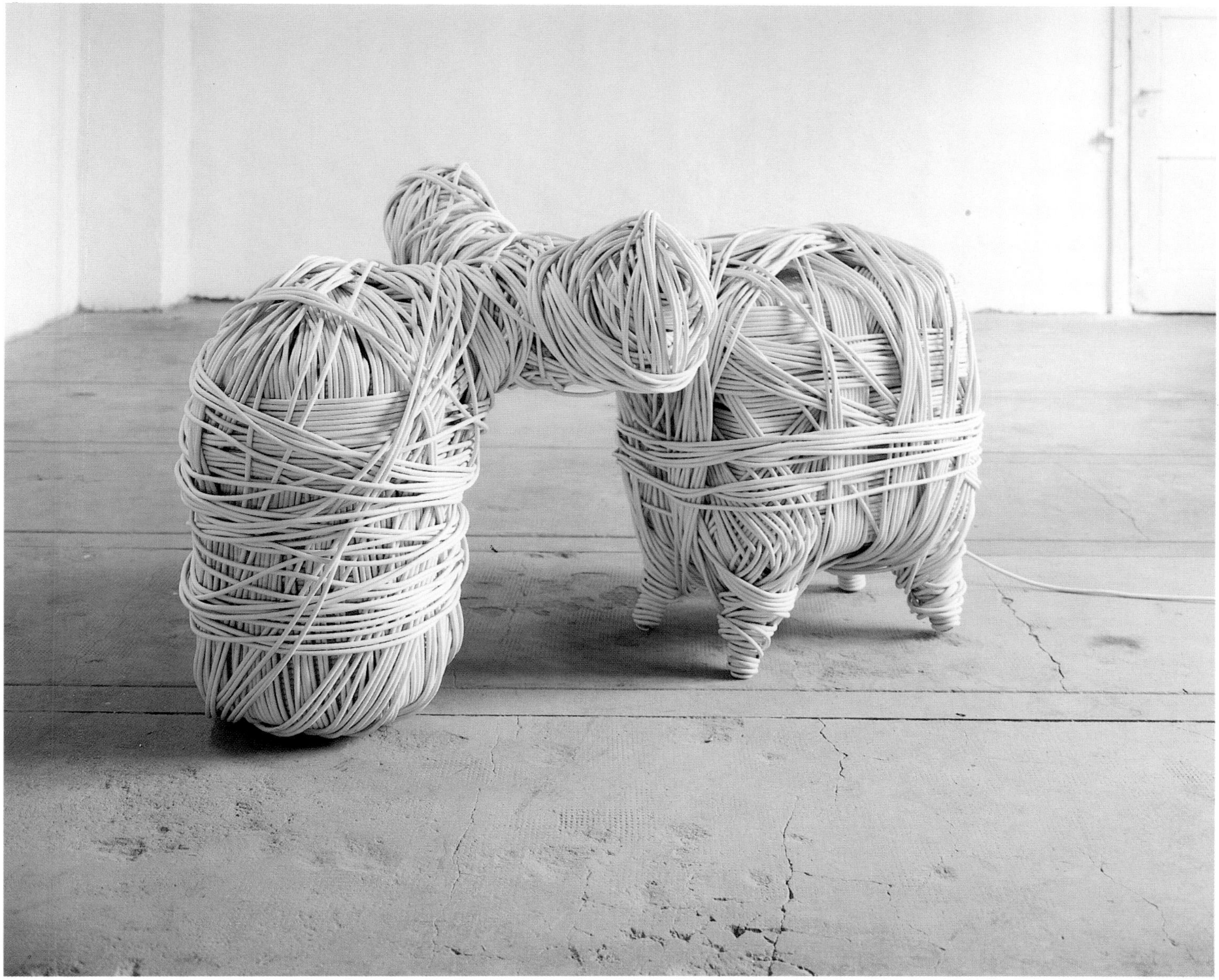

53. *Shore Landscape*, 1985

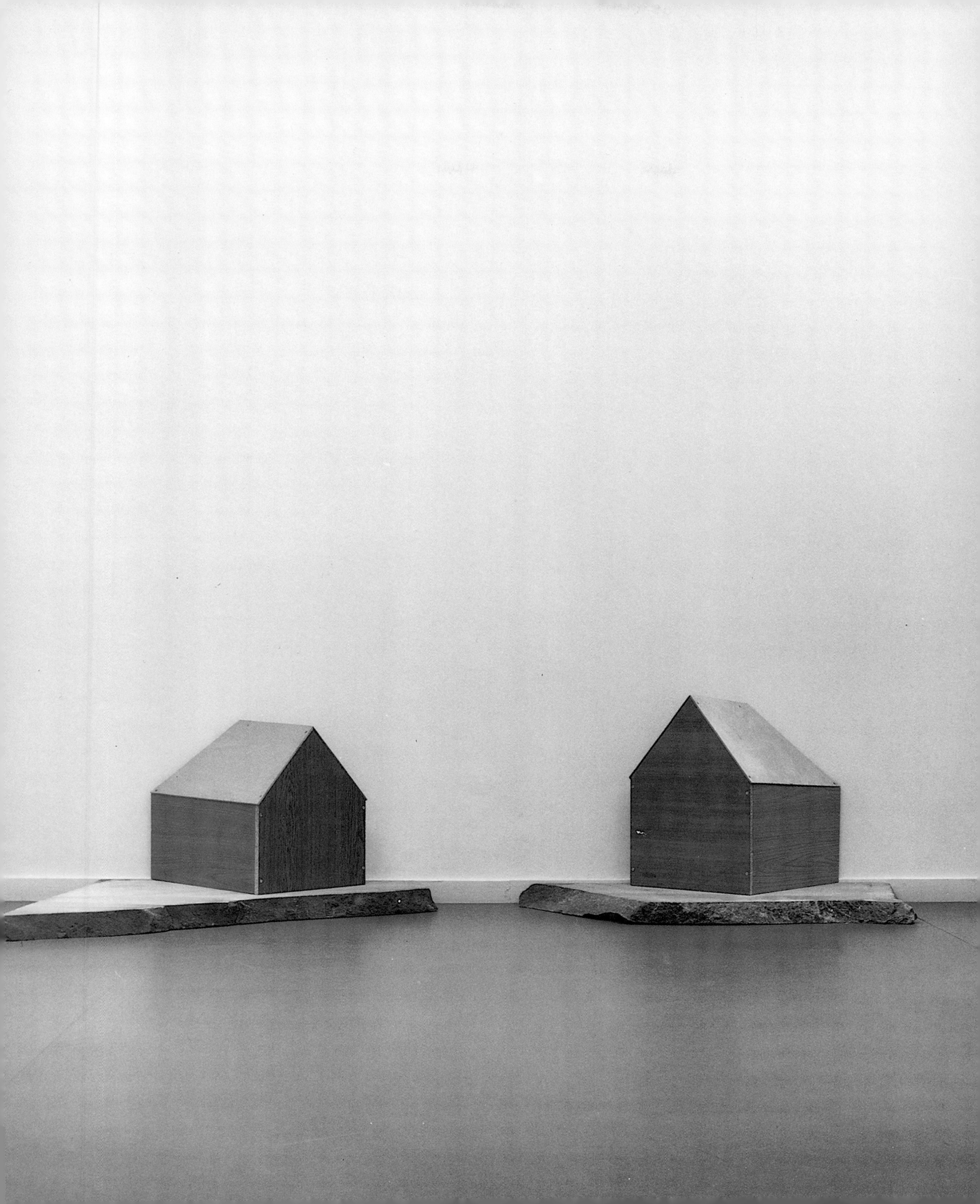

54. *Houses in Fjord*, 1985

55. *Lens*, 1985

56. *Tools*, 1986

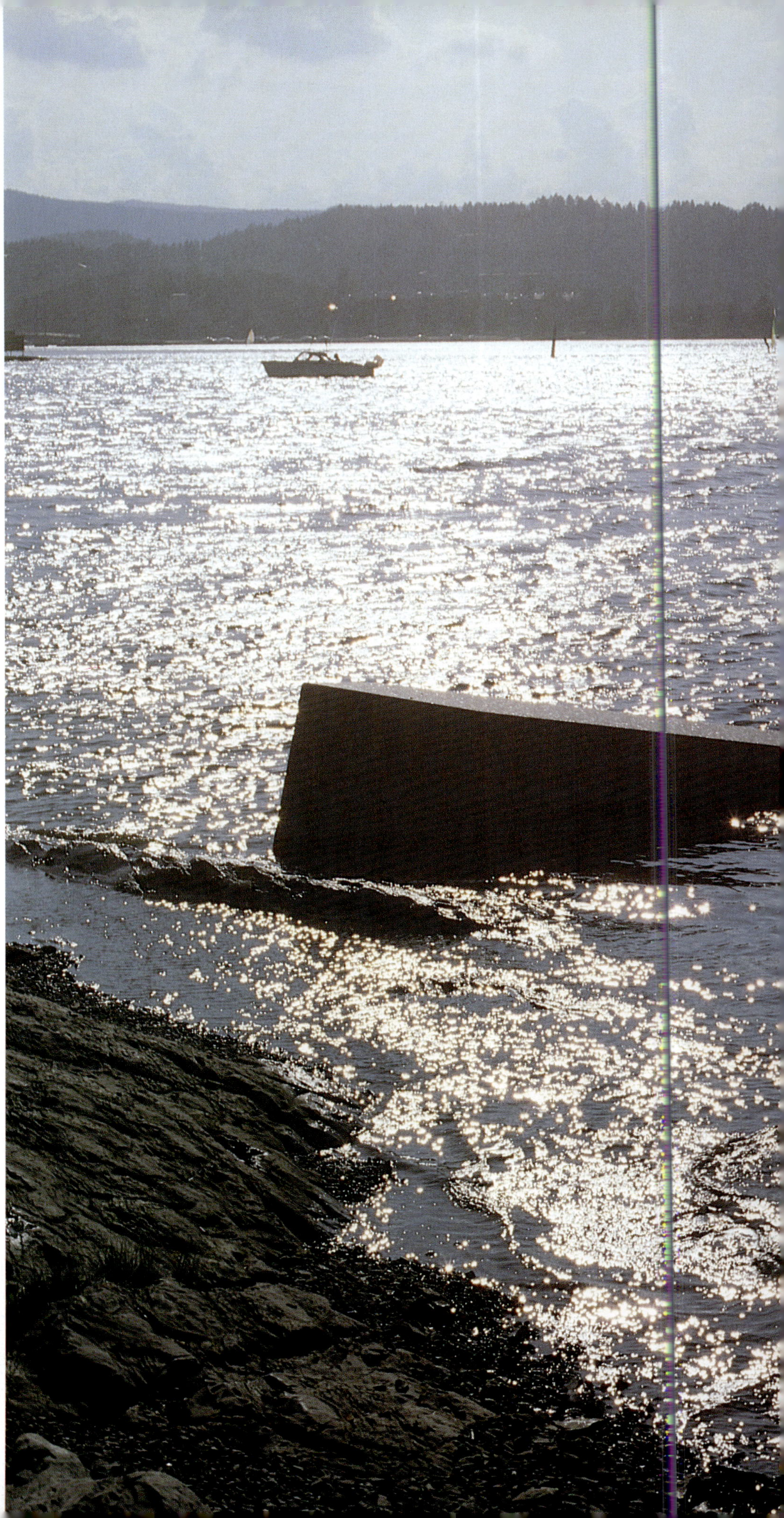

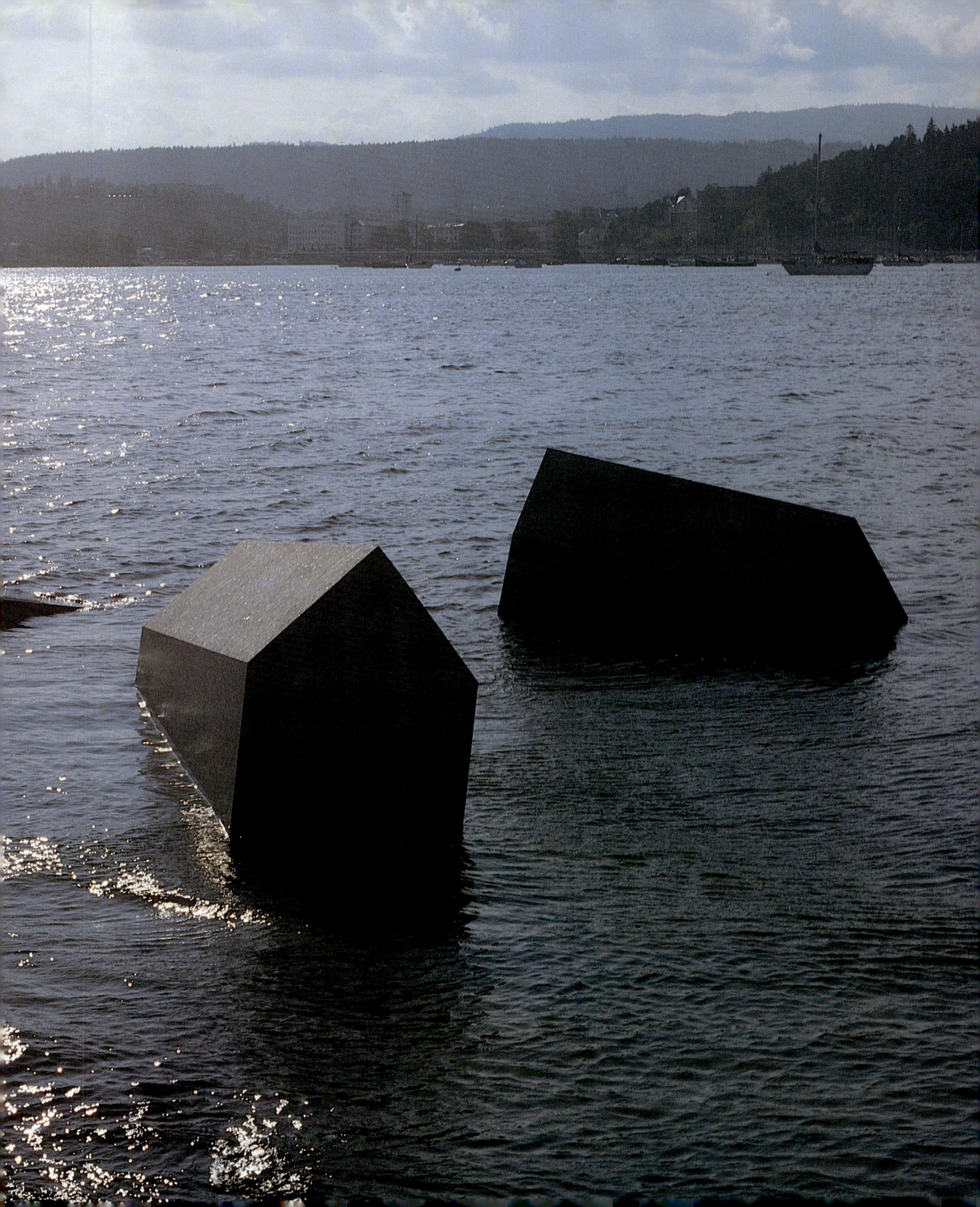

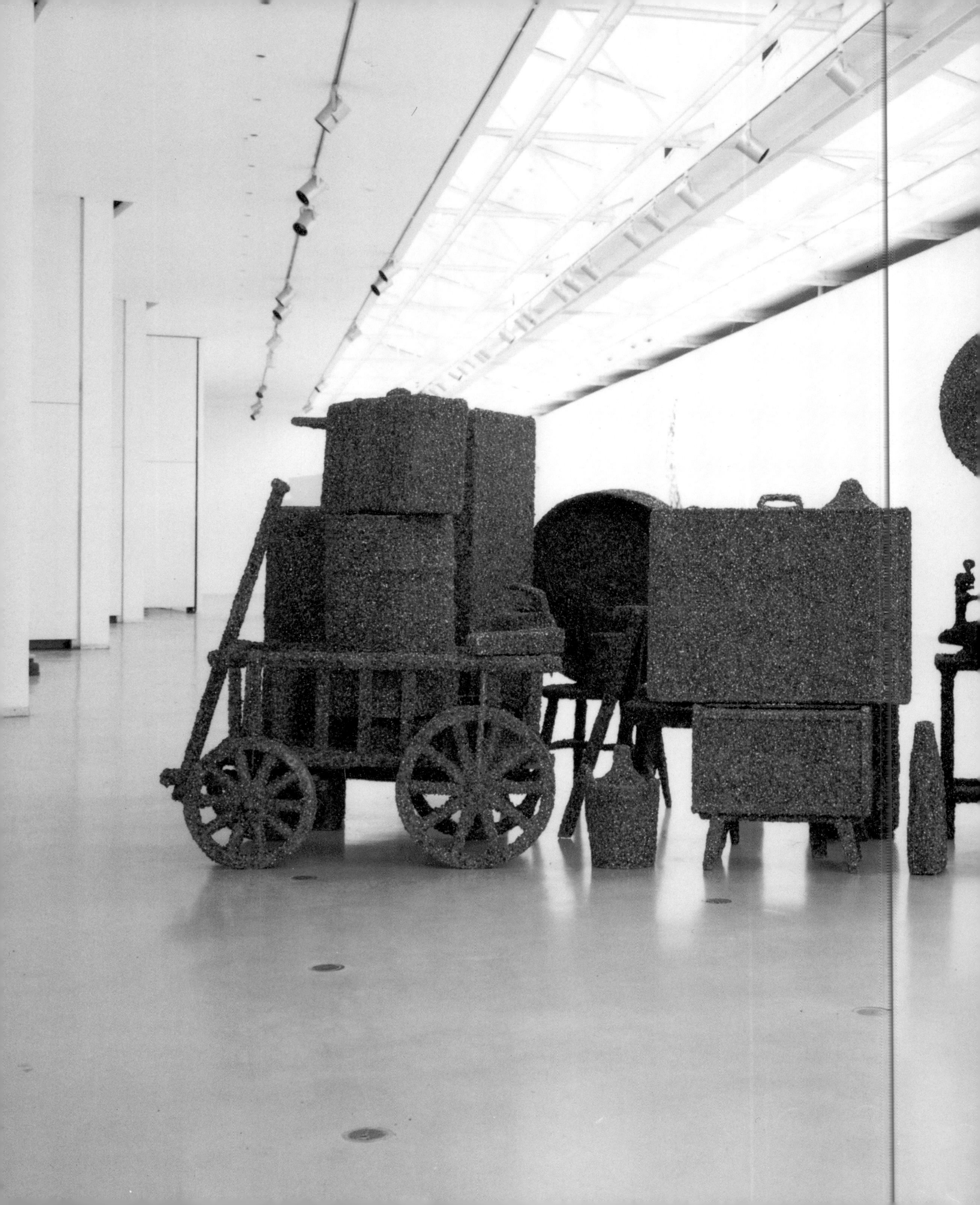

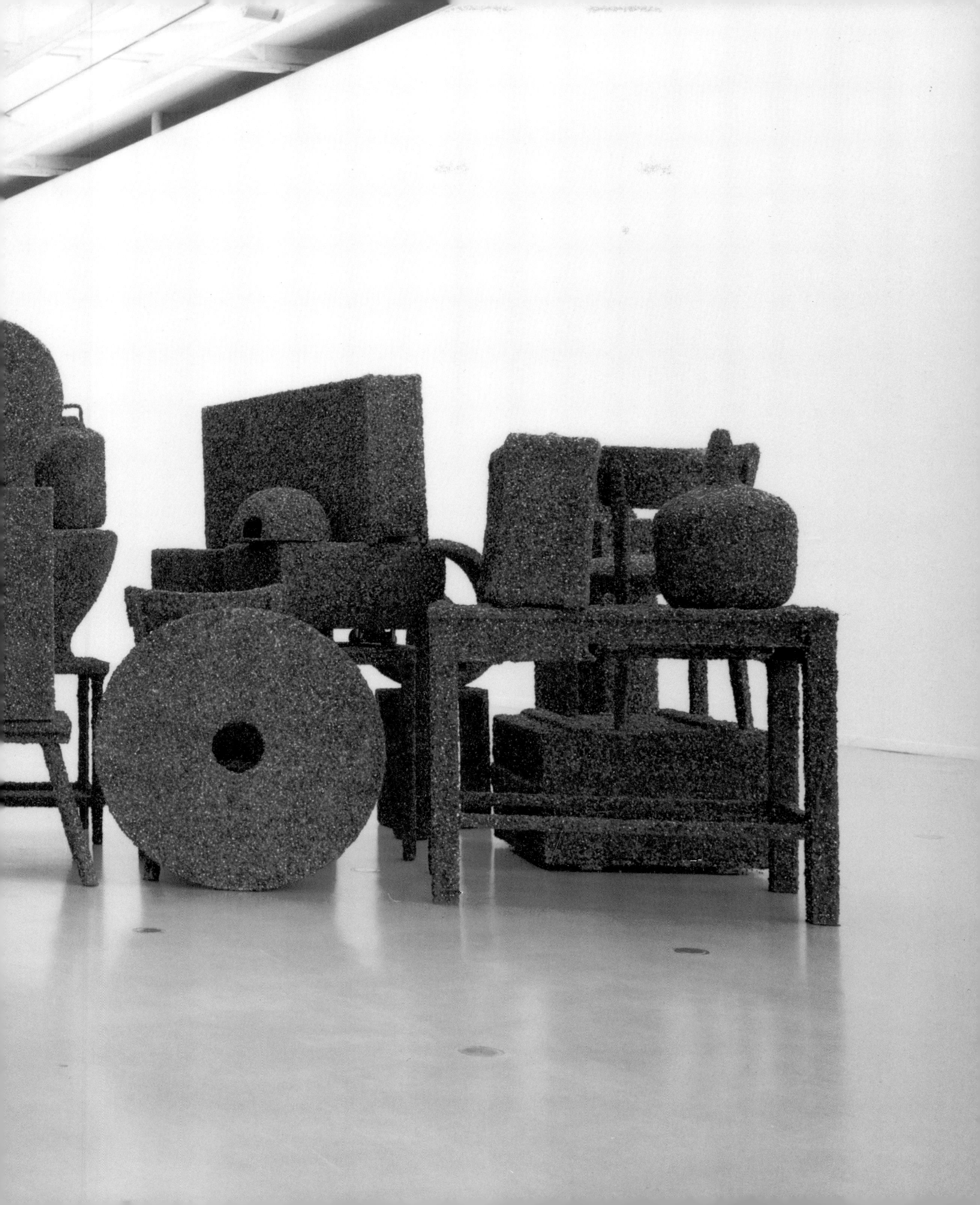

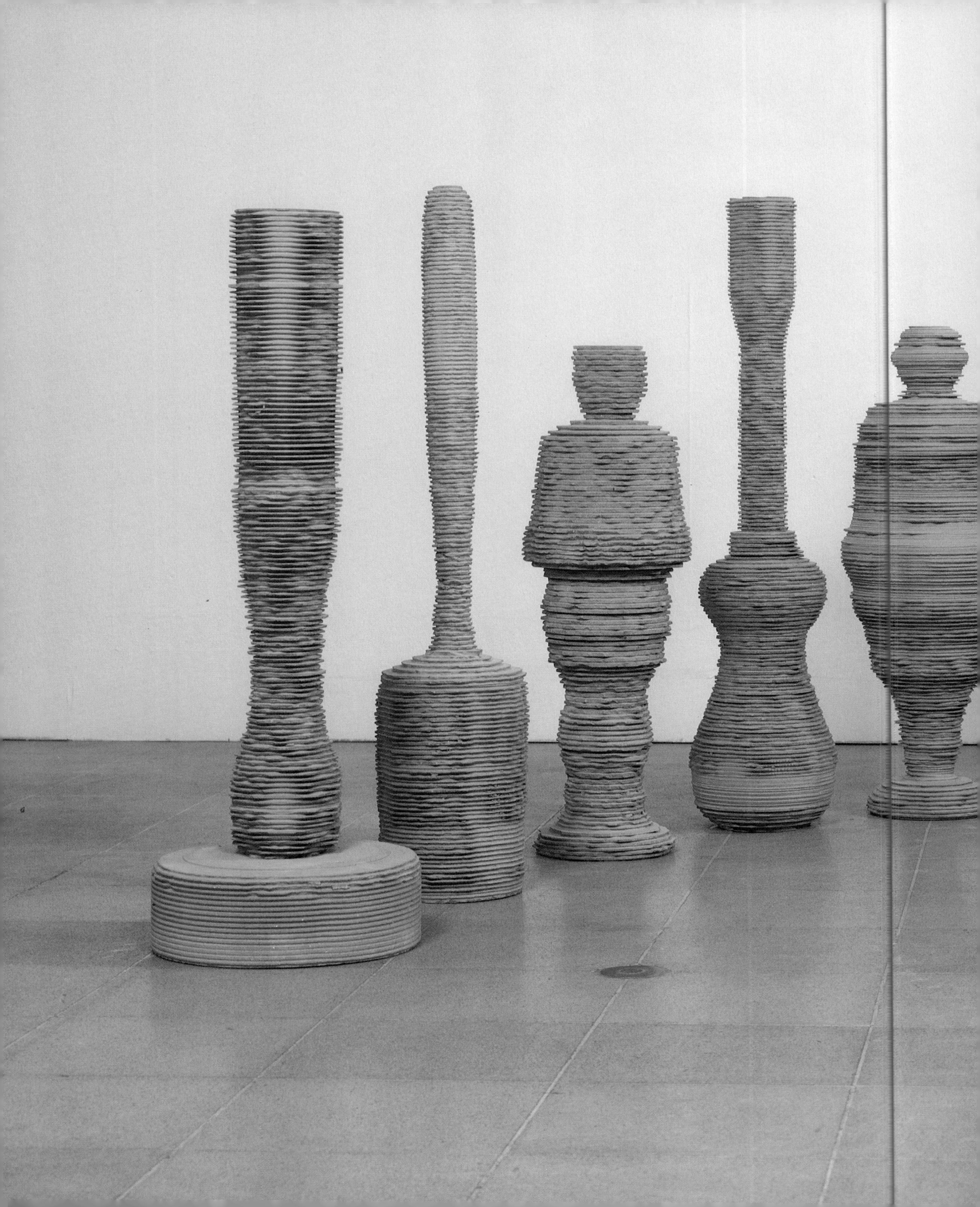

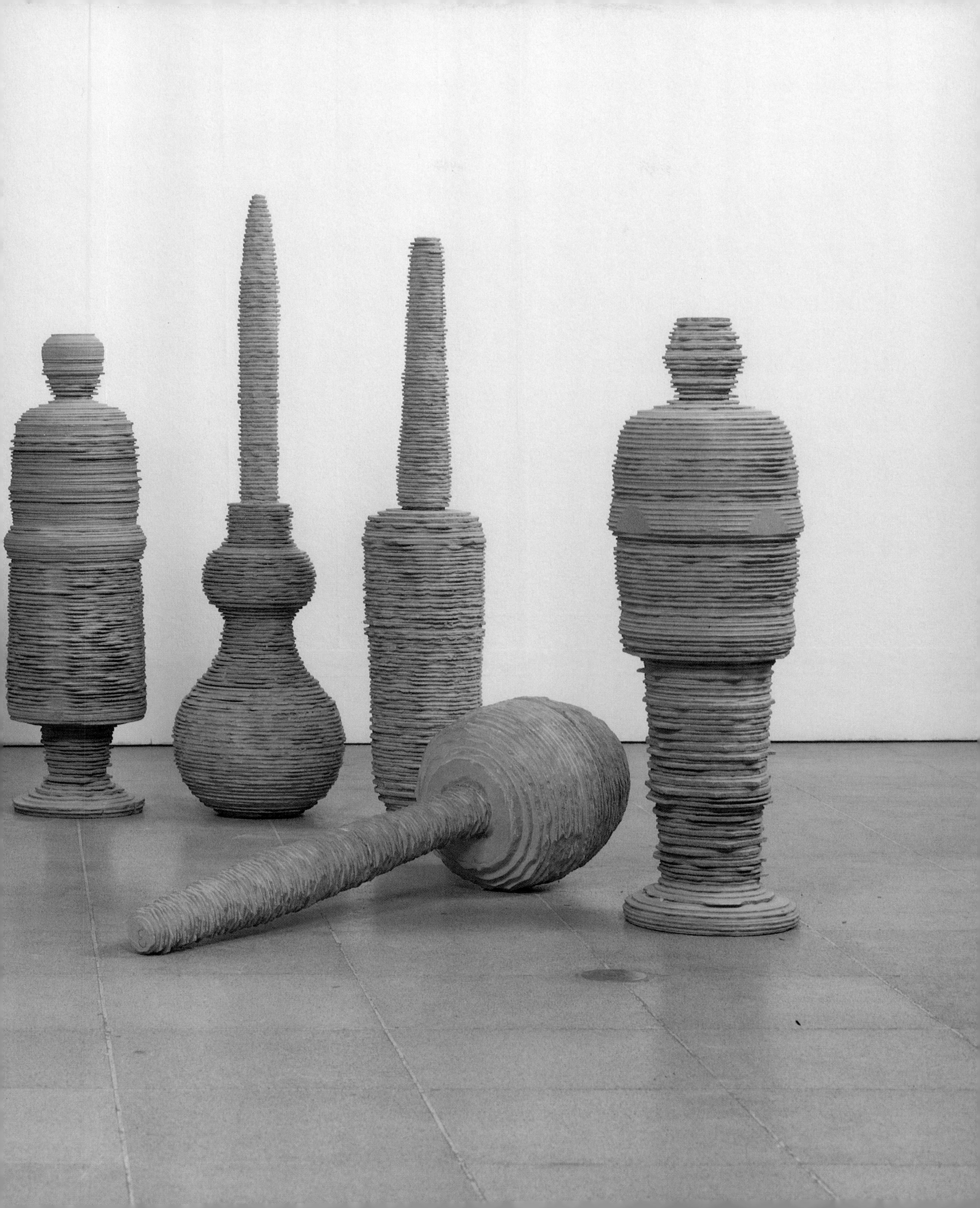

57. *Città*, 1986

Some artists like to exploit certain historical or cultural events. I prefer to use the world we live in. Everything on a beach is beautiful: the stones, nature, the plastic! Stone is a basic material, through our evolution. Plastic (what a beautiful material and what extraordinary colours) is a pure, man-made material. I do not disregard other materials. I use everything but preferably after they have been used by man. What interests me is the special critical appraisal which we apply to man-made objects and his activities.

First published in "Tony Cragg. Interview with Demosthène Davvetas." In *Tony Cragg*, exh. catalogue. Brussels: Palais des Beaux-Arts, 1985, p. 32.

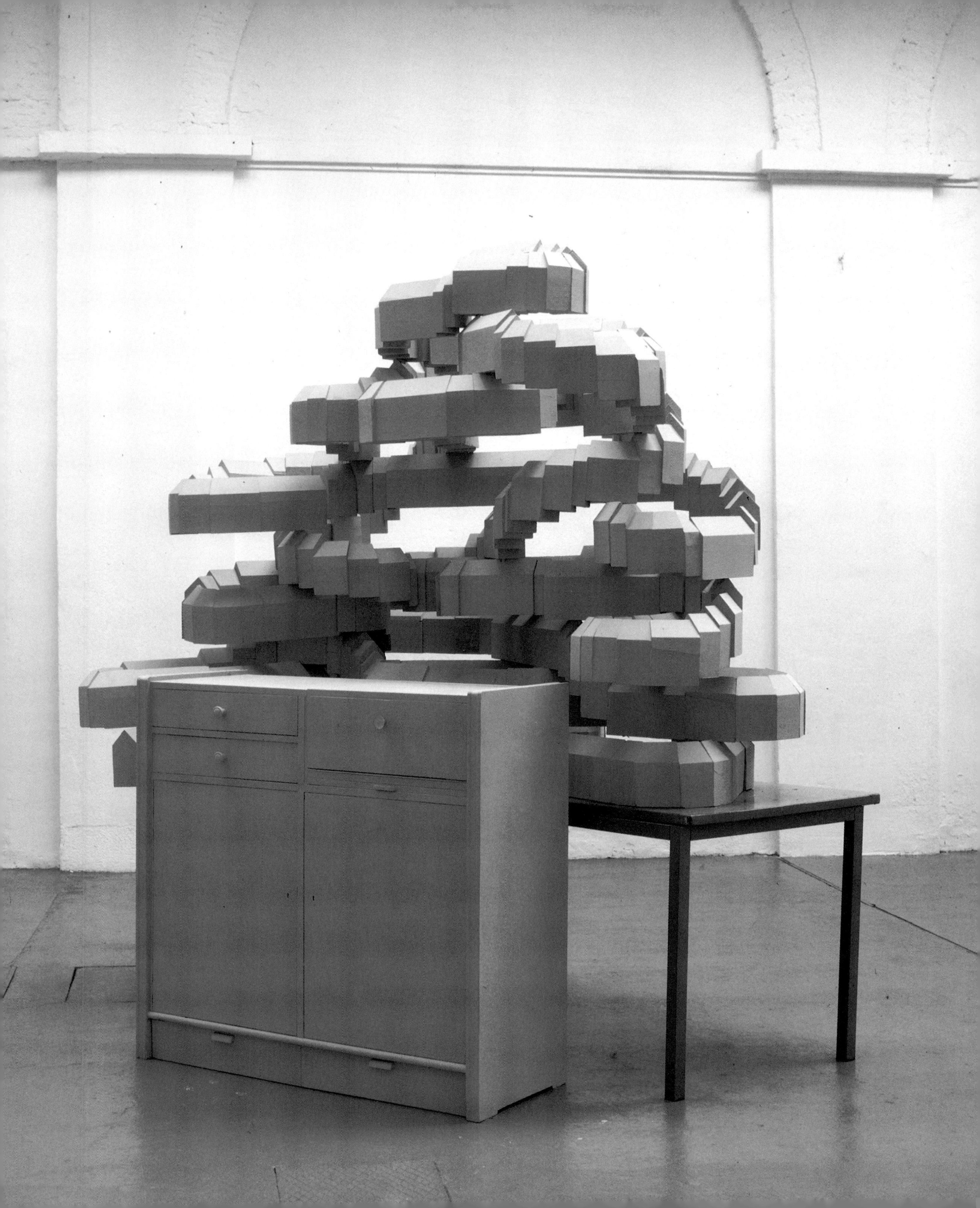

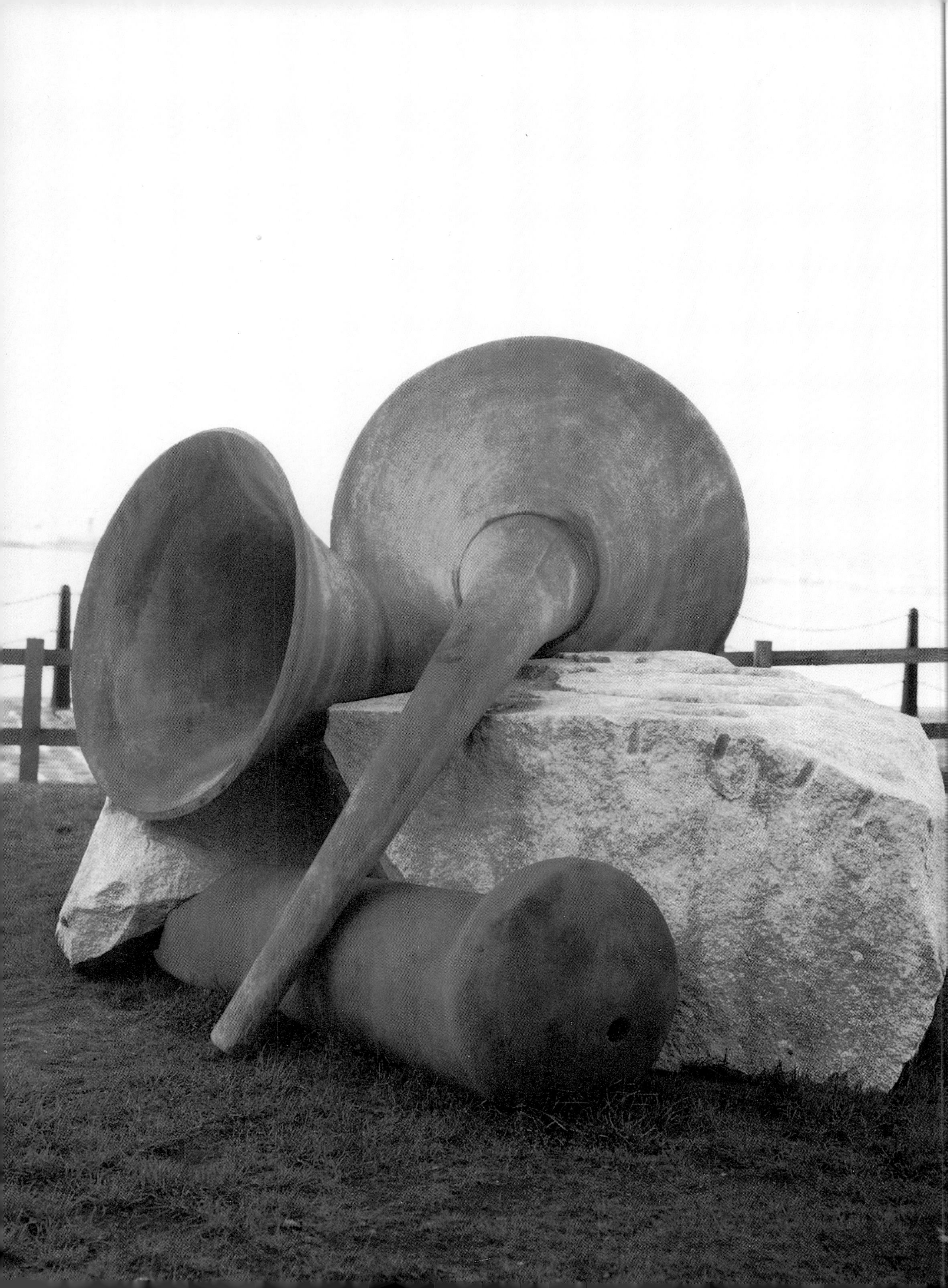

58. *Raleigh*, 1986

59. *Keymer*, 1986

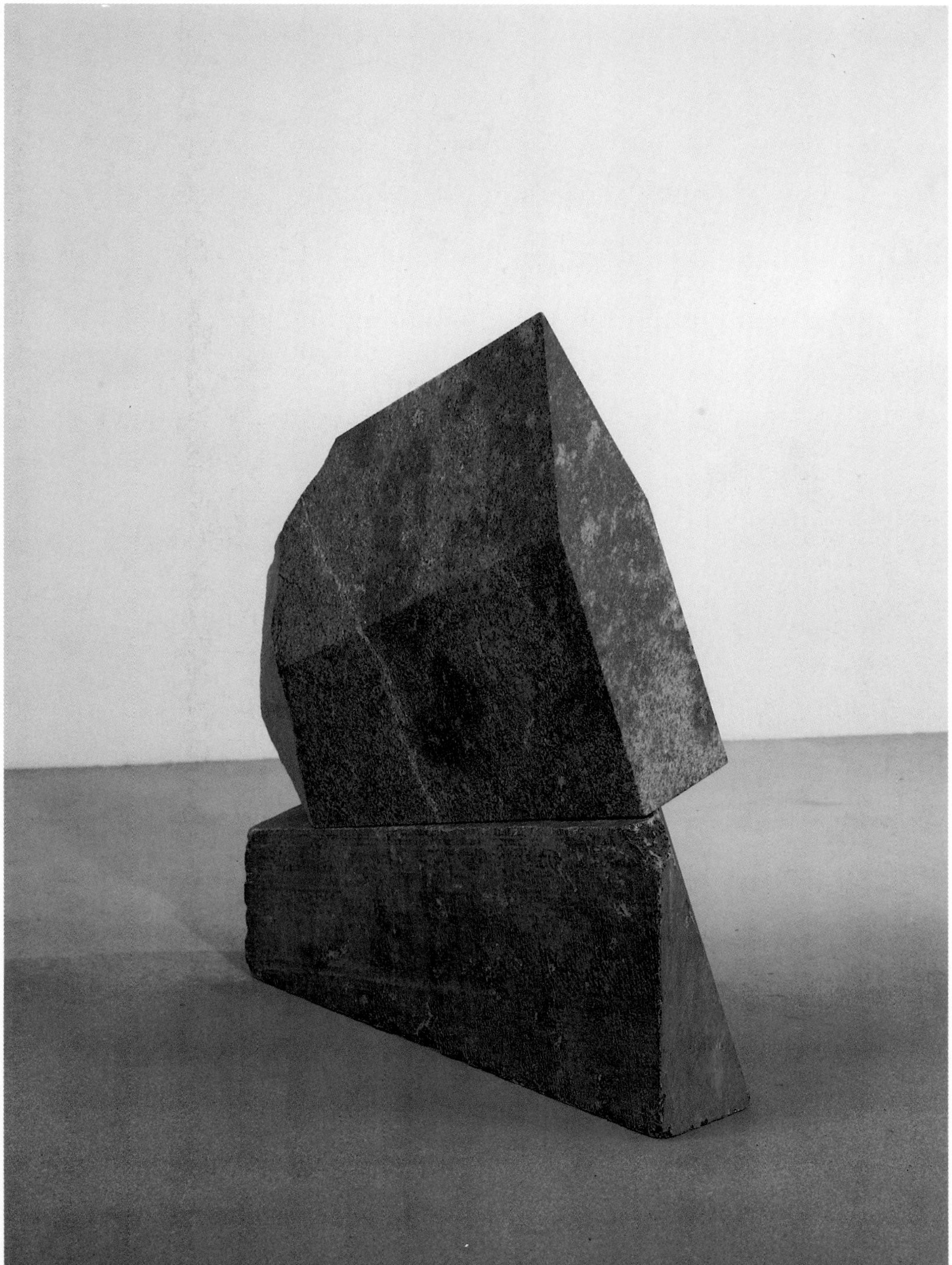

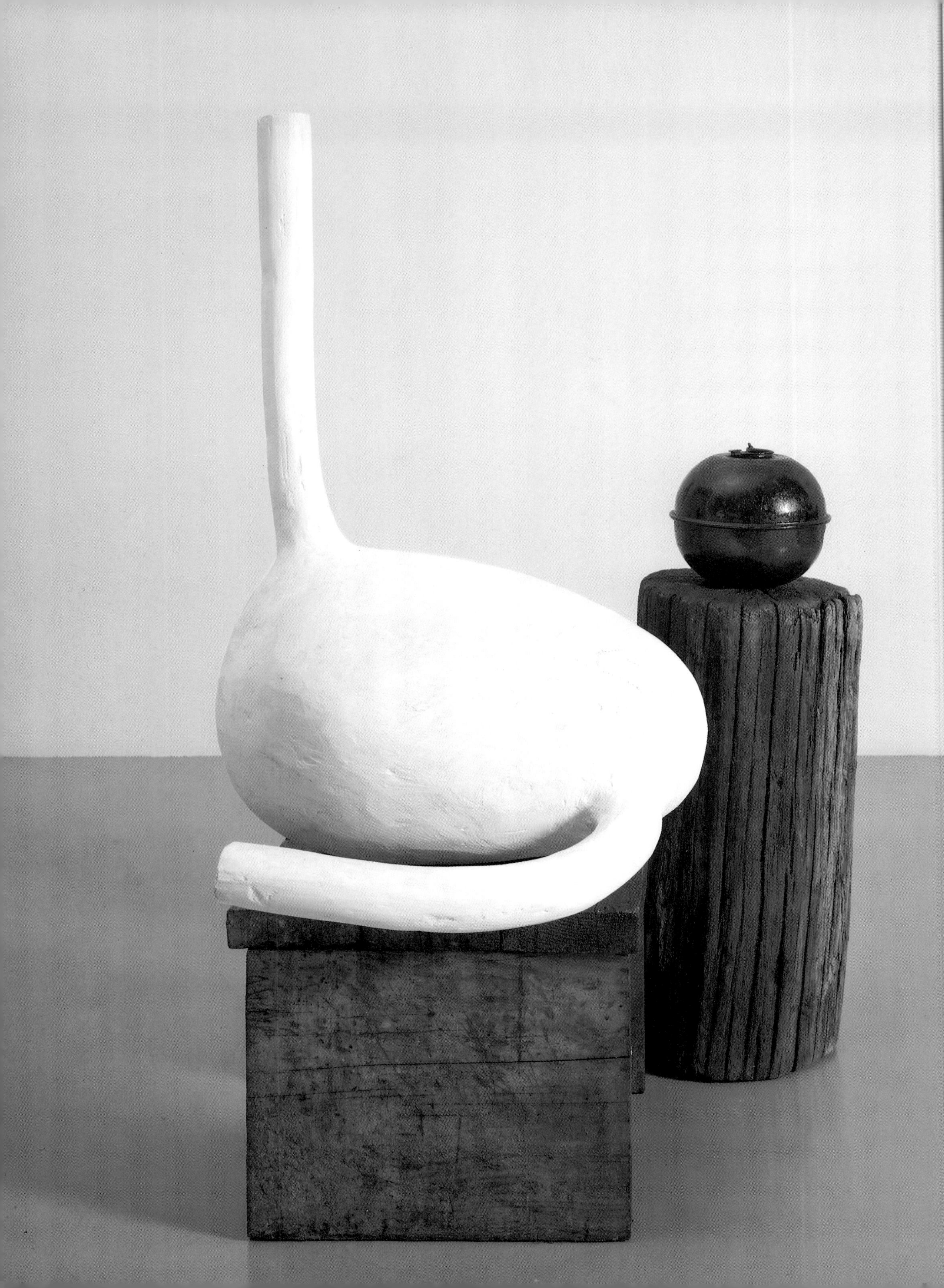

60. *Stomach*, 1986

61. *Eroded Glass*, 1986

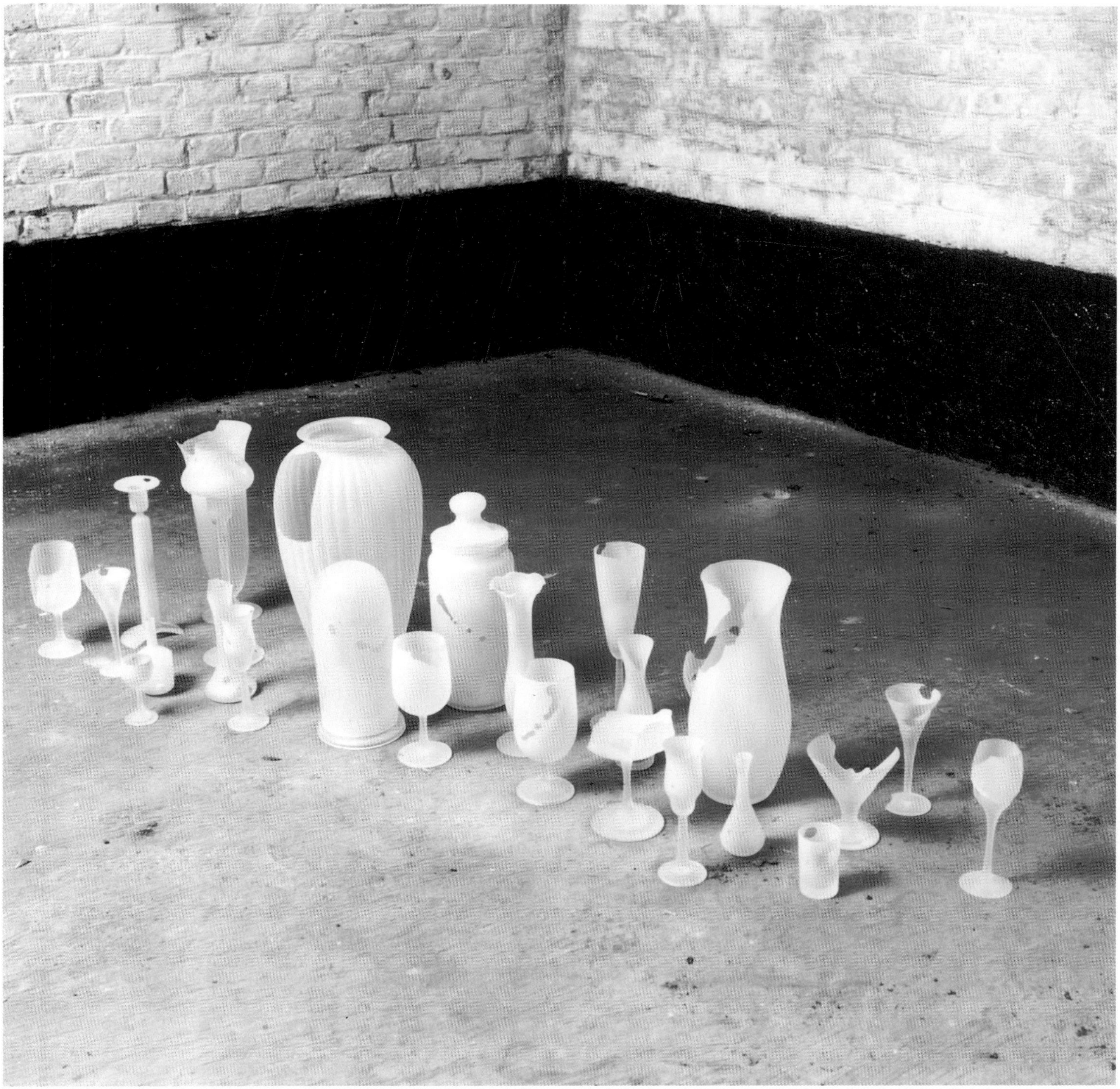

62. *Crackers Boxes*, 1986

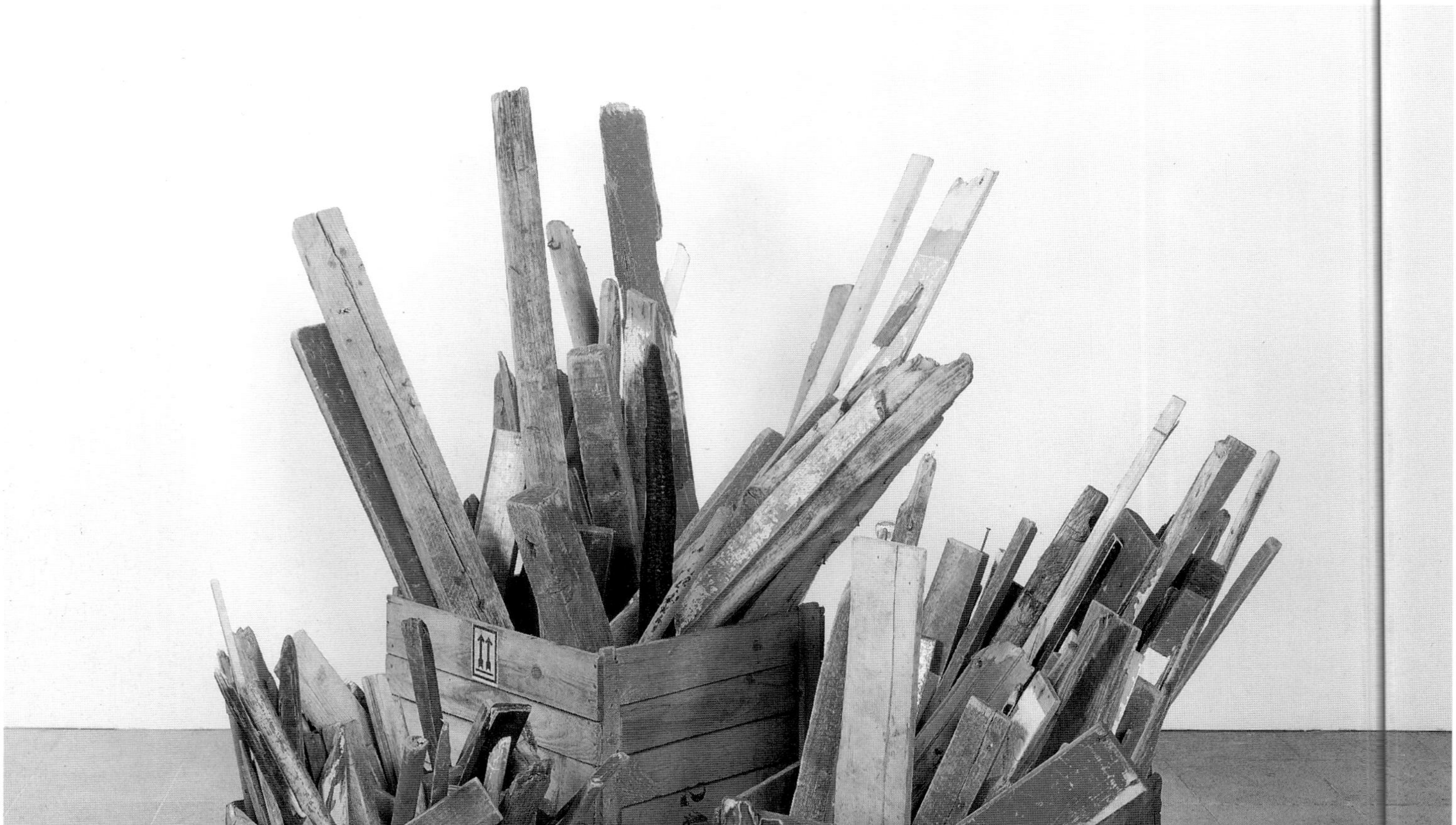

63. *Wooden Muscle*, 1986

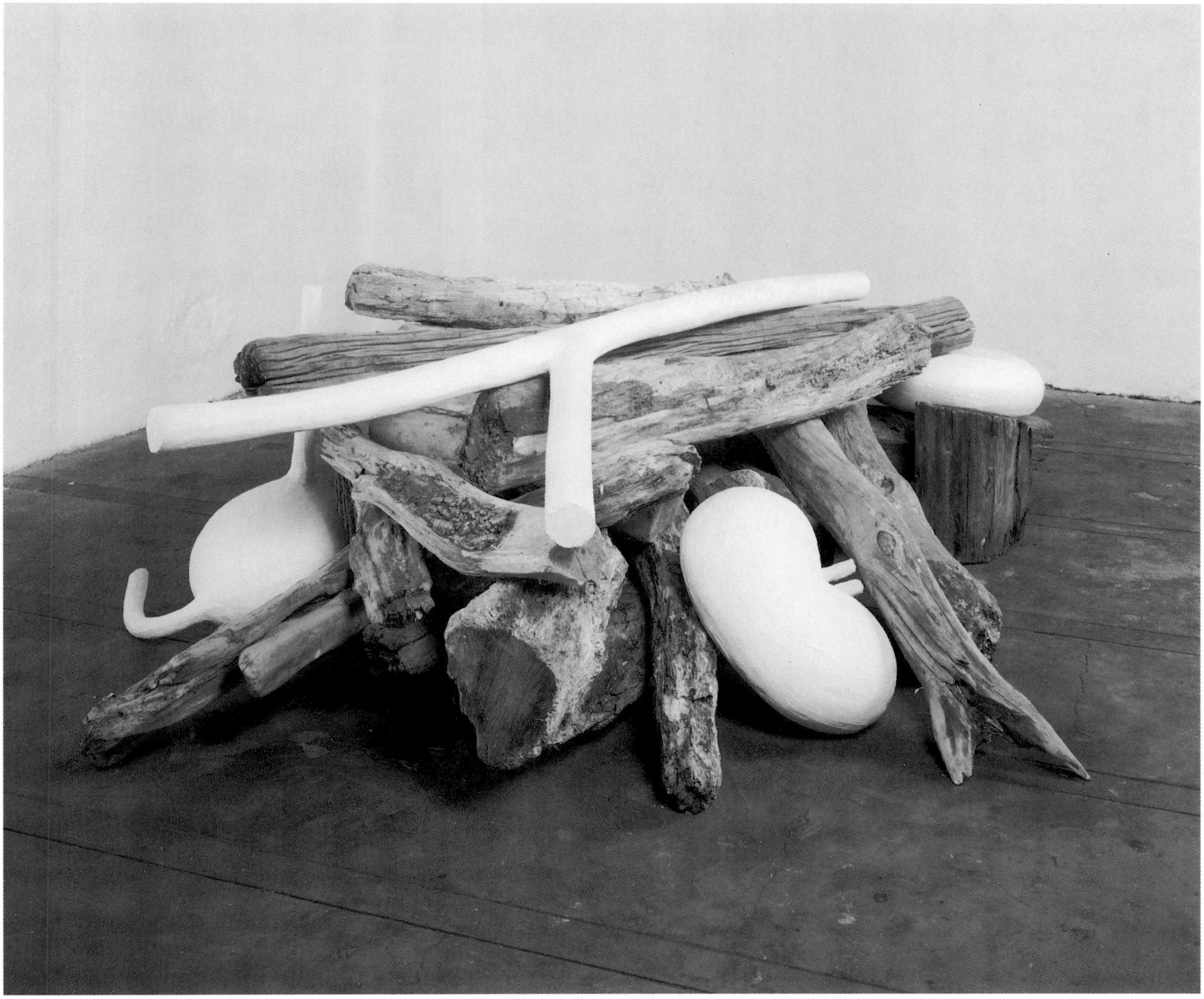

64. *Eroded Landscape*, 1987

65. *Riot*, 1987

The artist is a specialist in a field he defines for himself. This field is a mixture of objectivity, irrationality and subjectivity. In inventing a denser, more complex vocabulary, the artist contributes to an understanding of the world. He is simply a very small fragment of the universe. Torn between himself and his images, he is a grain of organic material in a universe where man cannot grasp his own insignificance ... He can observe the universe, and knows the value of an intellect which can reflect upon its own existence.
In fact it is a celebration of life, which, I think, is his main contribution.

First published in "Tony Cragg. Interview with Demosthène Davvetas." In *Tony Cragg*, exh. catalogue. Brussels: Palais des Beaux-Arts, 1985, p. 34.

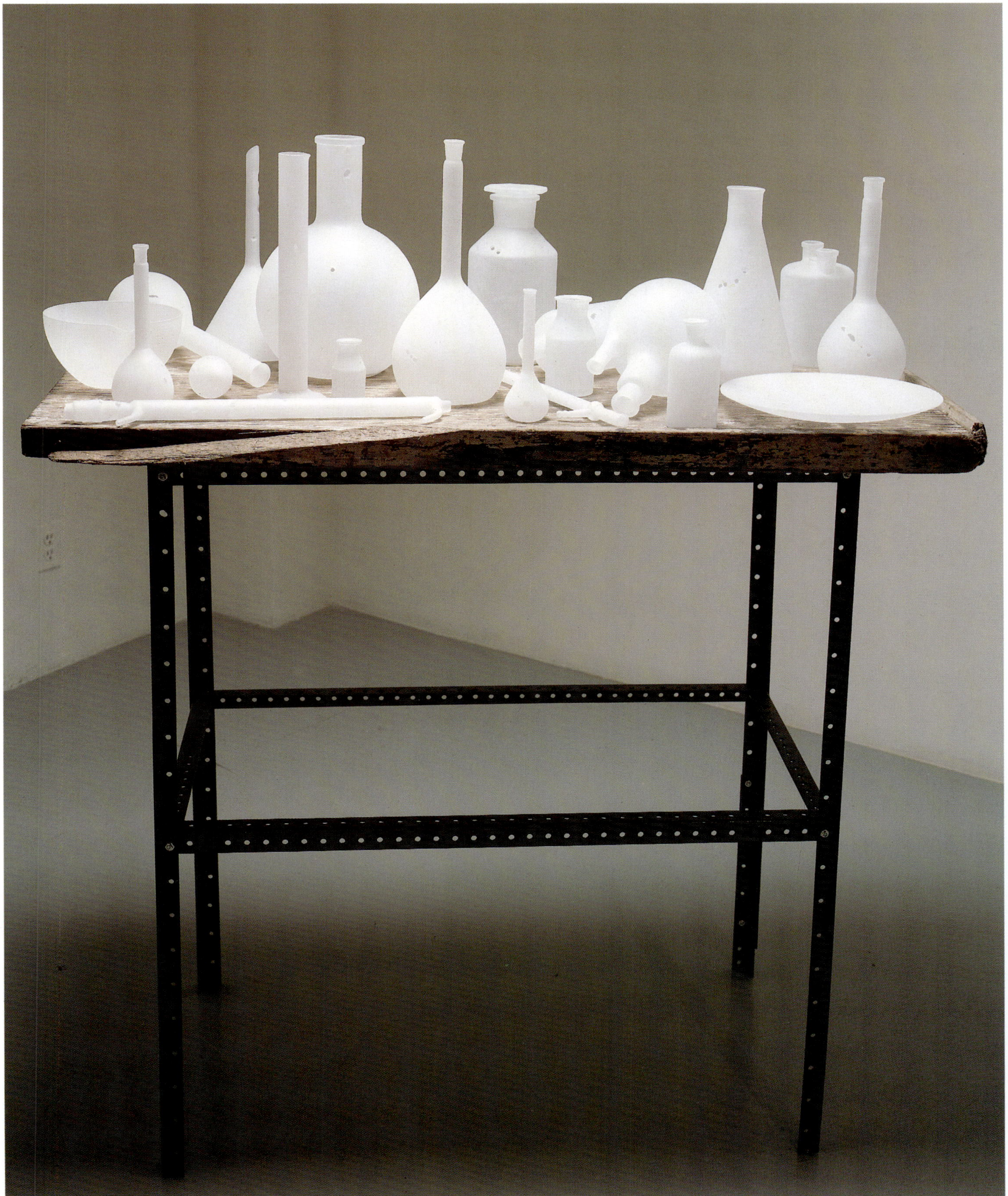

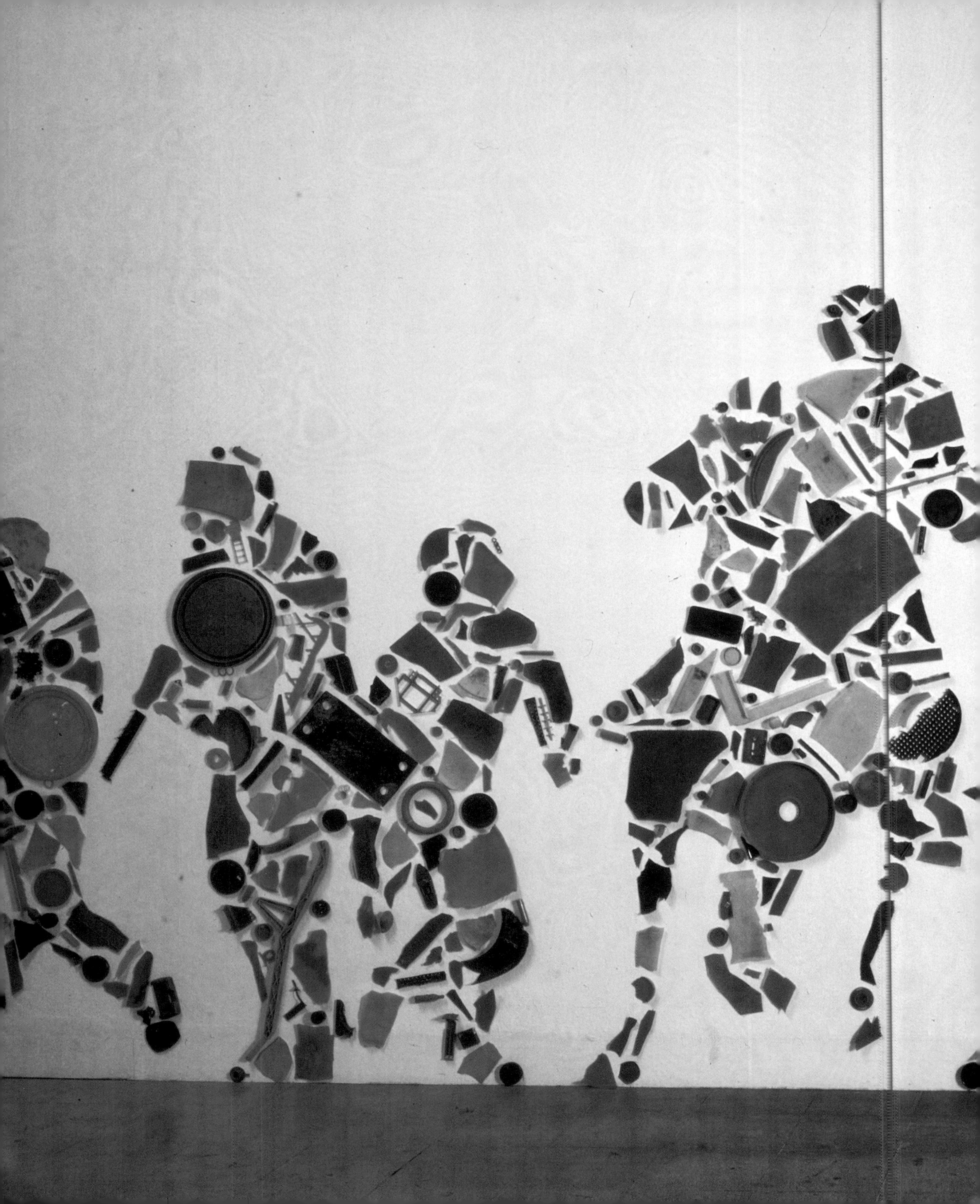

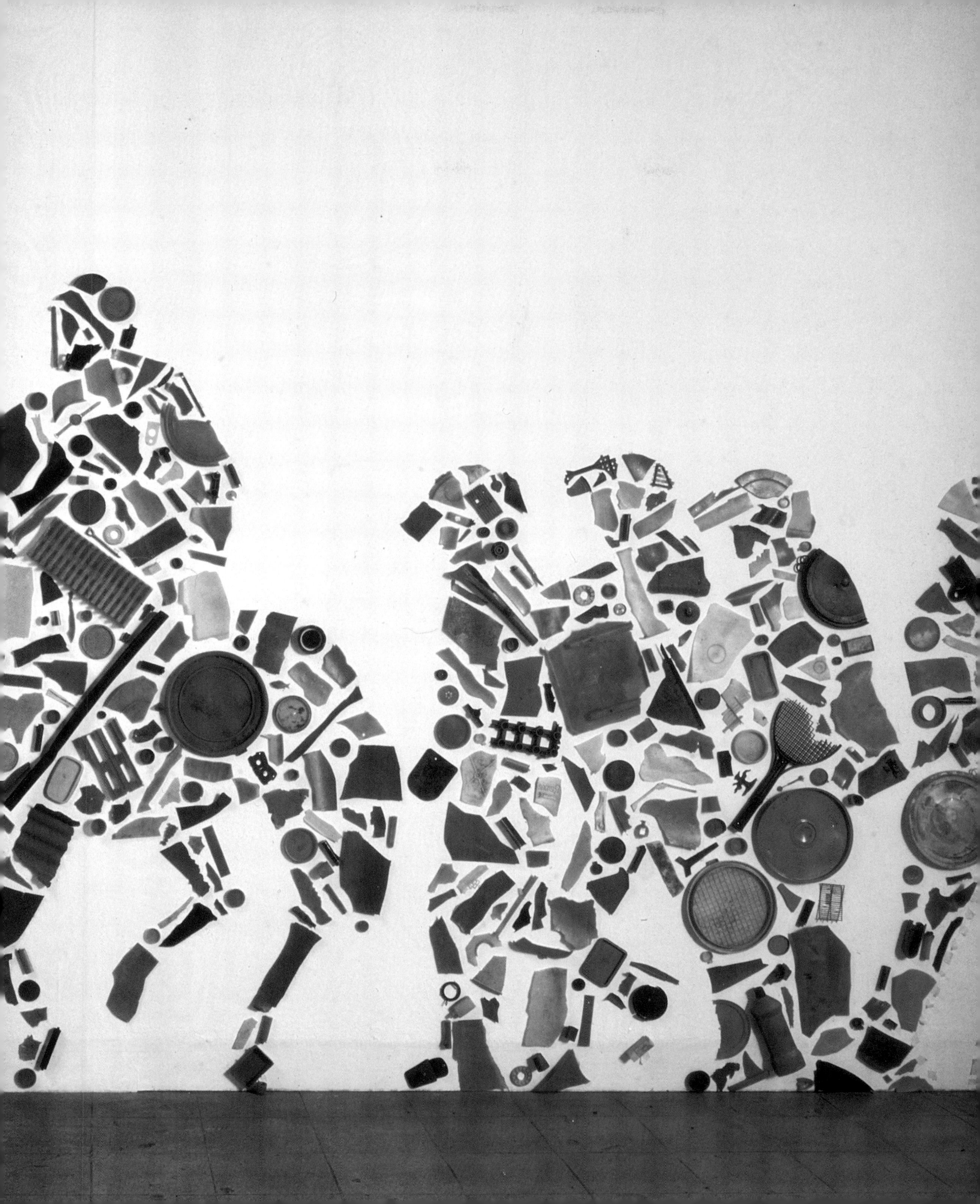

66. *Instinctive Reactions*, 1987

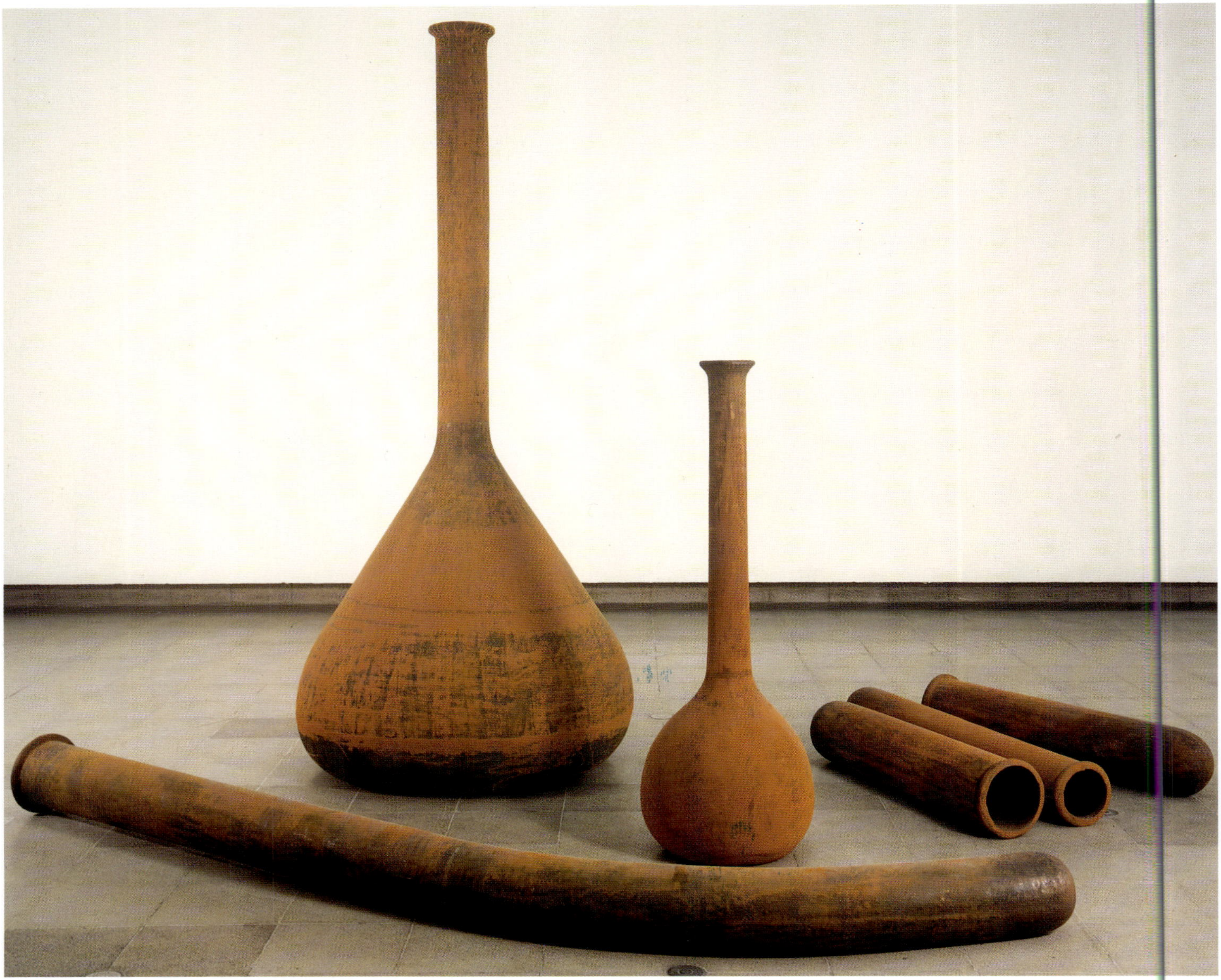

67. *Sedimenti cretacei*, 1987

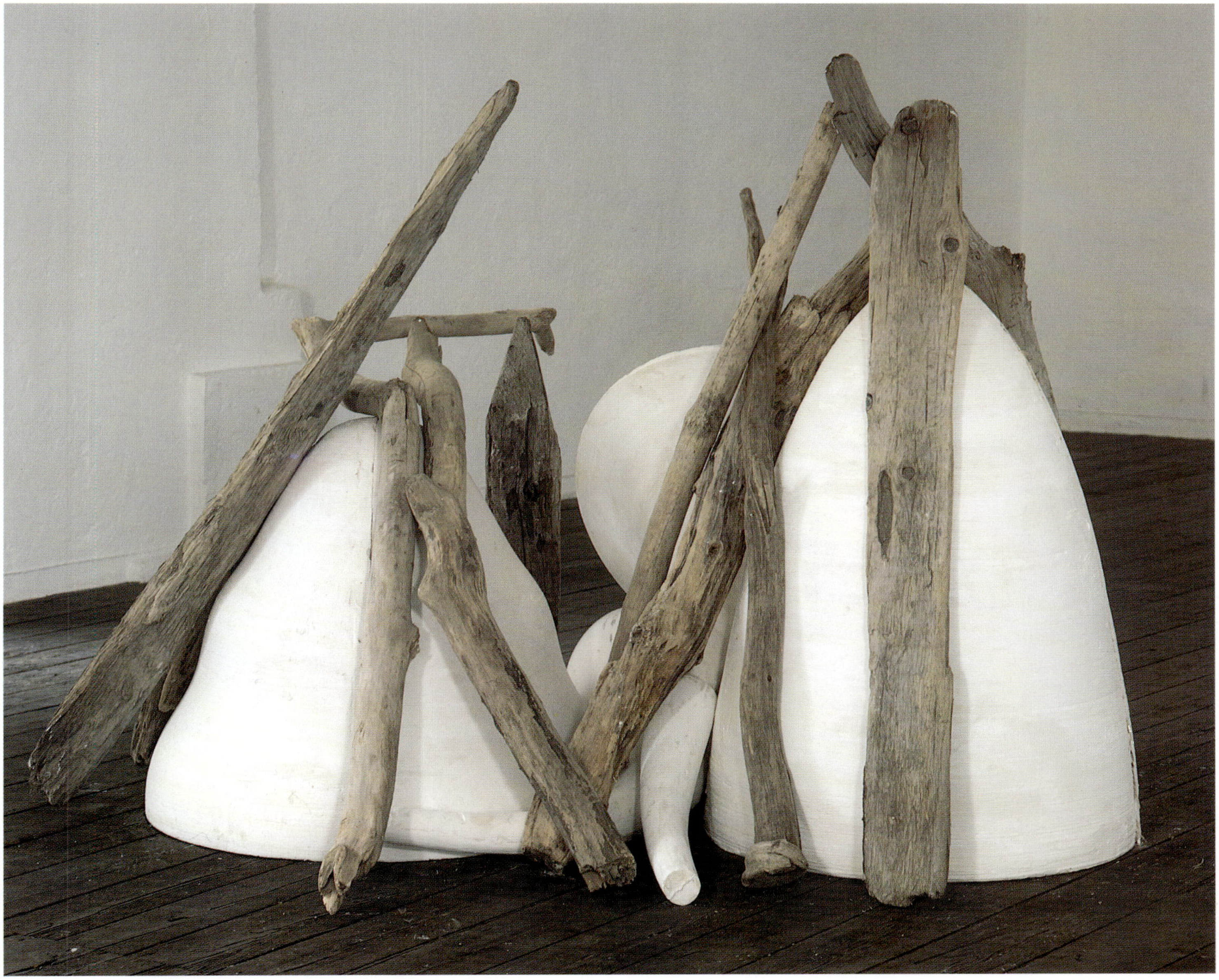

I don't want to glorify plastic. It's an interesting material because it is in many ways so far away from the organic, natural world that it actually underlines very strongly the problem of all man-made substances. It's the extreme case: the natural world is almost at the other end of the scale. The problem is more or less the same to varying degrees with all the artificial object world.

"Tony Cragg Interviewed by Lynne Cooke." In *Tony Cragg*, exh. catalogue. London: Arts Council of Great Britain, 1987, p. 16.

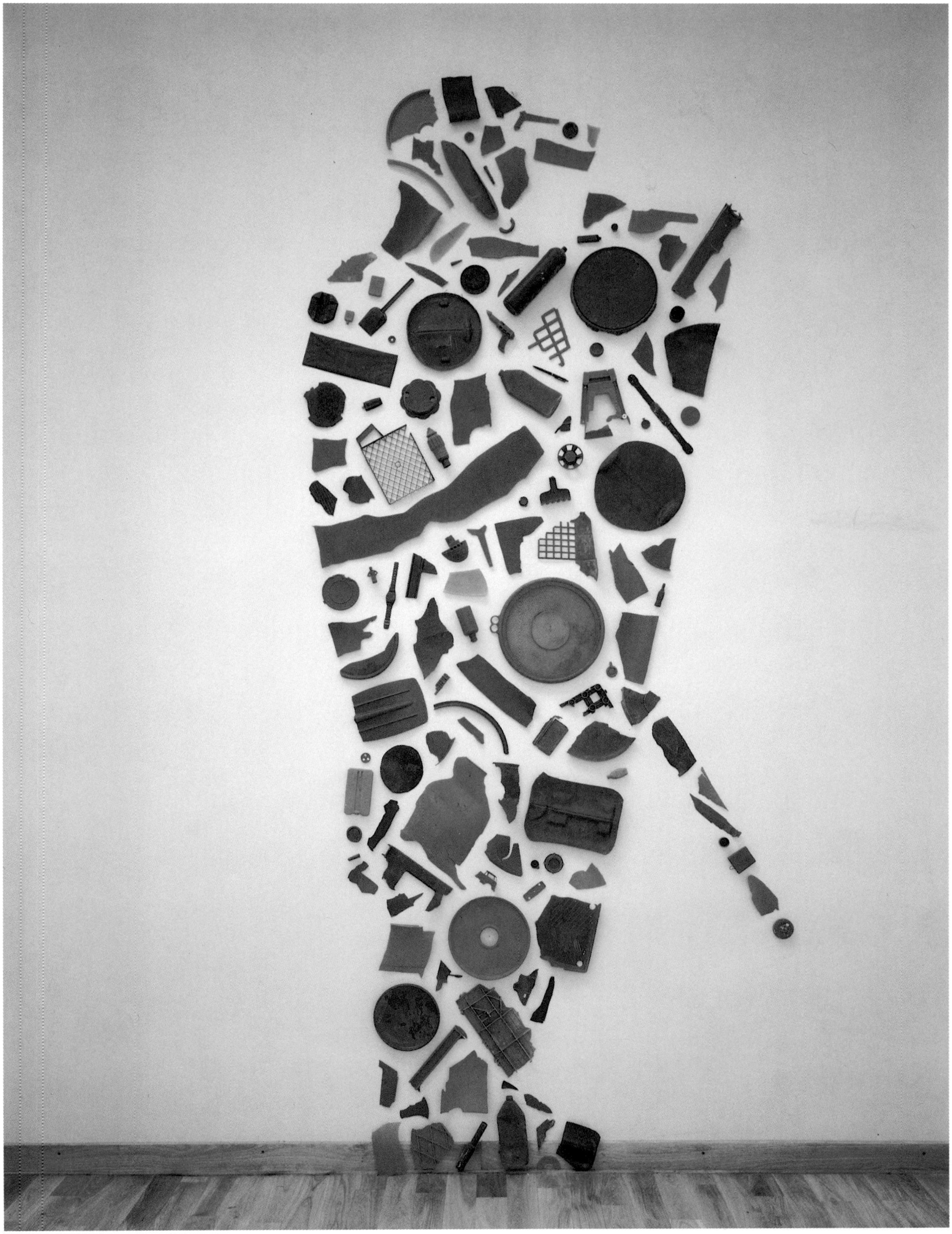

69. *Mortar and Pestle*, 1987

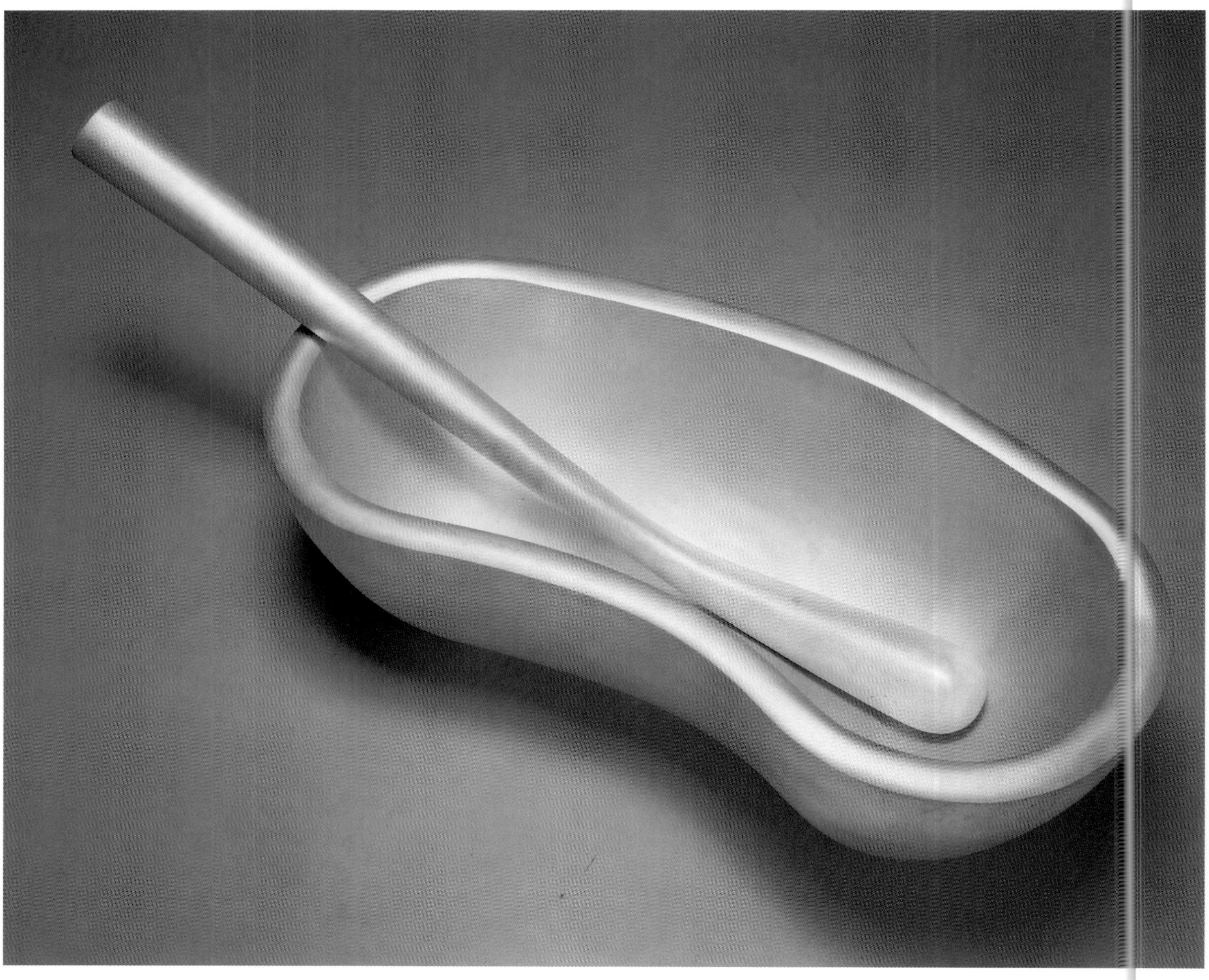

70. *Spill*, 1987

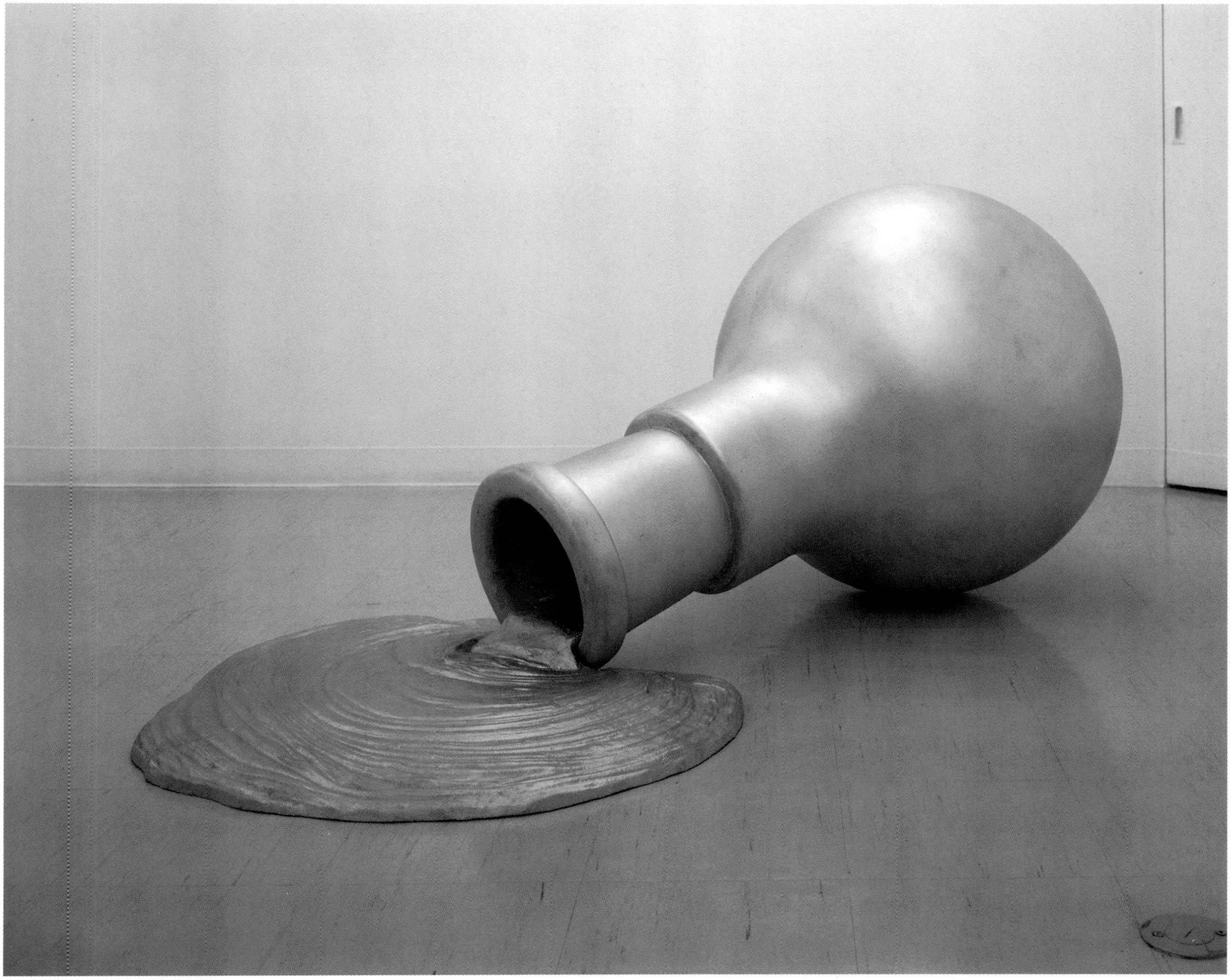

71. *Inverted Sugar Crop*, 1987

72. *Bestückung*, 1987–88

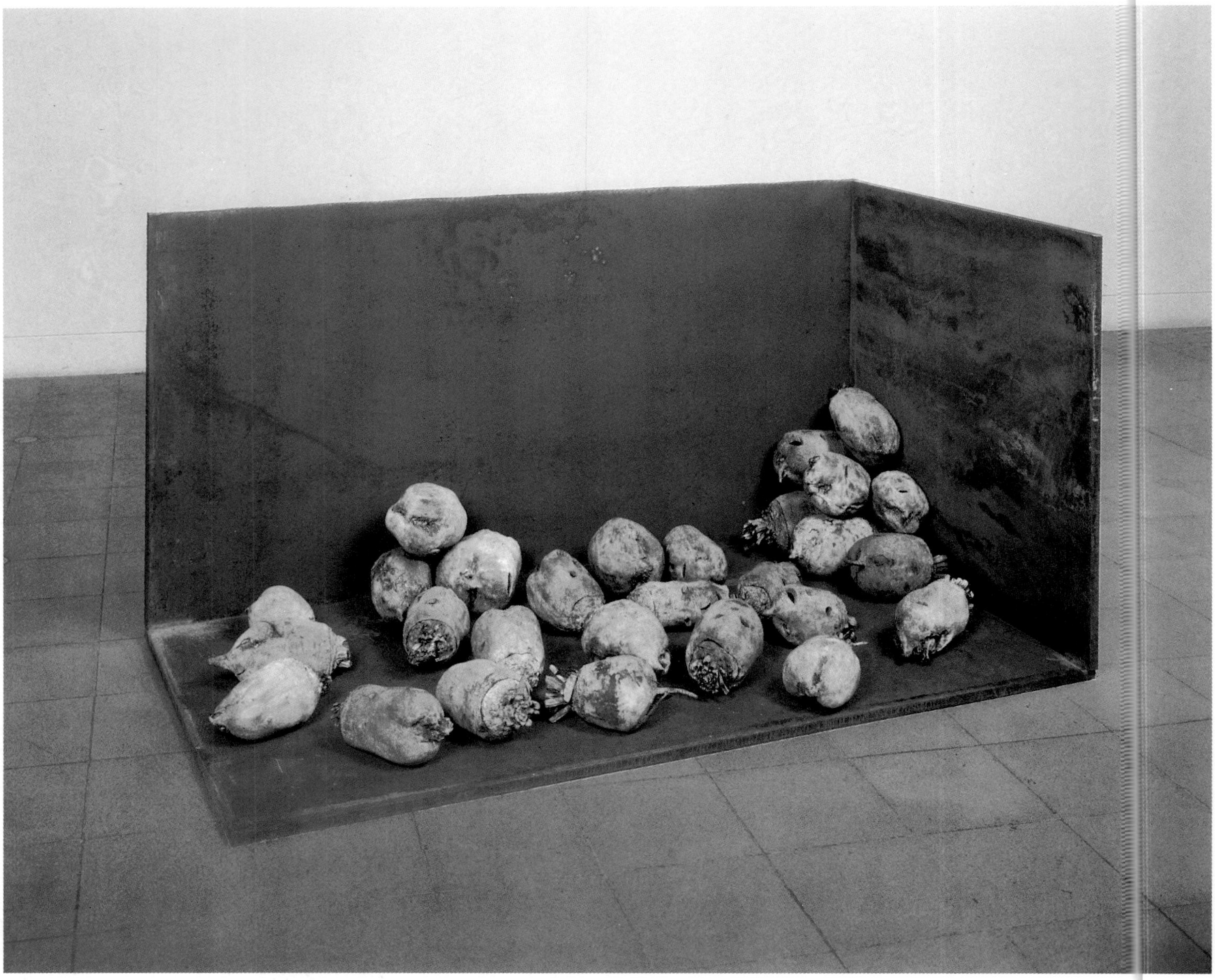

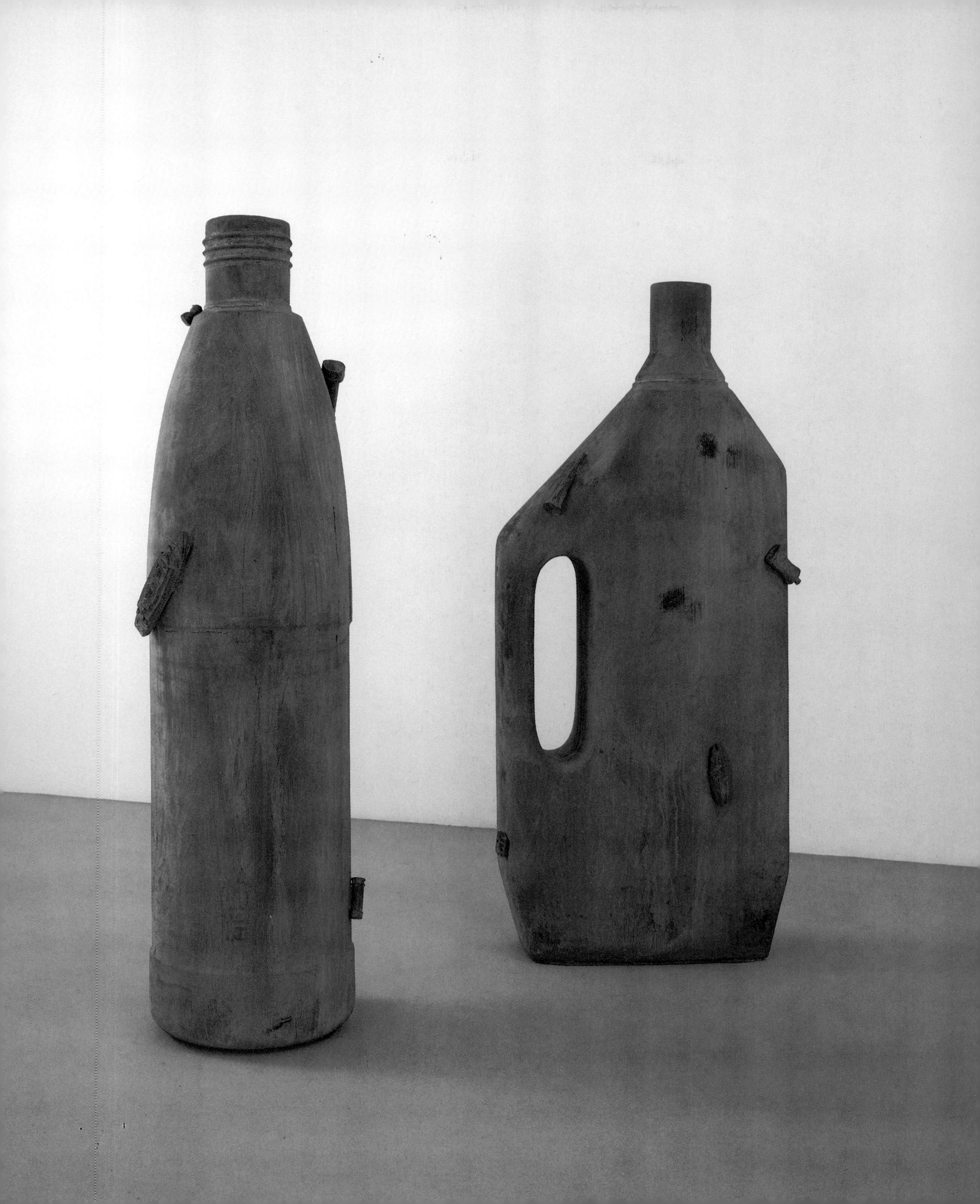

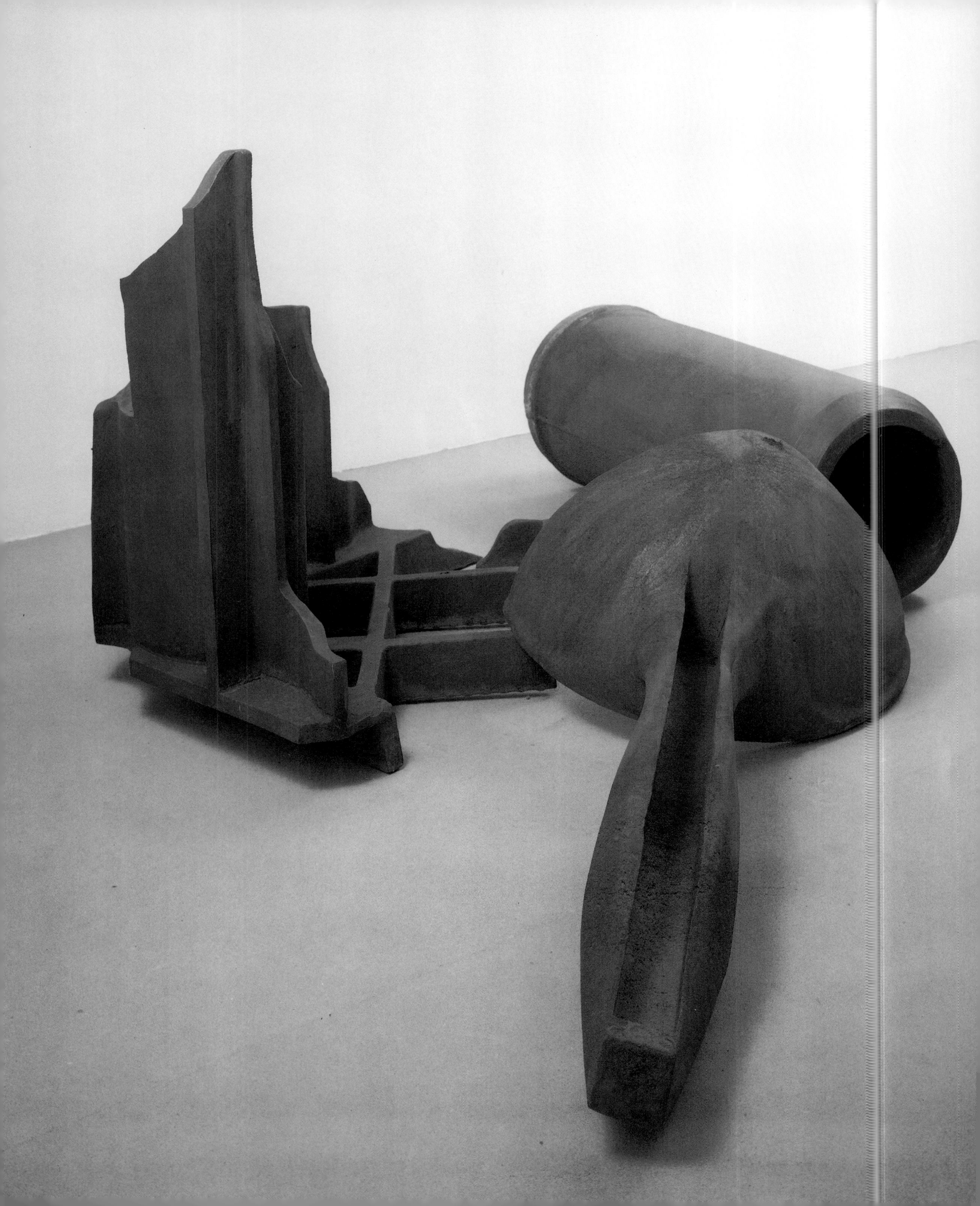

73. *Fragmente*, 1988

74. *Untitled (Shell)*, 1988

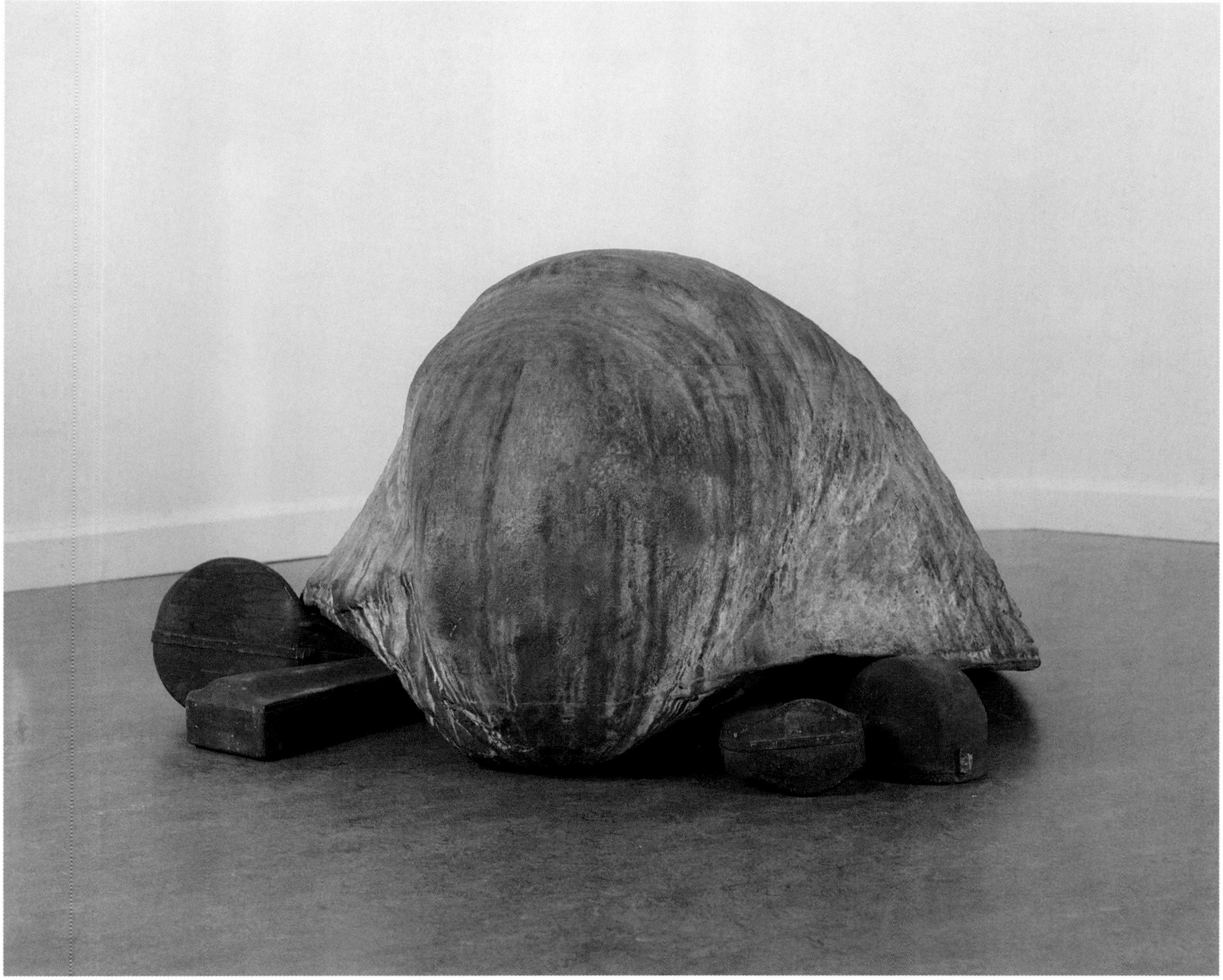

75. *Generations*, 1988

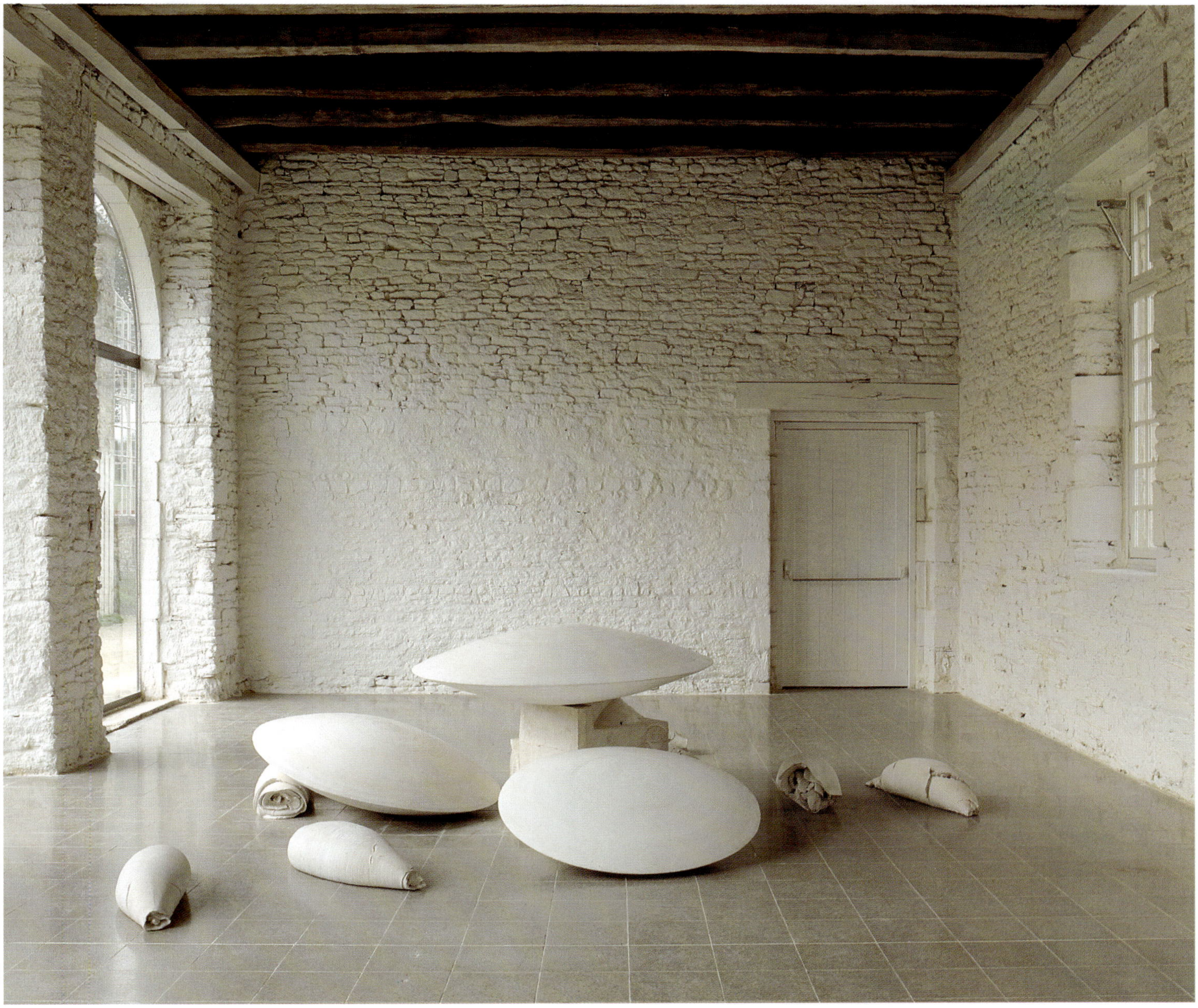

I think that objects have the capability to carry valuable information for us, to be important to us, but the fact is that most objects are made in ways which are irresponsible and manipulative. Irresponsible because people – the makers of this or that – don't really consider in any metaphysical way the meanings of the objects that they're making: and manipulative because things are made for a variety of commercial and power based reasons. My interest in the physical world, in this object world, is survivalistic at one level, but it will also lead me to dreams, to fantasy, and to speculation.

"Tony Cragg Interviewed by Lynne Cooke." In *Tony Cragg*, exh. catalogue. London: Arts Council of Great Britain, 1987, pp. 11-12.

76. *Fruits of Whose Labours*, 1989

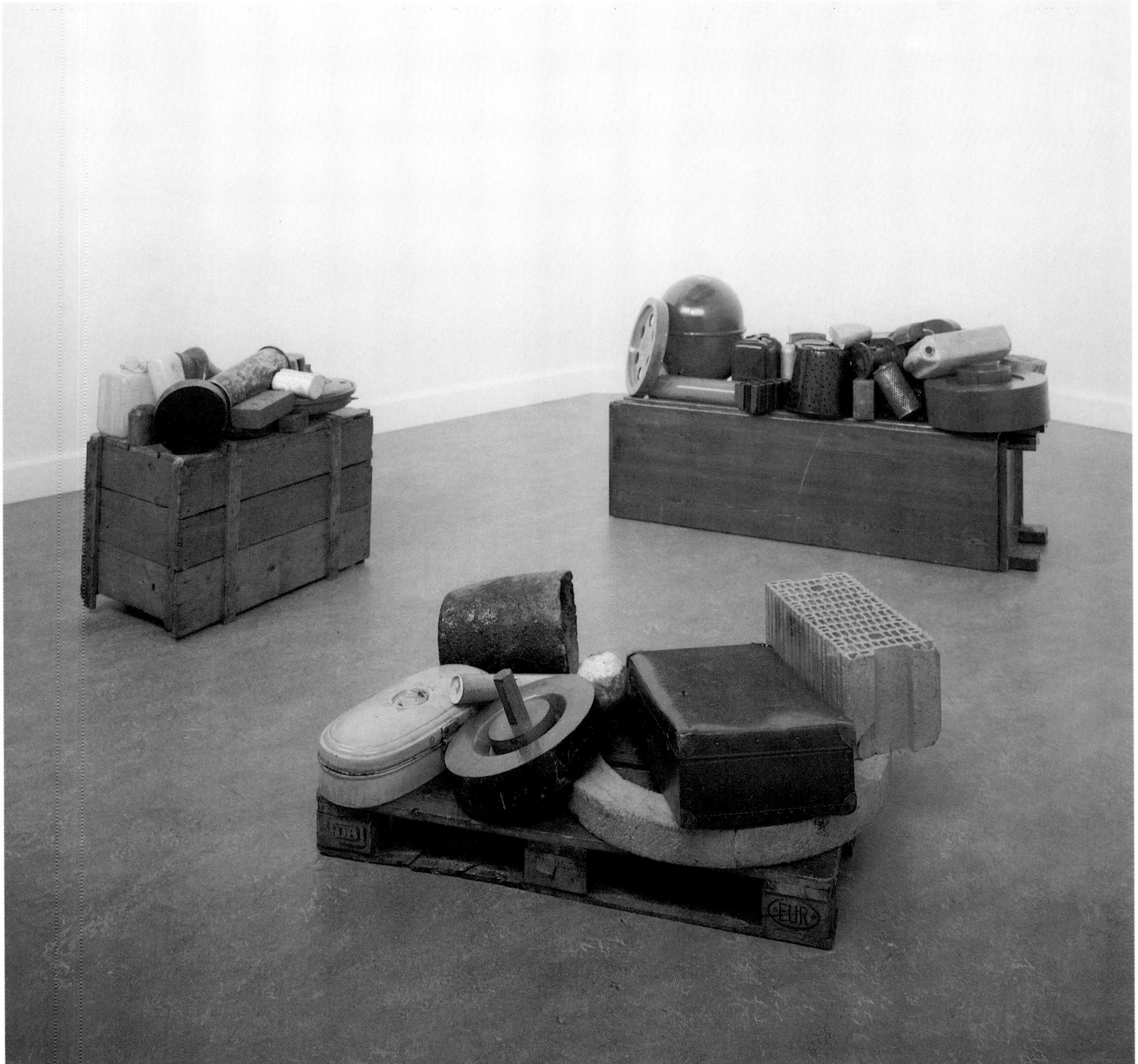

77. *Eroded Landscape*, 1990

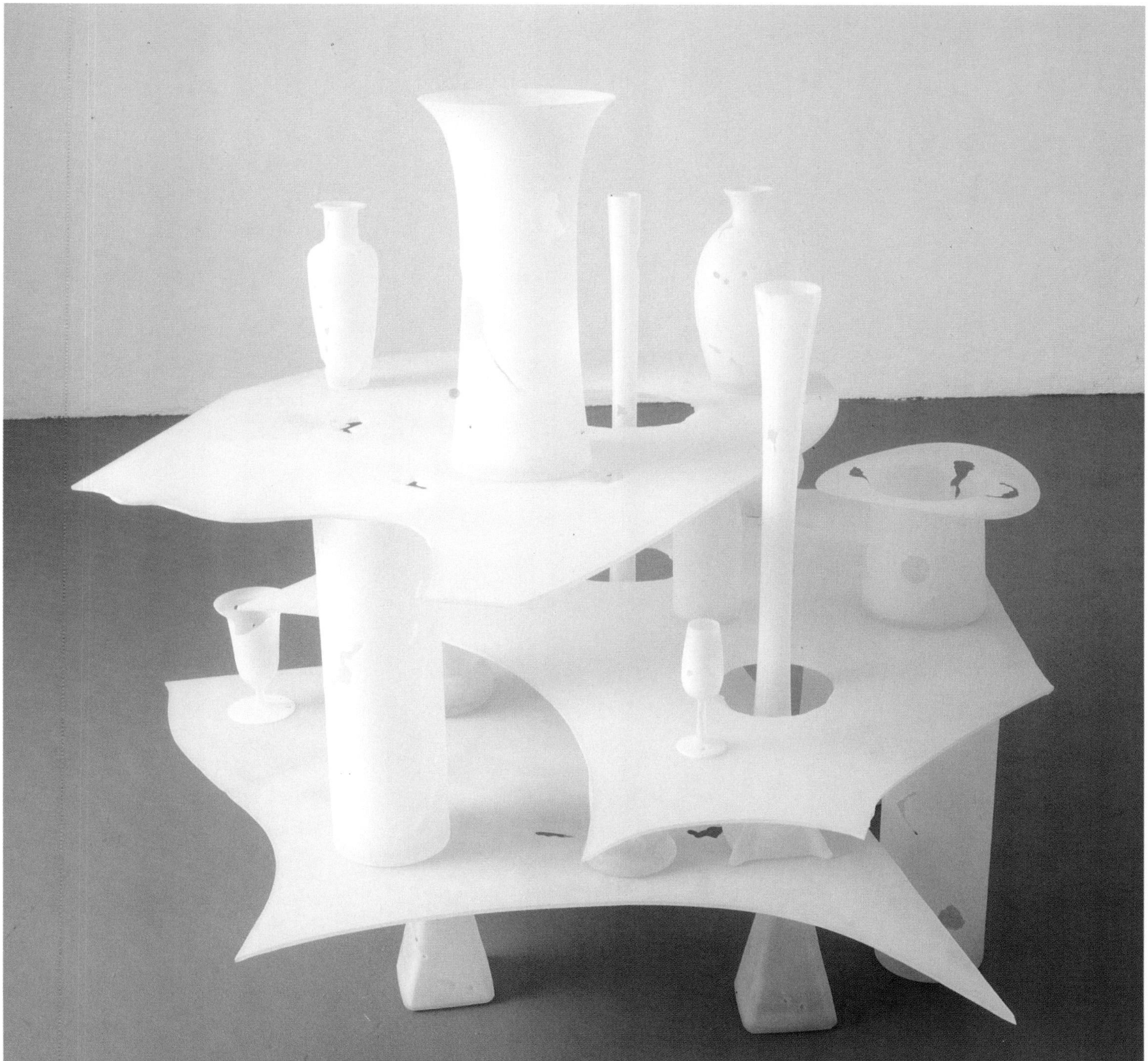

78. *Yard*, 1988

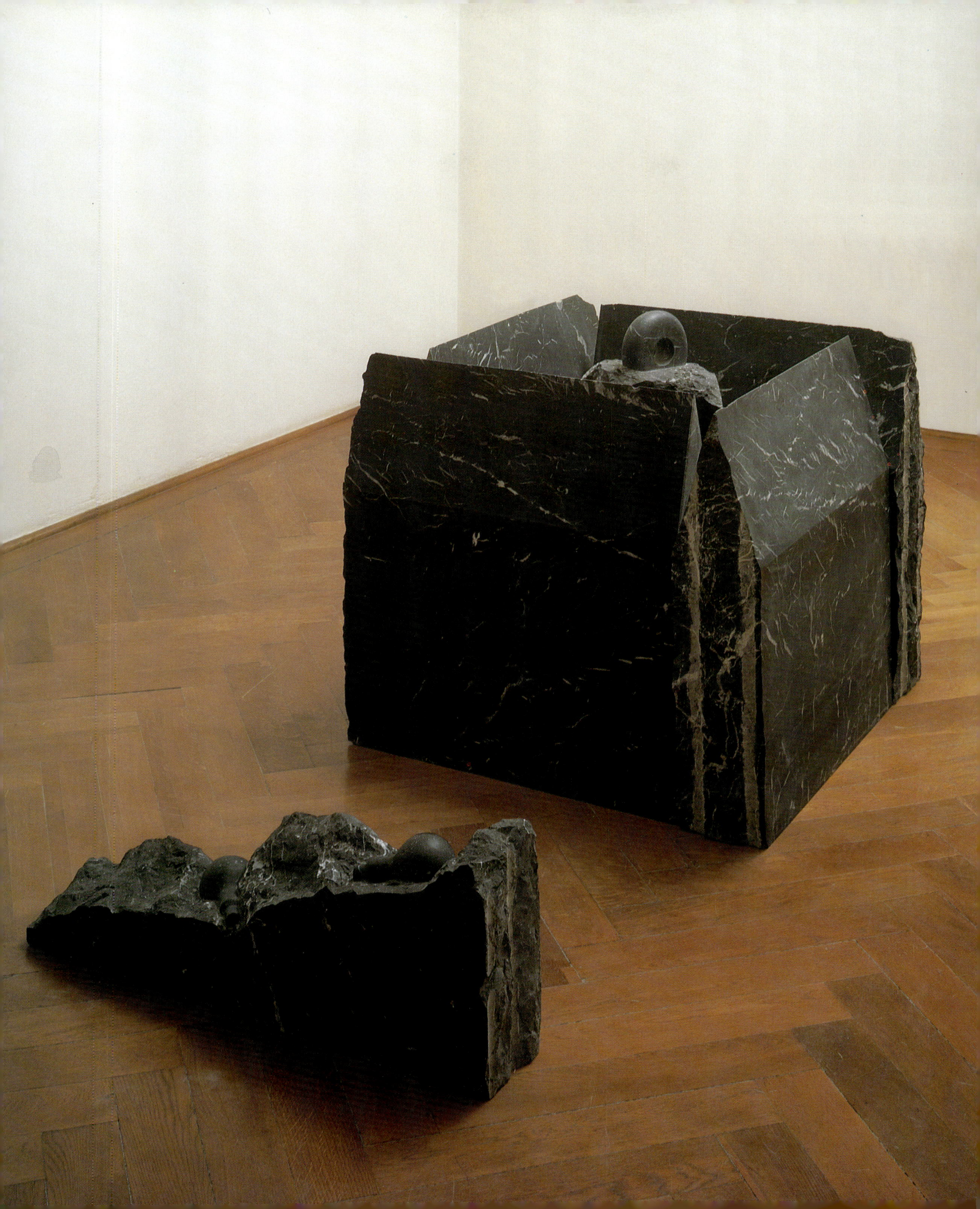

79. *Broken Landscape*, 1988

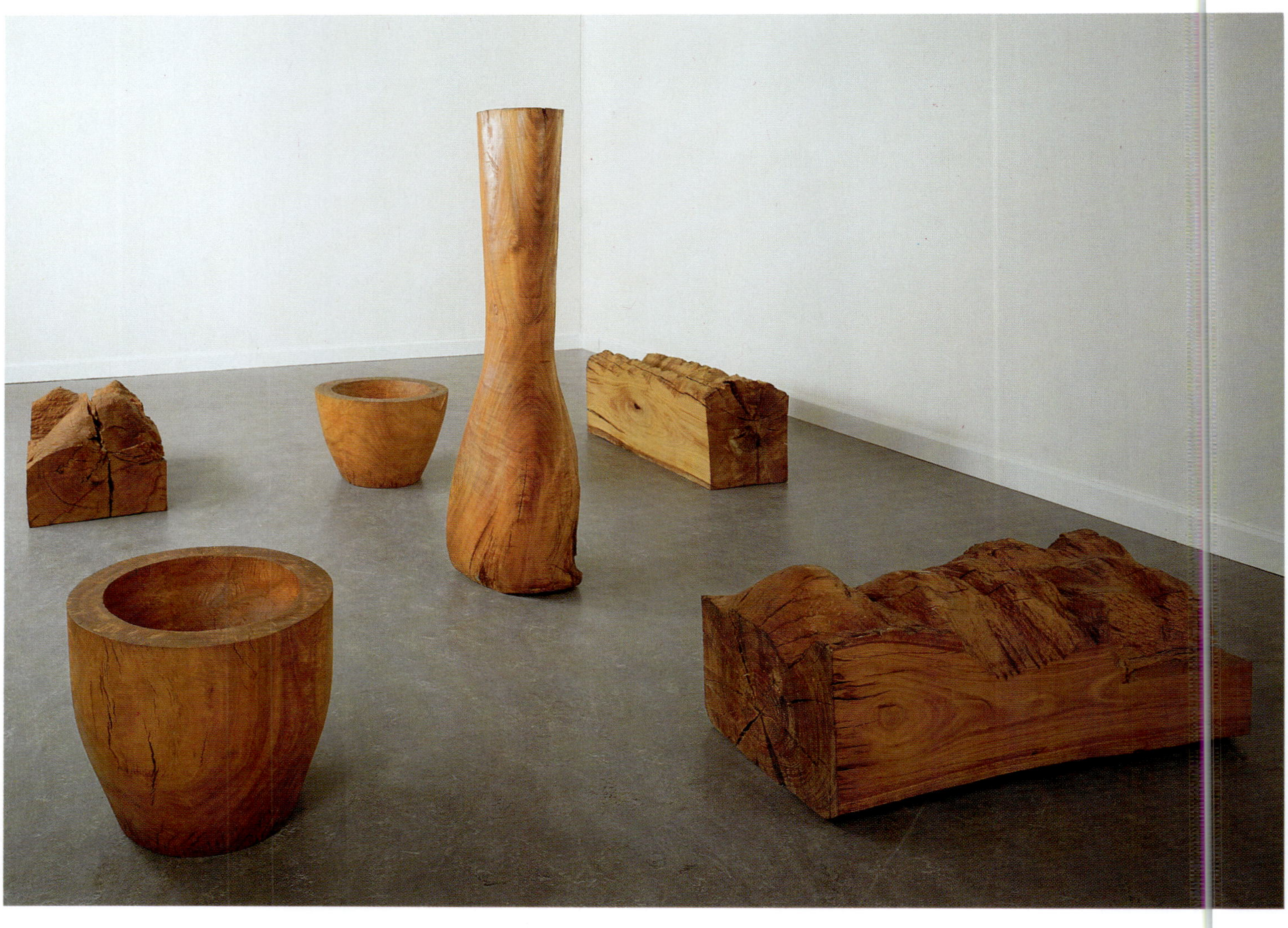

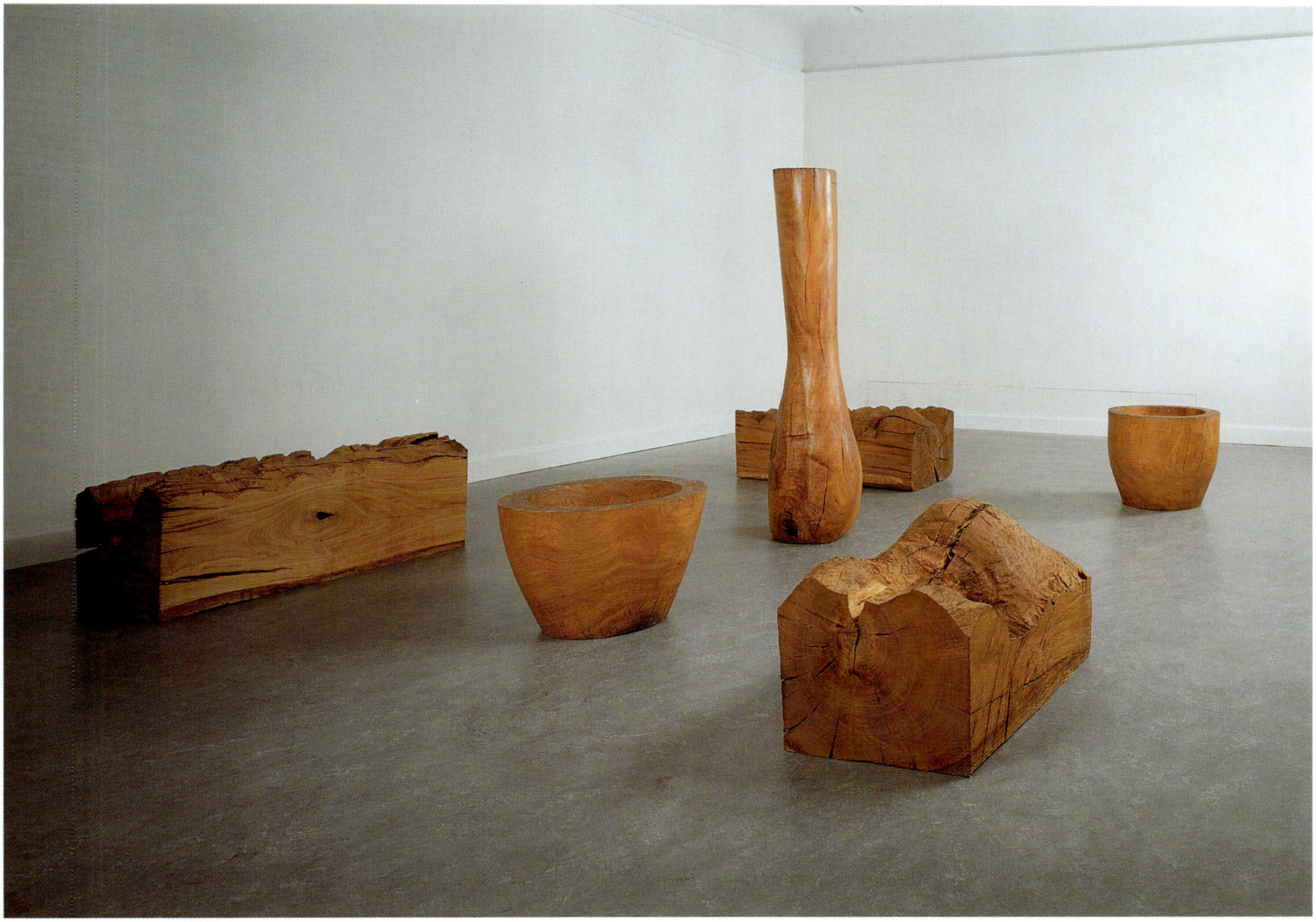

I want objects to stand there just like they should be there, like they have actually earned their place. So that it's a self-understood thing that they are there and that they have a particular visual quality. They're there and they want a dialogue on the basis of all the other things that are in the world, and not on the basis of a particular group of objects which one has called, in the past, "sculpture". That's a fundamental tenet of my approach to making sculpture. So one has to be very aware of formal qualities. For me a sculpture will only work if its form is right.

"Tony Cragg Interviewed by Lynne Cooke." In *Tony Cragg*, exh. catalogue. London: Arts Council of Great Britain, 1987, p. 14.

80. *Bodicea*, 1989

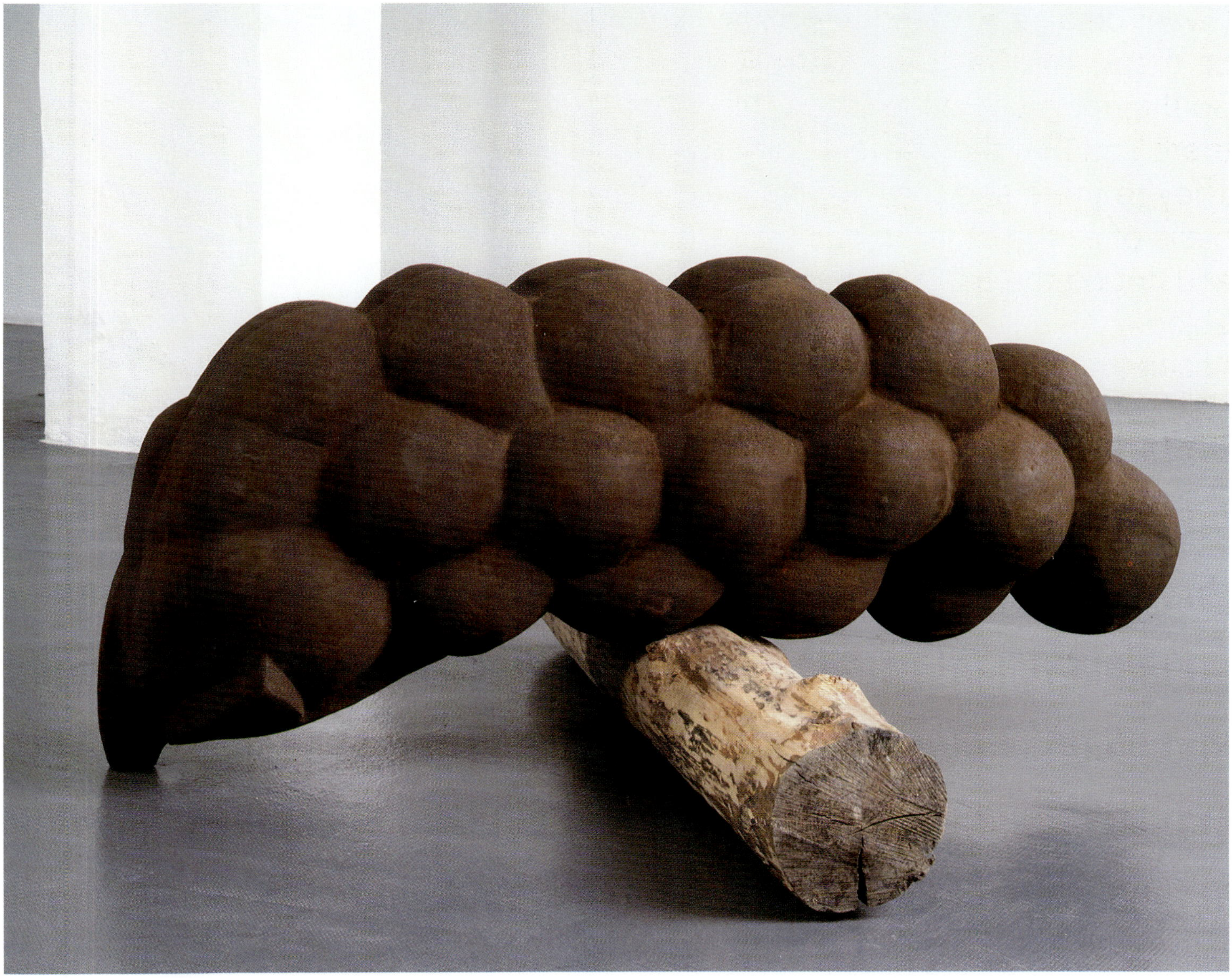

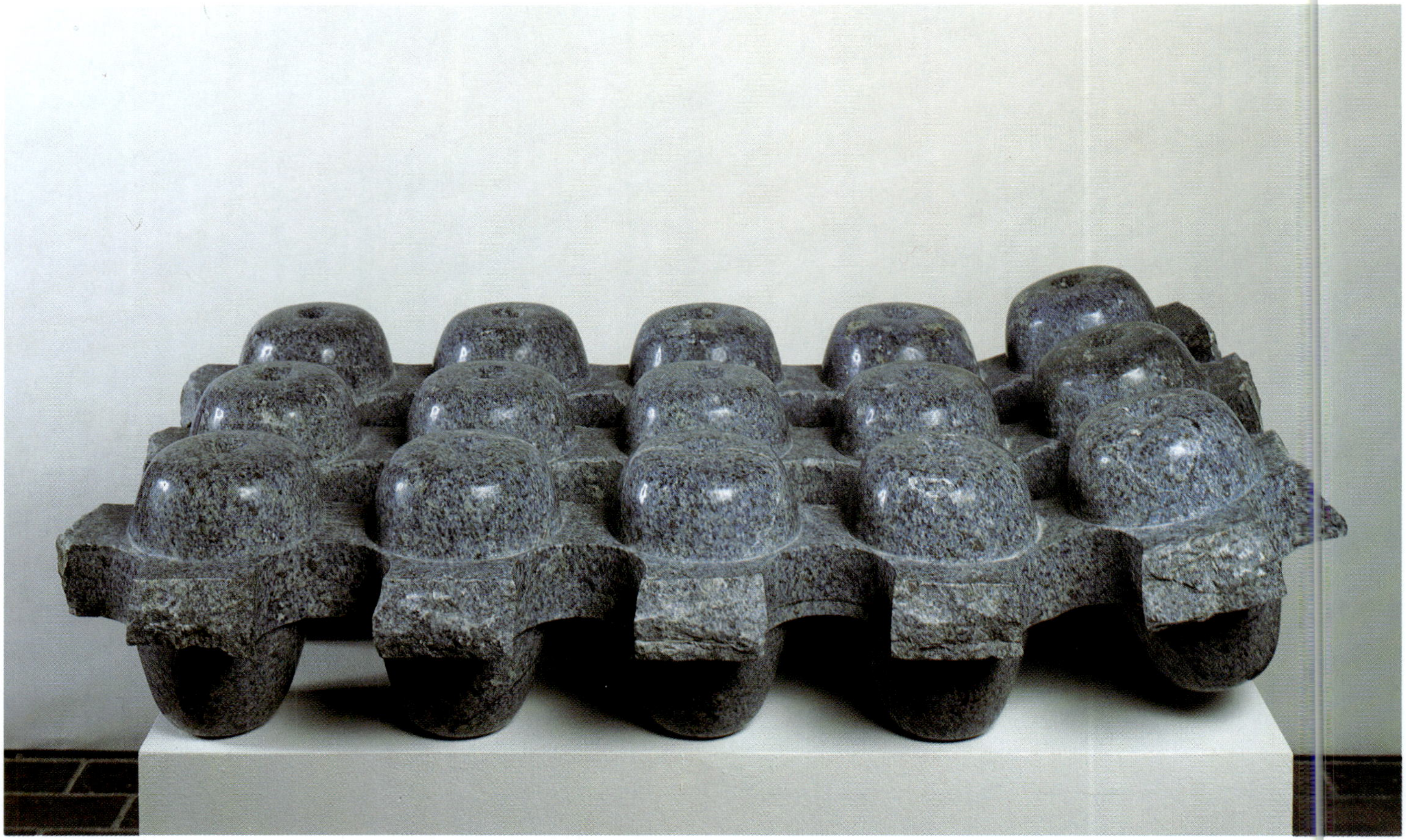

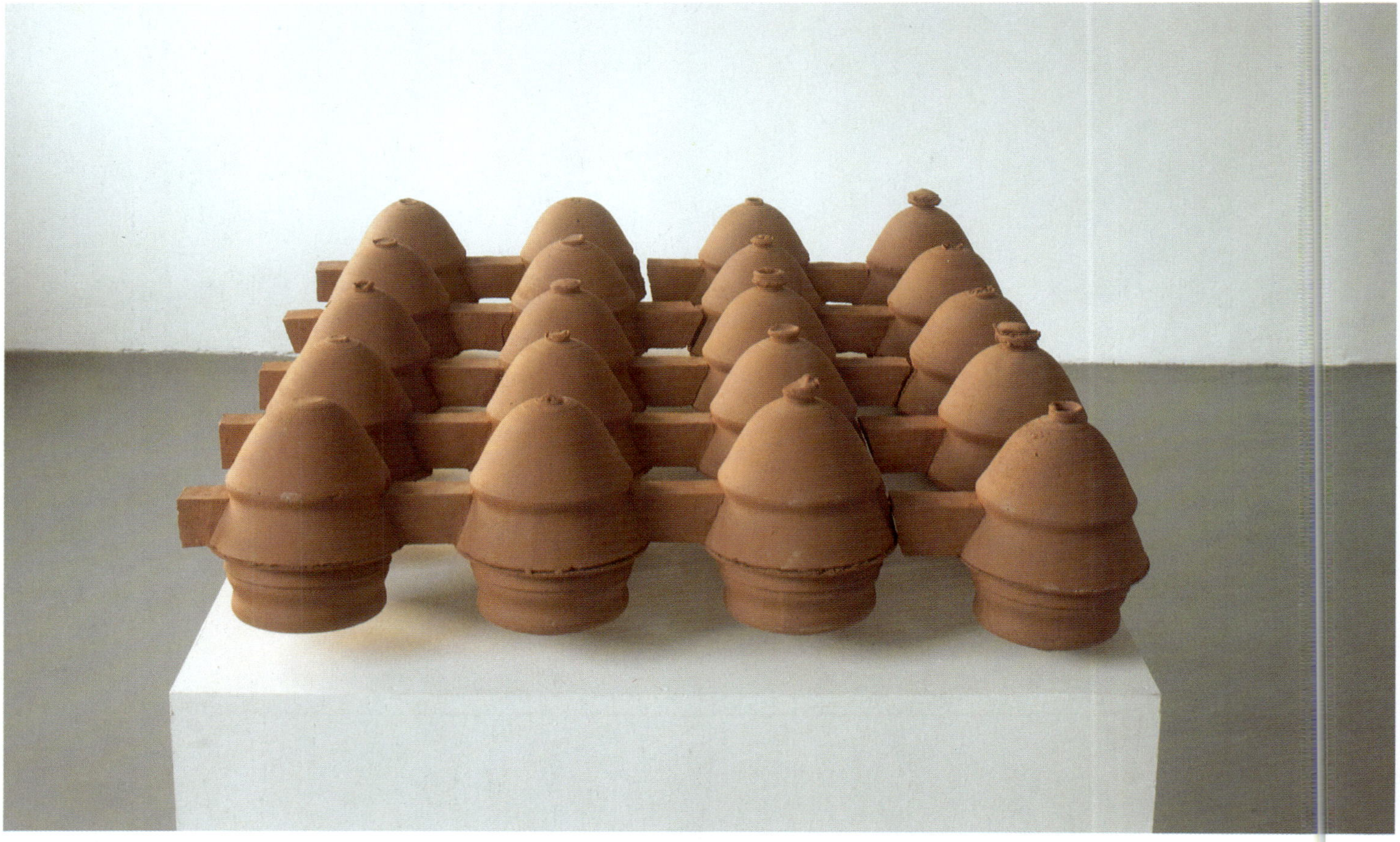

81. *Unit*, 1989

82. *Unit*, 1990

83. *Unit*, 1990

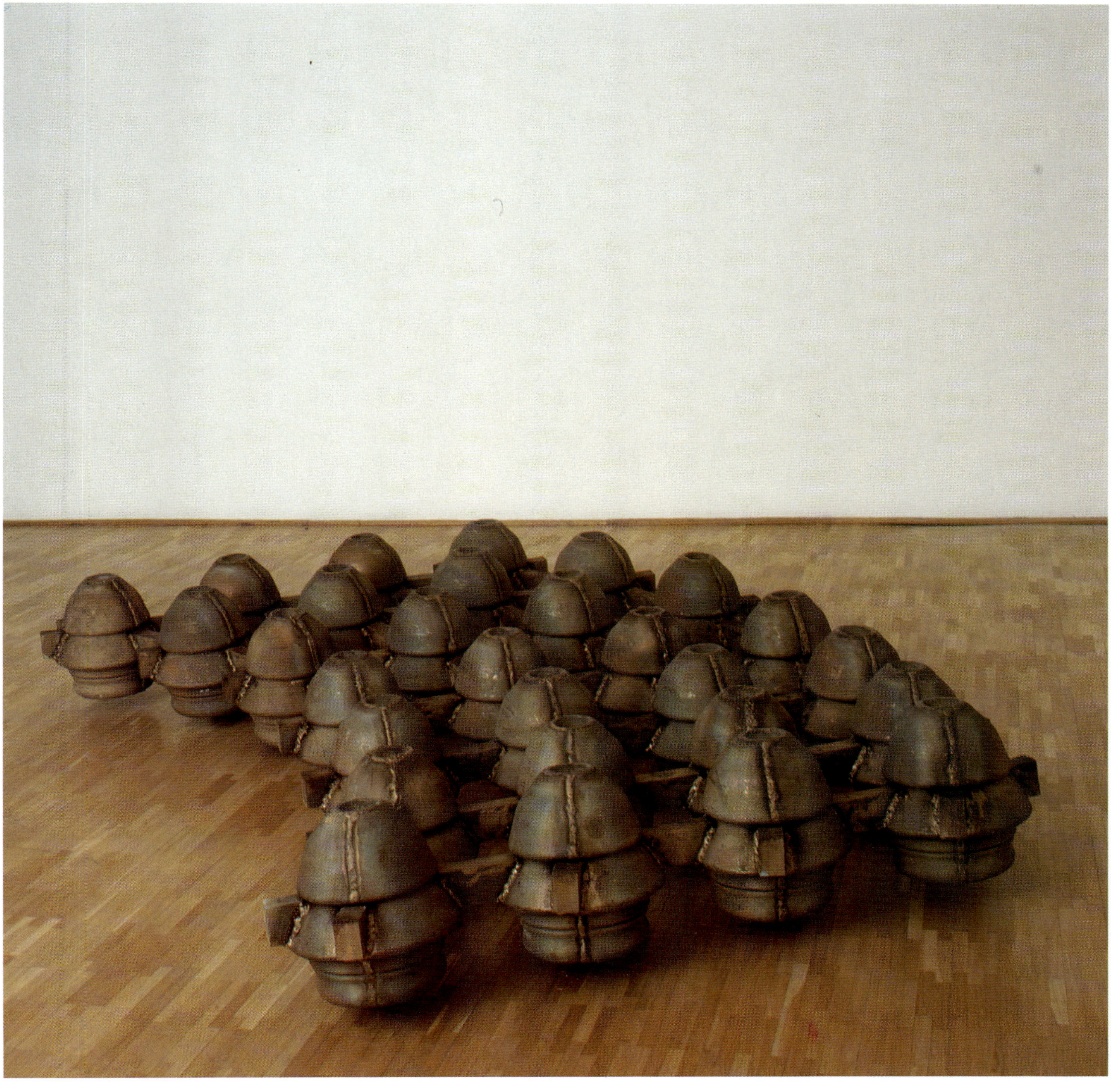

84. *Extrusion*, 1989

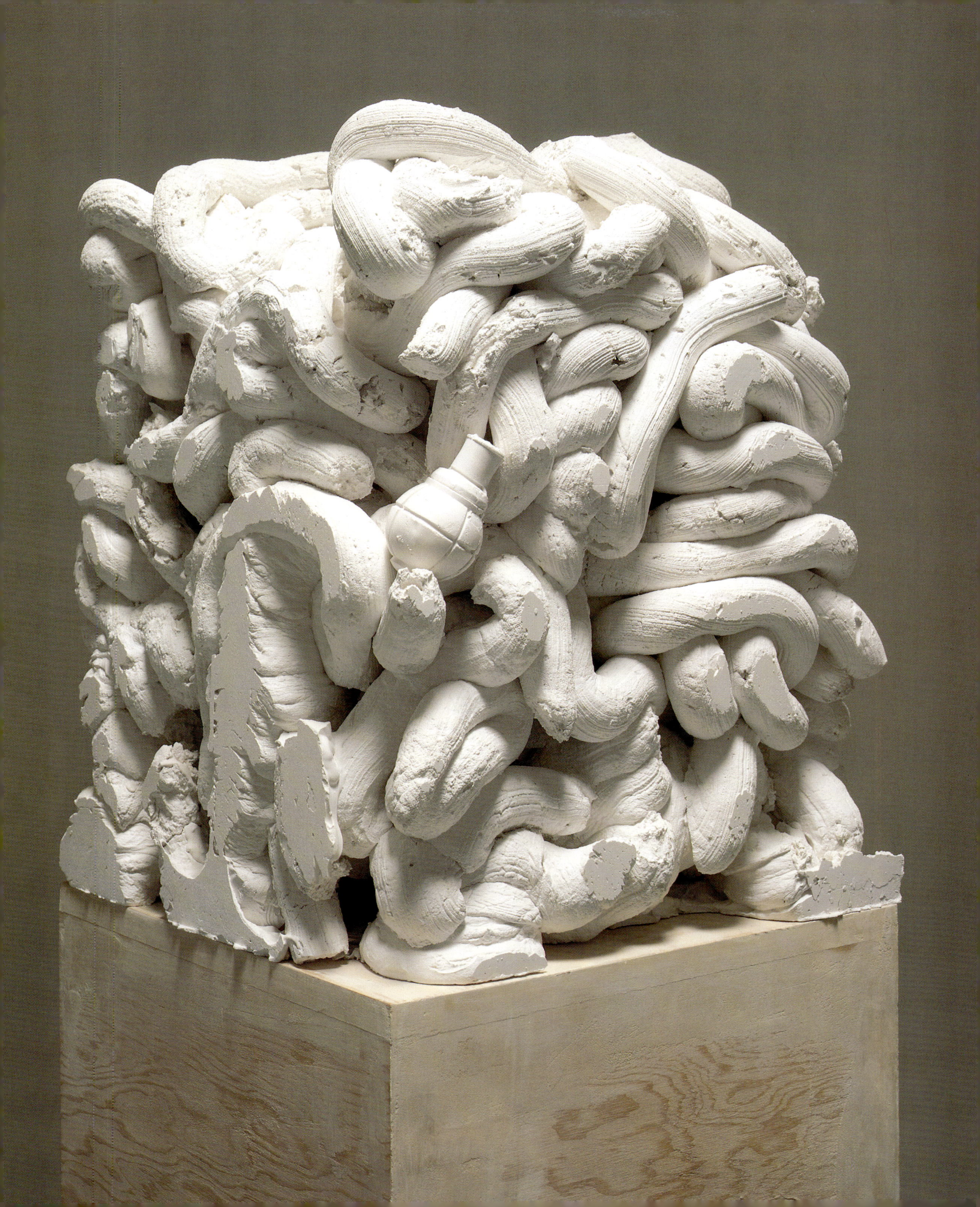

85. *Untitled*, 1988

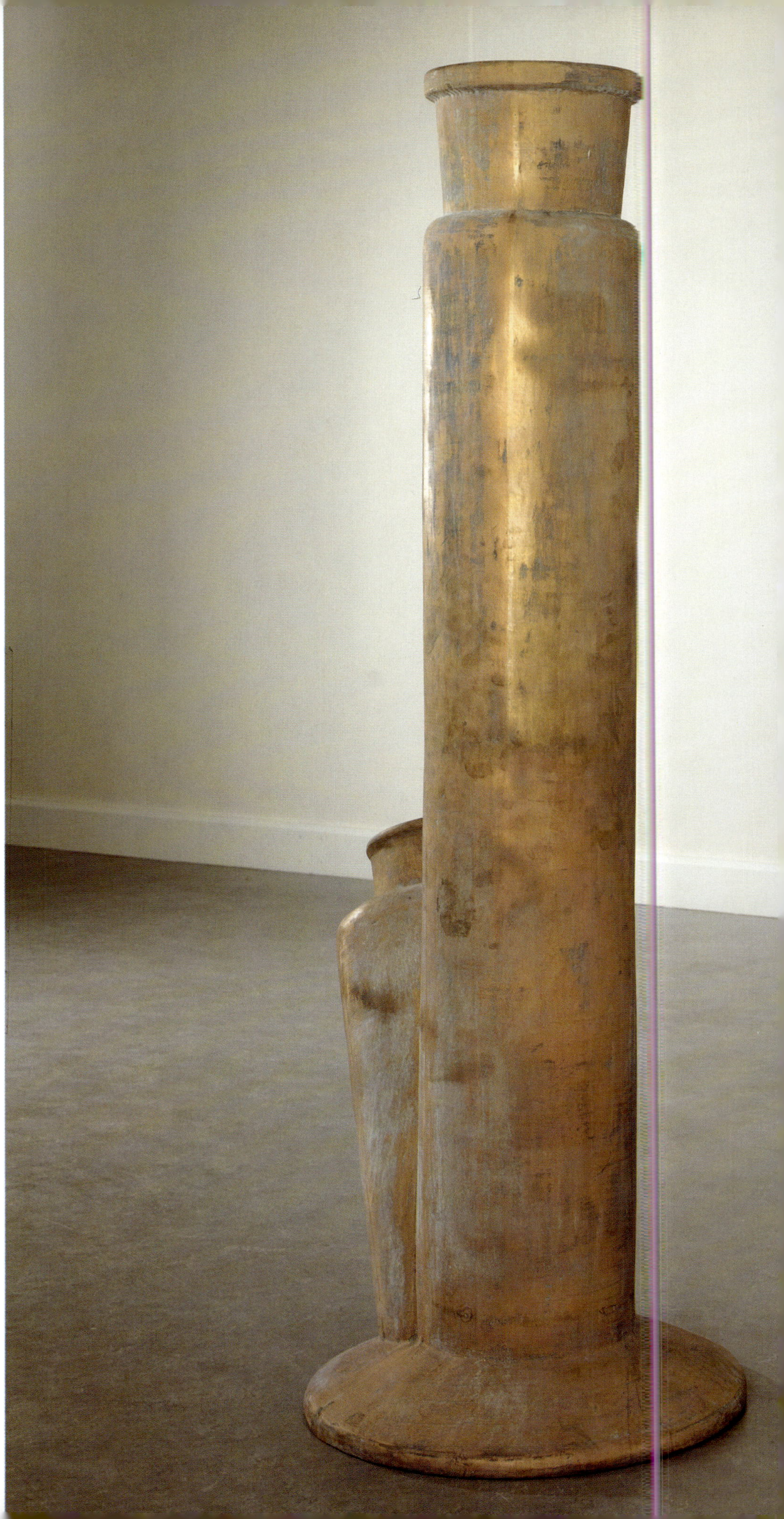

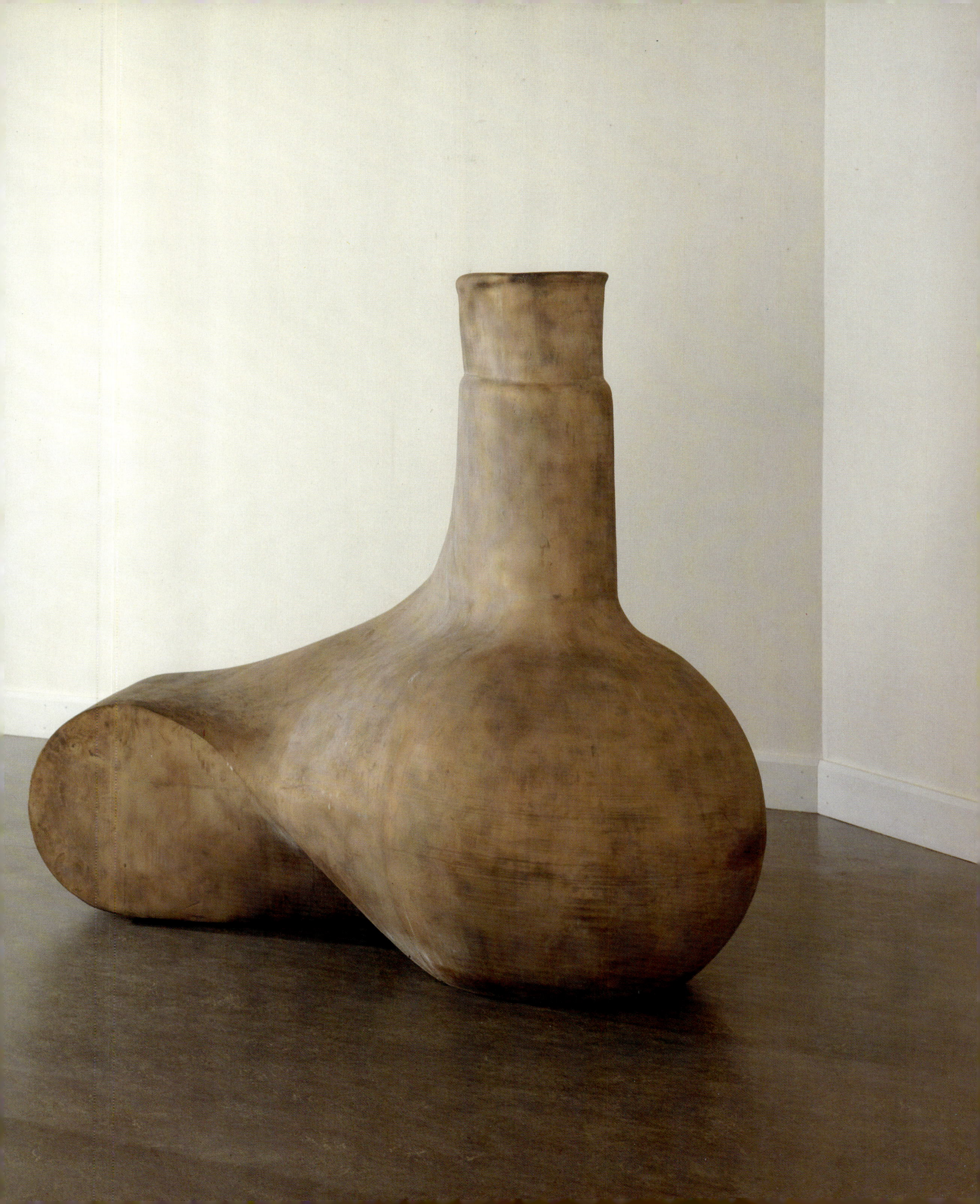

86. *Spill*, 1988

87. *Condensor*, 1989

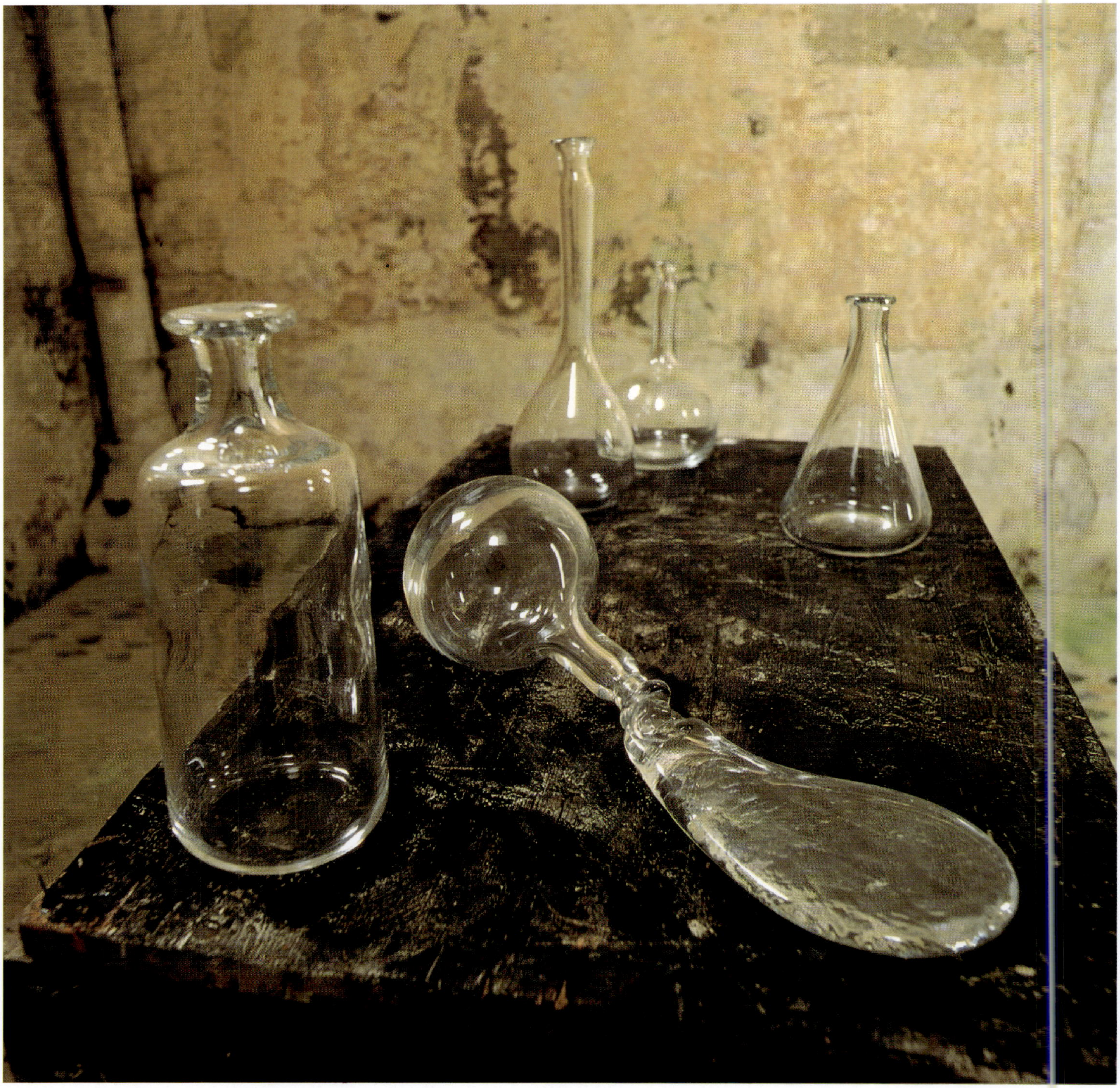

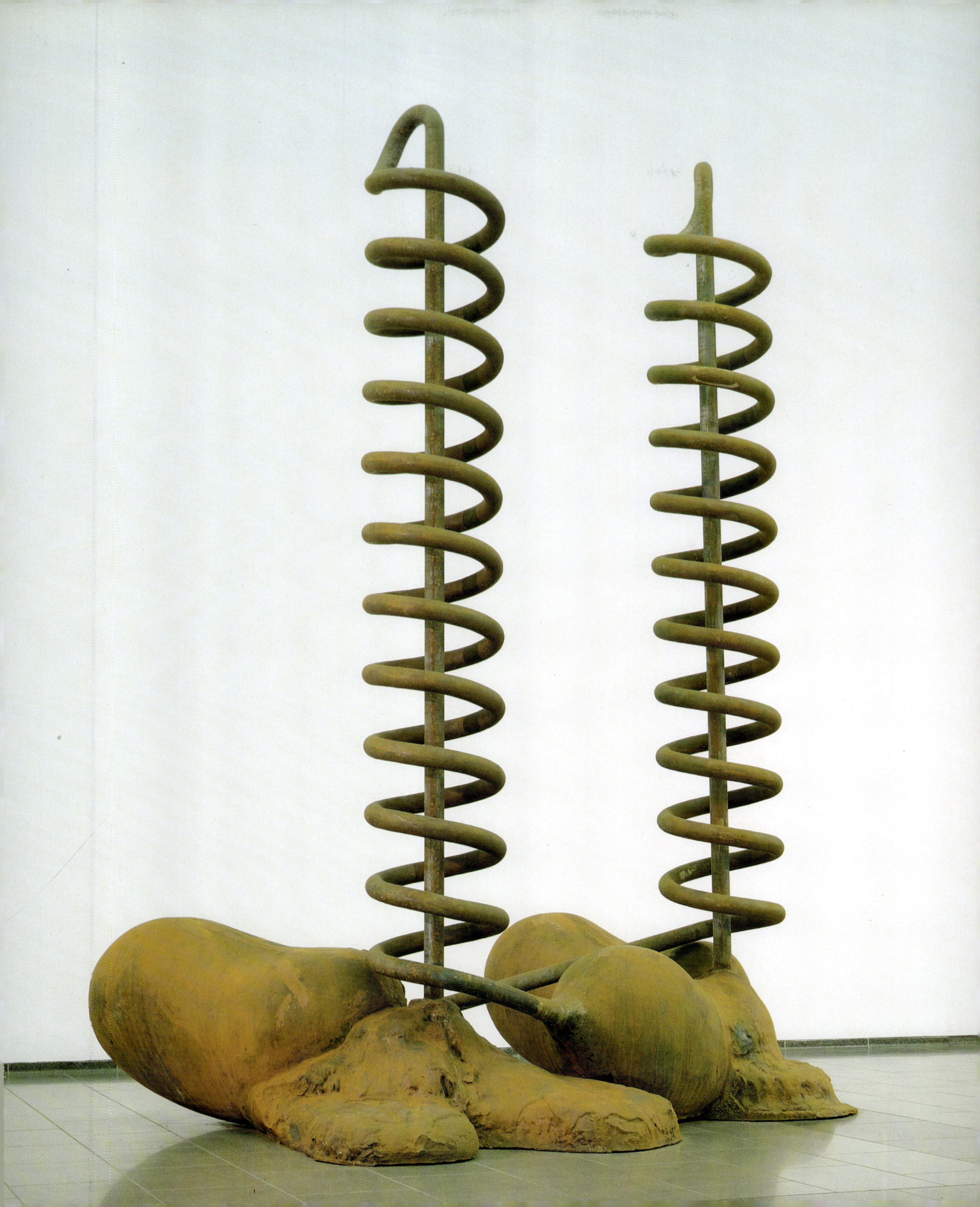

88. *Ordovician Pore*, 1989

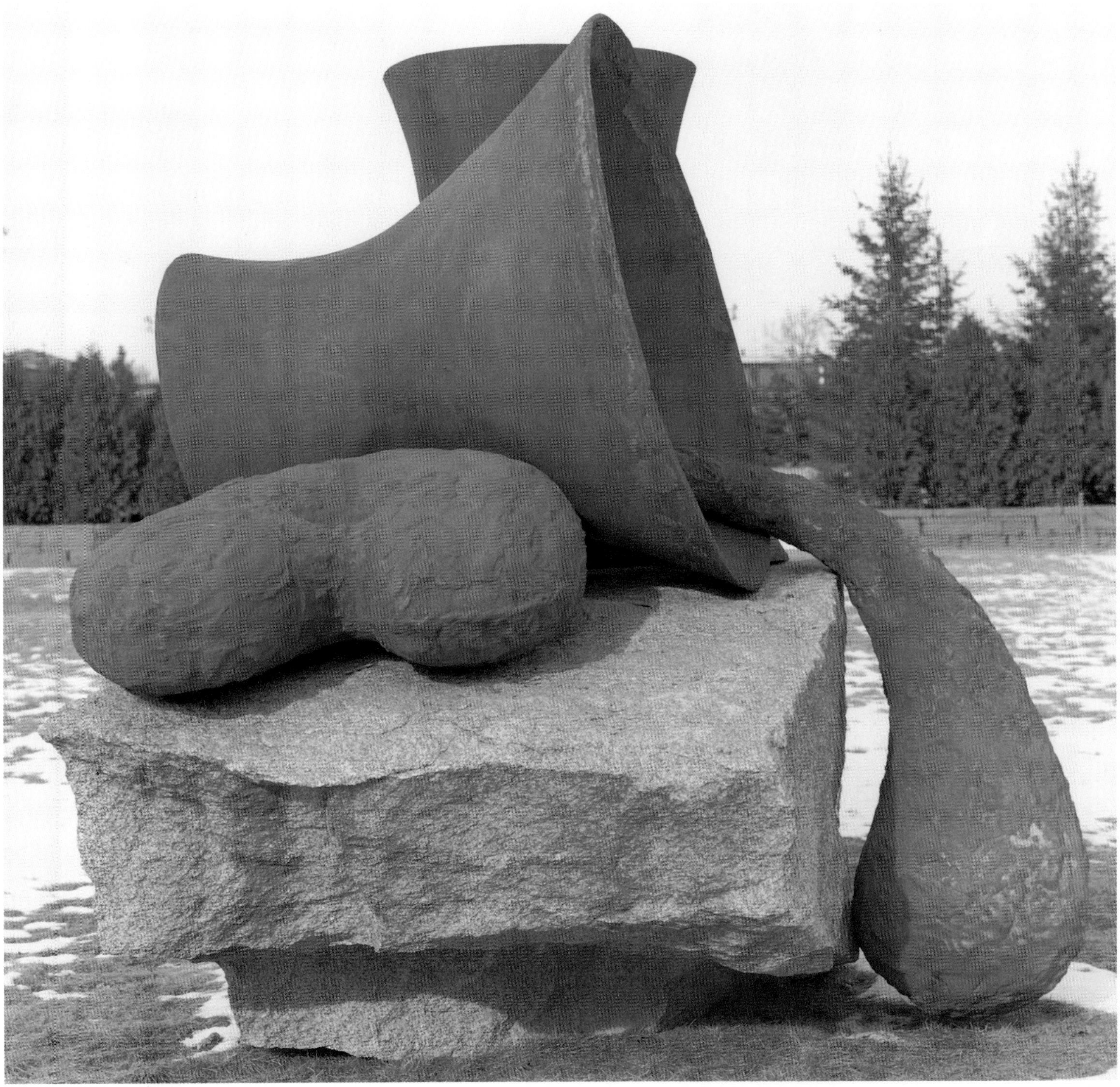

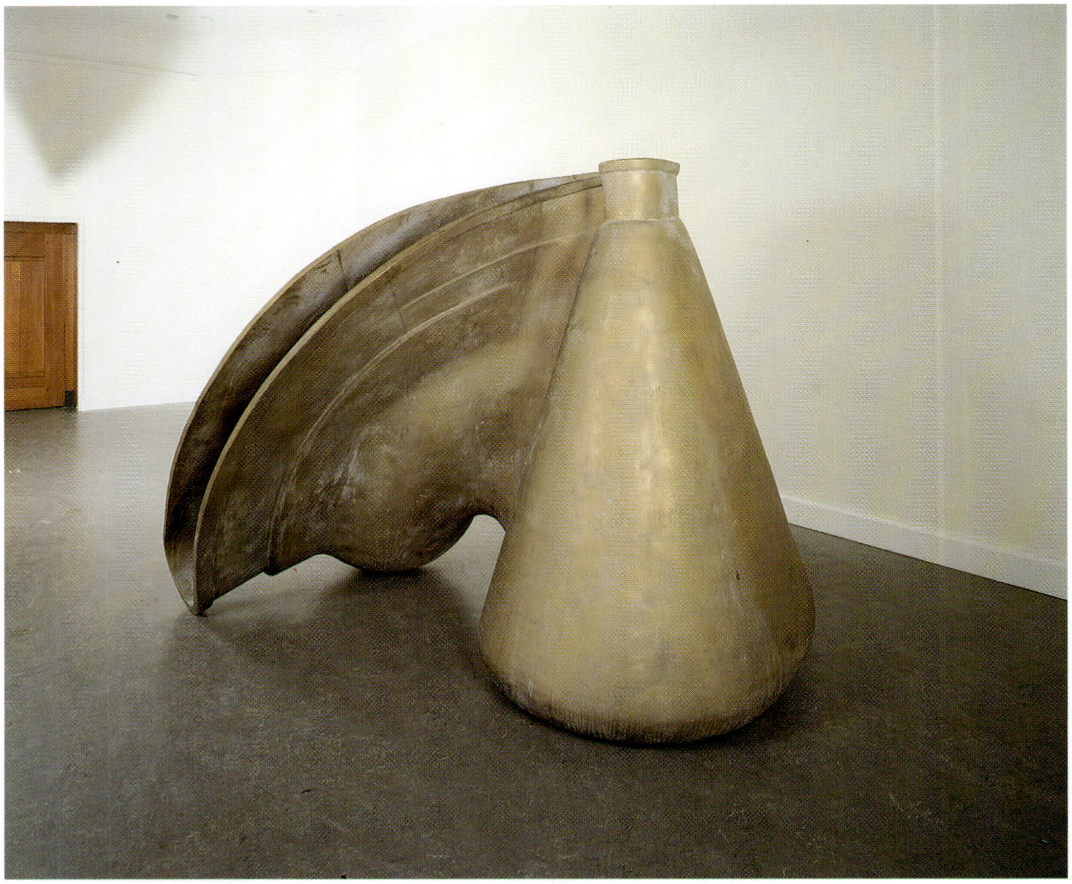

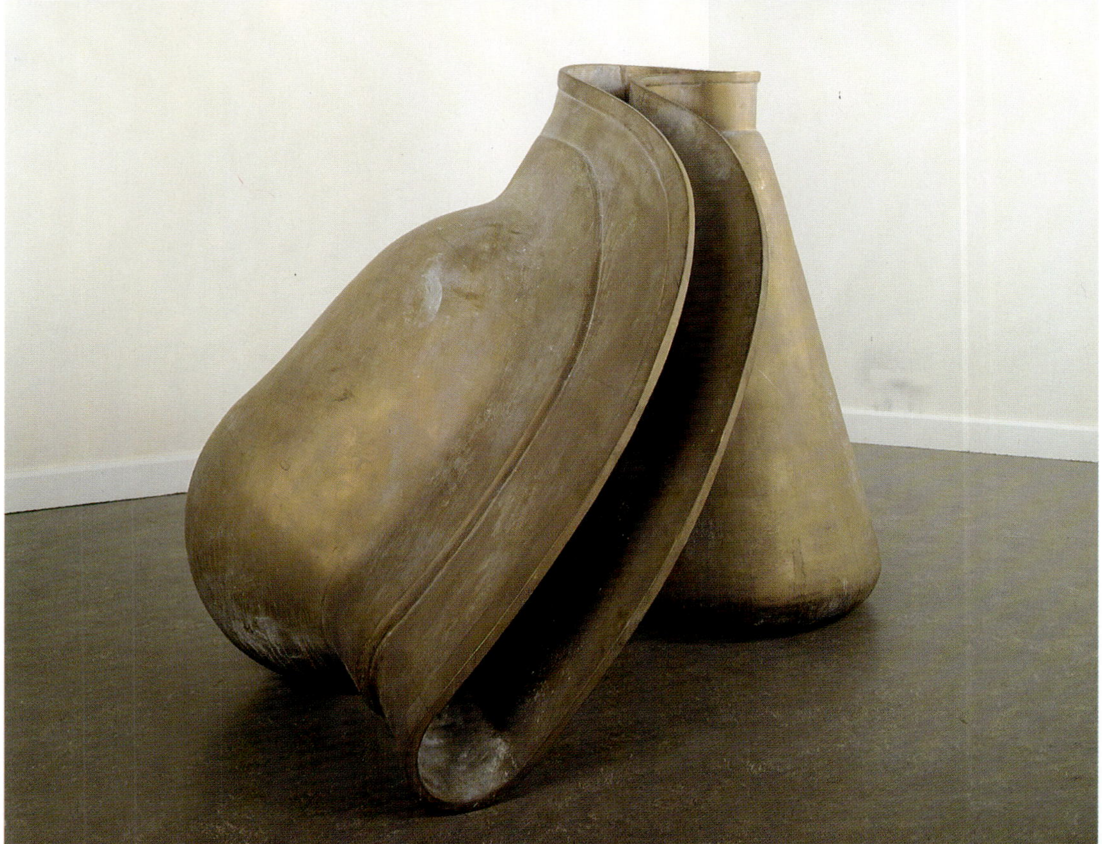

89. *Early Forms*, 1988

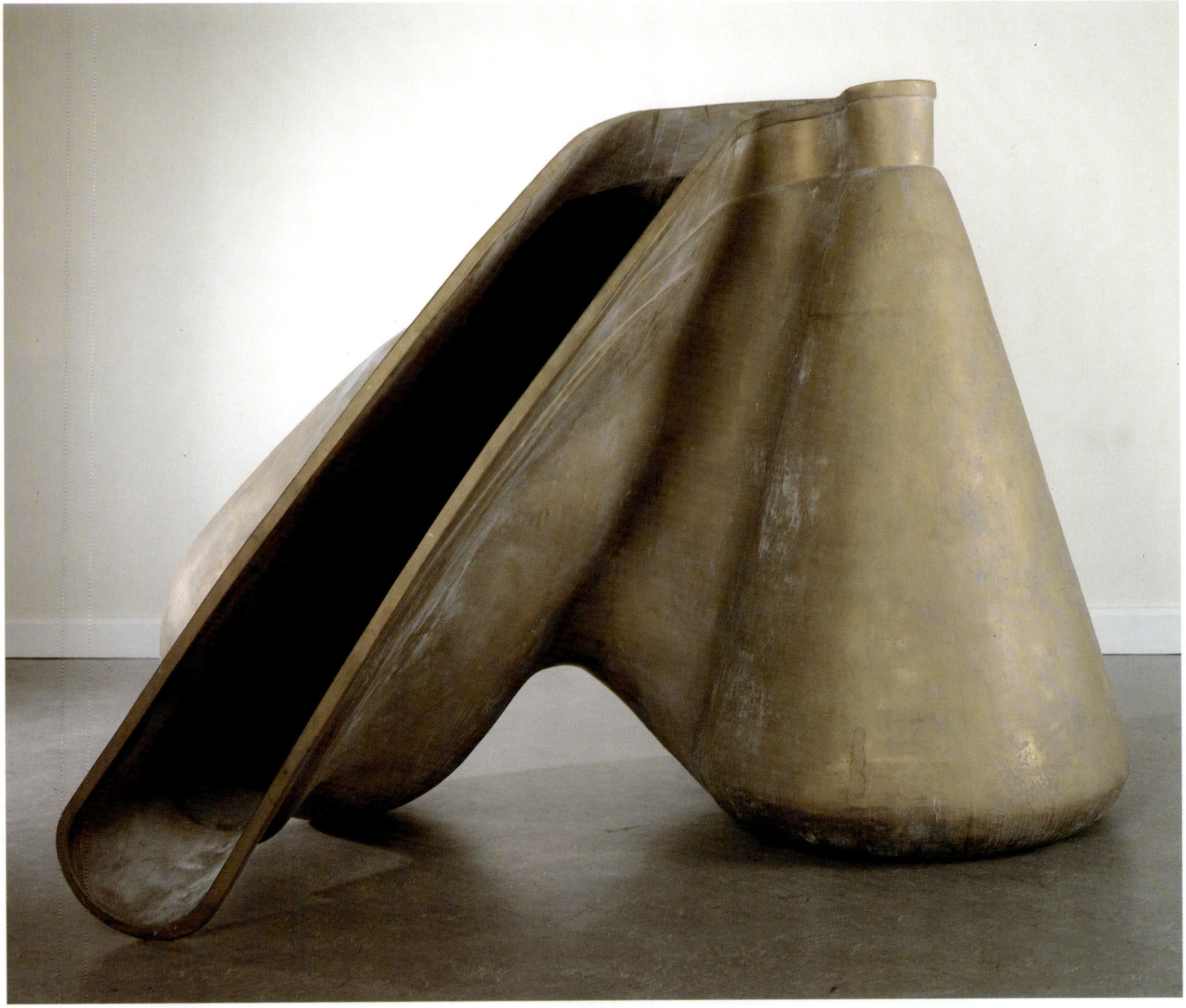

90. *Untitled*, 1988

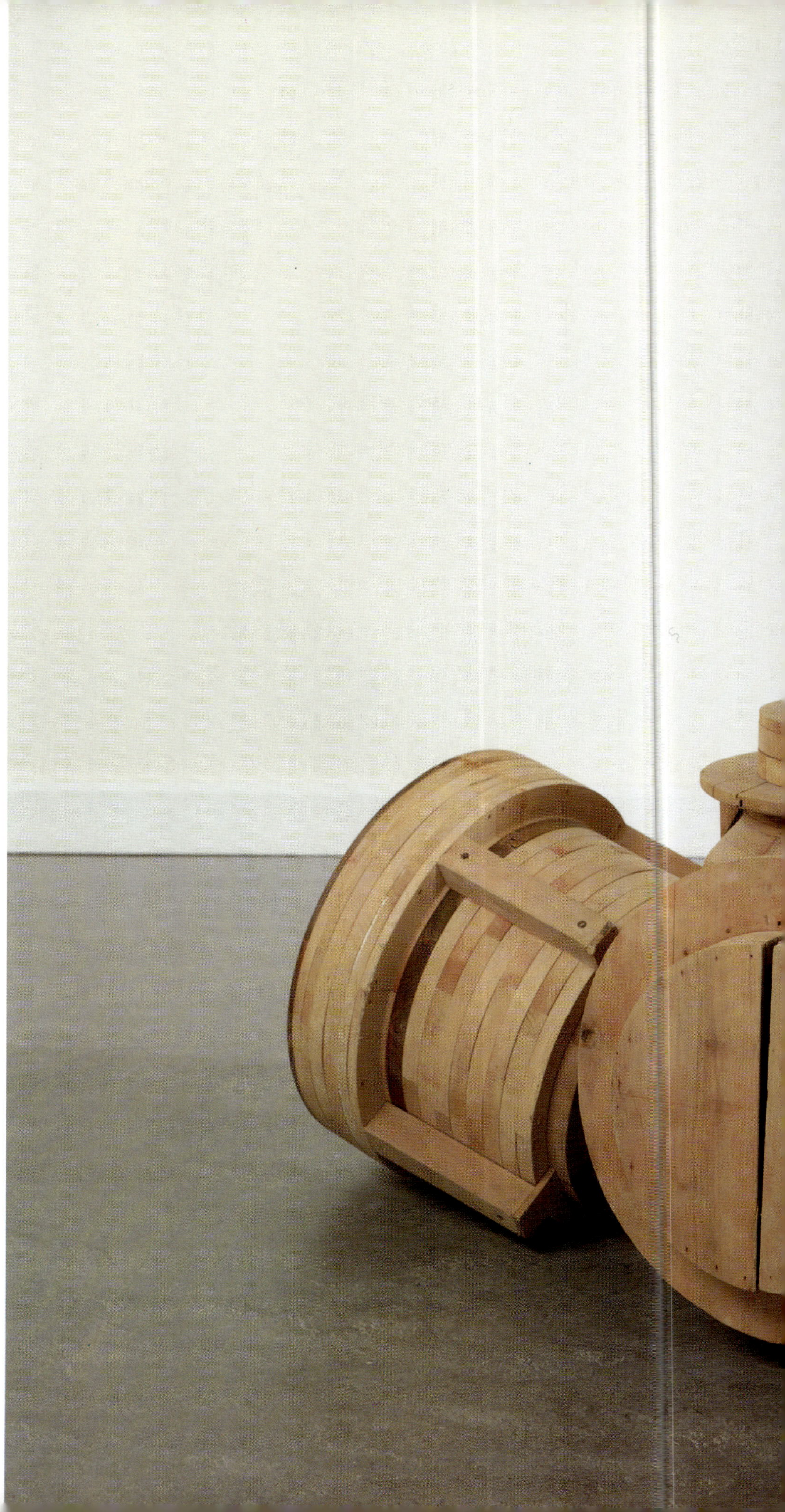

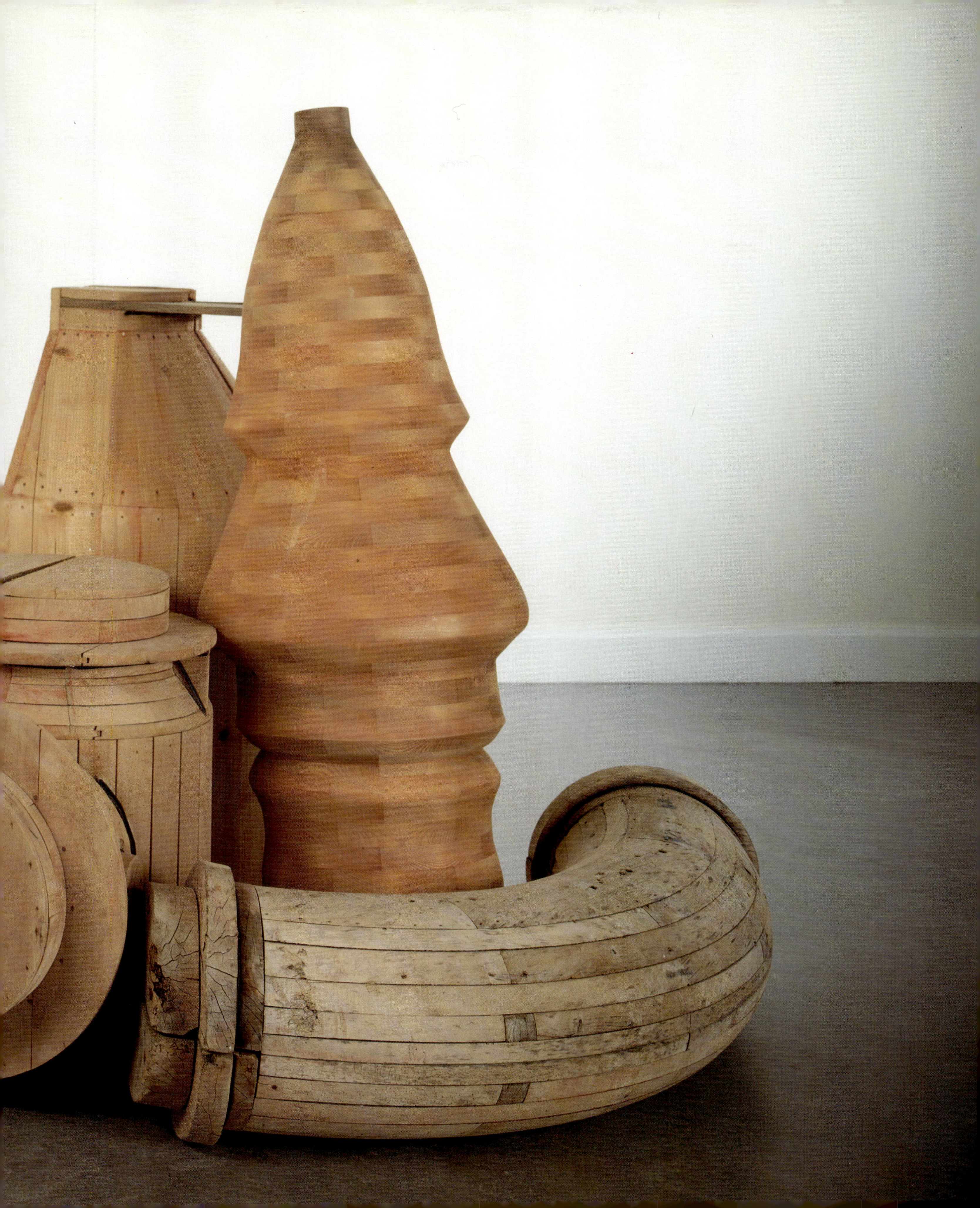

91. *Forminifera*, 1989

92. *Untitled*, 1989

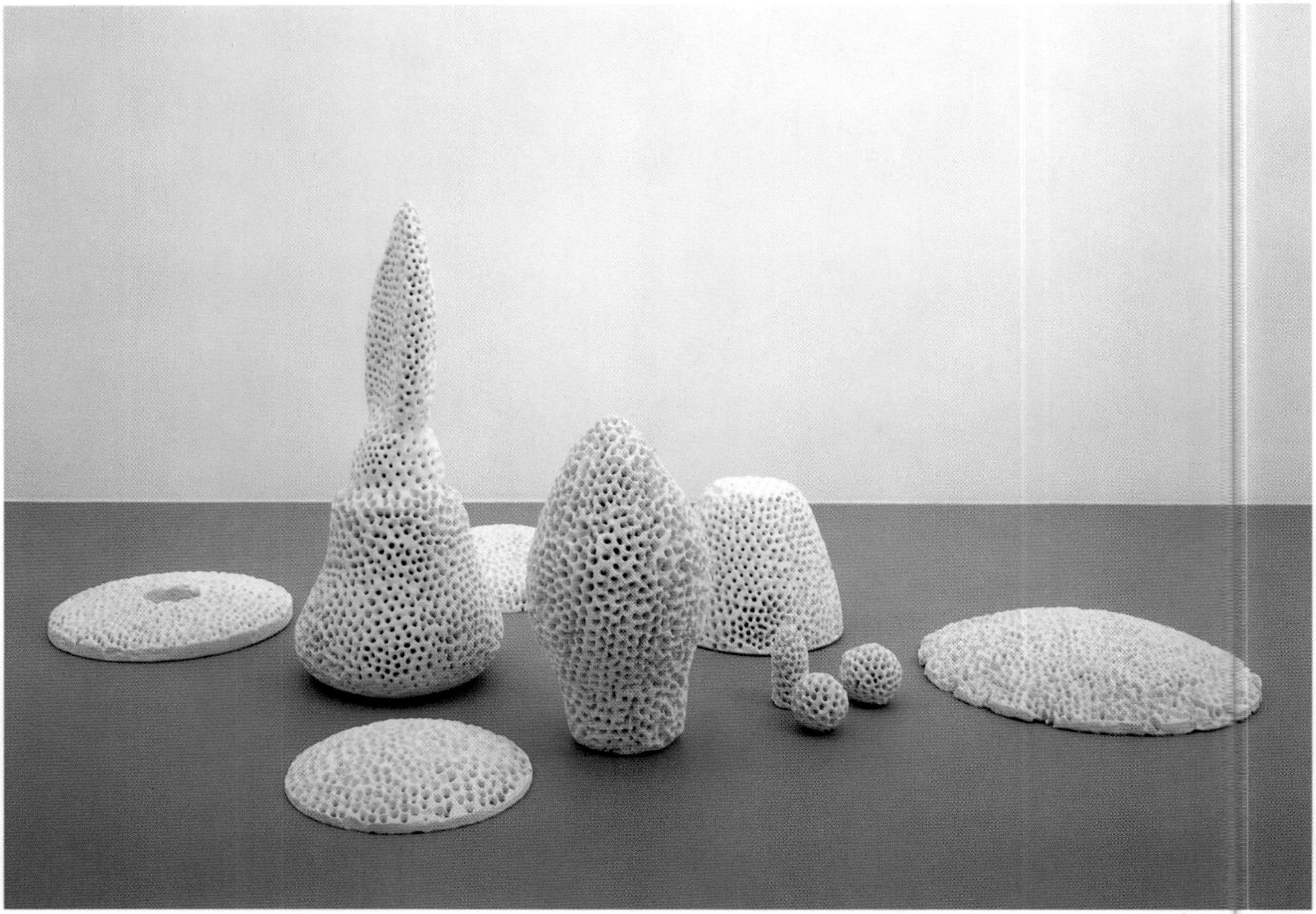

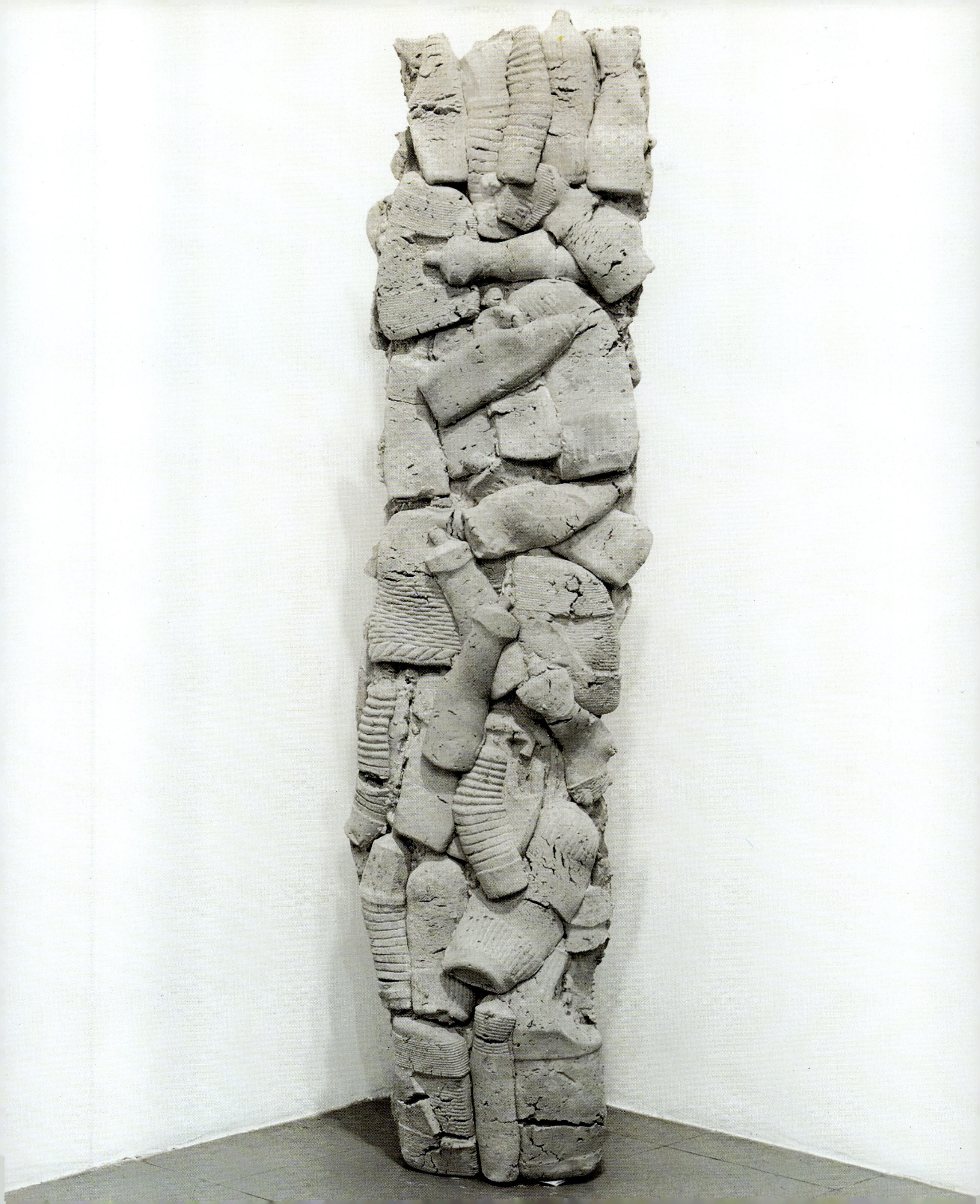

93. *Matruschka*, 1989

94. *Fruit Bottles*, 1989

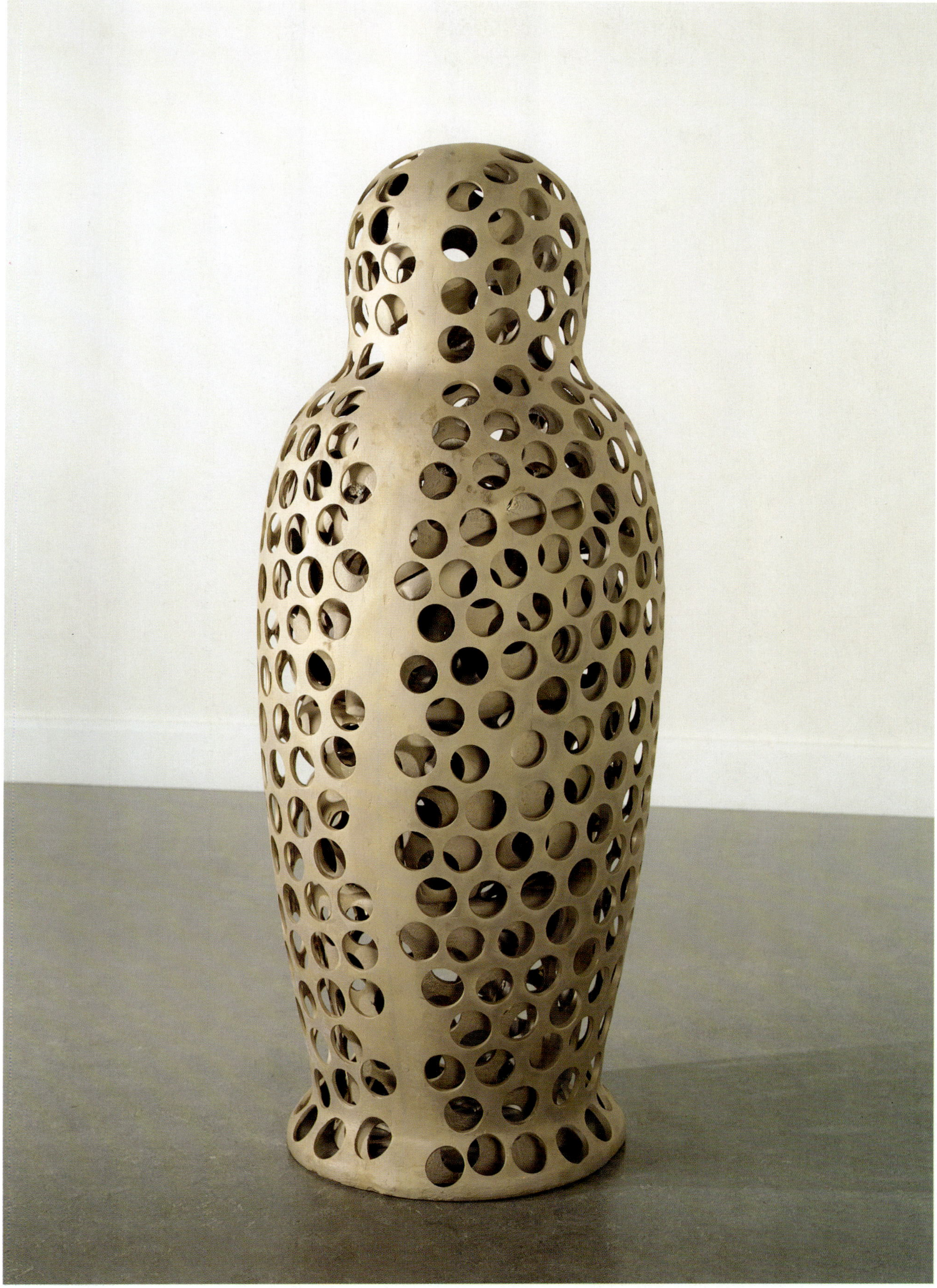

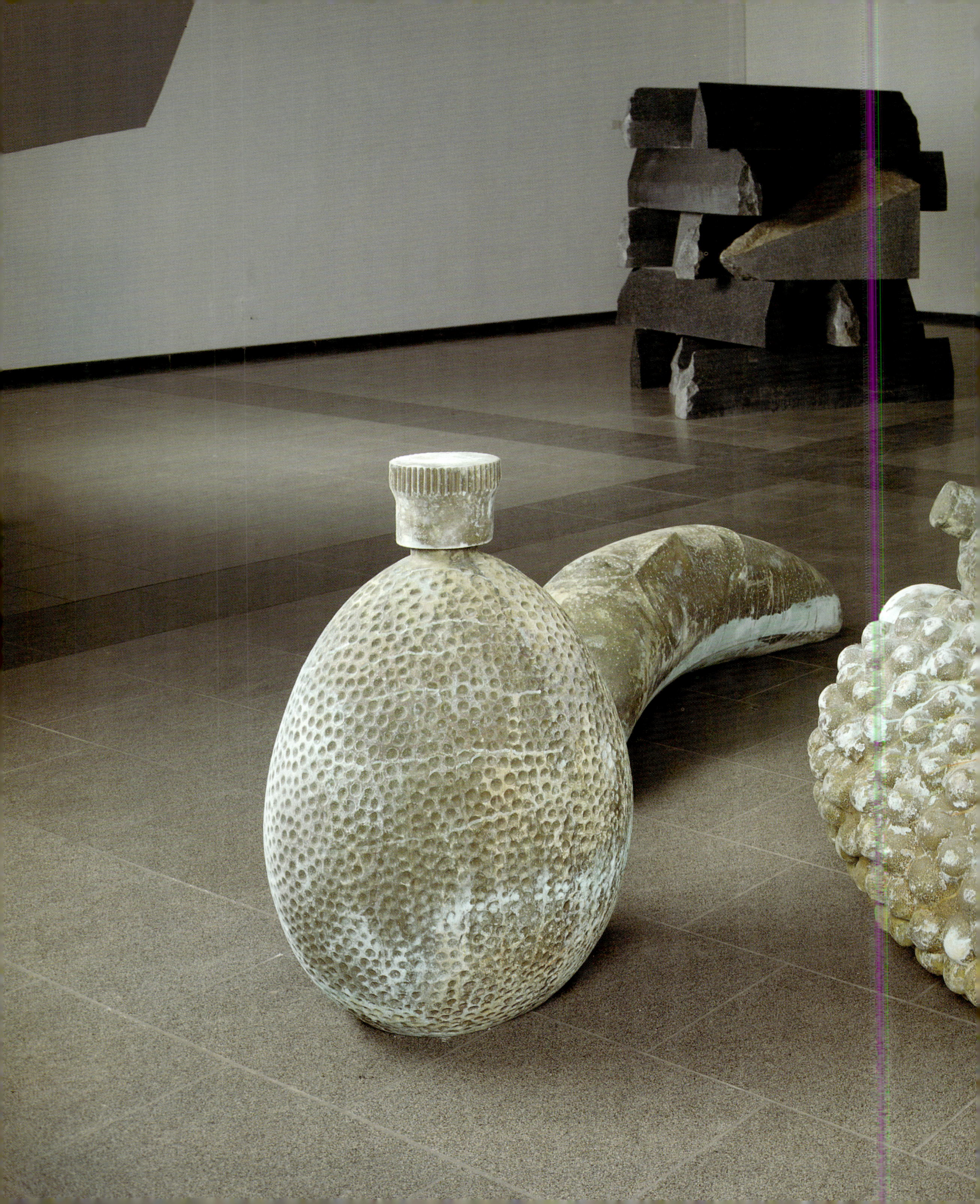

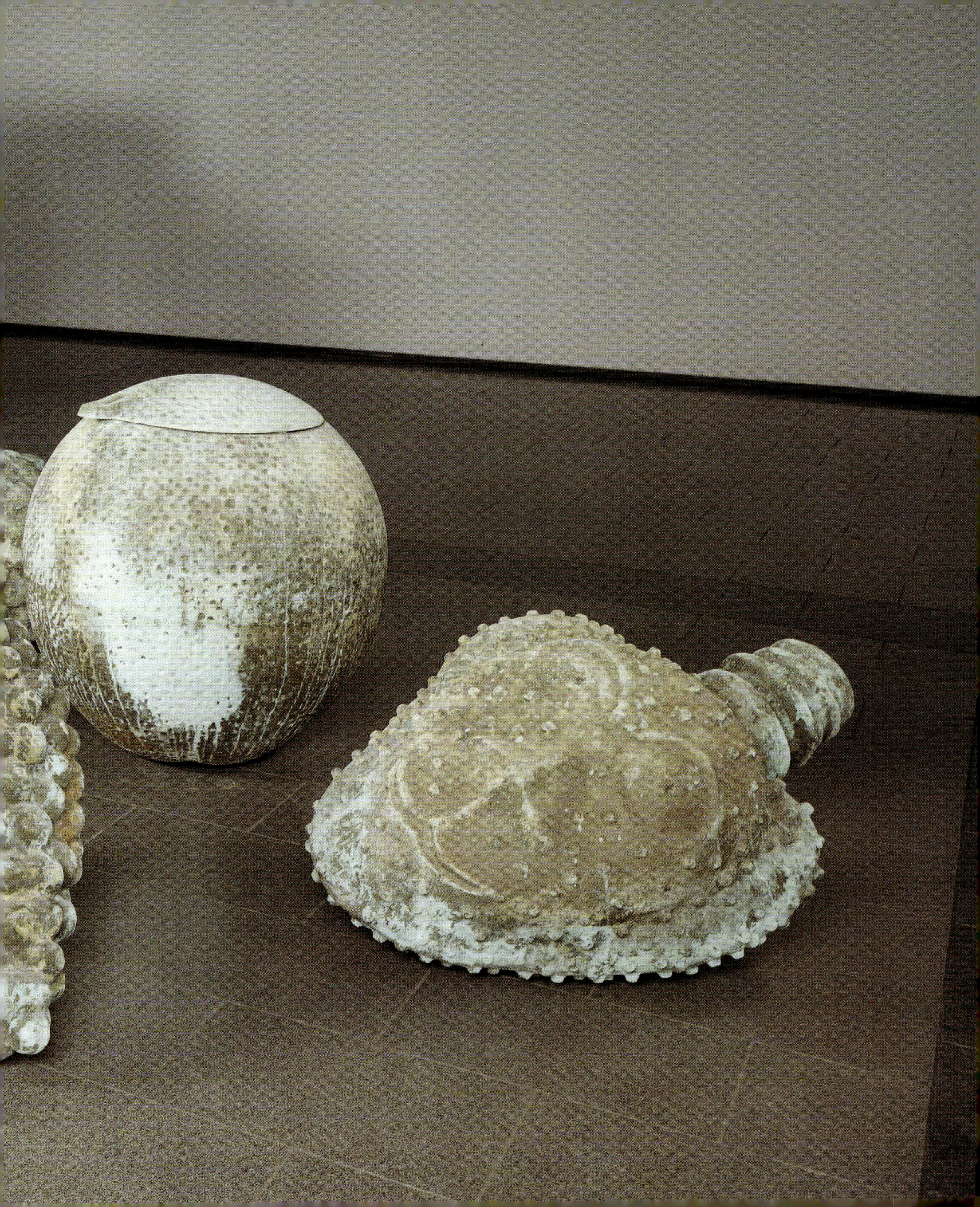

95. *Minster*, 1991

96. *Forminifera*, 1990

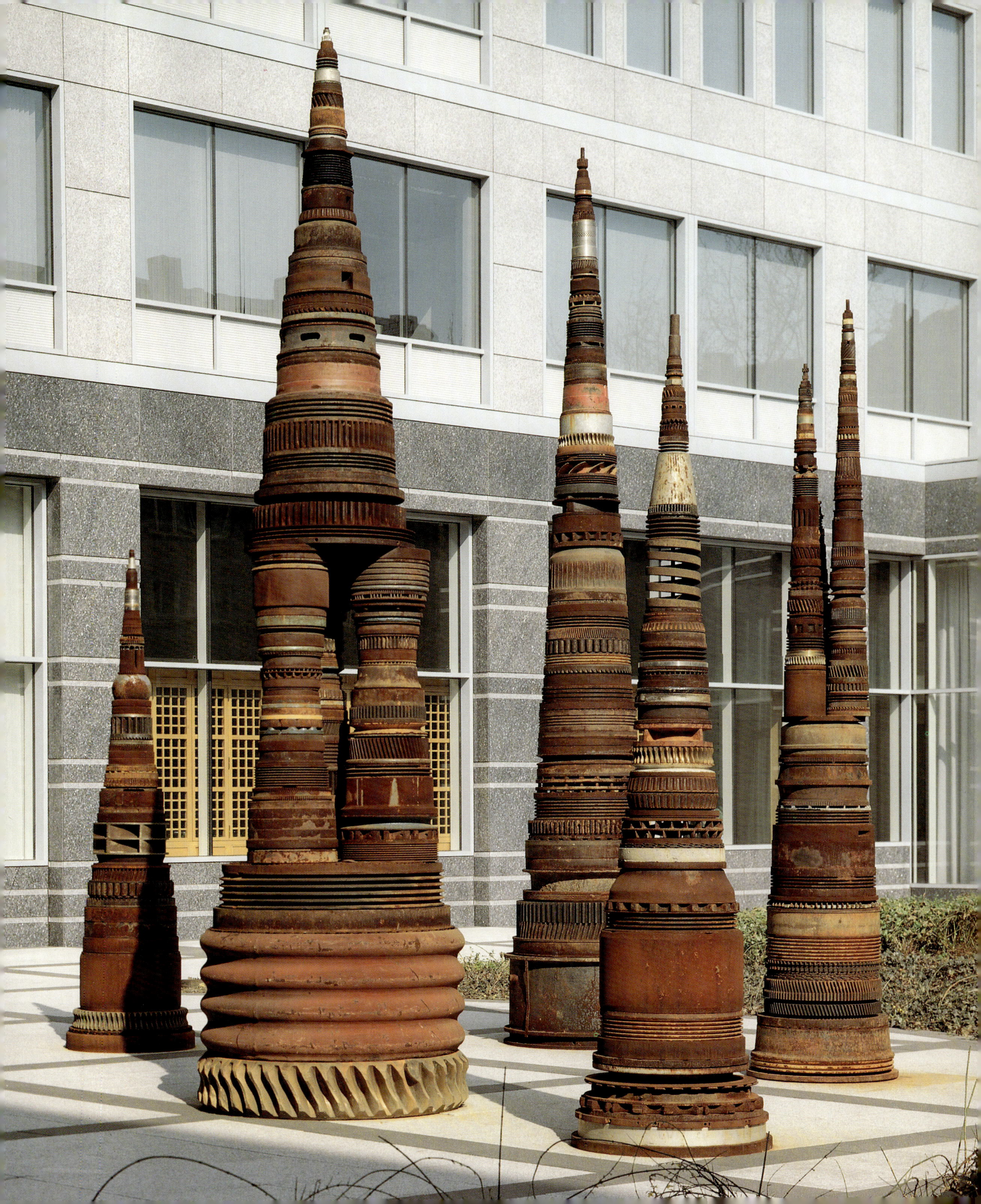

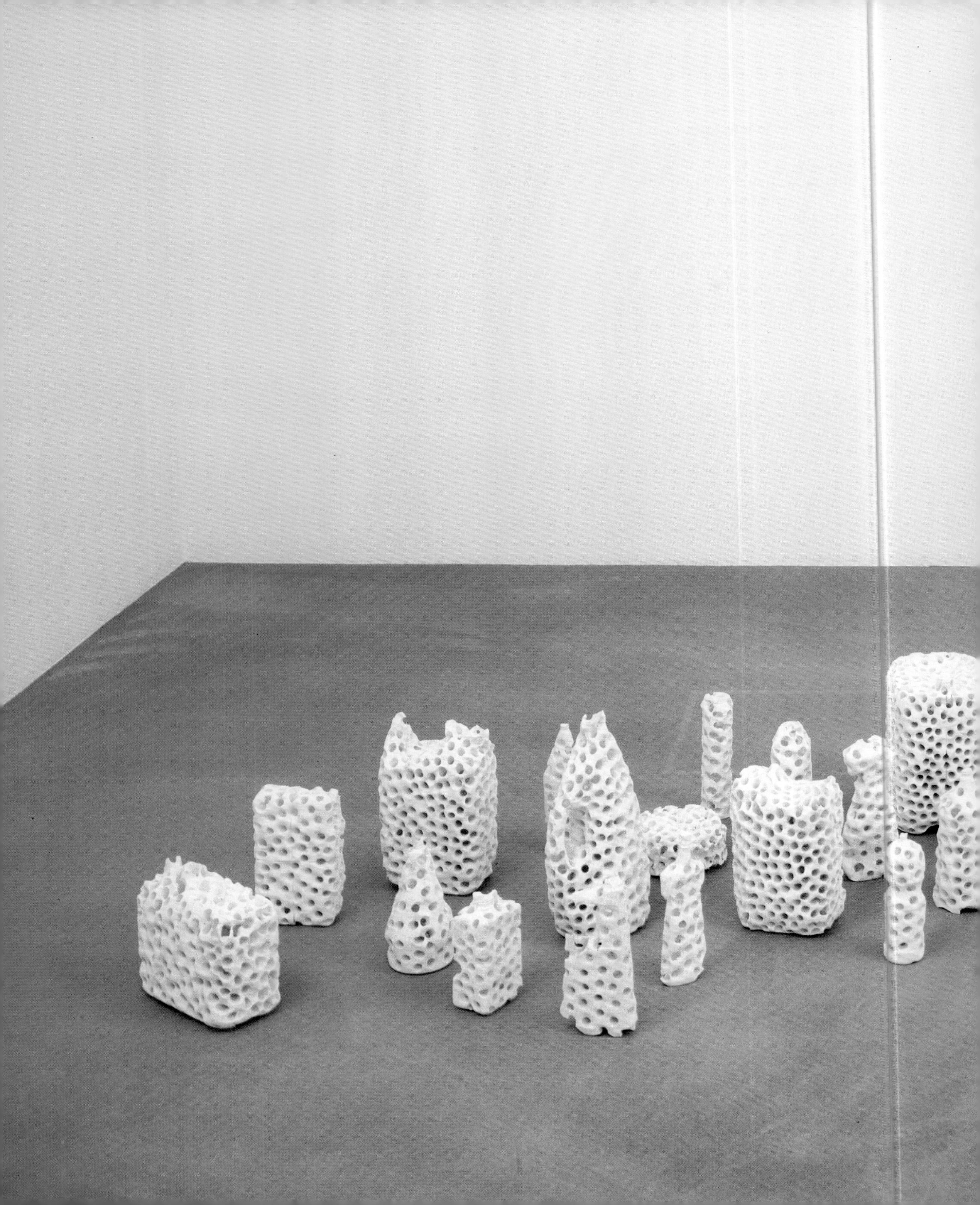

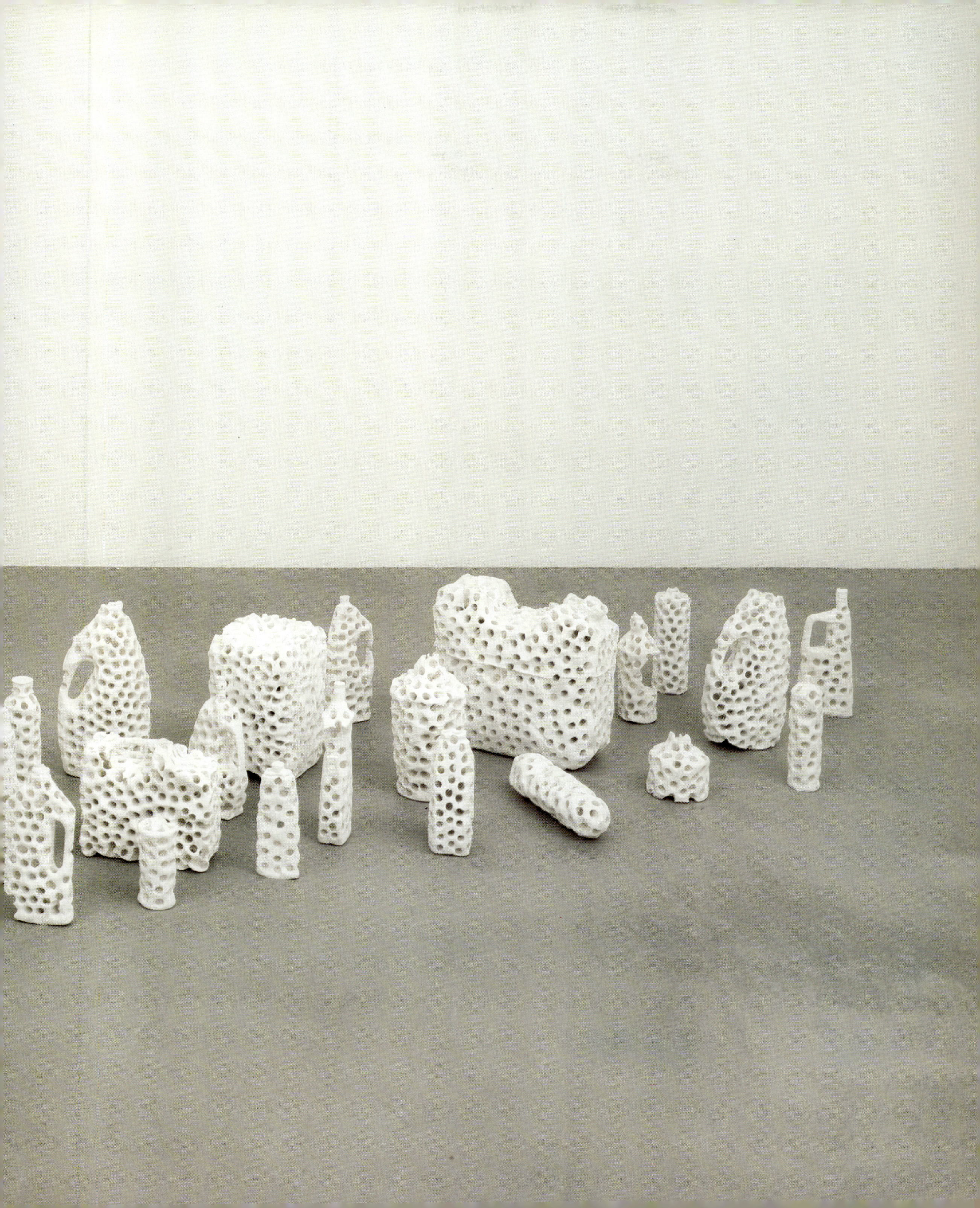

97. *The Complete Omnivore* (*Lucy's Teeth*), 1990

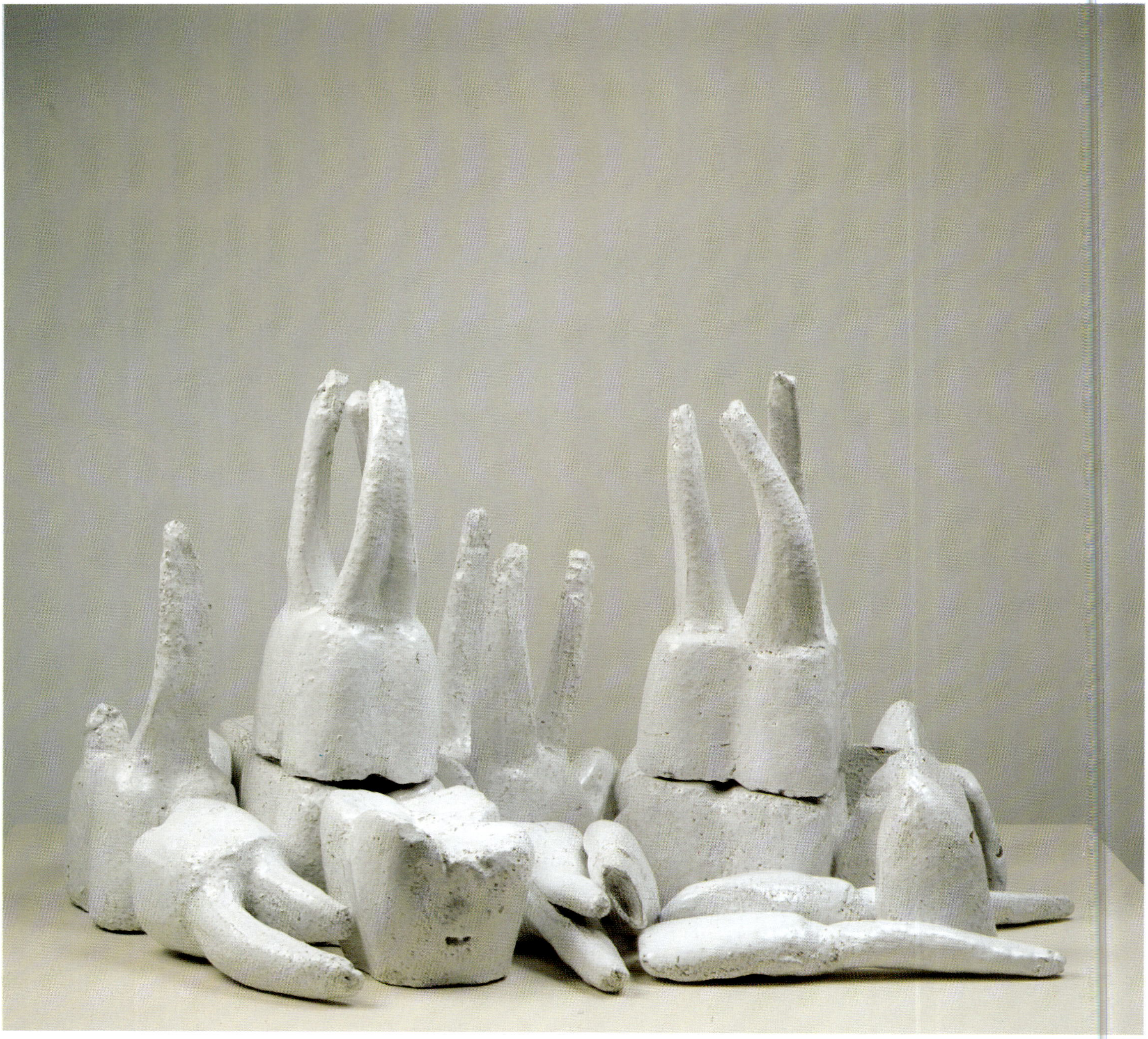

98. *Belgischer Hof*, 1990

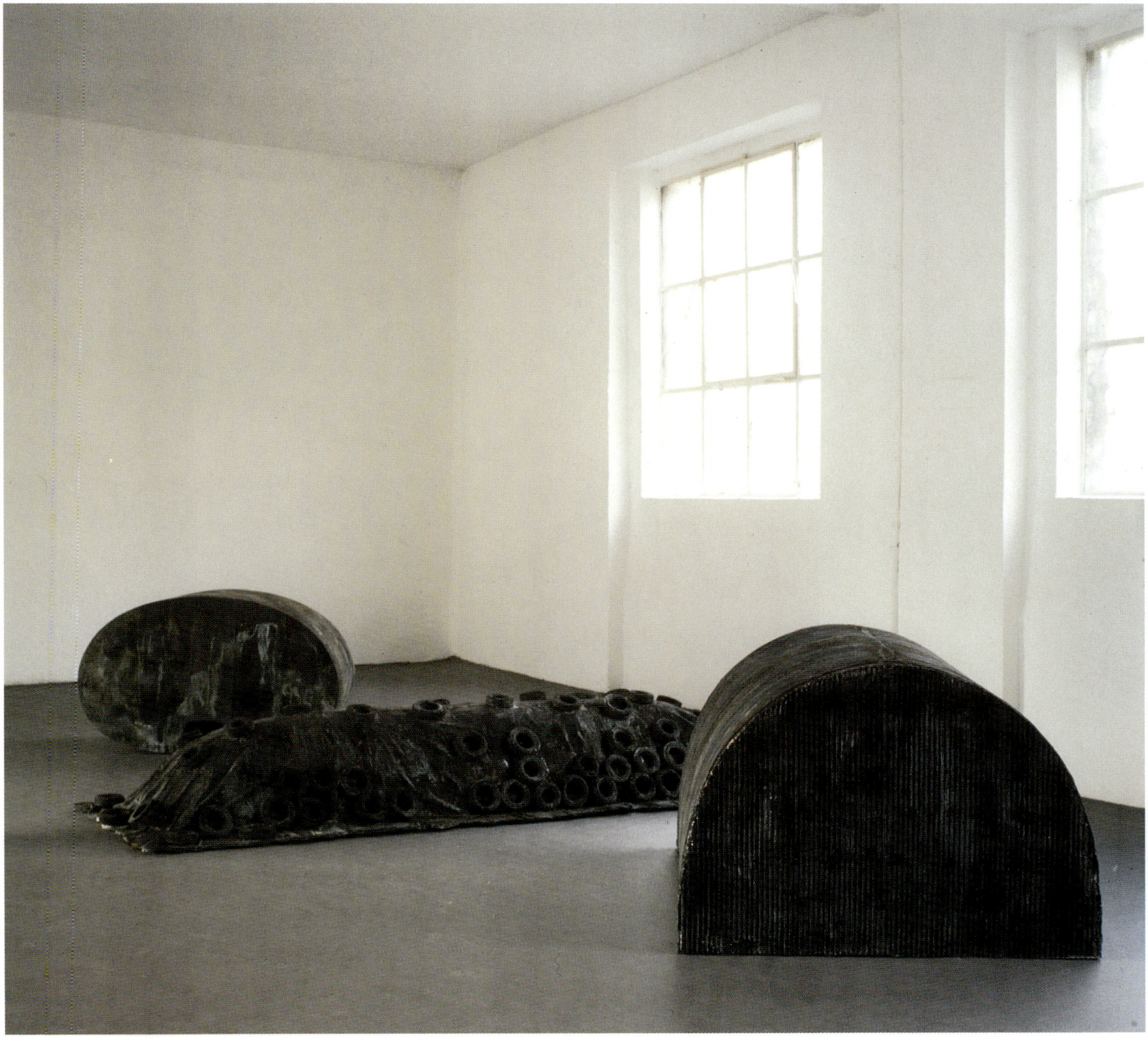

99. *Hildener Kreuz*, 1989

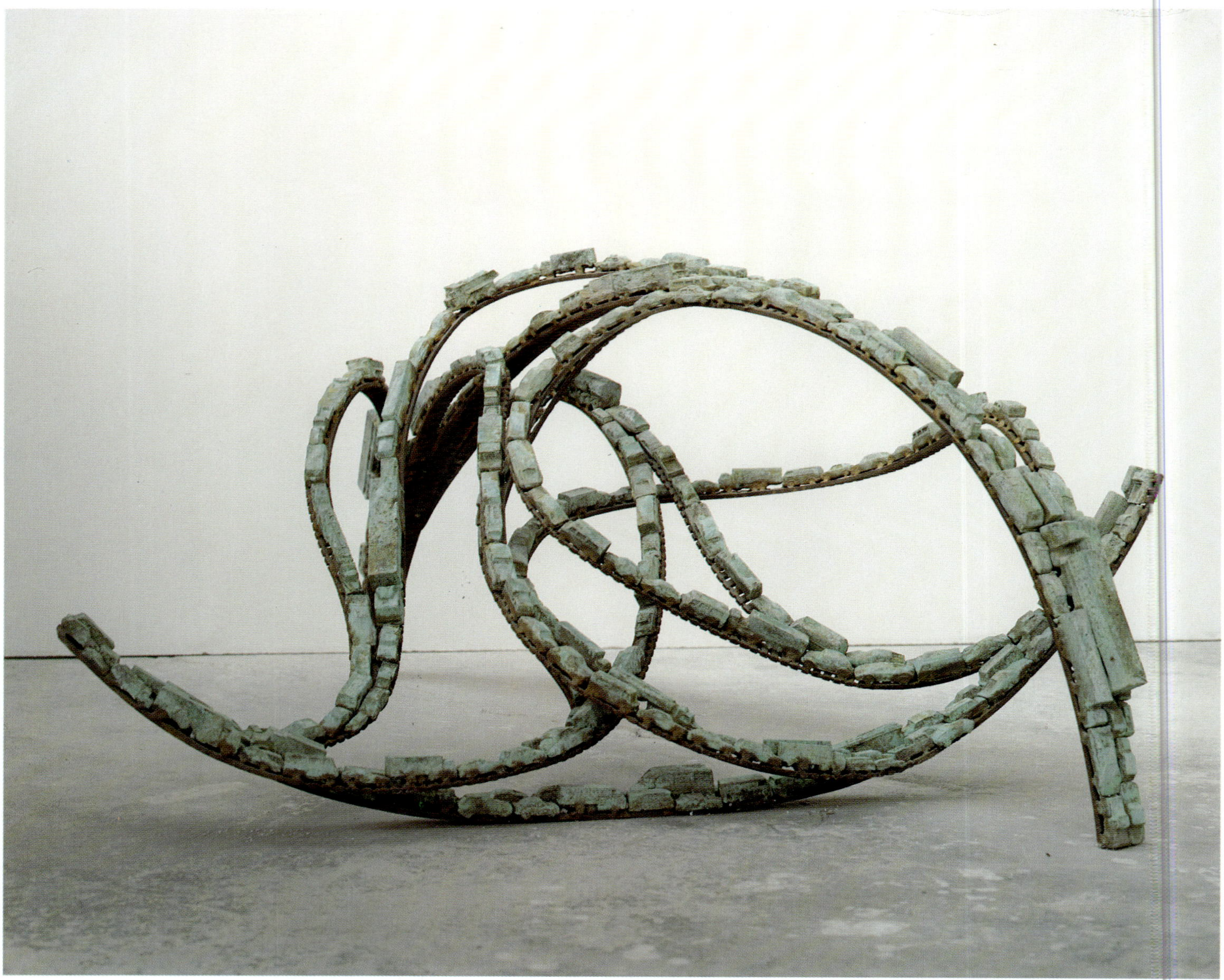

100. *Mineral Vein*, 1990

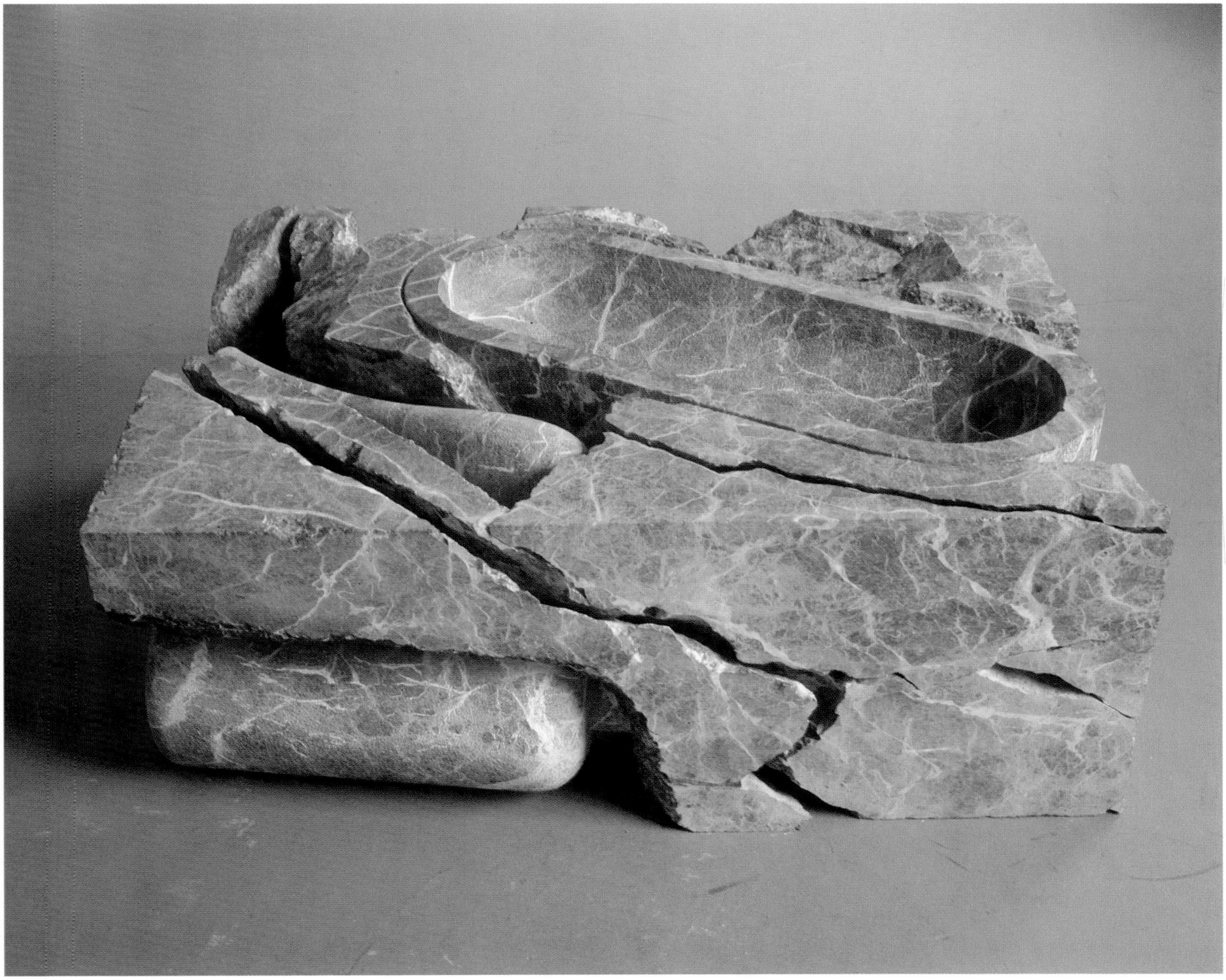

In a sense it's obvious that in terms of the physical world scientists make the more fundamental statements, but artists and philosophers don't have a less important job. They humanize, they find out what the significance of science is for human beings. At the point at which Einstein said there's no such thing as matter he didn't talk about the particles of things, he talked about things being a chain of events. If you're talking today about matter are you talking about substance? I've just said that there is a particular physical view of the world which is still an acceptable model for dealing with the world, but subsequent to Einstein there are alternatives. It takes a long time for philosophers and artists to pick up the pieces. I think you have to make images of objects which are like thinking models to help you get through the world.

"Tony Cragg Interviewed by Lynne Cooke." In *Tony Cragg*, exh. catalogue. London: Arts Council of Great Britain, 1987, pp. 34, 36.

101. *Trilobites*, 1989

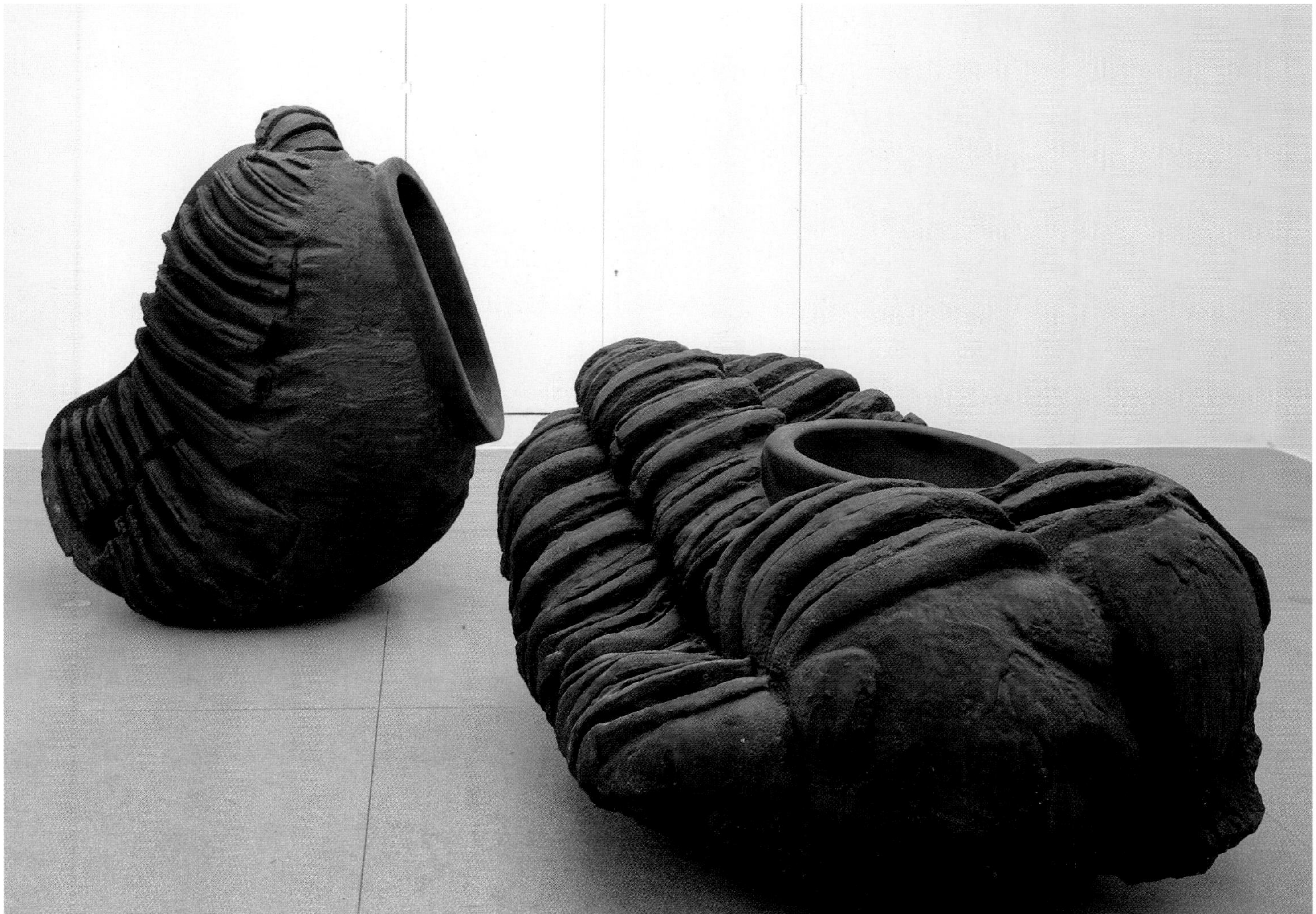

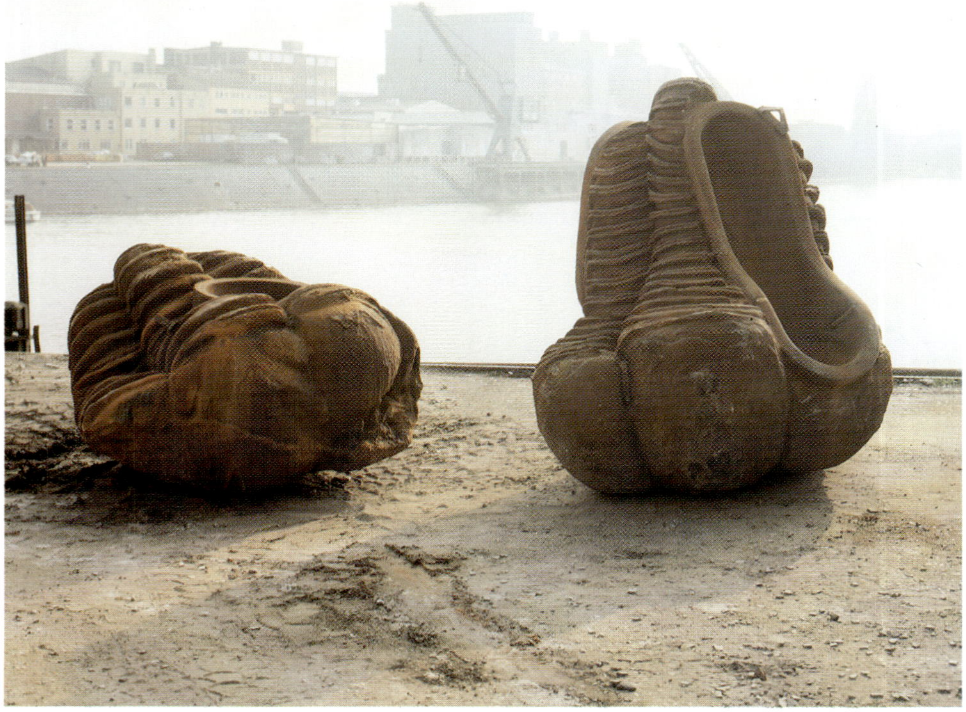

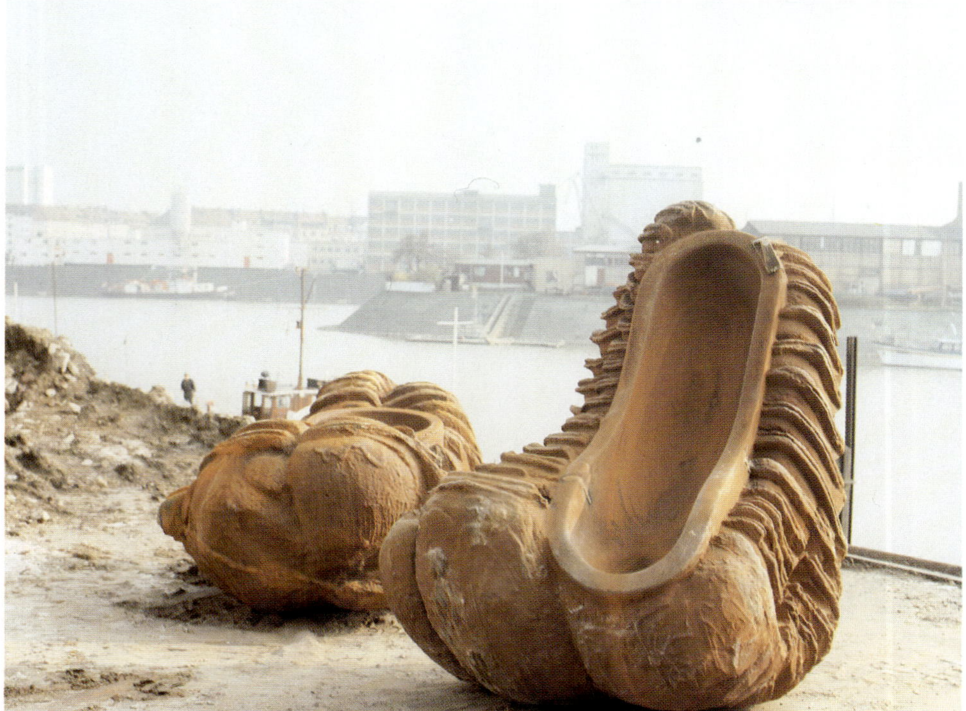

102. *Trilobites*, 1989

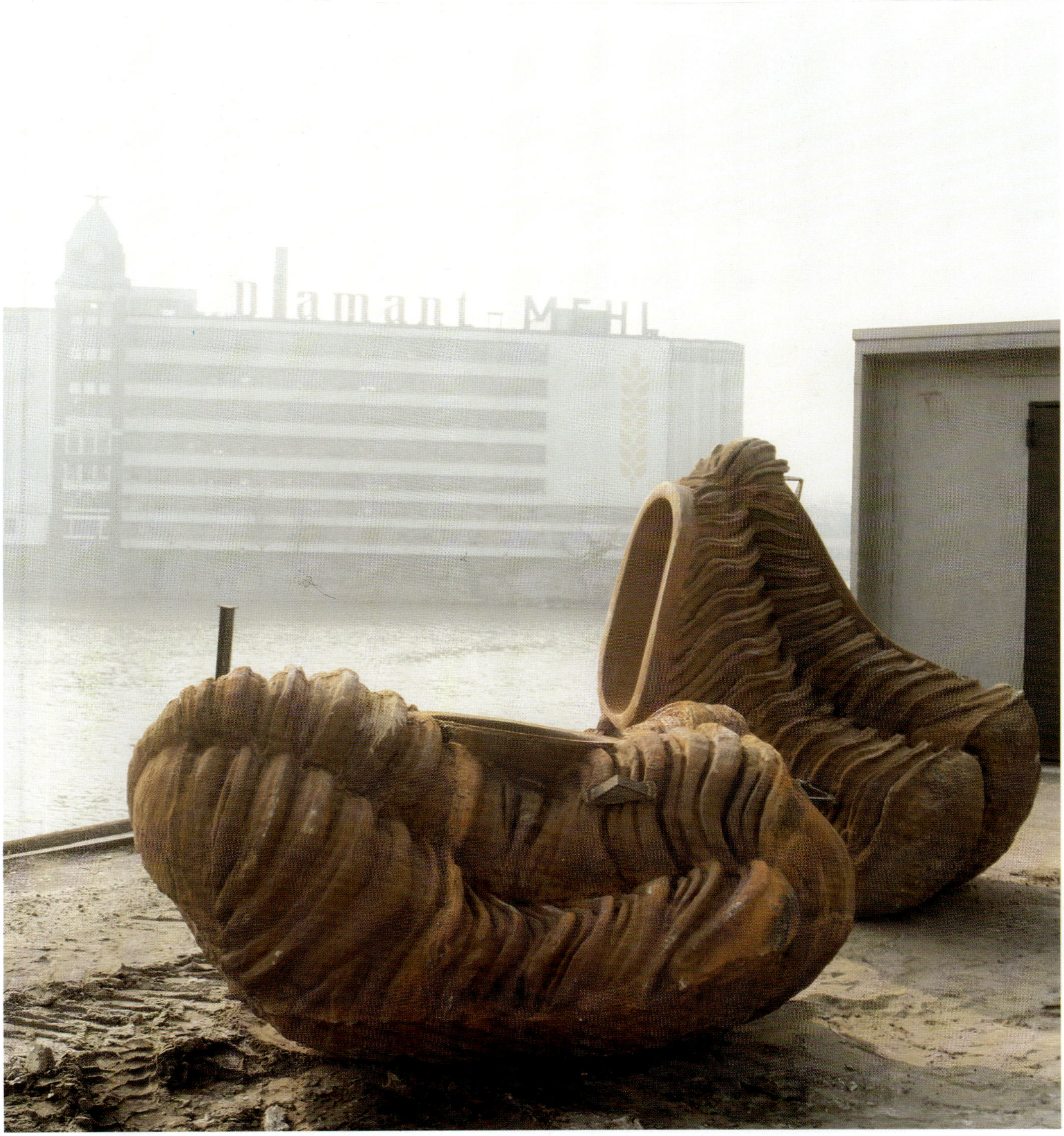

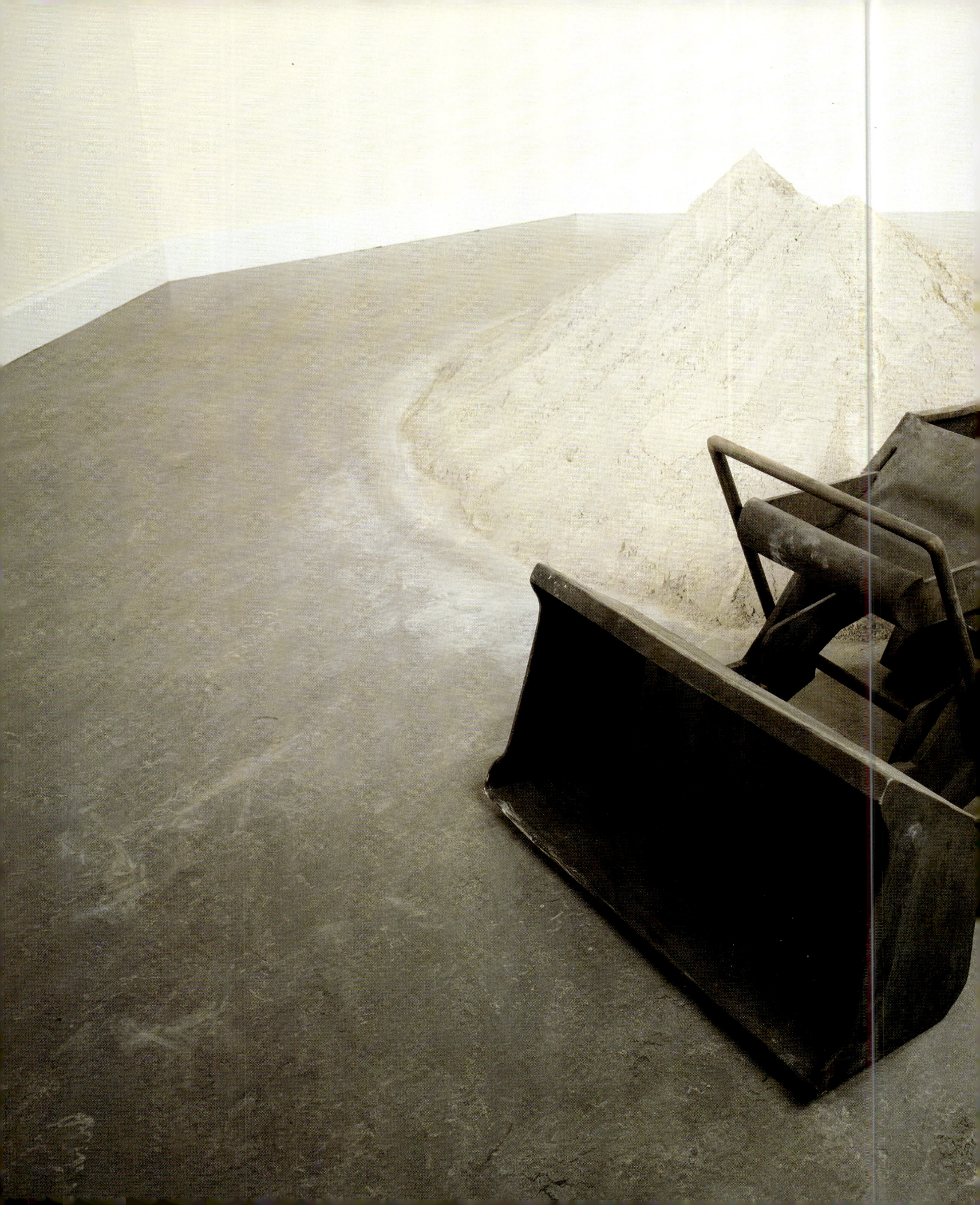

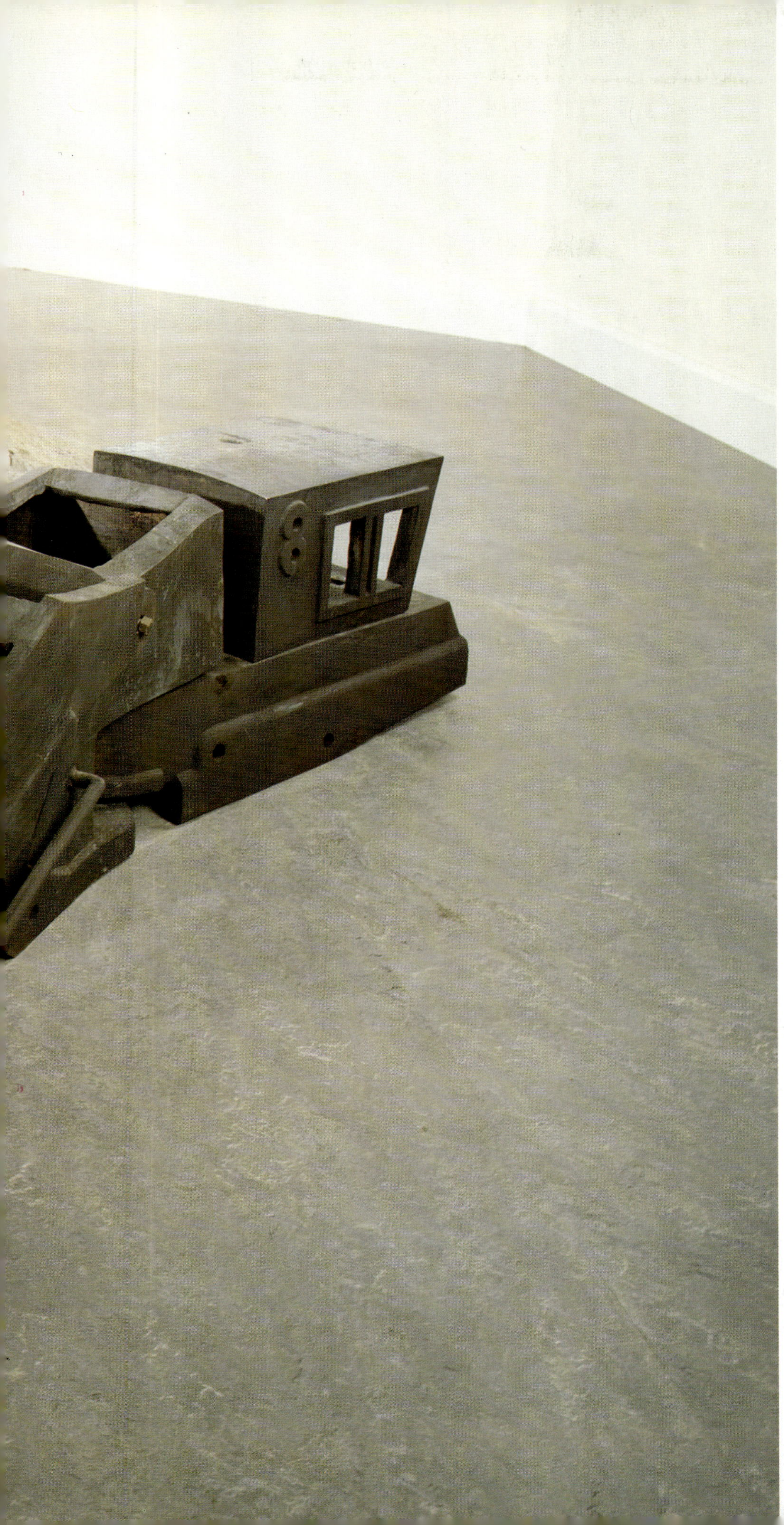

103. *Mountain Maquette* (*Quarry 'T'*), 1989

104. *Quarry Purofer*, 1990

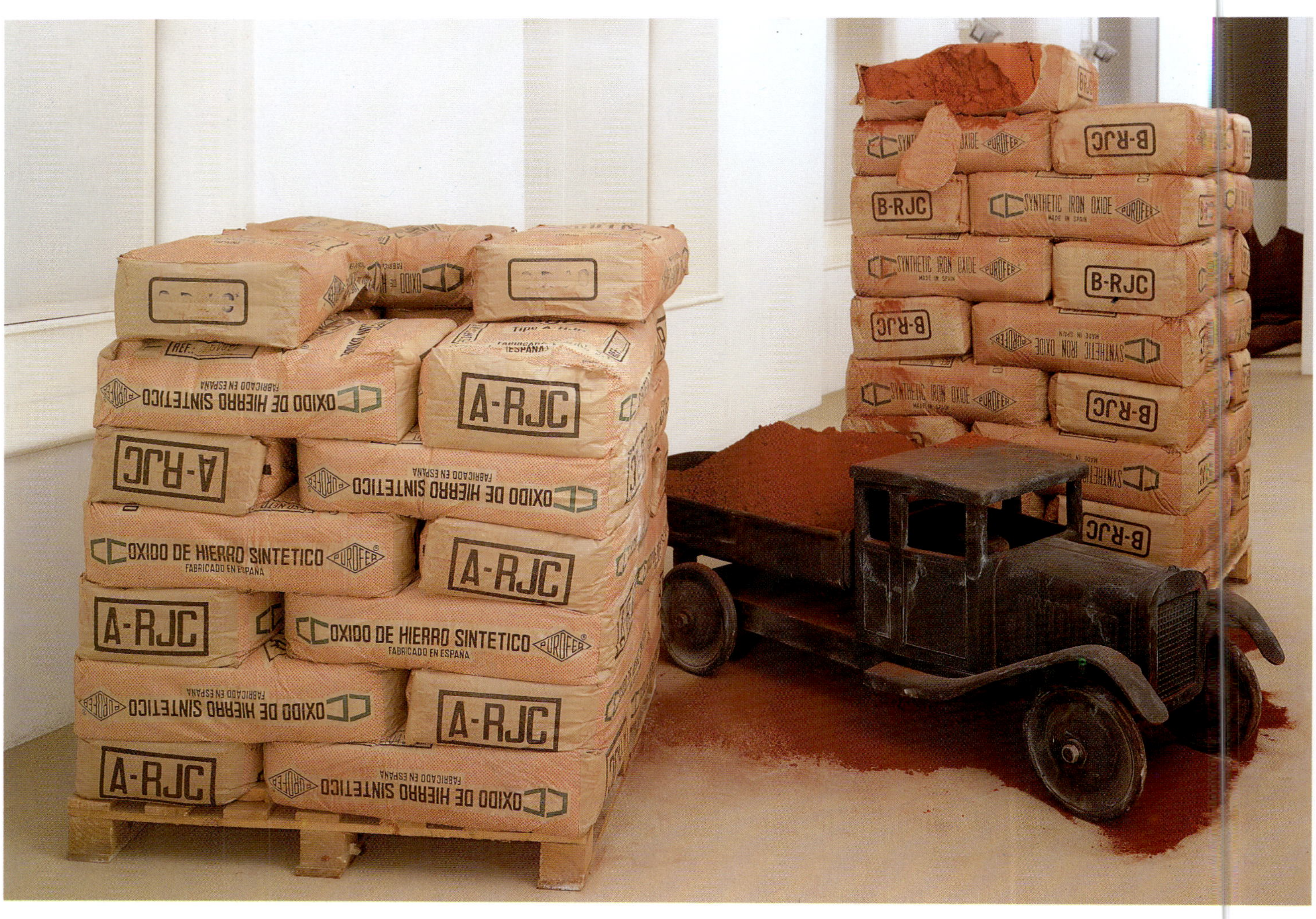

105. *Quarry*, 1990

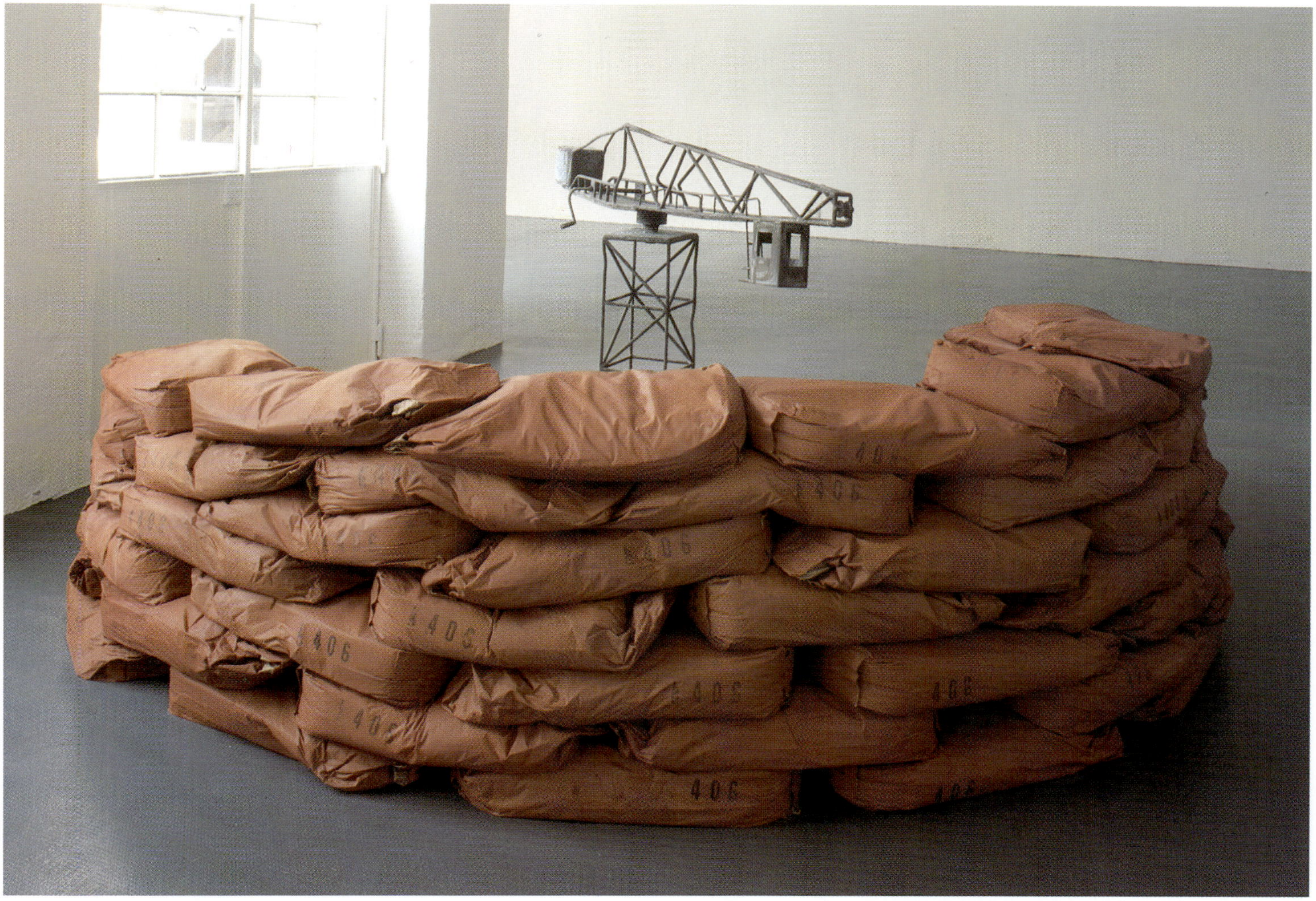

106. *Minster*, 1989-90

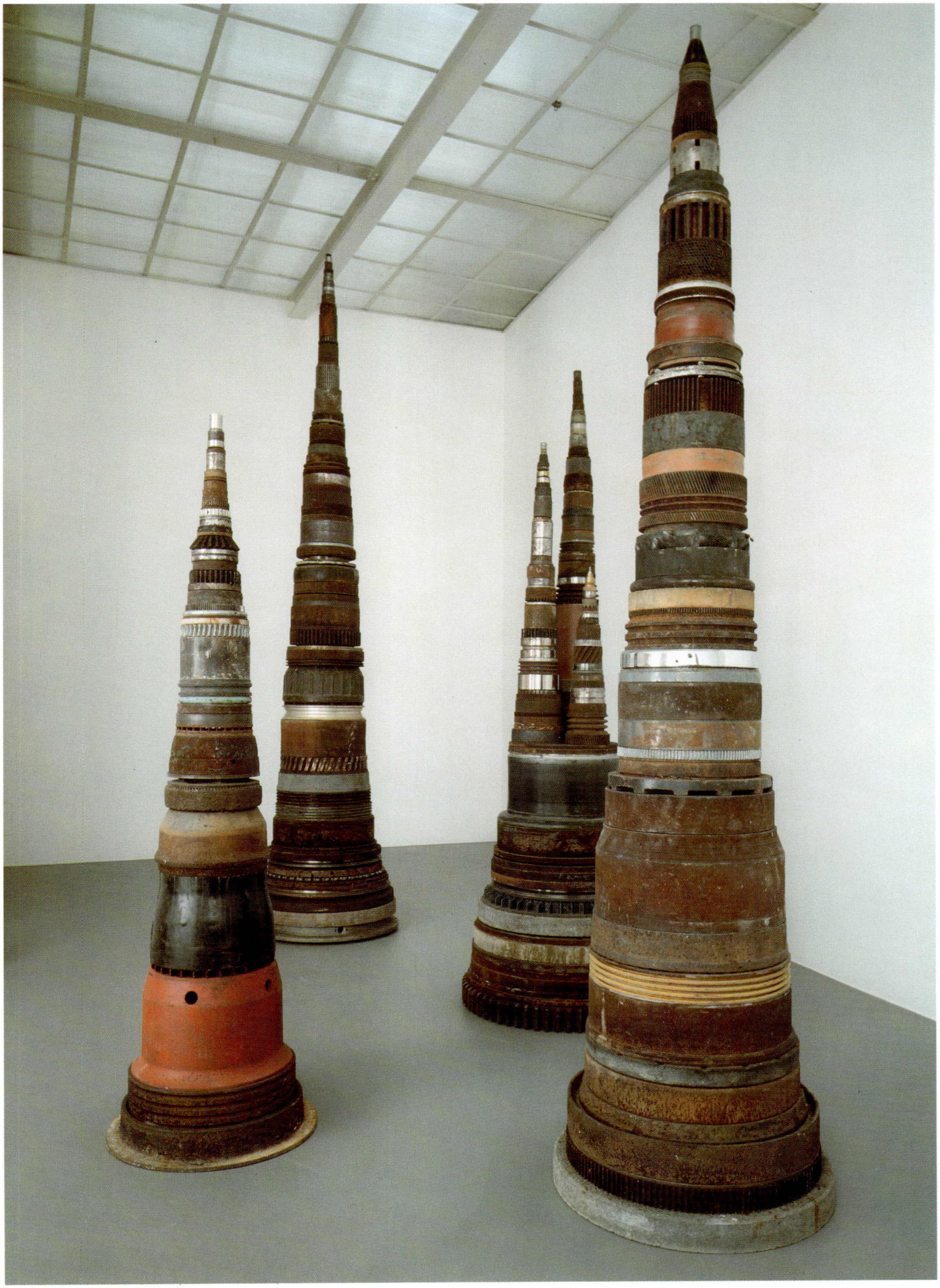

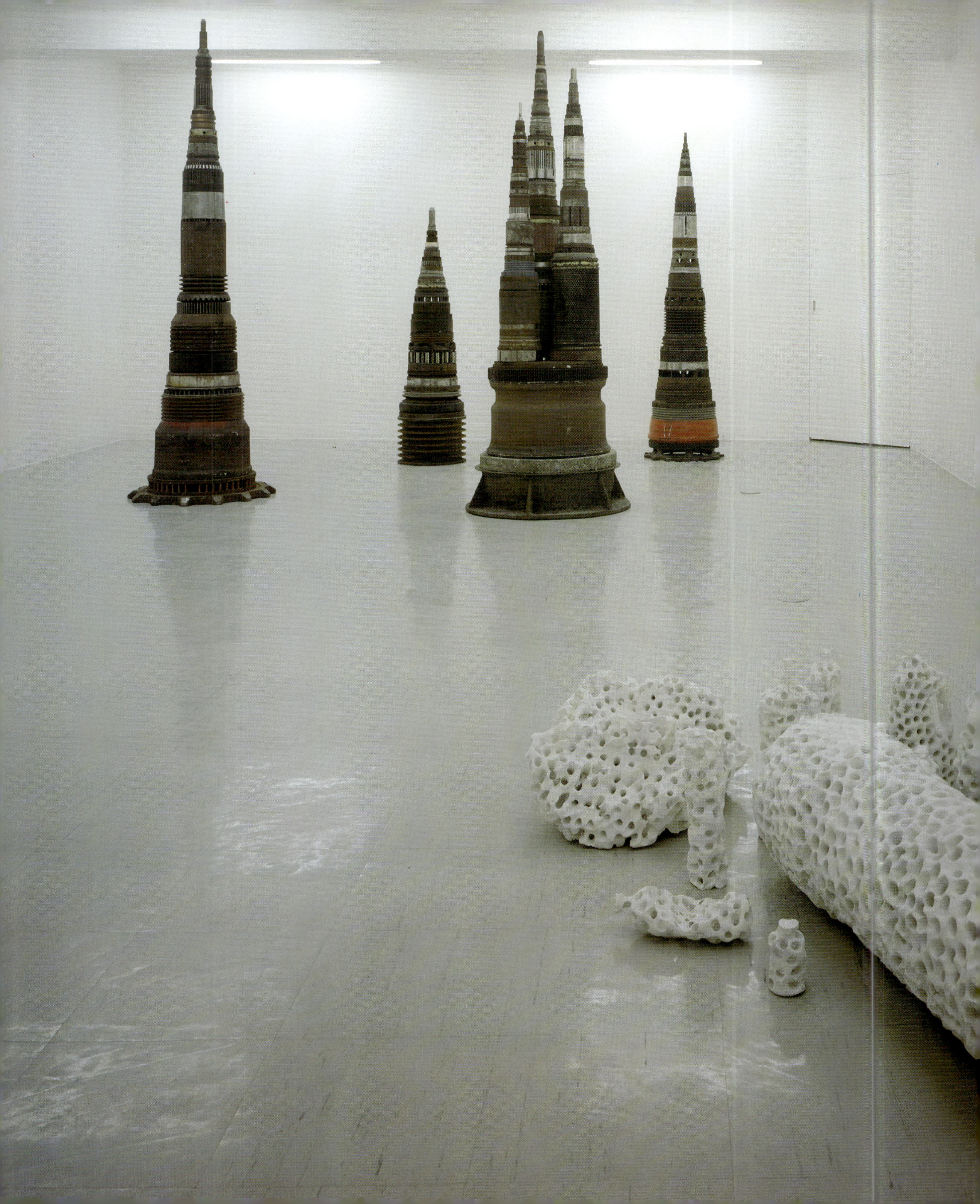

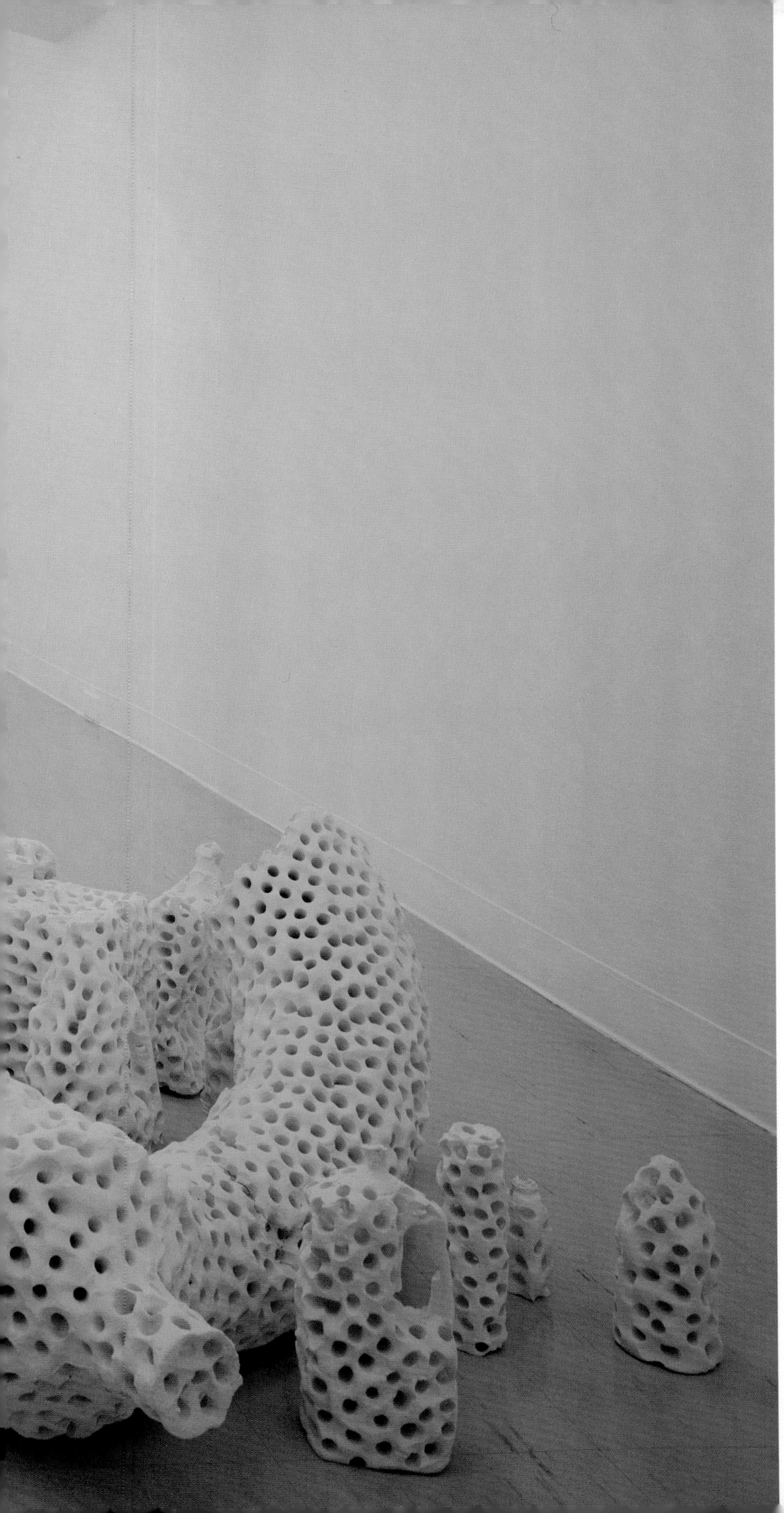

107. *Minster*, 1990

108. *Laibe*, 1991

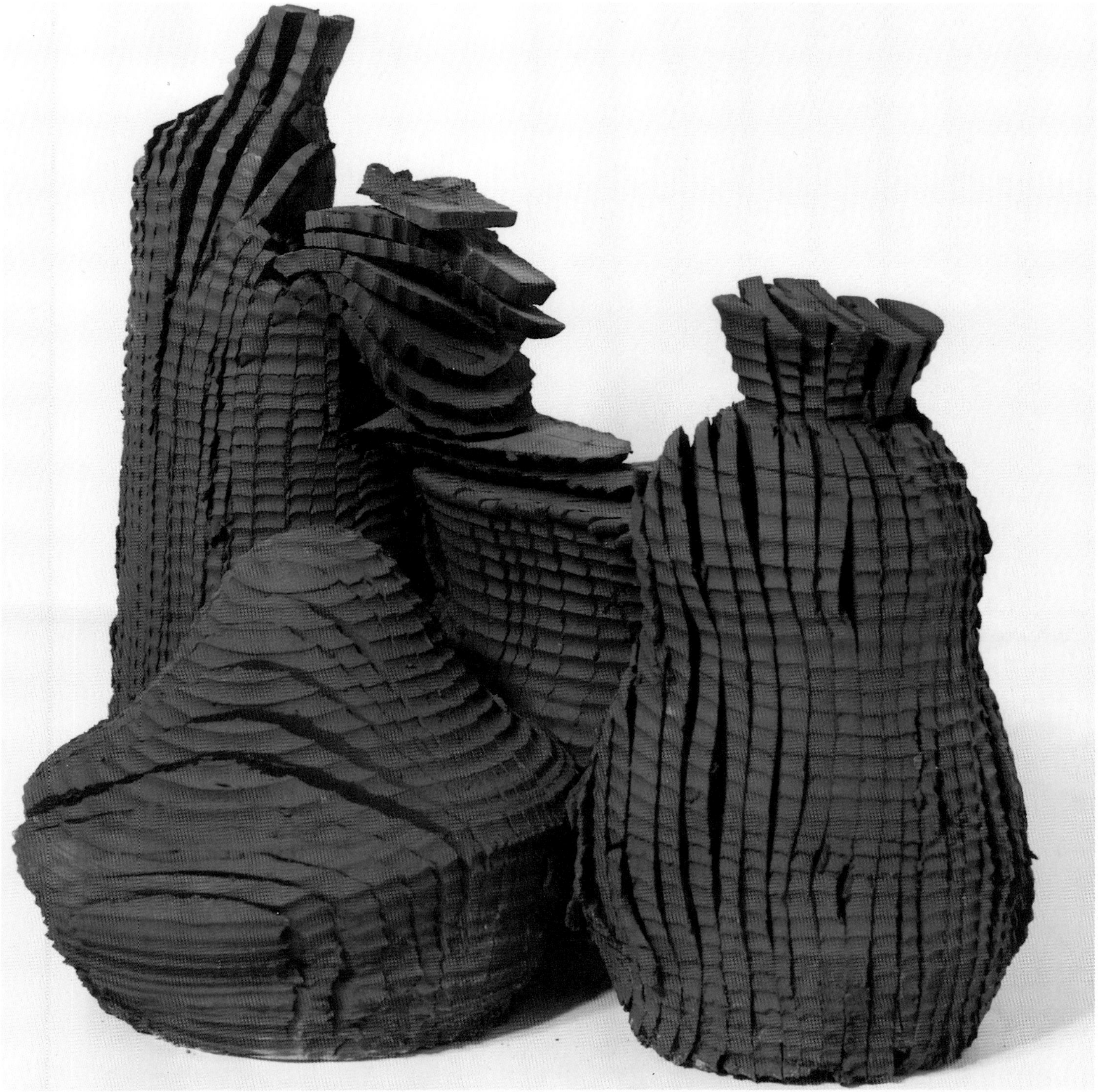

109. *Laibe*, 1990

110. *Laibe*, 1991

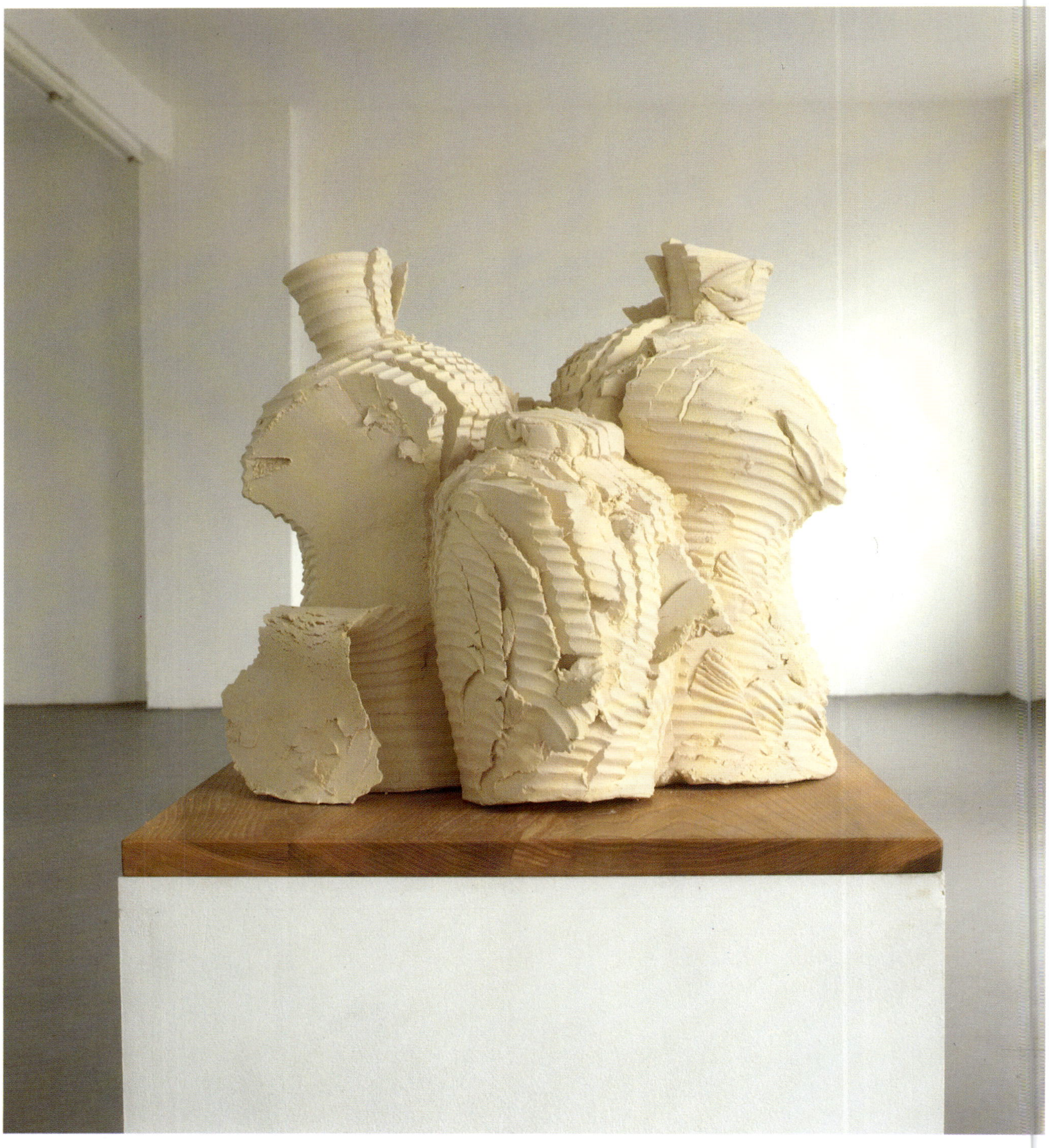

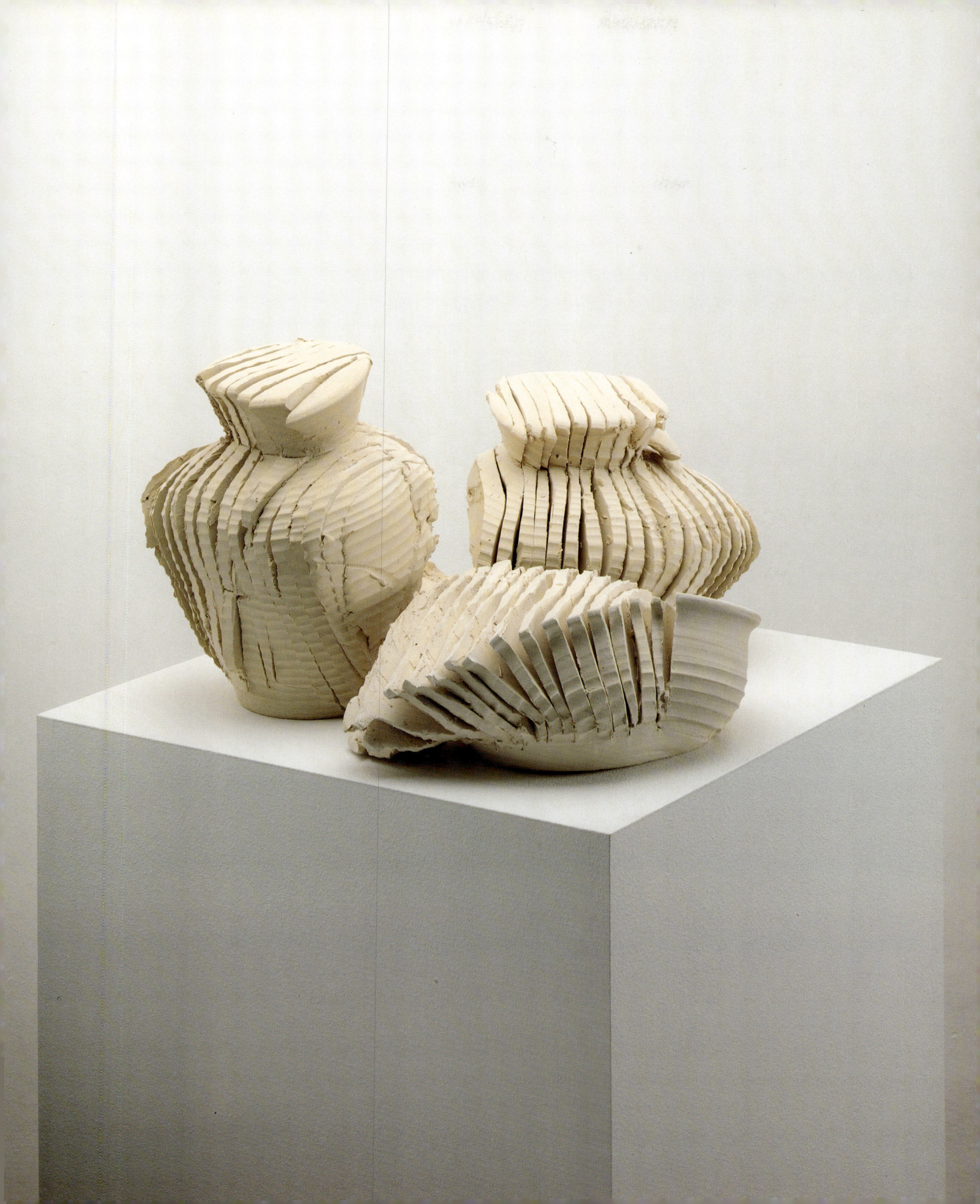

I'm trying to make natural materials and man-made materials have equal value. That's really the main concern. But I wouldn't say "I'm interested in plastic". There was a time in which I made more plastic works but now I'm using many other materials which are as artificial as plastic. A broader interest (and that's the central theme of the work) is the distinction between what is natural, or the world of nature, and the man-made and synthetic parts of the world. Traditionally it is a very clear divided convention. I think [this], for example, as we look at Central Europe, and it's difficult to maintain this absolute scale of nature, because we changed everything, we changed the plants, the animals, the water, the air. So, I think it's necessary to look at this border between natural and man-made. It is nothing concrete, so I continuously have to go across it to know where it is. That is one of the main concerns in the work rather than the idea that one takes a particular material and makes art out of it. It is an essential difference which is quite important.

Ludovico Pratesi, "A Conversation with Tony Cragg." In *Tony Cragg*, exh. catalogue. Rome: Valentina Moncada, 1990, p. 8.

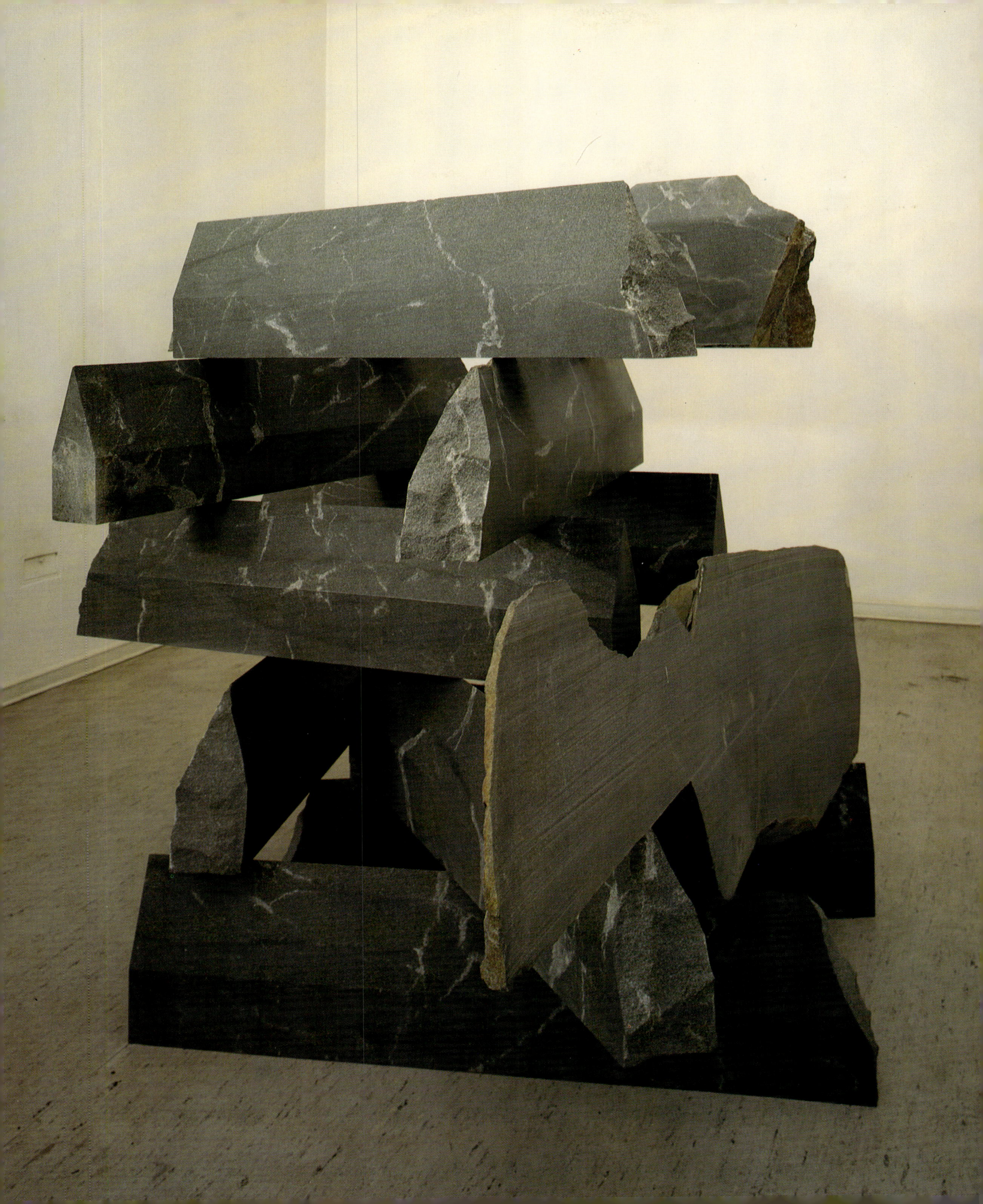

112. *Veil*, 1990

113. *Untitled*, 1990

114. *Larder*, 1990

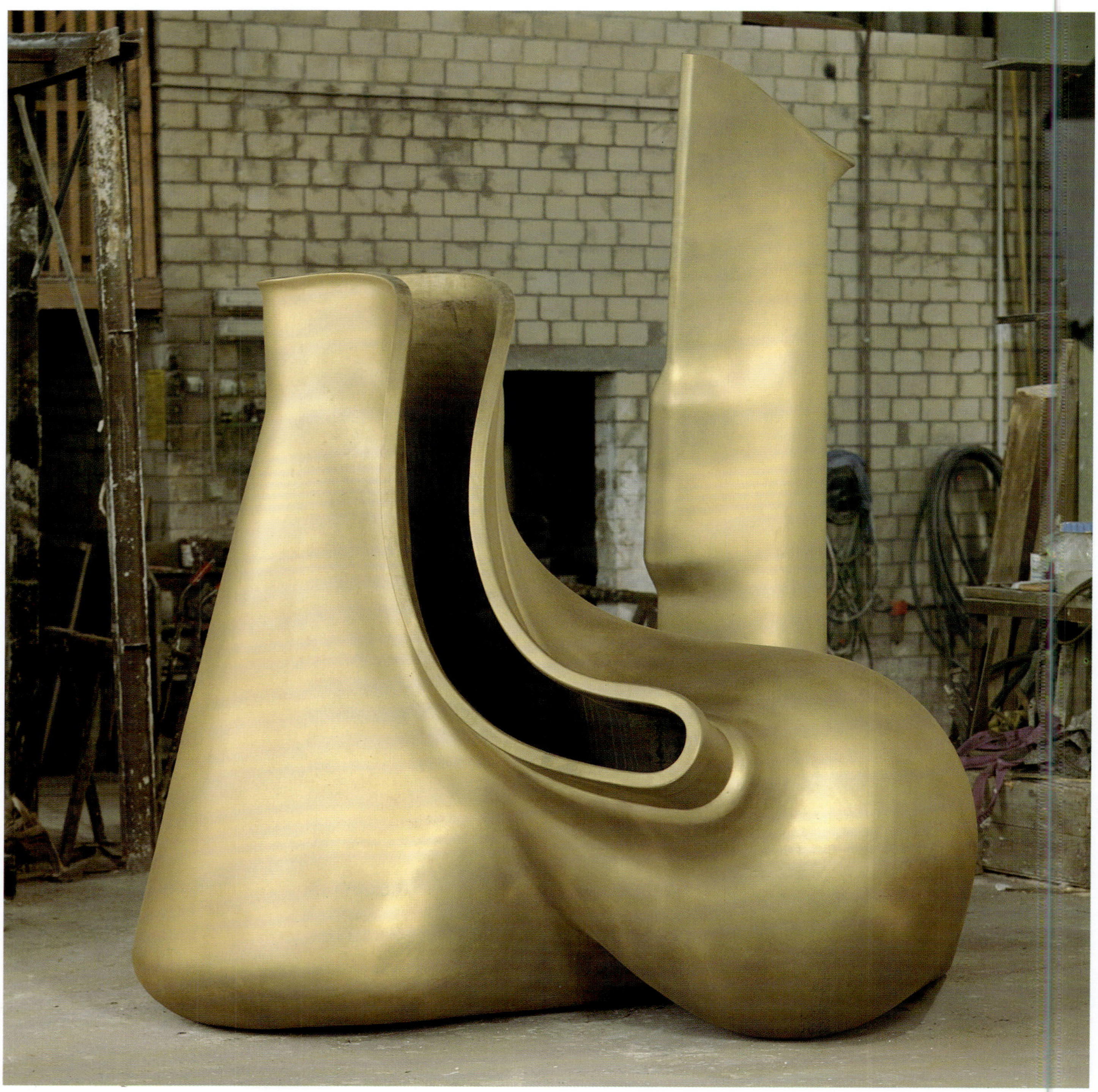

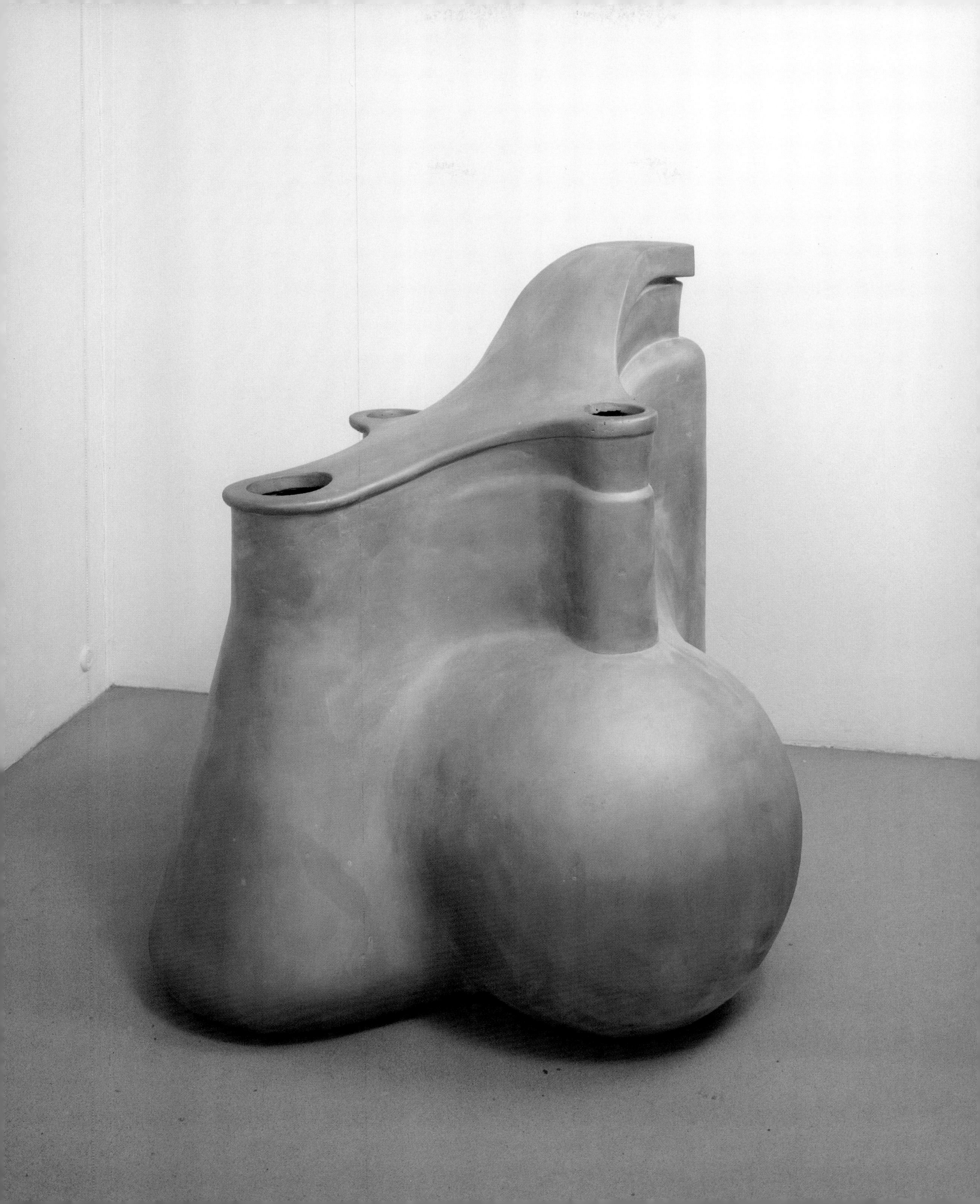

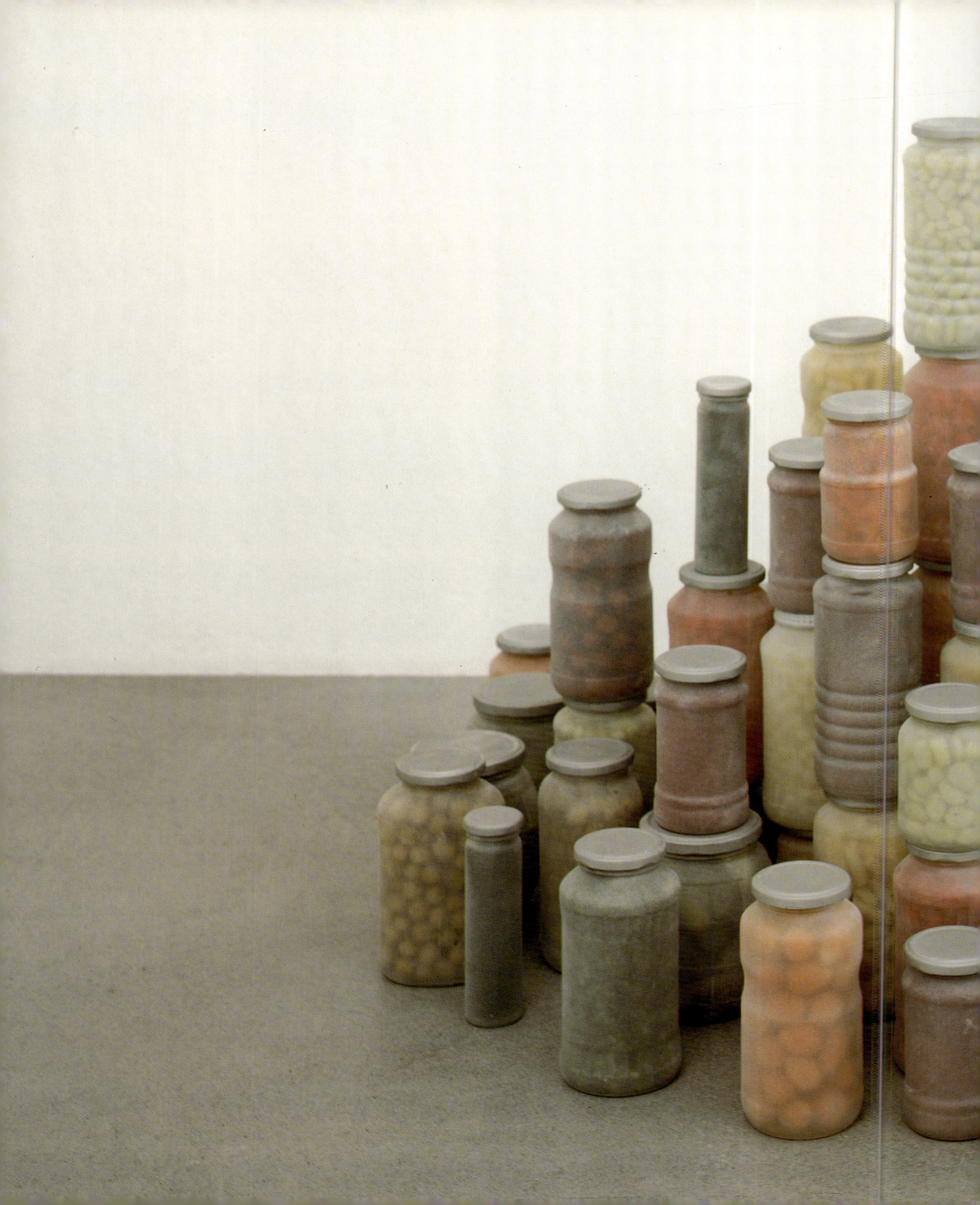

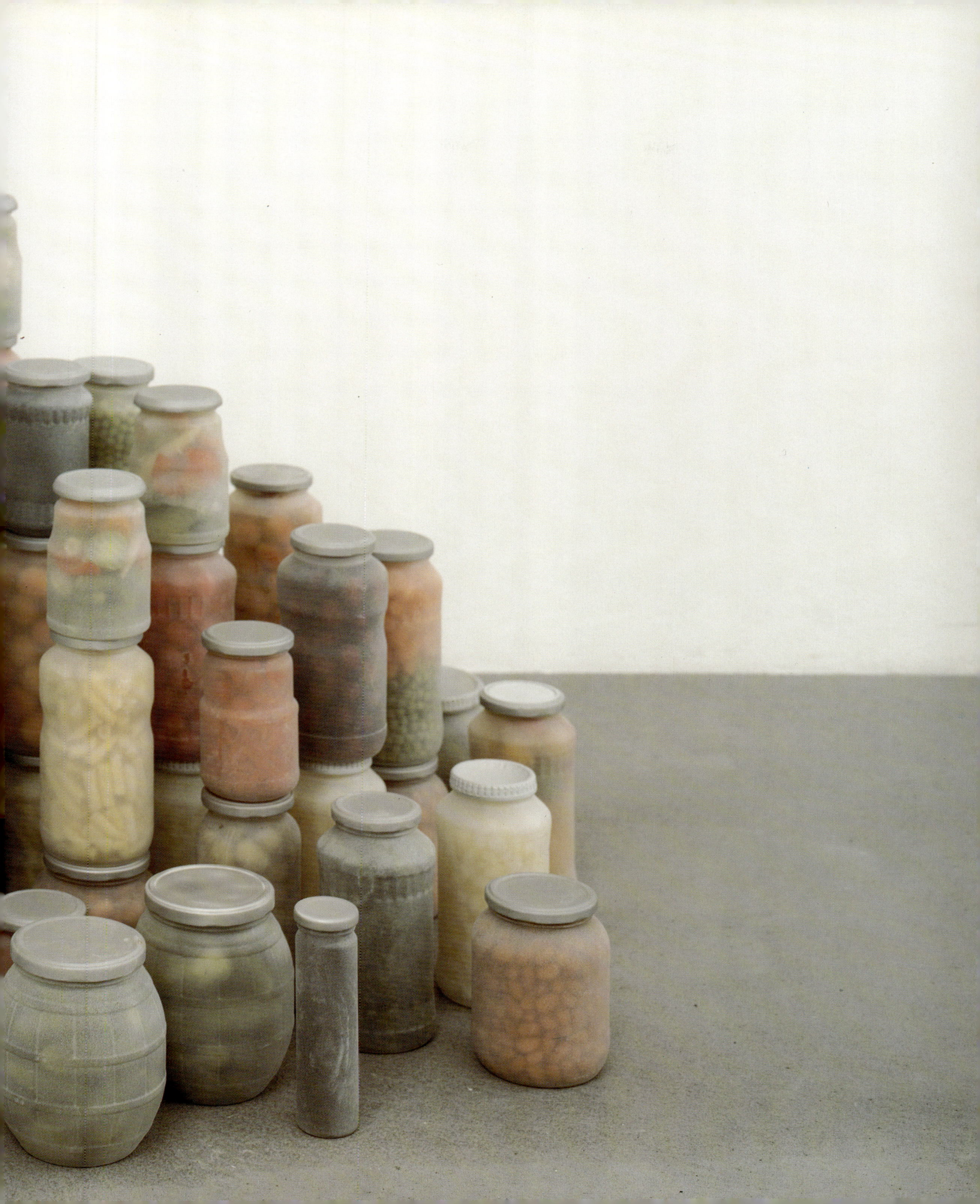

115. *Vessel*, 1991

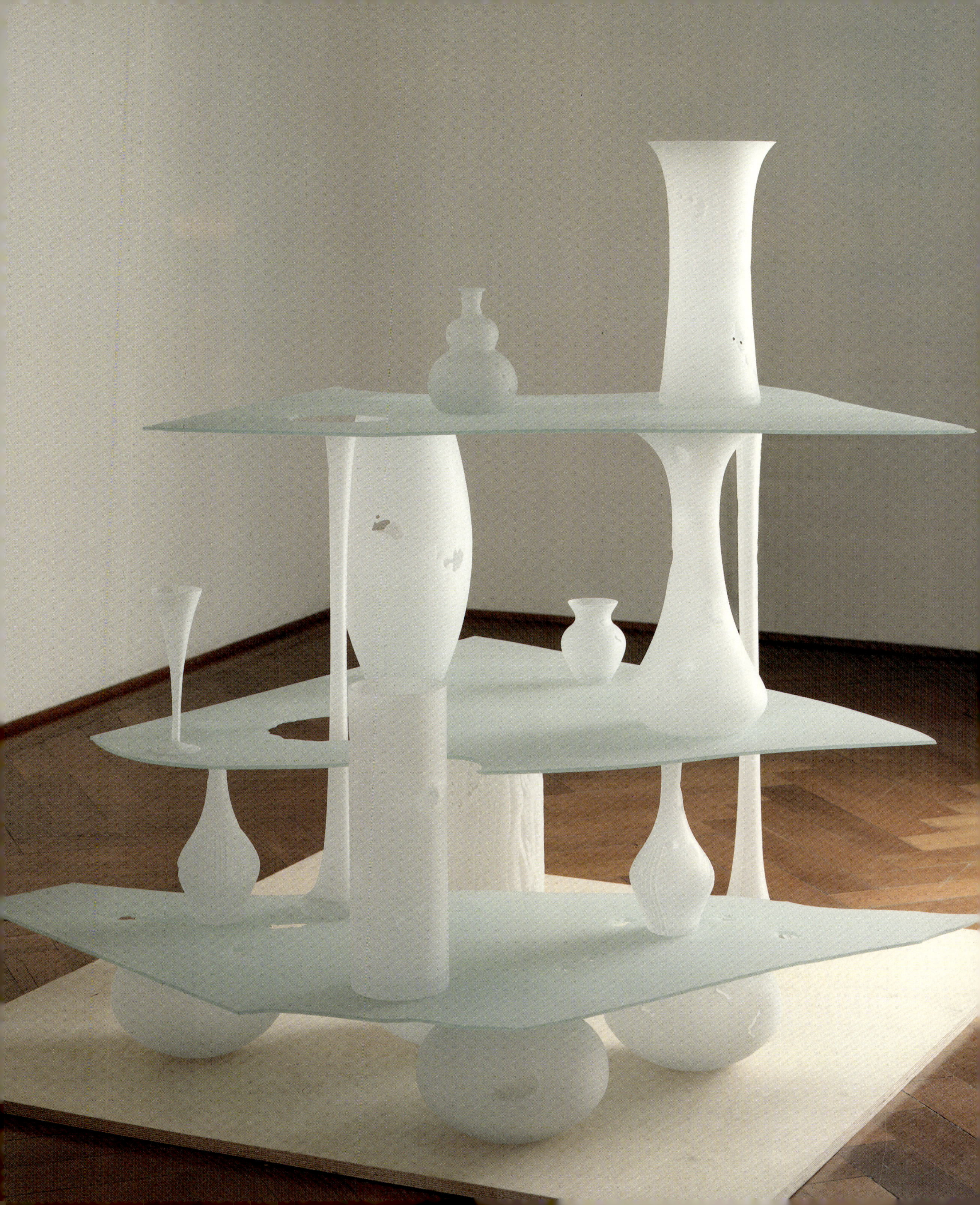

116. *Mineral Vein*, 1990

117. *Leguan*, 199[illegible]

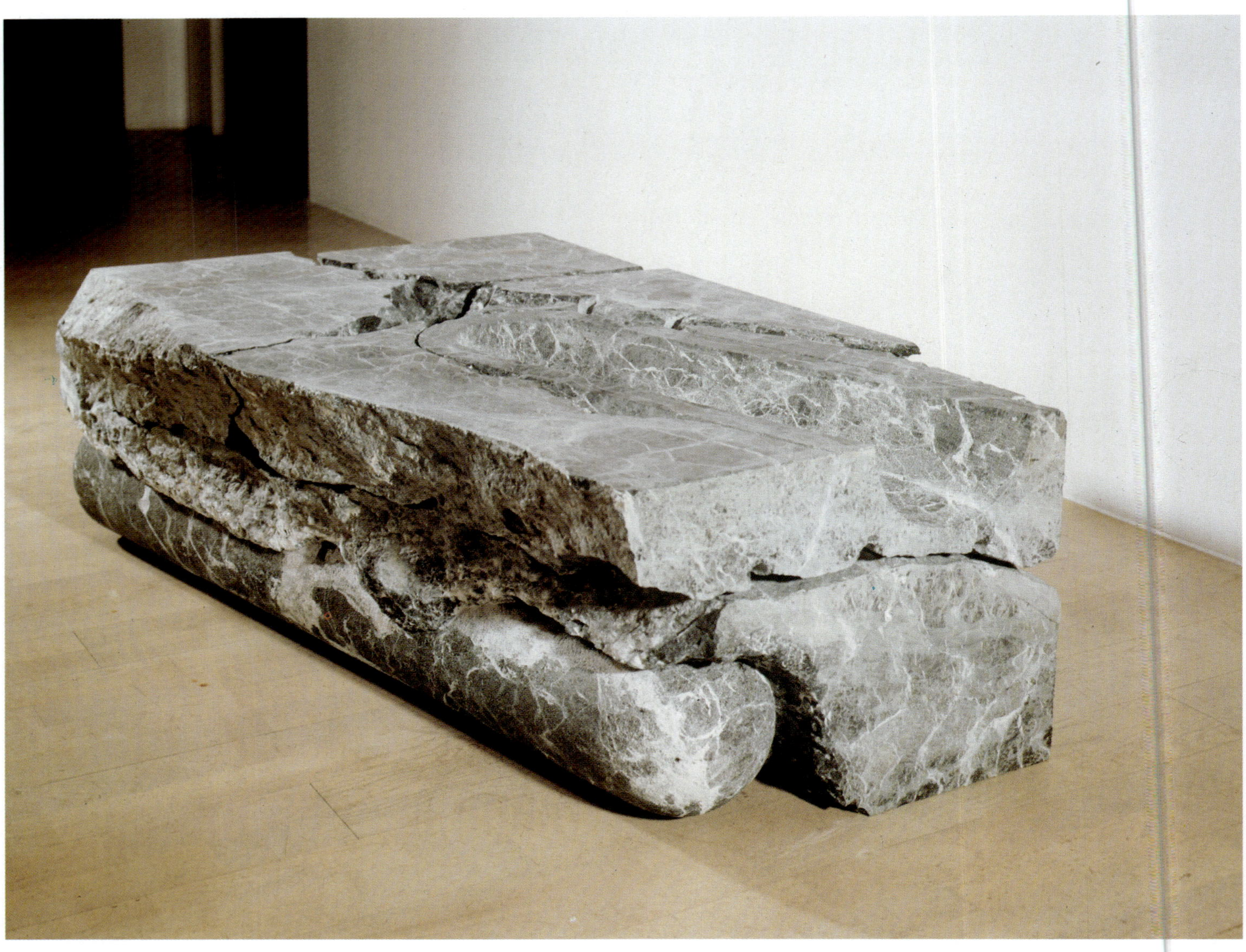

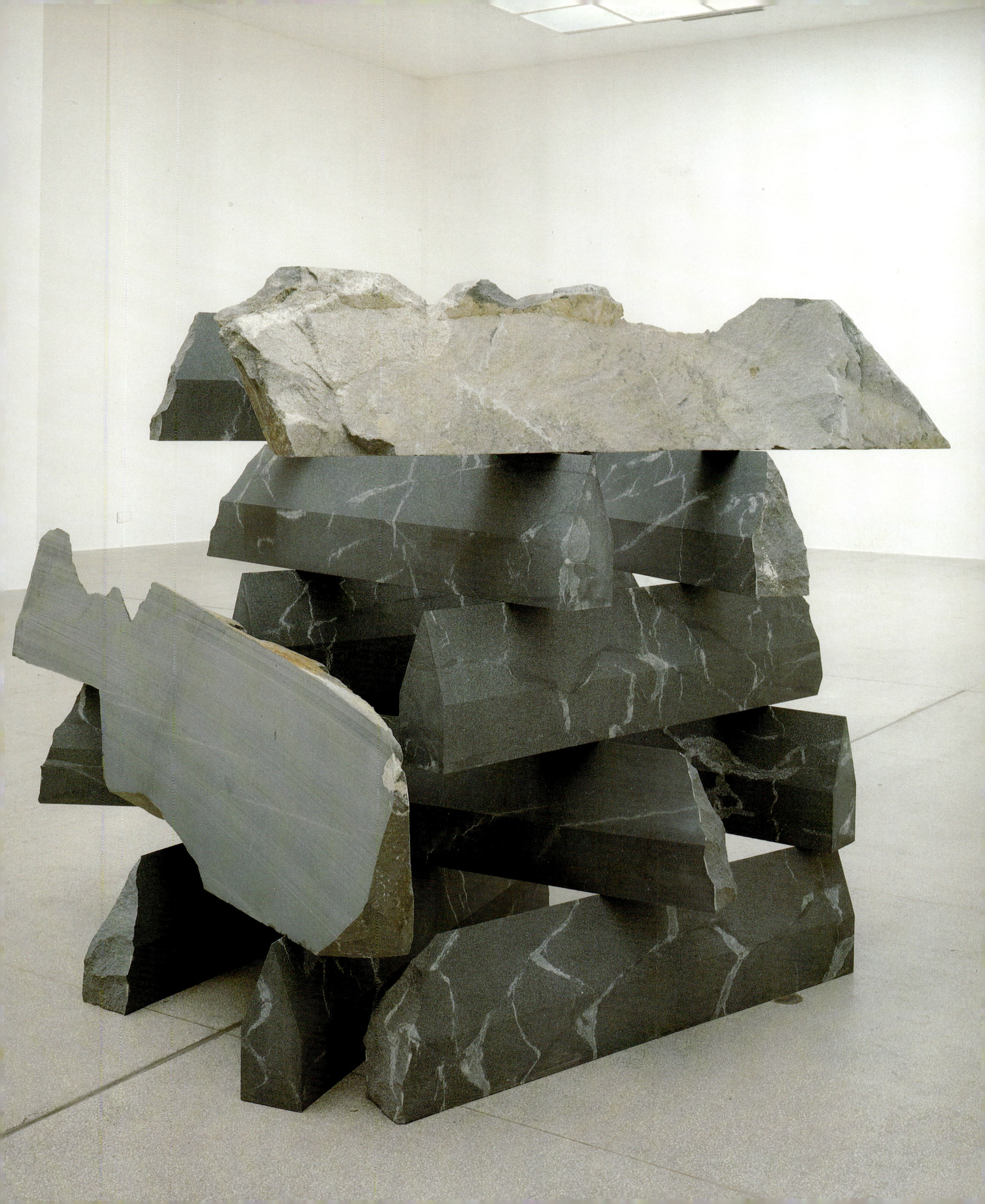

118. *Plant*, 1990

119. *Eichelhäher*, 1990

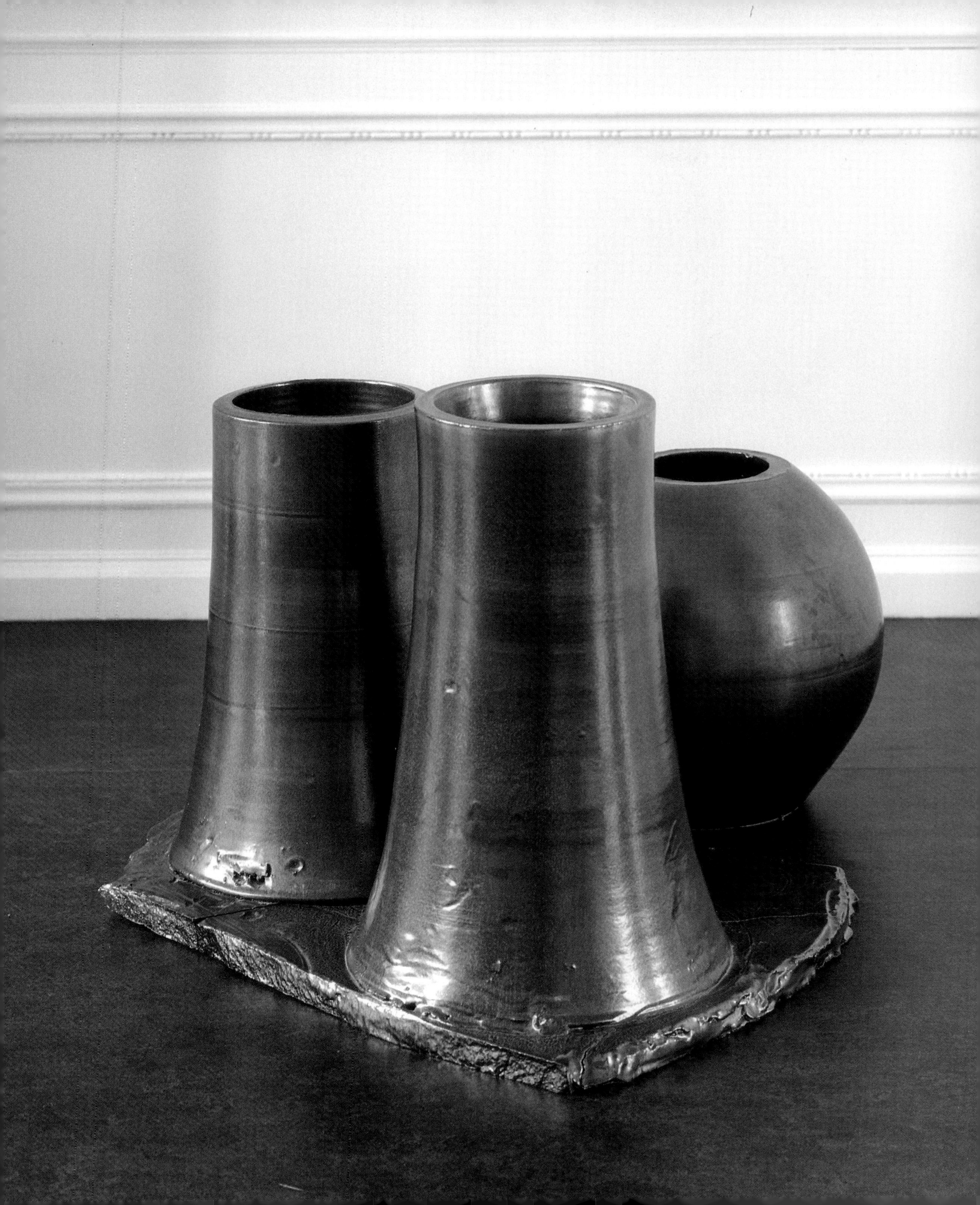

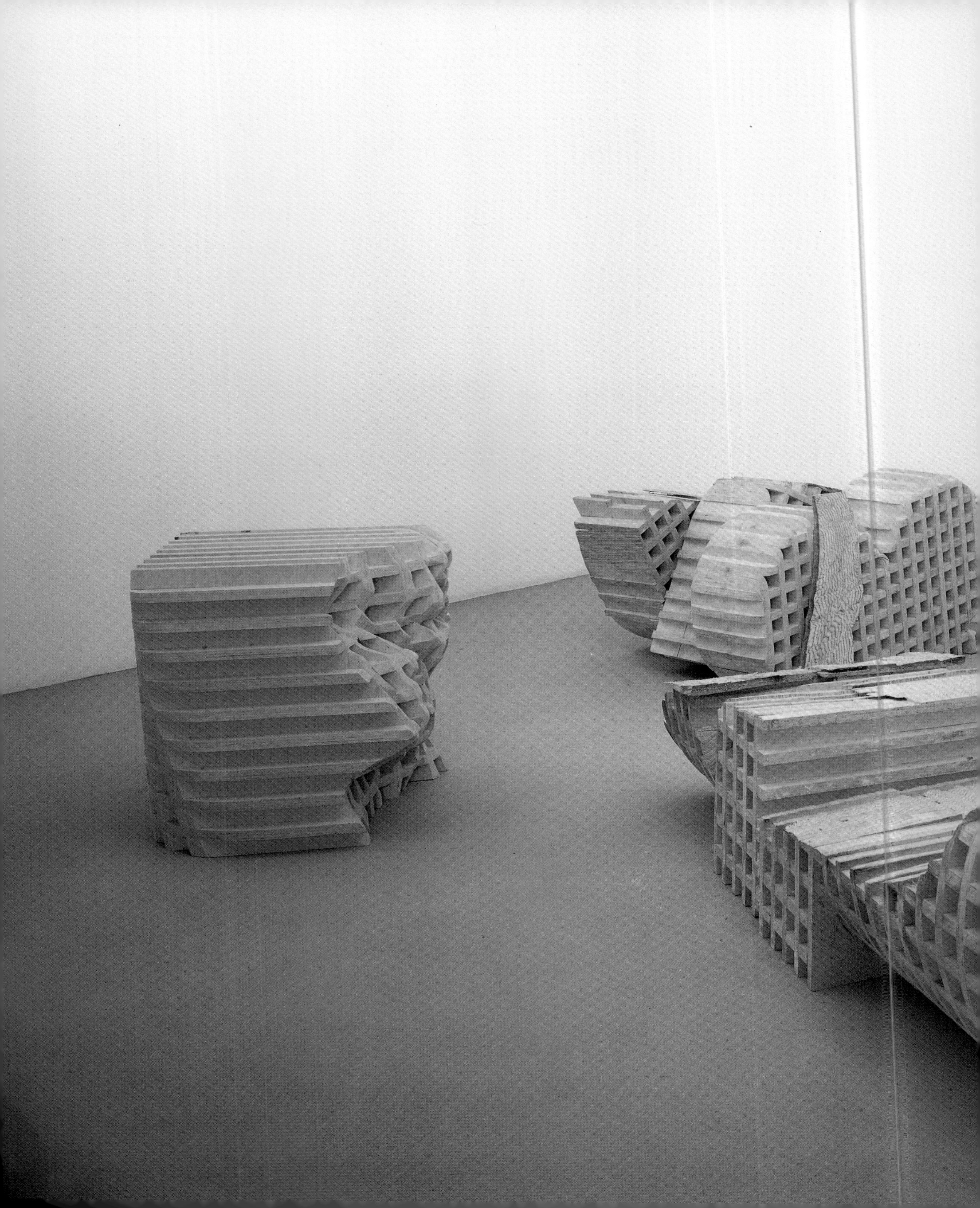

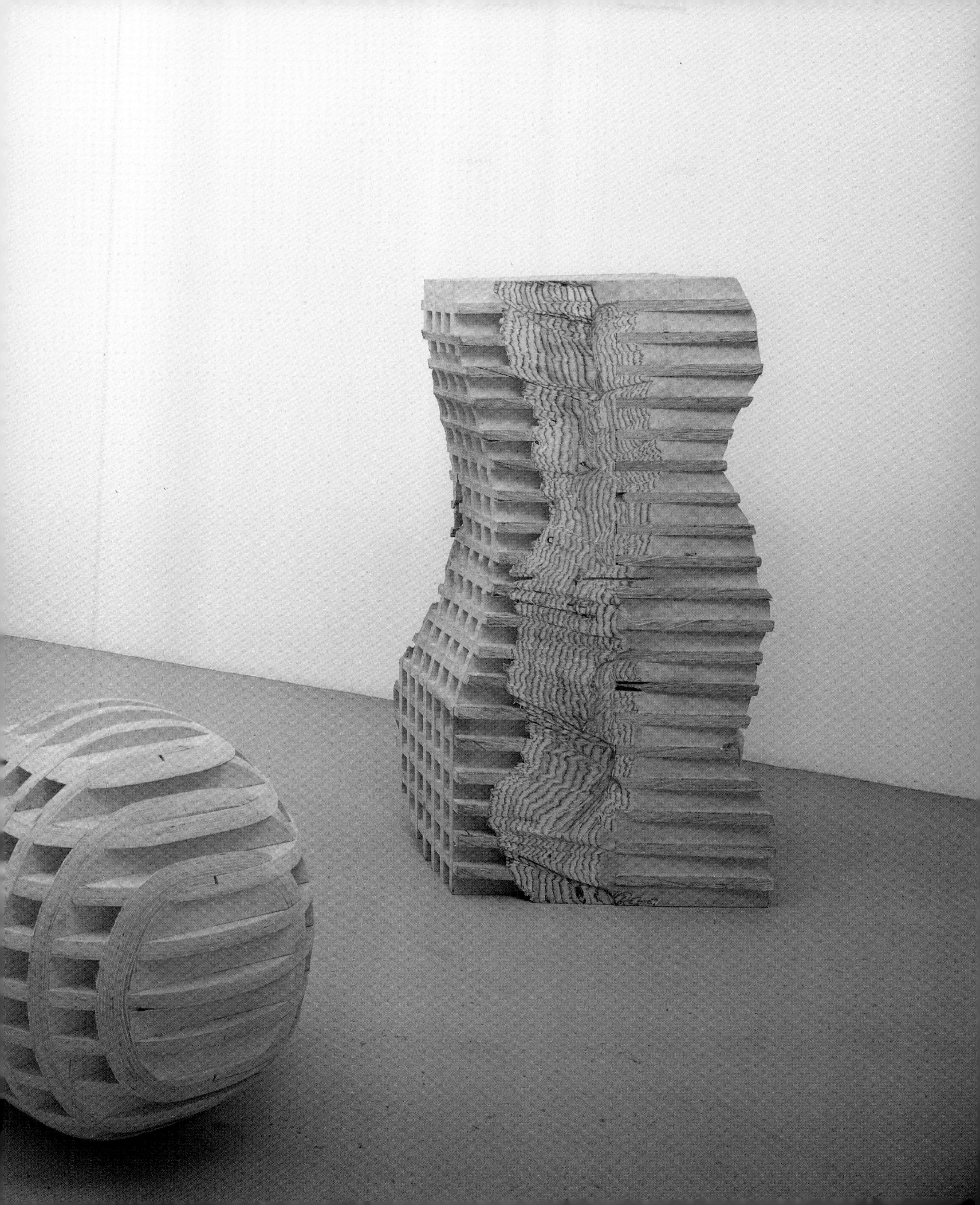

120. *Atmos*, 1990

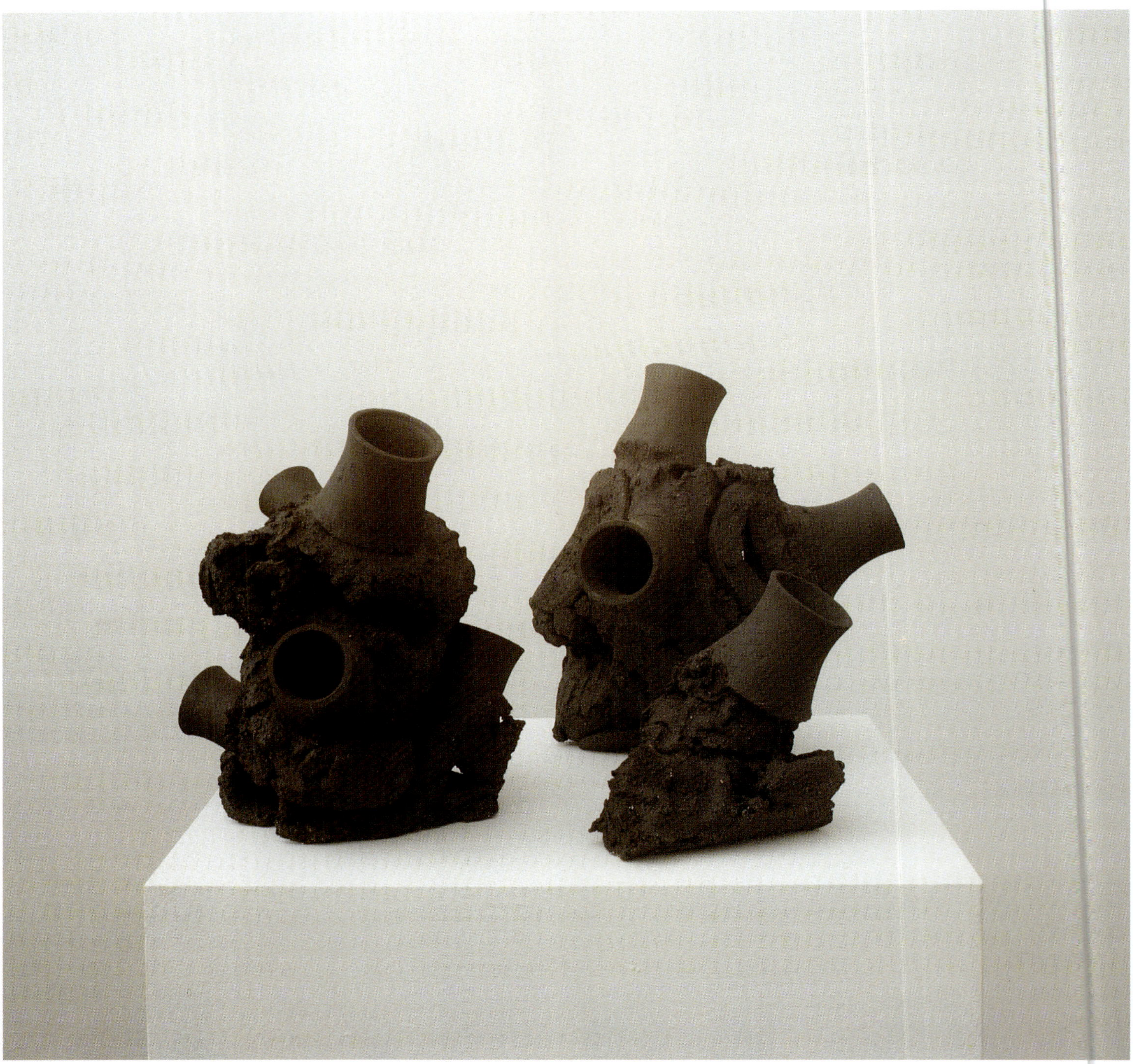

121. *Two Tigers*, 1990

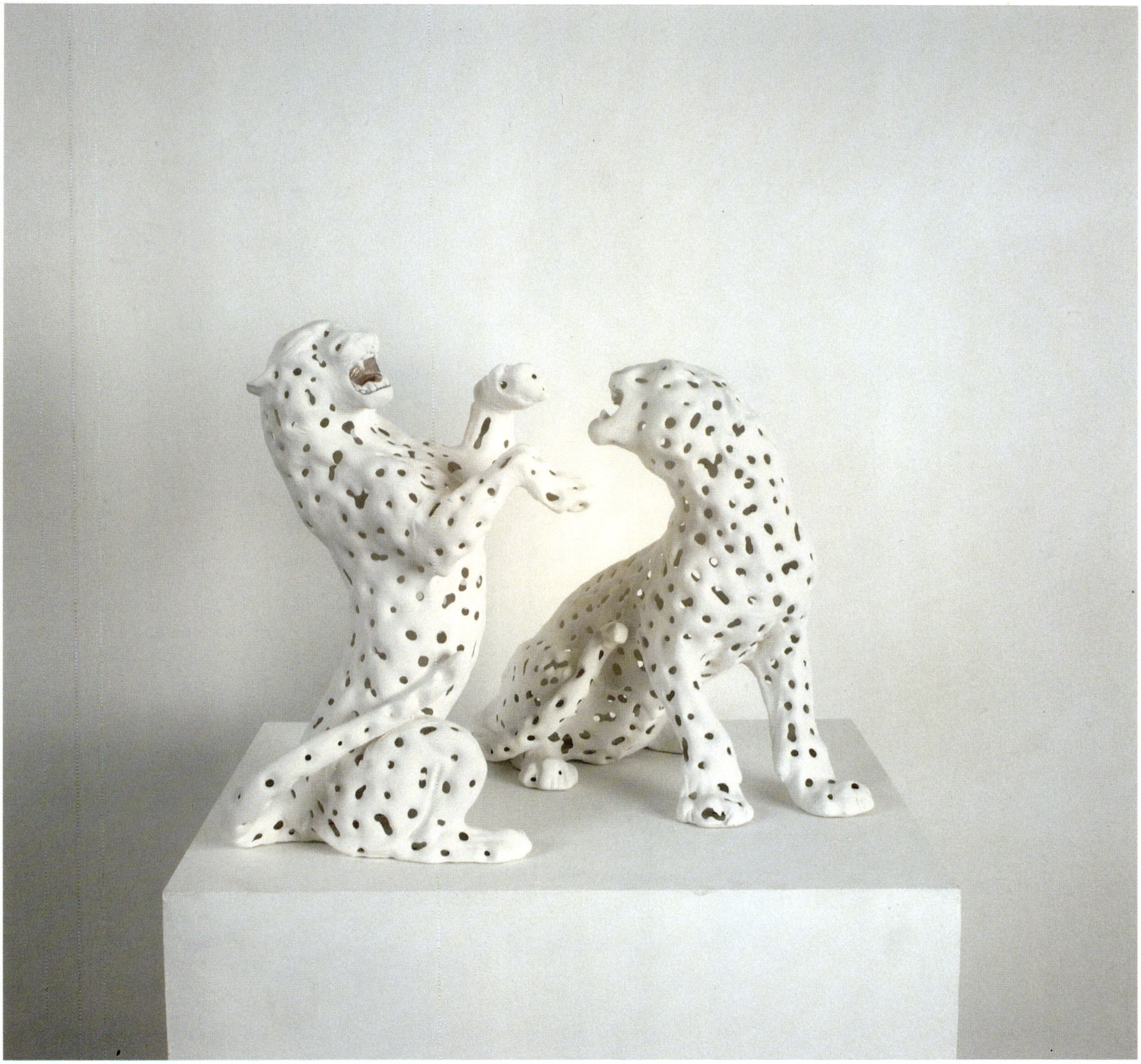

122. *Mixed Cylinders*, 1990

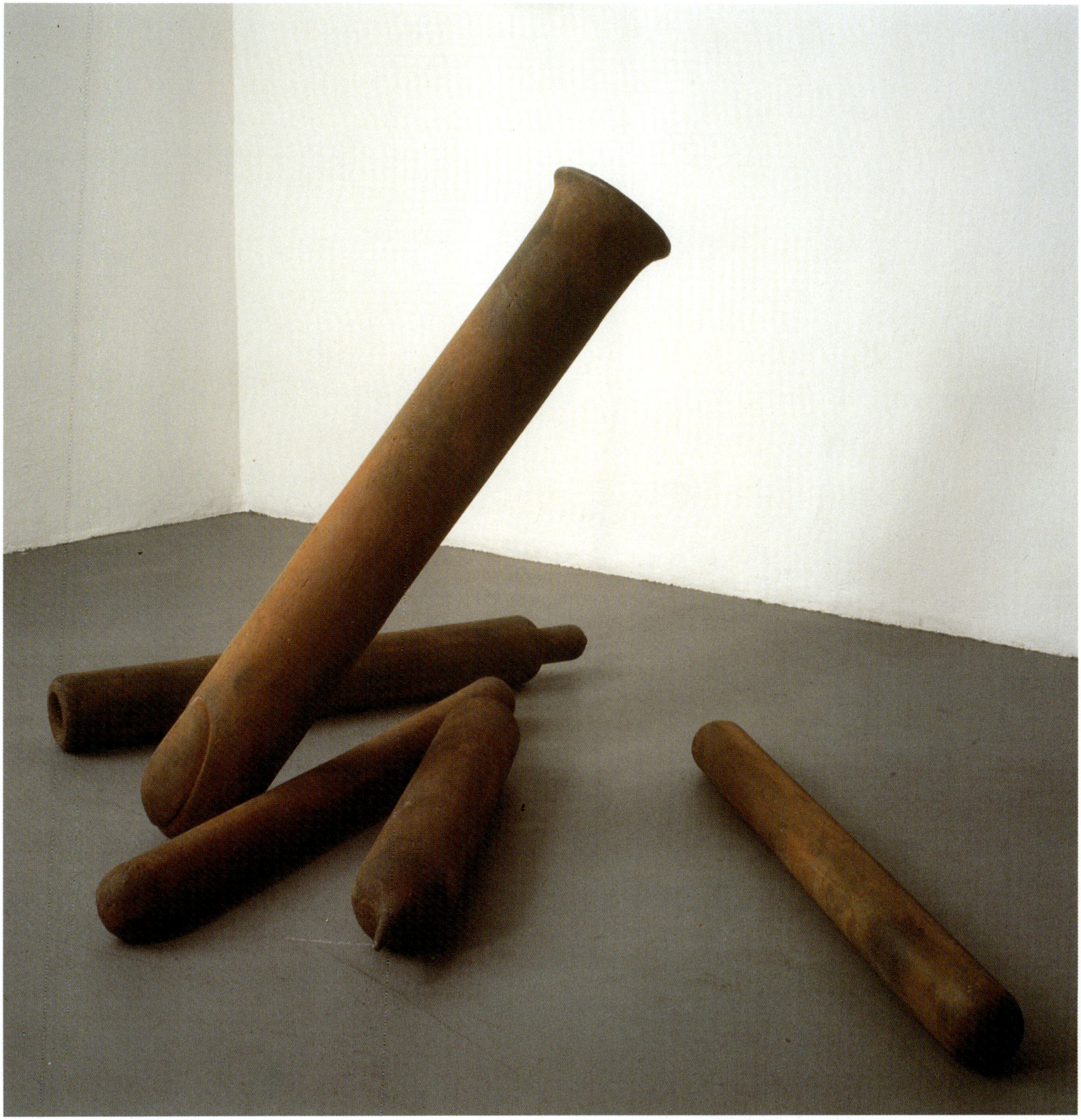

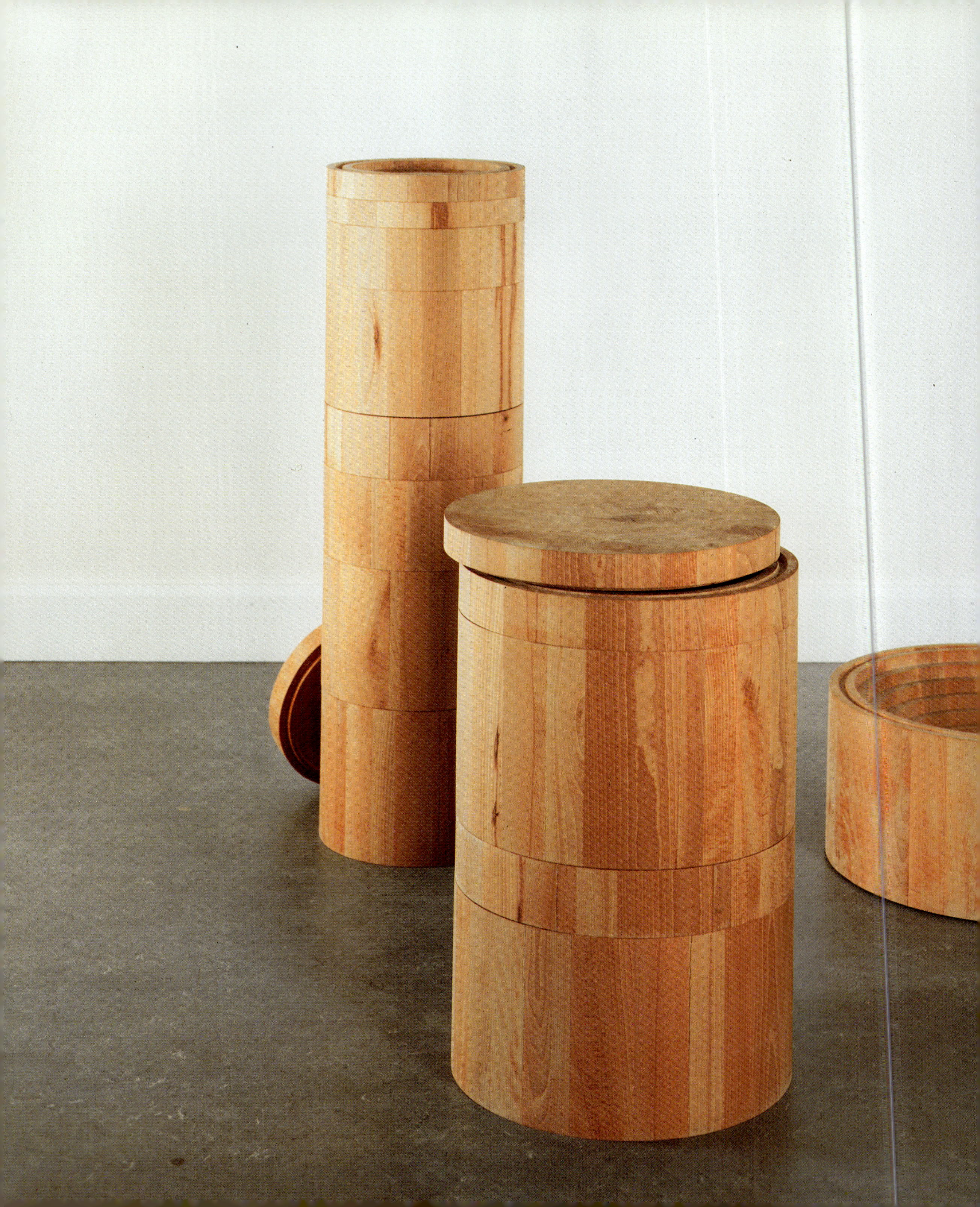

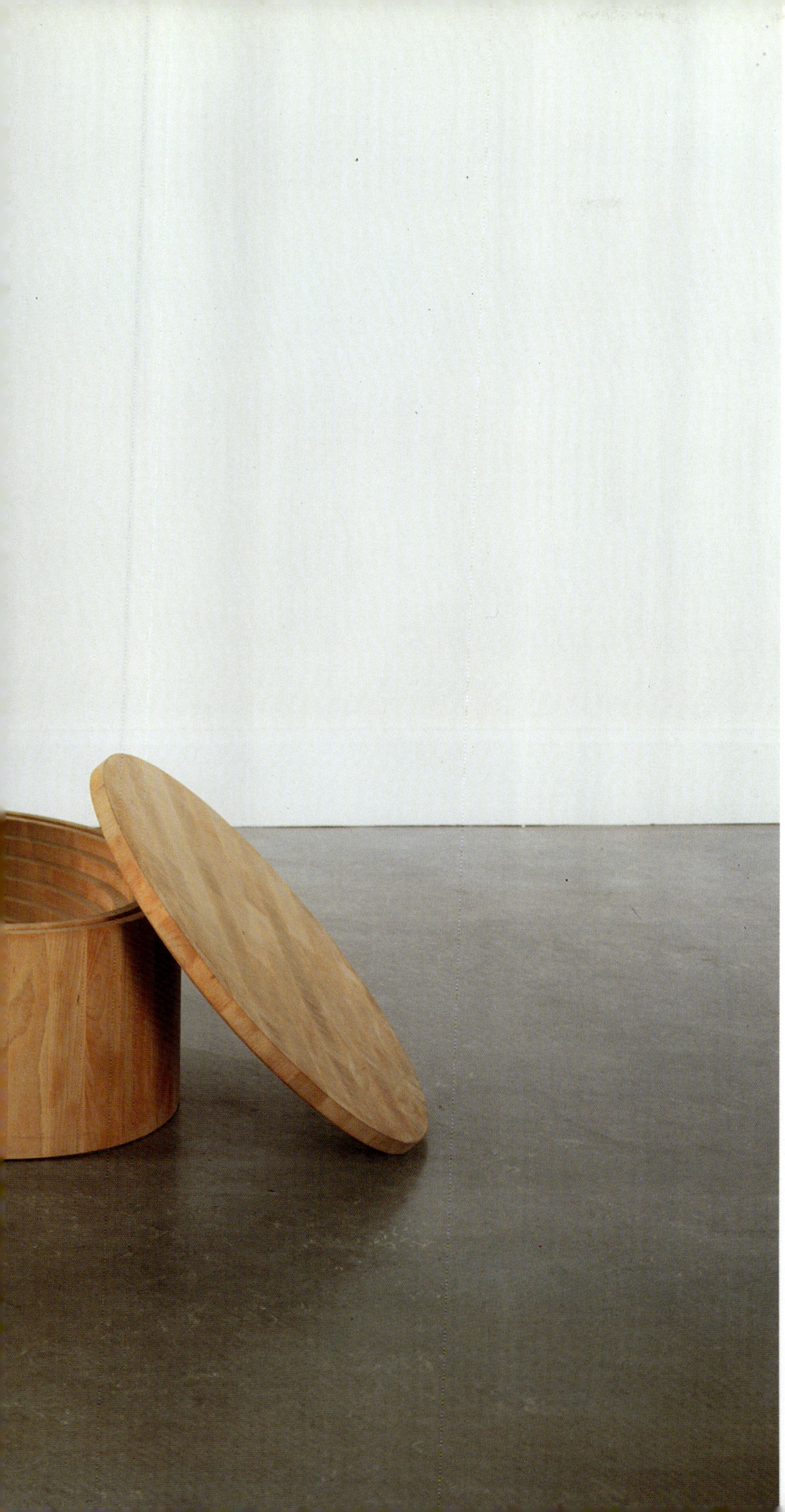

123. *Stock*, 1988

124. *Incubation*, 1990

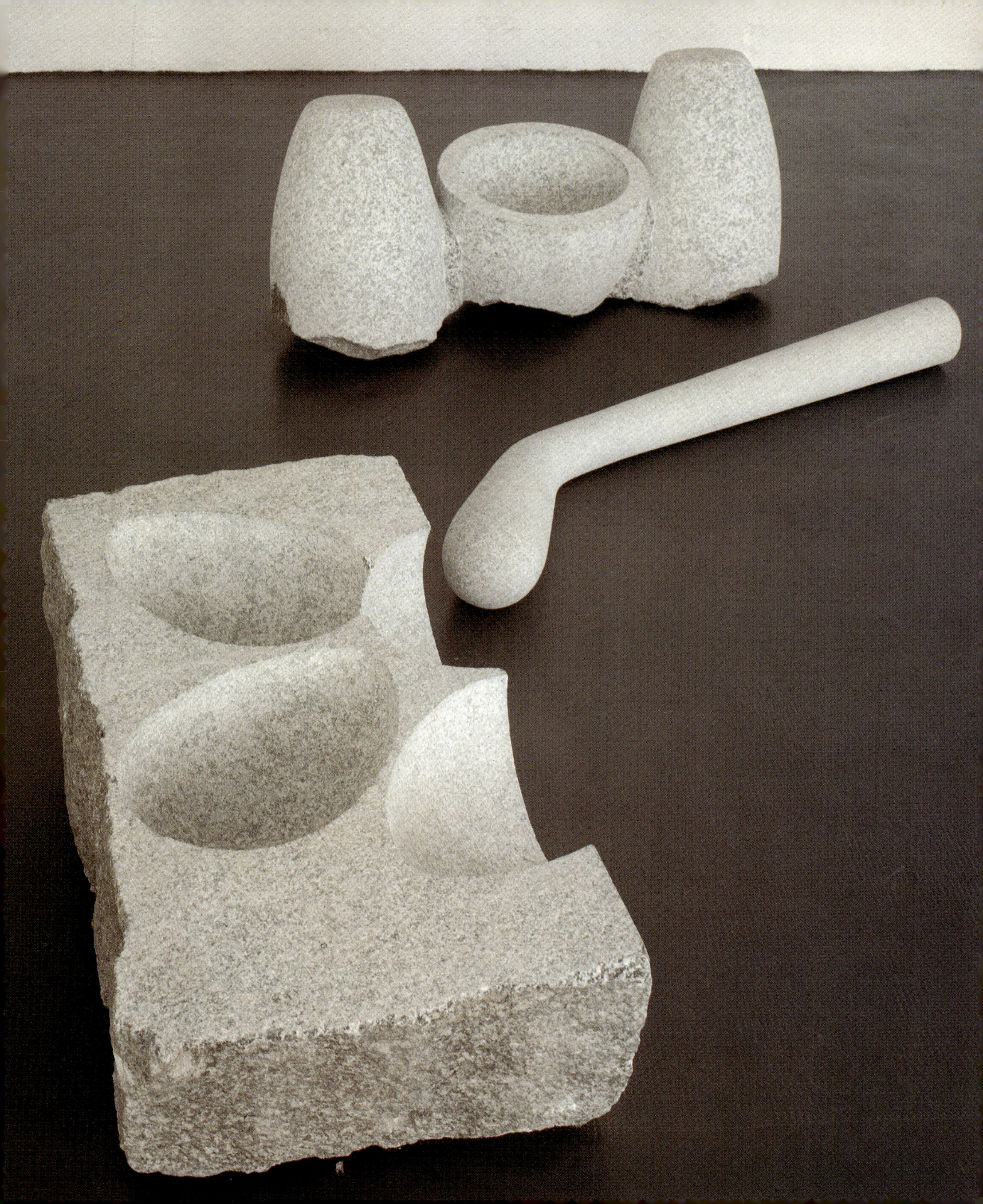

125. *Atmos*, 1990

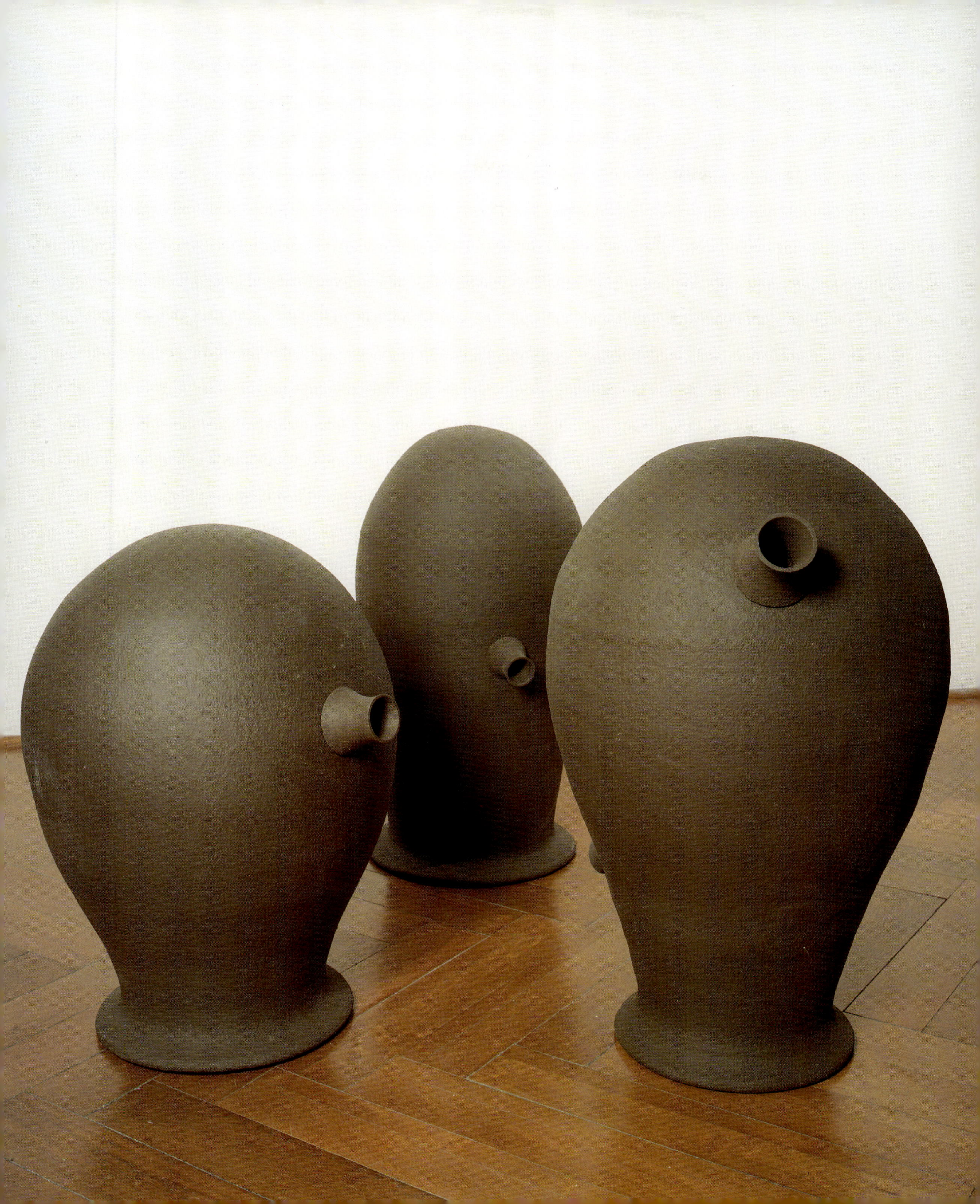

126. *Manipulations*, 1991

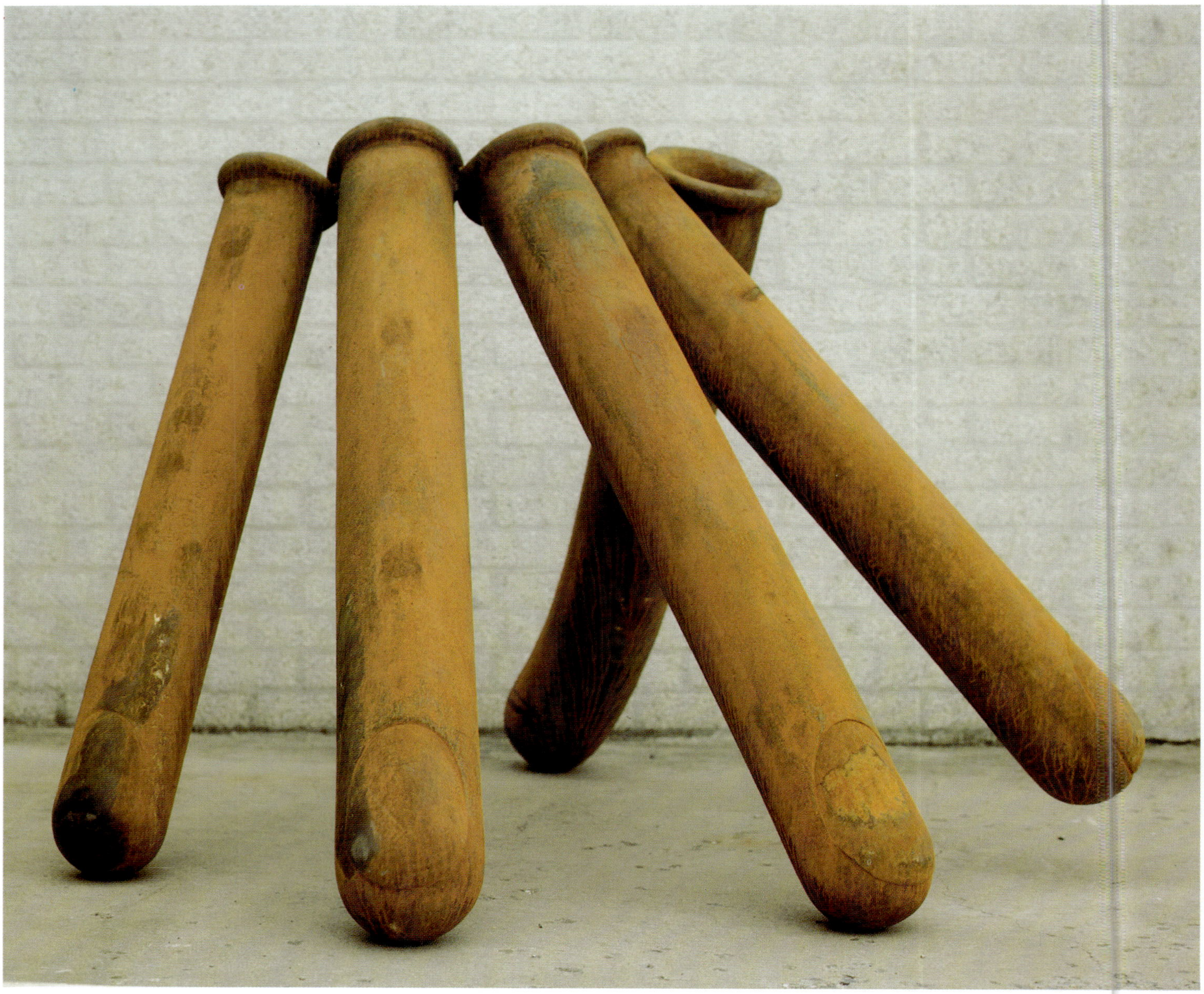

127. *Atmos*, 1991

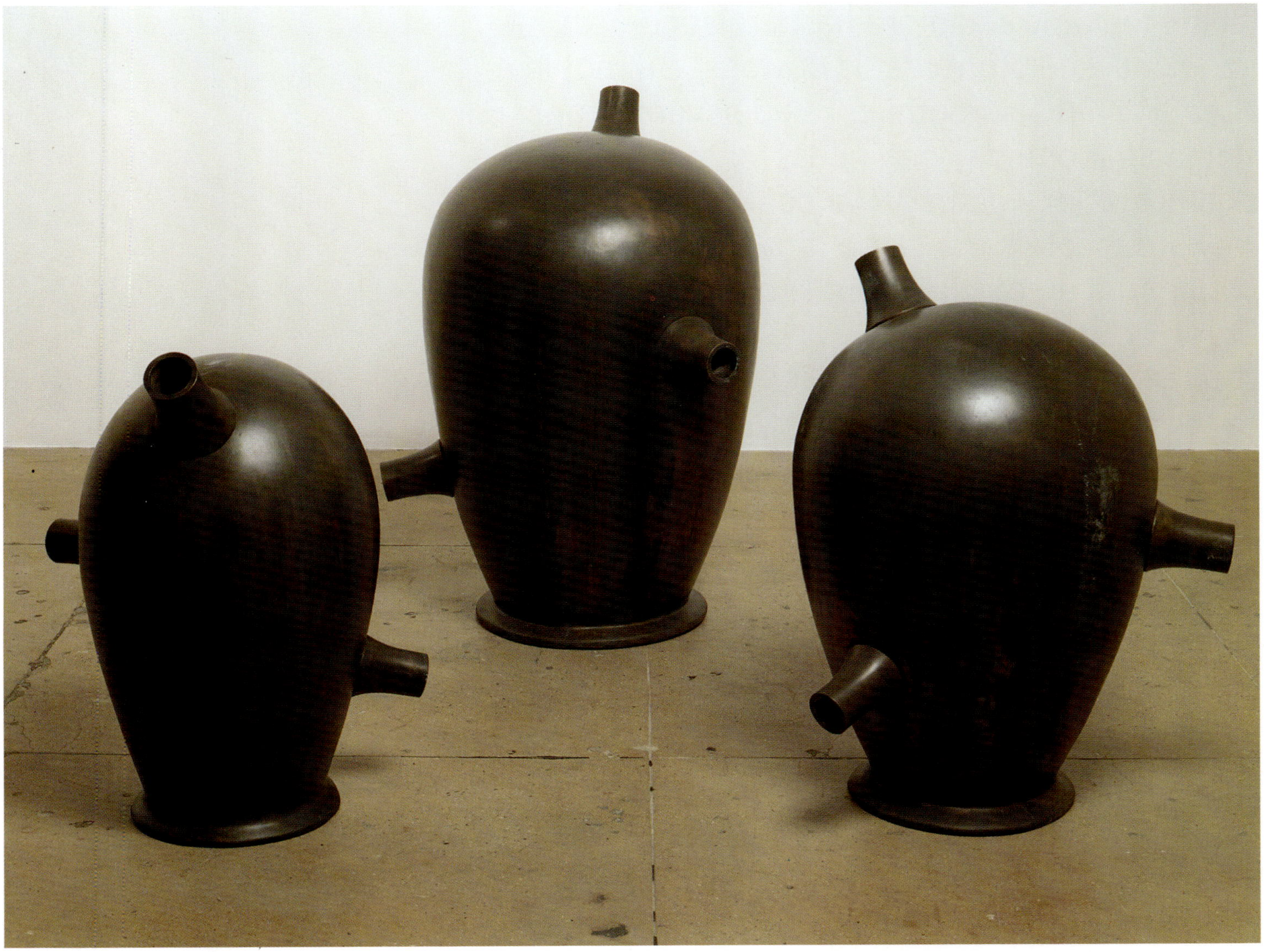

128. *Eroded Landscape*, 1991

I think that any sculpture has a relation with traditional sculpture that is obvious. But not in a direct way. It's something I said several times. For instance, if one day one finds, for example, a plastic bottle ... actually we could say it the other way around; it is the same if one finds a piece of pottery or ceramic, without knowing it is Roman, Greek or Etruscan. It has a special kind of *aura* about it; it has a special quality which is exciting, which generates myths, history and poetry ... but of course those things at the time may have just been for carrying oil, or something very banal, and when it was empty they threw it out. We then find it 3000 years later and of course we have a different feeling about it. Like the plastic vessels or the plastic bottles that we take and empty and throw out. Today we have the same sort of banal relationship with plastic containers. With glass, similarly, it's inevitable, the whole process of evolution of time, the landscape changing, all problems that sculpture is concerned with ... I think, finally, that traditional sculpture of any people starts from the point of the material. And so that remains a constant through all the making of sculpture.

Ludovico Pratesi, "A Conversation with Tony Cragg." In *Tony Cragg*, exh. catalogue. Rome: Valentina Moncada, 1990, pp. 6, 8.

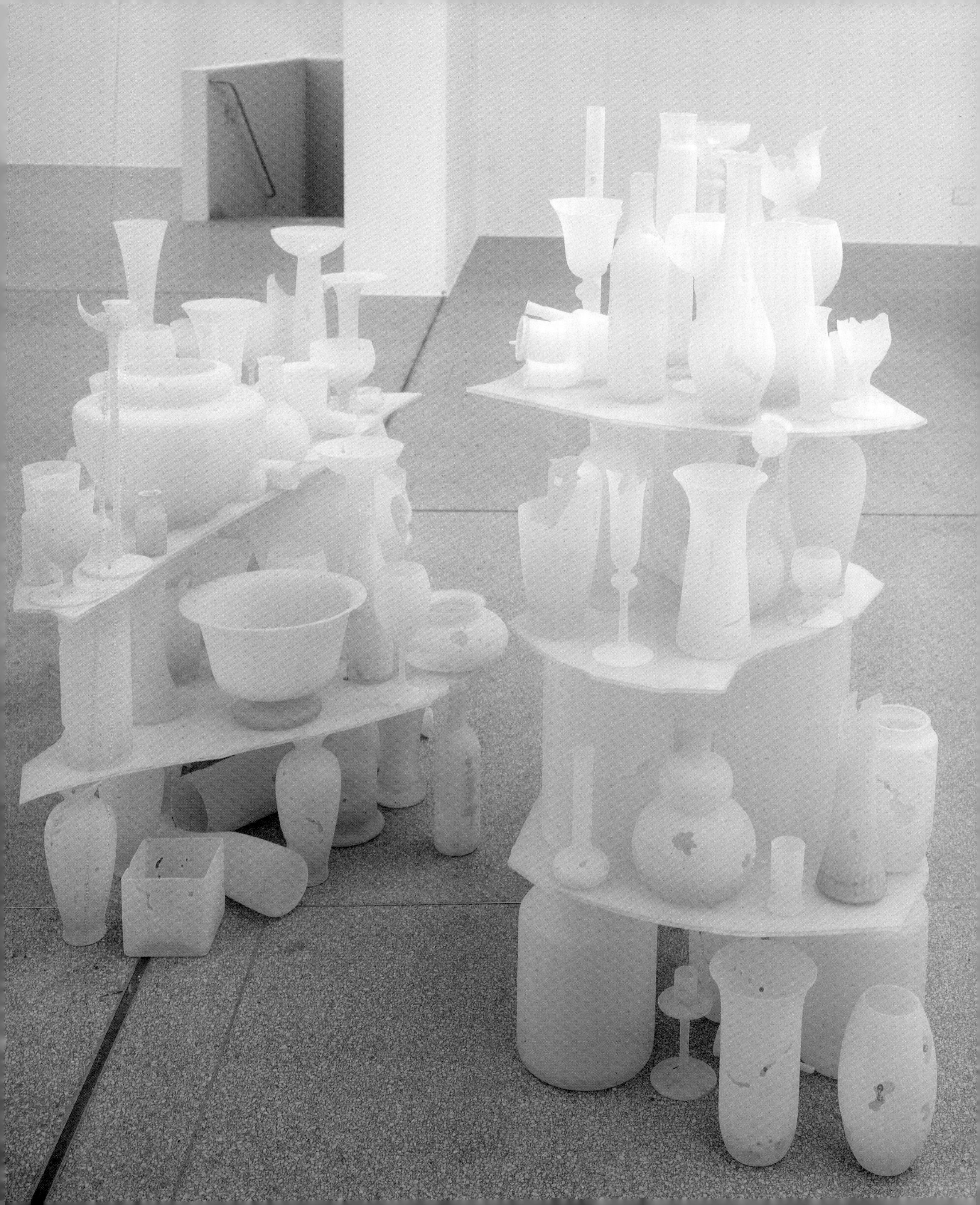

129. *Subcommittee*, 1991

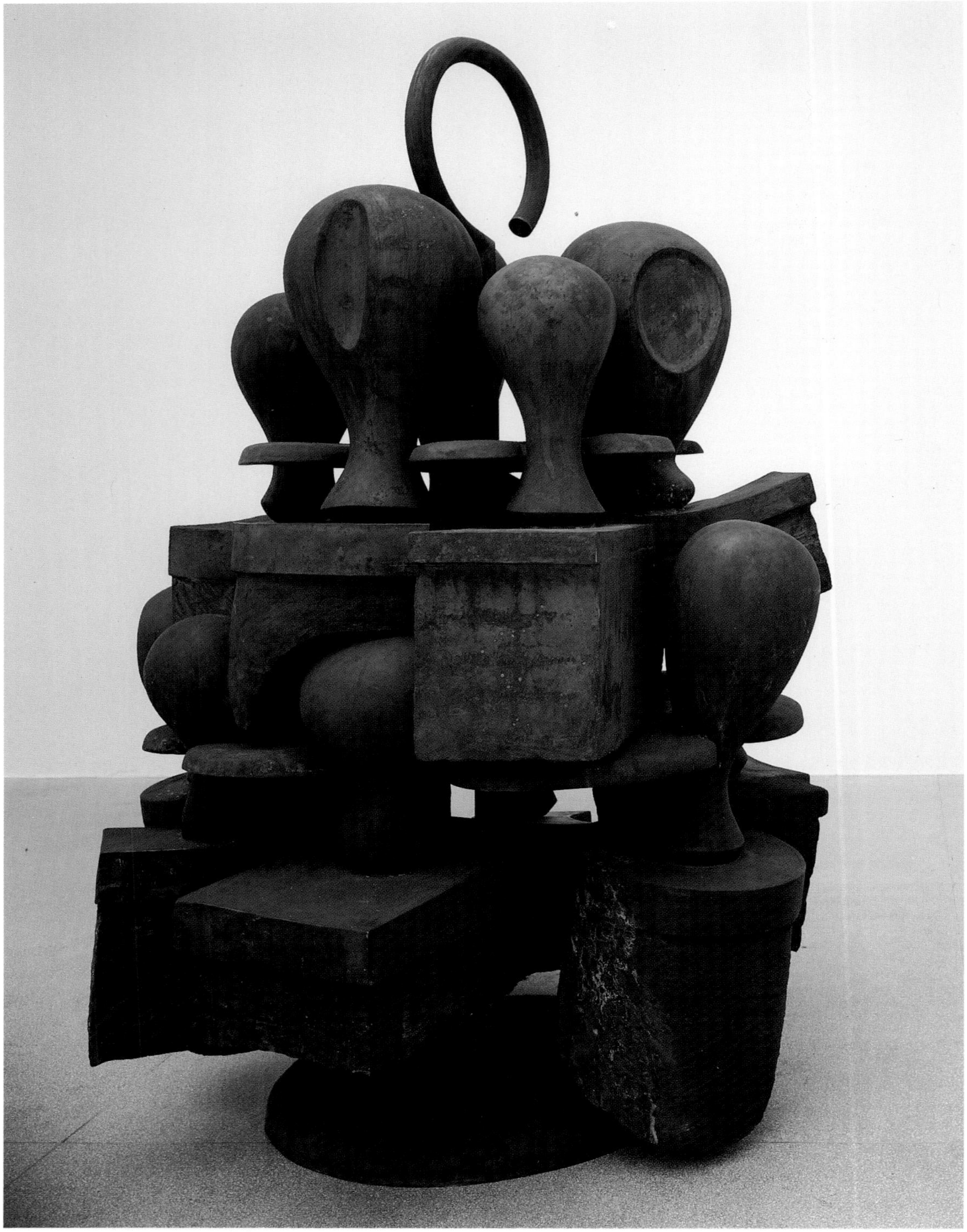

130. *Subcommittee*, 1991

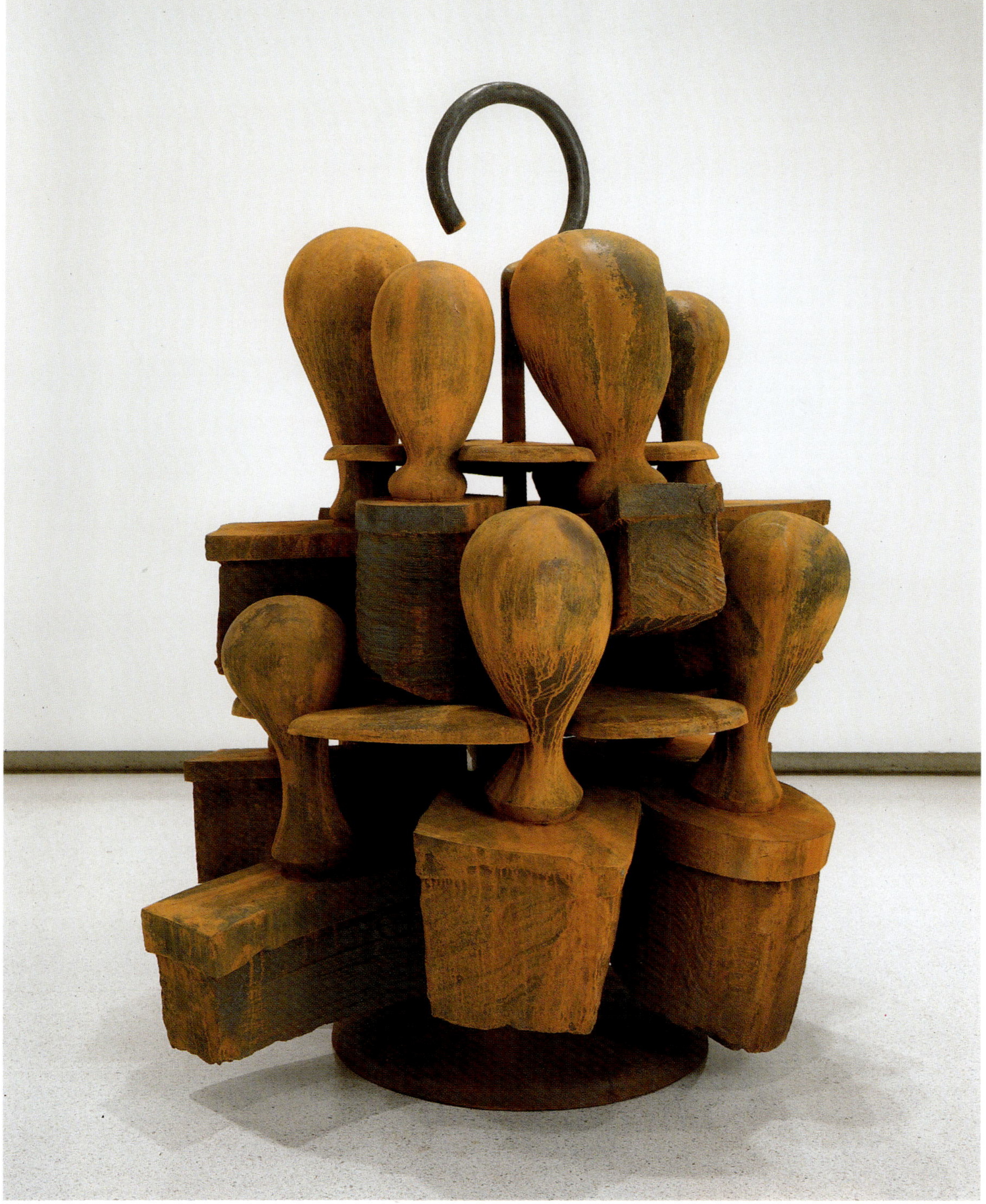

131. *Clearing*, 1991

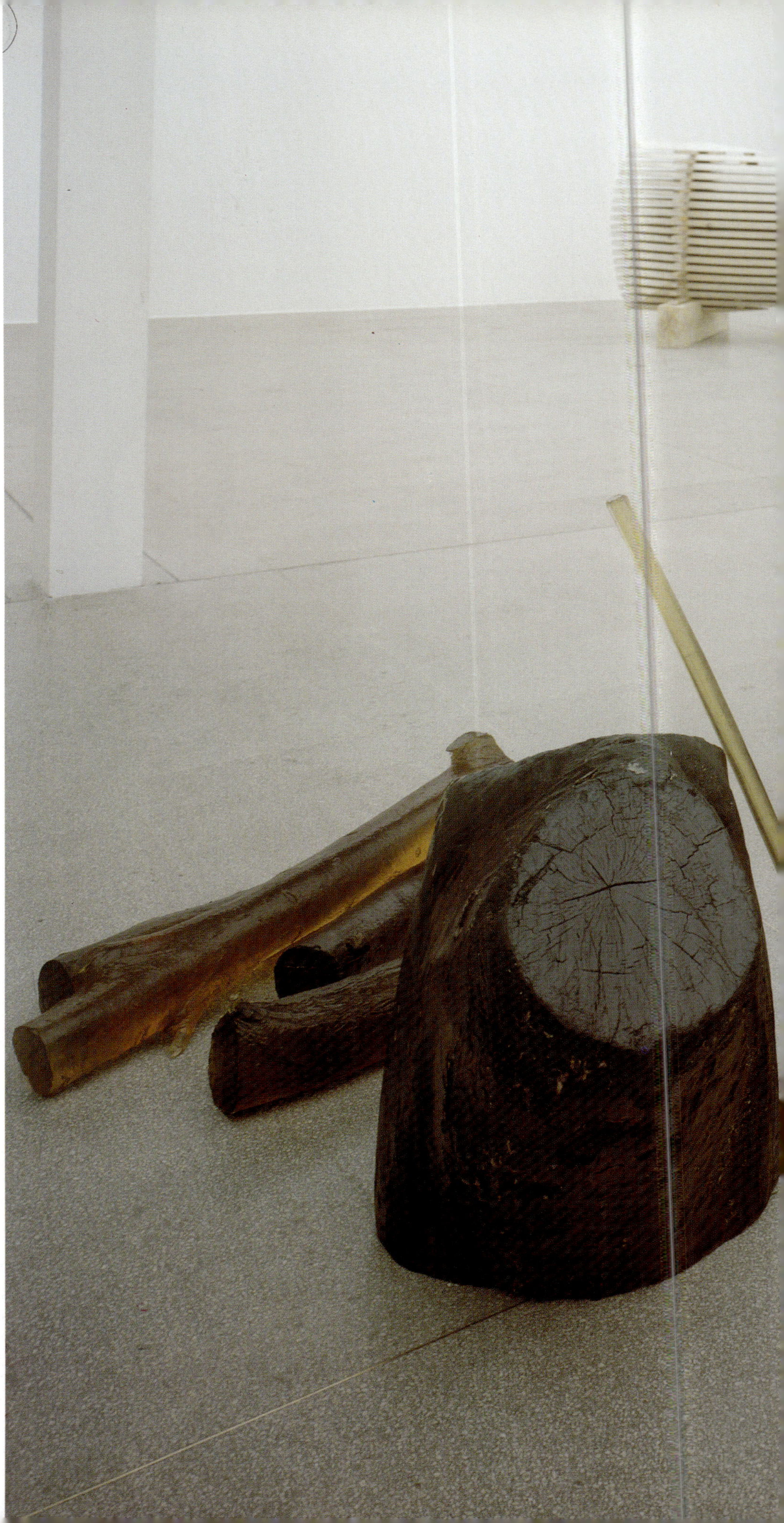

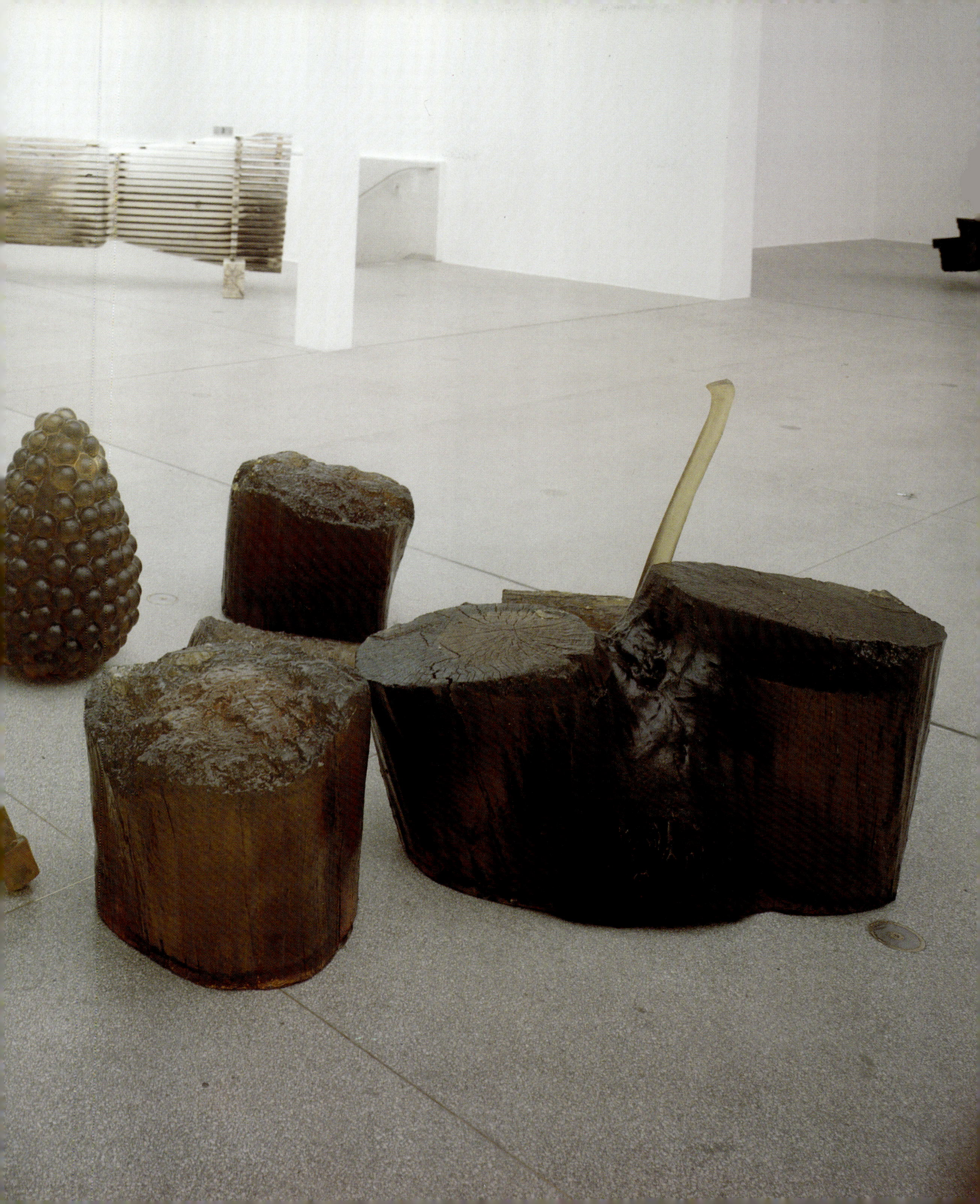

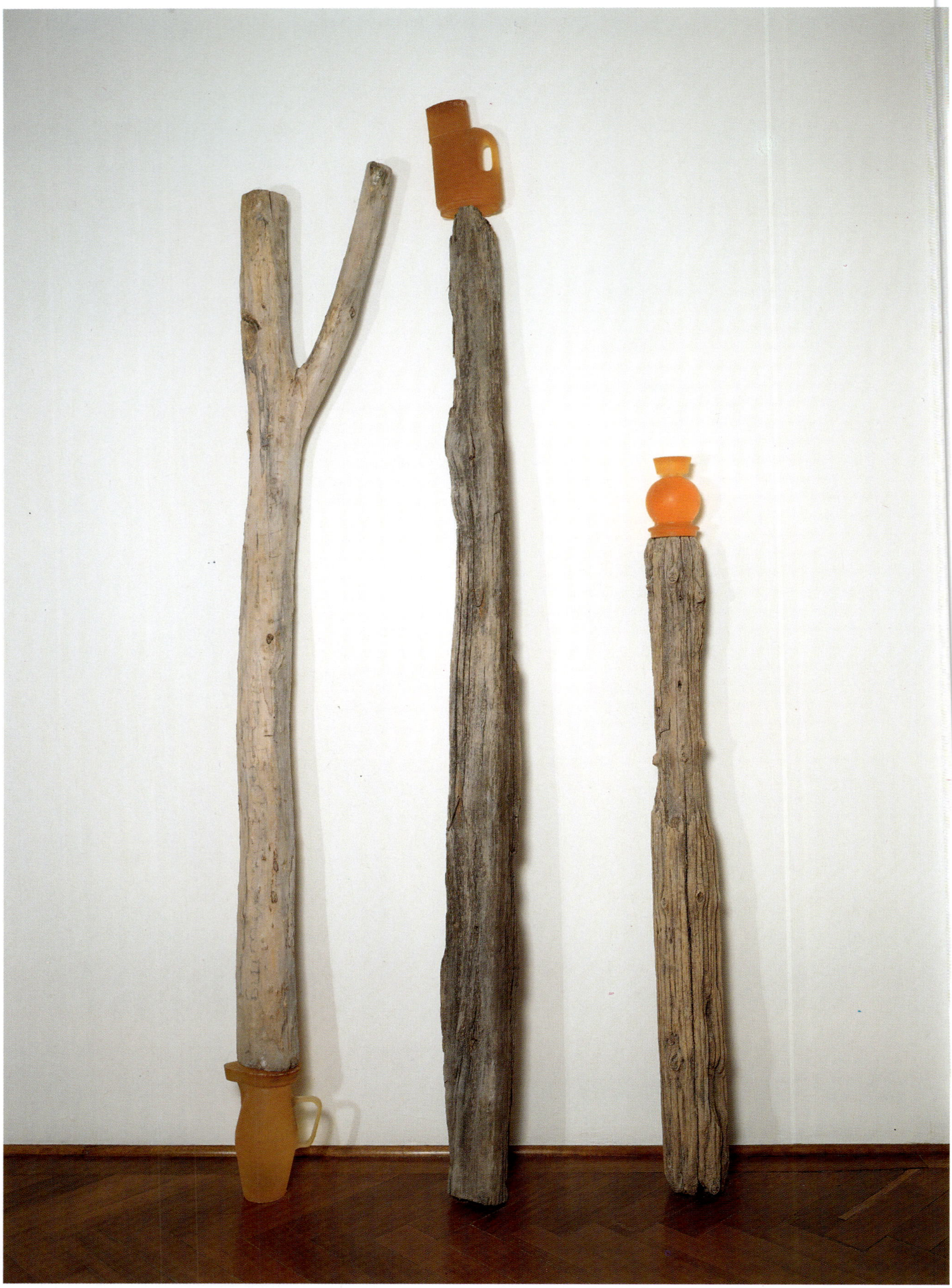

132. *Gold, Incense, Myrrh*, 1990

133. *Administered Landscape*, 1991

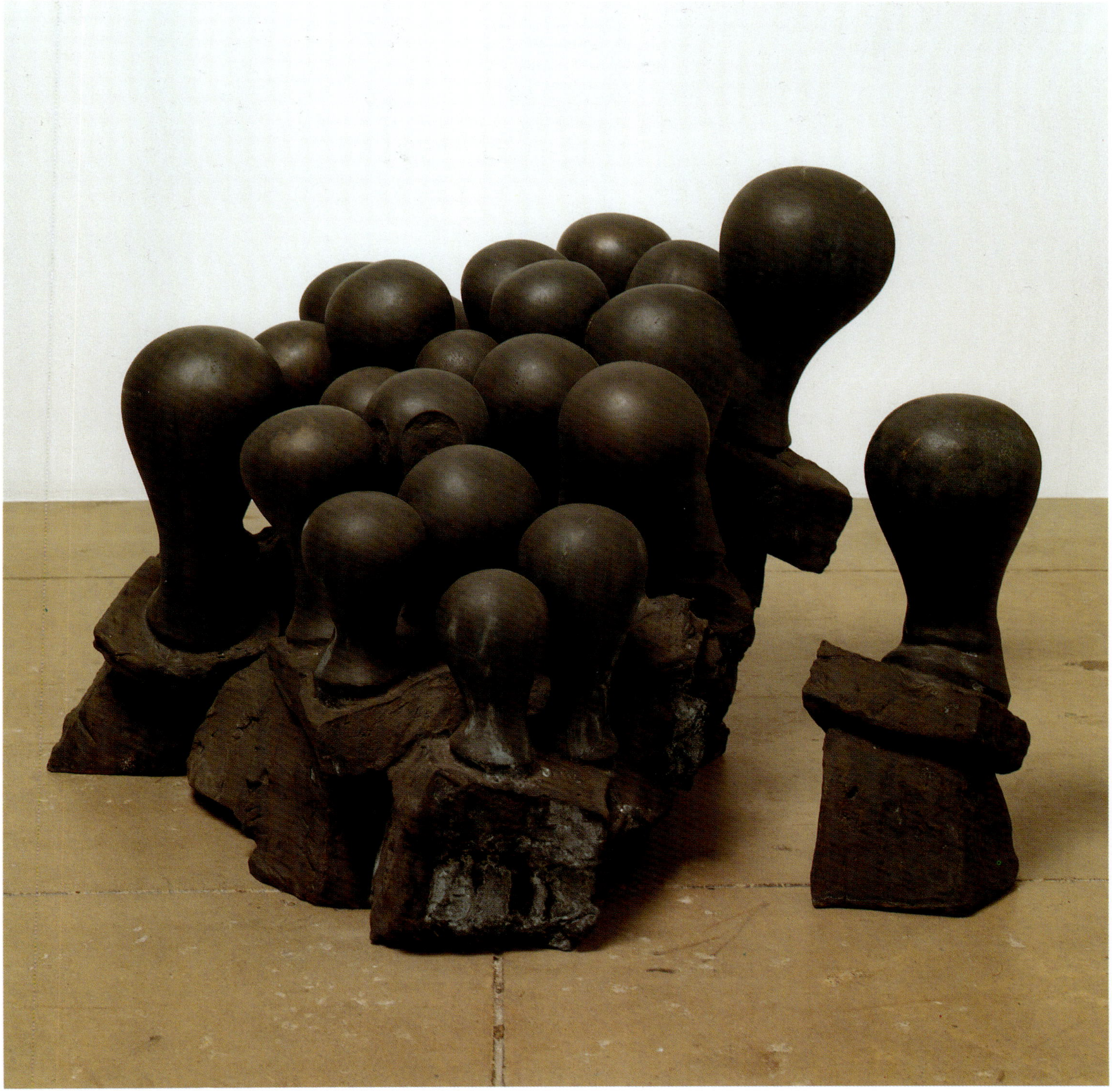

134. *Suburbs*, 1990

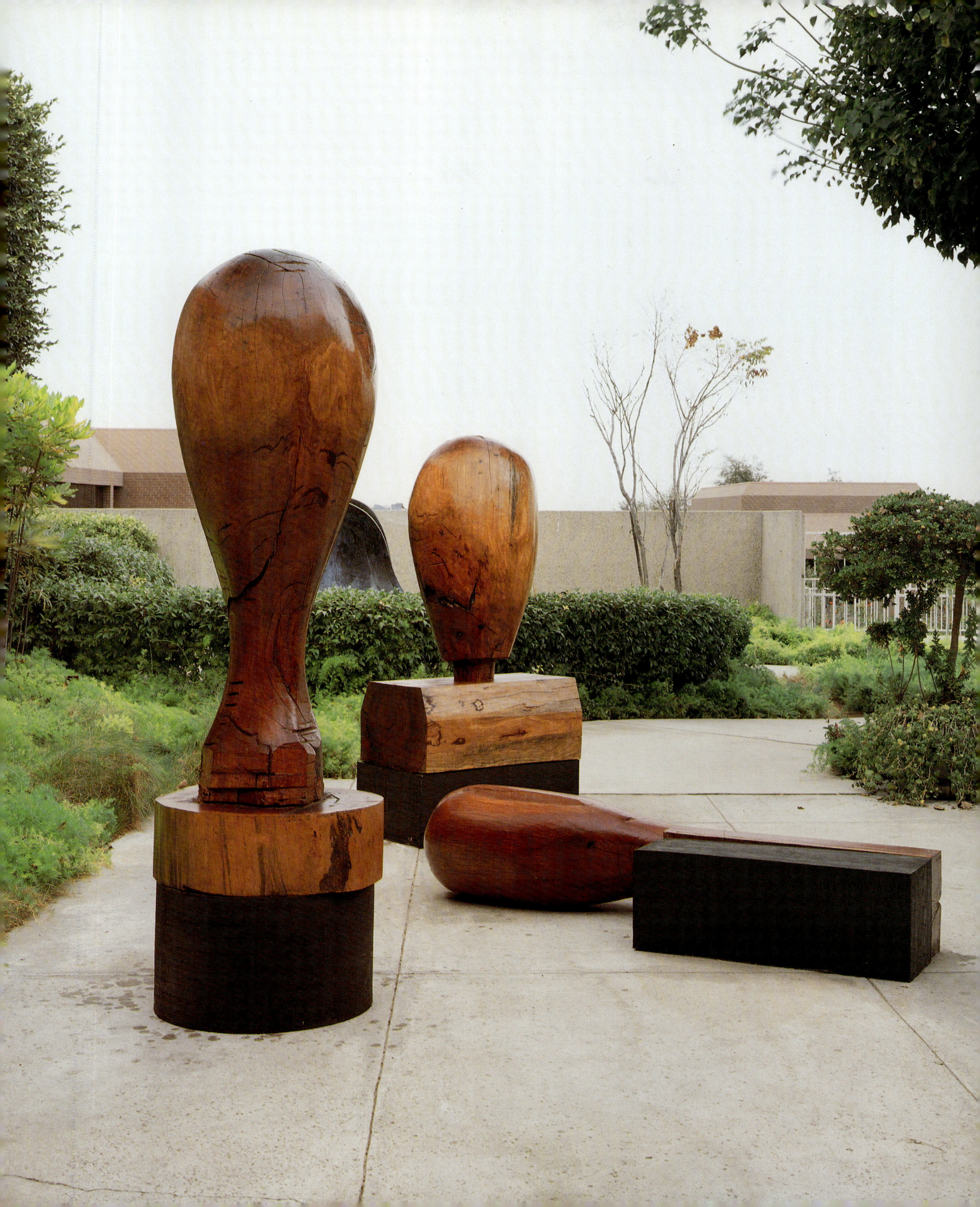

135. *Forminifera*, 1991

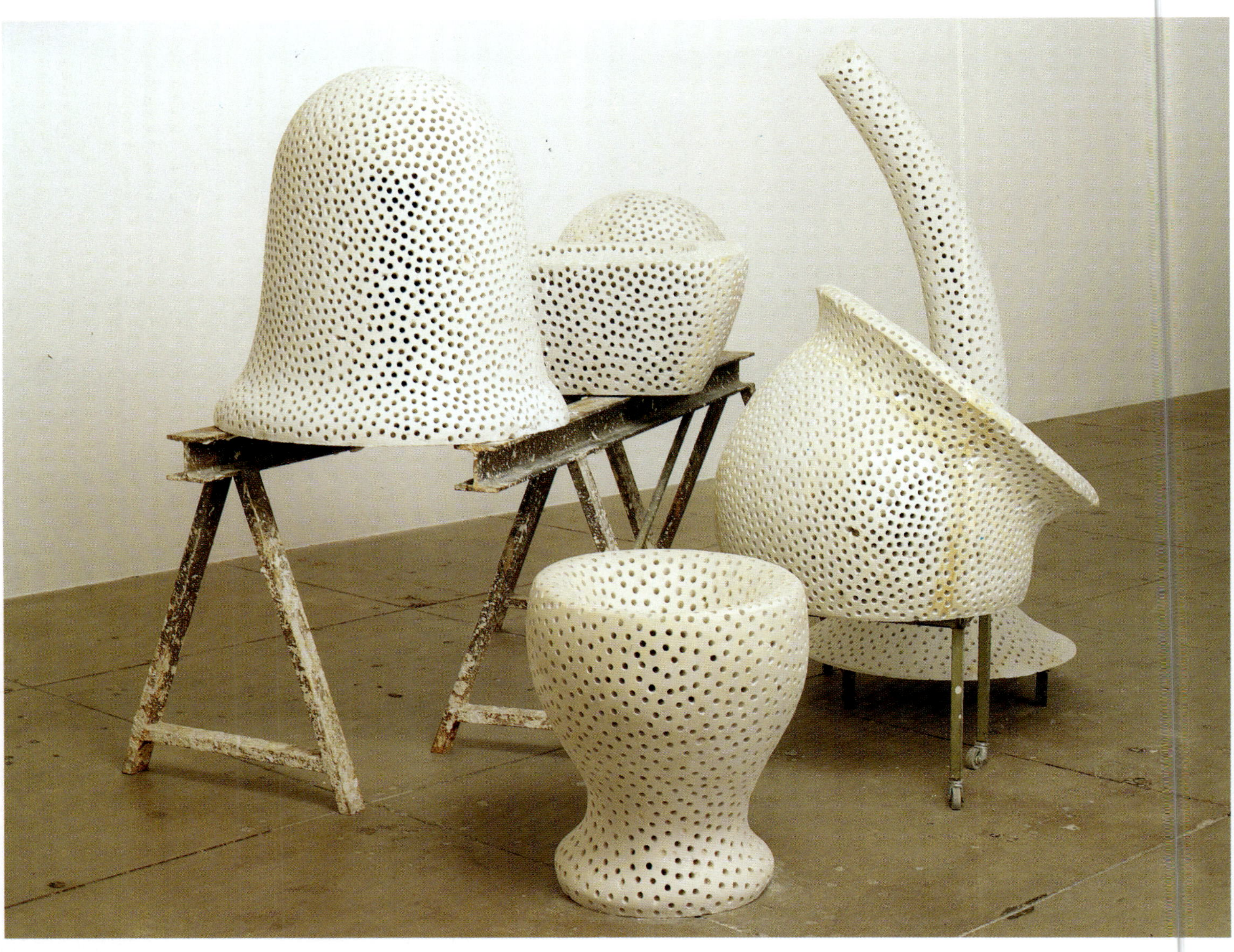

pp. 226-227
136. *Beasts of Burden*, 1991

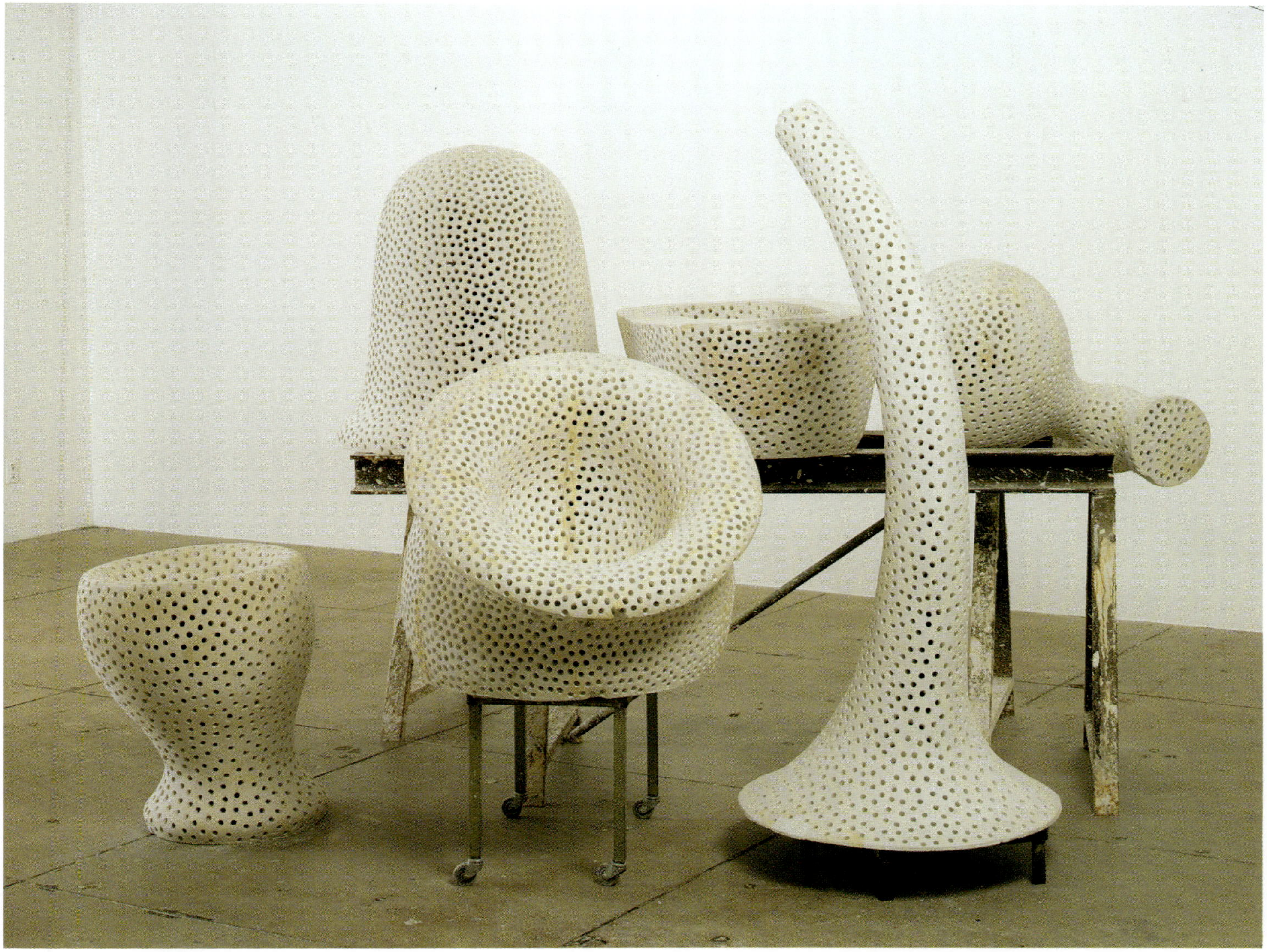

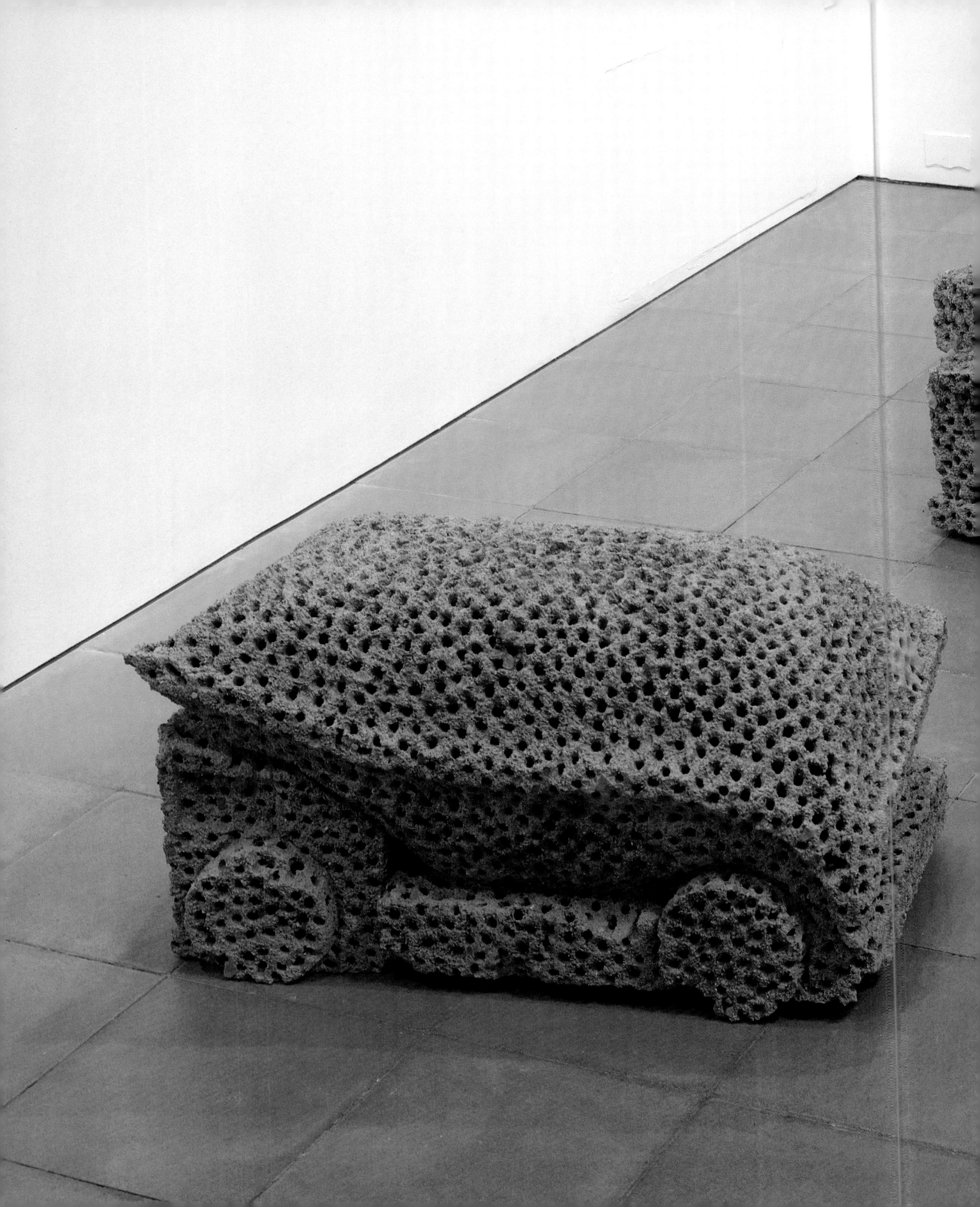

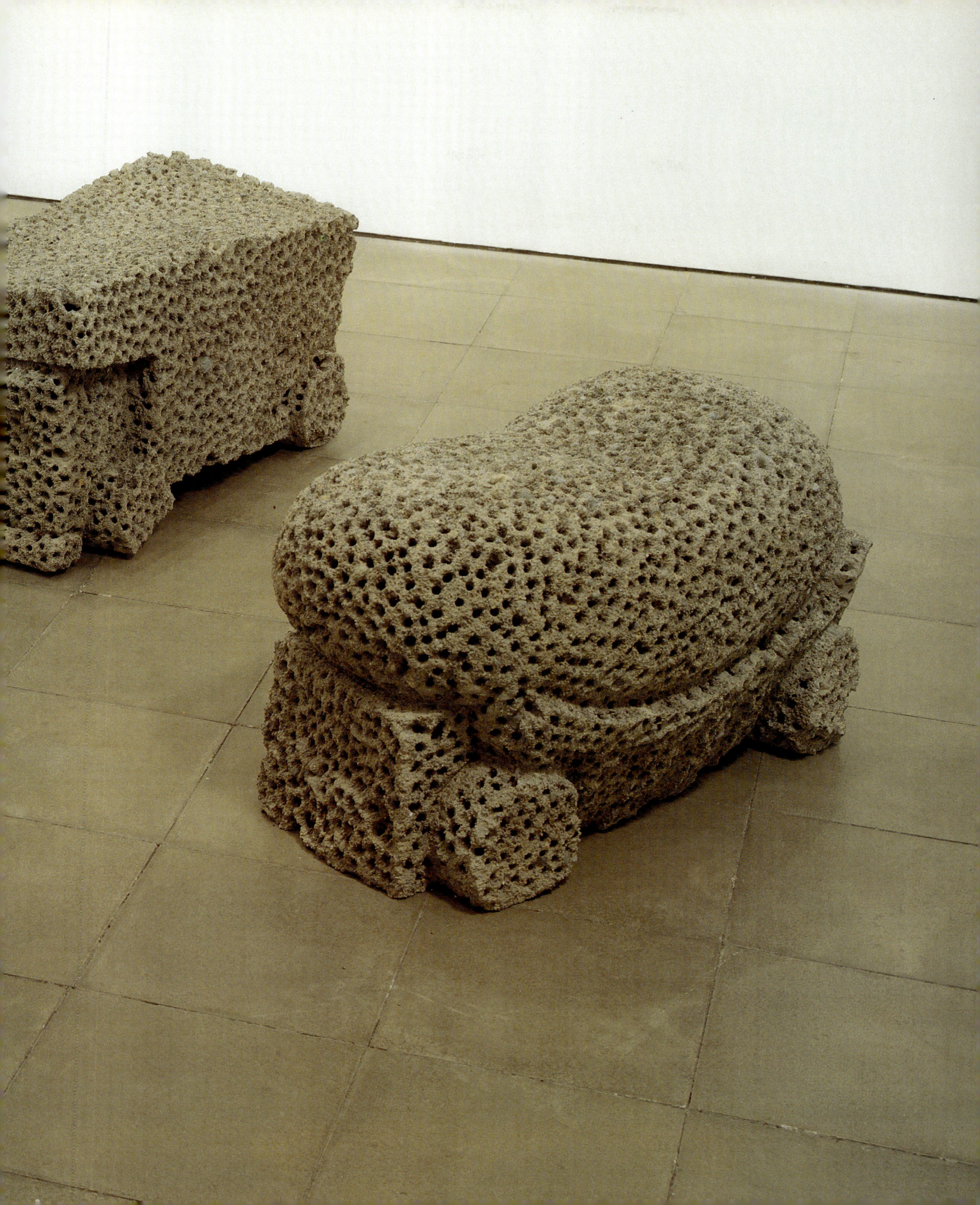

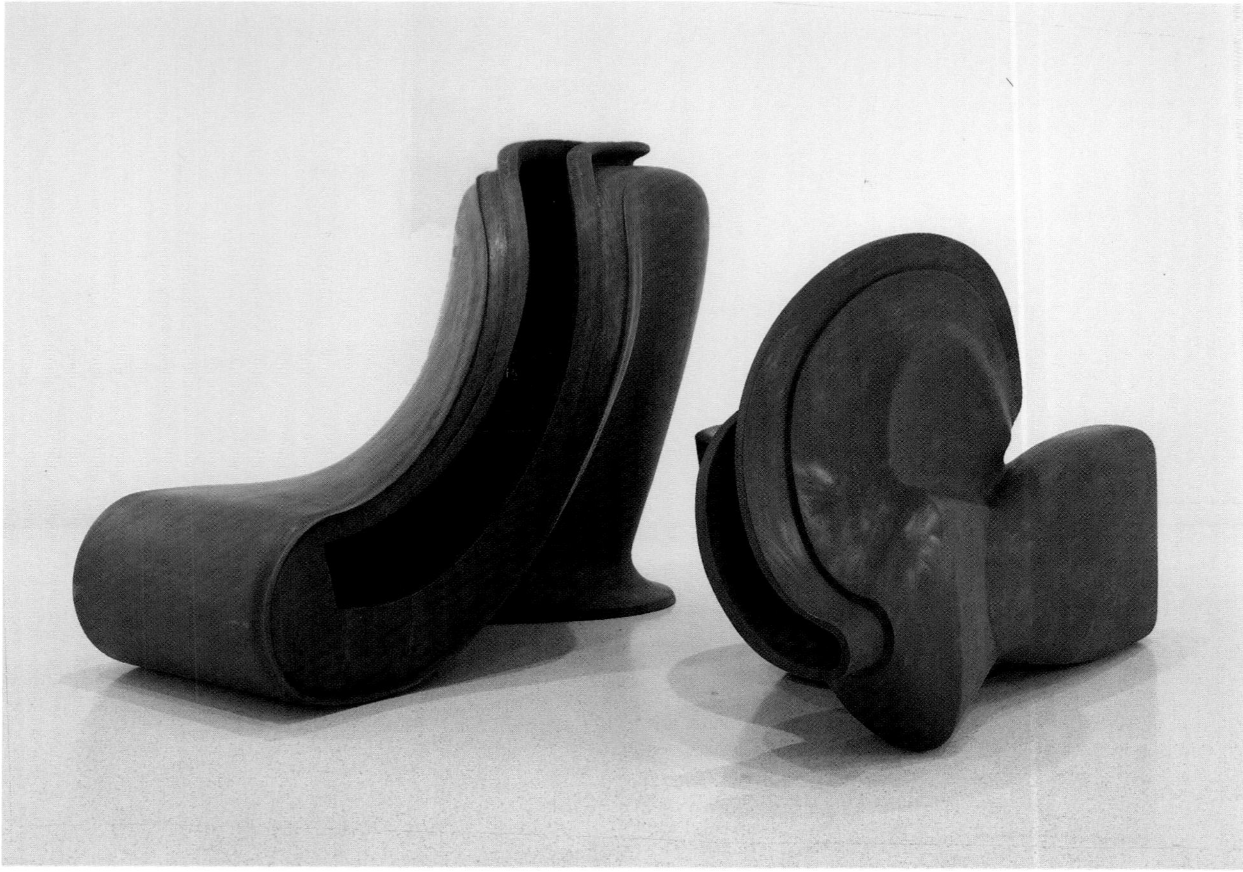

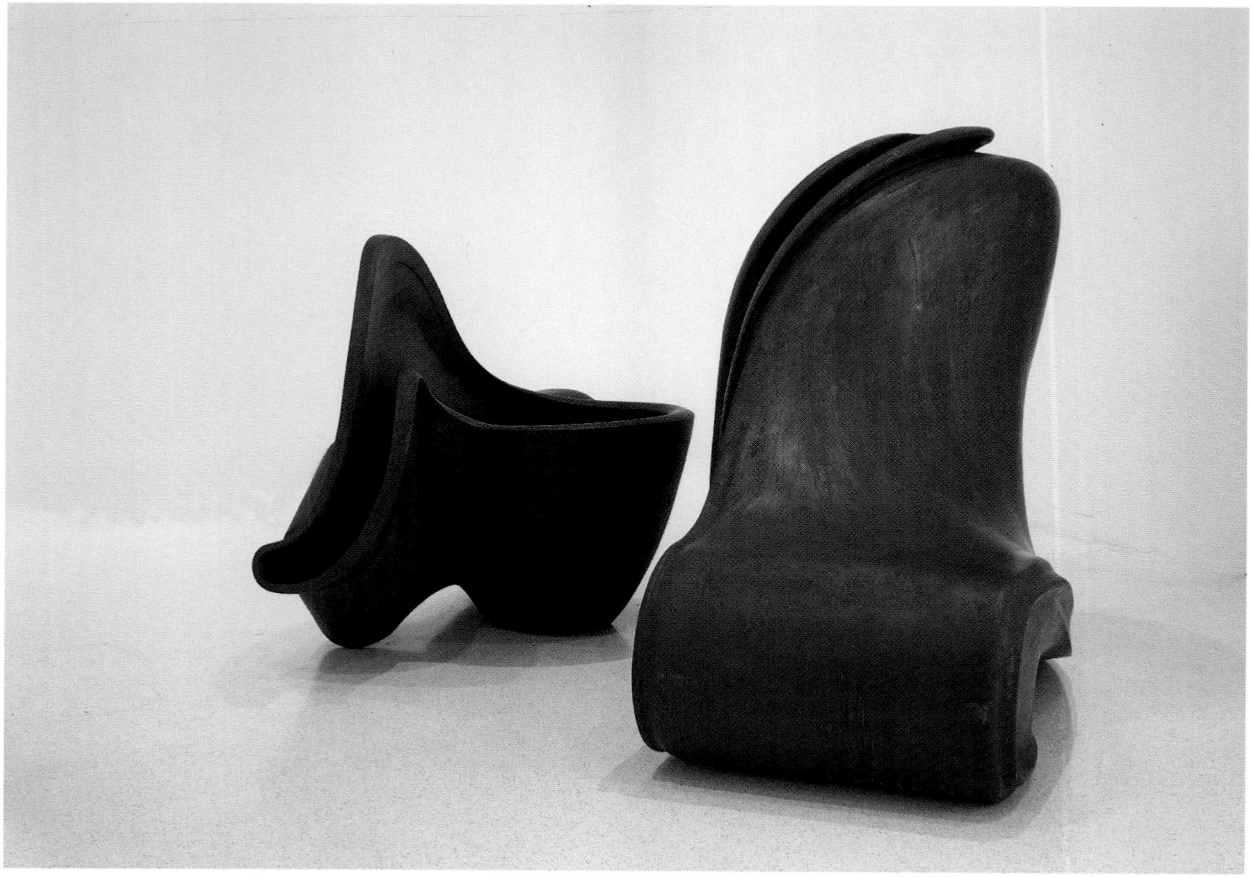

137. *Early Forms*, 1989

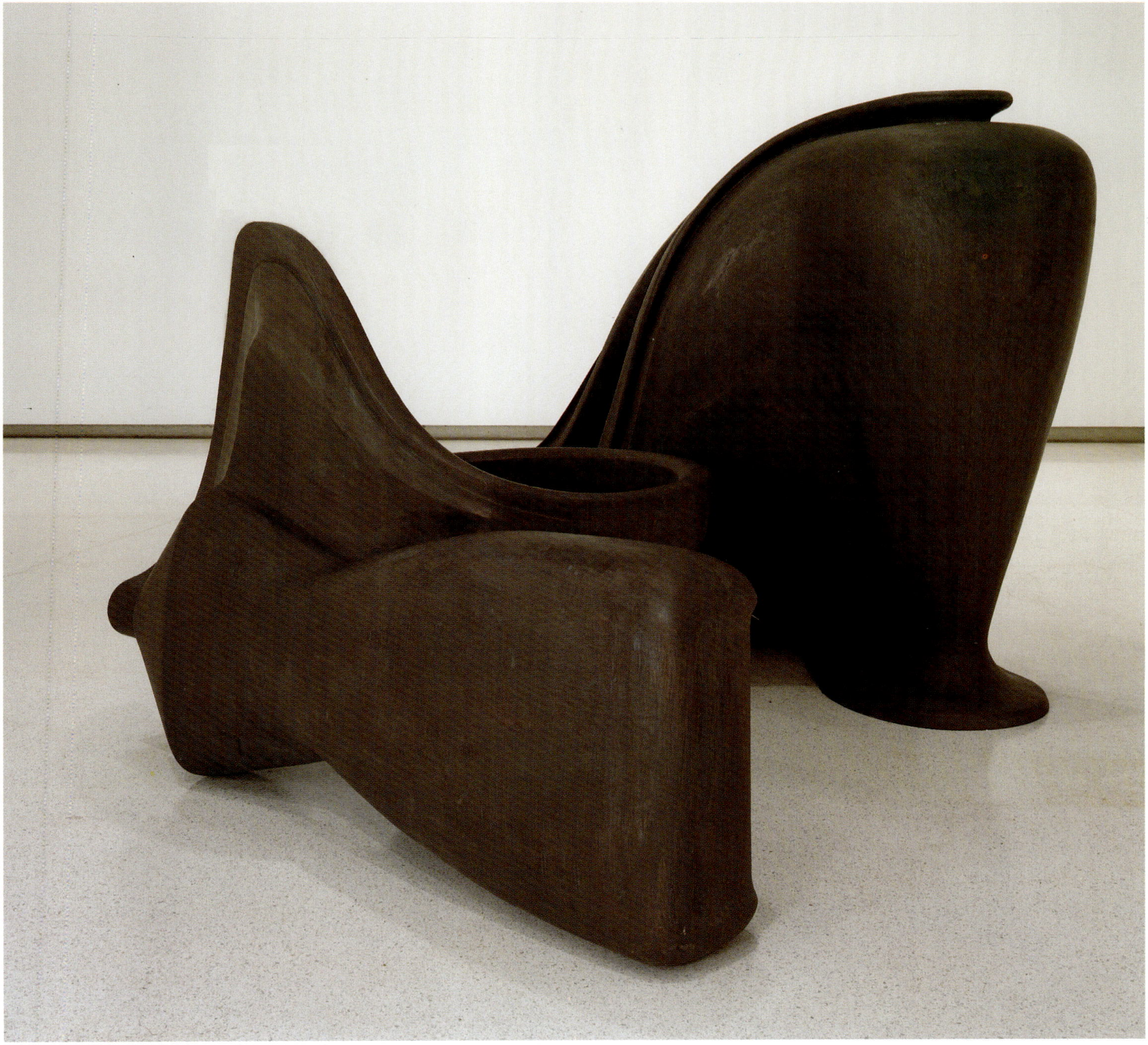

138. *Iron Mountain*, 1990

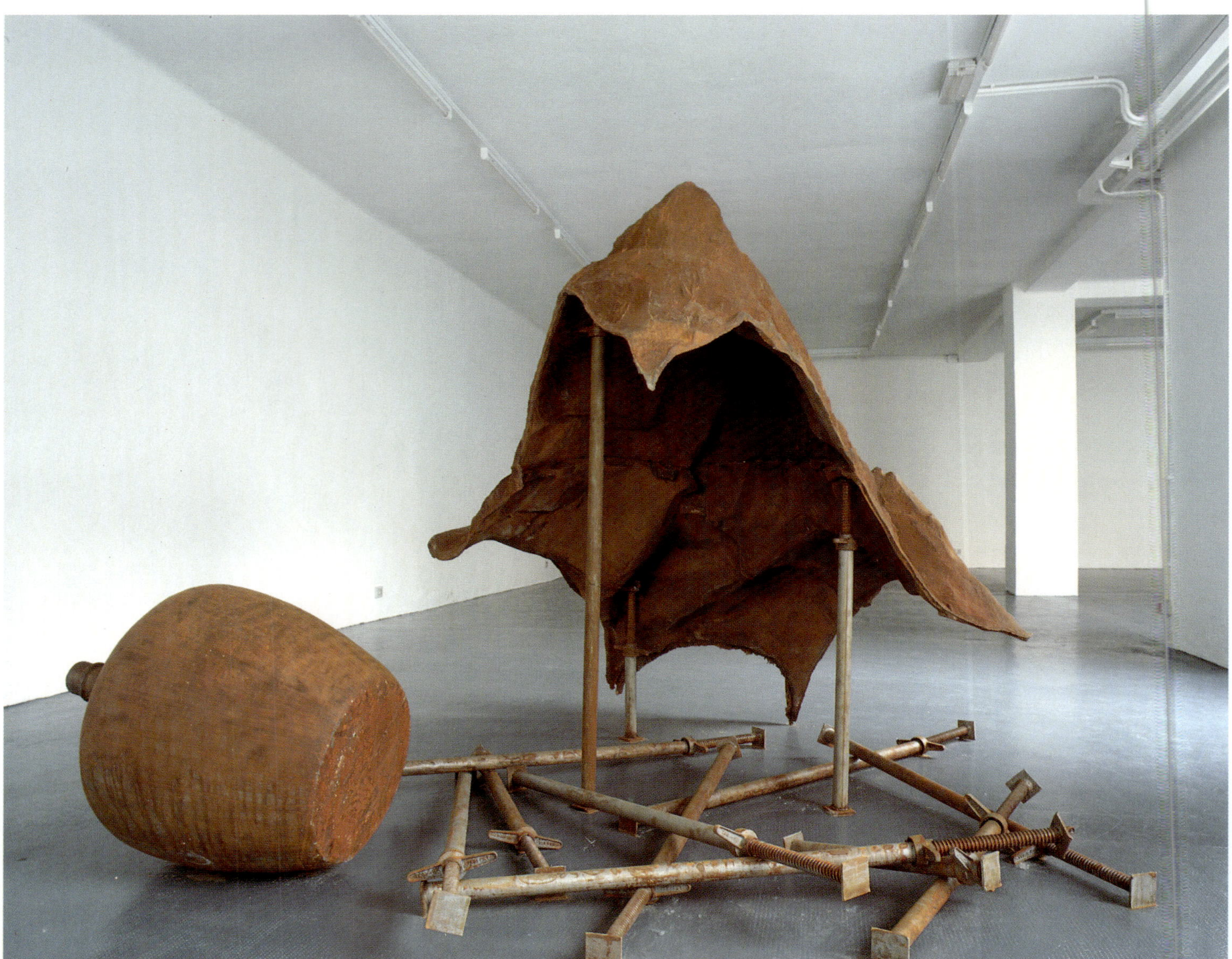

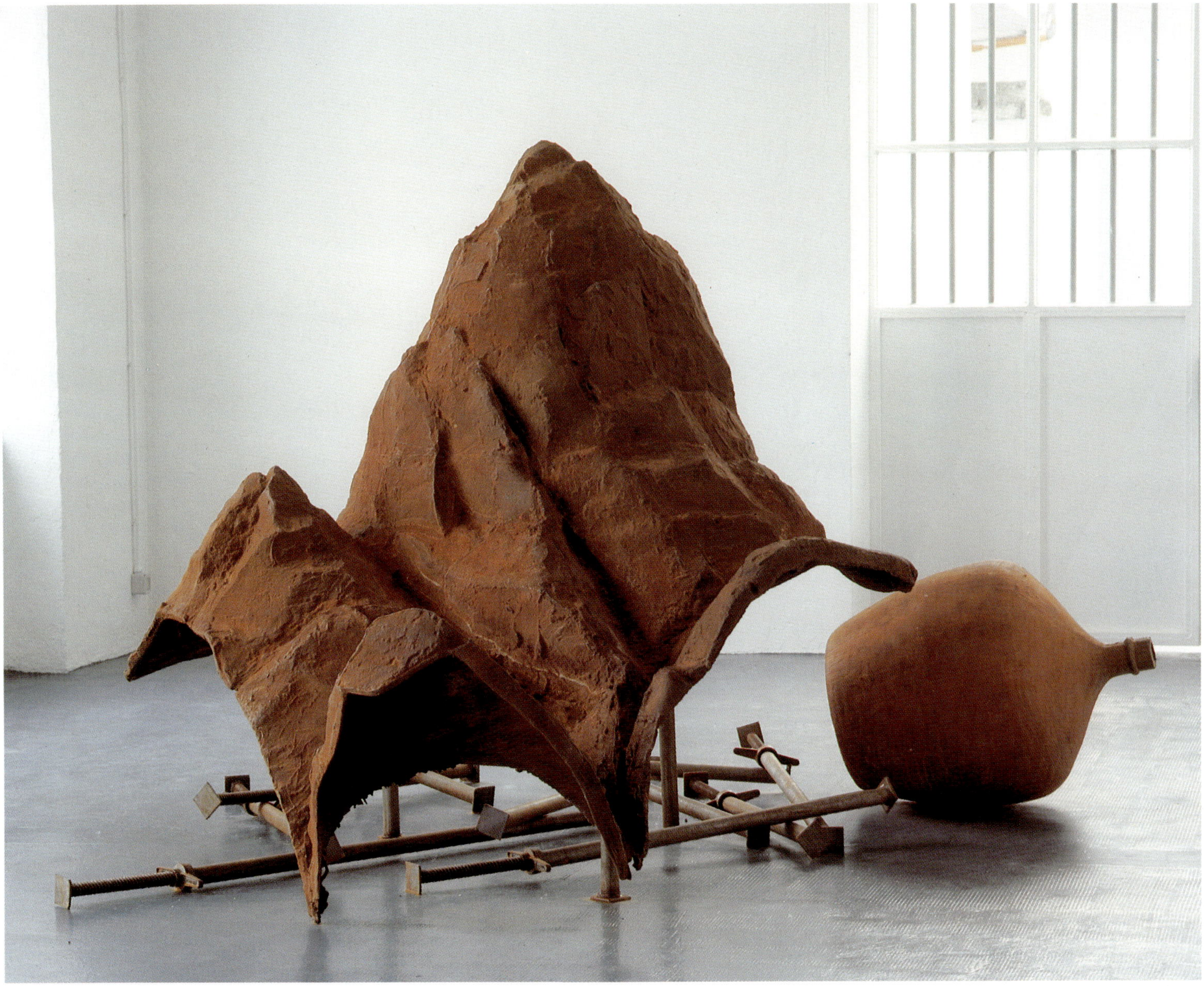

139. *Beasts of Burden*, 1991

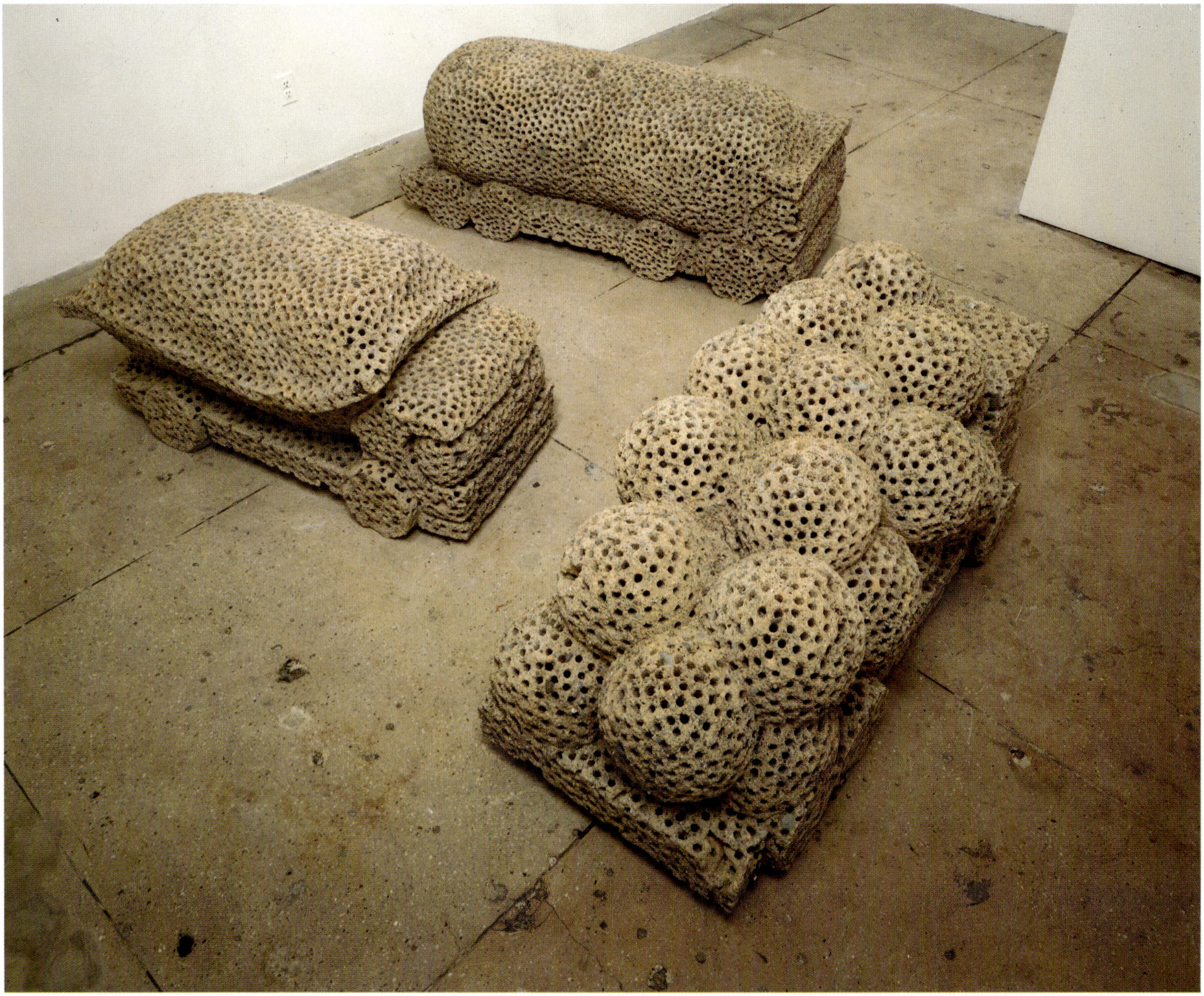

140. *Early Forms*, 1991

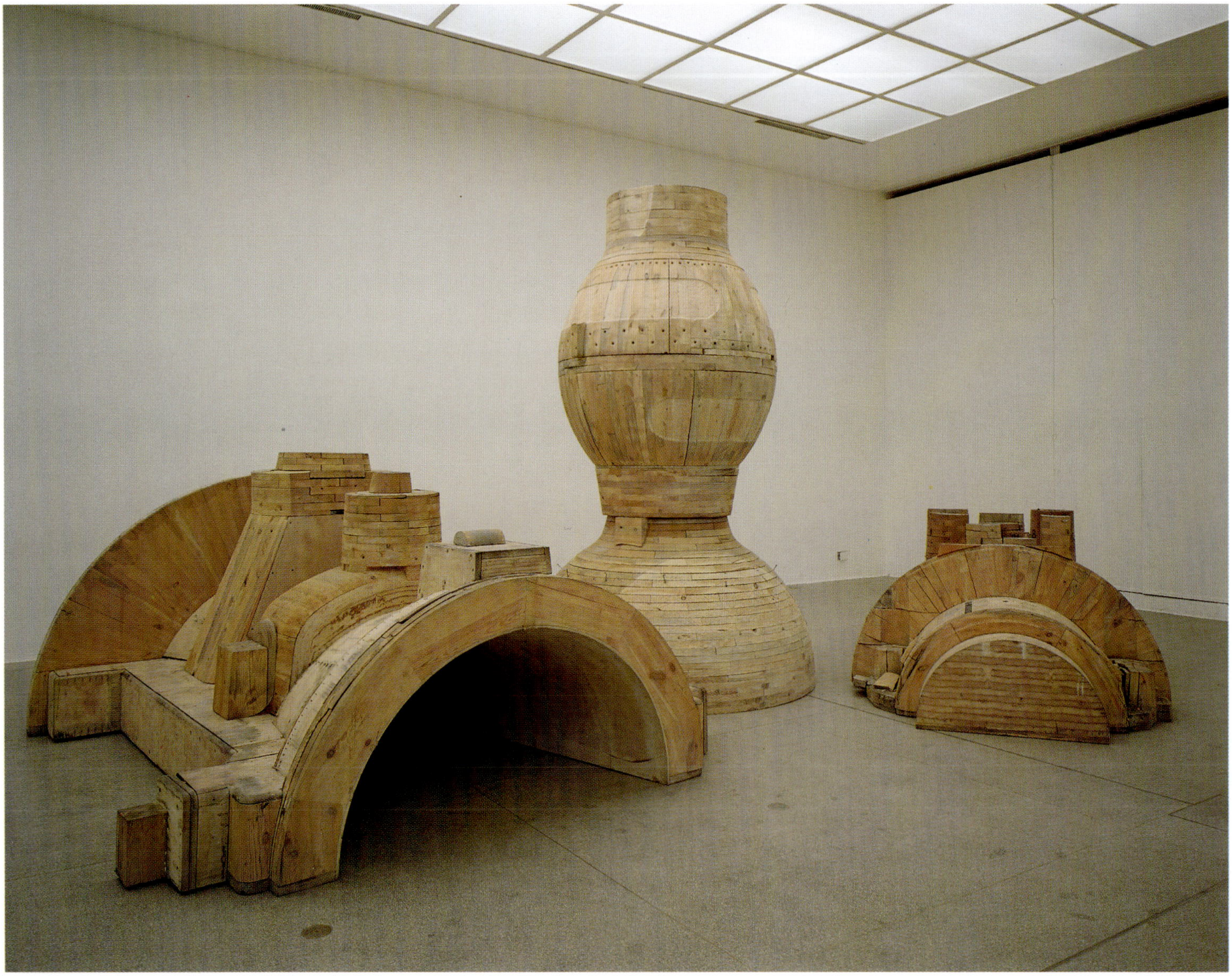

pp. 236-237
141. *Modern Types*, 1989

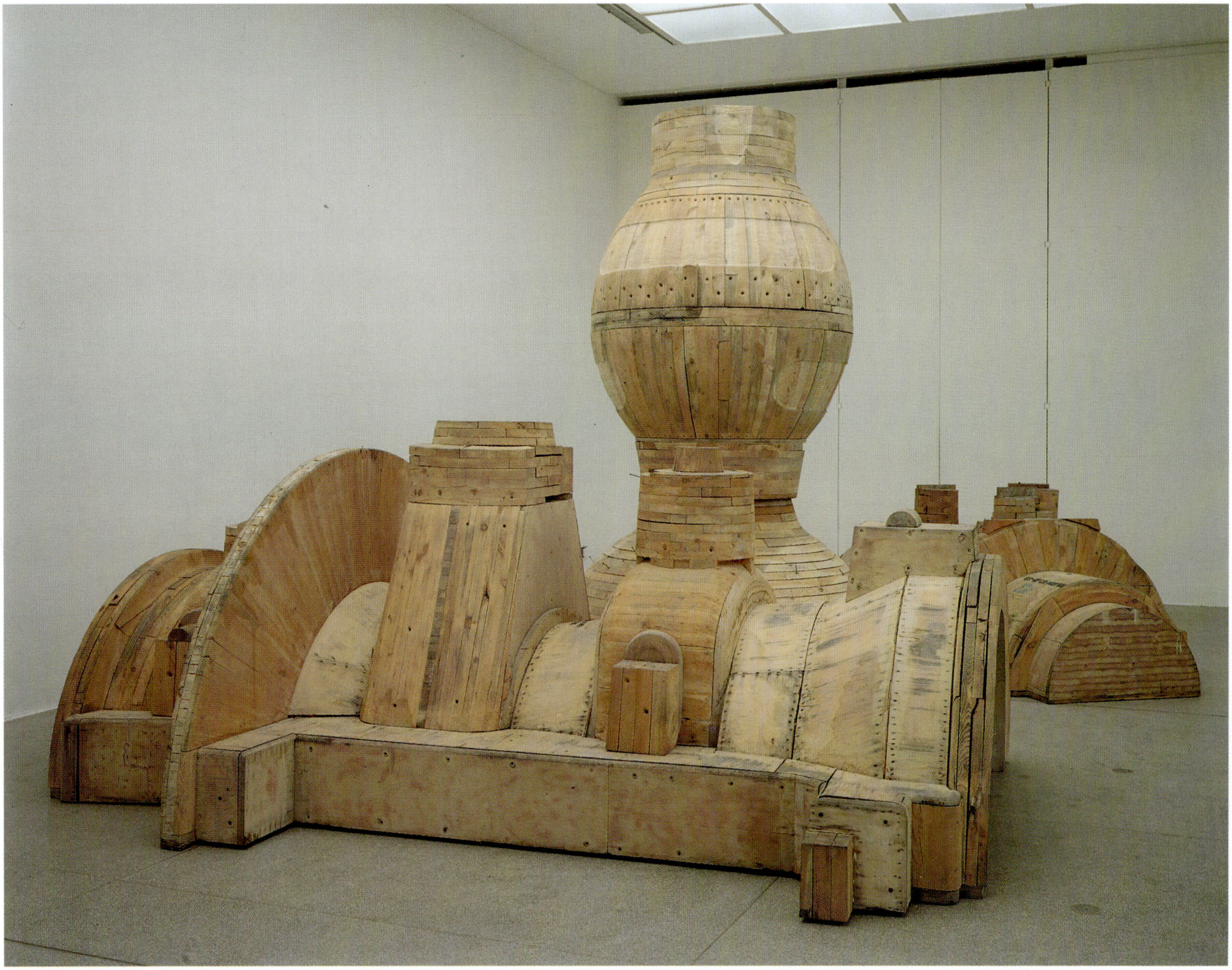

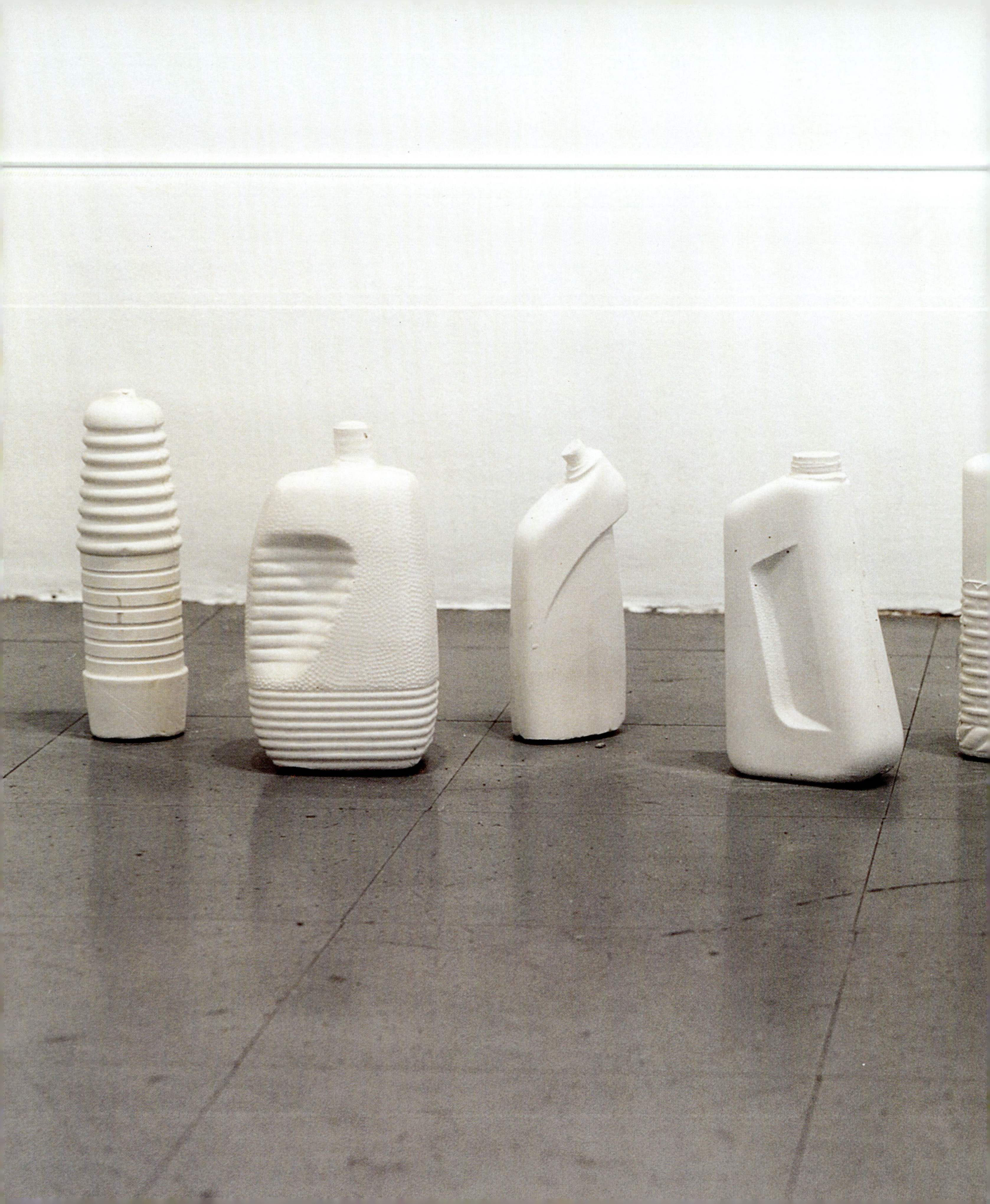

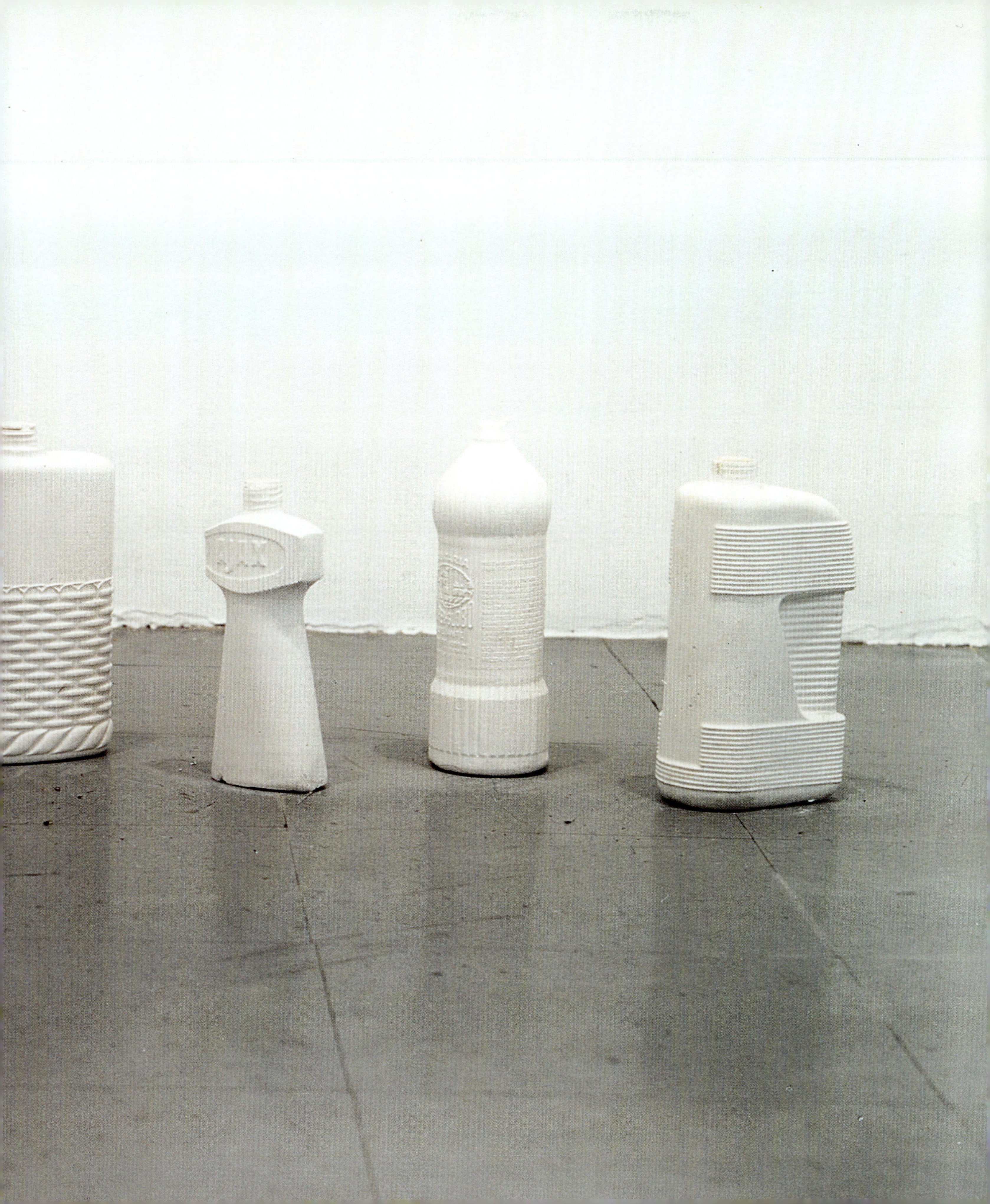
AJAX

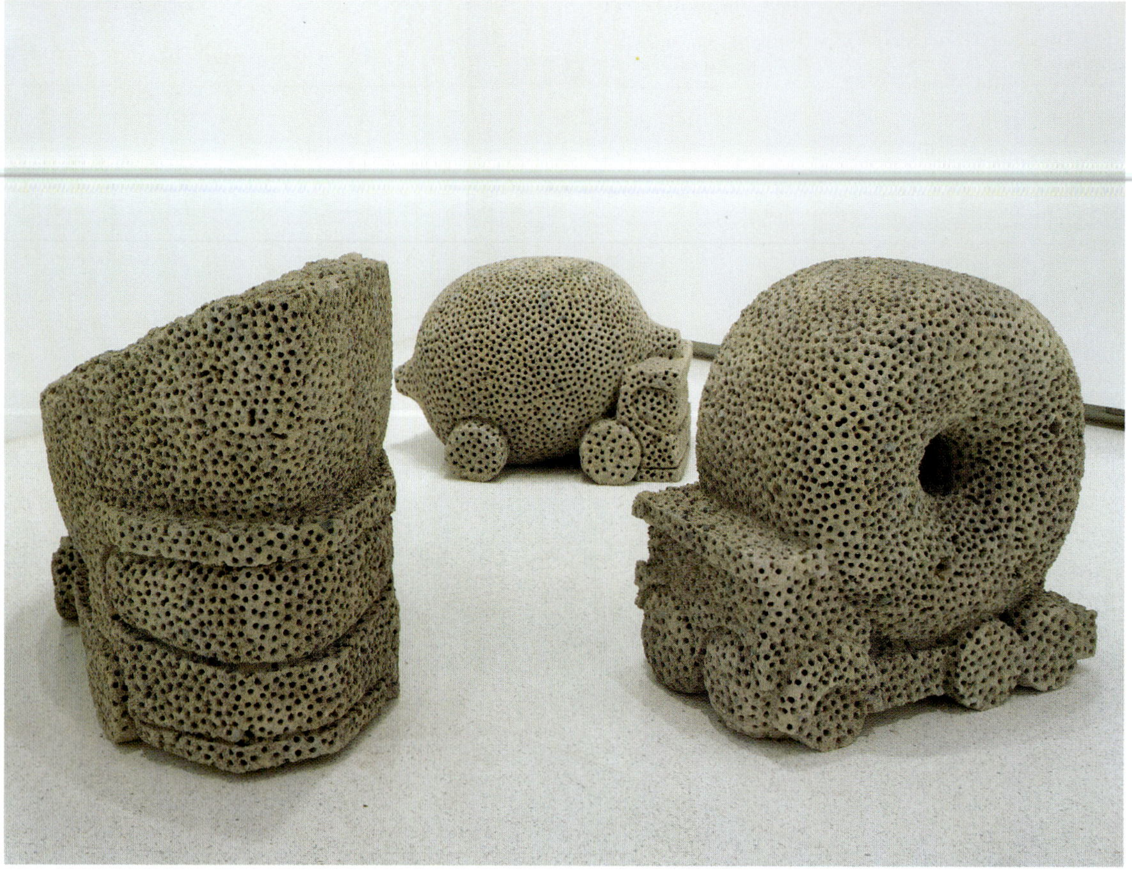

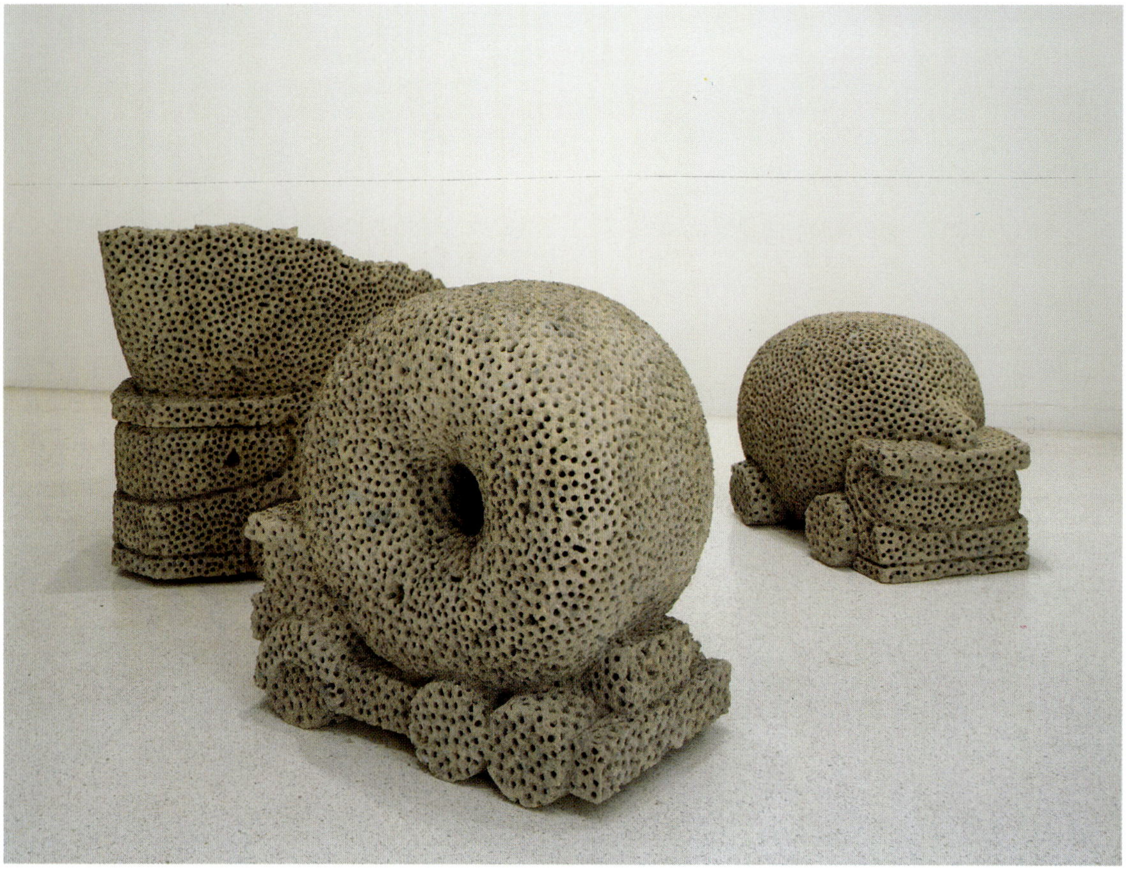

142. *Beasts of Burden*, 1992

143. *Shields*, 1991

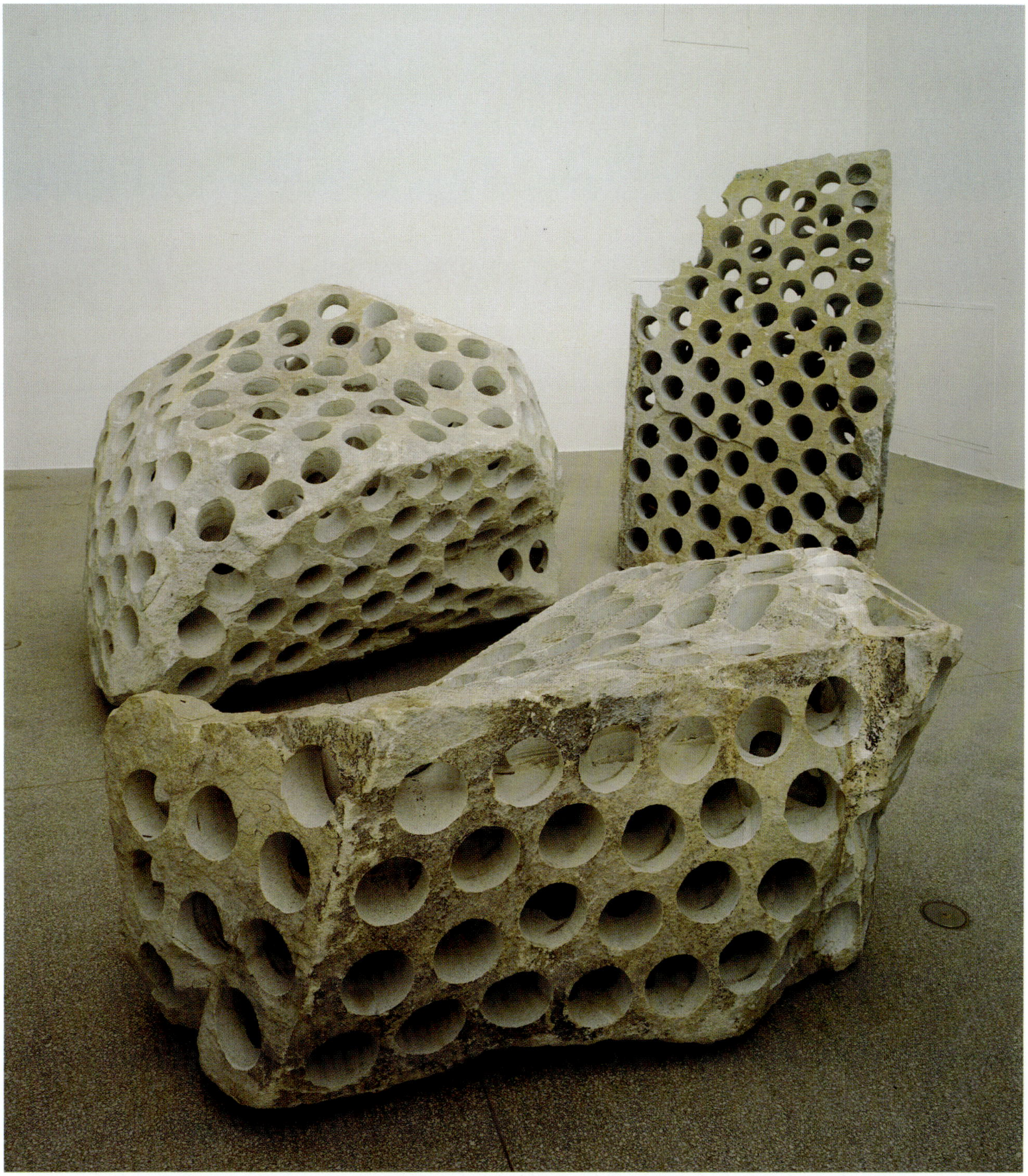

144. *Connecting Piece*, 1991

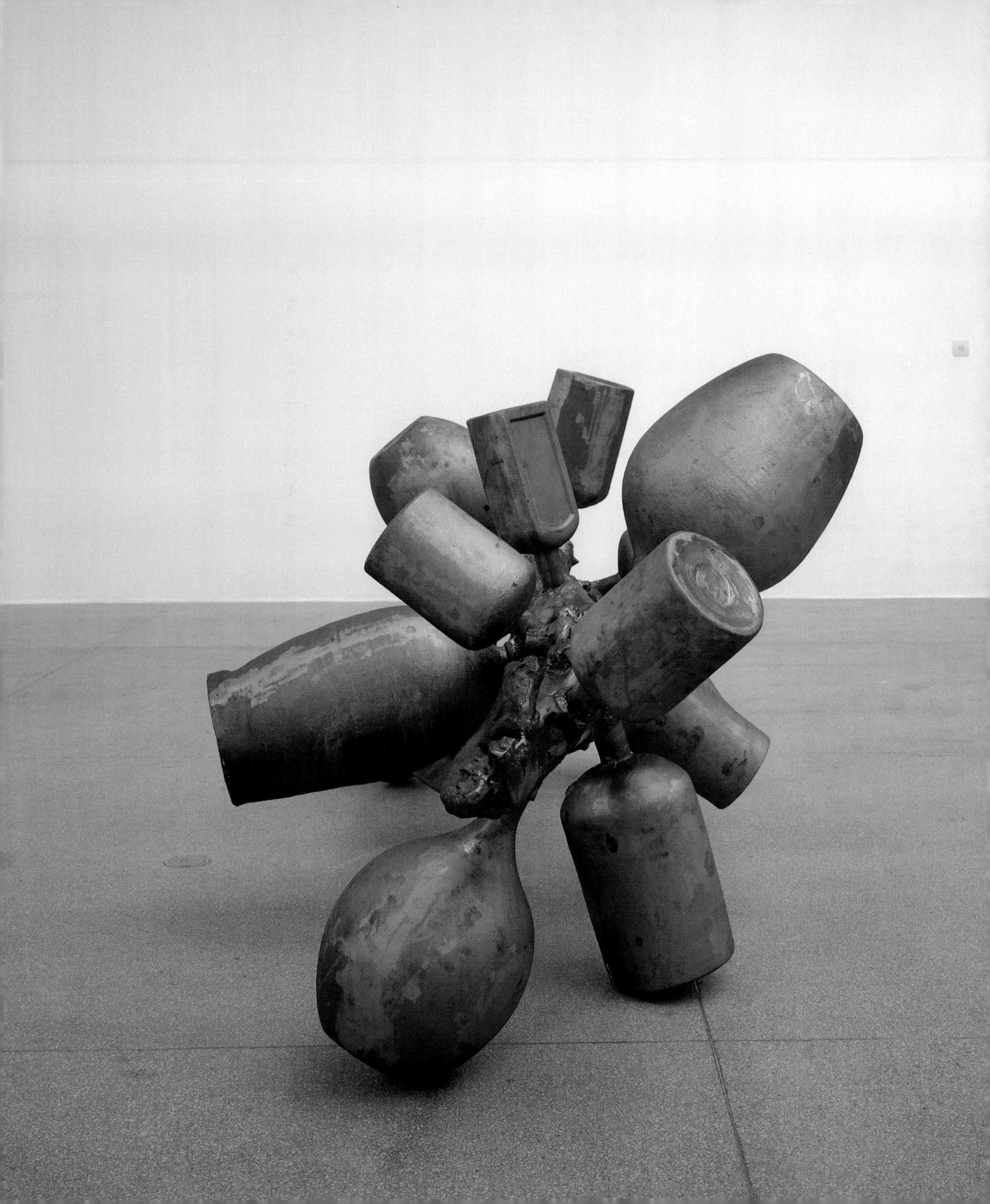

145. *Vulnerable Landscape: The Thin Skin*, 1991

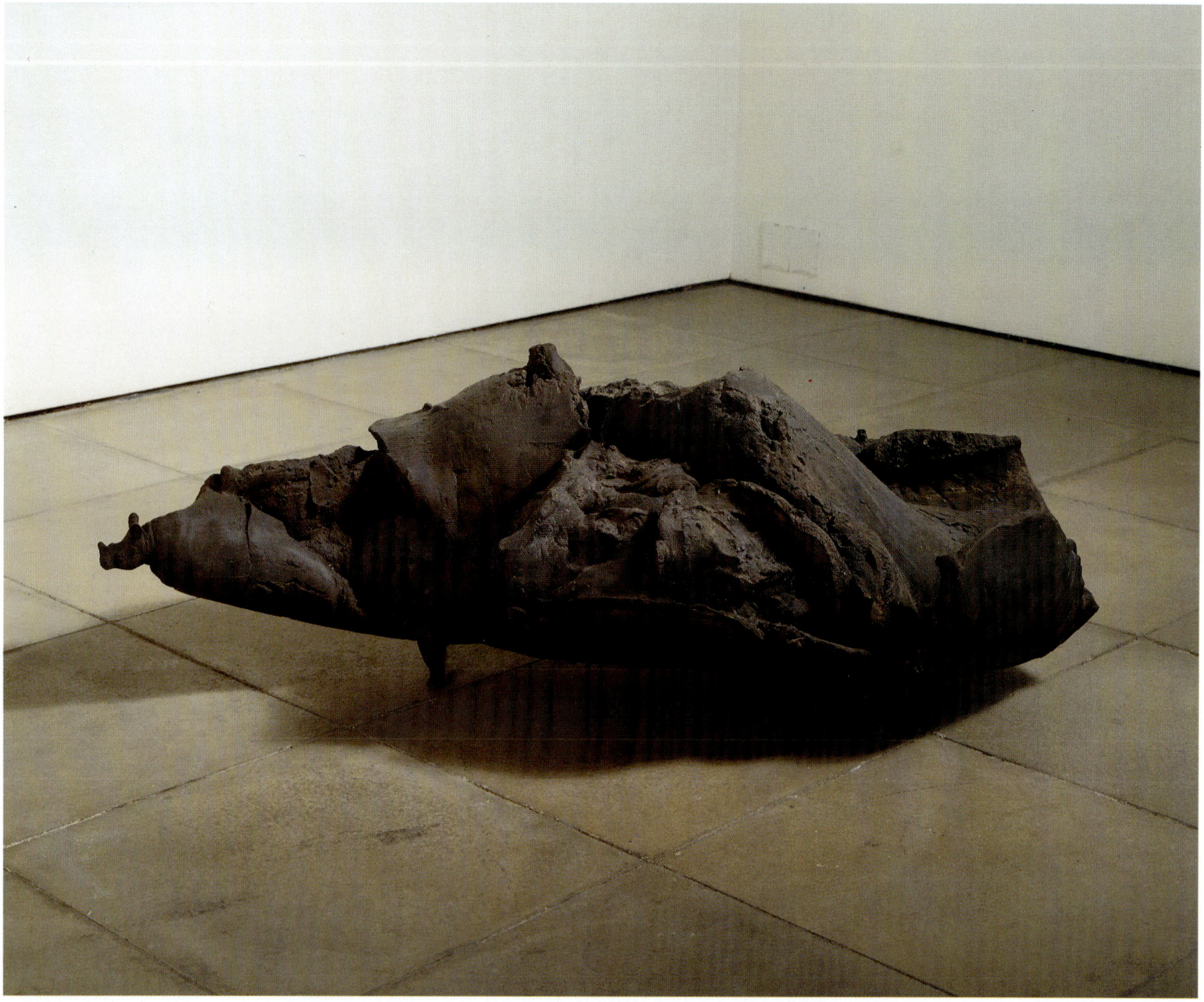

146. *Burden*, 1991

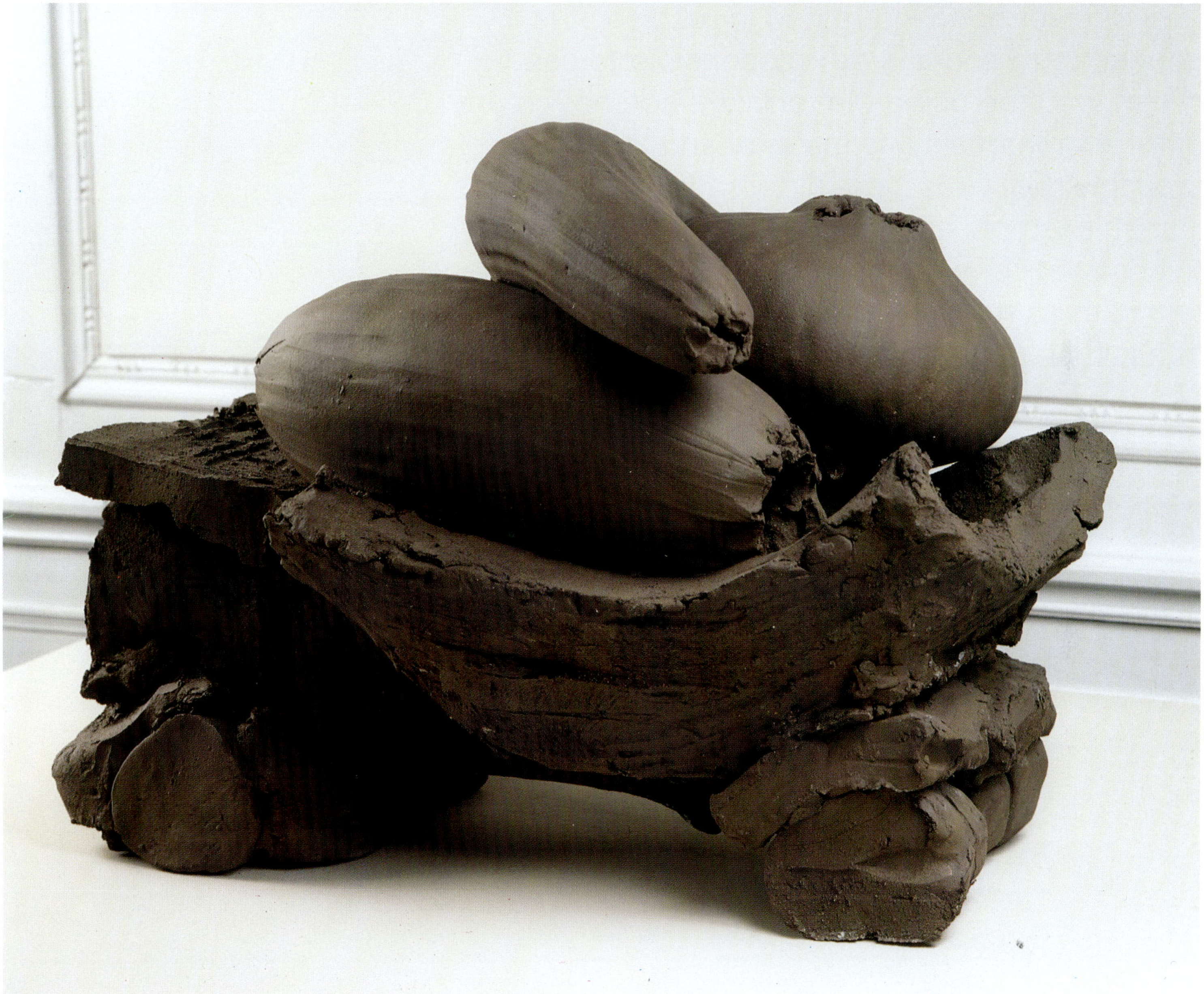

I have never been interested in rubbish; it is a generic term and it is so irresponsible to use it. When we stop using the term we see how many different materials it is made of and then we probably deal with them differently. It is true, it is just an example and a quick example of how things start to work, because one can either see this stuff as rubbish-on-the-beach or, as you say, one can start to think about it. Each one is beautiful, each one is ugly, or whatever. It depends on our set of criteria.

Ludovico Pratesi, "A Conversation with Tony Cragg." In *Tony Cragg*, exh. catalogue. Rome: Valentina Moncada, 1990, pp. 16, 18.

147. *Zooid*, 1991

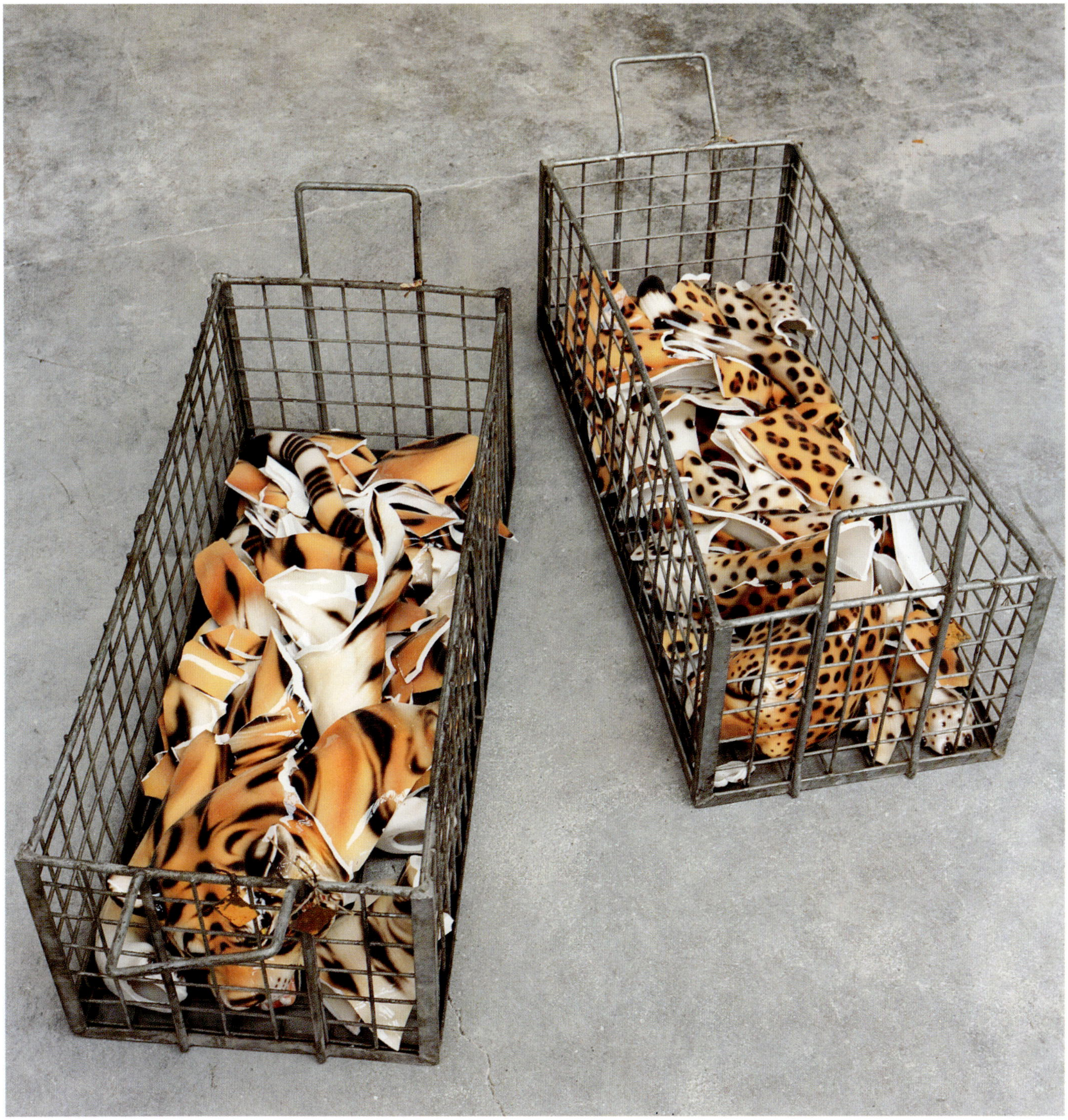

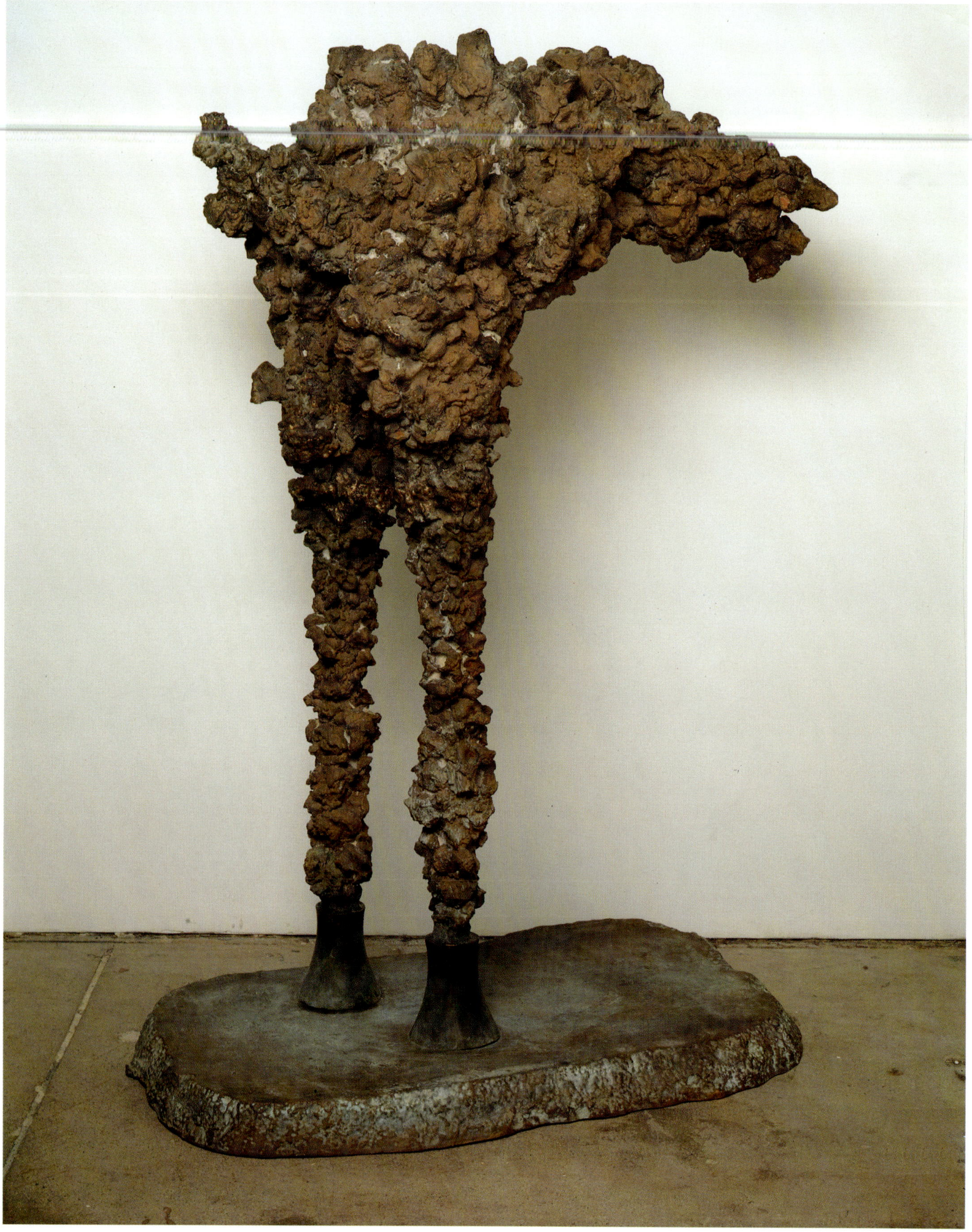

148. *Cloud*, 1991

149. *Plough*, 1990

150. *Species*, 1990

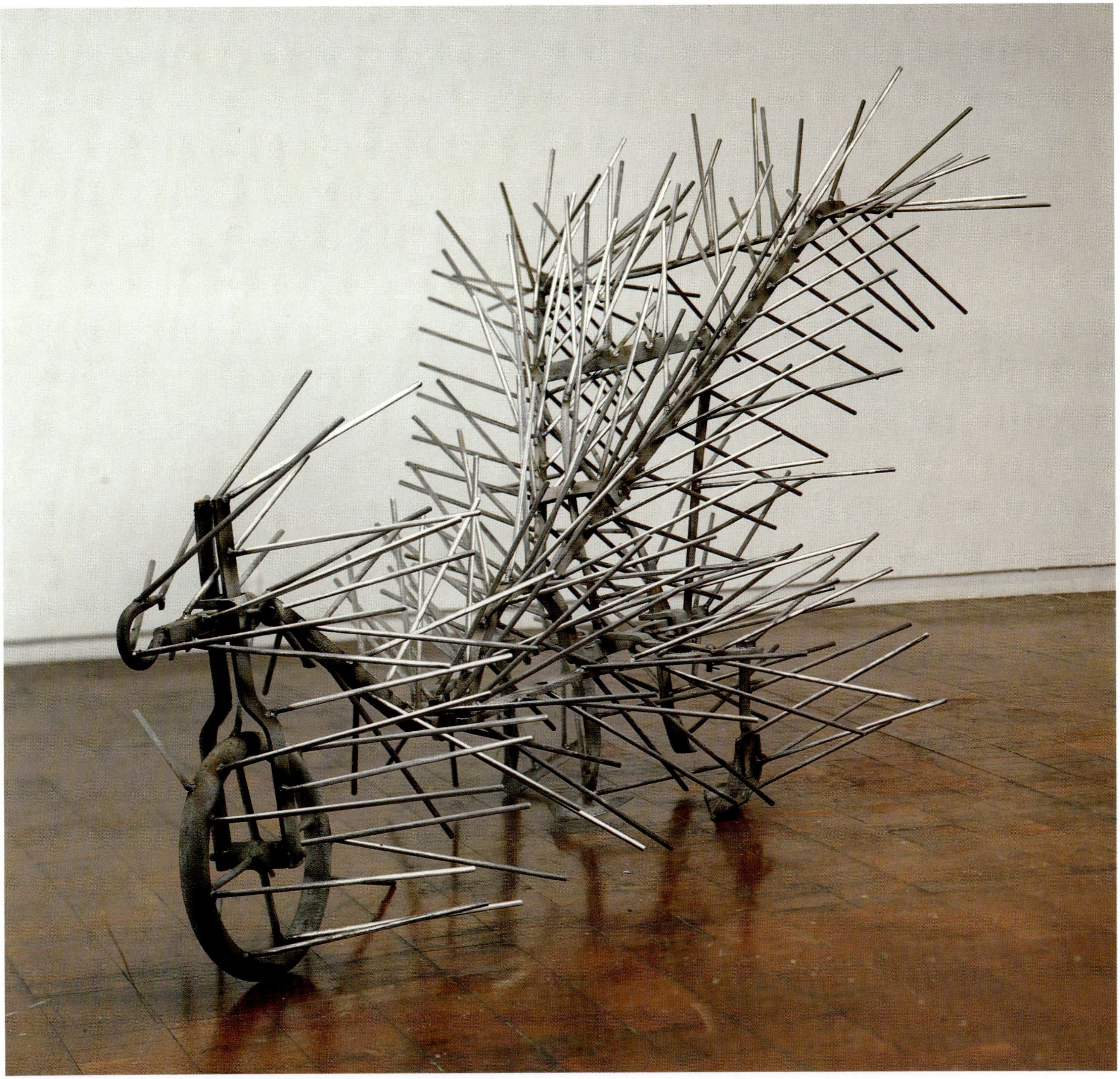

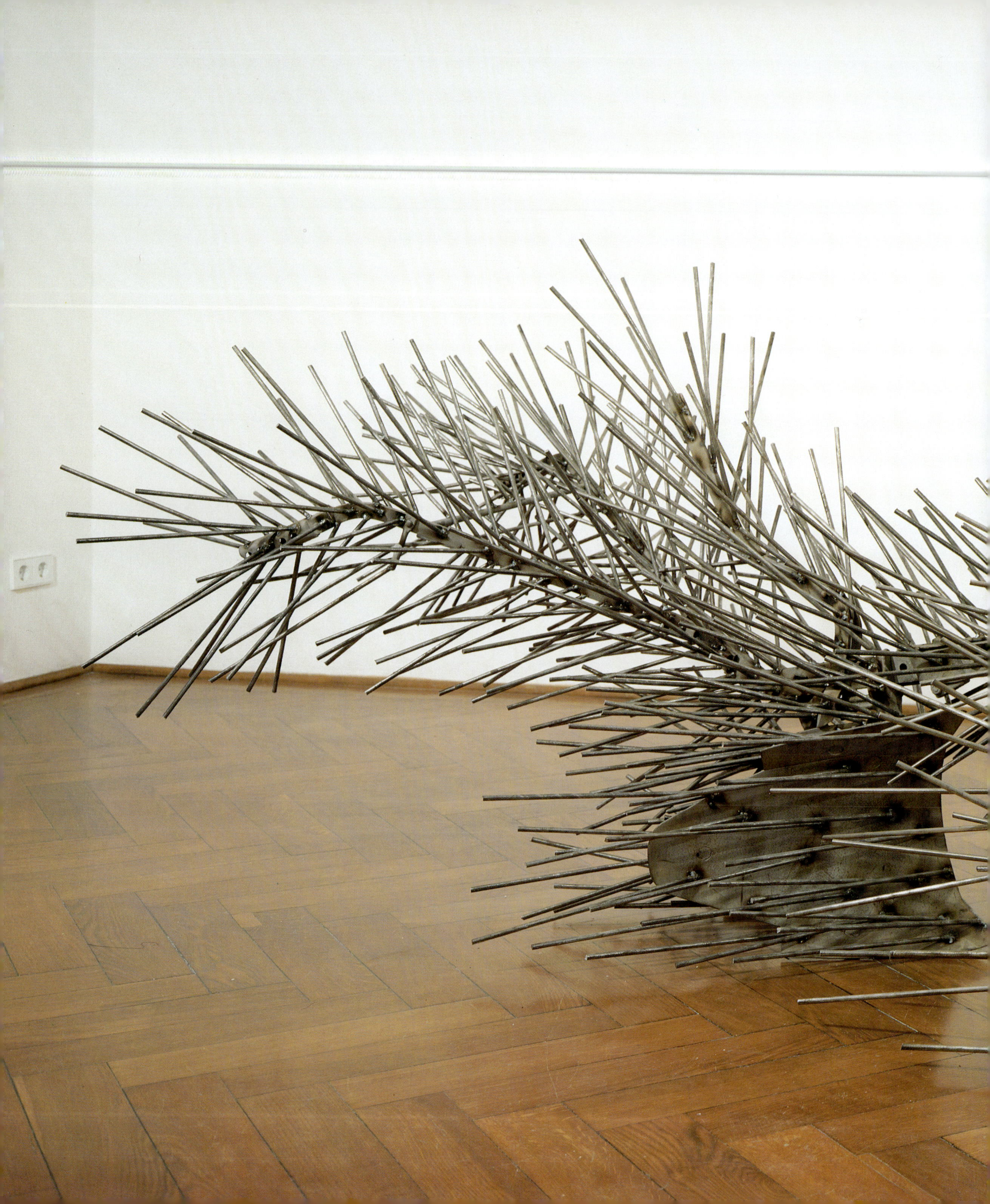

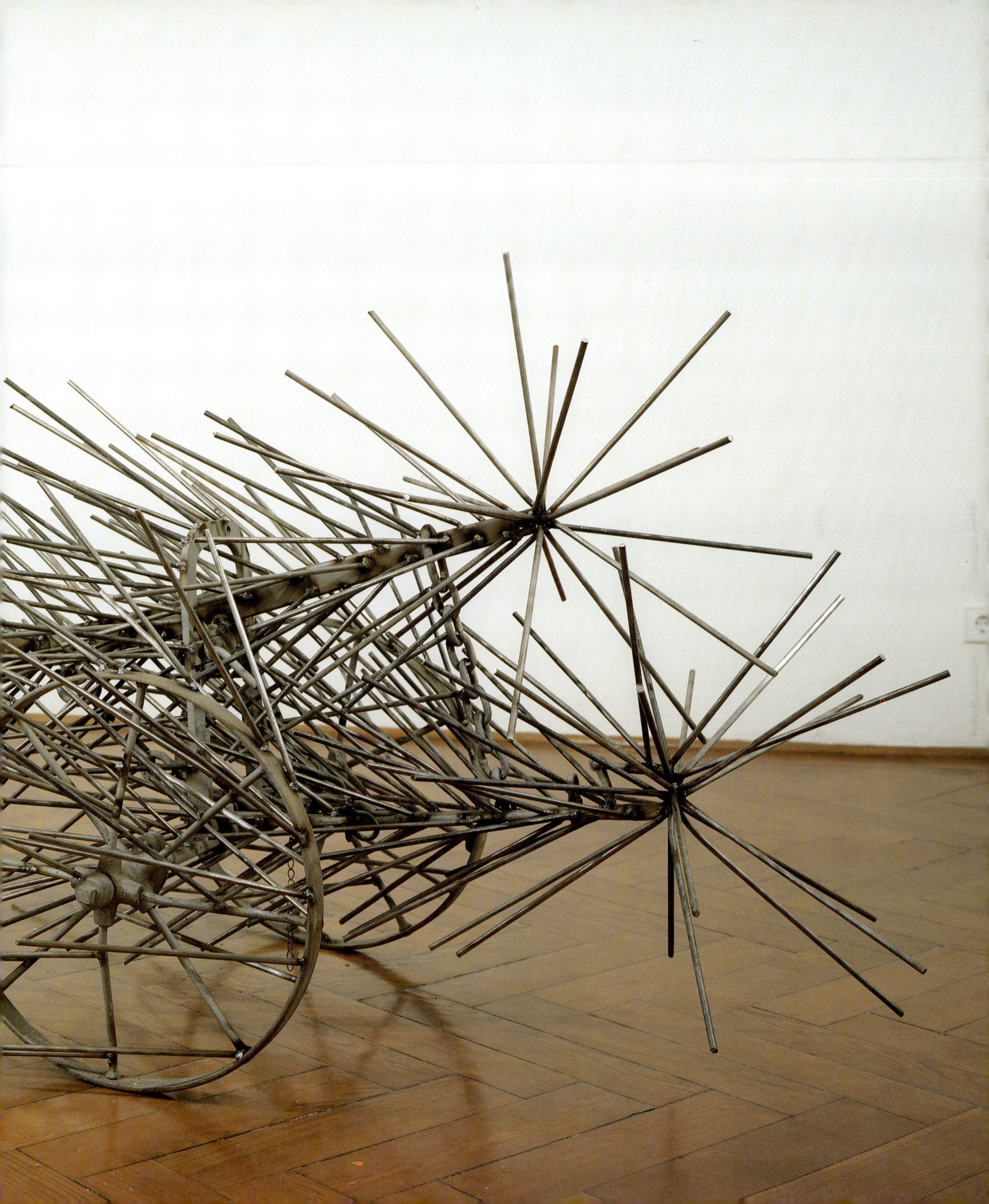

151. *Unschärferelation*, 1991

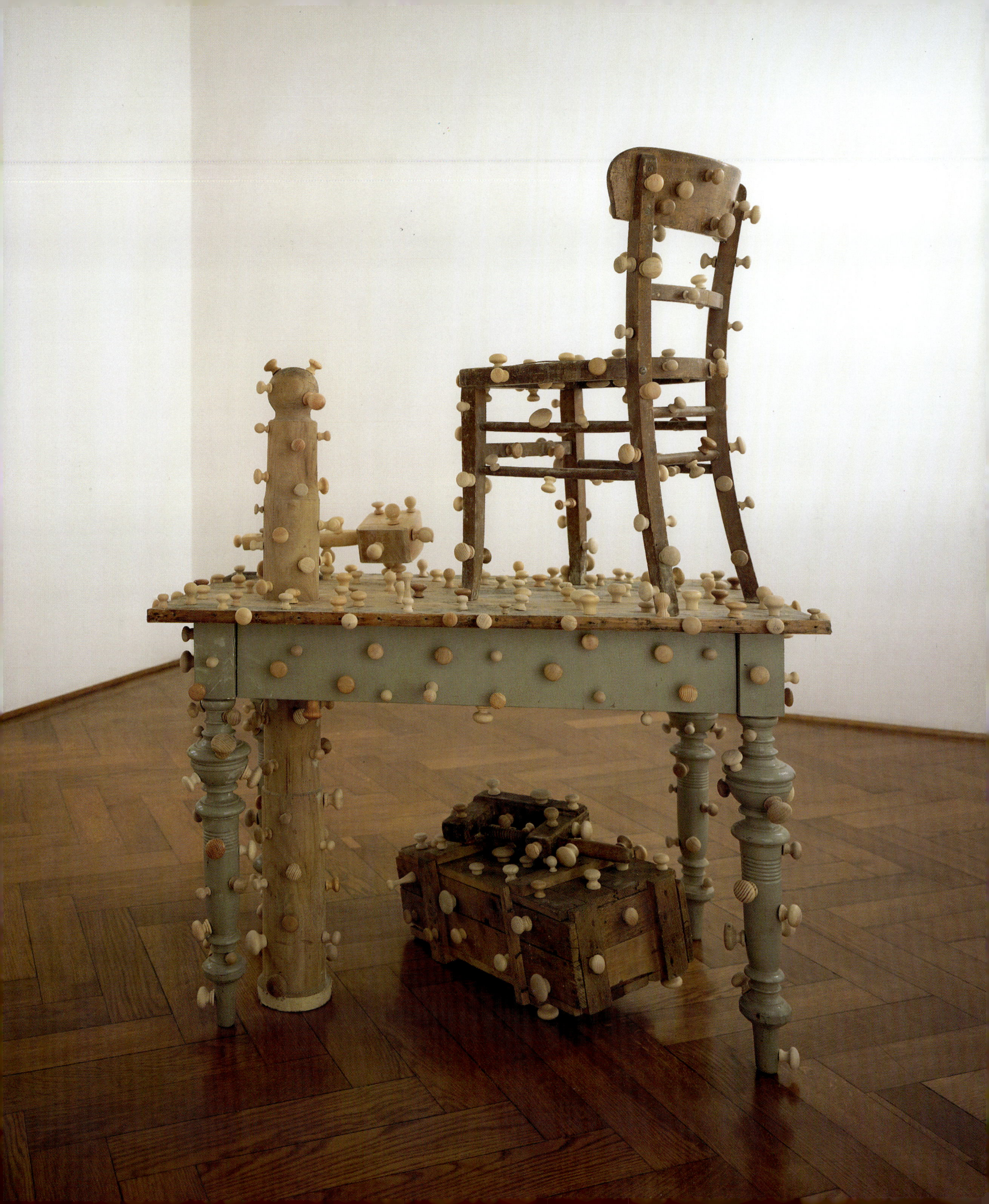

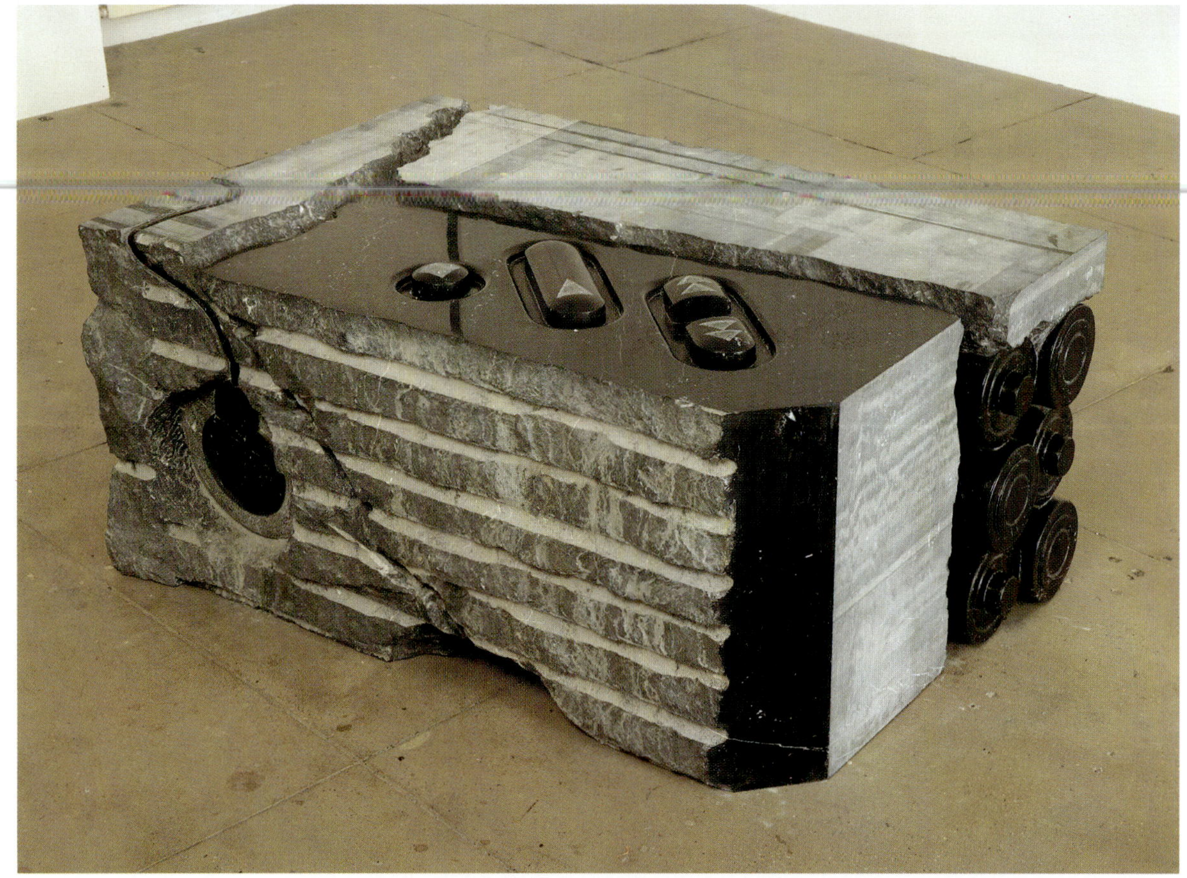

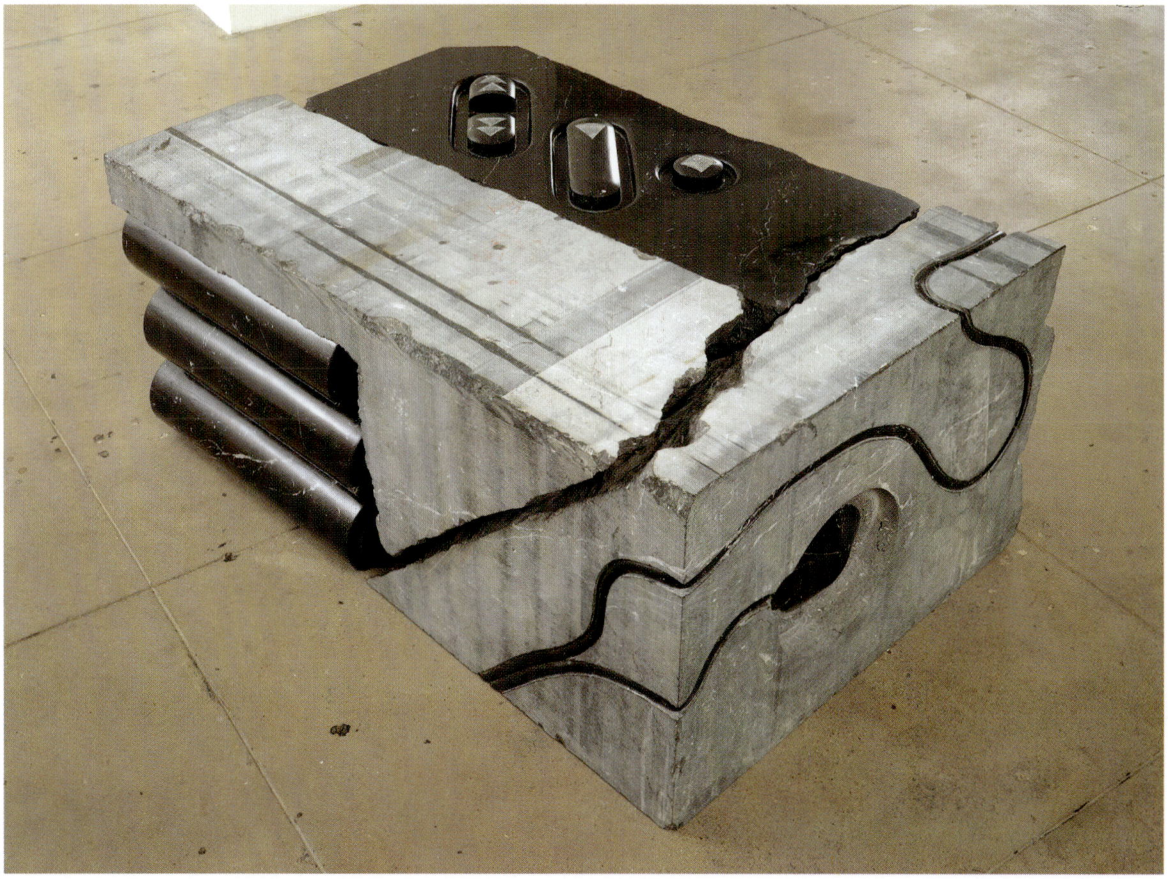

152. *For the Walking Man*, 1991 153. *Mineral Vein*, 1991 154. *Cellulose Memory*, 1991

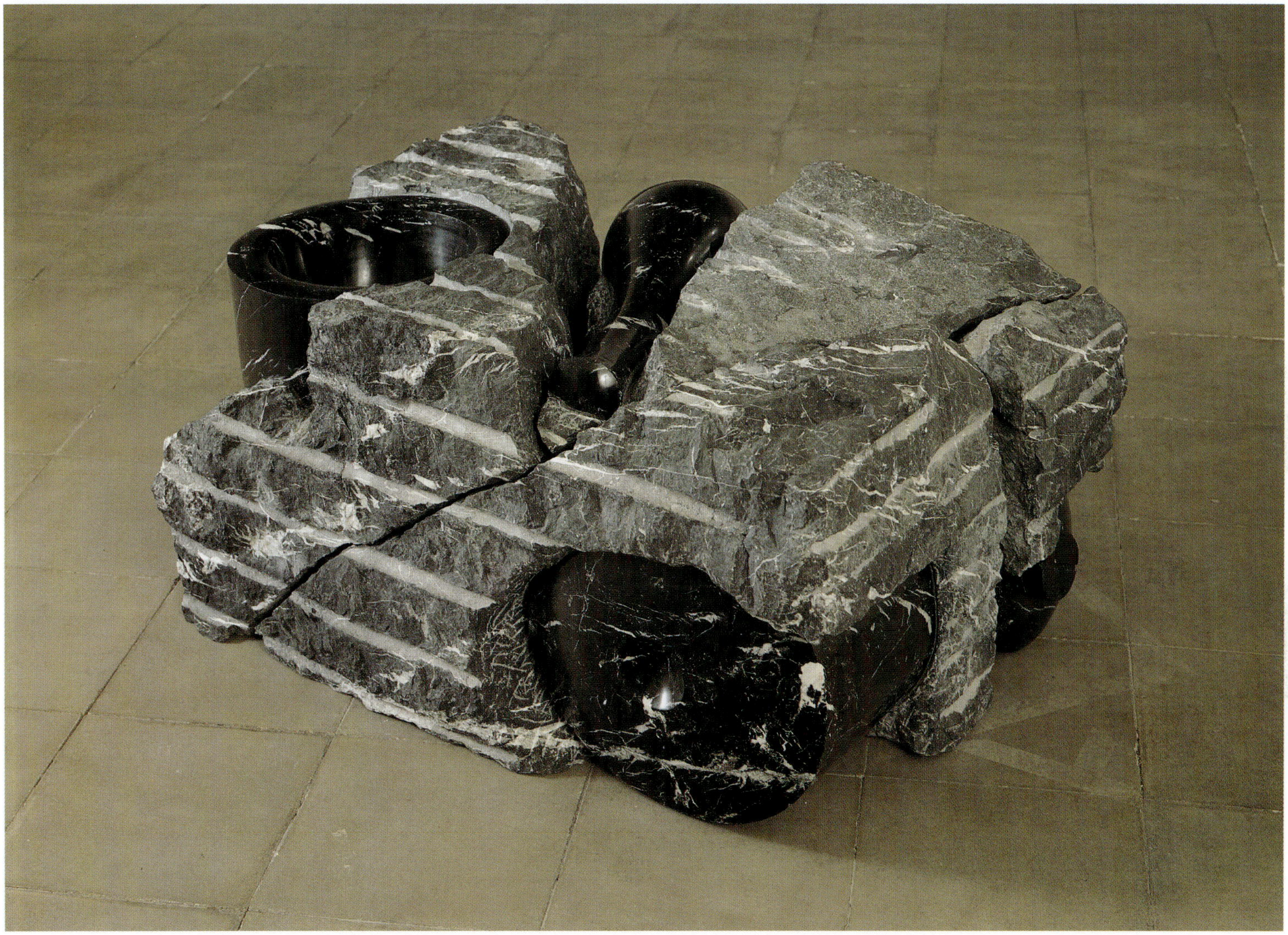

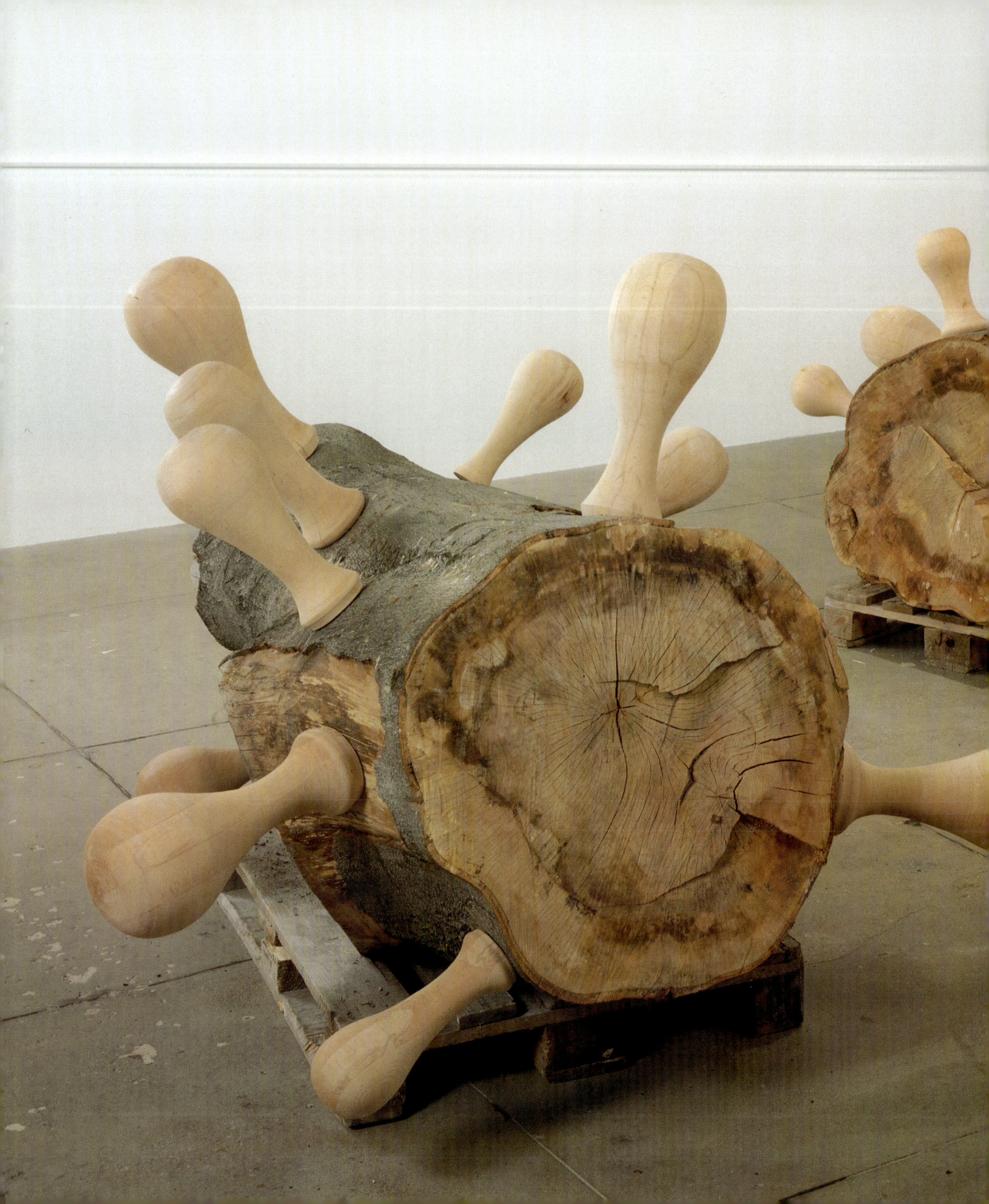

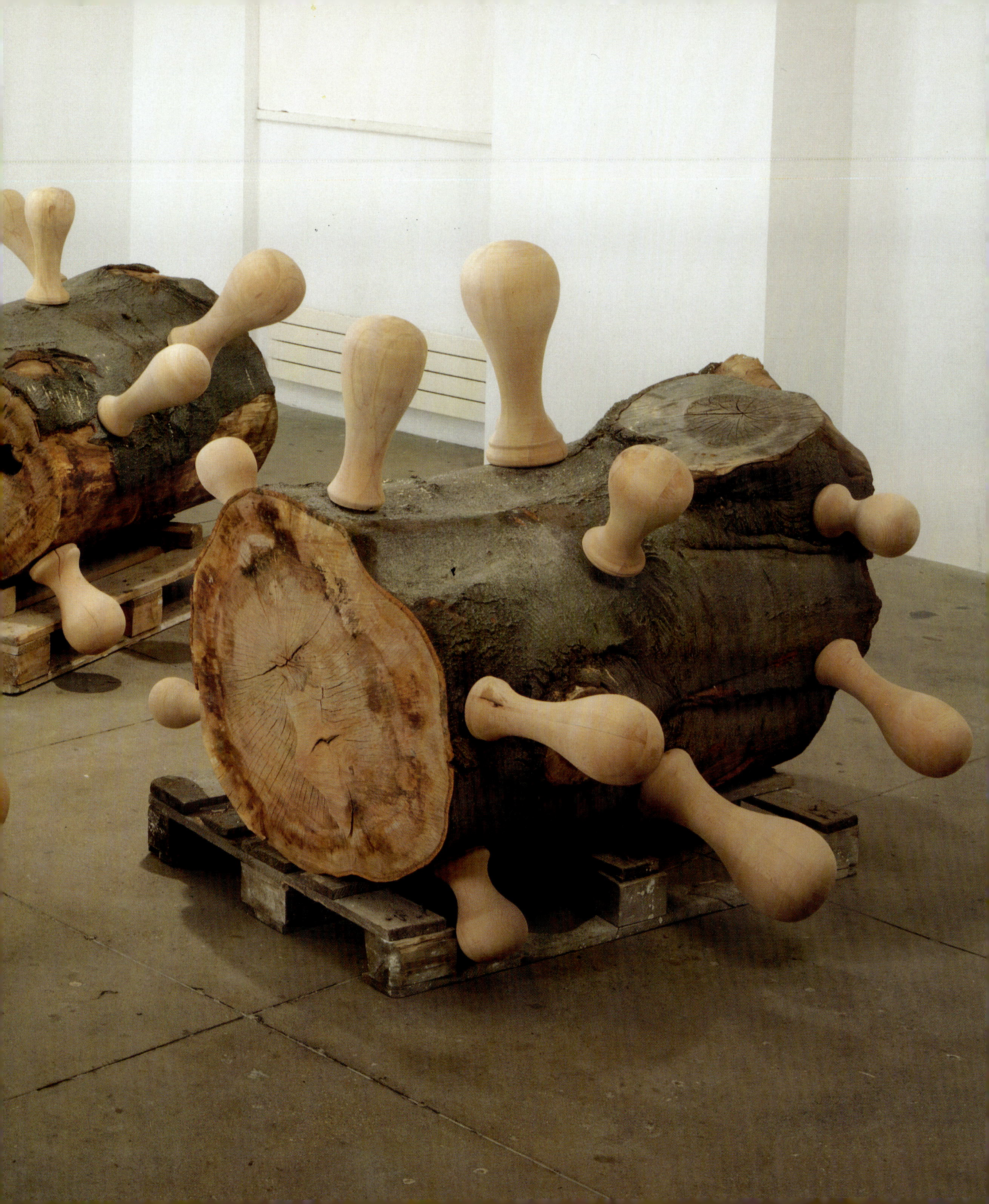

We are actually only at the very beginning. What if sculpture is just starting now? What if ideas about making sculpture are not about making some sort of adornment for the world, but about an investigative medium in a direct sense. Sculpture can bring about changes of all sorts in all areas of human life, I don't necessarily think there has to be some "good" moral quality in the working process. I feel one has to be free to make a lot of mistakes, as many as it takes for a new insight. I make a lot of experimental things and wreck a lot more as I'm going along.

"Extracts from an Interview with Tony Cragg in Glasgow, 24 July 1992." In *Tony Cragg. Sculpture*, exh. catalogue. Glasgow: Tramway, Centre for Contemporary Arts, 1992, pp. 5-6.

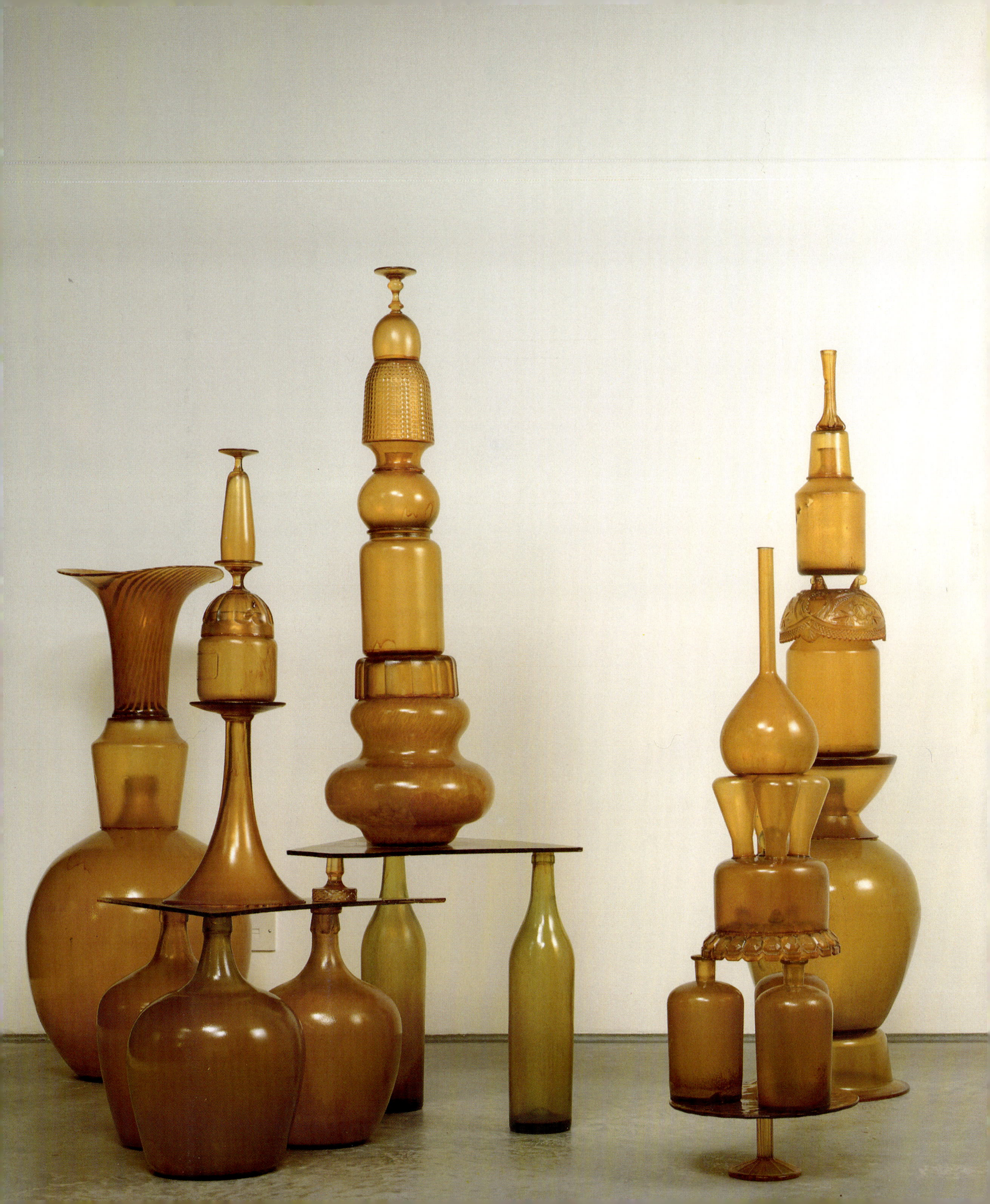

156. *Eroded Landscape*, 1992

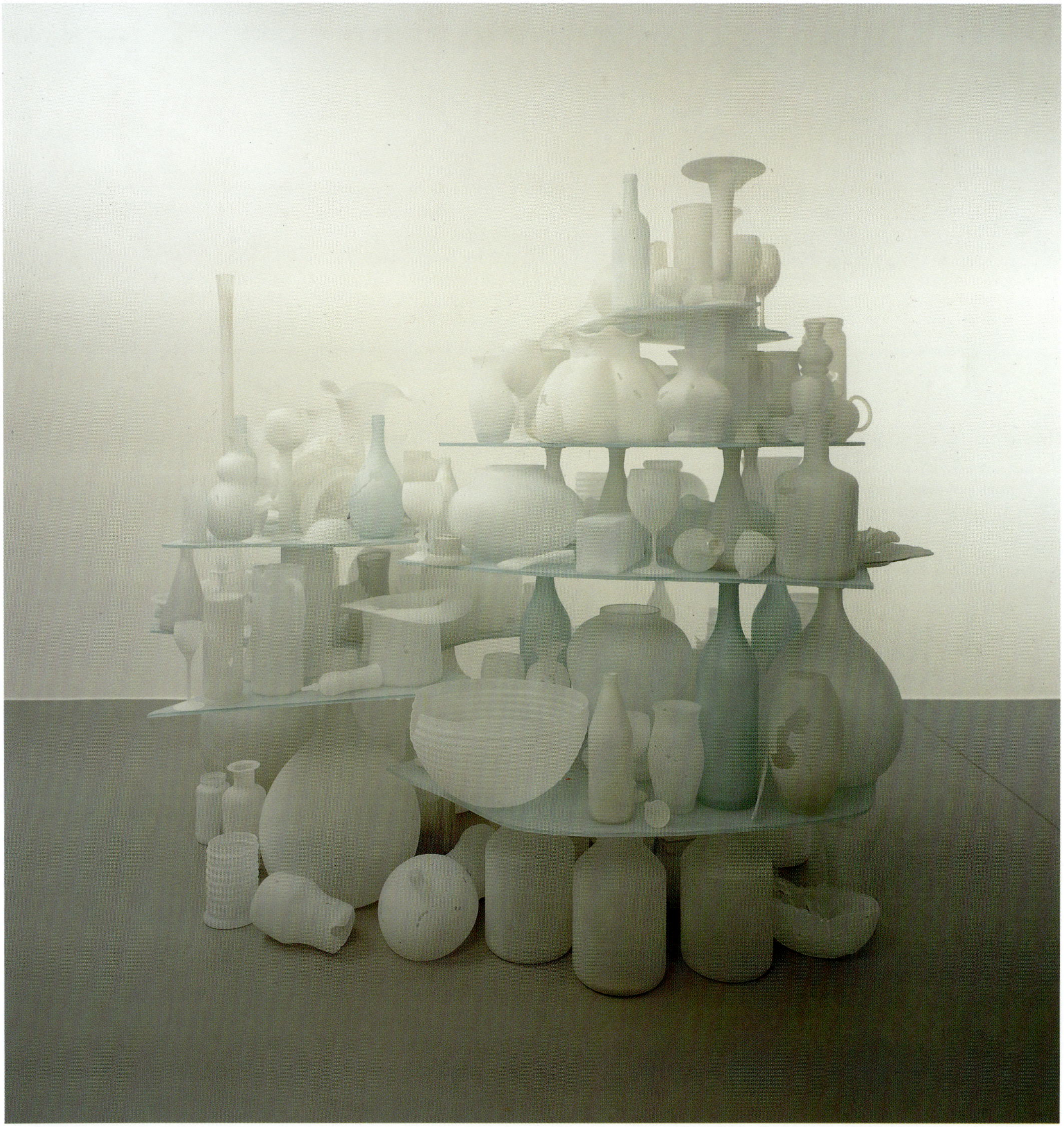

157. *Spyrogyra*, 1992

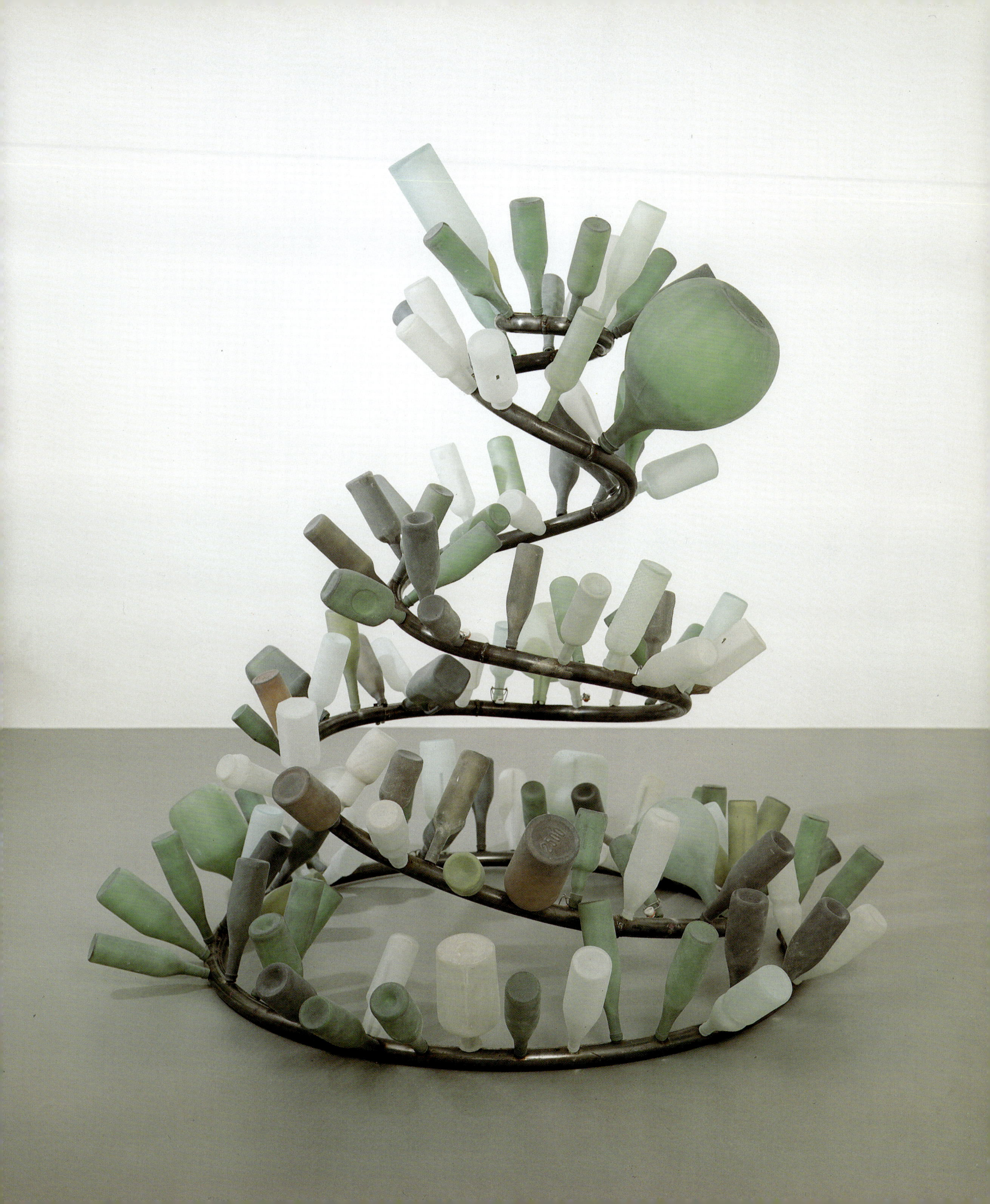

158. *Untitled*, 1990

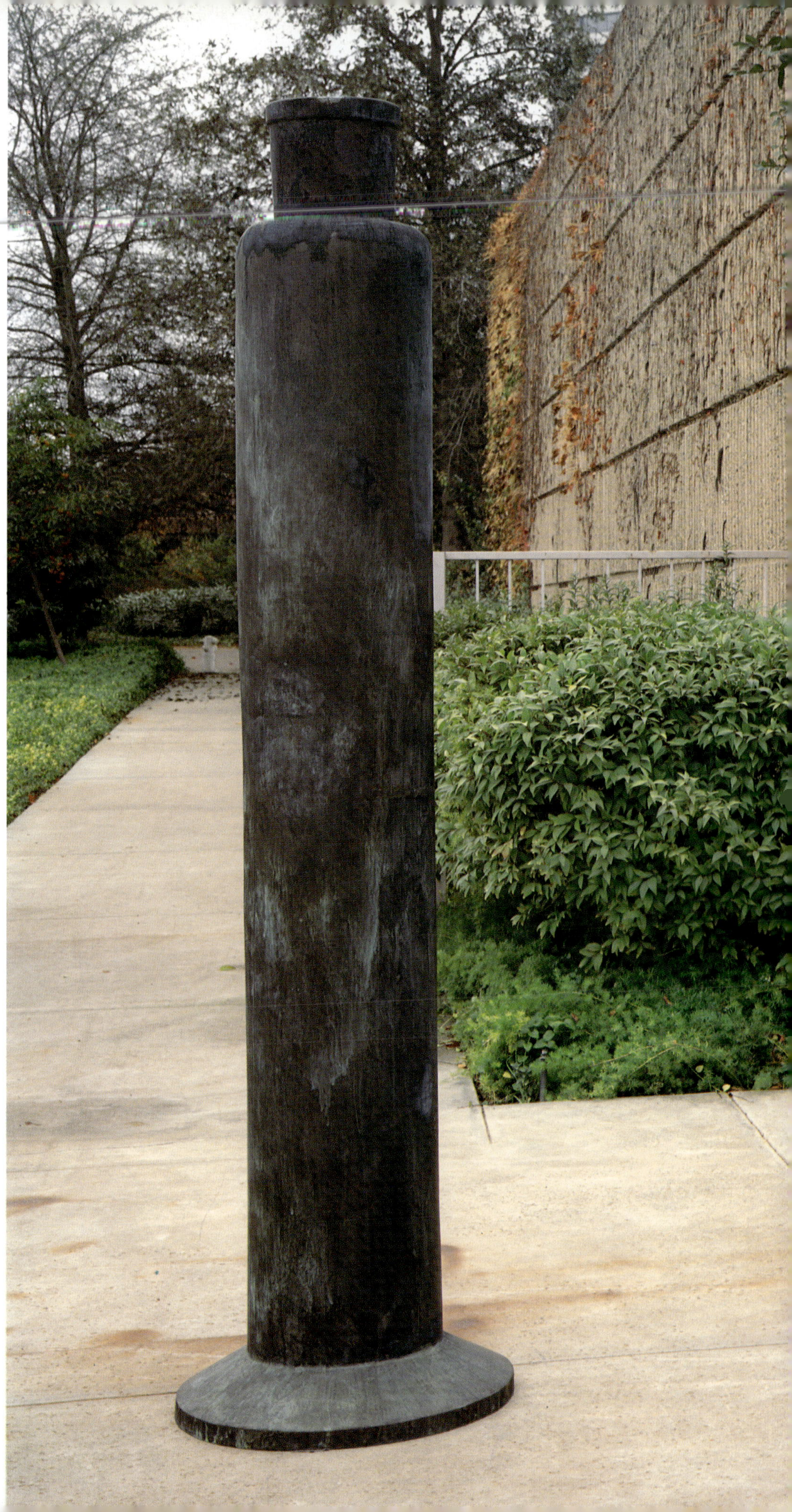

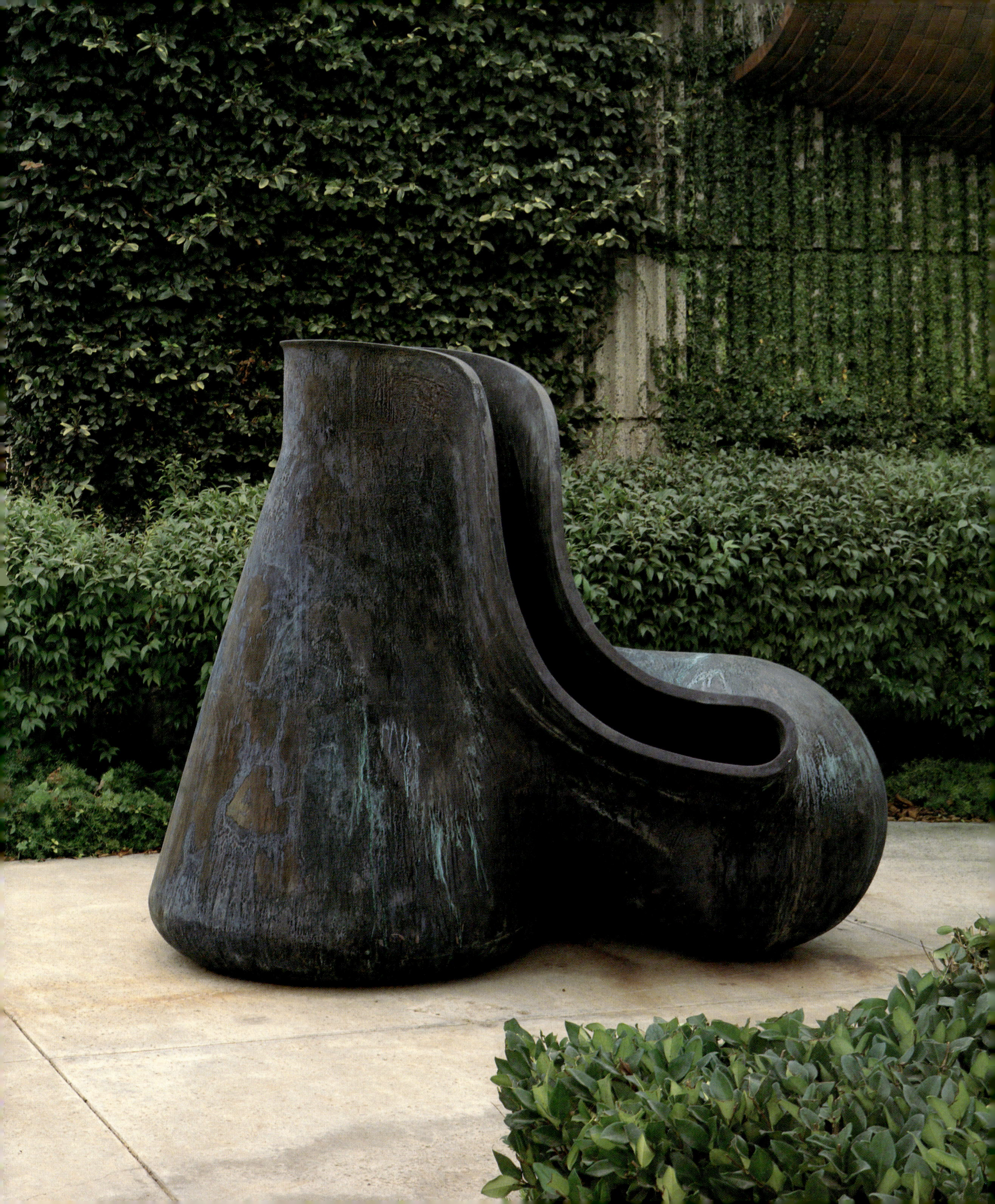

159. *Social Situation*, 1992

160. *Untitled*, 1992

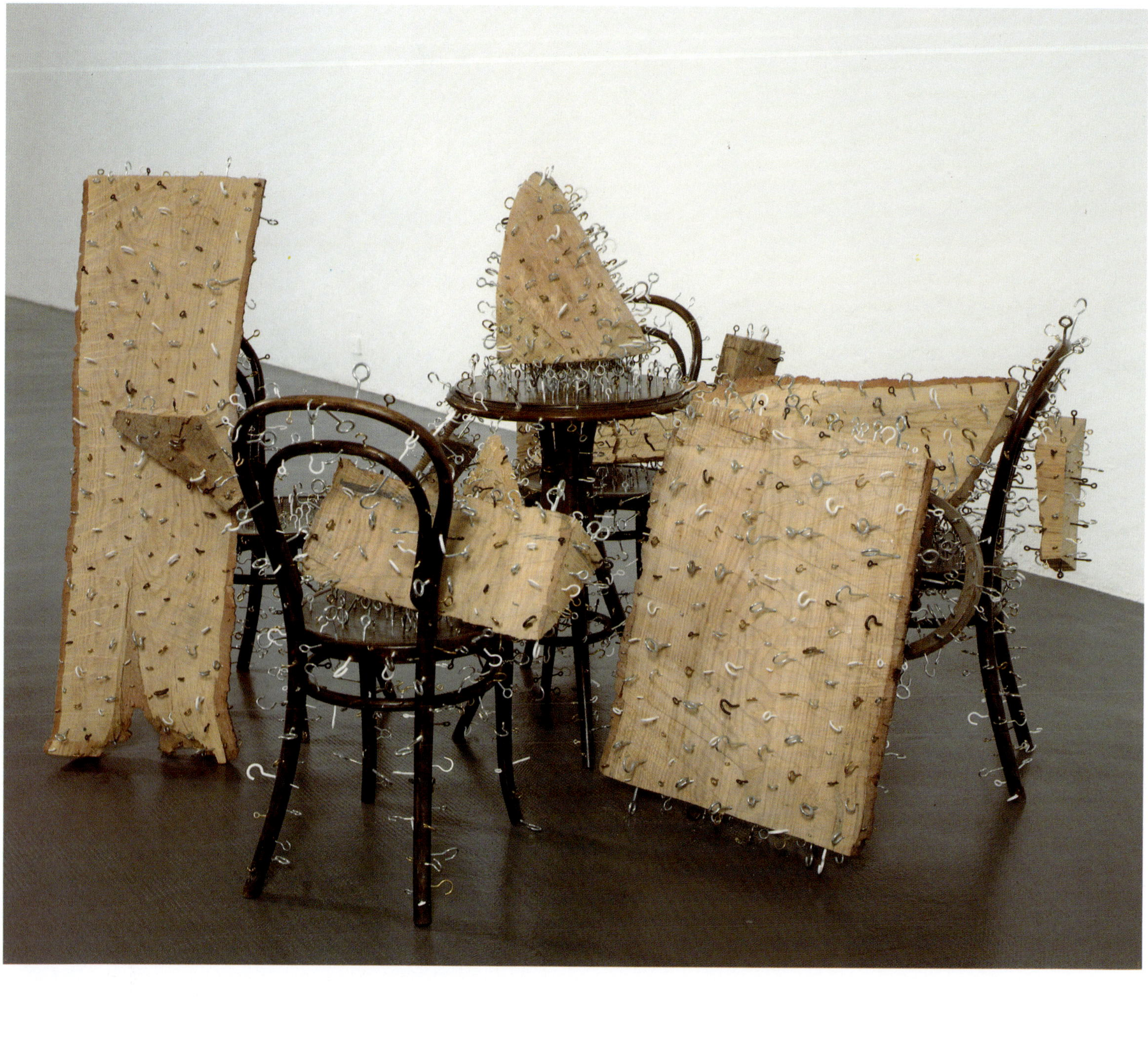

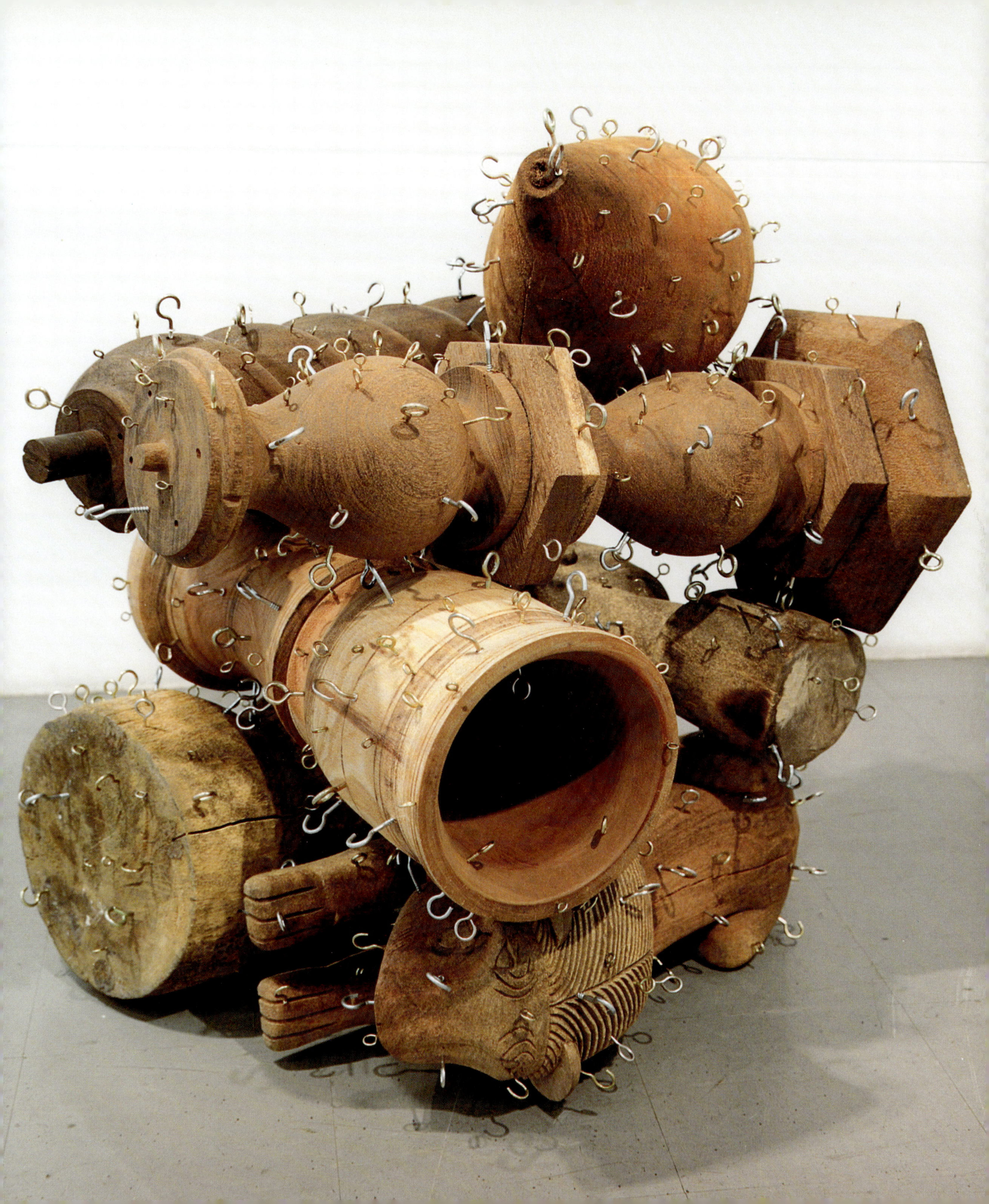

161. *Gazelle*, 1992

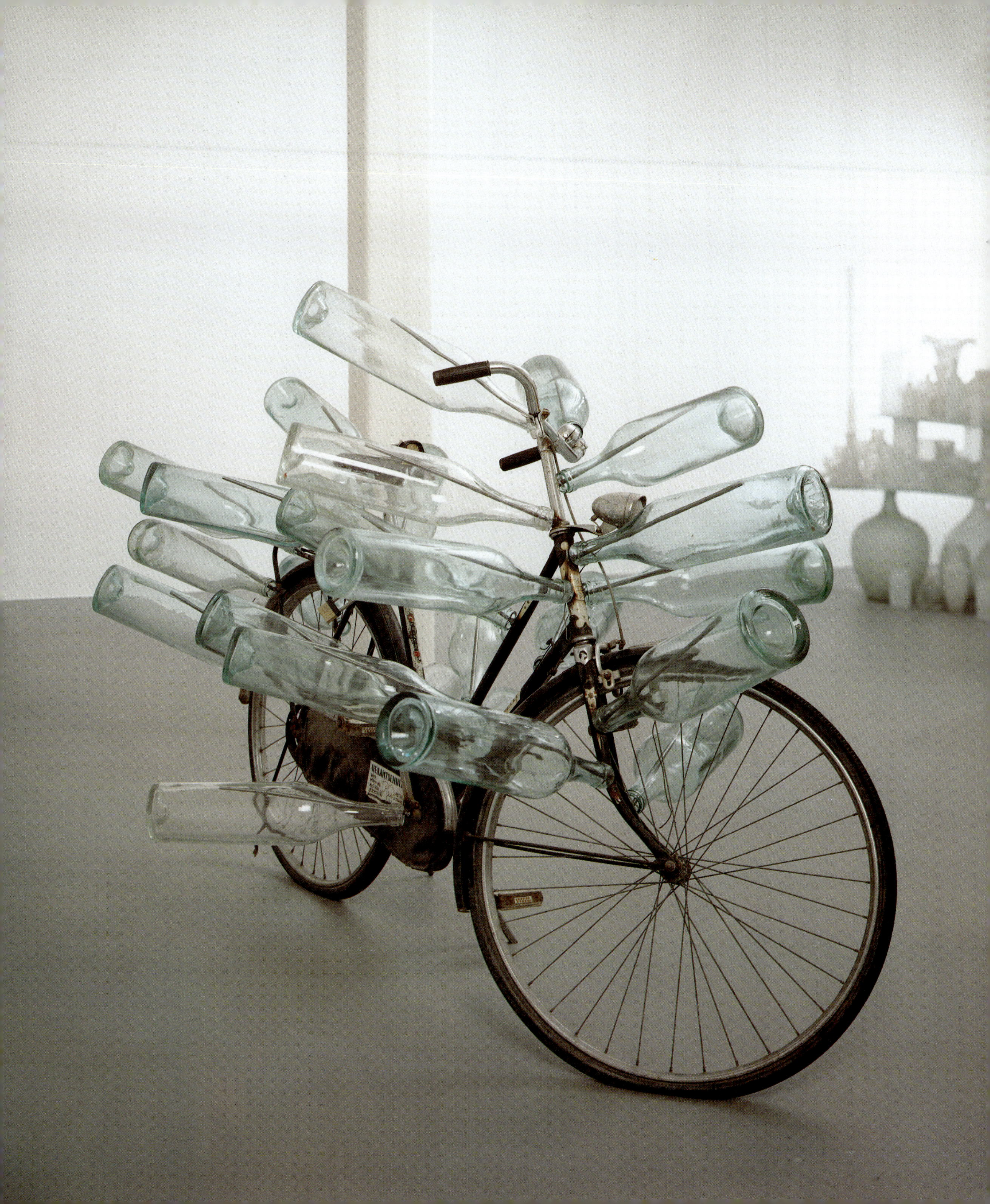

Paintings and sculptures are a very small category of objects in the world, given the mass of everything around us, and they have a very particular place in our lives. One of the important qualities that these objects have is that they don't belong to a certain productive, utilitarian power system. You look out onto the street and you say "It's awful architecture, it's a lousy design, it's awful media everywhere". So we're confronted with all these institutionally decided cultural things around us, and it is already what I call this terrible sinking down of any kind of quality and loss of authenticity.

"Extracts from an Interview with Tony Cragg in Glasgow, 24 July 1992." In *Tony Cragg. Sculpture*, exh. catalogue. Glasgow: Tramway, Centre for Contemporary Arts, 1992, p. 6.

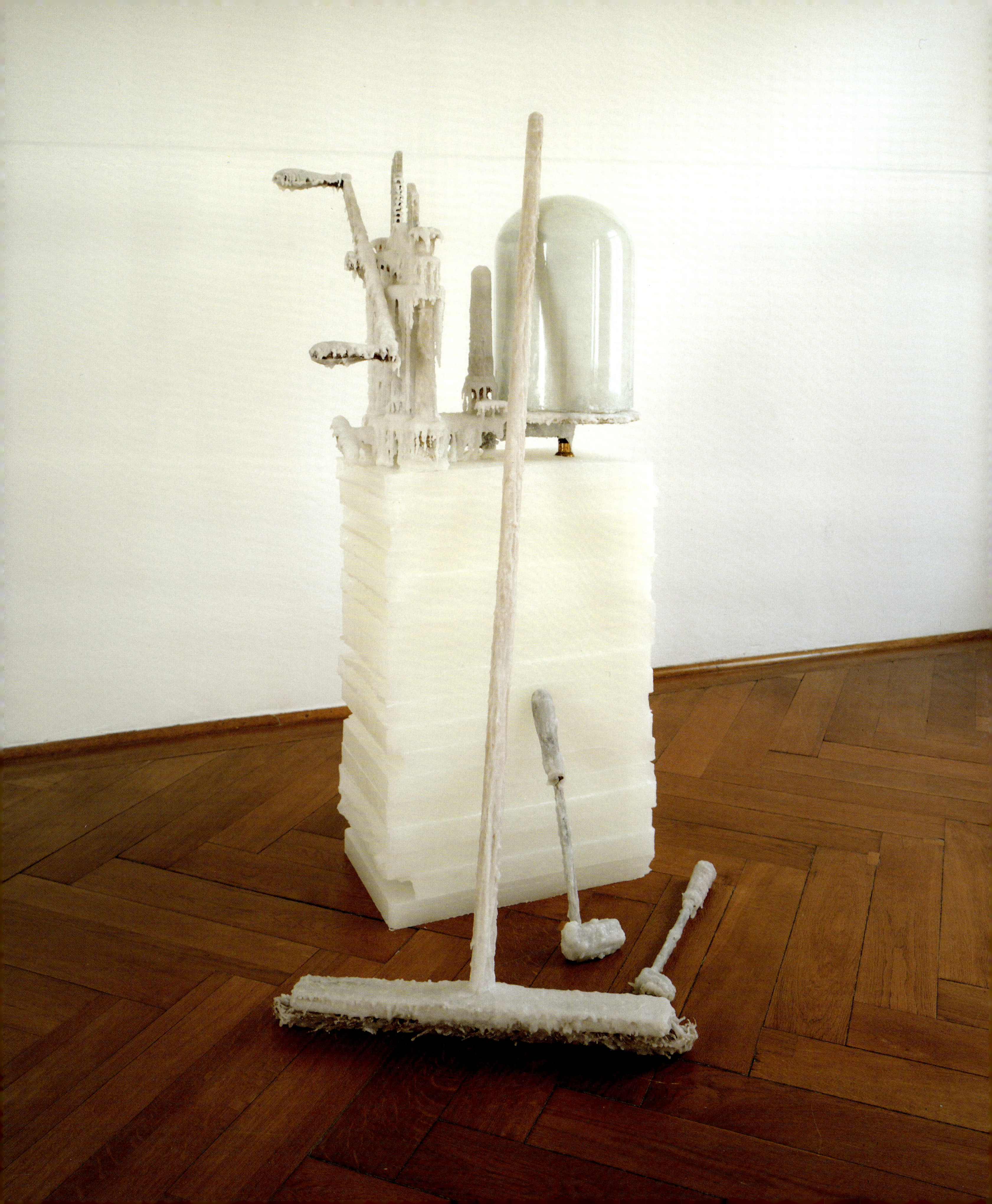

163. *Re-Forming*, 1992

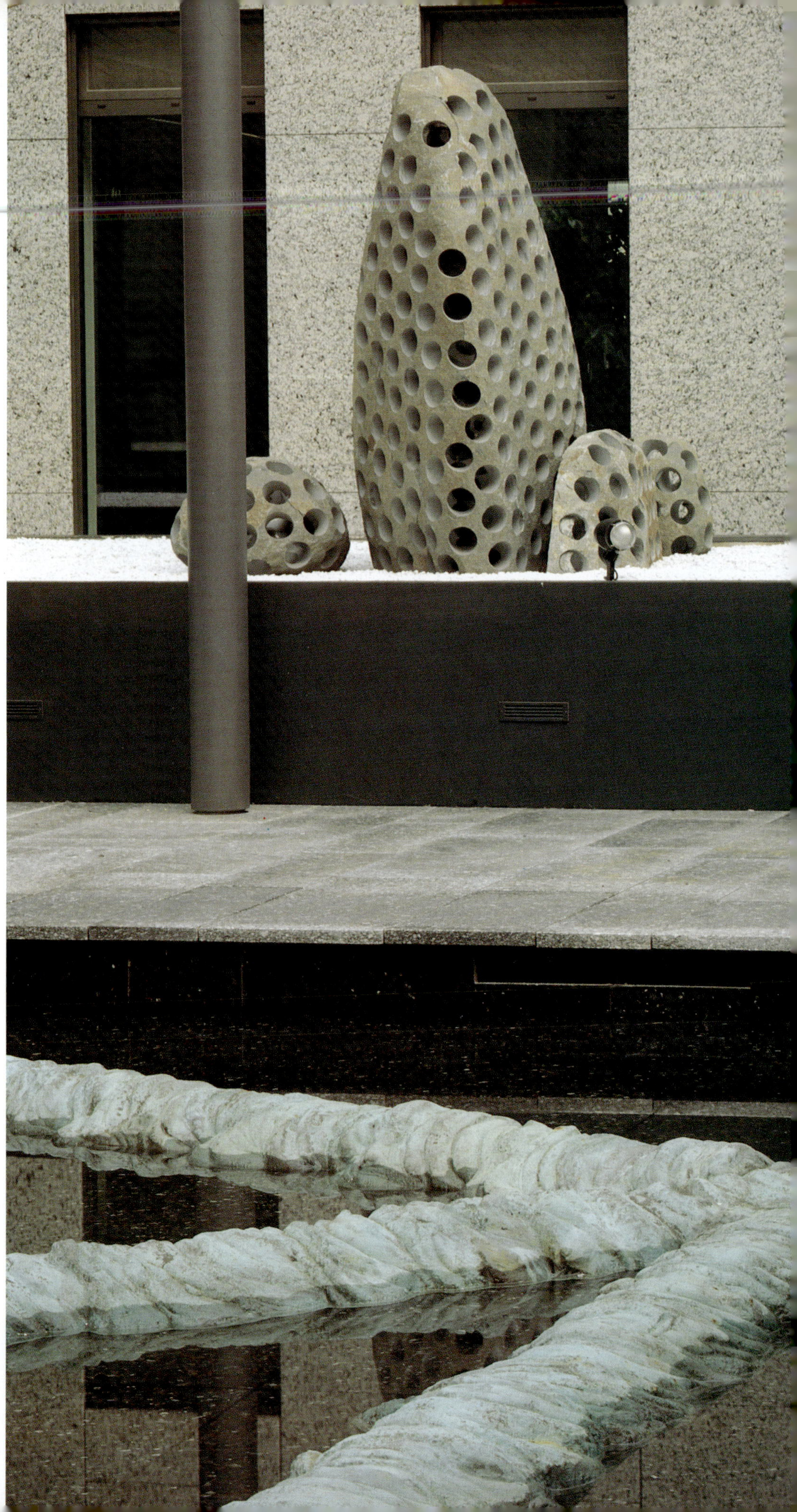

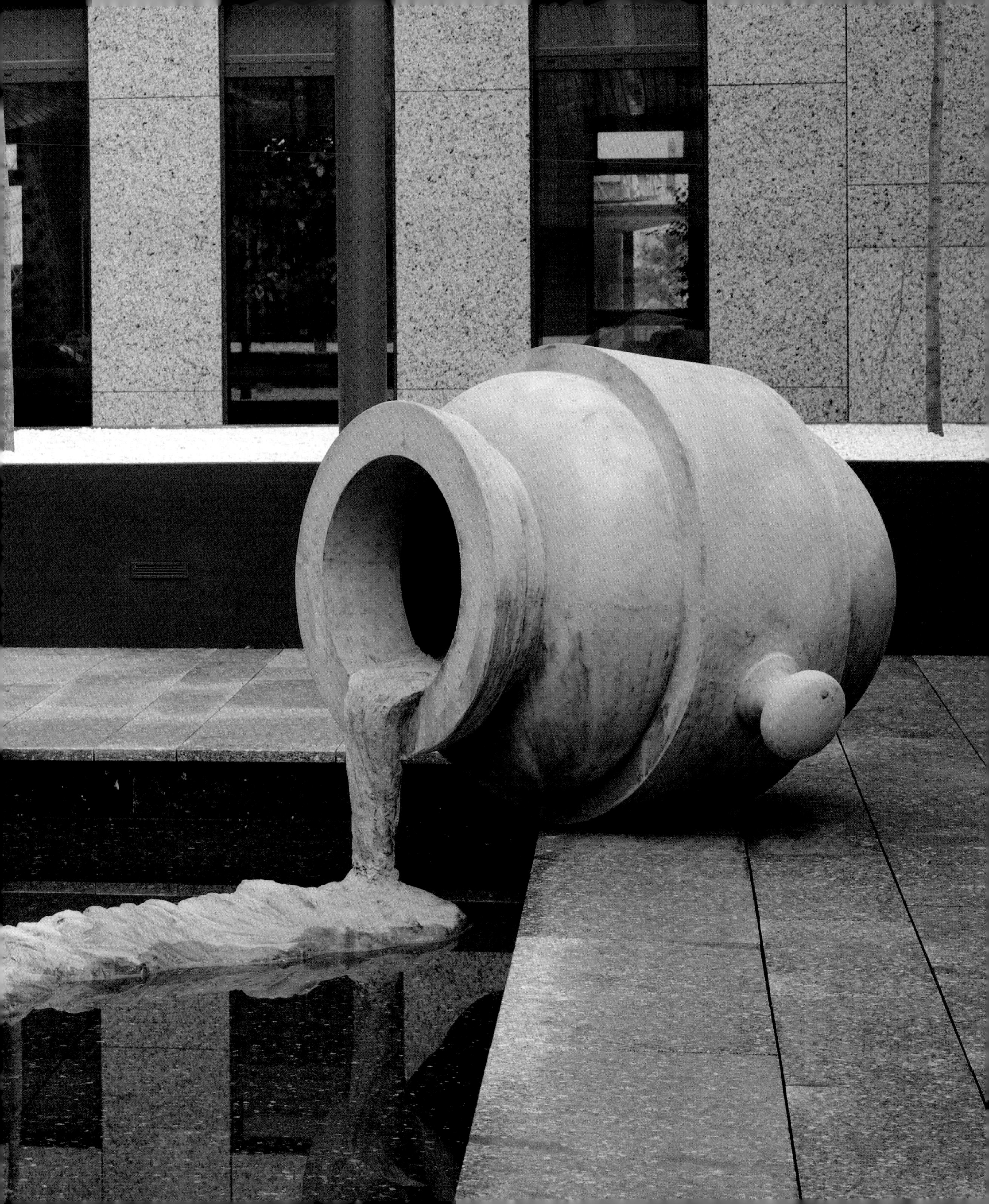

164. *Our Bolders*, 1992

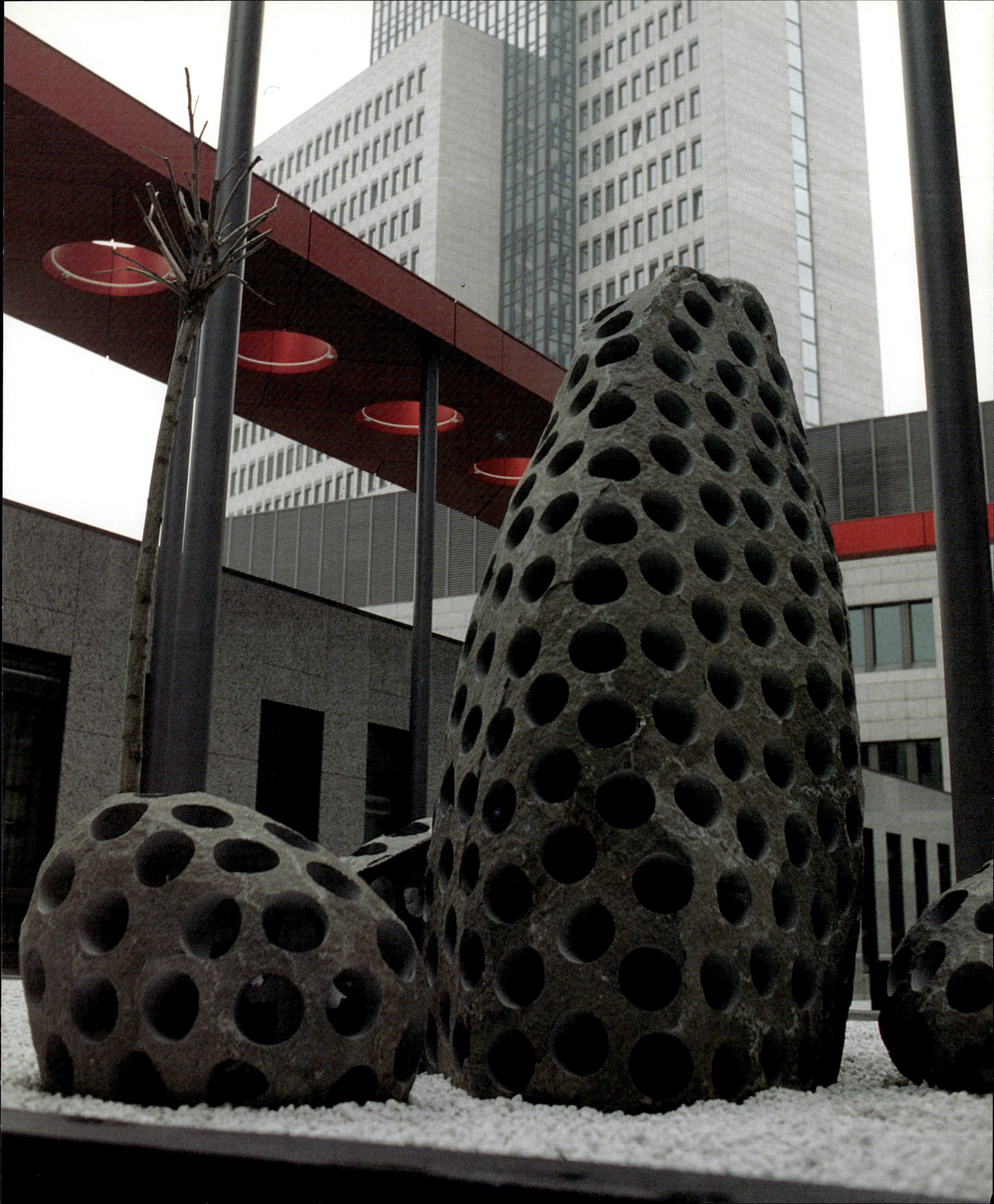

165. *Two Rivers*, 1992

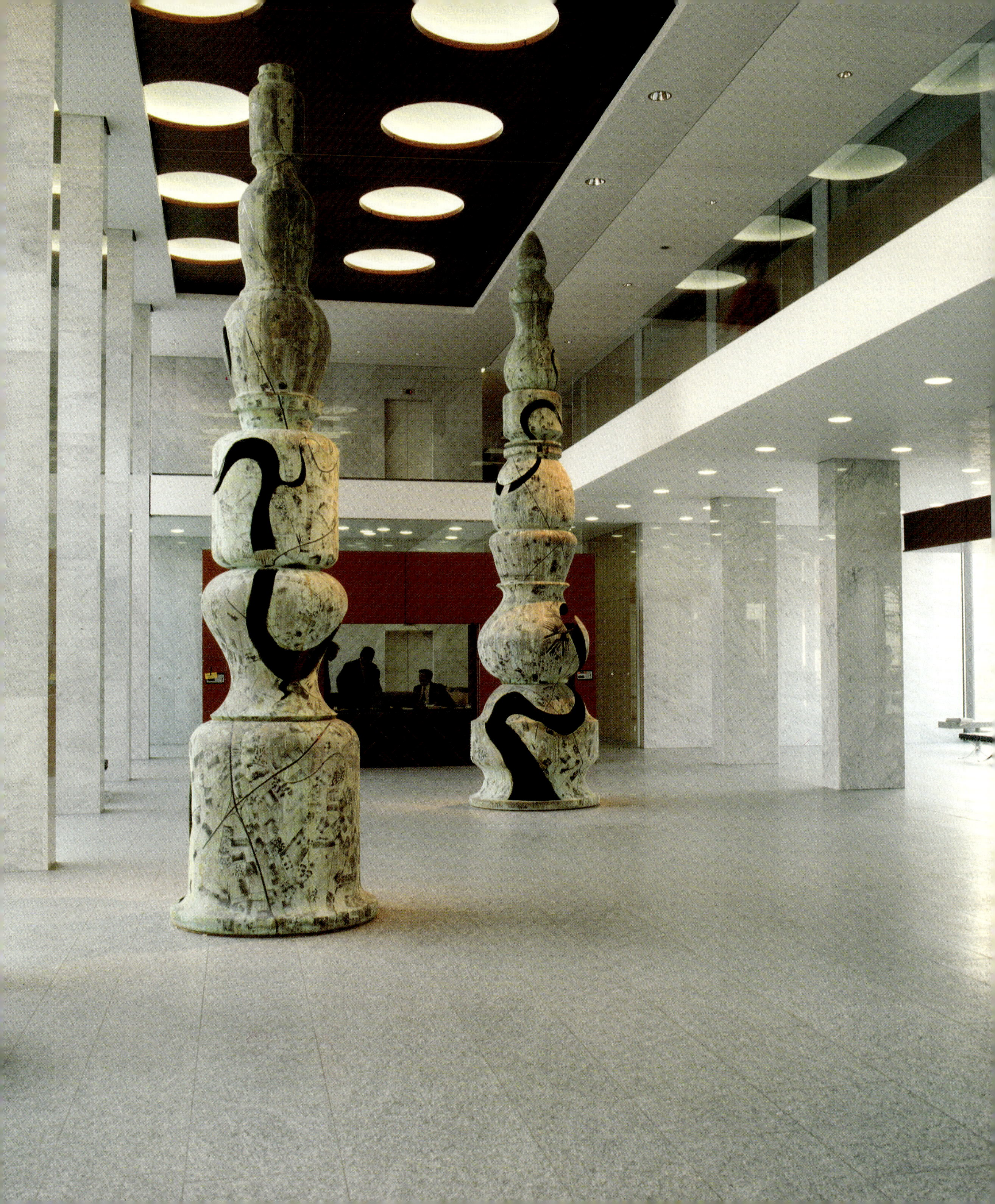

166. *Emergence*, 1992

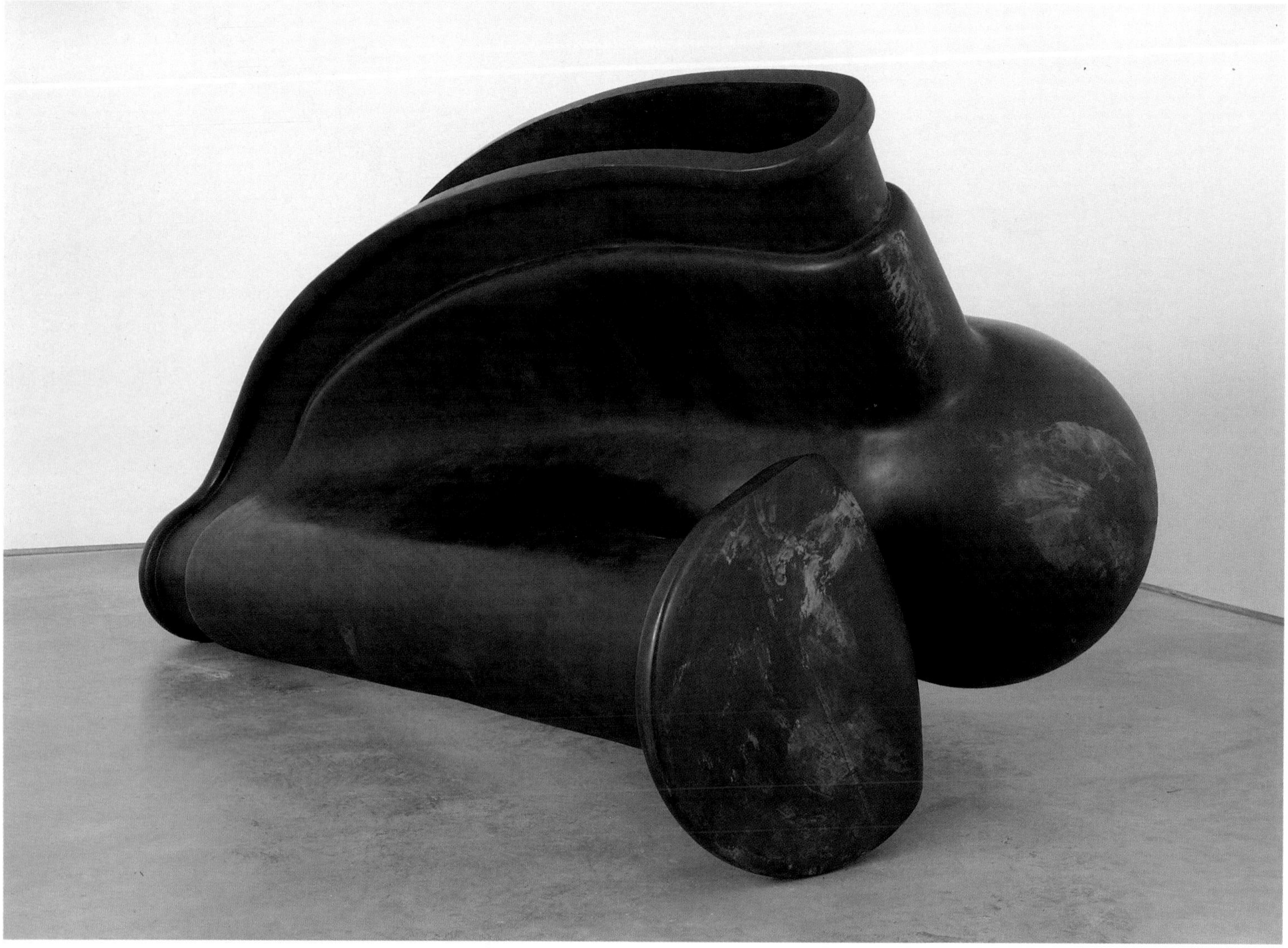

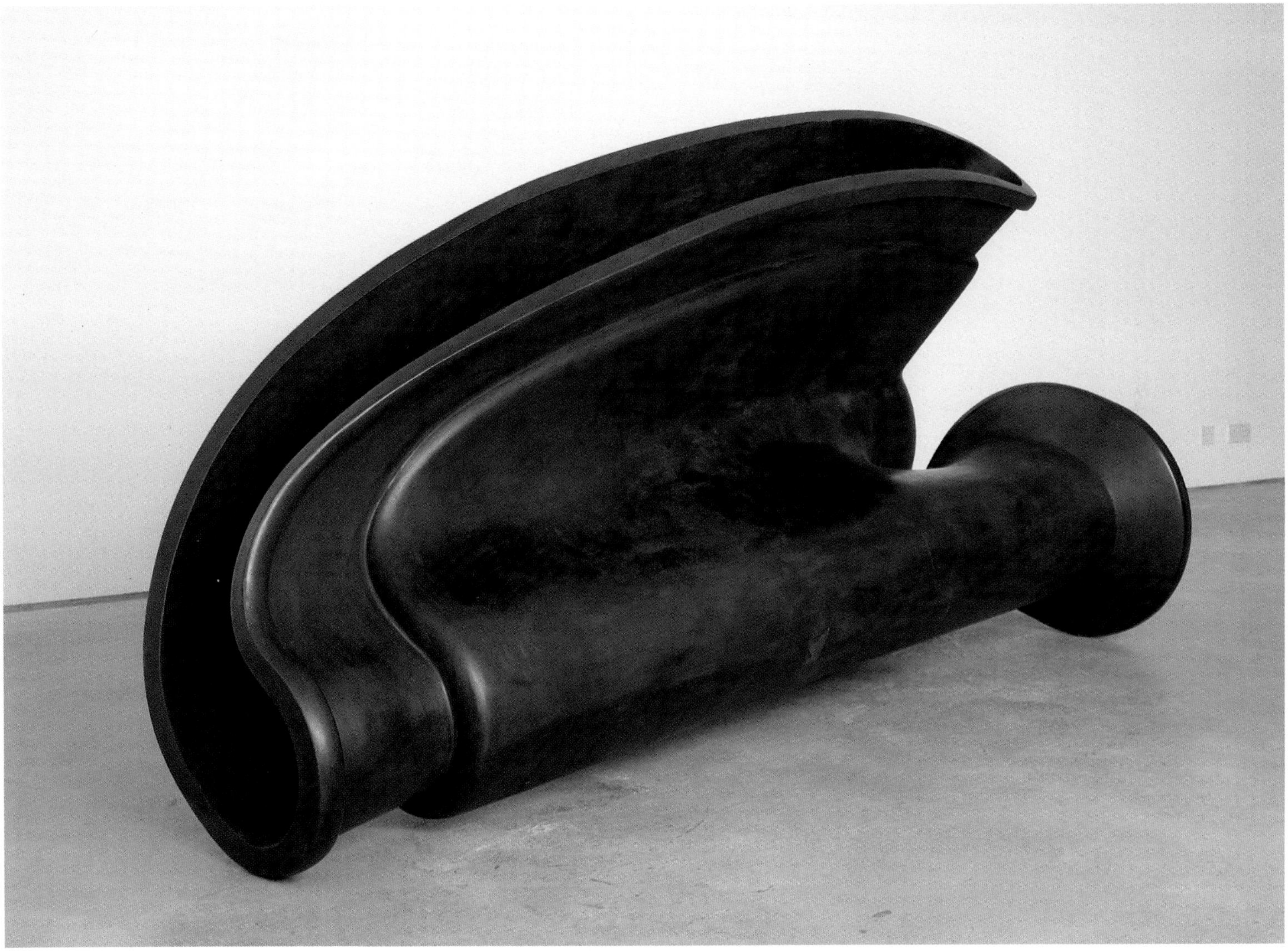

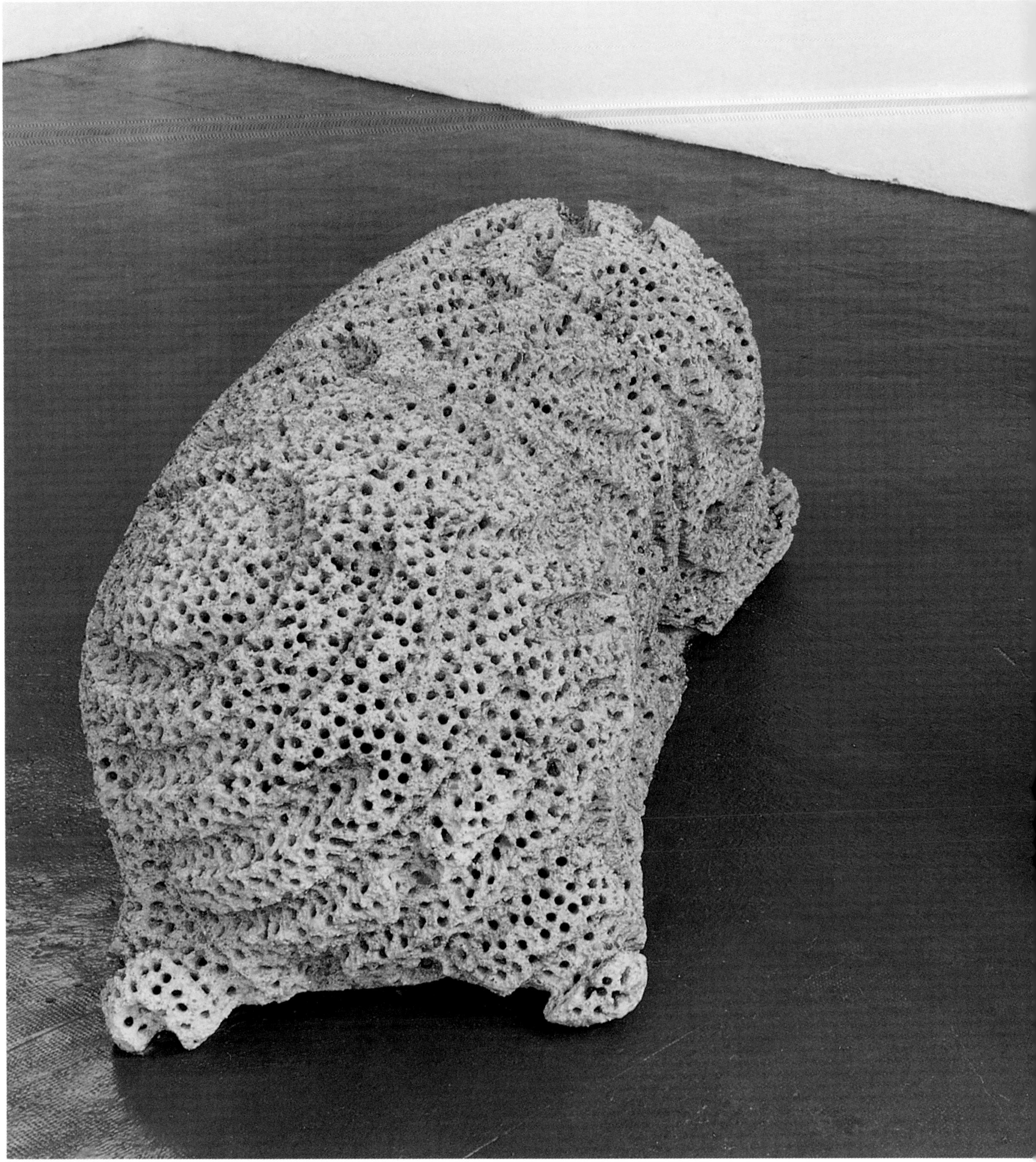

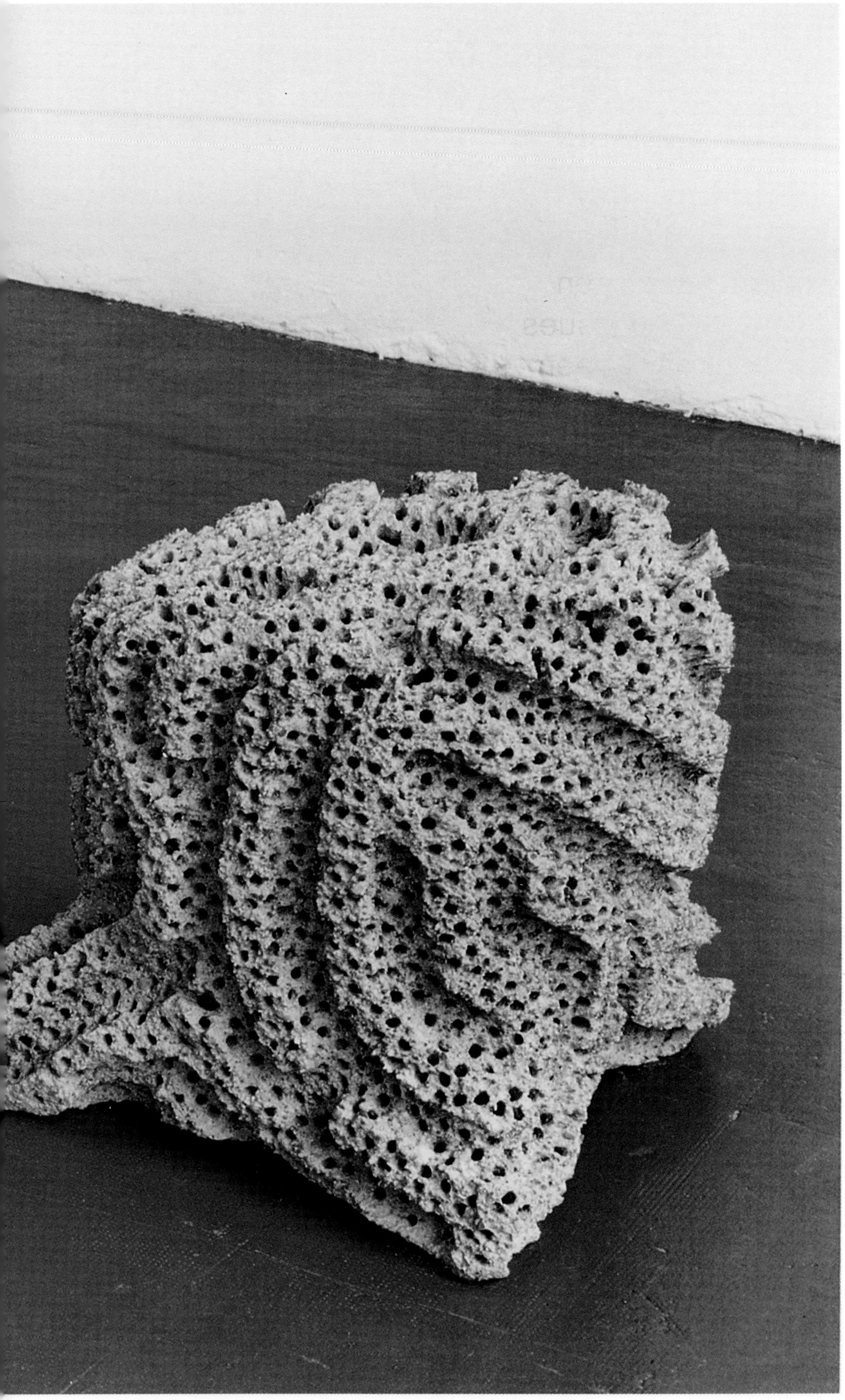

167. *Invertebrated Friends*, 1992

As formal possibilities many things have been named. Also, in terms of the content and issues about which one can make art there have been many important additions. The problem is that in a finite world there are only so many possibilities and at the moment it seems to me somewhat irrelevant to discover a new material to make art with. It still happens and it is nice when it happens but it doesn't seem a prime motivation any more.

In *Tony Cragg: In Camera*. 's-Hertogenbosch/Eindhoven: European Ceramics Work Centre/Stedelijk van Abbemuseum, 1993, p. 12.

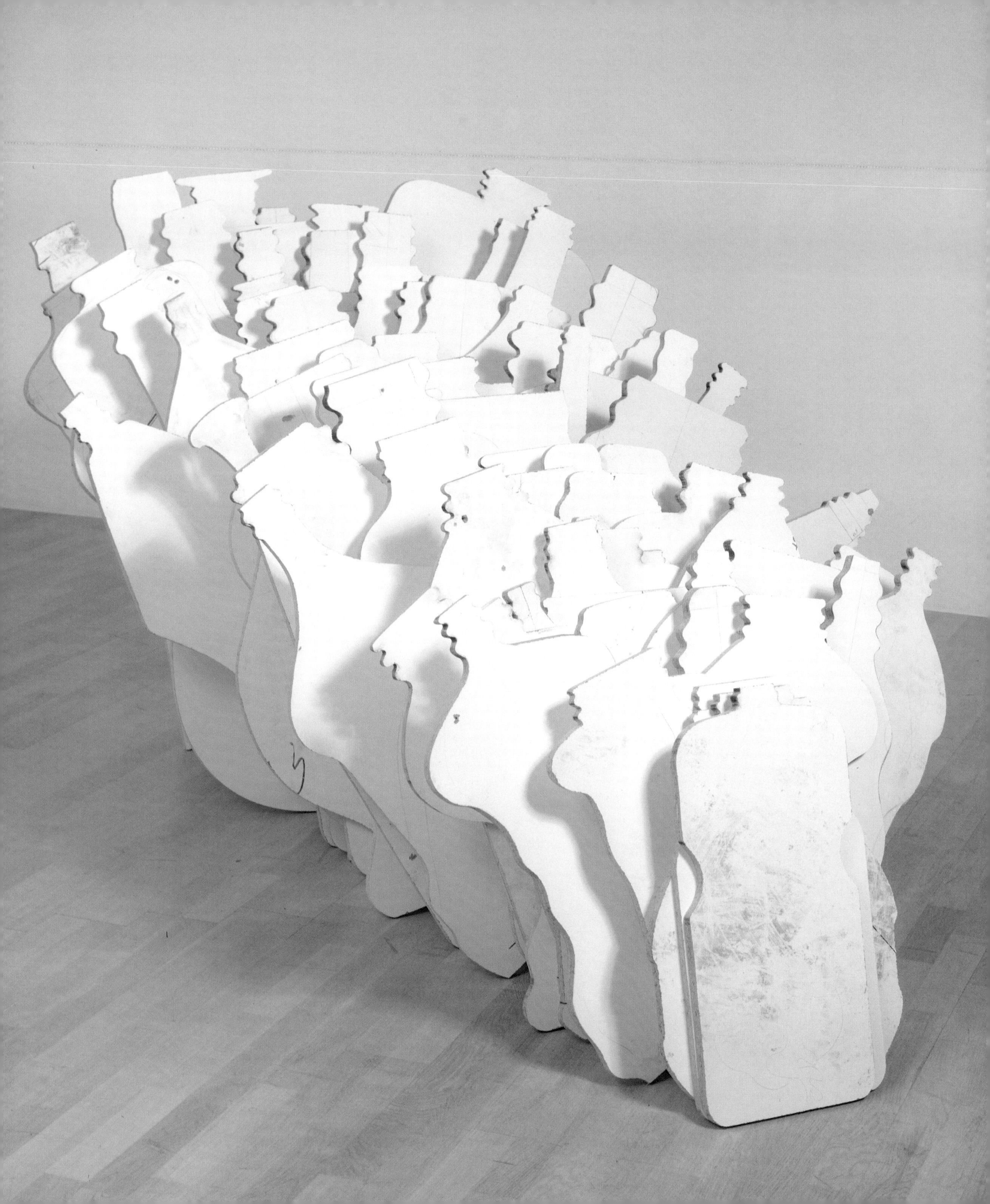

169. *In Camera*, 1993

170. *In Camera*, 1993

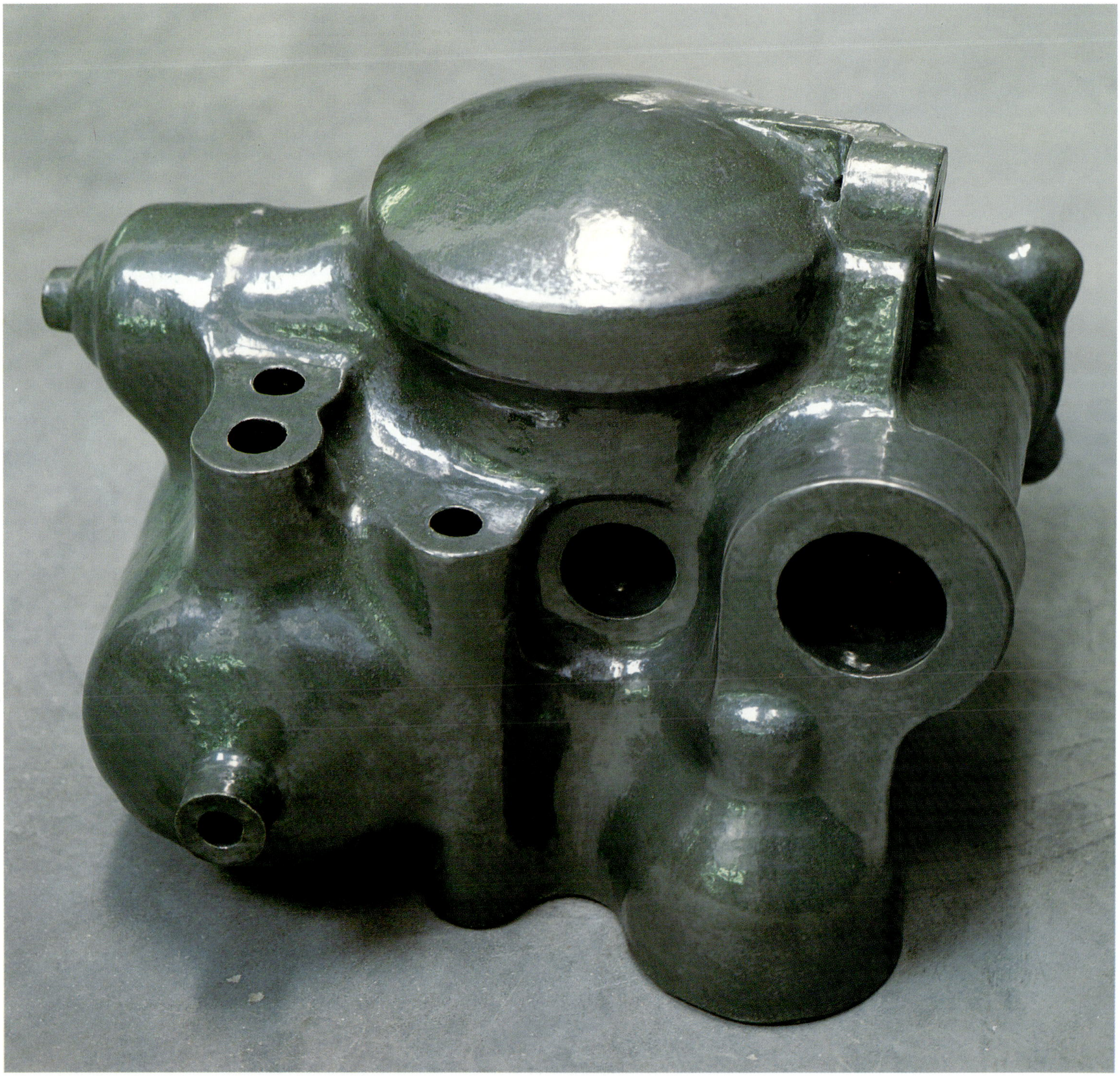

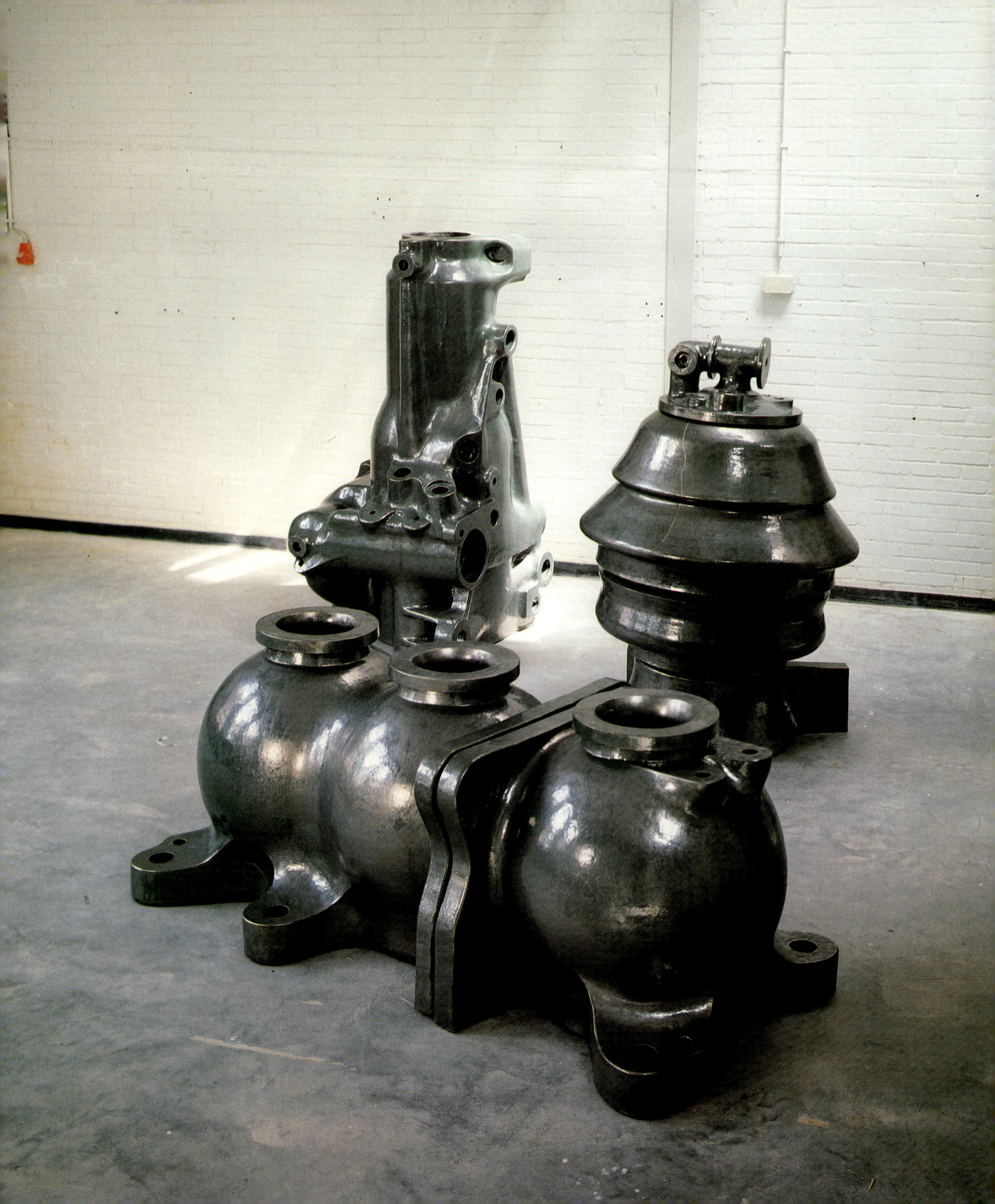

171. *Glass Hybrids*, 1992

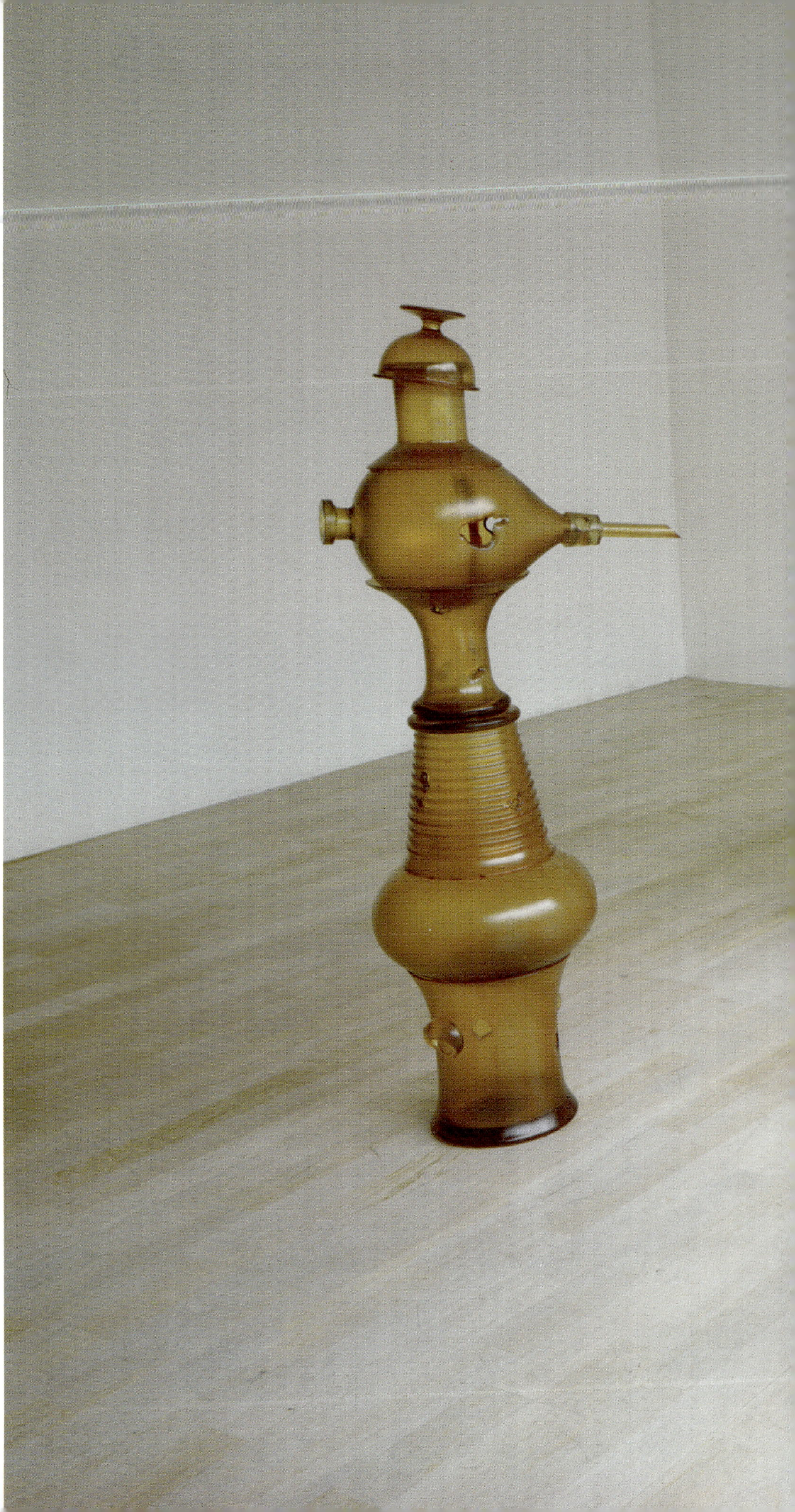

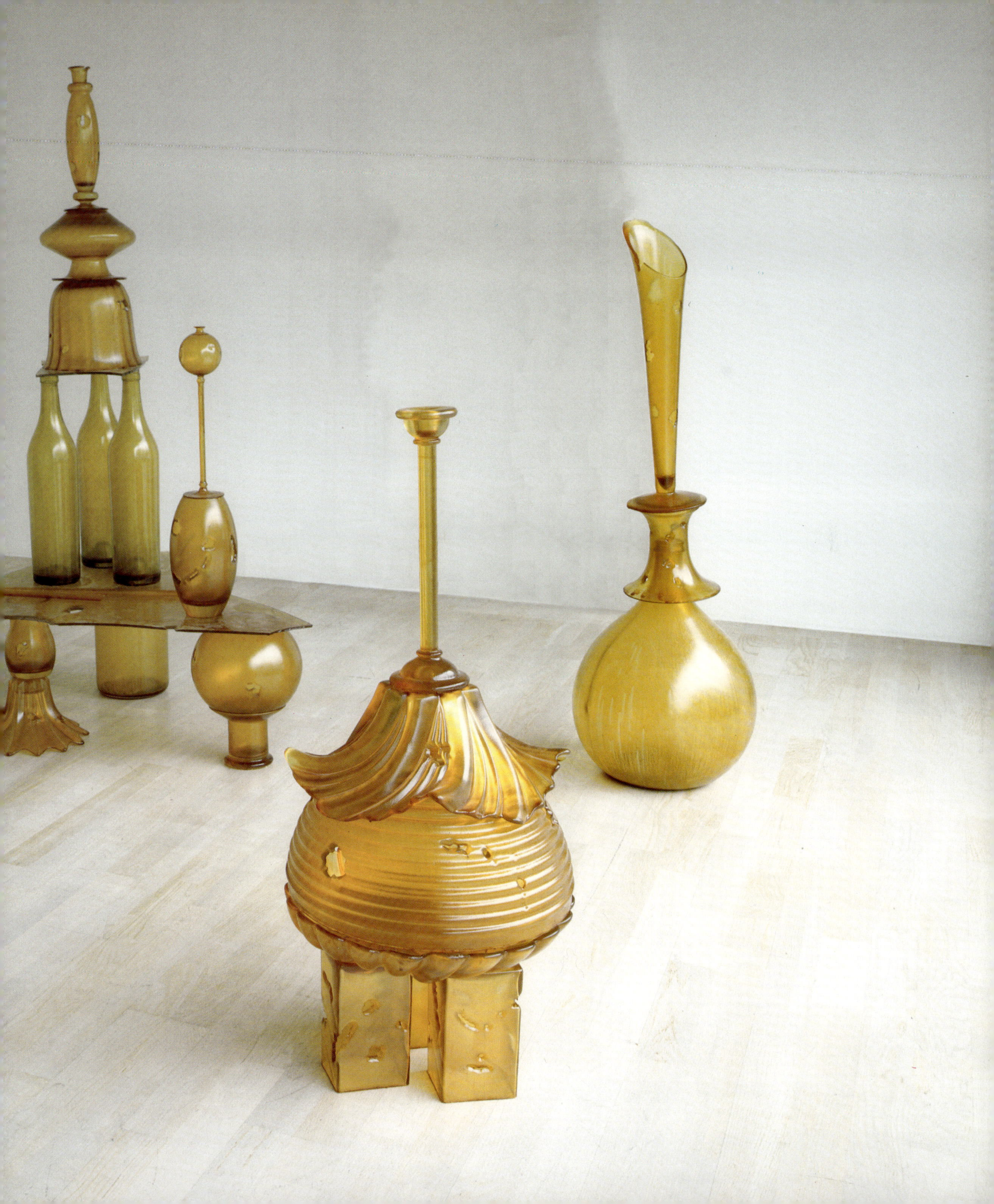

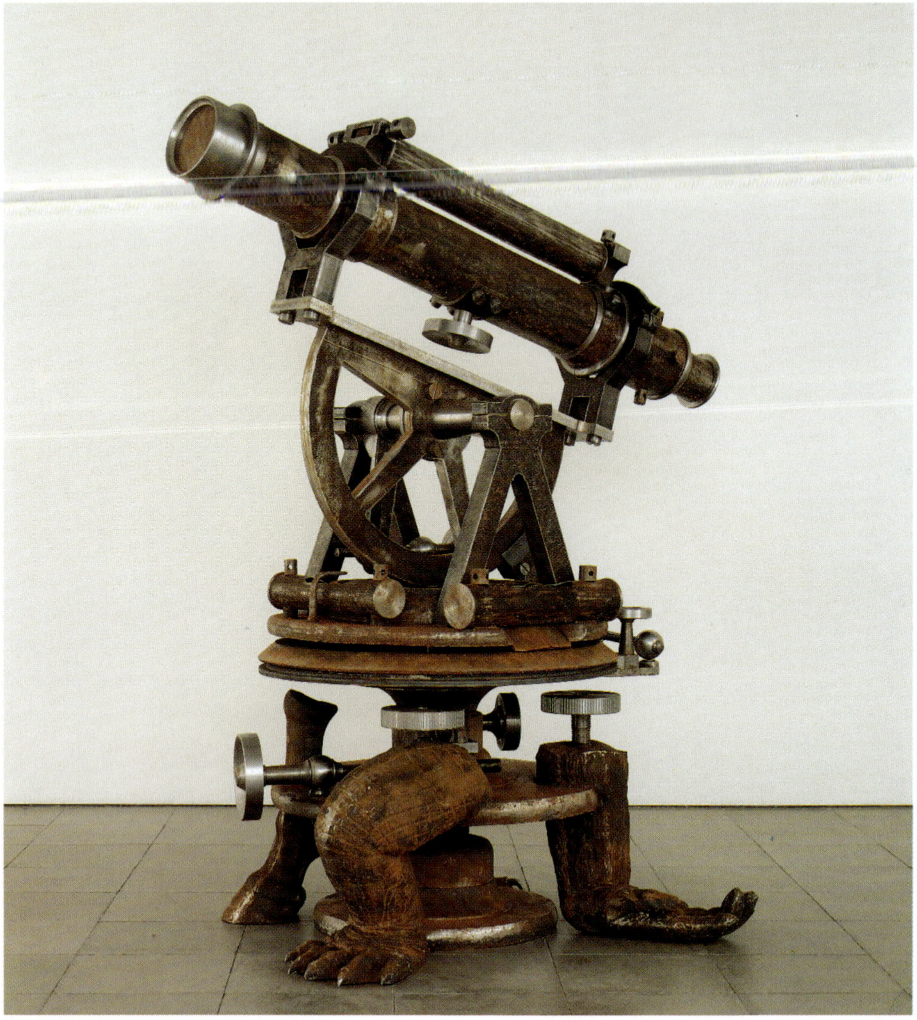

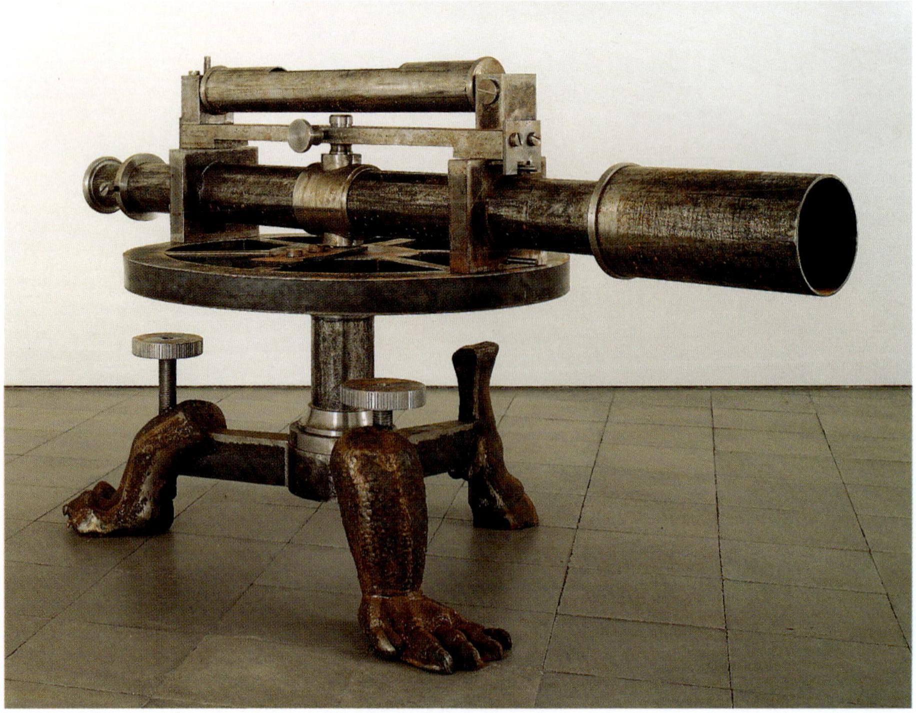

172. *Terris Novalis*, 1992

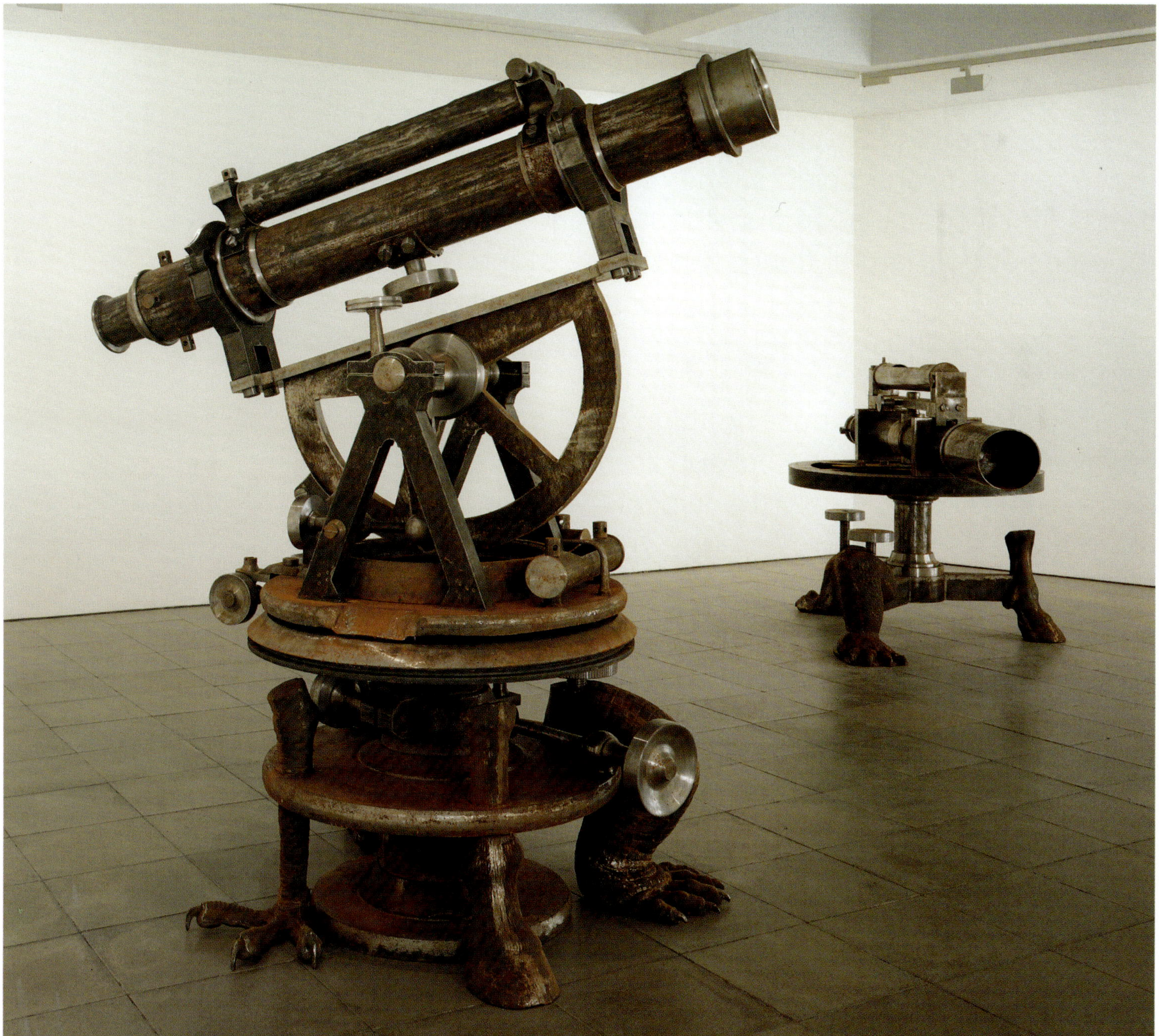

My concerns and interests lie in the objects and materials that we produce, that mankind has produced, apart from the natural world, to try and find out something about our relationship with these materials and objects. The reason for doing that is simply because in our language and our thoughts about natural things like wood, stone or fire, we have around these things a sort of balloon of information and associations. Natural things always have very substantial balloons of information around them. The thing has its physical qualities, but the balloon around contains its metaphysical qualities, the aspects we bring to that object, its history, mythology, meaning and aesthetic.

In *Tony Cragg: In Camera*. 's-Hertogenbosch/Eindhoven: European Ceramics Work Centre/Stedelijk van Abbemuseum, 1993, p. 11.

173. *Archimedes Screw*, 1993

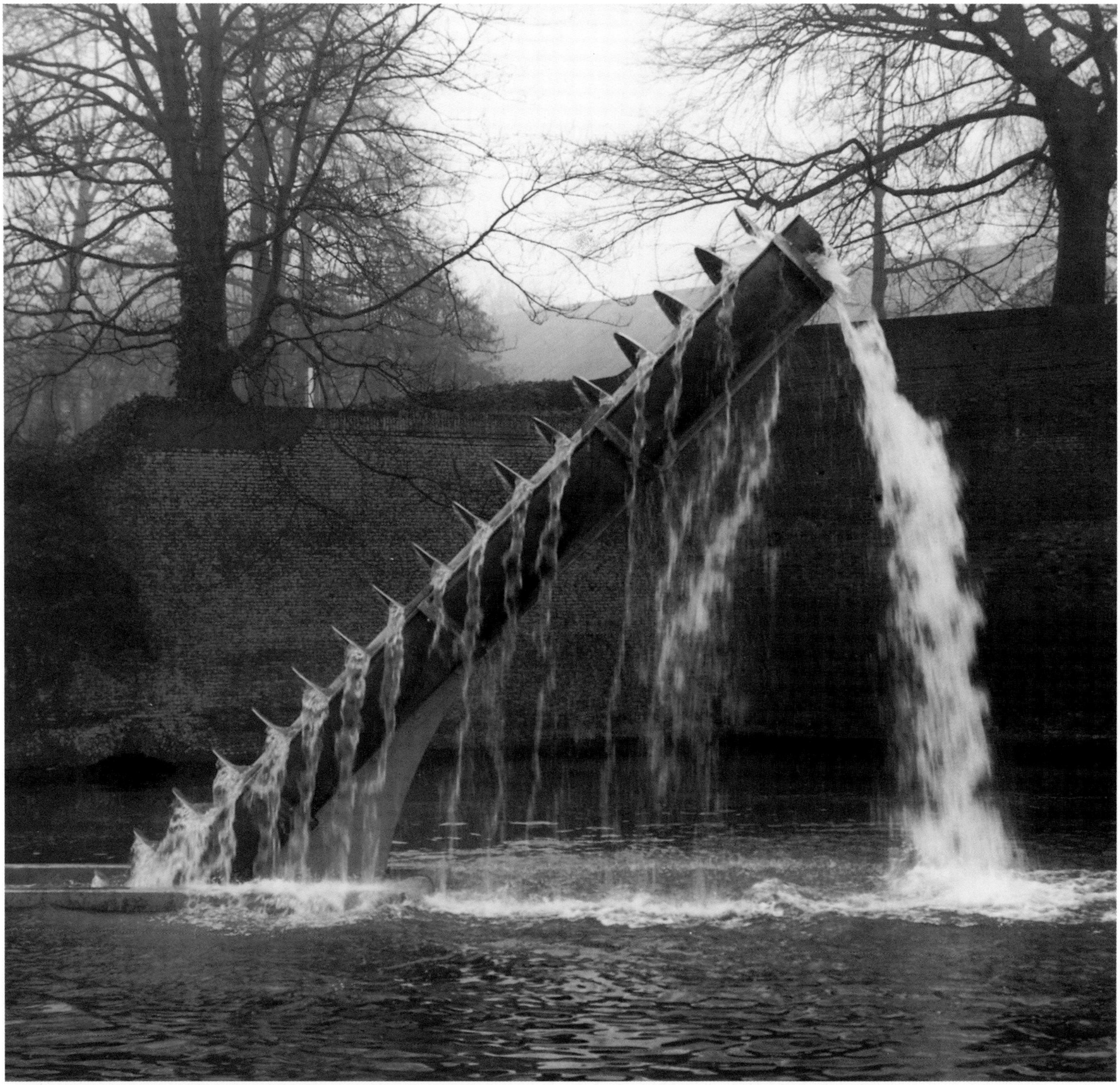

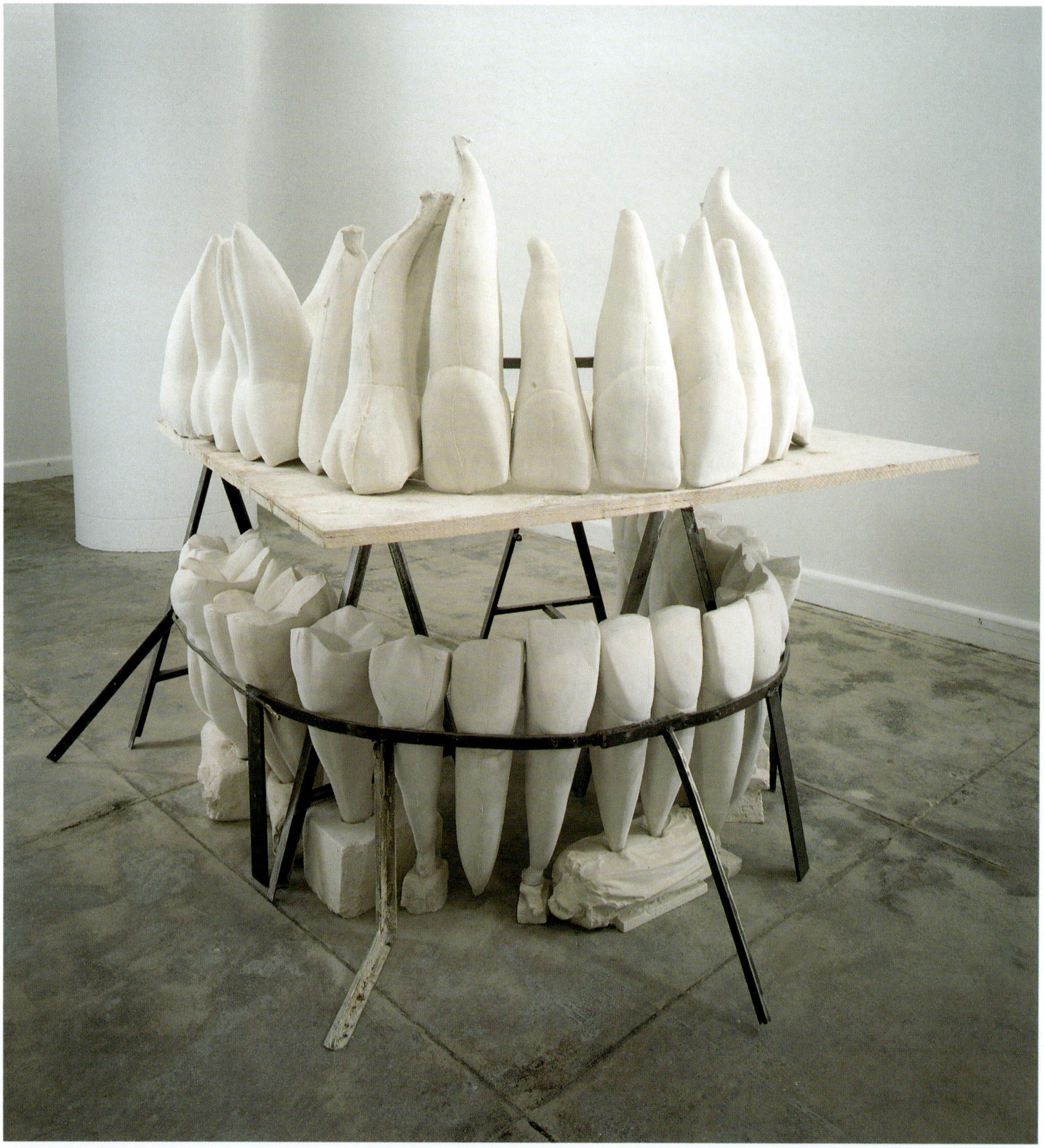

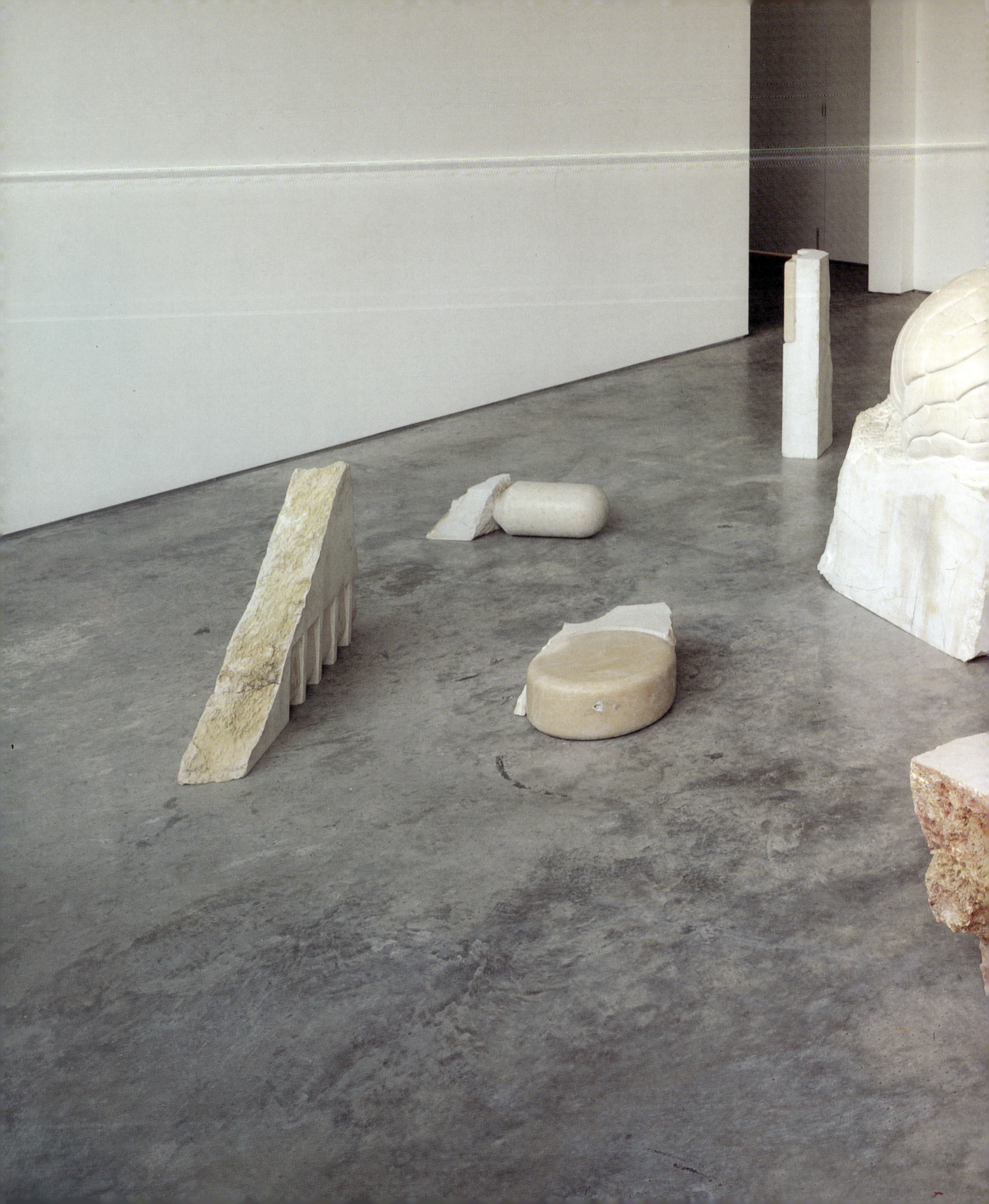

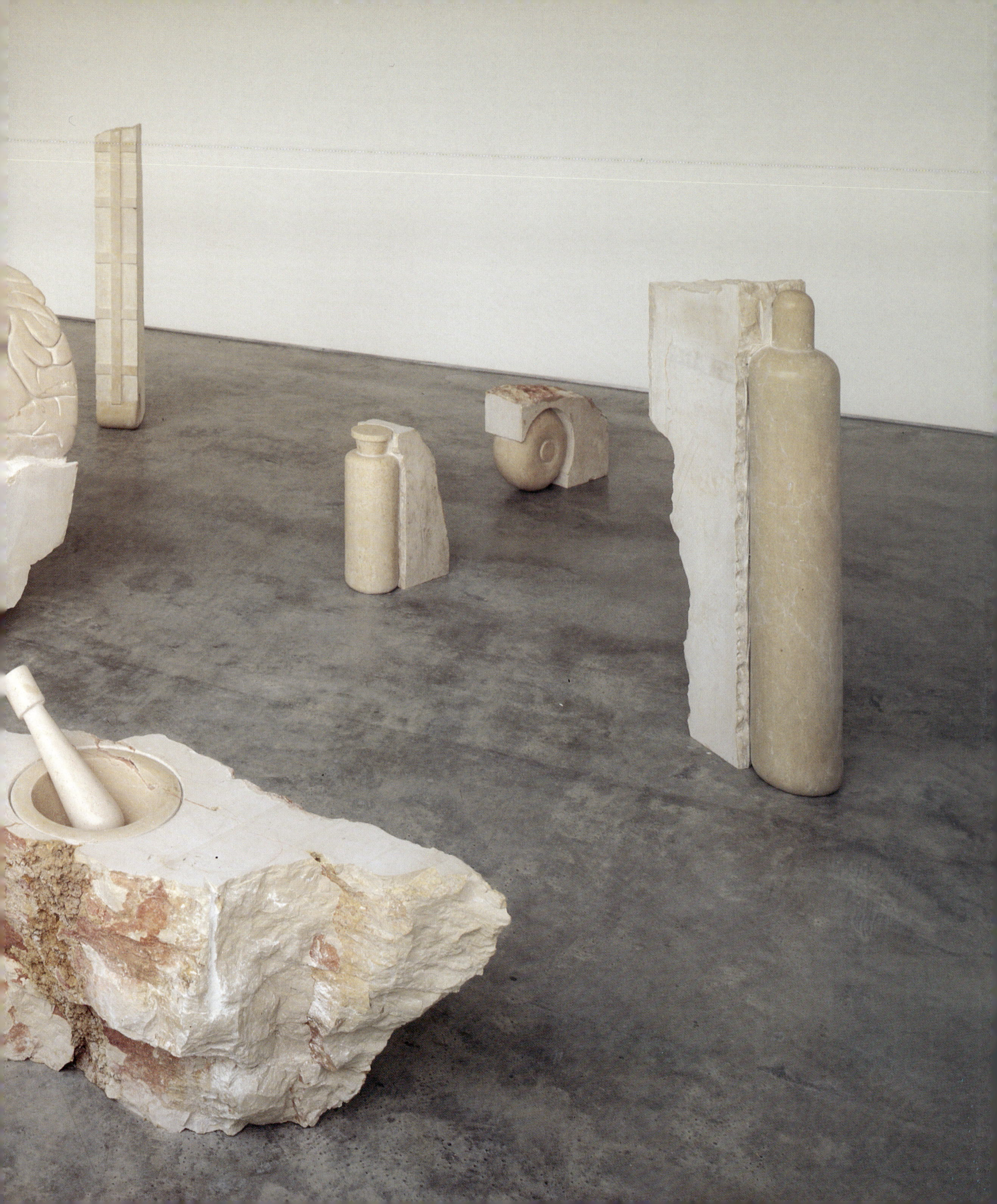

176. *Blood Sugar*, 1992

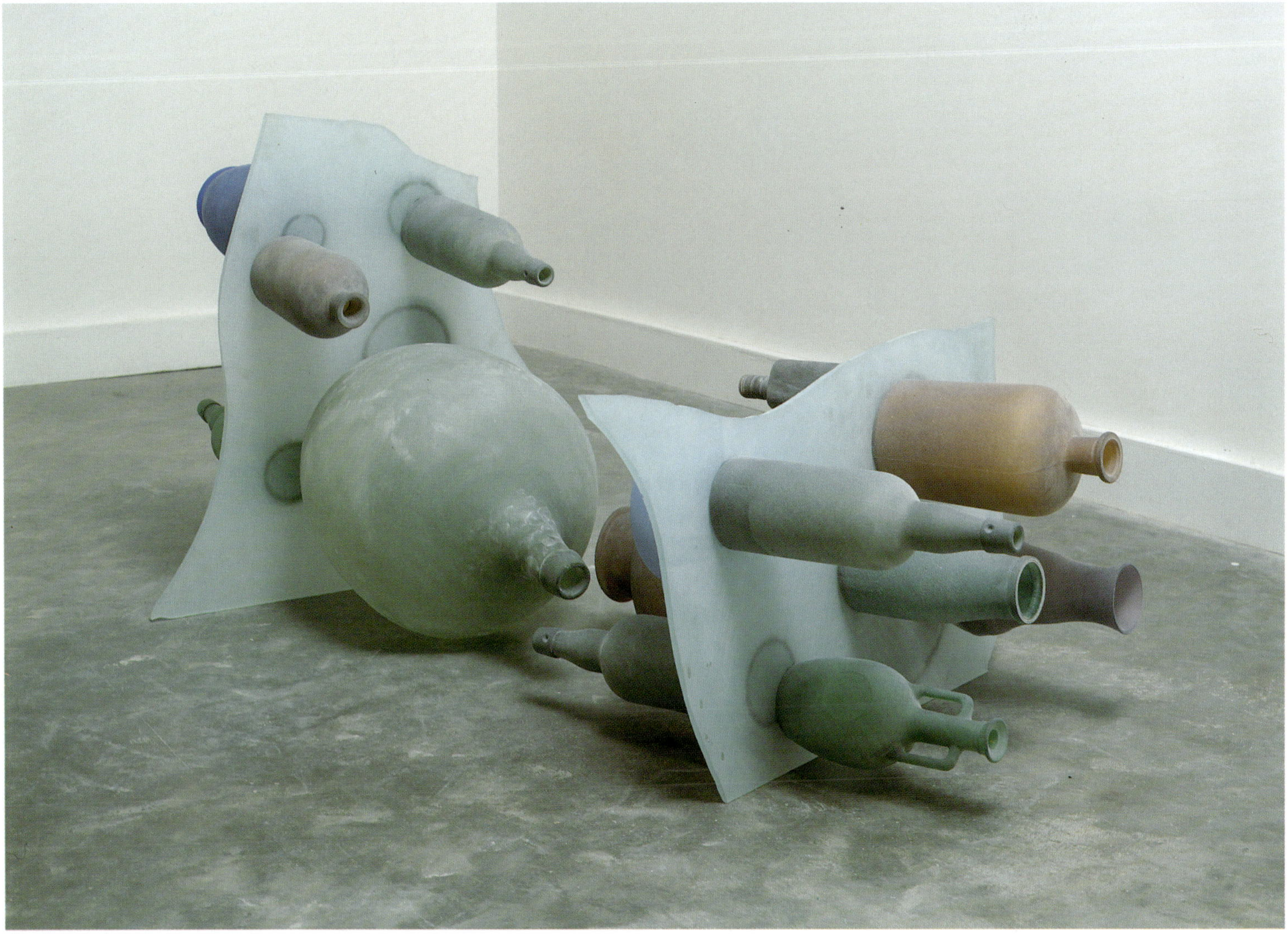

177. *Blood Sugar*, 1992

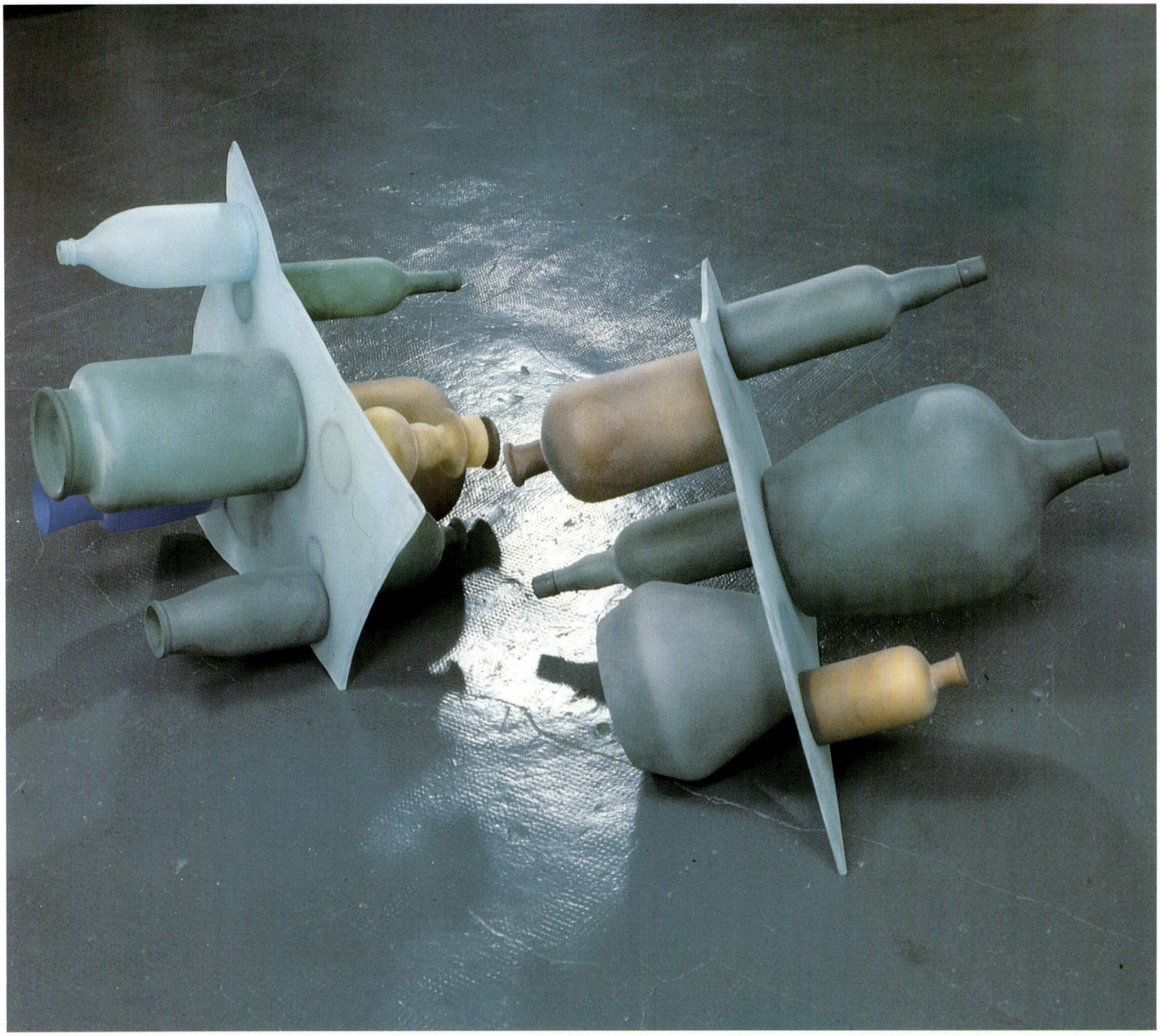

178. *Angels and Other Antibodies*, 1992

179. *Administrated Cellulose*, 1992

There exists a very beautiful letter from van Gogh to his brother that simply describes a walk through a fantastic landscape full of strange objects, forms and colours. This is a description of him walking across the local rubbish dump. So for artists even at the end of the 19th century there was already an awareness that there was not just a natural world but there was also a whole population of other objects. In fact, the products of the industrial society began to have an aesthetic impact.

In *Tony Cragg: In Camera*. 's-Hertogenbosch/Eindhoven: European Ceramics Work Centre/Stedelijk van Abbemuseum, 1993, p. 12.

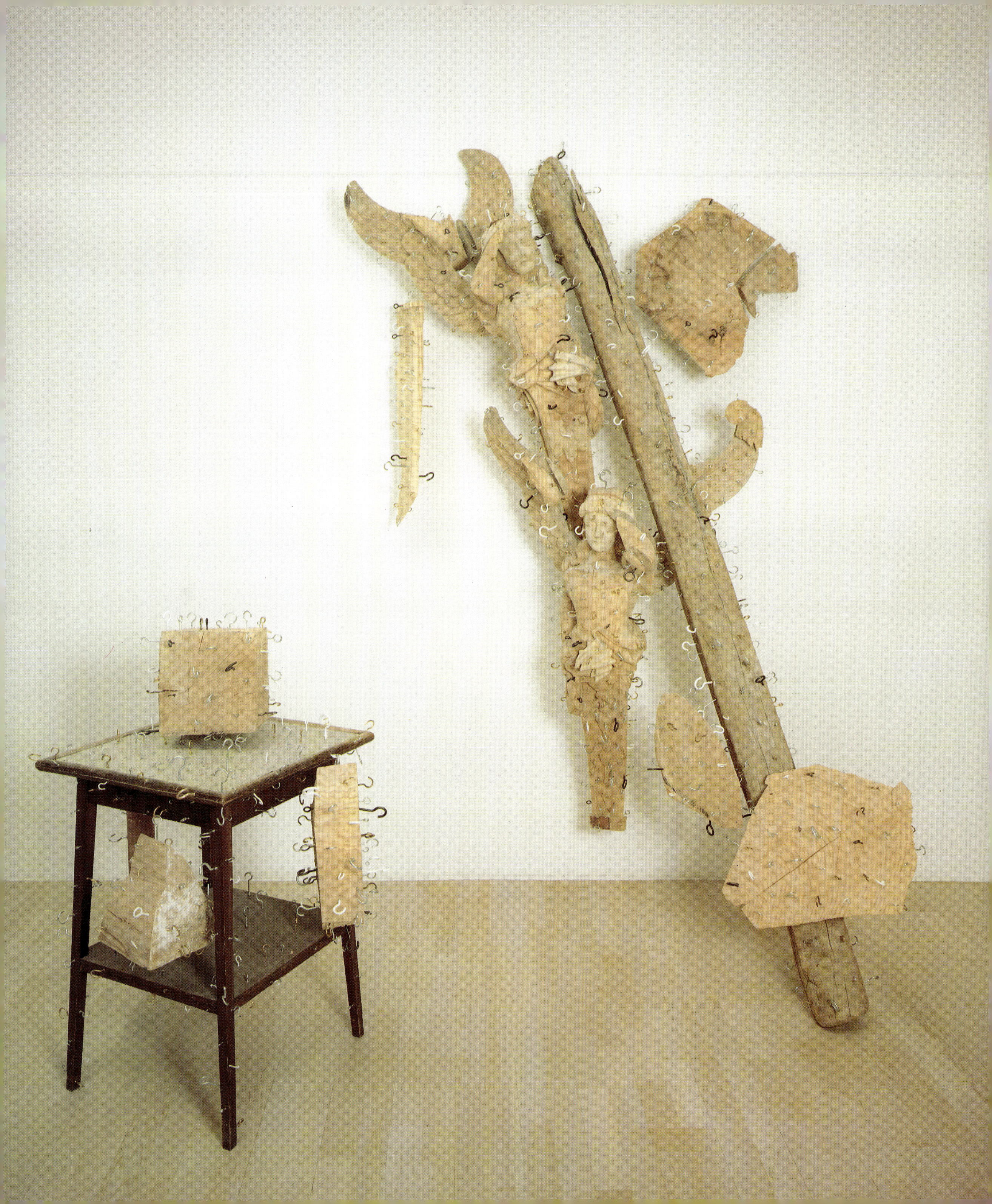

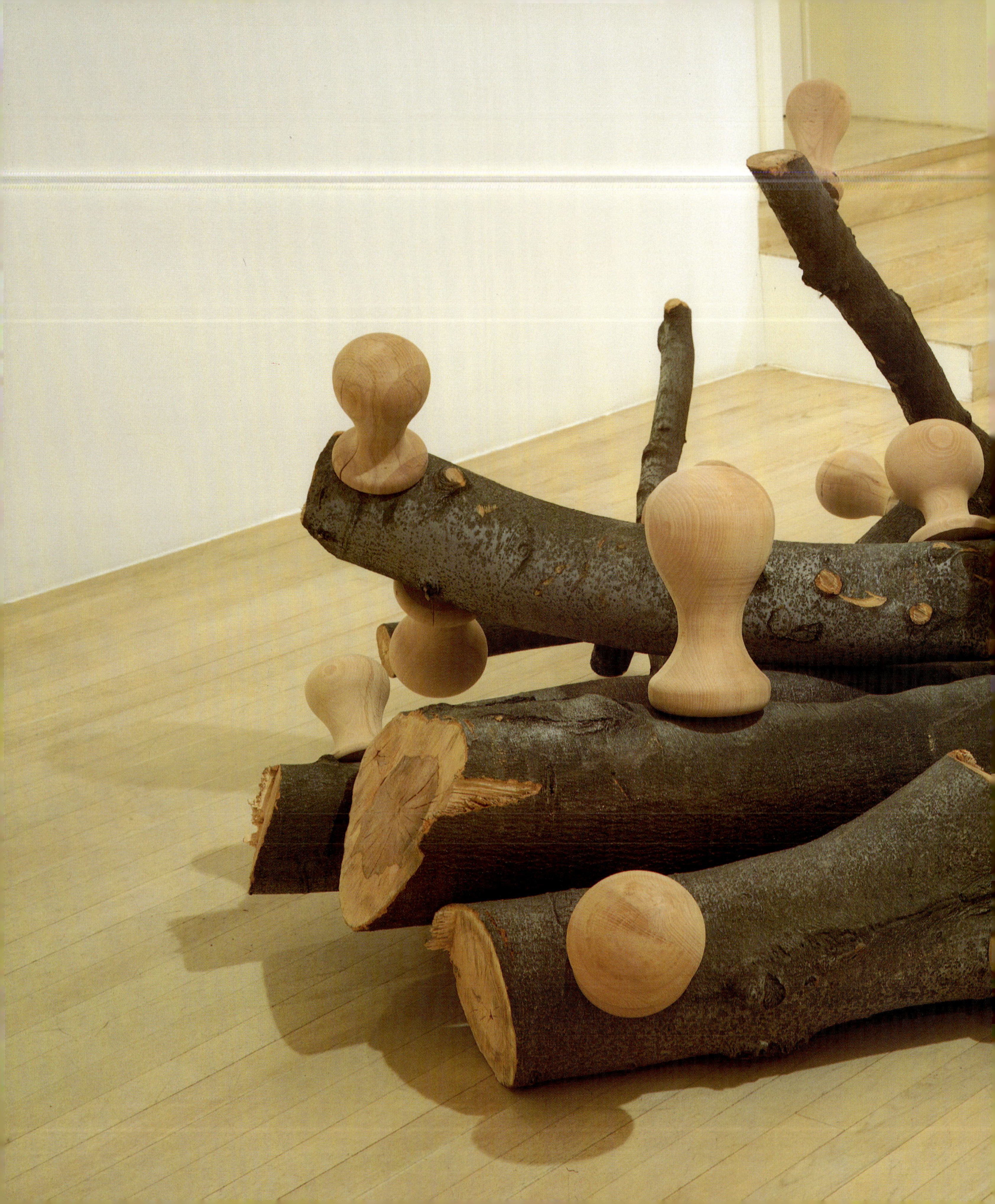

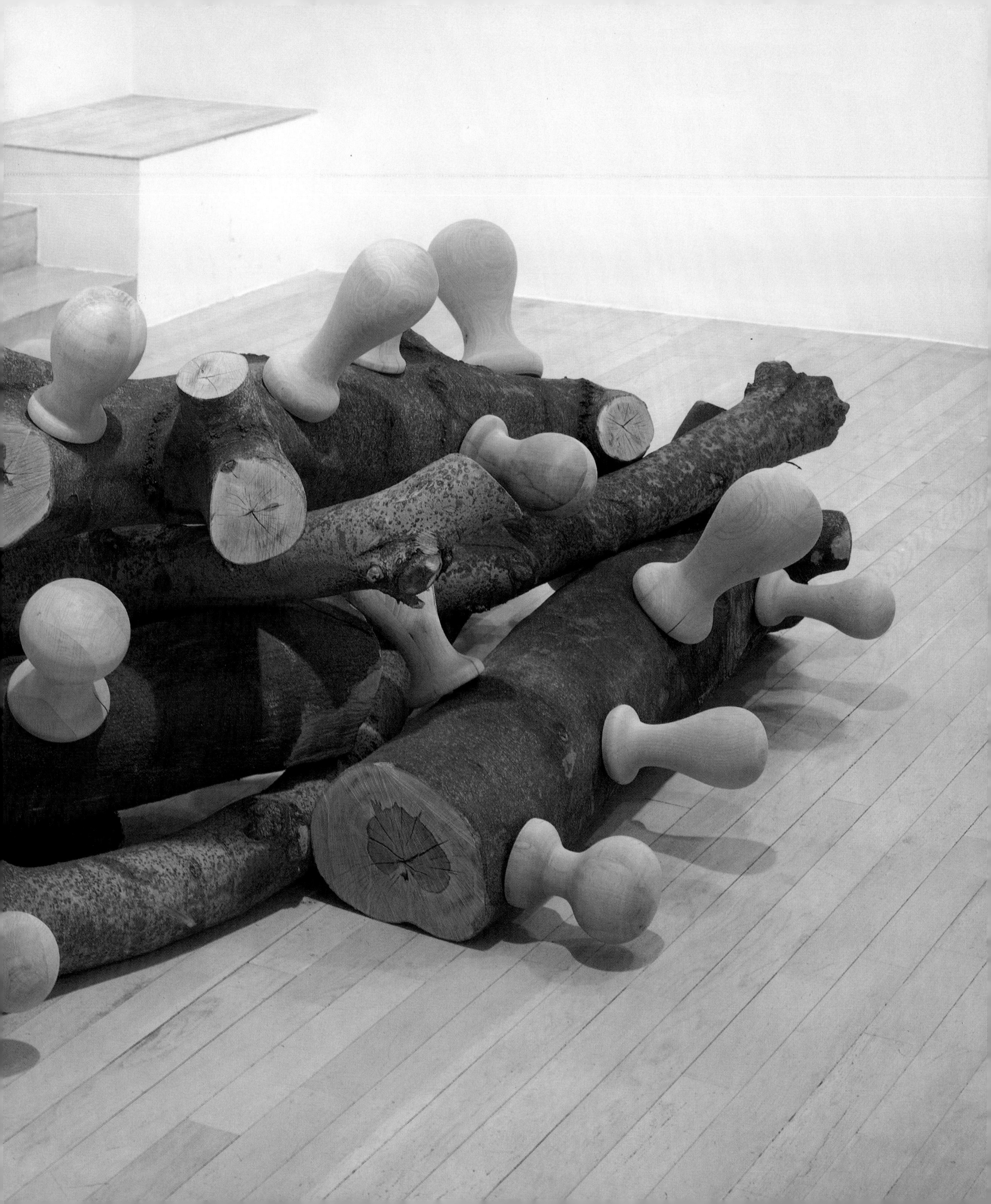

180. *Tool*, 1991

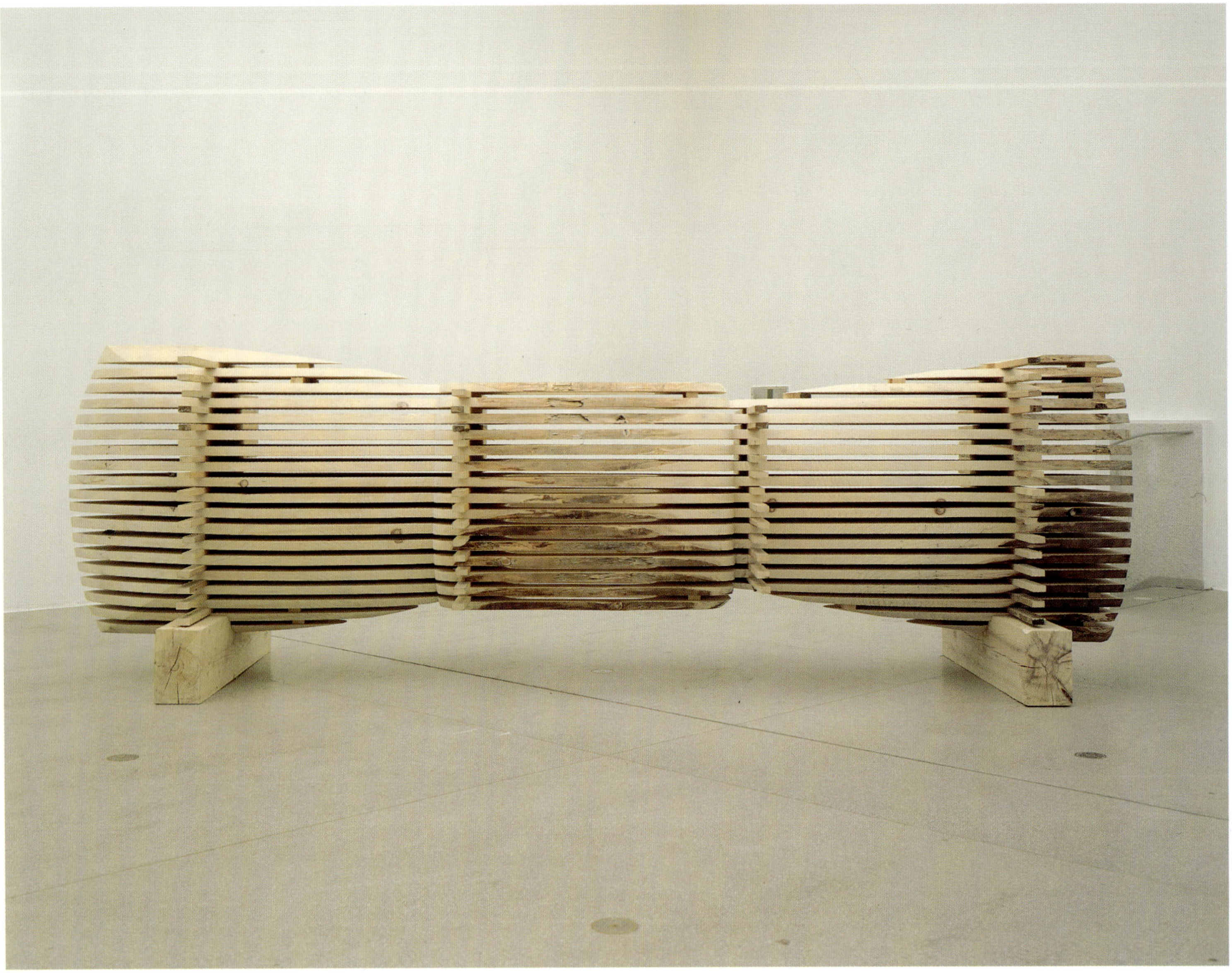

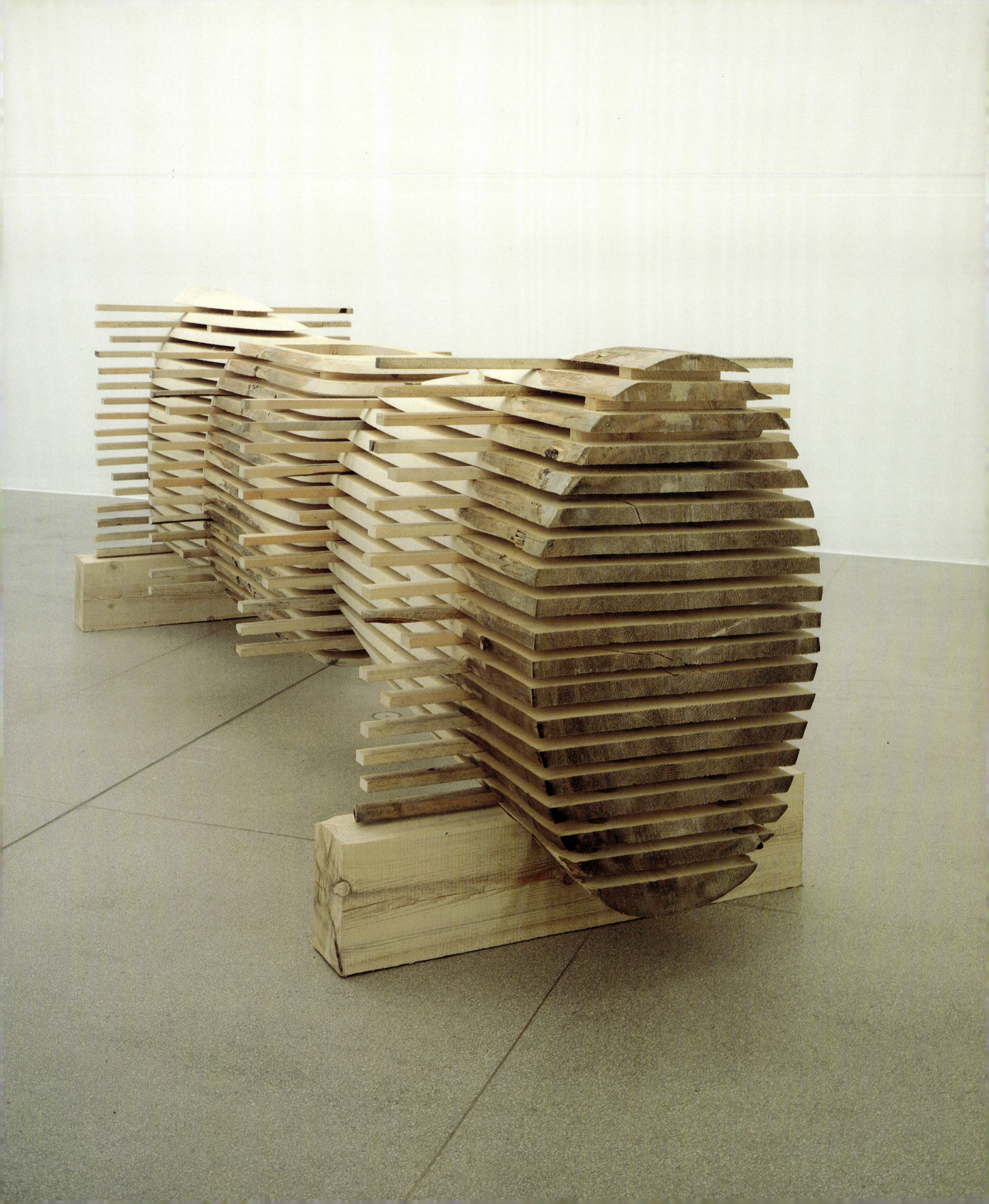

181. *Spear*, 1990

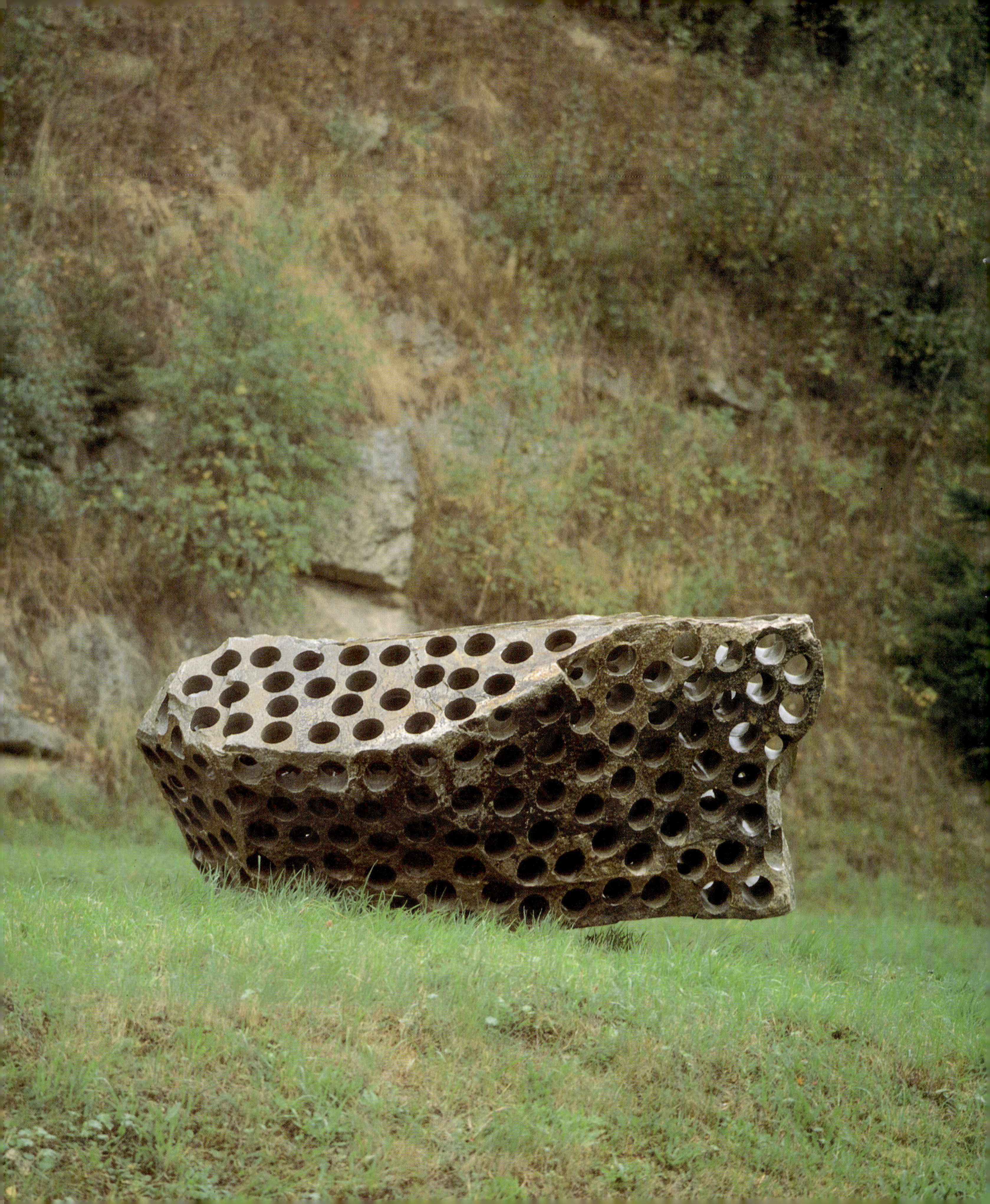

182. *Untitled*, 1993

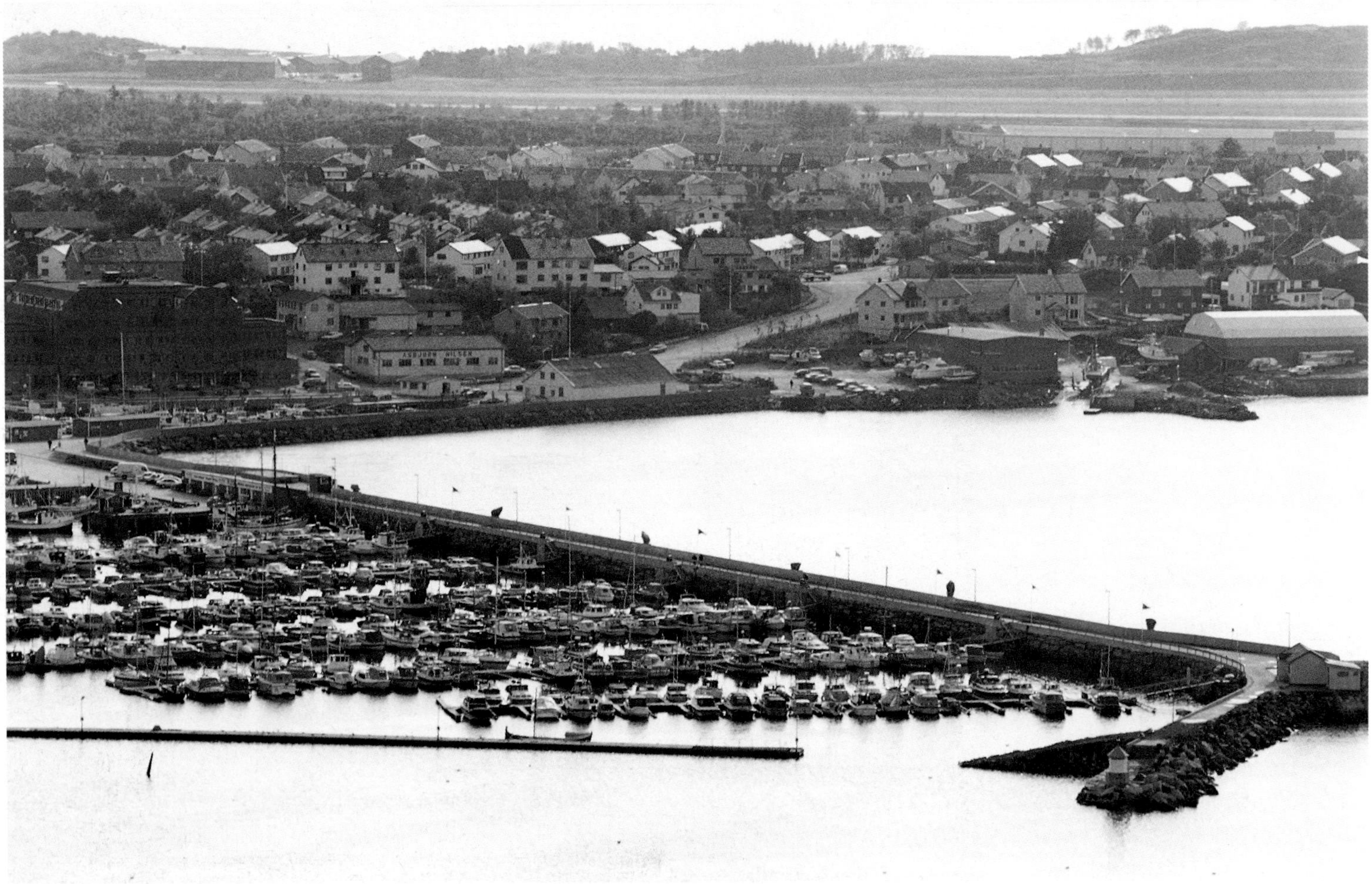

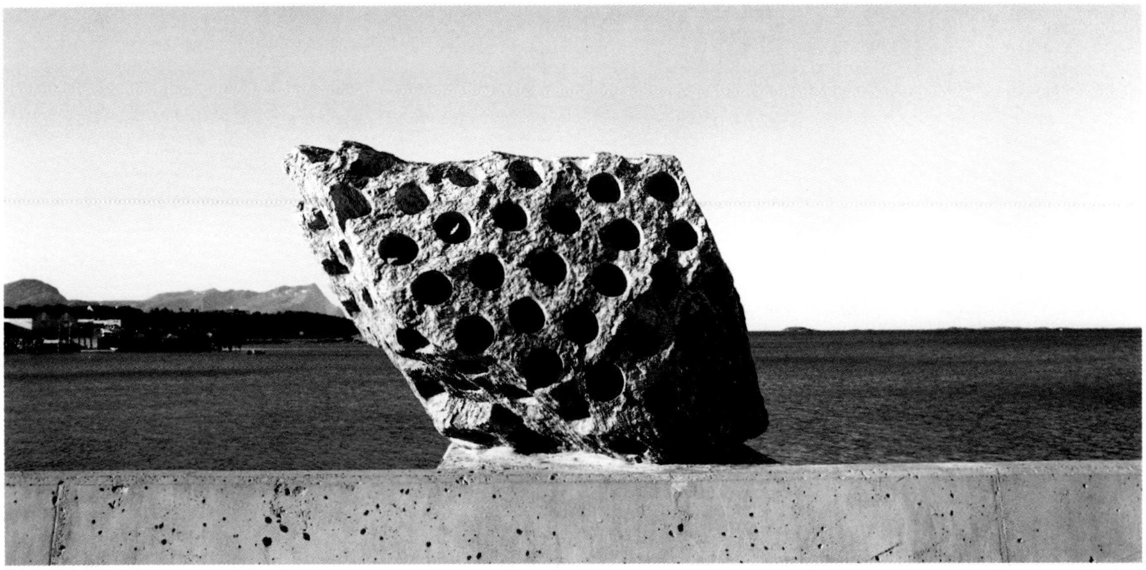

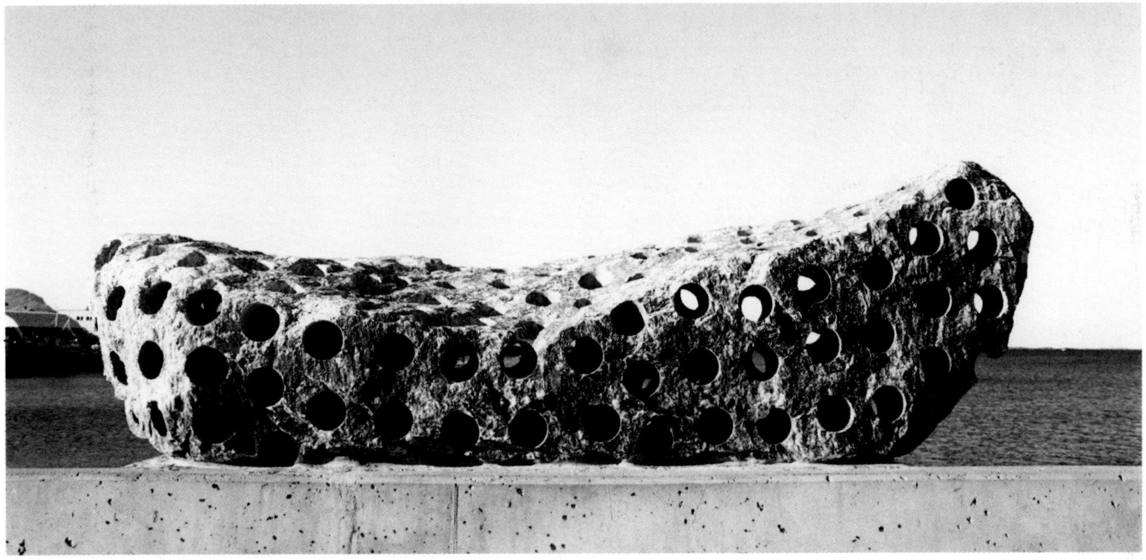

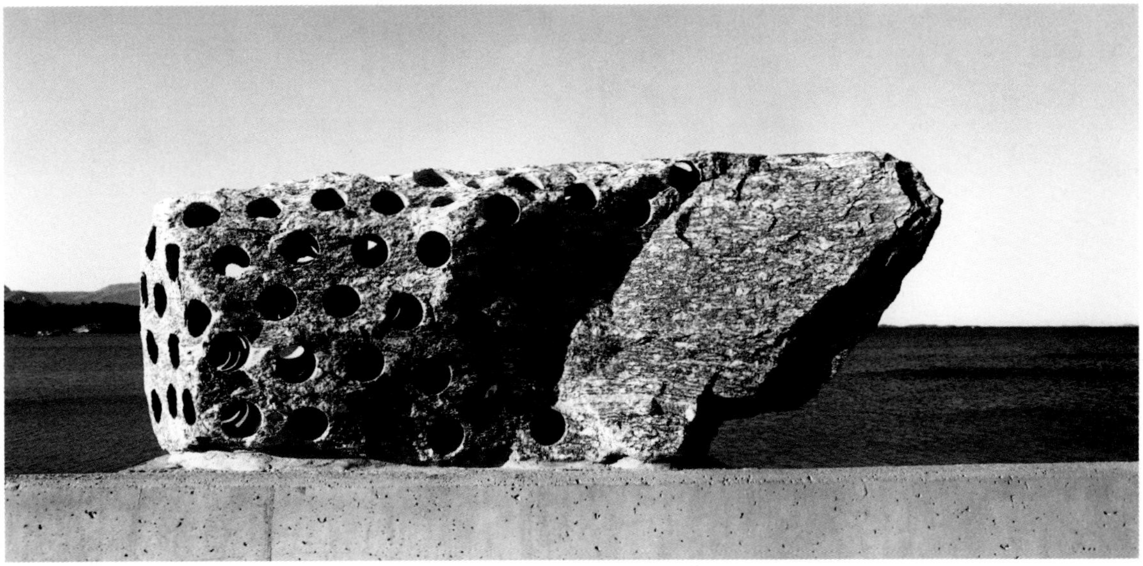

183. *Island*, 1993

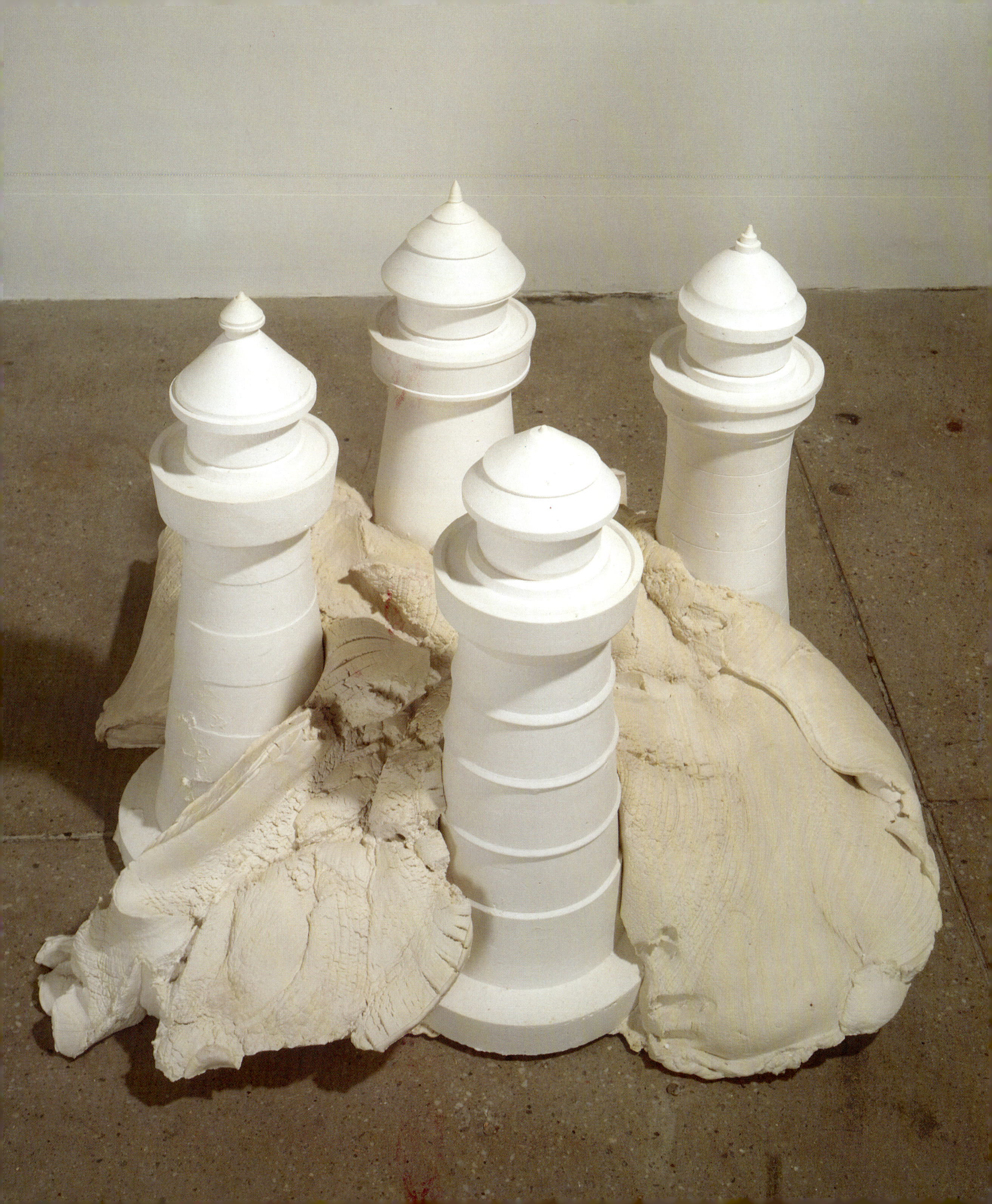

184. *Time Suds*, 1993

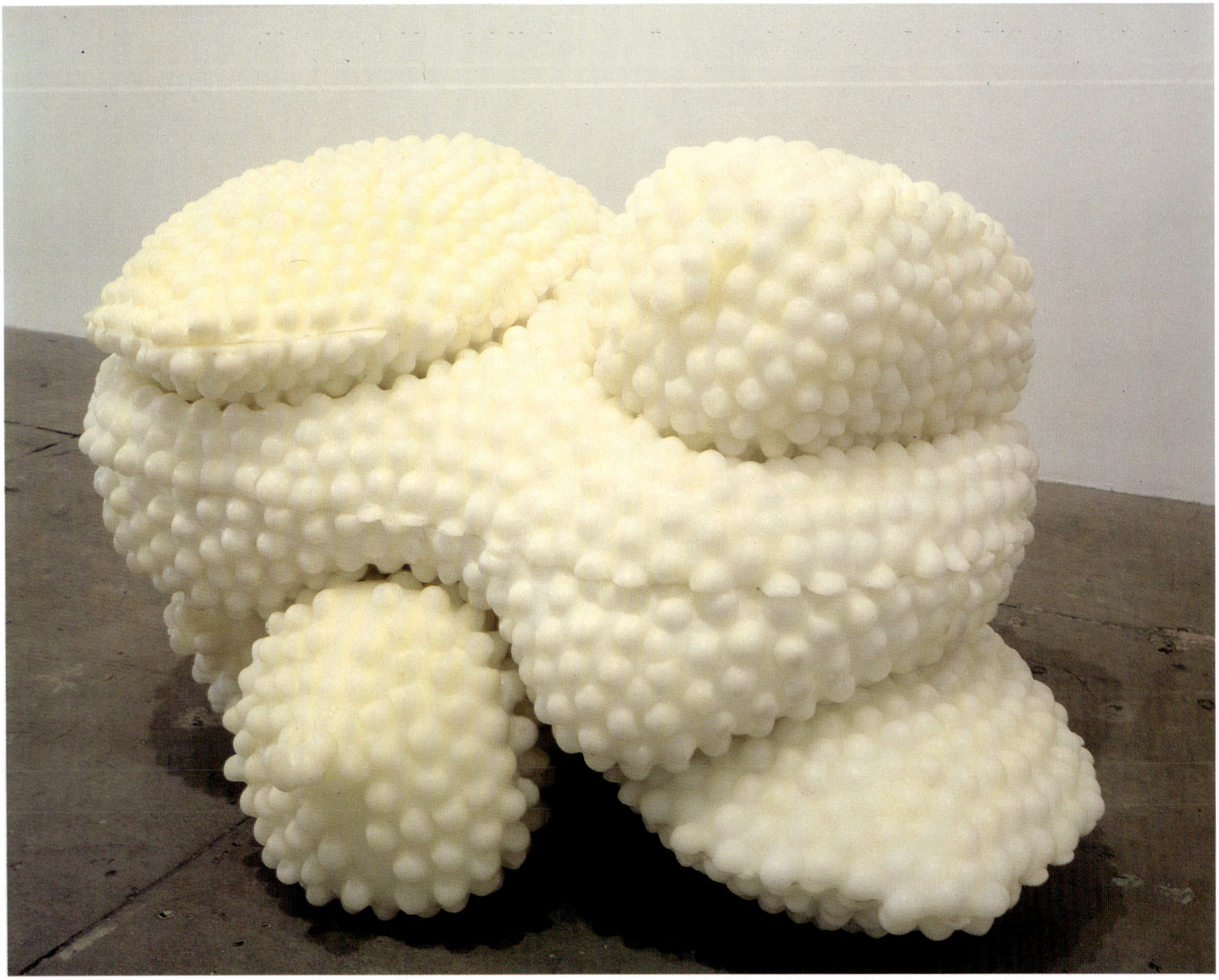

185. *Untitled*, 1993

186. *Messages*, 1993

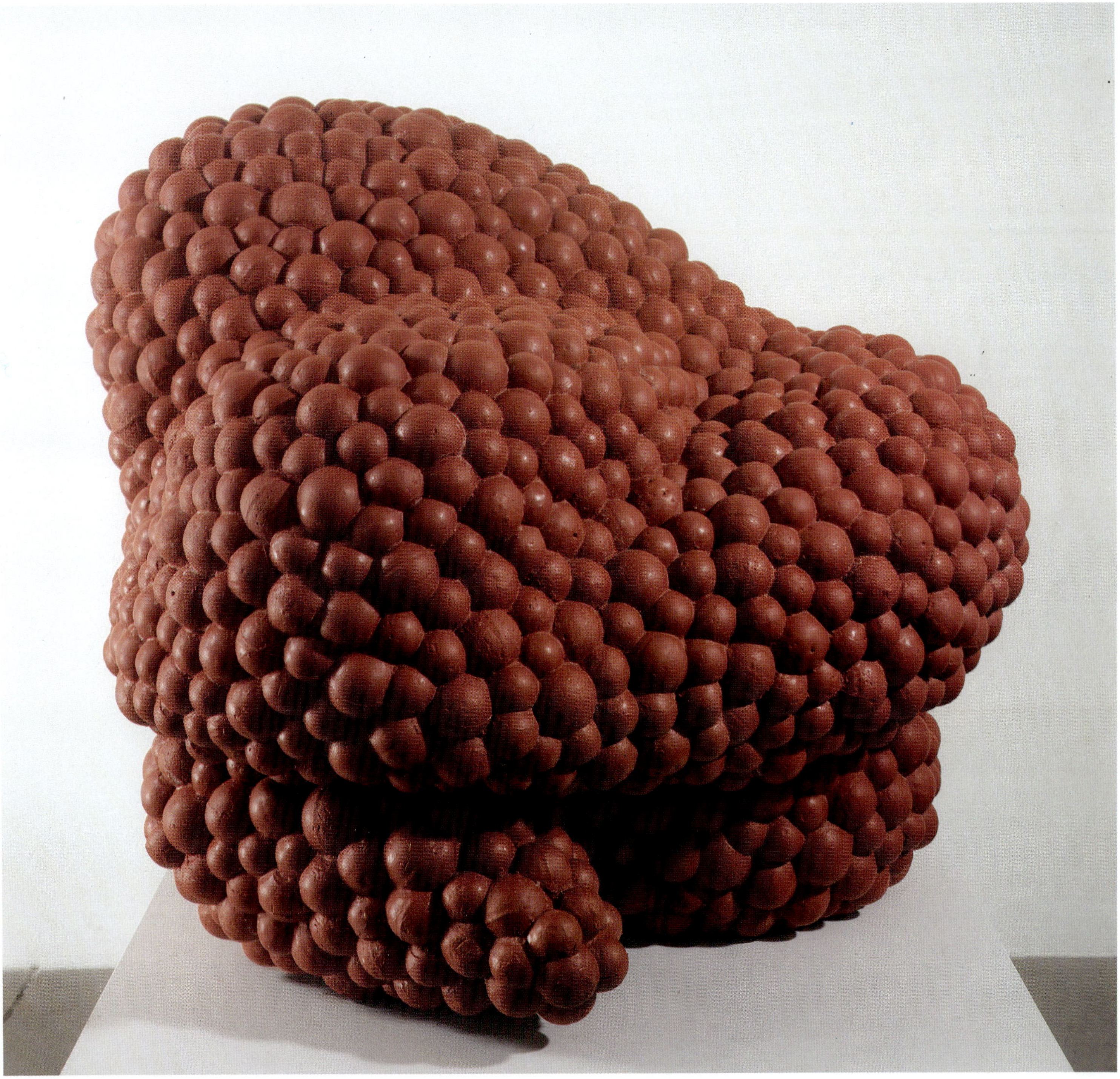

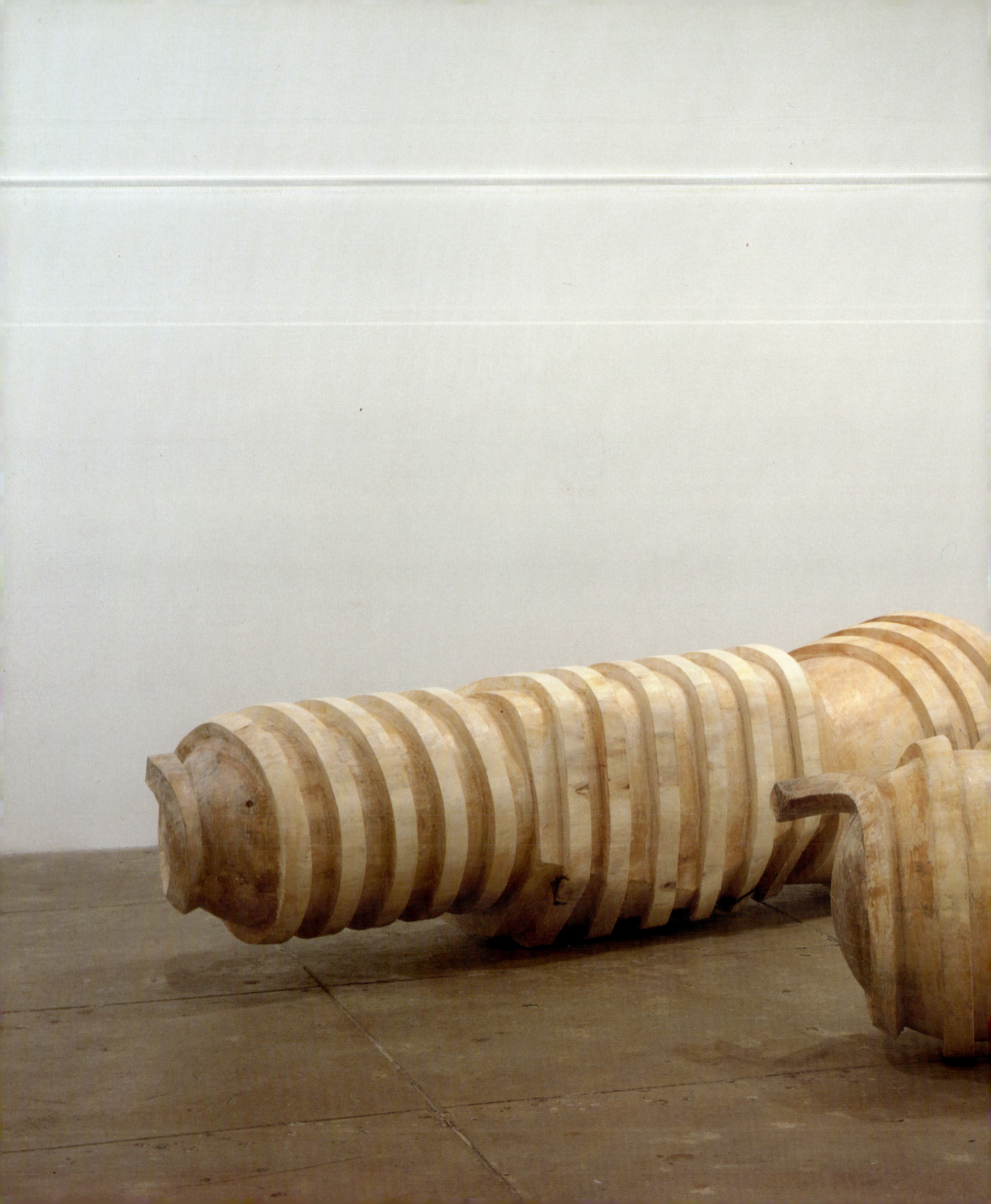

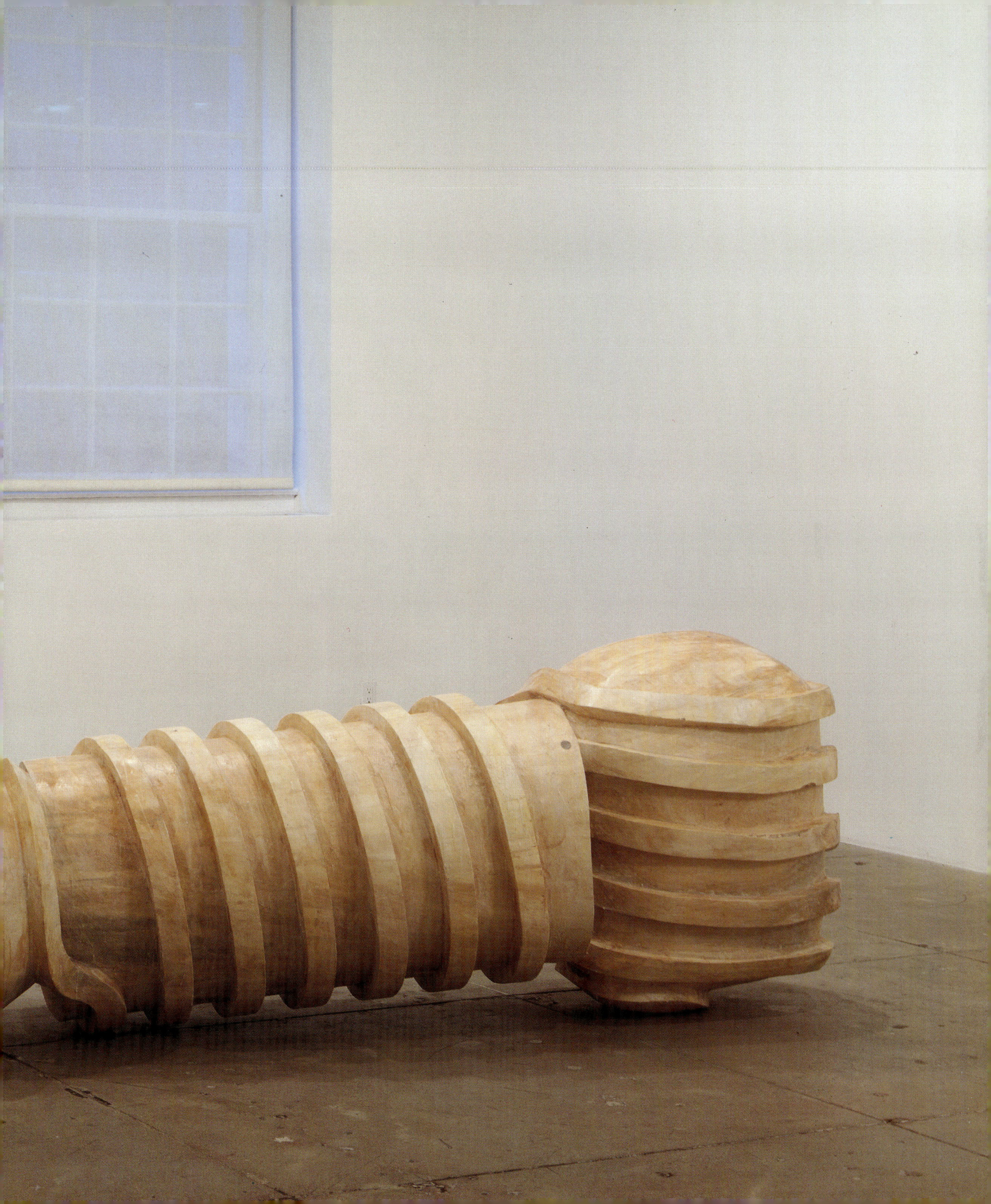

187. *Unholy Ghosts*, 1993

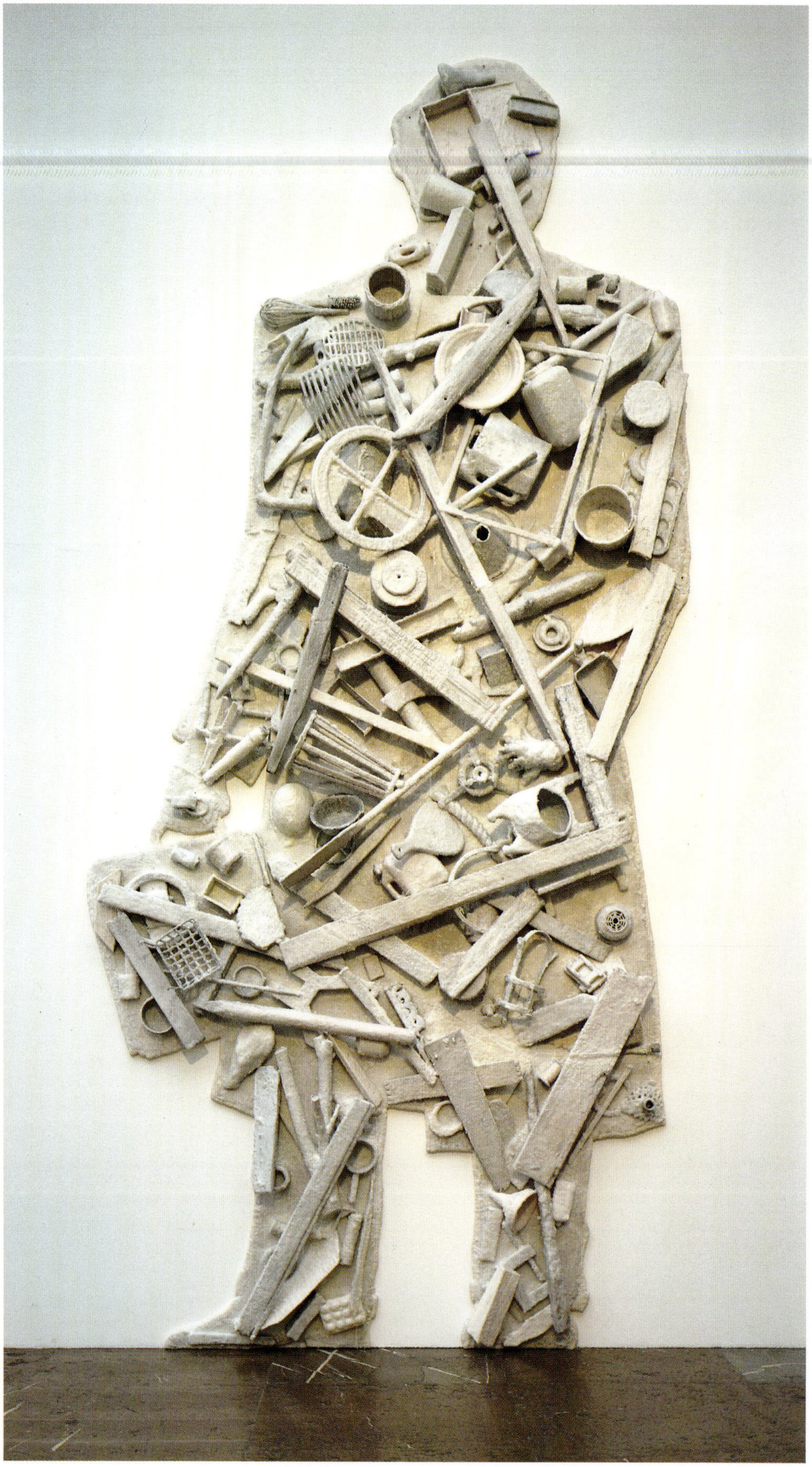

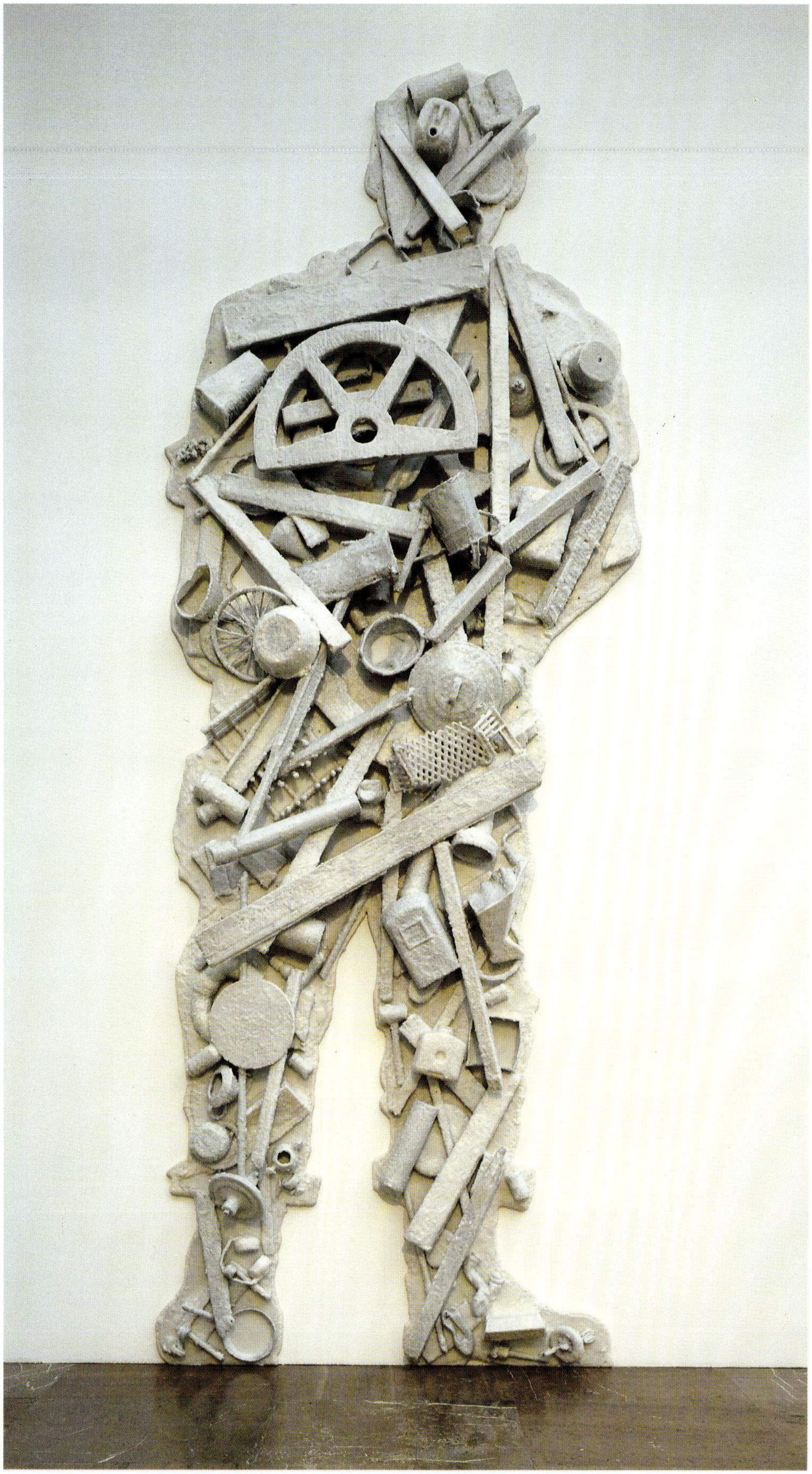

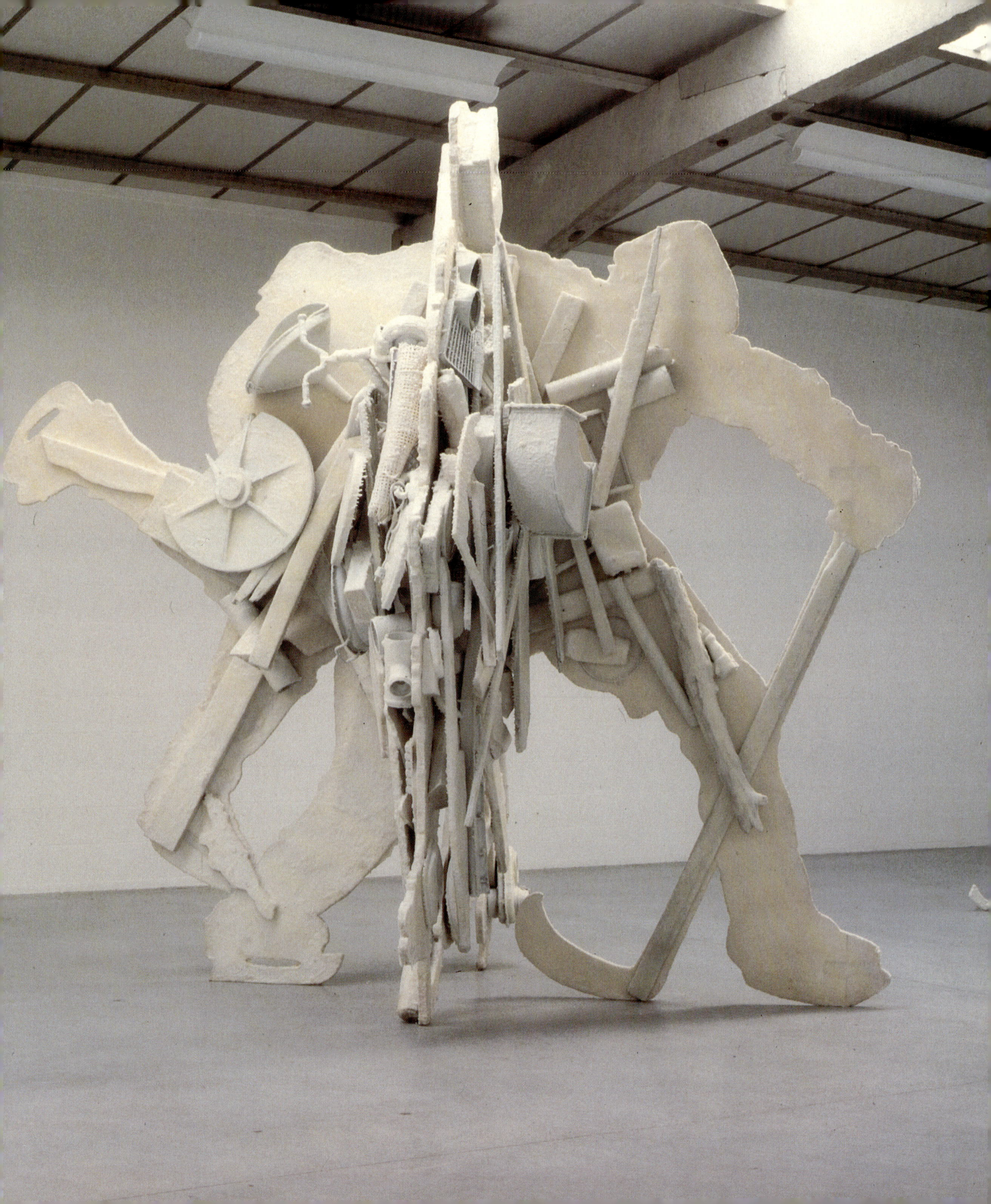

189. *Daily Bread*, 1994

A picture, an image or a form cannot be expressed with a thousand words – not even with a million. In addition, associated with our perception we have a huge vocabulary of responses even to the smallest and subtlest things, which are in a sense erotic responses to the world we live in. And that is really what making sculpture and looking at sculpture is all about. Trying to understand the physical world and to use it as a language is really a sign of the loving respect for the material we exist in and are made of.

In *Tony Cragg: In Camera*. 's-Hertogenbosch/Eindhoven: European Ceramics Work Centre/Stedelijk van Abbemuseum, 1993, p. 14.

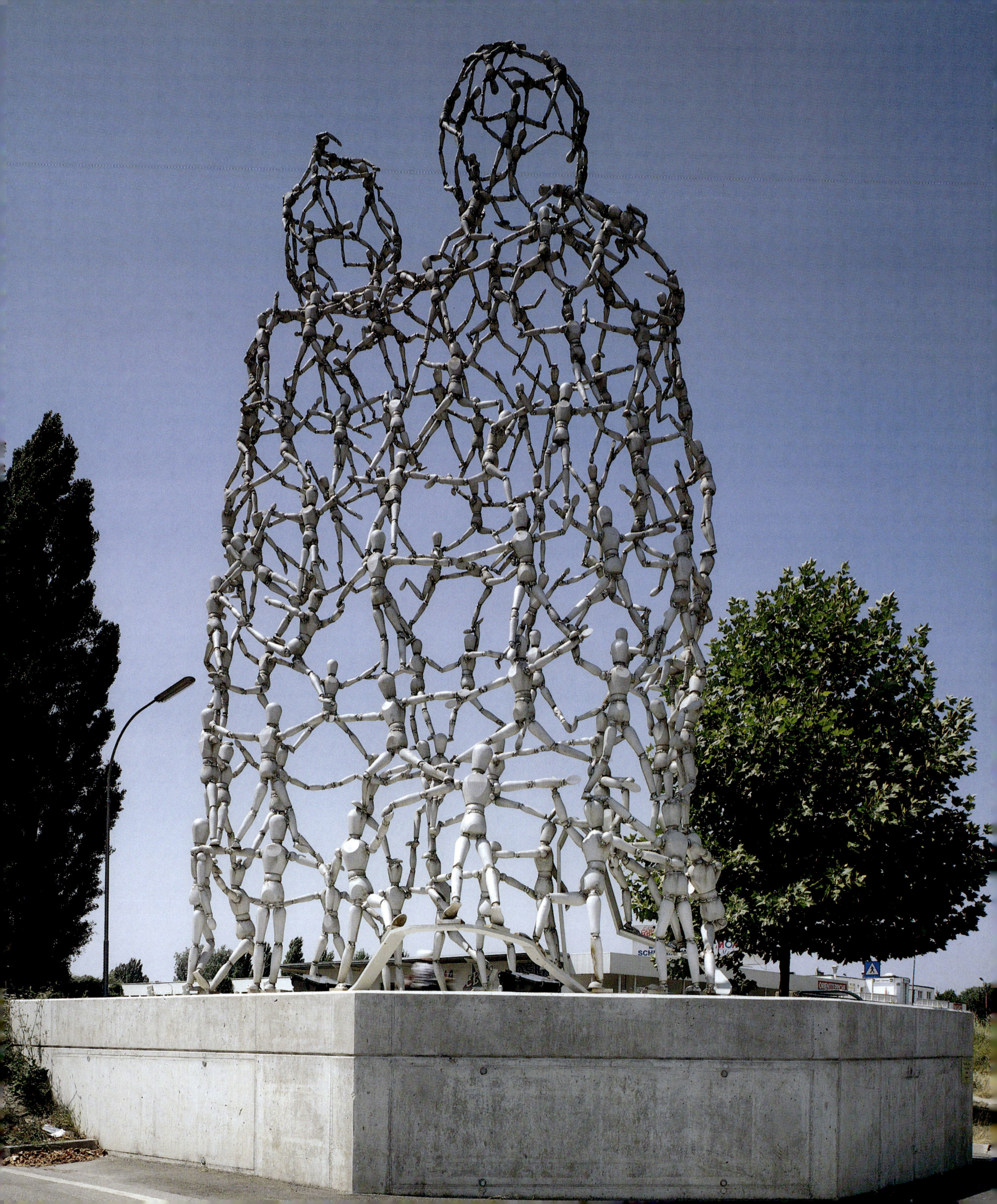

190. *Wildlife*, 1995

191. *Solid States*, 1995

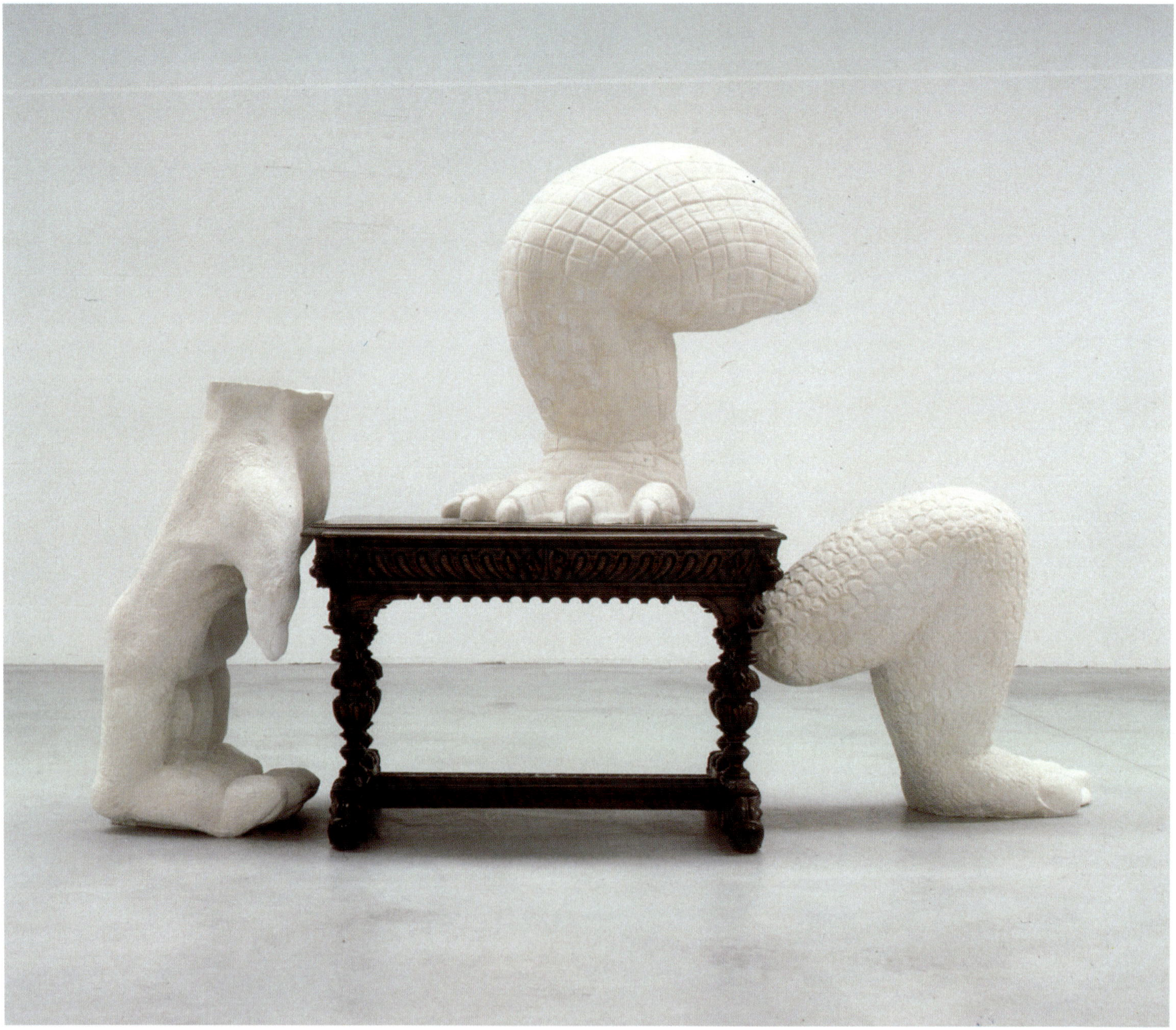

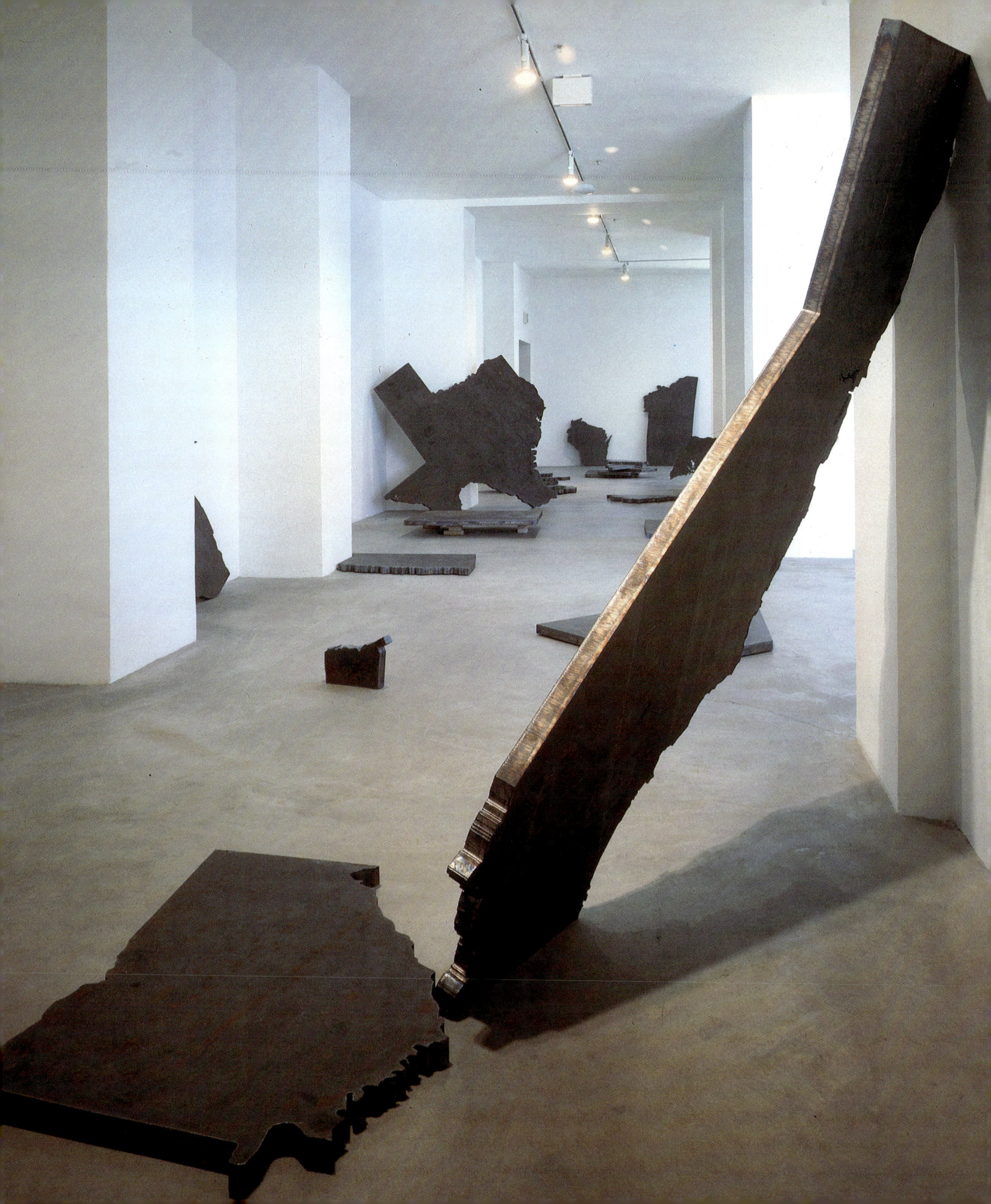

192. *Trade Wind*, 1995

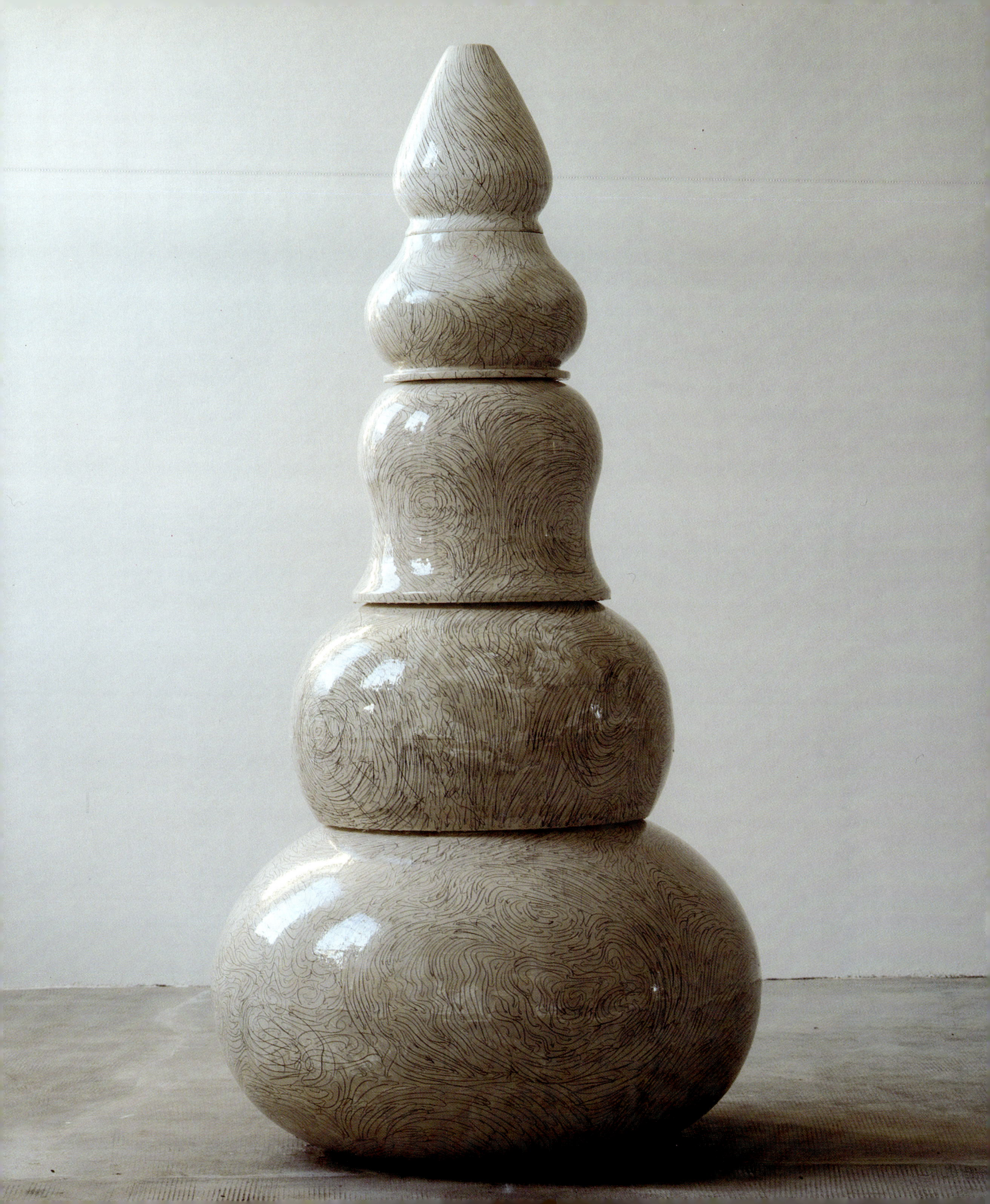

193. *Rational Beings*, 1995

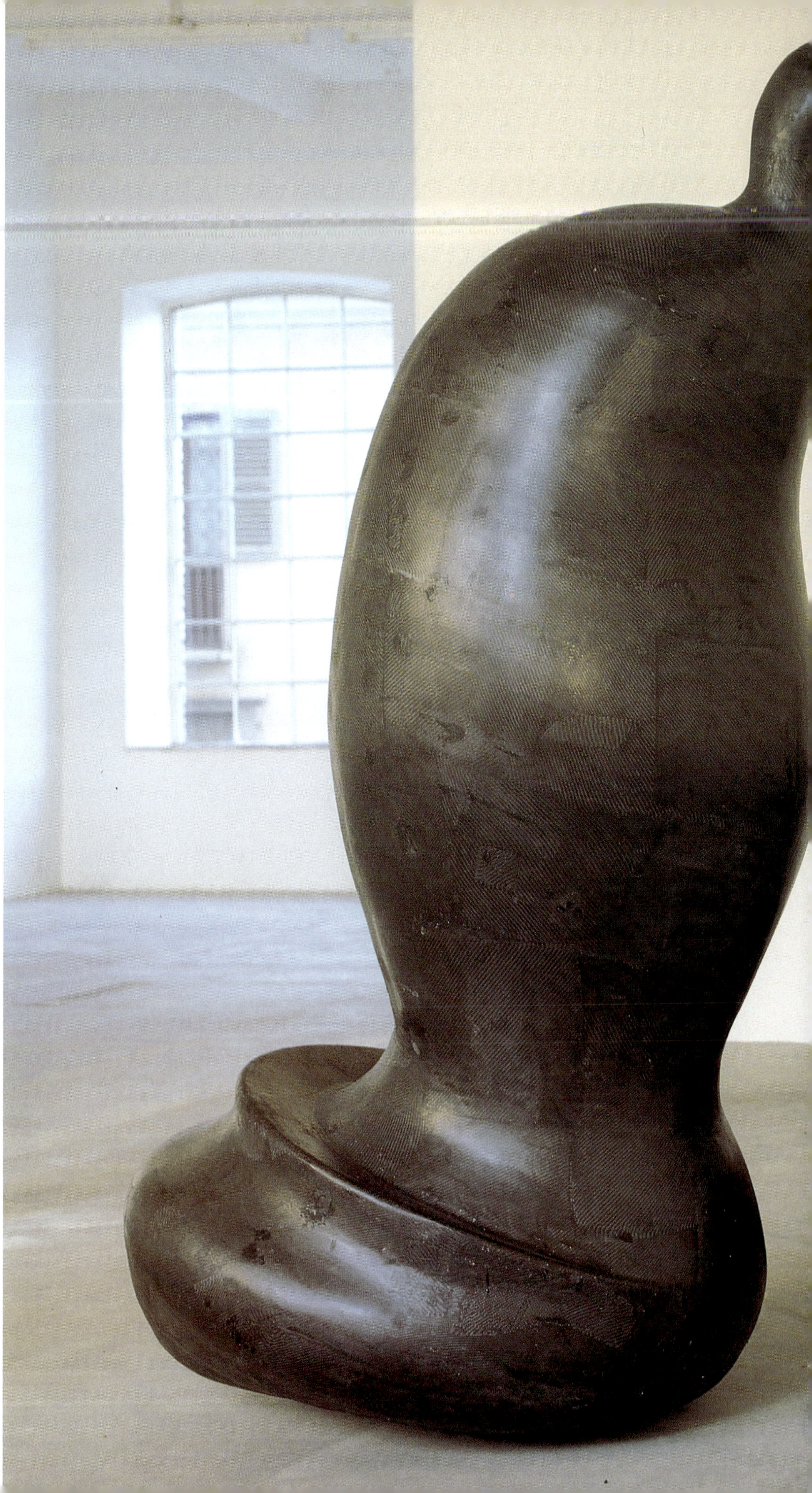

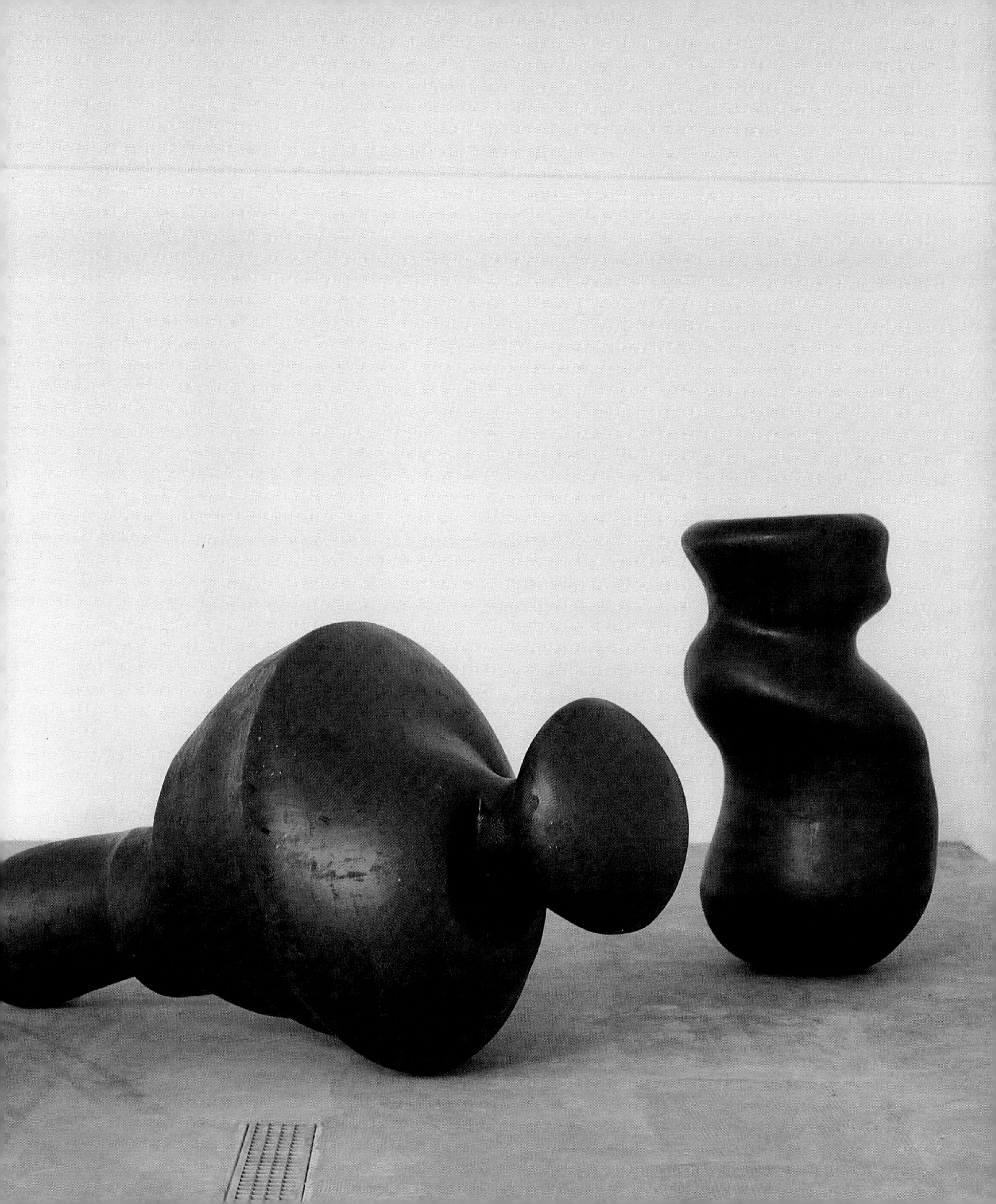

Catalogue of Works

1. *Untitled*, 1971
Shadow in sand

2. *Untitled*, 1972
Wood, 100x60x50 cm
Wimbledon, 1972

3. *Untitled*, 1973
Bricks, 300x300x30 cm
London, 1973

4. *Untitled*, 1974
Wood sticks, 30x500x200 cm

5. *Untitled*, 1975
Brick, cement rubble, 2 parts, 600x500 cm, 200x200 cm

6. *Stack*, 1976
Mixed media, 200x200x200 cm

7. *Untitled*, 1977
Chair, table, paper, 100x200x200 cm
London, 1977

8. *New Stones-Newton's Tones*, 1978
Found plastic fragments, 366x244x10 cm
Arts Council Collection, South Bank Centre, London

9. *Spectrum*, 1979
Found plastic fragments, 250x500 cm
Collection of the artist, Wuppertal
Photo Antje Zeis-Lois, Wuppertal

10. *Self-Portrait with Sack*, 1980
Found plastic fragments, canvas sack, 172x66x40 cm
Collection Sergio Bertola, Genoa

11. *Five Objects-Five Colors*, 1980
Mixed media
Green objects: Musée National d'Art Moderne, Centre Georges Pompidou, Paris
Installation: Museum van Hedendaagse Kunst, Ghent, 1980

12. *Self-Portrait on Chai*r, 1980
Found plastic fragments, h 244 cm
Collection Thomas Cohn, Rio de Janeiro
Installation: Lützowstrasse, Berlin, 1980

13. *Tree*, 1980
Found painted lengths of wood, 220x150 cm
Installation: Galerie Chantal Crousel, Paris, 1980

14. *The Streets Are Full of Cowboys and Indians*, 1980
Yellow found plastic fragments, 300x450 cm
Installation: Galleria Lucio Amelio, Naples, 1980

15. *Black and White Stack*, 1980
Mixed media, 200x300x60 cm
Installation: Lisson Gallery, London, 1980

16. *Boat*, 1980
Found painted lengths of wood, 150x400 cm
Collection Massimo Sandretto, Turin

17. *Bird*, 1980
Found painted lengths of wood
Installation: Galleria Lucio Amelio, Naples, 1980

18. *Polaris*, 1981
Found painted lengths of wood, 400x1100 cm
Installation: Whitechapel Art Gallery, London, 1981

19. *Policeman*, 1981
Green found plastic fragments, 320x160 cm

20. *Britain Seen from the North*, 1981
Mixed media, found plastic fragments,
Figure: 170x58 cm
Britain: 370x700 cm
Tate Gallery, London
Installation: Whitechapel Art Gallery, London, 1981

21. *Factory Fantasies I*, 1981
Cut-out wooden armoire, 175x64x47 cm
Fond Régional d'Art Contemporain, Rhône-Alpes, Lyon

22. *Farbfernseher*, 1981
Found painted lengths of wood

Installation: Galleria Civica, Modena, 1981

23. *Staubsauger*, 1981
Mixed media, 700x200 cm
Installation: Musée d'Art et d'Industrie, Saint-Etienne, 1981

24. *Postcard Union Jack*, 1981
Red and blue found plastic fragments, 250x400 cm
Leeds City Art Gallery, London

25. *Everybody's Friday Night*, 1981
Cut-out wooden armoire, 175x64x47 cm
Private collection, Belgium
Installation: Whitechapel Art Gallery, London, 1981

26. *Self-Portrait with Bottles and Bricks*, 1982
Mixed media, 850x200 cm
Installation: Badischer Kunstverein, Karlsruhe, 1982
Photo Walter Schmidt, Karlsruhe

27. *Indian Moon*, 1982
Yellow found plastic fragments, 250x220 cm
Installation: Fifth Triennale India, New Delhi, 1982

28. *Dining Motions*, 1982
White paint on found colored wood, 323x749 cm
Installation: Badischer Kunstverein, Karlsruhe, 1982

29. *Five Bottles on a Shelf*, 1982
Plastic, 33x58x14 cm

30. *Green Bottle II, Yellow Bottle II, Red Bottle II, Orange Bottle II, Blue Bottle II*, 1982
Found plastic fragments, h 250 cm
Installation: Metropolitan Art Museum, Tokyo, 1982

31. *House*, 1982
Mixed media on metal frame, 160x170x100 cm
Trough, 1982
Mixed media, 90x250x90 cm
Mercedes, 1982
Bricks, bottles, diam 300 cm
Collection Sylvia Pearlstein, Antwerp
Installation: Galerie Konrad Fischer, Düsseldorf, 1982-83

32. *Grey Container*, 1983
Bottles, wood board, wooden boxes, brick, paint, 200x280 cm
Courtesy Galleria Franco Toselli, Milan
Photo Salvatore Licitra, Milan

33. *Taxi!*, 1983
Mixed media, musical instrument cases, wooden boards, paint, 240x100x90 cm

34. *Large Mountain*, 1983
Mixed media, 230x200x150 cm
Courtesy Galleria Franco Toselli, Milan
Installation: Galleria Franco Toselli, Milan, 1983

35. *Untitled*, 1983
Lava, chairs, 200x80x100 cm
Collection Fondazione Amelio, Naples
Installation: Galleria Lucio Amelio, Naples, 1983

36. *Palette*, 1983
White paint on found colored boards
Installation: Galleria Lucio Amelio, Naples, 1983

37. *Element Plane*, 1983
Table, stones, 100x100x120 cm
Courtesy Galleria Franco Toselli, Milan
Installation: Galleria Franco Toselli, Milan, 1983

38. *Untitled*, 1983-84
Mixed media, wooden boards, wooden boxes, paint, 218x140x160 cm
Courtesy Galerie Chantal Crousel, Paris
Photo Kleinefenn, Paris

39. *Three Modern Buildings*, 1983
Clay, cement bricks, 210x300x400 cm
Private collection, Chiari

40. *Moonshadow*, 1983
Mixed media, 220x280 cm
Silent Garden, 1983
Mixed media, 450x400 cm
Collection Fondazione Amelio, Naples
Installation: Galleria Lucio Amelio, Naples, 1983

41. *Evensong*, 1984
Wood, paint, 209x210x175 cm
Courtesy Tucci Russo, Torre Pellice
Photo Enzo Ricci, Turin

42. *S*, 1984
Mixed media, 161x455x300 cm
Courtesy Galerie Chantal Crousel, Paris
Installation: Galerie Crousel-Hussenot, Paris, 1984

43. *Shed*, 1984
Stone, particle board, wood, 99x83.8x33 cm

44. *Village*, 1985
Wood, 70x200x220 cm

45. *Birnan Wood*, 1985
Found objects, plastic particles, 130x190x210 cm
Collection Eyck, Wylie
Courtesy Art&Project, Slootdorp
Installation: Art&Project, Amsterdam, 1985

46. *Mortus and Pestal*, 1985
Mixed media, 250x90x90 cm

47. *Circles*, 1985
Metal, wood, plastic, rubber, 185x300x300 cm

48. *Berg und Ring*, 1985
Wood, rubber, 220x200x150 cm

49. *New Figuration*, 1985
Found plastic fragments, 280x550 cm
Courtesy Marian Goodman Gallery, New York
Installation: Art&Project, Amsterdam, 1985

50. *Bacchus Drops*, 1985
Wood, glass, plastic, 130x70x70 cm
Collection of the artist, Wuppertal

51. *Twenty-four Hours Cycle*, 1984
Table, plastic piping, aluminum can, suitcase, 100x250x100 cm
Courtesy Tucci Russo, Torre Pellice
Photo Enzo Ricci, Turin

52. *VoltAmpOhm*, 1985
Electric wires, 100x100x210 cm

53. *Shore Landscape*, 1985
Wood, granite slabs, 50x180x60 cm

54. *Houses in Fjord*, 1985
Henie-Onstad Art Centre, Hovikodden
Installation: outskirts of Oslo, Norway

55. *Lens*, 1985
Found objects, plastic particles, 500x200x160 cm
Les Musées de la Ville de Strasbourg
Courtesy Galerie Buchmann, Basel/Cologne

56. *Tools*, 1986
Sandstone, 100x320x250 cm
Installation: Hayward Gallery, London, 1987

57. *Città*, 1986
Hardboard, wood, paint, 250x200x260 cm
Saatchi Collection, London

58. *Raleigh*, 1986
Cast iron, granite, 175x200x350 cm
Tate Gallery, London

59. *Keymer*, 1986
Lapis lazuli, serpentine, 81x70x17 cm

60. *Stomach*, 1986
Wood, metal, plaster, 110x100x90 cm
Photo Bill Jacobson Studio

61. *Eroded Glass*, 1986
Leerdam glass, 38x50x150 cm

62. *Crackers Boxes*, 1986
Wood, 150x170x160 cm
Private collection, New York

63. *Wooden Muscle*, 1986
Wood, plaster, 120x300x300 cm

64. *Eroded Landscape*, 1987
Glass, wood, steel, 145x125x60 cm
Private collection

65. *Riot*, 1987
Found plastic fragments, 235x1568x70 cm
Private collection, Switzerland
Courtesy Lisson Gallery, London
Installation: Hayward Gallery, London, 1987

66. *Instinctive Reactions*, 1987
Cast steel, 240x350x450 cm (overall)
Courtesy Lisson Gallery, London
Installation: Hayward Gallery, London, 1987

67. *Sedimenti cretacei*, 1987
Plaster, wood, 140x210x170 cm
Courtesy Tucci Russo, Torre Pellice
Installation: Galleria Tucci Russo, Turin, 1987
Photo Enzo Ricci, Turin

68. *Policeman*, 1988
Blue found plastic fragments, 400x120 cm

69. *Mortar and Pestle*, 1987
Aluminum, 94x1955x71 cm
Courtesy Marian Goodman Gallery, New York

70. *Spill*, 1987
Bronze, 90x330x115 cm
Collection Gerald S. Elliott, Chicago

71. *Inverted Sugar Crop*, 1987
Bronze, steel, 100x200x100 cm
Saatchi Collection, London

72. *Bestückung*, 1987-88
Cast iron, 2 parts, 210x220x80 cm (overall)
Collection Alfred and Mary Schands, Louisville
Courtesy Galerie Buchmann, Basel/Cologne

73. *Fragmente*, 1988
Steel, 3 parts, 123x250x220 cm (overall)
Courtesy Galerie Buchmann, Basel/Cologne

74. *Untitled (Shell)*, 1988
Steel, 110x220x200 cm
Saatchi Collection, London
Photo Jorg Sasse, Düsseldorf

75. *Generations*, 1988
Plaster, 13 parts, 90x300x350 cm (overall)
Courtesy Galerie Chantal Crousel, Paris
Photo Kleinefenn, Paris

76. *Fruits of Whose Labours,* 1989
Mixed media with shellac, 3 parts, 150x180x58 cm, 193x55x87 cm, 47x120x77 cm

77. *Eroded Landscape*, 1990
Glass, 120x150 cm
Courtesy Konrad Fischer, Düsseldorf
Photo Dorothee Fischer

78. *Yard*, 1988
Limestone, 6 parts, 81x96.5x190 cm (overall)
Collection Lenbachhaus, Munich
Photo Phillip Schönborn, Munich

79. *Broken Landscape*, 1988
Wood, 6 parts, 68x118x80 cm, 65x156x57 cm, 56x166x69 cm, 60x88.5 cm, 229x60 cm
Private collection, Augsburg

80. *Bodicea*, 1989
Iron, wood, 2 parts, 87x195x190 cm (overall)
Courtesy Tucci Russo, Torre Pellice
Photo Enzo Ricci, Turin

81. *Unit*, 1989
Lapis lazuli, 110x85x28 cm
Photo Chris Bliss

82. *Unit*, 1990
Ceramic, 10x140x28 cm
Courtesy Konrad Fischer, Düsseldorf
Photo Dorothee Fischer

83. *Unit*, 1990
Bronze, 18x210x35 cm
Courtesy Konrad Fischer, Düsseldorf
Photo Dorothee Fischer

84. *Extrusion*, 1989

Plaster, plywood, 160x40.6x40.6 cm
Courtesy Marian Goodman Gallery, New York

85. *Untitled,* 1988
Bronze, 2 parts, 80x50x215 cm (overall)
Musée National d'Art Moderne, Centre
Georges Pompidou, Paris
Photo Jorg Sasse, Düsseldorf

86. *Spill,* 1988
Glass, wood, 114x65x44 cm
Courtesy Galerie Chantal Crousel, Paris
Photo Gérard Rondeau

87. *Condensor*, 1989
Steel, 450x300x300 cm
Photo Andreas Jung, Düsseldorf

88. *Ordovician Pore*, 1989
Stone, steel, 315x244x228 cm
Walker Art Center, Minneapolis
Gift of Joanne and Phillip von Blon, 1989

89. *Early Forms,* 1988
Bronze, 210x210x285 cm
The Weltkunst Foundation, London
Photo Jorg Sasse, Düsseldorf and Bent
Weber, Hamburg

90. *Untitled,* 1988
Wood, 5 parts, 190x210x210 cm (overall)
Courtesy Galerie Chantal Crousel, Paris
Photo Jorg Sasse, Düsseldorf

91. *Forminifera*, 1989
Plaster, 10 parts, 150x400x300 cm (overall)
Courtesy Galerie Buchmann, Basel/Cologne

92. *Untitled*, 1989
Cement, 65x20x170 cm
Courtesy Thomas Cohn, Rio de Janeiro

93. *Matruschka*, 1989
Bronze, 190x80x80 cm
Collection Rivendell, New York
Photo Jorg Sasse, Düsseldorf

94. *Fruit Bottles*, 1989
Bronze, 6 parts, 80x166 cm (overall)
Private collection, Los Angeles
Photo Walter Klein, Gerresheim

95. *Minster*, 1991
Various metals, 5 parts, h 560 cm
Collection Mannheimer Versicherung AG
Photo Antje Zeis-Lois, Wuppertal

96. *Forminifera*, 1990
Plaster, 39 parts, 38x370x85 cm (overall)
Courtesy Galerie Buchmann, Basel/Cologne

97. *The Complete Omnivore (Lucy's Teeth)*, 1990
Ceramic, 83x92x51 cm
Photo Tom Haartsen, Ouderkerk a/d
Amstel

98. *Belgischer Hof,* 1990
Bronze, 3 parts, 71x135x62 cm,
40x270x105 cm, 76x144x11 cm
Courtesy Konrad Fischer, Düsseldorf
Photo Dorothee Fischer

99. *Hildener Kreuz*, 1989
Bronze, 100x170x150 cm
Courtesy Marian Goodman Gallery, New York

100. *Mineral Vein*, 1990
Marble, 47x134x107 cm
Courtesy Konrad Fischer, Düsseldorf
Photo Dorothee Fischer

101. *Trilobites*, 1989
Bronze, 2 parts, h 180 cm
Courtesy Bernd Klüser, Munich
Photo Walter Klein, Gerresheim
and Margherita Krischanitz, Vienna

102. *Trilobites*, 1989
Steel, 2 parts, h 180 cm
The Setagaya Art Museum, Setagaya

103. *Mountain Maquette (Quarry 'T')*,
1989
Bronze, cement
Bronze: 80x40x270 cm
Courtesy Marian Goodman Gallery, New York
Photo Jorg Sasse, Düsseldorf

104. *Quarry Purofer*, 1990
Bronze, ferric oxide, 200x380x300 cm
Courtesy Galerie Buchmann, Basel/Cologne
Photo Hans Gross, St. Gallen

105. *Quarry,* 1990
Bronze, ferric oxide, h 130 cm
Courtesy Tucci Russo, Torre Pellice
Photo Enzo Ricci, Turin

106. *Minster*, 1989-90
Various metals, 4 parts, 400x420x230 cm
(overall)
Courtesy Galerie Buchmann, Basel/Cologne

107. *Minster*, 1990
Various metals, 4 parts, 240x300x300 cm
(overall)
Courtesy Kanransha Gallery, Tokyo

108. *Laibe*, 1991
Ceramic, 60x65x60 cm
Photo Antje Zeis-Lois, Wuppertal

109. *Laibe*, 1990
Ceramic, 50x60x40 cm
Courtesy Konrad Fischer, Düsseldorf
Photo Dorothee Fischer

110. *Laibe*, 1991
Ceramic, 3 parts, 60x60x60 cm (overall)
Courtesy Bernd Klüser, Munich

111. *Newt*, 1990
Granite, 250x220x185 cm
Photo Margherita Krischanitz, Vienna

112. *Veil*, 1990
Bronze, 2 parts, 200x150x230 cm,
300x60 cm
Courtesy Galerie Chantal Crousel, Paris

113. *Untitled*, 1990
Bronze, 130x120x110 cm
Courtesy Galerie Buchmann, Basel/Cologne
Photo Hans Gross, St. Gallen

114. *Larder*, 1990
Glass, 90 parts, 65x100x90 cm (overall)
Courtesy Galerie Buchmann, Basel/Cologne

115. *Vessel*, 1991
Sandblasted glass, 19 parts,
148x146x153 cm (overall)
Courtesy Bernd Klüser, Munich
Photo Mario Gastinger, Munich

116. *Mineral Vein*, 1990
Marble, 41x130x90 cm
Courtesy Christine and Isy Brachot, Brussels

117. *Leguan*, 1990
Granite, h 237 cm
Collection Achenbach, Düsseldorf
Photo Antje Zeis-Lois, Wuppertal

118. *Plant*, 1990
Ceramic, 60x70x60 cm
Courtesy Art&Project, Slootdorp
Photo Tom Haartsen, Ouderkerk a/d Amstel

119. *Eichelhäher,* 1990
Wood, 4 parts, 152x450x310 cm (overall)
Courtesy Hachmeister Galerie, Münster
Photo Hans Gross, St. Gallen

120. *Atmos*, 1990
Ceramic, 3 parts, 30x50x50 cm (overall)
Courtesy Konrad Fischer, Düsseldorf
Photo Dorothee Fischer

121. *Two Tigers,* 1990
Sandblasted porcelain, 2 parts,
55x45x41 cm
Courtesy Konrad Fischer, Düsseldorf
Photo Dorothee Fischer

122. *Mixed Cylinders,* 1990
Steel, 5 parts, 200x200x110 cm (overall)
Courtesy Konrad Fischer, Düsseldorf
Photo Dorothee Fischer

123. *Stock,* 1988
Wood, 3 parts, 40x137 cm, 55x85 cm,
70x35 cm
Courtesy Werkstatt Kollerschlag, Vienna
Photo Margherita Krischanitz, Vienna

124. *Incubation,* 1990
Granite, 3 parts, 60x320x200 cm (overall)
Courtesy Tucci Russo, Torre Pellice
Photo Enzo Ricci, Turin

125. *Atmos*, 1990
Ceramic, 3 parts, 80x125x125 cm (overall)
Courtesy Bernd Klüser, Munich
Photo Mario Gastinger, Munich

126. *Manipulations,* 1991
Steel, 5 parts, 140x150x150 cm (overall)
Courtesy Deweer Art Gallery, Otegem

127. *Atmos,* 1991
Bronze, 3 parts, 116x101 cm, 101x78 cm,
89x76 cm
Courtesy Marian Goodman Gallery, New York
Photo Michael Goodman

128. *Eroded Landscape,* 1991
Sandblasted glass, 150x150x180 cm (overall)
Courtesy Galerie Buchmann, Basel/Cologne
Photo Margherita Krischanitz, Vienna

129. *Subcommittee,* 1991
Bronze, 250x200x200 cm
Photo Margherita Krischanitz, Vienna

130. *Subcommittee,* 1991
Steel, 240x140x185 cm
Hirshhorn Museum, Washington D.C.

131. *Clearing,* 1991
Polyurethane, 9 parts, 250x300x65 cm
(overall)
IVAM, Centre Julio Gonzalez, Valencia
Photo Margherita Krischanitz, Vienna

132. *Gold, Incense, Myrrh*, 1990
Wood, polyester, 3 parts,
300x130x30 cm (overall)
Courtesy Bernd Klüser, Munich

133. *Administered Landscape*, 1991
Bronze, 100x100x70 cm (overall)

134. *Suburbs*, 1990
Wood, rubber, 3 parts, 250x400x400 cm
(overall)
Courtesy Marian Goodman Gallery, New York
Photo Heidrun Lohr

135. *Forminifera,* 1991
Plaster with steel holders, 6 parts,
177x218x243 cm (overall)
Kunstmuseum Wolfsburg, Wolfsburg
Photo Michael Goodman

136. *Beasts of Burden*, 1991
Tufa stone, 3 parts, 60x110x60 cm each
Courtesy Lisson Gallery, London
Photo Gareth Winters, London

137. *Early Forms*, 1989
Bronze, 2 parts, 165.1x256.5x139.7 cm,
203.2x259.1x111.8 cm
New Academy for Art Studies, London

138. *Iron Mountain,* 1990
Cast iron, 190x255x280 cm
Collection Piero Fedeli, Milan
Courtesy Tucci Russo, Torre Pellice
Photo Enzo Ricci, Turin

139. *Beasts of Burden,* 1991
Bored and sandblasted volcanic ash,
3 parts, 66x140x63.5 cm, 61x114x61 cm,
58x152x61 cm
Courtesy Marian Goodman Gallery, New York
Photo Michael Goodman

140. *Early Forms,* 1991
Wood, 3 parts, 400x700x350 cm (overall)
Courtesy Werkstatt Kollerschlag, Vienna
Photo Margherita Krischanitz, Vienna

141. *Modern Types*, 1989
Plaster, 8 parts, 120x20x30 cm (overall)
Courtesy Thomas Cohn, Rio de Janeiro

142. *Beasts of Burden,* 1992
Tufa, 3 parts, 116.8x91.4x172.7 cm,
76.2x76.2x121.9 cm, 109.2x63.5x11.8 cm

143. *Shields,* 1991
Granite, 3 parts, 250x250x170 cm (overall)
Courtesy Werkstatt Kollerschlag, Vienna
Photo Margherita Krischanitz, Vienna

144. *Connecting Piece,* 1991
Steel, 90x250x120 cm
Photo Margherita Krischanitz, Vienna

145. *Vulnerable Landscape:*
The Thin Skin, 1991
Bronze, 35x112x54 cm
Courtesy Lisson Gallery, London
Photo Gareth Winters, London

146. *Burden,* 1991

Ceramic, 62x35x34 cm
Courtesy Art&Project, Slootdorp
Photo Tom Haartsen, Ouderkerk a/d Amstel

147. *Zooid,* 1991
Steel, ceramic, 2 parts, 30x93x37 cm (each)
Courtesy Lisson Gallery, London
Photo Marc Rader, Bochum

148. *Cloud,* 1991
Bronze, 116x68.5x45 cm
Courtesy Marian Goodman Gallery, New York
Photo Michael Goodman

149. *Plough*, 1990
Iron, 120x245x100 cm
Photo Gene Ogami

150. *Species*, 1990
Iron, 113x300x125 cm
Courtesy Bernd Klüser, Munich
Photo Mario Gastinger, Munich

151. *Unschärferelation,* 1991
Wood, 5 parts, 210x115x85 cm (overall)
Courtesy Bernd Klüser, Munich
Photo Mario Gastinger, Munich

152. *For the Walking Man,* 1991
Marble, metal, 3 parts, 66x139x94 cm (overall)
Courtesy Marian Goodman Gallery, New York
Photo Michael Goodman

153. *Mineral Vein,* 1991
Nero manquina, 80x146x102 cm
Courtesy Lisson Gallery, London
Photo Gareth Winters, London

154. *Cellulose Memory,* 1991
Beech wood, 3 parts, 137x373x356 cm (overall)
Courtesy Marian Goodman Gallery, New York
Photo Michael Goodman

155. *Bromide Figures,* 1992
Glass, shellac, 153x172x135 cm
Courtesy Lisson Gallery, London
Photo John Riddy, London

156. *Eroded Landscape,* 1992
Sandblasted glass, 200x140x160 cm
Courtesy Galerie Buchmann, Basel/Cologne

157. *Spyrogyra,* 1992
Sandblasted glass, metal, 210x210 cm
Courtesy Galerie Buchmann, Basel/Cologne

158. *Untitled*, 1990
Bronze, 2 parts, 200x150x230 cm, 300x60 cm
Courtesy Lisson Gallery, London

159. *Social Situation*, 1992
Wood, hooks, 130x200x200 cm
Courtesy Tucci Russo, Torre Pellice
Photo Enzo Ricci, Turin

160. *Untitled*, 1992
Wood, hooks, 105x100x105 cm
Courtesy Thomas Cohn, Rio de Janeiro

161. *Gazelle*, 1992
Bicycle, glass bottles, 130x200x130 cm
Courtesy Galerie Buchmann, Basel/Cologne

162. *Untitled*, 1992
Wax, mixed media, 137x78x75 cm
Courtesy Bernd Klüser, Munich
Photo Mario Gastinger, Munich

163. *Re-Forming*, 1992
Bronze, 1.5x15x18 m
Collection Landeszentralbank, Düsseldorf
Photo Axel Stoffers, Mulheim

164. *Our Bolders*, 1992
Granite, 200x180x200 cm (overall)
Collection Landeszentralbank, Düsseldorf
Photo Axel Stoffers, Mulheim

165. *Two Rivers*, 1992
Bronze, 2 parts, 720x128 cm, 610x110 cm
Collection Landeszentralbank, Düsseldorf
Photo Antje Zeis-Lois, Wuppertal

166. *Emergence*, 1992
Bronze, 135x250x143 cm
Courtesy Lisson Gallery, London
Photo John Riddy, London

167. *Invertebrated Friends*, 1992
Tufa, 2 parts, 80x230x100 cm, 80x90x90 cm
80x300x250 cm (overall)
Courtesy Tucci Russo, Torre Pellice
Photo Enzo Ricci, Turin

168. *Clear Microbe*, 1992
Wood, 120x210x140 cm
Courtesy Christine and Isy Brachot, Brussels

169. *In Camera,* 1993
Ceramic, 65x45x60 cm
Courtesy European Ceramics Work Centre, 's-Hertogenbosch

170. *In Camera*, 1993
Ceramic, 400x400x200 cm
Stedelijk van Abbemuseum, Eindhoven
Photo Peer van der Kruis

171. *Glass Hybrids*, 1992
Glass, 150x180x180 cm
Courtesy Christine and Isy Brachot, Brussels

172. *Terris Novalis*, 1992
Steel, 2 parts, 160x287x150 cm, 245x208x136 cm
Courtesy Lisson Gallery, London
Photo John Riddy, London

173. *Archimedes Screw*, 1993
Bronze, 120x120x800 cm
Courtesy Municipality of 's-Hertogenbosch
Photo Peer van der Kruis

174. *Complete Omnivore*, 1993
Plaster, wood, steel, 160x200x200 cm
Courtesy Marian Goodman Gallery, New York
Photo Tom Powel

175. *Mental Picture*, 1992
Jurassic limestone, 11 parts, 133x500x485 cm (overall)
Courtesy Lisson Gallery, London
Photo John Riddy, London

176. *Blood Sugar*, 1992
Glass, 2 parts, 64x187x85 cm (overall)
Courtesy Lisson Gallery, London
Photo John Riddy, London

177. *Blood Sugar*, 1992
Glass, 2 parts, 57x65x75 cm, 50x70x70 cm
57x130x80 cm (overall)

178. *Angels and Other Antibodies*, 1992
Wood, hooks, 225x240x150 cm
Courtesy Christine and Isy Brachot, Brussels

179. *Administrated Cellulose*, 1992
Wood, 105x270x220 cm
Courtesy Christine and Isy Brachot, Brussels

180. *Tool*, 1991
Wood, 110x400x130 cm
Courtesy Werkstatt Kollerschlag, Vienna
Photo Margherita Krischanitz, Vienna

181. *Spear*, 1990
Granite, 250x140x120 cm
Courtesy Werkstatt Kollerschlag, Vienna

182. *Untitled*, 1993
7 parts, total length 150 m
Courtesy Municipality of Bodo, Norway
Photo Werner Zellien, Bodo

183. *Island*, 1993
Plaster, 85x94x98 cm
Courtesy Marian Goodman Gallery, New York
Photo Tom Powel

184. *Time Suds*, 1993
Wax, 6 parts, 85x130x105 cm (overall)
Courtesy Marian Goodman Gallery, New York

185. *Untitled*, 1993
Polyurethane, 4 parts, 100x100x100 cm (overall)
Courtesy Marian Goodman Gallery, New York
Photo Tom Powel

186. *Messages*, 1993
Wood, 2 parts, 75x200x96 cm, 73x288x88 cm
Courtesy Marian Goodman Gallery, New York
Photo Tom Powel

187. *Unholy Ghosts*, 1993
Wax on mixed media, 2 parts, h 600 cm (each)
Photo Mario Gastinger, Munich

188. *Fast Particles,* 1994
Wood, object assemblage, wax
Courtesy Deweer Art Gallery, Otegem
Installation: Deweer Art Gallery, Otegem, 1995

189. *Daily Bread,* 1994
Aluminum, h 800 cm
Wiener Neustadt

190. *Wildlife,* 1995
Table, plaster
Courtesy Deweer Art Gallery, Otegem
Installation: Deweer Art Gallery, Otegem, 1995

191. *Solid States,* 1995
Steel, 48 Continental United States
Ace Contemporary Exhibitions, Los Angeles/New York

192. *Trade Wind,* 1995
Plaster, 240x115 cm
Courtesy Tucci Russo, Torre Pellice
Photo Enzo Ricci, Turin

193. *Rational Beings,* 1995
Carbon, 500x230x265 cm (overall)
Courtesy Tucci Russo, Torre Pellice
Photo Enzo Ricci, Turin

Bio-bibliographical Notes

Anna Costantini

Biography

Tony Cragg was born in Liverpool in 1949. His father was an electrical engineer who worked in the aircraft industry.
Perhaps then understandably, after his school studies which were science-oriented Cragg got a job in 1966 as a technician in the research laboratory of the Natural Rubber Producers Research Association.
It was during the two years he worked in the laboratory that he discovered his interest in art. He did his first drawings and began to consider the objects around him.
He attended the Gloucester College of Art and Design in Cheltenham in 1968-69 (at the same time working the night shift in a foundry near Bristol that produced parts for electric motors), then from 1969 to 1972 he attended the Wimbledon School of Art, where he was taught by Roger Ackling and Jim Rogers.
In 1972, he enrolled in the sculpture course at the Royal College of Art in London. At this time he became friends with Bill Woodrow and Richard Deacon. After graduating with the M.A. in 1977, he moved to Wuppertal in Germany where he still lives.
He started exhibiting in the late 1970s and was the first member of a new generation of British sculptors to appear in the 1980s.
In 1976 he taught at the École des Beaux-Arts in Metz.
In 1978 he started teaching at the Kunstakademie Düsseldorf and received a professorship in 1988.
He was awarded the Turner Prize 1988 and he has been a member of the Royal Academy since 1994.

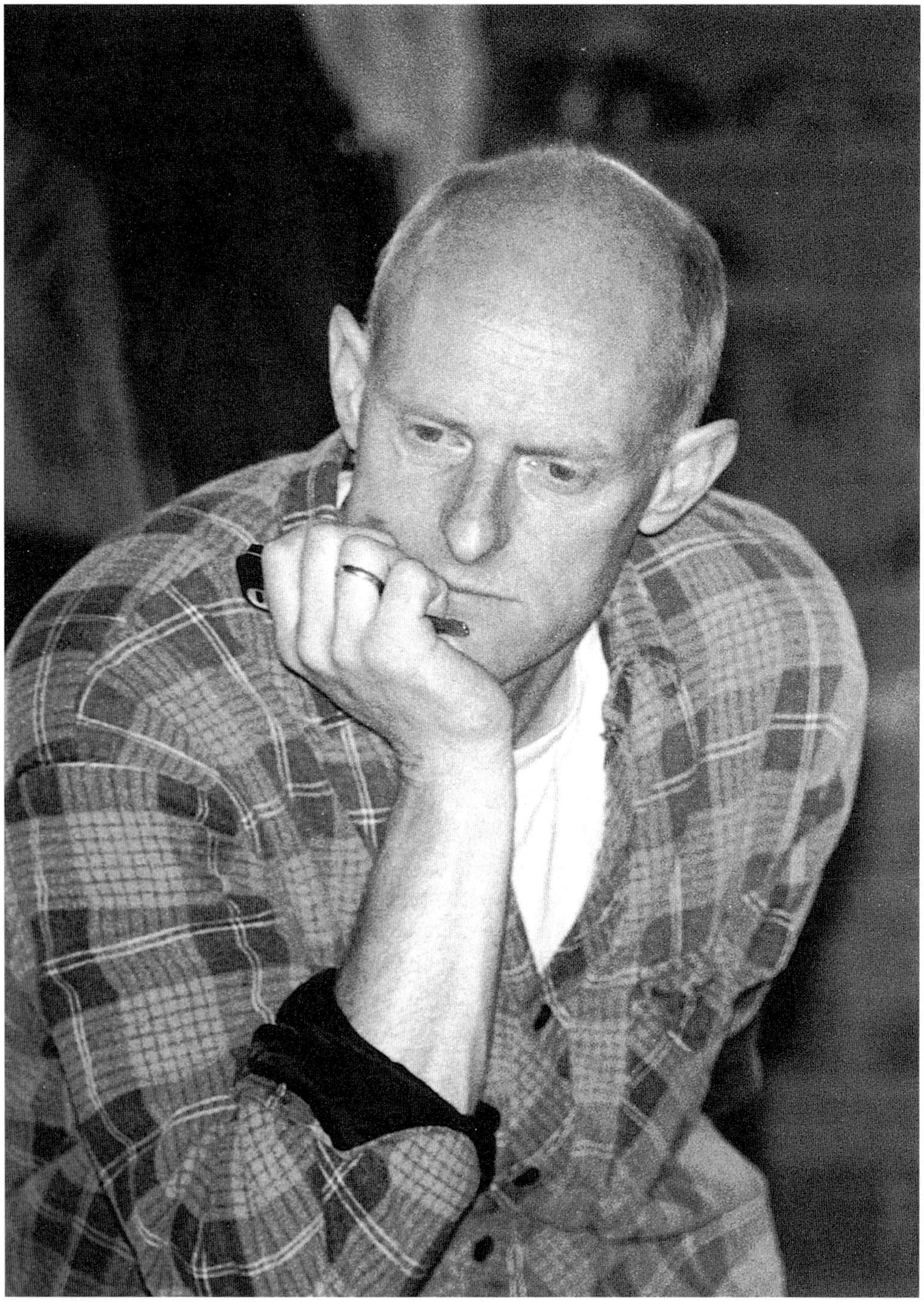

Selected Exhibition History

Solo Exhibitions and Reviews

1979
Lisson Gallery, London.
– S. Kent. *Time Out*, March 7, 1979.
– S. V. Winter. "Tony Cragg at Lisson." *Artscribe*, no. 17 (April 1979), pp. 30-31.

Lützowstrasse Situation, Berlin.

Künstlerhaus Weidenallee, Hamburg.

1980
Arnolfini Gallery, Bristol.
– L. Biggs. "Tony Cragg." *Arnolfini Review*, May-June, 1980.
– E. Phelps. "Joel Degen, Tony Cragg, Bruce McLean." *Arts Review* 32, no. 13 (July 4, 1980), p. 289.

Konrad Fischer, Düsseldorf.

Lisson Gallery, London. *Sculpture*. July 16-Aug. 9.
– S. Morgan. "Tony Cragg, Lisson Gallery." *Artforum* 19, no. 2 (Oct. 1980), pp. 85-86.

Chantal Crousel, Paris. *Tony Cragg*. Sept. 20-Oct. 23.
– C. Strasser. "Tony Cragg. Galerie Chantal Crousel." *Flash Art*, no. 100 (Nov. 1980), p. 50.

Lützowstrasse Situation, Berlin.

Lucio Amelio, Naples. Opened Oct. 18.

Franco Toselli, Milan. Opened Nov. 21.
– L. Somaini. "Tony Cragg/Franco Toselli." *Flash Art*, no. 101 (Jan.-Feb. 1981), pp. 58-59.
– L. Parmesani. "Milano/Galleria Toselli. Tony Cragg." *Segno*, no. 19 (Jan.-Feb. 1981), p. 25.

Samangallery, Genoa. Opened Nov. 25.

1981
Schellmann & Klüser, Munich. Opened Jan. 15.
– H. Weskott. "Tony Cragg. Abfallskulptur des Plastikzeitaters." *Kunstforum international*, no. 43 (Jan. 1981), pp. 165-166.

Musée d'Art et d'Industrie, Saint-Etienne. Jan. 23-March 8. Catalogue, with text by B. Ceysson.

The Whitechapel Art Gallery, London. Feb. 27-March 22.
– L. Cooke. "Tony Cragg at the Whitechapel." *Artscribe*, no. 28 (March 1981), pp. 54-55.

Le Nouveau Musée, Lyon.
– J. Rozier. "Tony Cragg invité à Lyon pour un an." *Le Journal*, June 1981.

Front Room, London. Oct. 3-17.

Von der Heydt Museum, Wuppertal. Oct. 20-Nov. 22. Catalogue, with text by U. Peters.

Vacuum, Düsseldorf.

1982
Badischer Kunstverein, Karlsruhe. *Tony Cragg. Skulpturen*. Jan. 12-Feb. 28. Curated by M. Schwarz. Catalogue, with text by M. Newman.
– R. Braxmeier. "Tony Cragg, Badischer Kunstverein, Karlsruhe." *Kunstwerk* 35, no. 2 (April 1982), p. 71.

Kanransha Gallery, Tokyo. Jan. 18-Feb. 20. Catalogue, with text by N. Nakamura.

Fifth Triennale India, New Delhi. March 15-April 7. Catalogue, with texts by J. Andrews, N. Lynton.

Chantal Crousel, Paris. *Tony Cragg*. April 15-May 15.
– M. Nuridsany. "Tony Cragg. Galerie Chantal Crousel." *Art press*, no. 60 (June 1982), p. 40.

Nisshin Gallery, Tokyo.

Marian Goodman Gallery, New York.

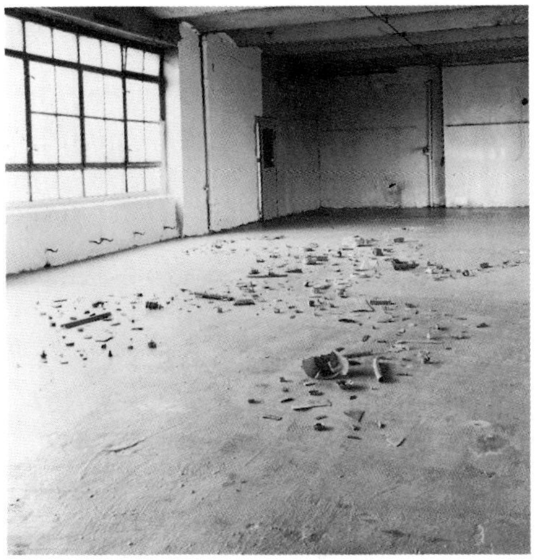

Redskin, *Lützowstrasse Situation, Berlin, 1979*

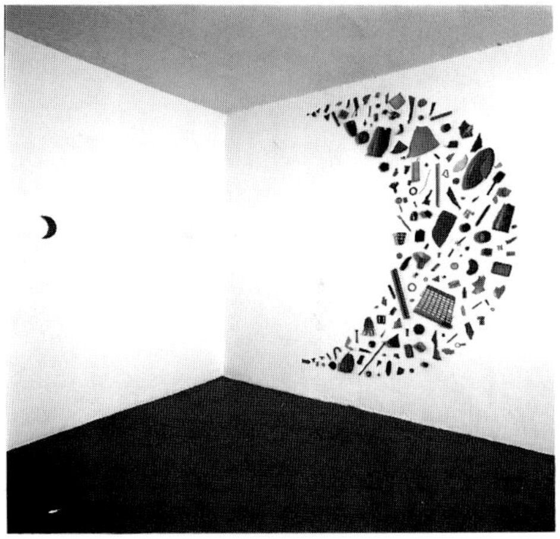

Blue Moon, *Galerie Chantal Crousel, Paris, 1980*

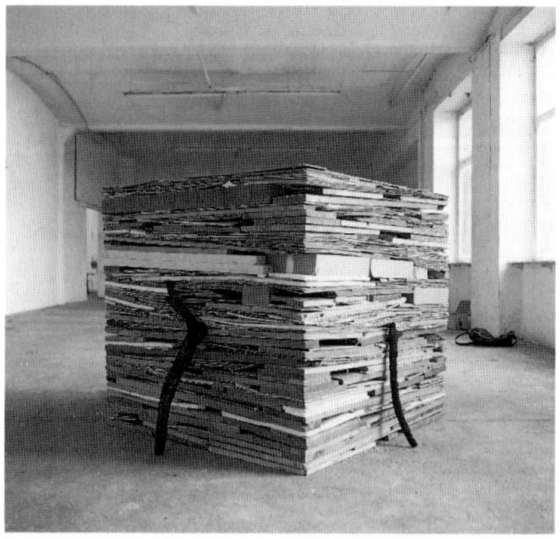

Stack, *Lützowstrasse Situation, Berlin, 1980*

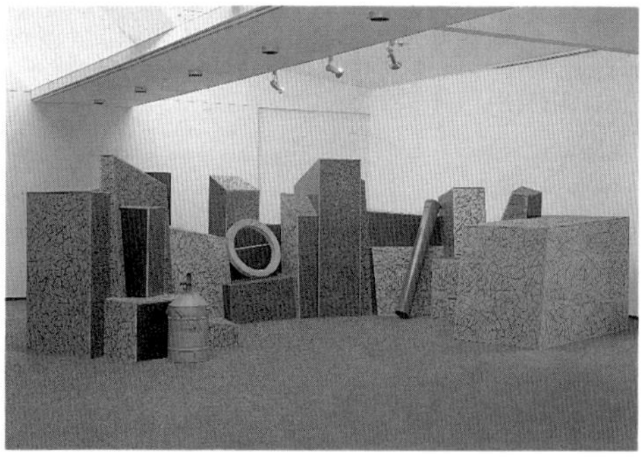

Echo, *Kölnischer Kunstverein, Köln, 1984*

Le Nouveau Musée, Lyon.

Schellmann & Klüser, Munich.

Konrad Fischer, Düsseldorf.
– A. Pohlen. "Hiroshima und danach. Ausstellungen im Rheinland." *Kunstforum international* 58, no. 2 (Feb. 1983), p. 182.

Lisson Gallery, London.
– J. Russel Taylor. "Timely mirror upon life's realities." *The Times*, Dec. 7, 1982.
– S. Kent. *Time Out*, Dec. 17, 1982.

Rijksmuseum Kröller-Müller, Otterloo. *Tony Cragg. Recente beelden*. Dec. 18-Jan. 23, 1983.

1983
Lucio Amelio, Naples. Opened March 5.

Marian Goodman Gallery, New York.
– *The New York Times*, April 24, 1983.
– C. Steelweg. "Tony Cragg: Marian Goodman (New York)." *ArtNews* 83, no. 6 (Summer 1983), p. 194.

Kunsthalle Bern, Bern. April 30-June 5. Catalogue, with texts by G. Celant, T. Cragg, J.-H. Martin.

Art&Project, Amsterdam.

Thomas Cohn, Rio de Janeiro.

Galerie Buchmann, St. Gallen. Sept. 24-Oct. 22. Catalogue, with text by A. Wildermuth.

Franco Toselli, Milan. Opened Oct. 15.
– L. Somaini. "Tony Cragg/Franco Toselli." *Flash Art* 17, no. 117 (Dec. 1983-Jan. 1984), p. 43.

1984
Yarlow & Salzmann Gallery, Toronto.
– G. M. Dault. *Vanguard*, April 1984.

De Vleeshal, Middelburg. Catalogue, with text by A. Wildermuth.

Louisiana Museum of Modern Art, Humlebaek.

Schellmann & Klüser, Munich. *Tony Cragg. Neue Skulpturen*. March 1-31.
– K. Hegewisch. *Kunstwerk*, June 1984.

Marian Goodman Gallery, New York.
– J. Russell. *The New York Times*, March 16, 1984.
– K. Baker. "Tony Cragg at Marian Goodman." *Art in America* 72, no. 8 (Sept. 1984), p. 206.
– V. Raynor. *The New York Times*, March 30, 1984.

Kanransha Gallery, Tokyo. March 26-April 28. Catalogue, with text by R. Kawaguchi.

Galerie Crousel-Hussenot, Paris. Sept. 15-Oct. 23.

Kölnischer Kunstverein, Cologne. *Tony Cragg. Vier Arbeiten*. Sept. 16-Oct. 28. Catalogue.
– N. Pohlen. "Julian Opie und Tony Cragg." *Kunstforum international*, no. 75 (Sept.-Oct. 1984).

Galleria Tucci Russo, Turin. Opened Nov. 9. Catalogue.
– G. Ciavoliello. "Tony Cragg/Tucci Russo Torino." *Juliet*, no. 18 (Feb.-March 1985), pp. 42-43.
– L. Rogozinski. "Turin. Tony Cragg, Galleria Tucci Russo." *Artforum* 23, no. 7 (March 1985), p. 107.

1985
Kunsthalle Waaghaus, Winterthur.

Staatsgalerie Moderner Kunst, Munich.

Donald Young Gallery, Chicago.
– J. Russi Kirshner. "Chicago. Tony Cragg, Richard Deacon, Donald Young Gallery." *Artforum* 23, no. 10 (Summer 1985), p. 113.

Lisson Gallery, London. *Tony Cragg. Recent Works*. March 20 – April 20.
– "No place for demarcation." *The Times*,

March 26, 1985.
– R. Cork. "Junk Mood." *The Listener*, April 11, 1985.
– M. R. Beaumont. *Arts Review*, no. 7 (April 12, 1985), p. 177.
– M. Vaizey. "Having fun with trash." *The Sunday Times*, April 14, 1985.
– M. Petzal. *Art Monthly*, May 1985.

Art&Project, Amsterdam. April 13-May 11.

Palais des Beaux-Arts, Brussels. June 21-July 28. Catalogue, with texts by A. G. Buzzi, K. J. Geirlandt, S. Pagé, A. Pohlen, interview by D. Davvetas. Traveled to Musée d'Art Moderne de la Ville de Paris, Paris. Oct. 9-Dec. 1, 1985.
– A. Pohlen. "Tony Cragg, Palais des Beaux-Arts, Brussels; ARC, Paris." *Financial Times*, April 16, 1985.

Bernd Klüser, Munich. *Tony Cragg. Neue Skulpturen*. Nov. 5-Jan. 15, 1986.

Kestner-Gesellschaft, Hanover. *Tony Cragg. Skulpturen*. Dec. 20-Feb. 9, 1986. Catalogue, with texts by T. Cragg, D. Davvetas, C. Haenlein.
– A. Pohlen. "Tony Cragg, Kestner-Gesellschaft." *Artforum* 24, no. 9 (May 1986), pp. 148-149.

1986

Galerie Buchmann, Basel. Jan. 18-March 1.

Marian Goodman Gallery, New York. March 11-April 5.
– J. Russel. *The New York Times*, March 21, 1986.
– N. Princenthal. "Tony Cragg at Marian Goodman." *Art in America* 74, no. 6 (June 1986), p. 127.

Joost Declercq, Ghent. May 3-June 7.

The Brooklyn Museum of Art, Brooklyn.

University Art Museum, University of California, Berkeley.

Het Geward, Ghent.

La Jolla Museum of Contemporary Art, La Jolla.
– R. McDonald. "Small But Choice La Jolla Exhibition." *Los Angeles Times*, Sept. 5, 1986.
– R. L. Pincus. "One Man's Discards Another Man's Art in La Jolla." *San Diego Union*, Aug. 28, 1986.
– L. Goldman. "Tony Cragg, La Jolla Museum of Contemporary Art." *ArtNews* 86, no. 1 (Jan. 1987), p. 62.

Pierre Huber, Geneva.

Konrad Fischer, Düsseldorf. *Tony Cragg. Cast Iron Works*. Dec. 12-Jan. 22, 1987.

1987

Hayward Gallery, South Bank Centre, London. March 5-June 7. Organized by C. Lampert. Catalogue, with text and interview by L. Cooke.
– W. Feaver. "Totter and a Pearly King." *The Observer*, March 8, 1987, p. 26.
– J. Bumpus. "Tony Cragg, Hayward Gallery." *Arts Review* 39, no. 5 (March 13, 1987), p. 158.
– M. Allthorpe-Guyton. "Tony Cragg." *Flash Art International*, no. 134 (May 1987), p. 76.
– J. McEwen. "Tony Cragg at the Hayward." *Art in America* 75, no. 7 (July 1987), pp. 36-37.
– J. Welchman. *Artscribe* (Summer 1987).

Galerie im Taxispalais, Innsbruck. March 3-April 12. Catalogue.

Corner House, Manchester.

Galleria Tucci Russo, Turin. Opened Sept. 25.
– M. T. Roberto, "Torino/Tony Cragg, Tucci Russo", *Flash Art*, no. 141 (Nov. 1987), p. 93.
– L. Parola, "Tony Cragg/Tucci Russo, Torino." *Juliet*, no. 34 (Dec.-Jan. 1988).

Kanransha Gallery, Tokyo. *Tony Cragg. New Works*. Dec. 1-26.

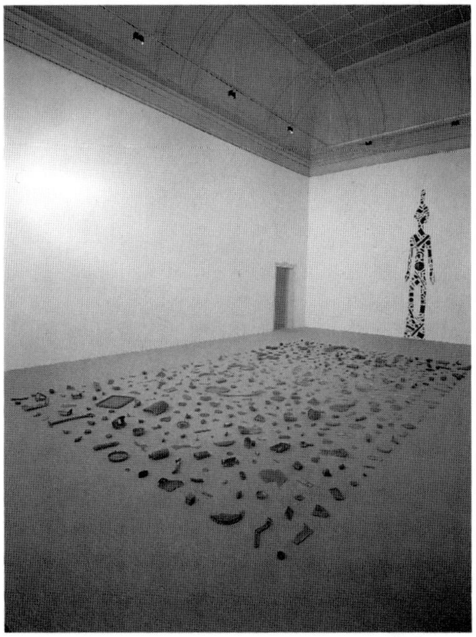

African Culture Myth, *1984*; Spectrum, *1983*
Kunsthalle Waaghaus, Winterthur, 1985

Marian Goodman Gallery, New York. Nov. 6-Dec. 5.
– K L[inker]. "Reviews. Tony Cragg/Marian Goodman Gallery." *Artforum* 26, no. 6 (Feb. 1988), pp. 146-147.

1988
XLIII Biennale Internazionale d'Arte, British Pavilion, Venice. Catalogue, with texts by D. Davvetas, H. M. Hughes, C. Lampert; in English and Italian.
– T. Hilton. "Dearth in Venice." *The Guardian*, June 29, 1988.
– A. Vettese. "Natura e esistenza maturano sculture." *Il Sole-24 ore*, July 31, 1988, p. 23.
– A. Graham-Dixon. "Biennale Bulletin." *Vogue*, July 1988.
– C. Millet. "La 43e biennale de Venise. Un art d'époque." *Art press*, no. 128 (Sept. 1988), p. 66.
– A. Dagbert. "Tony Cragg." *Ibidem*, p. 70.
– S. H. Madoff. "Venice Biennale: Calm Waters." *ArtNews* 87, no. 7 (Sept. 1988), pp. 178-180.
– P. Bickers. "New Models for Old: Tony Cragg at the 43rd Venice Biennale." *Art Monthly*, Sept. 1988.
– S. Schmidt-Wulfen. "Tony Cragg, British Pavilion." *Flash Art International*, no. 142 (Oct. 1988), pp. 107-108.
– L. Cooke. "Venice Biennale." *Art International*, Fall 1988.
– L. B. Bowen. "Venice: Sculpture Dominates the 43rd Venice Biennale." *Artpost* 6, no. 1 (Fall 1988), pp. 28-30.
– M. Vescovo. "Tony Cragg." *Tema Celeste*, no. 17-18 (Oct.-Dec. 1988), pp. 53-54.
– L. Camnitzer. "La XLIII Bienal de Venecia en sus 93 anos." *Arte en Columbia*, no. 38 (Dec. 1988), pp. 53-57, 137-138.

Marga Paz, Madrid.

Galerie Buchmann, Basel. Feb. 13-April 9.
– H.-J. Muller. "Dingfest: Neue Arbeiten von Tony Cragg in der Galerie Buchmann." *Basler Zeitung*, Feb. 18, 1988.

Galerie Crousel-Robelin, Paris. *Tony Cragg*. Oct. 15-Nov. 14.

Galerie Foksal, Warsaw.

Galerie Bernd Klüser, Munich. *Tony Cragg. Neue Arbeiten*. Oct. 4-Nov. 5.

Silo/Centre de création contemporaine, Val de Vesle. June 18-Aug. 30. Catalogue, with texts by T. Cragg and P. Piguet.
– P. Piguet. "Val de Vesle, Tony Cragg." *L'Oeil: revue d'art*, no. 396-397 (July-Aug. 1988), p. 68.
– A. Dagbert. "Tony Cragg." *Art press*, no. 128 (Sept. 1988), p. 70.

Lisson Gallery, London. Dec. 2-Jan. 28, 1989.
– R. Martin. "Tony Cragg/Lisson, London." *Flash Art International*, no. 145 (March-April 1989), p. 121.
– M. Archer. "Tony Cragg, Lisson Gallery." *Artforum* 27, no. 8 (April 1989), p. 180.
– D. Batchelor. *Artscribe*, no. 75 (May 1989), pp. 73-74.
– "Tony Cragg, u galerji Lisson." *Moment*, no. 15 (July-Sept. 1989).

1989
Konrad Fischer, Düsseldorf. Opened March 18.

Kanransha Gallery, Tokyo. *Tony Cragg. New Works*. March 13-April 8.

The Tate Gallery, London. *Tony Cragg. Winner of the 1988 Turner Prize*. April 26-June 25. Catalogue, with texts by T. Cragg and N. Serota.
– J. Norrie. "Tony Cragg, Tate Gallery." *Arts Review* 41, no. 10 (May 19, 1989), p. 384.
– R. MacDonald. *Contemporanea*, no. 6 (Sept. 1989), p. 92.

Stedelijk van Abbemuseum, Eindhoven. *Tony Cragg. Beelden/Sculptures*. May 14-July 2. Organized by J. Debbaut and S. Klein Essink. Catalogue, with texts by D. Batchelor, T. Cragg, J. Debbaut.

Thomas Cohn, Rio de Janeiro.

Marian Goodman Gallery, New York. *Tony Cragg. New Sculpture*. Nov. 9-Dec. 1.
– S. Hapgood. "Review/Tony Cragg at Marian Goodman." *Art in America*, March 1990.

Kunstsammlung Nordrhein-Westfalen, Düsseldorf. Nov. 18-Jan. 7, 1990. Catalogue, with text by M. Müller.
– H. Meister. "Kindergluck der kleinen Dinge." *WZ*, Nov. 18, 1989.
– P. Winter. "Spielzeug aus Goliaths Reich." *Frankfurter Allgemeine Zeitung*, Dec. 7, 1989.
– "Spuren von Natur und Zivilisation", *Haudelsblatt*, Dec. 8-9, 1989.

1990
Crown Point Press, San Francisco.

Galerie Buchmann, Basel. Feb. 3-March 3.
– "Ausstellungen in Basel", *Basler Zeitung*, Feb. 17, 1990.

Galleria Tucci Russo, Turin. May 11-Sept. 30.
– I. Mulatero. "Tony Cragg. Tucci Russo, Torino." *Juliet*, no. 49 (Oct.-Nov. 1990), p. 70.

Kanransha Gallery, Tokyo. *Tony Cragg. New Works*, Sept. 3-29.

Newport Harbor Art Museum, Newport Beach. *Tony Cragg: Sculptures 1975-1990*. Oct. 14-Dec. 30. Organized by P. Schimmel, Marilu Knode. Catalogue, with texts by L. Barnes, M. Francis, M. Knode, T. McEvilley, P. Schjeldahl. Traveled to The Corcoran Gallery of Art, Washington. Feb. 1-March 31, 1991; Power Plant, Toronto. Sept. 6-Oct. 27, 1991; Contemporary Art Museum, Houston. Nov. 16-Feb. 9, 1992.
– G. Harbrecht. "Artist creates behemoths of steel, bronze." *The Orange County Register*, Oct. 14, 1990, pp. 20-21.
– K. Baker. "Tony Cragg's Major Museum Show." *Datebook*, Oct. 28, 1990.
– R. L. Pincus. "Out of the rubble of our times he fashions art." *San Diego Union*, Nov. 25, 1990, p. E4-5.
– R. Wollheim. "Tony Cragg at forty-one at

Newport Beach." *Modern Painters*, Summer 1991, pp. 32-37.

Bernd Klüser, Munich. *Tony Cragg. Arbeiten*. Nov. 27-Feb. 15, 1991.
– D. Eichenauer. "Tony Cragg in der Galerie Klüser. Die Schule des Sehens." *Applaus*, no. 60-61 (Dec. 1990).

Konrad Fischer, Düsseldorf. Opened Dec. 8.

Valentina Moncada, Rome. Nov. 30-Jan. 15, 1991. Catalogue, with text by V. Moncada and interview by L. Pratesi.
– P. Balmas. "Tony Cragg." *Segno* 15, no. 100 (Jan. 1991), pp. 36-37.
– L. Pratesi. "Uno sguardo sugli oggetti." *Opening* (Jan.-Feb. 1991).
– G. Villa. "Tony Cragg. Valentina Moncada." *Flash Art* 24, no. 160 (Feb.-March 1991), p. 104.

1991
Galerie Crousel-Robelin, Paris. *Estampes*. Jan. 5-Feb. 9.

Stedelijk van Abbemuseum, Eindhoven. July 12-Sept. 15. Organized by J. Debbaut and S. Klein Essink. Catalogue, with texts by D. Batchelor, T. Cragg, J. Debbaut.

Galerie Crousel-Robelin, Paris. *Tony Cragg*. Oct. 10-Nov. 12.
– J-Y. Jouannais. "Tony Cragg, Galerie Crousel-Robelin Bama." *Art press*, no. 163 (Nov. 1991), pp. 92-93.

Werkstatt Kollerschlag, Kollerschlag.

Kunstverein Ruhr, Essen. Catalogue.

Wiener Secession, Vienna. Oct. 2-Nov. 3. Catalogue (2 vols), with texts by D. Karner, E. Kob, A. Krischanitz, M. Mittringer.

Bernd Klüser, Munich. *Tony Cragg. Die 1. Ära*. Nov. 5-Dec. 3.

Lisson Gallery, London. Closed Aug. 3.
– J. McEwen. "Still watching things tick and boil." *The Sunday Telegraph*, July 14, 1991.
– W. Feaver. "Issey gets busy." *The Observer*, July 21, 1991.
– S. Kent. "Mould Breaking." *Time Out*, July 24-31, 1991.
– R. Bevan. "The doldrums." *The Art Newspaper*, no. 10 (July-Sept., 1991), p. 21.
– M. Corris. "Tony Cragg, Lisson Gallery." *Artforum* 30, no. 3 (Nov. 1991), p. 152.
– M. Archer. "Tony Cragg, Lisson Gallery." *Artscribe*, no. 89 (Nov.-Dec. 1991), p. 89.

Marian Goodman Gallery, New York. *New Sculpture*. Oct. 31-Nov. 30.
– "Tony Cragg, Marian Goodman." *ArtNews*, Feb. 1992, p. 153.

Art&Project, Amsterdam.

1992
IVAM, Centre Julio Gonzalez, Valencia. Jan. 21-March 22.
– "Tony Cragg en el Ivam-Centro del Carmen." *Gente*, Jan. 27, 1992.
– "La lógica de la creación." *La mejor hoja de Valencia*, Jan. 31-Feb. 6, 1992.
– R. Prats Rivelles. "Tony Cragg: el reto que no cesa." *El mercantil Valenciano*, Feb. 1992.
– C. D. Marco. "Un ejemplo de buena lógica creativa." *Aqui Setmanari de Valencia*, Feb. 1992.
– "Tony Cragg al centro del Carme." *Perdre el Temps*, Feb. 10, 1992.
– "Tony Cragg en el IVAM." *Qué y Dondé*, Feb. 10, 1992.
– C. D. Marco. "Tony Cragg, IVAM." *Boom*, Feb. 1992.
– "Tony Cragg, singular exponente de la última escultura británica, en el Centro del Carmen." *Qué y Dondé*, Feb. 2-9, 1992.
– "Tony Cragg." *Diario 16*, March 3, 1992.
– P. Jimenez. "Tony Cragg, la intimidad de la escultura." *ABC*, March 6, 1992.
– "Escultura Británica." *Cambio 16*, March 23, 1992.
– "Tony Cragg y Susana Solano, principales atractivos de la nueva temporada escultorica en Valencia." *Martes*, March 1992.
– "El Centro del Carme albergara una muestra una interesante faceta del pintor." *Hoja de*

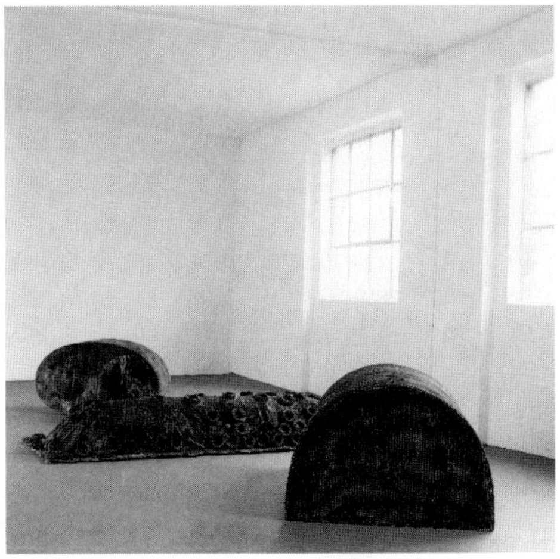

Belgischer Hof, *Galerie Konrad Fischer, Düsseldorf, 1990*
Photo Dorothee Fischer

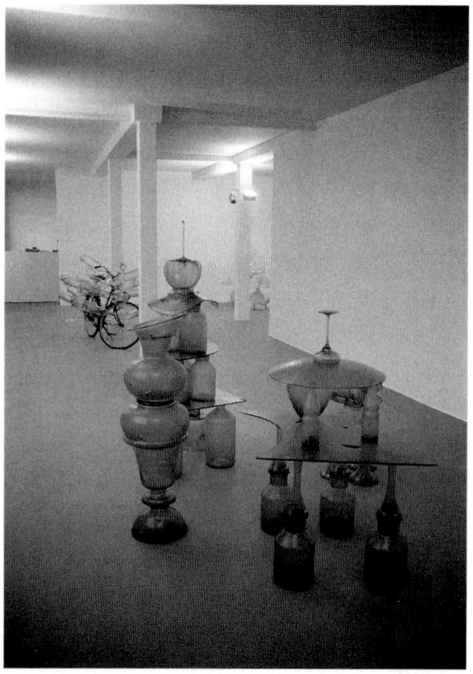

Glass Hybrids,
Gazelle, *Galerie Buchmann, Basel, 1992*

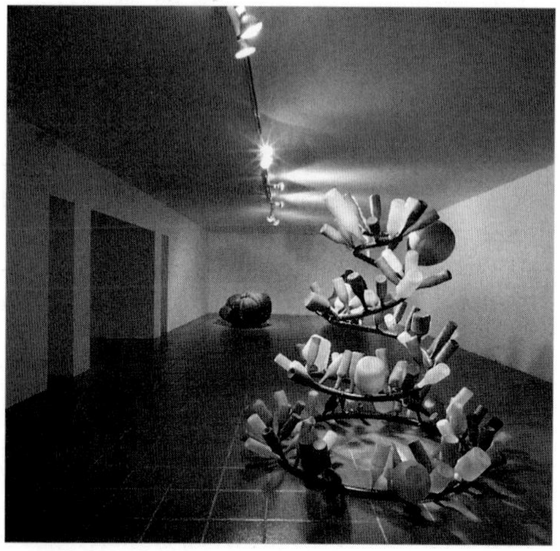

Spyrogyra, *1992*
Galleria Civica d'Arte Contemporanea, Trento, 1994

Valencia, April 8, 1992.
– "Muestra del escultor británico Tony Cragg en el IVAM." *Nacional*, April 24-30, 1992.
– "Gruyere de cemento en el IVAM." *Diario 16*, April 25, 1992.
– "El centro de El Carme cumple tres años con una muestra de Cragg." *El Pais*, April 25, 1992.
– "Tony Cragg: 'El arte puede devolver el sentido instintivo frente a los artificios'." *Hoja de Valencia*, April 25, 1992.
– "Tony Cragg expone en el Centro del Carmen sus ultimas esculturas." *El Mercantil Valenciano*, April 26, 1992.
– S. Dasca. "El escultor británico Tony Cragg expone en el IVAM sus ultimas creaciones." *Diario 16*, April 1992.

Basel, Galerie Buchmann. Jan. 18-March 14.
– C. Vogele. "Basel: Tony Cragg in der Galerie Buchmann." *Kunst-Bulletin*, no. 3 (March 1992).

Galerie Isy Brachot, Brussels. Feb. 6-March 28.

Musée départemental d'art contemporain, Château de Rochechouart. June 27-Oct. 4. Catalogue.

Centre d'art contemporain du Domaine de Kerguehennec, Bignan. *Tony Cragg, oeuvres des années '80*. July 4-Nov. 1. Catalogue.

Tramway and Centre for Contemporary Arts, Glasgow. July 25-Sept. 6. Catalogue, with text by T. Cragg.
– R. Mowe. "Master of plastic arts." *Scotland on Sunday*, July 26, 1992.
– M. France. "Rescuing plastic from screaming indignity." *The Sunday Times Scottish Section*, July 26, 1992.
– F. Byrne Sutton, M. MacDonald. *The Scotsman*, July 27, 1992.
– R. Dorment. "The beauty of old junk." *The Daily Telegraph*, July 29, 1992.
– M. France. "Banality rules. OK?" *The List*, July 31, 1992.
– J. McEwen. "The back of Cragg's hand." *The Sunday Telegraph*, Aug. 2, 1992.
– F. Whitford. "Subverting the banal." *The Sunday Times*, Aug. 2, 1992.
– T. Lubbock. "Metaphorically speaking." *The Independent on Sunday*, Aug. 2, 1992.
– A. G. Dixon. "Personal Stereo," *The Independent*, Aug. 4, 1992.
– R. Jennings. "Delicate and rather butch." *New Statesman*, Aug. 21, 1992.
– W. Feaver. "Metal guru's mighty faucets." *The Observer*, Aug. 23, 1992.
– M. R. Beaumont. "Life, near-death, sin and wickedness." *Financial Times*, Aug. 25, 1992.
– C. Henry. "Scotland." *Arts Review* (Sept. 1992).

Thomas Cohn, São Paulo.

Galleria Tucci Russo, Turin. Opened Nov. 27.
– G. Curto. "Tony Cragg. Uno sguardo contemporaneo affascinato dal passato." *Flash Art* 26, no. 172 (Feb. 1993), p. 99.

Lisson Gallery, London. Dec. 4-Jan. 16, 1993.
– R. Cork. "Surprises come in many forms." *The Times*, Dec. 11, 1992.
– G. Norman. "Expensive detour links science with Surrealism." *The Independent*, Dec. 14, 1992.
– W. Feaver. "The floors of perception." *The Observer*, Dec. 20, 1992.
– R. Bevan. "London." *The Art Newspaper*, Dec. 1992.
– S. Hubbard. "Tony Cragg, Lisson." *Time Out*, Jan. 6, 1993.
– M. Gayford. "Gallery Round-up." *The Daily Telegraph*, Jan. 6, 1993.
– S. Corbin. "Tony Cragg, Lisson Gallery." *What's On in London*, Jan. 6, 1993.
– R. Bevan. "Gilbert and George and Cragg star shows." *The Art Newspaper*, no. 24 (Jan. 1993), p. 27.

Moderna Galerija, Ljubljana. Dec. 18-Jan. 10, 1993. Catalogue.

1993
Museum Het Kruithuis, 's-Hertogenbosch. *Archimedes Screw*. March 21-May 31.

Catalogue, with text by M. van Rooy and interview by R. Steenbergen.
– "Tony Cragg Starts up Fountain Plan." *Flash Art International* 25, no. 166 (Oct. 1992), p. 118.

Knoll Galeria, Budapest.
– "British sculpture invades Budapest galleries." *The Hungarian Times*, June 25, 1993.

Ganserhaus, Wasserburg Inn, Aug. 1993. Catalogue.

Galerie Hachmeister, Münster.

Galerie Buchmann, Basel. *Minster*. Sept. 3-Oct. 23.
– S. Gebhardt. "Ausstellungen in Basel." *Basler Zeitung*, Oct. 2, 1993.

1994

Marian Goodman Gallery, New York, Jan. 11-Feb. 19.
– H. Cotter. "Tony Cragg at Marian Goodman." *The New York Times*, Feb. 4, 1994.
– J. Dector. "Reviews. Tony Cragg/Marian Goodman." *Artforum* 32, no. 8 (April 1994), p. 94.
– T. Eccles. "Reviews. Tony Cragg at Marian Goodman." *Art in America*, April 1994.
– J. Goodman. "Tony Cragg at Marian Goodman." *ArtNews* 93, no. 4 (April 1994).
– M. Ritchie. "Tony Cragg. Marian Goodman." *Flash Art International* 27, no. 176 (May-June 1994), pp. 113-114.

Musée des Beaux-Arts, Nantes. *Tony Cragg. Dessins*. Jan. 22-April 25. Organized by J. Storsve. Traveled to Stadtgalerie, Saarbrucken; Kunstmuseum, St. Gallen.
– "Dessins de Tony Cragg." *Presse-Océan*, Jan. 20, 1994.
– "Cent dessins inédits." *Ouest-France*, Jan. 22-23, 1994.
– E. Foucher. "Les dessins de Tony Cragg." *Nantes Poche*, Feb. 2-8, 1994.
– P. Dagen. "Molecules, mollusques protozoaires." *Le Monde*, March 16, 1994.
– M. J. "Tony Cragg à la recherche du dessin." *Beaux-Arts*, no. 121 (March 1994).
– D. Arnaudet. *Voir*, no. 105 (April 1994).
– "Kunstmuseum St. Gallen: Das Werk von Tony Cragg." *Neue*, Dec. 2, 1994.
– U. Hane. "Tony Cragg im Kunstmuseum." *St. Galler Tagblatt*, Dec. 3, 1994.
– "Arbeiten von Tony Cragg im Kunstmuseum-Voller Asthetik." *Die Ostschweiz*, Dec. 6, 1994.
– "St. Gallen Kunstmuseum-Tony Cragg: Skulpturen und Zeichnungen." *Werk, Bauen +Wohnen*, Jan.-Feb. 1995.

Galerie Chantal Crousel, Paris. *Sculptures récentes, Tony Cragg*. May 12-July 16, 1994.
– *Art press*, no. 194 (Sept. 1994), p. 17.

Galleria Civica d'Arte Contemporanea, Trento. *Tony Cragg*. May 28-July 10. Catalogue, with texts by G. Celant, T. Cragg, D. Eccher, C. Schulz-Hoffmann.
– G. Nicoletti. "Magica inquietudine." *L'Adige*, April 15, 1994.
– "Tony Cragg." *Segno* 18, no. 133 (May-June 1994), p. 4.
– L. Serravalli. "Scolpire le cose." *Alto Adige*, May 28, 1994, p. 12.
– G. Nicoletti. "Vive intuizioni." *L'Adige*, May 28, 1994, p. 48.
– L. Bortolon. "Cragg: sculture per gli anni Novanta." *Grazia* 67, no. 21 (June 1, 1994), p. 55.
– A. Vettese. "Alchimia di oggetti quotidiani." *Il Sole-24 ore*, June 12, 1994.
– M. Meneguzzo. "Cragg, il nuovo ordine della pattumiera." *Avvenire*, June 25, 1994, p. 4.
– E. Bovo. "Il dualismo scienza-natura nelle creazioni sorprendenti dell'alchemico Tony Cragg." *L'Arena*, June 27, 1994, p. 34.
– "Tony Cragg e un'estate trascendentale." *Il Giornale dell'Arte*, no. 123 (June 1994).
– S. Cagol. *U.C.T.* 19, no. 222-223 (June-July 1994).
– N. Pallini. "Le forme e la materia." *Gioia*, July 4, 1994.
– A. Madesani. "Tony Cragg in Italia." *Abitare*, no. 331 (July-Aug. 1994), p. 40.
– L. Meneghelli. "Tony Cragg." *Flash Art* 27, no. 187 (Oct. 1994), p. 96.
– M. Bertoni. "Tony Cragg. Modelli di pensiero e fantasia nel soffio lieve della creazione." *Segno* 18, no. 136 (Oct. 1994), pp. 28-31.

Gesellschaft für Gegenwartskunst, Augsburg. *Tony Cragg: Silikate*. Catalogue.

Espaço Cultural BMW, São Paulo. *Tony Cragg*. July 26-Aug. 27.

Galerie Bernd Klüser, Munich. *Tony Cragg. Skulpturen*. Nov. 22-Jan. 27, 1995.

1995

Deweer Art Gallery, Otegem. *Tony Cragg*. Feb. 4-March 5. Catalogue, with text by J. Coucke.

Museo Nacional Centro de Arte Reina Sofia, Madrid. *Anthony Cragg*. Opened March 21. Catalogue, with texts by C. Alborch, F. Castro Florez, T. Cragg, F. Duque, J. Guirao, H. N. Jocks, B. Pinto de Almeida, M. A. Ramos.
– F. Calvo Serraller. "Para allegar la pesadez." *El Pais*, March 21, 1995.
– S. Quinones. "Contemplar una escultura es una experencia intelligente y sensual." *La información de Madrid*, March 21, 1995.
– "Las mil caras de la escultura." *Epoca*, March 21, 1995, p. 86.
– F. Castro Florez. "Metamorfosis del material." *Diario 16*, March 22, 1995.
– J. Ramon Danvila. "Anthony Cragg, el escultor que 'suena los materiales', llega al Reina Sofia." *El Mundo*, March 22, 1995.
– P. Ortega. "Tony Cragg: 'Es muy importante ampliar el vocabulario del arte'." *Ya*, March 22, 1995.
– Efe. "El escultor Anthony Cragg expone en el Reina Sofia." *La Vanguardia*, March 22, 1995.
– R. Valdelomar. "Los reportes obligan al Reina Sofia a aplazar dos exposiciones y reducir las adquisiciones." *ABC*, March 22, 1995.
– "Obra de Anthony Cragg en el Museo Reina Sofia." *El Diario Vasco*, March 22, 1995.
– Efe. "El centro de Arte Reina Sofia acoge la primera exposición individual del escultor británico Anthony Cragg en Madrid." *El Correo Espanol*, March 22, 1995.

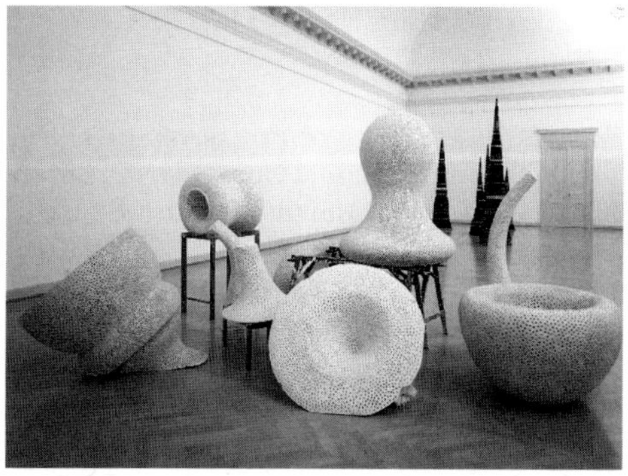

Forminifera, *1991;* Minster, *1990*
Kunstmuseum St. Gallen, St. Gallen, 1994-95

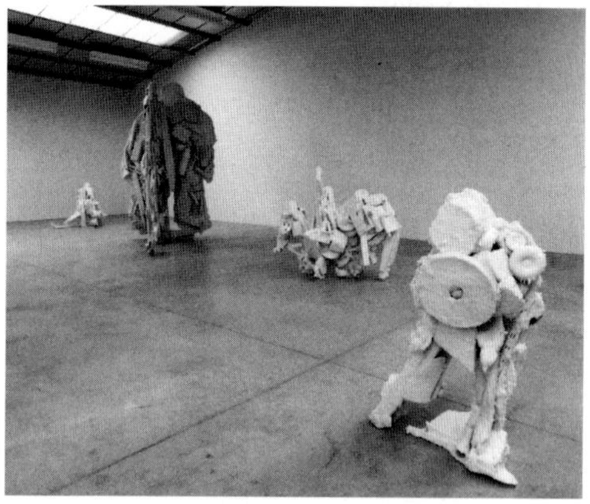

Fast Particles, *1994-95*
Deweer Art Gallery, Otegem, 1995

– dpa. "Anthony Cragg in Madrid." *Neue Osnabrucker Zeitung*, March 30, 1995.

Galleria Effe Arte Contemporanea, Lecco. Closed April 30.
– "Un grande artista inglese a Lecco. Alla Effe Contemporanea il britannico Tony Cragg e la sua arte della materia." *Il Giornale di Lecco*, no. 10 (March 6, 1995).
– C. Piccoli. "Tony Cragg a Lecco. Quando urlano i lupi è venuto il momento di darsi alla scultura." *La Repubblica/Tutto Milano & Lombardia*, March 16-22, 1995.
– "Lecco. Tony Cragg." *Flash Art* 28, no. 191 (April-May 1995), p. 52.

Nova Sin, Prague. *Tony Cragg*. Catalogue.

Galerie Hachmeister, Münster.

Valdsteinska jizdarna v Praze, Prague. June 20-July 23. *Tony Cragg. Sochy*. Catalogue.

Dum umeni mesta Brna, Brno. June 26-Aug. 13.

Galerie Buchmann, Basel. *Installation: Crowd*. Oct. 3-Nov. 24; *Zeichnungen*. Nov. 28-Dec. 20.

Tucci Russo, Torre Pellice. Oct. 28-Jan. 15, 1996.

1996
Musée National d'Art Moderne, Centre Georges Pompidou, Paris. Jan. 23-April 8. Catalogue.

Galerie Karsten Greve, Paris. *Tony Cragg. Dessins*. Jan. 24-March 30.

Group Exhibitions and Reviews

1975
Brunel University, Uxbridge.

Royal College of Art, Gulbenkian Hall, London.

1976
Ecole des Beaux-Arts, Metz.

1977
Lisson Gallery, London and Ninth Floor, The Fine Arts Building, New York. Feb. 5-March 1. Catalogue.

Royal College of Art, London. *RCA Degree Show*.

Battersea Park, London. *Silver Jubilee Sculpture Show*.

1978
Paris. *JA-NA-PA III*.

1979
Lisson Gallery, London. *Summer Show*.

Stuttgart. *Europa-Kunst der 80er Jahre*.

1980
Cambridge, *B. Meadows at the Royal College of Art*.

XVI Triennale, Palazzo della Triennale and Galleria del Disegno, Milan. *Nuova immagine/New Image*. April-July. Catalogue, with texts by G. M. Accame, F. Caroli, C. Cerritelli, A. D'Elia, F. Gualdoni, D. Paparoni, L. Parmisani, M. Pleynet, M. Vescovo.

Basel. *A Perspective*.

XXXIX Biennale Internazionale d'Arte, Magazzini del Sale alle Zattere, Venice. *Aperto '80*. June-Oct. Catalogue, with texts by A. Bonito Oliva and H. Szeemann.
– W. J. Hennessey. "Reflections on the 39th Venice Biennale." *Art Journal* 41, no. 1 (Spring 1981), p. 72.

Museum van Hedendaagse Kunst, Ghent. *Kunst in Europa na '68*. June 21-Aug. 31. Catalogue, with texts by G. Celant, J. Cladders, R. Dubois, K. Geirlandt, J. Hoet, S. Nairne, P. Van Daalen, J. P. Van Tieghem.
– B. Marcelis. "I muri di Gent. 'Kunst in Europa na '68'." *Domus*, no. 609 (Sept. 1980), pp. 48-51.

1981
Galleria Civica, Modena. *Il magico primario in Europa*. Catalogue, with text by F. Caroli.
– E. Bargiacchi. "Modena/Galleria Civica. Il magico primario in Europa." *Segno*, no. 20 (March-April 1981), p. 14.

Lisson Gallery, London. *Summer Show*.

Front Room, London. *The Motor Show*.

The Whitechapel Art Gallery, London. *British Sculpture in the Twentieth Century*. Catalogue, with text by F. Crichton.

1982
Metropolitan Art Museum, Tokyo. *Aspects of British Art Today*. Feb. 27-April 11. Catalogue, with texts by D. Brown, J. Burgh, K. Okamoto. Traveled to Utsonomiya, 1982; Osaka, 1982; Fukuoka, 1982; Sapporo, 1982.

Centre d'art contemporain, Geneva. *De la catastrophe*. April-May. Catalogue, with texts by C. Ferrari, A. von Furstenberg, A. Lukinovich, F. Salvadori, R. Thom.

Institute of Contemporary Art, London. *Art and Architecture*.

Nachst St. Stephan, Vienna. *Neue Skulptur*.

Kunsthalle, Bern. *Leçons des choses*. June 9-July 25. Catalogue, with an interview by J.-H. Martin. Traveled to Chambery, 1982; ARC, Musée d'Art Moderne de la Ville de Paris, Paris. *Truc et Troc, Leçons des choses*. Opened Jan. 26, 1983.
– C. Gintz. "La sculpture et ses objects, l'objet de la sculpture." *Art press*, no. 66 (Jan. 1983), pp. 24-27.

Museum Fridericianum, Kassel. *Documenta 7*. June 19-Sept. 28. Catalogue (2 vols.), with texts by G. Celant, R. Fuchs, J. Gachnang, C. van Bruggen.
– M. R. Beaumont. "Kassel: Documenta 7." *Arts Review* 34, no. 15 (July 16, 1982), p. 385.
– G. Celant. "Dall'Alfa Trainer alla Subway." *Segno* 6, no. 28 (Sept.-Oct. 1982), pp. 12-19.

Kunsthalle, Luzern. *Englische Plastik Heute/ British Sculpture Now*. July 11-Sept. 12. Catalogue, with texts by M. Kunz, M. Newman.
– B. Stutzer. "Englische Plastik Heute." *Pantheon* 40, no. 3 (July-Sept. 1982), p. 258.
– H. Zellweger. "Englische Plastik Heute." *Kunstwerk* 35, (Oct. 1982), pp. 30-31.

Neue Nationalgalerie, Berlin. *Kunst wird Material*.

Fruitmarket Gallery, Edinburgh. *Objects and Figures. New Sculpture in Britain*. Nov. 20-Jan. 8, 1983. Catalogue, with text by M. Newman.

1983
Museo civico d'arte contemporanea, Gibellina. *Tema Celeste*. Jan. 22-March 30. Catalogue, with text by D. Paparoni.

Rotterdamse Kunststichting, Rotterdam. *Beelden/Sculpture 1983*. May 13-June 22. Catalogue, with text by P. Heftig.
– P. Groot. "'Sculpture '83' Rotterdam Art Foundation." *Artforum* 22, no. 1 (Sept. 1982), p. 83.

Galerie Crousel-Hussenot, Paris. *Boltanski, Cragg, Cucchi, Disler, McLean, Sherman*.

Hayward Gallery and Serpentine Gallery, London. *The Sculpture Show*. Aug. 13-Oct. 9. Catalogue, with texts by K. Blacker, F. Crichton, P. de Moncheaux, N. Dimitrijrvic, S. Morgan, D. Petherbridge, B. Robertson, N. Serota.

Museo del Sannio, Benevento. *Arcaico Contemporaneo con Tony Cragg, Mario Merz, Bill Woodrow, nella Terra dei Sanniti*. Sept. 3-Oct. 8. Catalogue, with text by E. R. Comi.
– E. R. Comi. "Arcaico contemporaneo." *Lo Spazio Umano*, no. 9 (Oct.-Dec. 1983), pp. 57-66.

The Tate Gallery, London. *New Art*. Sept. 14-Oct. 23. Catalogue.

36, Rue d'Ulm, Paris. *A Pierre et Marie. Une exposition en traveaux*. Curated by D. Buren, M. Claura, J.-H. Martin, Sarkis, S. Selvi. Opened Sept. 26.

XVII Bienal de São Paulo, São Paulo. *Transformations. New Sculpture from Britain*. Oct. 14-Dec. 18. Catalogue, with texts by J. Andrews, L. Biggs, L. Cooke, M. Francis, T. Gleadowe, J. McEwen, S. Morgan, J. Roberts, N. Serota. Traveled to Museu de Arte Moderna, Rio de Janeiro. Jan. 20-Feb. 20, 1984; Museo de Arte Moderna, Mexico City. March 15-May 15, 1984; Fundaçao Calouste Gulbekian, Lisbon, 1984.

Kunstmuseet Ateneum, Helsinki. *Ars '83*.

Kanransha Gallery, Tokyo. *Summer Show*.

1984
Musée des Beaux-Arts, Rouen. *Sol-Mur*.

Zem, Martigues. *Plastiques et Plasticiens*.

Musée de Nantes, Nantes. *Tilt. L'art à l'oeuvre*.

Art Gallery of New South Wales, Sydney. *The Fifth Biennale of Sydney*.

The Museum of Modern Art, New York. *An International Survey of Recent Painting and Sculpture*. May 17-Aug. 19. Catalogue, with texts by K. McShine and R. E. Oldenburg.

St. Jakob Merian Park, Basel. *Skulptur im 20. Jahrhundert*. June 3-Sept. 30. Catalogue, with texts by A. Franzke, L. Glozer, S. Gossa, A. Kaiser, W. Jehle, F. Meyer, W. Rotzler, M. Schwander, K. Turr, T. Vischer, A. von Graevenitz, J. H. Waldegg, A. G. Wilkinson.
– C. Idone. "Sculpture in the 20th Century. Merian-Park, Basel." *Flash Art International*, no. 119 (Nov. 1984), pp. 46-47.
– M. Heller. "Skulptur als Reiz Klima." *Artefactum*, no. 6 (Nov.-Dec. 1984), pp. 93-94.

Villa Campolieto, Ercolano. *Terrae Motus. Fondazione Amelio*. July 6-Dec. 31. Catalogue, with texts by L. Amelio, G. C. Argan, J. Beuys, B. Blistène, A. Bonito Oliva, M. Bonuomo, L. Cherubini, B. Corà, D. Cortez, F. Durante, G. Galasso, M. Newman, F. Piemontese, C. Pinto, F. Ramondino, D. Robbins, B. Rose, D. Smith, B. Tosi, H. Vasconcelos, S. Vassalli, P. Weiermair. Traveled to Grand Palais, Paris. March 28-May 11, 1987.

Galerie Buchmann, Basel. *Anzinger, Cragg, Lavier*. July 10-Aug 31.

Château des Ducs d'Eperon, Cadillac. *Histoire de sculpture*. Summer. Catalogue, with text by B. Marcadé. Traveled to Villeneuve d'Ascq, 1984; Nantes, 1984-1985.

Galerie Schellmann & Klüser, Munich. *Arbeiten zu Skulpturen*. Oct. 4-Nov. 3. Catalogue.

Birmingham, Birmingham Museum and Art Gallery and Ikon Gallery. *The British Art Show: Old Allegiances and New Directions 1979-1984*. Nov. 2-Dec. 22. Catalogue, with texts by M. Allthorpe-Guyton, A. Moffat, J. Thompson. Traveled to Royal Scottish Academy, Edinburgh. Jan. 19-Feb. 24, 1985; Mappin Art Gallery, Sheffield. March 16-May 4, 1985; Southampton Art Gallery, Southampton. May 18-June 30, 1985.
– A. Brighton. *Art Monthly*, Dec. 1984-Jan. 1985.

The Guinness Hop Store, Dublin. *ROSC '84*. Catalogue.

1985

Musée d'art contemporain, Montreal. *Les vingt ans du musée à travers sa collection*. Jan. 27-April 21. Catalogue, with texts by P. Gagnon, P. Landry, A. Ménard.

Oslo, *Aureola Borealis*.

The Tate Gallery, London. *Turner Prize Exhibition of Shortlisted Artists*.

Kunsthaus Zürich, Zürich. *Spuren, Skulpturen und Monumente. Ihren präzisen Reise*. Catalogue, with text by H. Szeemann.
– R. Kurzmeyer. *Nike* 3, no. 12 (March-April 1986), p. 38.
– C. Schenker. "Traces, Sculptures and Monuments of their Exact Voyage." *Flash Art International*, no. 126 (Feb.-March 1986), p. 59.

Kunsthalle, Tübingen. *7000 Eichen*. March 2-April 14. Catalogue, edited by H. Bastian. Traveled to Kunsthalle, Bielefeld. June 2-Aug. 11, 1985.

Von der Heydt Museum, Wuppertal. *Die sich Verselbständigenden Möbel. Objekte und Installationen von Künstlern*. March 24-April 30. Catalogue.

Antwerp, *18th Biennial*.

Kunsthalle, Bern. *Alles und noch viel mehr*.

Galleria Comunale d'Arte Moderna, Bologna. *Anniottanta*. July 4-Sept. 30. Catalogue, with texts by D. Abadie, R. Barilli, F. Caroli, L. Cooke, Z. Felix, C. Pozzati, T. Sokolowski, C. Spadoni *et al.*

Centre d'art contemporain, Geneva. *20 oeuvres de la collection Rhône-Alpes*. Nov. 21-Dec. 14.

Art Gallery of Western Australia, Perth, *The British Show*. Feb. 19-March 24. Catalogue, with text by M. Newman. Traveled to Art Gallery of New South Wales, Sydney. Apr. 23-June 9; Queensland Art Gallery, Brisbane. July 5-Aug. 11; The Exhibition Hall, Melbourne; National Art Gallery, Wellington, New Zealand.
– V. Lynn. "New British Sculpture." *Art and Australia* 23, no. 2 (Summer 1985), pp. 226-230.
– T. Snell. "Relevance strikes a blow for the British." *The Australian*, Feb. 21, 1986.

Hayward Gallery, London. *Hayward Annual*.
– C. Harrison, J. Annear. "View of Hayward Annual." *Art Monthly*, June 1985.

1986

Palacio de Velázquez, Madrid. *Entre el objecto y la imagen. Escultura Británica contemporánea*. Jan. 28-April 20. Catalogue, with texts by J. Andrews, L. Biggs, J. Munoz. Traveled to Centre Cultural de la Caixa de Pensions, Barcelona. *Entre l'objecte i la image*. June 3-July 17, 1986 (catalogue).

Corcoran Gallery of Art, Washington D.C. *The Generic Figure*.

Wiener Festwochen, Messepalast, Vienna. *De Sculptura "Tu sculptura felix nube-spatium."* Opened May 16. Catalogue, with text by H. Szeemann.
– M. Bruderlin. "De Sculpture. Messepalast-Wiener Festwochen." *Flash Art International*, no. 130 (Oct.-Nov. 1986), pp. 82-83.

Park Sonsbeek, Arnhem. *Sonsbeek '86. International Sculpture Exhibition*. June 18-Sept. 14. Catalogue (2 vols.), with texts by G. F. Boreel, S. Bos, M. Brouwer, A. von Graevenitz, and artists' statements.

XLII Biennale Internazionale d'Arte, Padiglione Centrale, Giardini di Castello, Venice. *Wunderkammer*. June 29-Sept. 28. Catalogue, with text by A. Lugli.

Städtische Galerie im Lenbachhaus, Munich. *Beuys zu Ehren*. July 16-Nov. 2. Catalogue, with texts by L. Amelio, J. Cladders, R. Feldman, K. Gallwitz, L. Glozer, G. Jappe, B. Klüser, T. M. Messer, A. and A. d'Offay, J. Schellmann, R. Speck, G. Ulbricht, F. J. van der Grinter, A. Zweite.

Frankfurter Kunstverein and Schirn Kunsthalle Frankfurt, Frankfurt. *Prospect '86*. Sept. 9-Nov. 2. Catalogue.

Galerie Harold Behm, Hamburg. *Englische Bildhauer*.

Städtische Kunsthalle, Düsseldorf. *Skulptur Sein*.

1987

The Museum of Contemporary Art, Chicago. *A Quiet Revolution: British Sculpture since*

1965. Jan. 23-April 5. Catalogue, with texts by G. Beal, L. Cooke, I. M. Danoff, C. Harrison, H. T. Hopkins, M. J. Jacob, D. A. Nawrocki. Traveled to San Francisco, 1987; Newport Beach, 1987; Washington, 1987; Buffalo, 1988.
– V. Lautman. "British sculptors stage a 'Quiet Revolution'." *USA Today*, Jan. 26, 1987.
– M. Carroll. "Artist carves niche in nature." *Chicago Tribune*, Feb. 4, 1987.
– S. Taylor. "Scavenging artists send a message." *Chicago Sun-Times*, Feb. 12, 1987.
– M. C. Frey. "British modern art on display here is just smashing." *Chicago Sun-Times*, Feb. 15, 1987.
– S. Conn. "British sculpture exhibition illuminates nonsensical world." *Crain's Chicago Business*, Feb. 23, 1987.
– "The Quiet Revolutionaries." *The Independent*, March 9, 1987.

Liljevalchs Kosthall, Stockholm. *British Art of the 1980s*. Catalogue, with text by L. Cooke. Traveled to Sara Hilden Art Museum, Tampere. *Britannia. Paintings and Sculpture from the 1980s*. June 16-Aug. 23, 1987.

P.S. 1, The Institute for Art and Urban Resources, Long Island. *Juxtapositions. Recent Sculpture from England and Germany*. April 26-June 21. Catalogue, with texts by J. Decter, A. Heiss, D. Zacharopoulos.

Musée National d'Art Moderne, Centre Georges Pompidou, Paris. *L'époque, la mode, la moral, la passion*. May 21-Aug. 17. Catalogue, with texts by B. Blistène, C. David, A. Pacquement *et al*.

Museum Haus Lange, Krefeld. *Anderer Leute Kunst*. May 24-July 26. Catalogue, with text by J. Heynen.

Kassel. *Documenta 8*. June 12-Sept. 20. Catalogue (3 vols.), with texts by V. Fagone, E. F. Fry, W. Herzogenrath, L. Romain, M. Schneckenburger, A. Zweite.
– *Wolkenkratzer*, no. 4 (June-Aug. 1987), p. 78.

Kanransha Gallery, Tokyo. *Drawing*.

Royal Scottish Academy, Edinburgh. *Edinburgh International*.

1988

FRAC Rhône-Alpes, Ville du Parc. *Présentation & Propositions*.

Museum van Hedendaagse Kunst, Antwerp. *De Verzameling*.

Centre d'art contemporain, Geneva. *Sculptures de chambre*. March 15-April 8.

Valeria Belvedere, Milan. *Tony Cragg Dan Flavin Donald Judd Richard Long*. May 26-July 16.

Museo d'arte contemporanea Luigi Pecci, Prato. *Europa oggi/Europe now. Arte contemporanea nell'Europa Occidentale*. June 25-Oct. 20. Catalogue, with texts by A. Barzel, M. Bellandi, C. Bertelli, A. Bonito Oliva, B. Corà, G. Dorfles, H. Draxler, K. Jensen, J. Kosuth, D. Kuspit, P. Ludwig, G. Maragliano, J.-H. Martin, B. Merz, T. M. Messer, G. Panza di Biumo, A. von Graevenitz *et al*.
– H. Kontova. "Prato Museum." *Flash Art International*, Oct. 1988.

Carlisle Museum and Art Gallery, Carlisle. *Still Life, A New Life*.

Musée St. Pierre, Lyon. *La couleur seule. L'expérience du monochrome*. Oct. 7-Dec. 5. Catalogue, with texts by M. Besset, T. De Duve, T. McEvilley, T. Raspail *et al*.

Musée des Beaux-Arts André Malraux, Le Havre, Ecole d'Architecture de Normandie, Rouen, Musée de l'Evêche, Evreux. *Britannica*. Oct. 15-Dec. 12. Catalogue, with texts by F. Cohen, L. Cooke, C. Grenier. Traveled to Museum van Hedendaagse Kunst, Antwerp, 1989; Centre régional d'art contemporain, Labege Innopole, 1989.
– F. Bataillon. "Britannica." *Art press*, no. 131 (Dec. 1988), p. 64.

Musée d'art contemporain, Montreal. *British Now: sculpture et autres dessins*. Catalogue, with text by S. G. Marchand.

Scottish Art Council, Third Eye Centre, Glasgow. *Camouflage*.

The Tate Gallery, Liverpool. *Starlit Waters: British Sculpture. An International Art 1968-1988*. Catalogue, with texts by L. Cooke, C. Harrison, M. Kunz.

The Tate Gallery, London. *Turner Prize Exhibition*.

1989

Hirschl&Adler Modern, New York. *Repetition*. Feb. 25-March 25. Catalogue.

Château d'Oiron, Thouars. *Collection du FNAC*.

Le Case d'Arte, Milan. *Mondi possibili*. Opened Feb. 16.

Palais des Beaux-Arts, Charleroi. *Un choix dans les collections du Nouveau Musée de Villeurbanne*. March 11-April 16.

Galerie Buchmann, Basel. *Tony Cragg, Willi Kopf, Richard Tuttle*. April 8-May 20.

Centre de la Vieille Charité, Marseilles. *Dimension Jouet*. April 20-June 18. Traveled to Maison du Jouet de Moirans, Moirans-en-Montagne. Oct.-Nov. 1989.

Marga Paz, Madrid. *Complex Object*. Curated by A. Melo. Opened April 21.

Musée National d'Art Moderne, Centre Georges Pompidou, Paris. *Magiciens de la terre*. May 18-Aug. 14. Catalogue, with texts by H. Bhabha, M. Francis, P. Gaudibert, A. Luque, A. Magnin, B. Marcadé, J.-H. Martin, T. McEvilley, J. Soulillon.

Galerie Crousel-Robelin, Paris. *Journeys 1970-1989. Tony Cragg, Jochen Gerz, Annette Messager, Sigmar Polke*. Oct. 21-Nov. 22.

Nicola Jacobs Gallery and Donald Young Gallery, Chicago. *Subject: Object.*

Freedman Gallery, Albright College, Reading, Pennsylvania. *The European Avant-Garde.*

Grob Gallery, London. *Sculpture.*

Galerie JGM, Paris. *Fers.*

Feigen Gallery, Chicago. *Filling in the Gap.*

1990

Galerie 1990-2000, Paris. *Marché libre marchands bienvenus.* Jan. 8-30.

Galeria Comicos, Lisbon. *Je est un autre, Part II.* March 29-April 28. Catalogue, with texts by P. Fadre, C. Matossian, J. Yau.

Art Gallery of New South Wales, Sydney. *The Eighth Biennial of Sydney, The Readymade Boomerang. Certain Relations in 20th Century Art.* April 11-June 3. Catalogue, with texts by R. Block, L. Cooke, A. M. Freybourg, D. Higgins, B. Murphy.

Hirshhorn Museum and Sculpture Garden, Washington. *Culture and Commentary: An '80s Perspective.* Closed May 6. Catalogue, with text by K. Halbreich.

Richard Kuhlenschmidt Gallery, Santa Monica. *Werkstatt Kollerschlag: Sculpture Show.* June 9-July 7.

Institute of Contemporary Art, University of Pennsylvania, Philadelphia. *Signs of Life. Process and Materials, 1960-1990.* June 15-Aug. 12. Catalogue.

Messepalast, Vienna. *Von der Natur in der Kunst.* Closed July 15.

The Art Institute of Chicago, Chicago. *Affinities and Intuitions. The Gerald S. Elliott Collection of Contemporary Art.* May 5-July 29. Catalogue, edited by N. Benezra, with text by L. Cooke.

Setagaya Museum, Tokyo. *British Art Now: A Subjective View.* Aug. 25-Oct. 7. Catalogue, with texts by A. Graham-Dixon, H. M. Hughes, A. Obigane, J. Shioda. Traveled to Fukuoka Art Museum, Fukuoka, 1990; Nagoya City Art Museum, Nagoya, 1990; Tochigi Prefectural Museum of Fine Arts, Tochigi, 1991; Hyogo Prefectural Museum of Modern Art, Hyogo, 1991; Hiroshima City Museum of Contemporary Art, Hiroshima, 1991.

Marian Goodman Gallery, New York. *Group Show October 1990.* Oct. 18-Nov. 30.

Gallery Paule Anglim, San Francisco. *John Baldessari, Tony Cragg, John McCracken.* November.

Hayward Gallery, London. *Now for the Future. Purchases of the Arts Council Collection since 1984.*

Jack Tilton Gallery, New York. *Detritus: Transformation and Reconstruction.*

Galerie Crousel-Robelin, Paris. *Keys for a Building.*

Galerie Isy Brachot, Brussels. *Perspectives-Prospectives.* Nov. 15-Dec. 15.

Galerie Isy Brachot, Brussels. *Made of Stone.* Dec. 19-Jan. 1991. Catalogue.

Moderna Galerija, Ljubljana. *Art of the Eighties from the Thomas Collection.* Dec. 20-Jan. 20, 1991.

1991

Musée de la Roche-sur-Yon and Musée de Poitiers. *L'insoutenable légèreté de l'art.*

Galerie Bernd Klüser, Munich. *Selected Works.*

Ecole Régionale des Beaux-Arts, Rennes. *Restes: des humeurs colorée.*

Fondation Daniel Templon, Fréjus. July 4-Sept. 29. *La sculpture contemporaine après 1970.* Catalogue, with texts by P. Cabanne, D. Dobbels, S. Gohr, D. Paparoni, C. Ratcliff, C. Smulders.

Serpentine Gallery, London. *Object for the Ideal Home. The Legacy of Pop Art.* Catalogue.

Marian Goodman Gallery, New York. *Summer Group Show.* June 14-Aug. 2.

Stedelijk van Abbemuseum, Eindhoven. *Zomeropstelling eigen collectie: nieuwe aanwinsten.* July 12-Sept. 15.

Kettle's Yard, University of Cambridge, Cambridge. *Excavating the Present: Art in Ruins.* July 13-Sept. 29.

Castello di Volpaia, Radda in Chianti. *Imprevisto.* Sept. Organized by L. Pistoi. Catalogue, with texts by S. Benni, L. Cherubini, G. Di Pietrantonio, F. Fossati, L. Frisa, C. Levi, F. Piquè, L. Pratesi, M. A. Zanarotti.

Fundación "la Caixa", Barcelona. *Qué se n'ha fet dels 80?*

Rencontres Art-Public Gare de Paris-Est, Paris. *Grandes lignes.*

Donald Young Gallery, Seattle.

Valentina Moncada, Rome.

The Carnegie Museum of Art, Pittsburgh. *51st Carnegie International.* Oct. 19-Feb. 16, 1992. Catalogue.
– J. Saltz. "Pittsburgh, Carnegie International." *Galeries Magazine*, Dec. 1991-Jan. 1992.
– D. Deitcher. "Art on the installation plan." *Artforum* 30, no. 5 (Jan. 1992), pp. 83-84.
– A. Jinkner-Lloyd. "Report from Pittsburgh. Musing on Museology." *Art in America* 80, no. 6 (June 1992).

Museum Haus Lange und Haus Esters, Krefeld. *In anderen Raumen.* Catalogue.

Deweer Art Gallery, Otegem. *To Return to*

Base. Oct. 26-Dec. 15. Catalogue, with texts by J. Coucke, M. Deweer.

Dum umeni mesta Brna, Brno. Nov.-Jan. 1992.

Galleria Gian Ferrari Arte Contemporanea, Milan. *Parallele. Linee della scultura contemporanea*. Dec. 4-Jan. 26, 1992. Catalogue, with text by F. Gallo.

1992

Galerie Gérard Delsol et Laurent Innocenzi, Paris. *Giulio Paolini, Tony Cragg, Curtis Mitchell*.

Galerie Crousel-Robelin, Paris.

Galerie Bernd Klüser, Munich. *Der Gefrorene Leopard/The Frozen Leopard Part I*. April-May. Catalogue, with texts by A. Bonito Oliva, B. Klüser.

Marian Goodman Gallery, New York. *Summer Group Show*. June-Aug.

Tramway, Centre for Contemporary Arts, Glasgow. July-Sept.

Kanransha Gallery, Tokyo. *White*.

Werkstatt Kollerschlag, Vienna.

Musée Communal, Ixelles. *The Binary Era: New Interactions*. Closed Nov. 30. Catalogue.

Centre de Conférences Albert Borschette, Brussels. *New Voices, New Works for the British Council Collection*. Sept. 23-Dec. Catalogue, with text by G. Hedley.

Galerie Ludwig, Krefeld. *Skulptur-Konzept*.

The Tate Gallery, Liverpool. *Natural Order: Recent European Sculpture from the Tate's Collection*. Opened July 3. Catalogue, with text by P. Curtis.
– R. Bevan. "Natural Order: contemporary sculpture collection of the Tate Gallery." *Galeries*, Aug.-Sept. 1992.

Donald Young Gallery, Seattle.

1993

Kunsthalle Zacheta, Warsaw. *Détente*. Catalogue, with texts by O. Breicha, Rainer Fuchs, L. Hegyi, J. Kosuth, M. Mattringer, D. Rabinowitch, G. Rombold, J. Sevcik, J. Valoch, H. Weskott. Traveled to Moderna Galerija, Ljubljana, 1993; Museum Moderner Kunst Stiftung Ludwig, Wien. Closed Jan. 9, 1994.

Valentina Moncada and Pino Casagrande, Rome. *Visione britannica*. Feb. 23-March 30.

Galerie Heinz Holtmann, Cologne. *Skulptur Heute*. March-April.

Portland Art Museum, Portland. *Material Identity. Sculpture between Nature and Culture*. April 20-June 27. Catalogue, with text by John S. Weber.

Leo Castelli, New York. *Sculpture*. Opened May 29.

Marian Goodman Gallery, New York. *Summer Group Show*. June-Aug.

XLV Esposizione Internazionale d'Arte, Peggy Guggenheim Collection, Venice. *Art against AIDS*. Catalogue, with text by J. Cheim, D. Cortez, C. Gimenez, K. Kertess.
– W. Trager. "Biennale Venedig '93." *Kunstforum*, Nov.-Dec. 1993.

Raanana, Israel. *Sculpture in the Little Forest*.

Münster. *Gegenbilder*.

Werkstatt Kollerschlag, Vienna. *Sommerausstellung*.

Stedelijk van Abbemuseum, Eindhoven. *The Collection*. July 17-Sep. 5.

Galerie Crousel-Robelin, Paris. *Briques*. Oct. 30-Nov. 27.

1994

Museum of Modern Art, Oxford. *The Raw and the Cooked: New Work in Clay in Britain*. Jan. 23-April 10. Catalogue, with texts by A. Britton, M. Margetts.

Ferenc Art Gallery, Hull. *Recent British Sculpture*. Traveled to Oriel Mostyn Gallery, Llandudno. Jan. 29-March 12.

Kunsthaus, Murzzuschlag.

Musée d'art moderne et d'art contemporain, Nice. *Aspects d'une collection*.

Galerie Ficheroulles, Brussels.

Sprengel Museum, Hanover. *Figur Natur*.

Le Nouveau Musée, Villeurbanne. *Toujours: Moderne*.

Kunstmuseum, Luzern. *Prospect/Retrospect*.

Galleria Manuela Allegrini, Brescia.

Museum für Gestaltung, Zürich.

Centro Atlántico de Arte Moderno, Las Palmas de Gran Canaria. *Entre la Presencia y la Representación. La Colección de Arte Contemporáneo Fundación "la Caixa" en diálogo con el arte canario*. May 17-July 16. Catalogue, with texts by N. Bisbe, M. Chirino, L. Monreal, P. L. Montalvo.
– "Entre la Presencia y la Representación". *Panorama. Fundación "la Caixa"*, Sept. 1994.

Kunstmuseum, Wolfsburg. *Tuning up-Einsatz für eine Sammlung in Wolfsburg*. May 29-Sept. 25. Catalogue.

Marian Goodman Gallery, New York. *A Sculpture Show*. June 3-Summer.

Leopold Hoesch Museum, Duren. *Paper Art*.
– A. Bosetti. "Besser denn je-5. Internationale Biennale der Papierkunst in Duren." *Durener Nachrichten*, June 10.

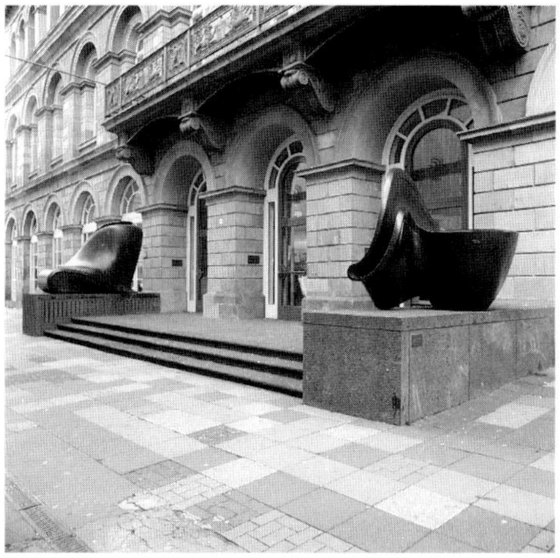

Early Forms, *1989*
Von der Heydt Museum, Wuppertal

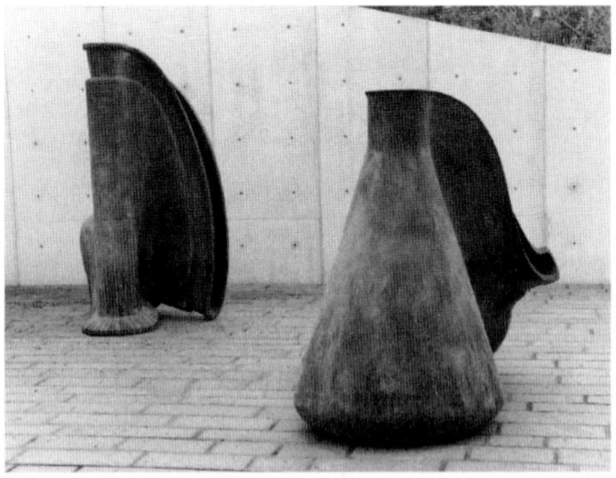

Untitled, *1991-92*
From the Schissler Foundation to The Museum of Fine Arts, Houston

Castel Ivano, Ivano Fracena, Val Sugana. *L'Incanto e la Trascendenza*. July 10-Aug. 28. Curated by D. Eccher. Catalogue, with texts by A. Bonito Oliva, D. Eccher, E. Olmi, C. Valenziano.
- G. Nicoletti. "Incanto e disagio." *L'Adige*, July 9, 1994.
- A. Vettese. "Un castello d'artisti, con Nitsch in cantina e Vedova in chiesa." *Il Sole-24 ore*, July 24, 1994, p. 25.
- M. Vescovo. "Trento. Verso la trascendenza." *La Stampa*, July 25, 1994.
- L. Serravalli. "Trascendenza e incanti nel castello." *Alto Adige*, July 26, 1994, p. 13.
- G. Nicoletti. "Atmosfera magica." *L'Adige*, Aug. 7, 1994, p. 9.

Stabilimento Radiomarelli, S. Antonino di Susa. *Collezione Agostino e Patrizia Re Rebaudengo-Massimo Sandretto*. Sept. 24-Nov. 18.

Palazzo Reale, Caserta. *Terrae Motus Terrae Motus*. Opened Dec. 9. Curated by A. Bonito Oliva. Catalogue.

Castello di Rivoli, Museo d'arte contemporanea, Rivoli. *L'Orizzonte. Da Chagall a Picasso. Da Pollock a Cragg*. Dec. 19-April 23, 1995. Catalogue, with texts by R. Fuchs, I. Gianelli, G. Imanse.
- F. Pasini. "Rivoli, festa di compleanno al museo con gli amici Chagall, Kandinsky..." *Il Secolo XIX*, Dec. 18, 1994, p. 11.
- P. Giangaspro. "Per Rivoli festa di compleanno con capolavori." *Il Giorno*, Dec. 28, 1994.
- M. Bonuomo. "Un secolo d'arte." *Grazia*, no. 1 (Jan. 8, 1995), pp. 54-55.
- A. Vettese. "Stedelijk festeggia Rivoli." *Il Sole-24 ore*, no. 7 (Jan. 8, 1995).
- P. Rizzi. "Dall'avanguardia in avanti." *Il Gazzettino*, no. 7 (Jan. 10, 1995).
- M. Vescovo. "Le fiabe di Chagall e i nudi di Picasso." *L'Informazione* 2, no. 11 (Jan. 14, 1995).
- G. C. "Grandi maestri al Castello." *Lombardia oggi*, no. 81 (Jan. 29, 1995).
- A. Berruti. "Castello di Rivoli. Cronaca di un futuro restituito." *Art Leader* 4, no. 22 (March-April 1995), pp. 32-33.
- M. Bertoni. "Un magnifico orizzonte." *Segno*, no. 139 (March-April 1995).
- L. Pratesi. "Visioni dall'Olanda." *Quadri& Sculture*, no. 13 (March-April 1995).

1995

Museet for Samtidskunst, Oslo. *Referanser*. Jan. 26-Feb. Traveled to Kunstmuseum, Lillehammer. Feb. 18-March 5, 1995; Kunstforening, Bergen. March 18-April 2, 1995.

La Lonja, Zaragoza.

Auditorio de Galicia, Santiago de Compostela. *De Henry Moore os anos 90. Escultura britanica contemporanea*. June 3-July 25. Catalogue. Traveled to Fundação de Serralves, Oporto. Sept. 7-Nov. 5, 1995.

Bonnefanten Museum, Maastricht.

Royal Academy of Arts, London.

FRAC Rhône-Alpes, Ville du Parc, Annemasse. *L'objet*.

The Irish Museum of Modern Art, Dublin. *British Art of the 1980s & 1990s. The Weltkunst Collection*. May 17-Oct. 5.

Galleria Civica, Palazzo dei Giardini, Modena. *Arte inglese d'oggi nella raccolta Re Rebaudengo-Sandretto*. May 21-July 31. Curated by G. Cochrane, F. Gualdoni. Catalogue, with text by F. Gualdoni.
- A. Vettese. "Giovani inglesi crescono." *Il Sole-24 ore*, May 28, 1995, p. 31.

Casino Luxembourg, Luxembourg. *Swinging Sixties/Sparkling Nineties. Contemporary art collection of the Banque Bruxelles Lambert*. May 23-July 9. Catalogue, with texts by D. Cardon de Lichtbuer, P. De Peuter.

Marian Goodman Gallery, New York. *A Summer Show*. June 17-Summer.

Serpentine Gallery, London. *Here & Now*.

British Sculptors at the Serpentine Gallery from 1970 to the Present. June 19-July 2. Catalogue, with text by S. Kent.

Museum van Hedendaagse Kunst, Citadelpark, Ghent. *Corpus delicti*. July 1-Sept. 3. Catalogue, with texts by J. Hoet, S. Jacobs, G. Verzotti.

Lisson Gallery, London. *Ideal Standard Summertime*. July 17-Sept. 30.

Le Domaine de Kerguéhennec, Centre d'art contemporain, Bignan. *Le domaine du diaphane*. Sept. 30-Jan. 28, 1996.

Lisson Gallery, London. *Postscript* (Ideal Standard Summertime). Oct. 6-21.

Stedelijk van Abbemuseum, Eindhoven. (*Entr'Acte 4*). Nov. 25-Jan. 21, 1996.

Marian Goodman Gallery, New York. *Group Show*. Dec. 1-Jan. 13, 1996.

Castello di Rivoli, Museo d'arte contemporanea, Rivoli. *Collezionismo a Torino*. Feb. 16-April 21. Curated by I. Gianelli.

Commissions

Realms and Neighbours. Merian Park, Basel. Commissioned by Kunstmuseum Basel, 1984. The gift of Christoph Merian Collection.

Jurassic Landscape. Private Collection, Bottmingen.
Commissioned by Galerie Buchmann, Basel/Cologne, 1986.

Fossils. The British Oxygen Company, Windlesham, Surrey, 1987.
Commissioned by The British Oxygen Company Group.

Ordovician Pore. Minneapolis Sculpture Garden, Minneapolis, USA, 1989.
Commissioned by Walker Art Center. The gift of Joanne and Phillip von Blon.

Neue Formen. Museum Von der Heydt, Wuppertal, 1989.
Commissioned by Museum Von der Heydt.

Unsere Broken. Umgestaltung. Licht-Dichtung. 2 Flusse. Landeszentralbank. Nordrhein-Westfalen, Düsseldorf, 1991.
Commissioned by Landeszentralbank.

Untitled. The Lillie and Hugh Roy Cullen Sculpture Garden, Museum of Fine Arts, Houston, USA, 1992.
Commissioned by the Museum of Fine Arts. The gift of The Schissler Foundation.

Archimedes Screw, Corner of Hekelaan and Pettelaarseweg, 's-Hertogenbosch, The Netherlands, 1993.
Commissioned by the Municipality of 's-Hertogenbosch. Sponsored in part by Lips B.V. in Drunen and Koninklijke van Drunen B.V., 's-Hertogenbosch.

Untitled, 7 parts. Bodo, Norway, 1993.
Commissioned by Artscape Nordland.

Daily Bread. Wiener Neustadt, 1994.
Commissioned by Merkur Werenhandels-AG.

Selected Bibliography

Books by the Artist

Tony Cragg: Eine Werkauswahl. Basel: Galerie Buchmann, 1990.

Ecrits/Writings/Geschriften. Brussels: Editions Isy Brachot, 1992.

Tony Cragg: In Camera. 's-Hertogenbosch/Eindhoven: European Ceramics Work Centre/Stedelijk van Abbemuseum, 1993. Text by Tony Cragg.

Tony Cragg. Dibujos/Drawings 1991-92. Valencia: IVAM Collecció Centre del Carme, 1993. Text by Manuel Costa.

Tony Cragg. Dessins/Zeichnungen. Basel/Ostfildern: Galerie Buchmann/Cantz Verlag, 1993. Texts by Henry-Claude Cousseau, Bernd Schulz, Roland Wäspe, Armin Wildermuth.

Tony Cragg. "Early Forms". Basel: Galerie Buchmann, 1994. Text by Armin Wildermuth.

Writings, Statements, Projects and Interviews for Periodicals and Catalogues by the Artist

"Einfache arbeitsvorgange...." In *Tony Cragg*, exh. catalogue. Wuppertal: Von der Heydt Museum, 1981.

"Street Life." *Furor*, no. 5 (Jan. 1982).

"The Interests.../Die Interessen...." In *Documenta 7*, exh. catalogue. Kassel: 1982, pp. 340-341.

"Vous prenez quel apart?" *Actuel*, no. 47 (1983). Project.

"Da un'intervista con Laura Cherubini e Barbara Tosi." In *Terrae Motus*, exh. catalogue. Naples: Electa, 1984, p. 65.

"Tony Cragg. Interview with Demosthène Davvetas." In *Tony Cragg*, exh. catalogue. Brussels: Société des Expositions du Palais des Beaux-Arts, 1985, pp. 31-34.

"Pre-conditions." In *Tony Cragg. Skulpturen*, exh. catalogue. Hanover: Kestner-Gesellschaft, 1985, pp. 37-40.

I. Lemaitre. "Interview with Tony Cragg." *Artefactum* 2, no. 11 (Nov.-Dec. 1985/Jan. 1986), pp. 7-11.

R. Walser. "Weil, die Welt ist halt so. Interview mit Tony Cragg." *Nike* 3, no. 13 (May-June 1986), pp. 10-12.

"De evolutie van de mens.../The evolution of human beings..." In *Sonsbeek '86*, exh. catalogue. Arnhem, 1986, p. 300.

"Tony Cragg Interviewed by Lynne Cooke." In *Tony Cragg*, exh. catalogue. London: Arts Council of Great Britain, 1987, pp. 11-36.

"Tony Cragg:" *Artforum* 26, no. 7 (March 1988), pp. 120-122. Project for *Artforum*.

"Tony Cragg. Interview by Constance Lewallen." *View* 6, no. 1 (Winter 1988-89).

L. Pratesi. "A Conversation with Tony Cragg." In *Tony Cragg*, exh. catalogue. Rome: Valentina Moncada, 1990, pp. 4-18.

"Somewhere in a moment..." In *51st Carnegie International*, exh. catalogue. Pittsburg: The Carnegie Museum of Art, 1991.

"Extracts from an interview with Tony Cragg in Glasgow, 24 July 1992." In *Tony Cragg*, exh. catalogue. Glasgow: Tramway, Centre for Contemporary Arts, 1992, pp. 5-7.

"Kunst aus Mull." *Internationales Forum für Gestaltung: Gemeinsam nutzen statt Einzeln verbrauchen*. Ulm: 1992, pp. 76-81.

"I am English..." In *Tony Cragg: In Camera*. 's-Hertogenbosch/Eindhoven: European Ceramics Work Centre/Stedelijk van Abbemuseum, 1993, pp. 7-14.

H.-N. Jocks. "Tony Cragg: 'Dieses Kleinzeug wirkt dann wie ein Augenfang, vergleichbar den Warzen auf der Haut'." *Kunstforum international*, no. 122, 1993, pp. 354-375.

A. Wildermuth. "Die Entdeckung der Zeichnung. Interview mit Tony Cragg." In *Tony Cragg. Zeichnungen/Dessins*. Basel: Galerie Buchmann, 1993, pp. 10-23.

R. Steenbergen. Interview with Tony Cragg. In *Tony Cragg. Archimedes' Screw*. 's-Hertogenbosch/Amsterdam: Museum Het Kruithuis/Municipality of 's-Hertogenbosch/Kunst en Bedrijf of Amsterdam, 1993.

Exhibition Catalogues

Tony Cragg. Saint-Etienne: Musée d'Art et d'Industrie, 1981.

Tony Cragg. Wuppertal: Von der Heydt Museum, 1981. Texts by Tony Cragg and Ursula Peters.

Tony Cragg. Fifth Triennale India. London: The British Council, 1982. Texts by Julian Andrews and Norbert Lynton.

Tony Cragg. Skulpturen. Karlsruhe: Badischer Kunstverein e.V., 1982. Text by Michael Newman.

Tony Cragg. Tokyo: Kanransha Gallery, 1982. Text by Nobuo Nakamura; in English and Japanese.

Tony Cragg. St. Gallen and de Vleeshal: Galerie Buchmann, 1983. Text by Armin Wildermuth.

Tony Cragg. Bern: Kunsthalle Bern, 1983. Texts by Germano Celant, Tony Cragg, Jean-Hubert Martin.

Tony Cragg. Turin: Galleria Antonio Tucci Russo, 1984.

Tony Cragg. Vier Arbeiten. Cologne: Kölnischer Kunstverein, 1984.

Tony Cragg. Tokyo: Kanransha Gallery, 1984. Text by Reiji Kawaguchi; in Japanese and English.

Tony Cragg. Skulpturen. Hannover: Kestner-Gesellschaft, 1985. Texts by Tony Cragg, Demosthène Davvetas, Carl Haenlein.

Tony Cragg. Brussels/Paris: Palais des Beaux-Arts/ARC Musée d'Art Moderne de la Ville de Paris, 1985. Texts by Annelie Pohlen, interview by Demosthène Davvetas; in French, English and Dutch.

Tony Cragg. London: Arts Council of Great Britain, 1987. Interview and text by Lynne Cooke.

Tony Cragg. Exhibition Guide. London: Hayward Gallery, South Bank Centre, 1987.

Tony Cragg. Innsbruck: Galerie im Taxispalais, 1987.

Tony Cragg. Sculptures. Val de Vesle: Silo/Centre de création contemporaine, 1988. Texts by Tony Cragg, Philippe Piguet; in French and English.

Tony Cragg. XLIII Biennale di Venezia. London: The British Council, 1988. Texts by Demosthène Davvetas, Henry Meyric Hughes, Catherine Lampert.

Tony Cragg. Winner of the 1988 Turner Prize. London: The Tate Gallery & Patrons of New Art, 1989. Texts by Tony Cragg, Nicholas Serota.

Tony Cragg. Düsseldorf: Kunstsammlung Nordrhein-Westfalen, 1989. Text by M. Müller.

Tony Cragg: Eine Werkauswahl. Basel: Galerie Buchmann, 1990. Text by Armin Wildermuth.

Tony Cragg. Rome: Valentina Moncada, 1990. Texts by Valentina Moncada, interview by Ludovico Pratesi; in Italian and English.

Tony Cragg. Sculpture 1975-1990. Newport Beach/London, New York: Newport Harbor Art Museum/Thames & Hudson, 1990/1991. Texts by Lucinda Barnes, Mark Francis, Marilu Knode, Thomas McEvilley, Pater Schjeldahl.

Tony Cragg. Eindhoven: Van Abbemuseum [1991]. Texts by David Batchelor, Tony Cragg, Jan Debbaut; in English and Dutch.

Tony Cragg. Vienna: Wiener Secession, 1991. Texts by Dietrich Karner, Edelbert Kob, Adolf Krischanitz, Markus Mittringer.

Tony Cragg. Essen: Kunstverein Ruhr, 1991.

Tony Cragg. Rochechouart/Bignan: Musée départemental d'art contemporain/Centre d'art contemporain du Domaine de Kerguehennec, 1992.

Tony Cragg. Sculpture. London/Glasgow: Lisson Gallery/Tramway, Centre for Contemporary Arts, 1992. Text by Tony Cragg.

Tony Cragg. Ljubljana: Moderna Galerija, Mala Galerija, 1992.

Tony Cragg: de schroef van Archimedes/Archimedes Screw. 's-Hertogenbosch/Amsterdam: Museum Het Kruithuis/Municipality of 's-Hertogenbosch/Kunst en Bedrijf of Amsterdam, 1993. Text by Max van Rooy, interview by Renee Steenbergen; in Dutch and English.

Tony Cragg. Milan/Trento: Charta/Galleria Civica di Arte Contemporanea, 1994. Texts by Germano Celant, Danilo Eccher, Carla Schulz-Hoffmann; in Italian and German.

Tony Cragg: Silikate. Augsburg: Gesellschaft für Gegenwartskunst e.V., 1994.

Tony Cragg. Prague: Nova sin, 1995.

Cragg. Madrid: Museo Nacional Centro de Arte Reina Sofia, 1995. Texts by Carmen Alborch, Fernando Castro Florez, Tony Cragg, Felix Duque, Jose Guirao, Heinz Norbert Jocks, Bernardo Pinto De Almeida, Miguel Angel Ramos.

Tony Cragg. Sochy. Prague/Brno: Valdsteinska jizdarna v Praze/ Dum umeni mesta Brna, 1995.

Tony Cragg. Otegem: Deweer Art Gallery, 1995. Text by Jo Coucke; in Dutch and French.

Articles and Essays about the Artist

Artscribe, no. 8 (Sept. 1977).

L. L. P[onti]. "Tony Cragg." *Domus*, no. 611 (Nov. 1980), pp. 50-51.

G. Celant. "Tony Cragg and Industrial Platonism." *Artforum* 20, no. 3 (Nov. 1981), pp. 40-46.

J. L. Maubant. *Découpage/Collage. A propos de Tony Cragg*, Cahiers du Cric, Le Nouveau Musée, no. 4 (May 1982).

P. Cuvelier. "Le Système anglo-panique des objets, Tony Cragg: objets perdus." *Libération*, May 4, 1982, pp. 24-25.

P. Winter. "Tony Cragg. Puzzlespiel und Superzeichen." *Kunstforum international*, no. 62 (June 1983), pp. 56-65.

"Tony Cragg: Element Plane." Domus, no. 641 (July-Aug. 1983), p. 67.

C. Besson. "Tony Cragg." *Public*, no. 1 (1984).

P. Turner. "Tony Cragg's Axehead." *Tate New Art/The Artist's View*, 1984.

D. Semin. "Tony Cragg. Des outils pour la pensée." *Art press*, no. 116 (July-Aug. 1987), pp. 22-25.

D. Davvetas. "Tony Cragg, bris d'images."

Beaux-Arts Magazine, no. 57 (May 1988), pp. 36-41.

P. Sterckx. "Tony Cragg. Présentation de la Sculpture." *Artstudio* (*La sculpture "à l'anglaise"*), no. 10 (Fall 1988), pp. 105-119.

L. Cooke. "Tony Cragg: Darkling Light." *Parkett*, no. 18 (Dec. 1988), pp. 96-102.

"El Premio Turner 1988 para Tony Cragg." *Lapiz*, no. 50 (1988), p. 90.

"Tony Cragg wins Turner Prize 1988." *Flash Art News*, *Flash Art International*, no. 144 (Jan.-Feb. 1989).

A. G. Dixon. "Cragg's Way." *ArtNews*, March 1989.

M. Castello. "Scolpire a memoria. Tony Cragg." *Tema Celeste*, no. 21 (July-Sept. 1989).

A. Obigane. "Profile/Tony Cragg." *Atelier. Fine Arts Magazine*, no. 760 (June 1990), pp. 2-36.

A. Wildermuth. "Tony Cragg. Ding-Skulpturen." *Artis*, Dec. 1990-Jan. 1991.

E. Shanes. "Tony Cragg. Sculpture 1975-1990." *Art Book News*, Jan. 1992.

J.-Y. Jouannais, ed. "Tony Cragg. Dans le paysage de l'atelier." *Art press*, no. 173 (Oct. 1992), pp. 16-23.

E. McArthur. "Tony Cragg. Neither a technological optimist nor post-industrial pessimist." *Art Monthly*, Oct. 1992, pp. 9-10.

C. Donn. "Sculture urbane." *Vogue Italia*, Aug. 1994, pp. 177-180.

A. Claustres. "Tony Cragg. Sous la peau." *Art press*, no. 209 (Jan. 1996), pp. 10-12.

General Reference Books and Articles

M. Newman. "New Sculpture in Britain." *Art in America* 70, no. 8 (Sept. 1982), pp. 104-114, 177-179.

W. Januszczak. "The Pop, Skip and Junk Merchants of Sculpture." *The Guardian*, Dec. 15, 1982.

M. Nurissany. "Le 'je-ne-sais-quoi' et le 'presque-rien'." *Le Figaro*, Feb. 25, 1983.

J. Roberts. "Urban renewal. New British sculpture." *Parachute*, no. 30 (March-May 1983), pp. 12-17.

M. Newman. "Figuren und Objekte. Neue Skulptur in England." *Kunstforum international*, no. 62 (June 1983), pp. 22-35.

P. Bloch and L. Pesenti. "Nouvelle sculpture: la culture de l'objet." *Beaux-Arts Magazine*, no. 3 (June 1983), pp. 40-45.

L. Cooke. "Reconsidering the 'New Sculpture'." *Artscribe*, no. 42 (Aug. 1983), pp. 25-29.

M. Newman. "Discourse and Desire: Recent British Sculpture." *Flash Art International*, Jan. 1984.

W. Feaver. "The New British Sculpture." *ArtNews* 83, no. 1 (Jan. 1984), pp. 71-75.

N. Dimitrijevic. "Sculpture after evolution." *Flash Art International*, no. 117 (April-May 1984), pp. 22-31.

U. Bischoff. "Skulptur im 20. Jahrhundert." *Pantheon* 42, no. 4 (Oct.-Dec. 1984), p. 390.

W. Januszczak. "The Church of the New Art." *Flash Art International*, no. 120 (Jan. 1985), pp. 28-32.

G. P. "Interview with Nicholas Logsdail." *Flash Art International*, *ibidem*, pp. 34-35.

R. Cork. "Sculpture Junk." *Vogue*, Aug. 1985.

M. R. Beaumont. "Beyond tradition: Sculpture since Caro." *Art & Design* 3, no. 1-2 (Feb. 1987), pp. 68-73.

M. Currah. *City Limits*, March 12, 1987.

M. Lothian. "Art in the space age." *The Guardian*, May 15, 1987.

P. Bonaventura. "An Introduction to Recent British Sculpture." *Artefactum* 4, no. 20 (Sept.-Oct. 1987), pp. 3-7, 67-72.

P. Overy. "The Britishness of sculpture." *Studio International* 200, no. 1018 (Nov. 1987), pp. 8-13.

E. Heartney. "Born Again Object." *Art in America*, Feb. 1988.

C. Ferbos. "Sculptures 'in between' – le paysage." *Artstudio* (*La sculpture "à l'anglaise"*), no. 10 (Fall 1988), pp. 21-25.

A. Hicks. *New British Art in the Saatchi Collection*. London: Thames and Hudson, 1989.

M. Livingstone, ed. *British Object Sculptors of the '80s I*. Kyoto: Art Random, 1989.

H. Gercke, ed. *Blau: Farbe der Ferne*. Heidelberg: Wuderhorn, 1990.

J. Shioda. "Here's to Art! The Spirit of John Bull." *Geijutsu Shincho*, Oct. 1990, p. 12.

"For Love or for Money." *ArtNews*, Dec. 1990.

"Sculpture des années '80/Sculpture of the 80's." *Eighty Magazine*, 1990.

T. Godfrey. *Drawing Today. Draughtsmen in the Eighties*. Oxford: Phaidon Press, 1990.

D. Von Dratlin. "Art&Pub 1890-1990: un siècle de creation." *Kunstforum*, no. 111 (Jan.-Feb. 1991).

K. Baker. "All things considered." *Artforum* 29, no. 7 (March 1991), pp. 105-108.

W. Packer. "Controversial reputations." *Financial Times*, July 20, 1991.

J. Hall. "Perfunctory eulogising." *The Art Newspaper*, no. 10 (July-Sept. 1991), p. 16.

G. Norman. "Eighties for sale." *The Independent on Sunday*, May 3, 1992.

G. Barker. "One man who isn't counting the cost." *The Daily Telegraph*, May 11, 1992.

Aanwinsten/Acquisitions 1989-1993. Een Selectie/A Selection. Eindhoven: Stedelijk Van Abbemuseum, 1993.

C. Henry. "Bouquets and brickbats for annus horribilis of art world." *Glasgow Herald*, Jan. 8, 1993.

S. Fairbrass. "A Modern Restoration Tragedy." *Art Review*, Nov. 1993, pp. 59-62.

P. Corrias. "Looking to the future: contemporary art in London." *The Society of London Art Dealers (1994/5 Yearbook & Directory of Members)*, pp. 44-45.

C. Gleadell. "Still Tough at the Top." *Art Monthly*, no. 177 (June 1994), pp. 42-43.

"Luis Monreal, Director of La Caixa, Has a National Sized Budget to Spend." *The Art Newspaper* 5, no. 41 (Oct. 1994).

G. Norman. "British Set Trend with Pickled Bulls and Subversive Vases." *The Independent*, Nov. 21, 1994.

N. de Oliveira, N. Oxley, and M. Petry. *Installation Art*. Texts by M. Archer. London: Thames and Hudson, 1994, pp. 142-143.

M. Archer. "The Cologne Art Fair." *Art Monthly*, Dec. 1994-Jan. 1995, p. 29.

P. Bickers. "La sculpture britannique: générations et tradition". *Art press*, no. 202 (May 1995), pp. 31-39.

J. Fineberg. *Art since 1940. Strategies of Being*, Englewood Cliffs: Prentice Hall, 1995.